American Language Hub

LEVEL 3
Teacher's Book

BOBBY DUNNETT

macmillan education

Macmillan Education Limited
4 Crinan Street
London N1 9XW

Companies and representatives throughout the world

American Language Hub Level 3 Teacher's Book
ISBN 978-0-230-49720-7
American Language Hub Level 3 Teacher's Book with Teacher's App
ISBN 978-0-230-49721-4

Written by Bobby Dunnett

First published 2020

Teacher's Book credits:
Original design by emc design ltd
Page make-up by SPi Global
Illustrated by Pablo Gallego (Beehive Illustration)
Cover design by The Restless
Cover image by Getty Images/Peathegee Inc.

Author's acknowledgements
The author would like to thank Tabbie, Dulcie and Felix.

The author and publishers would like to thank the following for permission to reproduce their photographs:

Bananastock W20; **Brand X** W39(m); **Corbis** W39(tl); **Getty Images** W38(b), Getty Images/Thinkstock Images/altrendo images W5(tr), Getty Images/Eric Audras Onoky W31, Getty Images/Levi Bianco W10(ml), Getty Images/iStockphoto/Thinkstock/Joggie Botma W5(m), Getty Images/Caiaimage/Paul Bradbury W17, Getty Images/Caiaimage W28, Getty Images/Nancy R. Cohen W37, Getty Images/E+/bo1982 W2, Getty Images/iStockphoto/Daniel Ernst W3(t), Getty Images/FatCamera W27, Getty Images/Food Collection W1(b), Getty Images/Fotosearch W16(tl), Getty Images/funstock W36, Getty Images/Fuse W21(tl), W34; Getty Images/Thinkstock Images/GOTO_TOKYO W26, Getty Images/Michael Haegele W8(tl), Getty Images/Hero Images Inc W22(tr), W31(r), Getty Images/kali9 W39(mr), Getty Images/Darren Muir/EyeEm W38(t), Getty Images/iStockphoto W30(tl), Blend Images/Jetta Productions/Blend Images W4(m), Getty Images/Blend Images/KidStock W5(tl), Getty Images/Brian A Jackson/iStockphoto W8(tr), Getty Images/jaroszpilewski W40, Jupiterimages W10(tr), Getty Images/Maskot W1(t), Getty Images/Emir Memedovski W23(tl), Getty Images/Photodisc W10(b), W16(mr), W29(tr), Getty Images/Compassionate Eye Foundation/Justin Pumfrey W24, Getty Images/EyeEm Ronik Rawat W16(ml), Getty Images/iStockphoto/Thinkstock/Luiz Rocha W11, Getty Images/Caiaimage/David Schaffer W6, W39(tm), Getty Images/Elisabeth Schmitt/Flickr W3(b), Getty Images/skynesher W30(tr), Getty Images/iStockphoto/STEEX W4(t), Getty Images/visualspace W22(tl), vm W18; Getty Images/Westend61 W31(l), Getty Images/iStockphoto Thinkstock Images/XiXinXing W21(tr); **Guardian News and Media** XV(tr); **Image Source** W4(b), Jasper White CM W13, W23(tr); **Macmillan Education Limited** Paul Bricknell W19; W39(ml); Creative Listening XV(mr); **Stockbyte** W39(tr); **Superstock** W29(tl).

The author and publisher are grateful for permission to reprint the following copyright material:

Extracts from '700 Classroom Activities New Edition' © David Seymour and Maria Popova 2005, published by Macmillan Education Limited. Used with permission. All rights reserved.

Extracts from 'Learning Teaching 3rd Edition Student's Book' © Jim Scrivener 2011, published by Macmillan Education Limited. Used with permission. All rights reserved.

Extracts from 'Teaching English Grammar' © Jim Scrivener 2010, published by Macmillan Education Limited. Used with permission. All rights reserved.

Student's Book credits:
Text, design and illustration © Macmillan Education Limited 2020
Written by Jeremy Day and Gareth Rees
With thanks to Edward Price for additional authoring and to Signature Manuscripts for the Grammar Hub pages.

Designed by emc design ltd
Illustrated by Rasmus Juul (Lemonade Illustration Agency) and Daniel Limon (Beehive Illustration)
Cover design by Restless
Cover image by Peathegee Inc/Getty Images
Picture research by Emily Taylor and Victoria Gaunt
Café Hub videos produced by Creative Listening
Café Hub video scripts written by James and Luke Vyner

The authors and publishers are grateful for permission to reprint the following copyright material:

p8 Extract from 'Why being bilingual helps keep your brain fit' by Gaia Vince. Originally published in Mosaic Science, 06 August 2016. © The Wellcome Trust Limited 2018. Republished under a Creative Commons licence. https://mosaicscience.com/bilingual-brains/

p18 Extract from 'War veteran, 89, posts ad for job to stop him 'dying of boredom'' by Alexandra Topping. Originally published in The Guardian, 29 November 2016. Copyright © Guardian News & Media Ltd 2018. Reprinted with permission of The Guardian.

p18 Extract from 'Eager 89-year-old seeks job: café snaps him up' by Alexandra Topping. Originally published in The Guardian, 01 December 2016. Copyright © Guardian News & Media Ltd 2018. Reprinted with permission of The Guardian.

p28 Epley, N., & Schroeder, J. (2014). Mistakenly seeking solitude. Journal of Experimental Psychology: General, 143(5), 1980–1999.

Full acknowledgements for photographs in the facsimile pages can be found in the Student's Book ISBN 978-1-380-01715-4.

Printed and bound in Brazil

2022
11

Contents

Student's Book Introduction

American Language Hub is a new six-level general English course for adult learners, which takes the complexity out of teaching English. It is designed to promote effective communication and helps to build learners' confidence with regular opportunities for meaningful practice. With its firm pedagogic foundation and syllabus aligned to the revised CEFR, American Language Hub has clear learning outcomes which make it easy to use in a variety of teaching situations.

1 COMMUNICATION

Wise men speak because they have something to say; fools because they have to say something.
Plato

A young woman enjoys her walk outdoors

OBJECTIVES

- update your status on social media
- make a short podcast
- plan and conduct an interview
- use rhetorical questions in a presentation
- ask for, offer and respond to help
- write a report about trends

Work with a partner. Discuss the questions.

1 How does 21st century technology make it easier or harder to communicate with other people?
2 Read the quote. To what extent do you agree with Plato?
3 Which forms of communication do you use most often: face-to-face or electronic; written or spoken communication? Which do you prefer and why?

COMMUNICATION 1

The engaging photograph and famous quote help teachers to focus students and familiarize themselves with the ideas in the unit. Teachers can also encourage students to label the picture.

Student's Book unit opener
The first page of every American Language Hub unit is the unit opener. It is an exciting visual opportunity for students to engage with the theme of the unit and see at a glance the CEFR learning objectives for each lesson.

There is a quick warm-up speaking activity. Teachers can use this time to prepare the class for their lesson and delay the main start for five minutes until all the students arrive.

Student's Book lessons 1 and 2 first spread

Reading and Listening

Reading and listening sections allow students to practice their receptive skills. All sections have tasks that move from global to detailed understanding so students can achieve a good overall comprehension. The key skills focus is clearly marked in the activity titles. The texts and scripts also present target vocabulary, grammar or pronunciation.

Grammar

The American Language Hub approach to grammar is inductive. Students are exposed to new language in context. Each grammar section prompts the student to notice the feature in context and to discover its form and use. Students then have further opportunities for controlled practice before using their new language in more authentic spoken or written output.

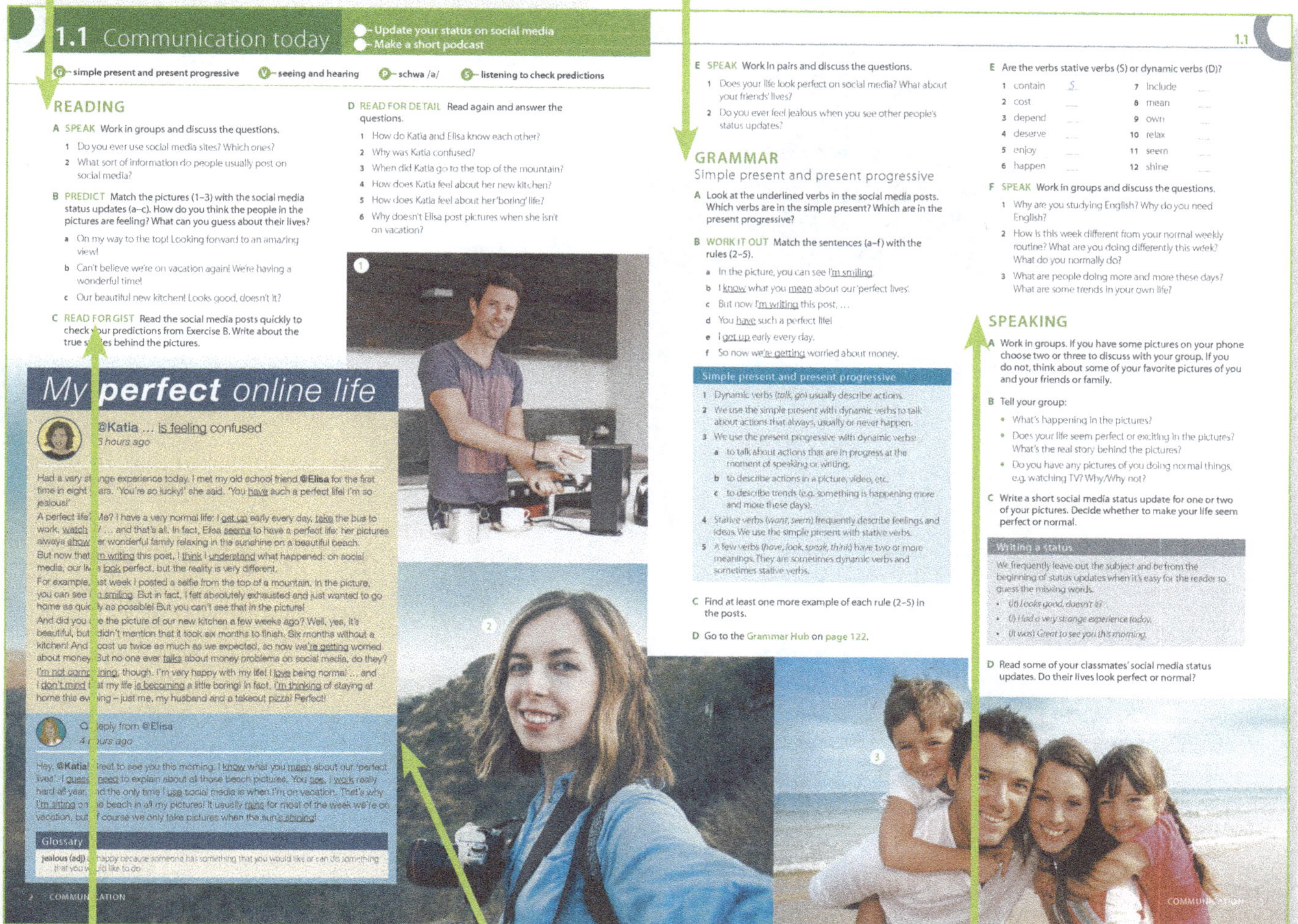

1.1 Communication today

- Update your status on social media
- Make a short podcast

G – simple present and present progressive V – seeing and hearing P – schwa /ə/ S – listening to check predictions

READING

A SPEAK Work in groups and discuss the questions.
1 Do you ever use social media sites? Which ones?
2 What sort of information do people usually post on social media?

B PREDICT Match the pictures (1–3) with the social media status updates (a–c). How do you think the people in the pictures are feeling? What can you guess about their lives?
a On my way to the top! Looking forward to an amazing view!
b Can't believe we're on vacation again! We're having a wonderful time!
c Our beautiful new kitchen! Looks good, doesn't it?

C READ FOR GIST Read the social media posts quickly to check your predictions from Exercise B. Write about the true stories behind the pictures.

D READ FOR DETAIL Read again and answer the questions.
1 How do Katia and Elisa know each other?
2 Why was Katia confused?
3 When did Katia go to the top of the mountain?
4 How does Katia feel about her new kitchen?
5 How does Katia feel about her 'boring' life?
6 Why doesn't Elisa post pictures when she isn't on vacation?

My perfect online life

@Katia ... is feeling confused
3 hours ago

Glossary
jealous (adj) unhappy because someone has something that you would like or can do something that you would like to do

E SPEAK Work in pairs and discuss the questions.
1 Does your life look perfect on social media? What about your friends' lives?
2 Do you ever feel jealous when you see other people's status updates?

GRAMMAR

Simple present and present progressive

A Look at the underlined verbs in the social media posts. Which verbs are in the simple present? Which are in the present progressive?

B WORK IT OUT Match the sentences (a–f) with the rules (2–5).
a In the picture, you can see I'm smiling.
b I know what you mean about our 'perfect' lives.
c But now I'm writing this post, ...
d You have such a perfect life!
e I get up early every day.
f So now we're getting worried about money.

Simple present and present progressive
1 Dynamic verbs (tell, go) usually describe actions.
2 We use the simple present with dynamic verbs to talk about actions that always, usually or never happen.
3 We use the present progressive with dynamic verbs:
a to talk about actions that are in progress at the moment of speaking or writing.
b to describe actions in a picture, video, etc.
c to describe trends (e.g. something is happening more and more these days).
4 Stative verbs (want, seem) frequently describe feelings and ideas. We use the simple present with stative verbs.
5 A few verbs (have, look, speak, think) have two or more meanings. They are sometimes dynamic verbs and sometimes stative verbs.

C Find at least one more example of each rule (2–5) in the posts.

D Go to the Grammar Hub on page 122.

E Are the verbs stative verbs (S) or dynamic verbs (D)?

1 contain	S	7 include	
2 cost		8 mean	
3 depend		9 own	
4 deserve		10 relax	
5 enjoy		11 seem	
6 happen		12 shine	

F SPEAK Work in groups and discuss the questions.
1 Why are you studying English? Why do you need English?
2 How is this week different from your normal weekly routine? What are you doing differently this week? What do you normally do?
3 What are people doing more and more these days? What are some trends in your own life?

SPEAKING

A Work in groups. If you have some pictures on your phone choose two or three to discuss with your group. If you do not, think about some of your favorite pictures of you and your friends or family.

B Tell your group:
- What's happening in the pictures?
- Does your life seem perfect or exciting in the pictures? What's the real story behind the pictures?
- Do you have any pictures of you doing normal things, e.g. watching TV? Why/Why not?

C Write a short social media status update for one or two of your pictures. Decide whether to make your life seem perfect or normal.

Writing a status
We frequently leave out the subject and be from the beginning of status updates when it's easy for the reader to guess the missing words.
- (It) Looks good, doesn't it?
- (I) Had a very strange experience today.
- (It was) Great to see you this morning.

D Read some of your classmates' social media status updates. Do their lives look perfect or normal?

2 COMMUNICATION   COMMUNICATION 3

Skill labels

By focusing students' attention on the skill labels next to each exercise number, teachers can highlight which skills are being practiced and recycled.

Topics

American Language Hub topics contextualize the language input for the lesson. They have been selected to allow opportunities for personalization.

Speaking

Each lesson starts with a CEFR unit objective which the lesson is designed to address. Students will usually use the grammar, vocabulary and pronunciation from the lesson to complete a speaking activity linked to the unit objective. American Language Hub allows students to safely practice speaking in pairs after most sections. This ensures that they feel confident to take an active role in the final speaking task.

American Language Hub for Teachers

Student's Book lessons 1 and 2 second spread

Reading and Listening Skill

Every unit includes a task designed to practice a key reading or listening skill. This ensures students are given the tools they need to effectively process a wide variety of texts and scripts. By the end of each book, students will have been exposed to 20 different skills for reading or listening.

Pronunciation

In American Language Hub, lessons focus on both word level and sentence level pronunciation. This not only allows students to improve their accuracy, but also fluency through sentence level intonation, which helps students understand how to add meaning through their pronunciation.

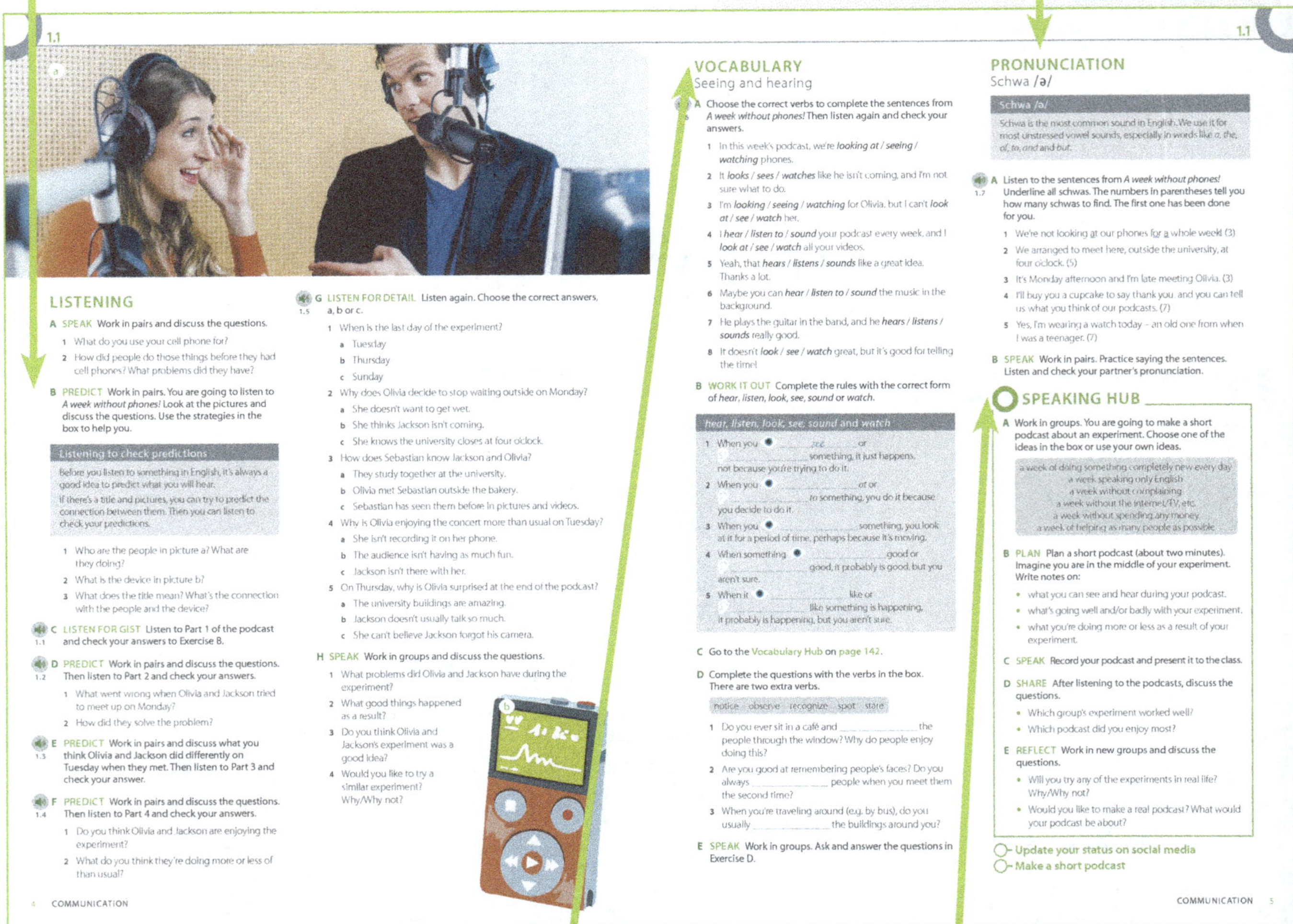

1.1

a

LISTENING

A SPEAK Work in pairs and discuss the questions.

1 What do you use your cell phone for?
2 How did people do those things before they had cell phones? What problems did they have?

B PREDICT Work in pairs. You are going to listen to *A week without phones!* Look at the pictures and discuss the questions. Use the strategies in the box to help you.

Listening to check predictions

Before you listen to something in English, it's always a good idea to predict what you will hear.

If there's a title and pictures, you can try to predict the connection between them. Then you can listen to check your predictions.

1 Who are the people in picture a? What are they doing?
2 What is the device in picture b?
3 What does the title mean? What's the connection with the people and the device?

1.1 C LISTEN FOR GIST Listen to Part 1 of the podcast and check your answers to Exercise B.

1.2 D PREDICT Work in pairs and discuss the questions. Then listen to Part 2 and check your answers.

1 What went wrong when Olivia and Jackson tried to meet up on Monday?
2 How did they solve the problem?

1.3 E PREDICT Work in pairs and discuss what you think Olivia and Jackson did differently on Tuesday when they met. Then listen to Part 3 and check your answer.

1.4 F PREDICT Work in pairs and discuss the questions. Then listen to Part 4 and check your answers.

1 Do you think Olivia and Jackson are enjoying the experiment?
2 What do you think they're doing more or less of than usual?

1.5 G LISTEN FOR DETAIL Listen again. Choose the correct answers, a, b or c.

1 When is the last day of the experiment?
 a Tuesday
 b Thursday
 c Sunday
2 Why does Olivia decide to stop waiting outside on Monday?
 a She doesn't want to get wet.
 b She thinks Jackson isn't coming.
 c She knows the university closes at four o'clock.
3 How does Sebastian know Jackson and Olivia?
 a They study together at the university.
 b Olivia met Sebastian outside the bakery.
 c Sebastian has seen them before in pictures and videos.
4 Why is Olivia enjoying the concert more than usual on Tuesday?
 a She isn't recording it on her phone.
 b The audience isn't having as much fun.
 c Jackson isn't there with her.
5 On Thursday, why is Olivia surprised at the end of the podcast?
 a The university buildings are amazing.
 b Jackson doesn't usually talk so much.
 c She can't believe Jackson forgot his camera.

H SPEAK Work in groups and discuss the questions.

1 What problems did Olivia and Jackson have during the experiment?
2 What good things happened as a result?
3 Do you think Olivia and Jackson's experiment was a good idea?
4 Would you like to try a similar experiment? Why/Why not?

b

4 COMMUNICATION

VOCABULARY

Seeing and hearing

A Choose the correct verbs to complete the sentences from *A week without phones!* Then listen again and check your answers.

1 In this week's podcast, we're *looking at / seeing / watching* phones.
2 It *looks / sees / watches* like he isn't coming, and I'm not sure what to do.
3 I'm *looking / seeing / watching* for Olivia, but I can't *look at / see / watch* her.
4 I *hear / listen to / sound* your podcast every week, and I *look at / see / watch* all your videos.
5 Yeah, that *hears / listens / sounds* like a great idea. Thanks a lot.
6 Maybe you can *hear / listen to / sound* the music in the background.
7 He plays the guitar in the band, and he *hears / listens / sounds* really good.
8 It doesn't *look / see / watch* great, but it's good for telling the time!

B WORK IT OUT Complete the rules with the correct form of *hear, listen, look, see, sound* or *watch*.

hear, listen, look, see, sound and watch

1 When you ___*see*___ or ___ something, it just happens, not because you're trying to do it.
2 When you ___ *at* or ___ *to* something, you do it because you decide to do it.
3 When you ___ something, you look at it for a period of time, perhaps because it's moving.
4 When something ___ good or ___ good, it probably is good, but you aren't sure.
5 When it ___ like or ___ like something is happening, it probably is happening, but you aren't sure.

C Go to the Vocabulary Hub on page 142.

D Complete the questions with the verbs in the box. There are two extra verbs.

notice observe recognize spot stare

1 Do you ever sit in a café and ___ the people through the window? Why do people enjoy doing this?
2 Are you good at remembering people's faces? Do you always ___ people when you meet them the second time?
3 When you're traveling around (e.g. by bus), do you usually ___ the buildings around you?

E SPEAK Work in groups. Ask and answer the questions in Exercise D.

1.1

PRONUNCIATION

Schwa /ə/

Schwa /ə/

Schwa is the most common sound in English. We use it for most unstressed vowel sounds, especially in words like *a, the, of, to*, and *and but*.

1.7 A Listen to the sentences from *A week without phones!* Underline all schwas. The numbers in parentheses tell you how many schwas to find. The first one has been done for you.

1 We're not looking at our phones for a whole week! (3)
2 We arranged to meet here, outside the university, at four o'clock. (5)
3 It's Monday afternoon and I'm late meeting Olivia. (3)
4 I'll buy you a cupcake to say thank you, and you can tell us what you think of our podcasts. (7)
5 Yes, I'm wearing a watch today – an old one from when I was a teenager. (7)

B SPEAK Work in pairs. Practice saying the sentences. Listen and check your partner's pronunciation.

SPEAKING HUB

A Work in groups. You are going to make a short podcast about an experiment. Choose one of the ideas in the box or use your own ideas.

a week of doing something completely new every day
a week speaking only English
a week without complaining
a week without the internet/TV, etc.
a week without spending any money
a week of helping as many people as possible

B PLAN Plan a short podcast (about two minutes). Imagine you are in the middle of your experiment. Write notes on:

- what you can see and hear during your podcast.
- what's going well and/or badly with your experiment.
- what you're doing more or less as a result of your experiment.

C SPEAK Record your podcast and present it to the class.

D SHARE After listening to the podcasts, discuss the questions.

- Which group's experiment worked well?
- Which podcast did you enjoy most?

E REFLECT Work in new groups and discuss the questions.

- Will you try any of the experiments in real life? Why/Why not?
- Would you like to make a real podcast? What would your podcast be about?

Update your status on social media
Make a short podcast

COMMUNICATION 5

Vocabulary

American Language Hub teaches vocabulary in topic-related sets to help students categorize the new words they learn. Key vocabulary sets are built on and reviewed in the back of the book.

Speaking Hub

At the end of each lesson, students perform a longer speaking turn which is staged to allow planning and idea creation. Students should apply their learning from the whole unit in the performance of their long speaking turn.

Student's Book Lesson 3

Functional Language

Each video provides a model for functional language so that students are able to access an ever-expanding bank of phrases. This language helps students to communicate effectively in a range of real-world situations.

Café Hub

The final lesson in each unit focuses on a video. Café Hub is an amusing situation comedy series. Meet Milly, Sam, Neena, Zac and Gaby as they take you through their adventures in London. Find out how they start their journey as complete strangers but become the best of friends.

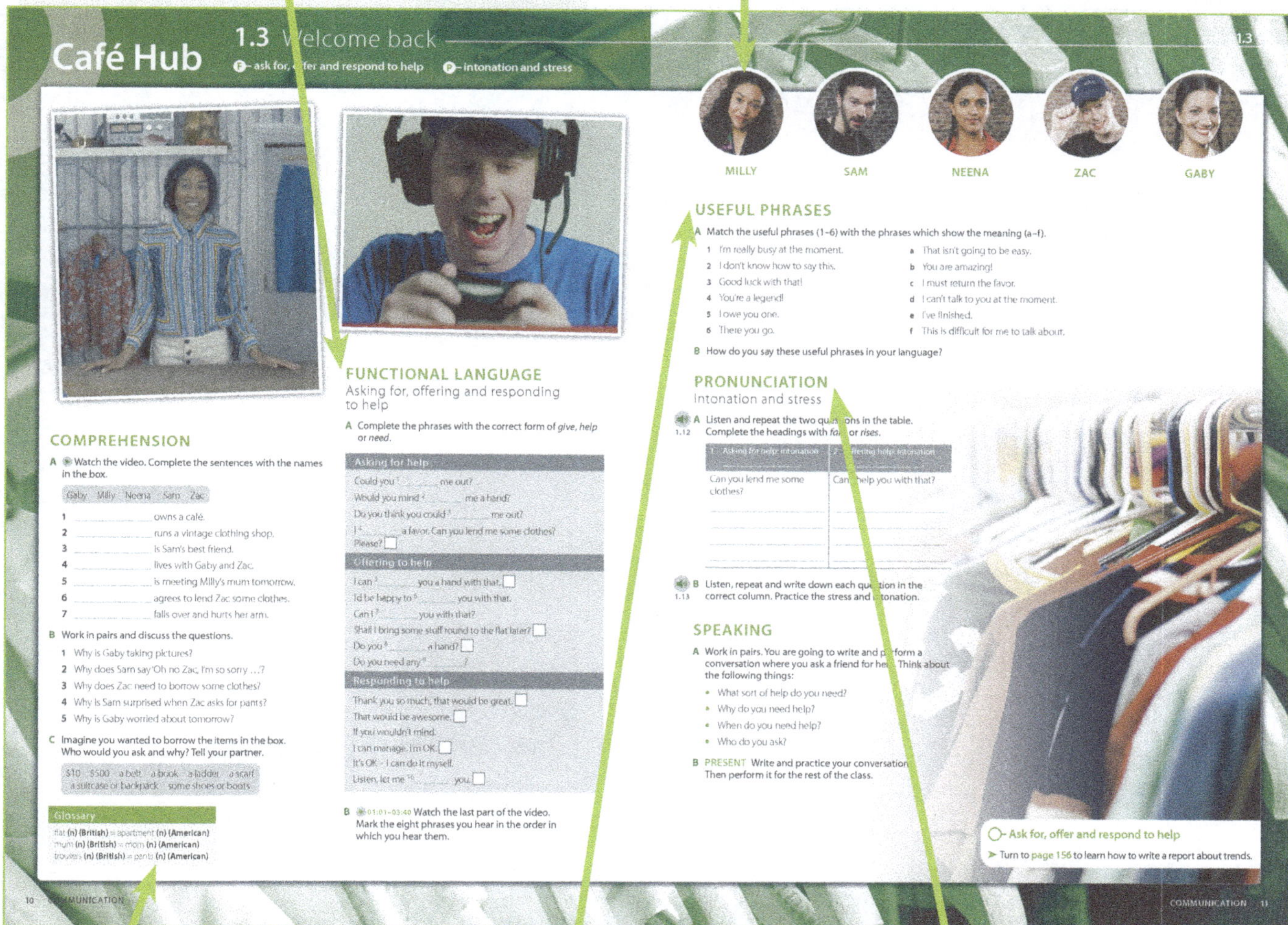

Café Hub

1.3 Welcome back

F – ask for, offer and respond to help   P – intonation and stress

COMPREHENSION

A Watch the video. Complete the sentences with the names in the box.

Gaby Milly Neena Sam Zac

1 ________ owns a café.
2 ________ runs a vintage clothing shop.
3 ________ is Sam's best friend.
4 ________ lives with Gaby and Zac.
5 ________ is meeting Milly's mum tomorrow.
6 ________ agrees to lend Zac some clothes.
7 ________ falls over and hurts her arm.

B Work in pairs and discuss the questions.

1 Why is Gaby taking pictures?
2 Why does Sam say 'Oh no Zac, I'm so sorry …'?
3 Why does Zac need to borrow some clothes?
4 Why is Sam surprised when Zac asks for pants?
5 Why is Gaby worried about tomorrow?

C Imagine you wanted to borrow the items in the box. Who would you ask and why? Tell your partner.

$10 $500 a belt a book a ladder a scarf a suitcase or backpack some shoes or boots

Glossary

flat (n) (British) = apartment (n) (American)
mum (n) (British) = mom (n) (American)
trousers (n) (British) = pants (n) (American)

FUNCTIONAL LANGUAGE

Asking for, offering and responding to help

A Complete the phrases with the correct form of *give*, *help* or *need*.

Asking for help
Could you [1] ________ me out?
Would you mind [2] ________ me a hand?
Do you think you could [3] ________ me out?
I [4] ________ a favor. Can you lend me some clothes? Please? ☐
Offering to help
I can [5] ________ you a hand with that. ☐
I'd be happy to [6] ________ you with that.
Can I [7] ________ you with that?
Shall I bring some stuff round to the flat later? ☐
Do you [8] ________ a hand? ☐
Do you need any [9] ________?
Responding to help
Thank you so much, that would be great. ☐
That would be awesome. ☐
If you wouldn't mind.
I can manage. I'm OK. ☐
It's OK – I can do it myself.
Listen, let me [10] ________ you. ☐

B 01:01–03:40 Watch the last part of the video. Mark the eight phrases you hear in the order in which you hear them.

MILLY SAM NEENA ZAC GABY

USEFUL PHRASES

A Match the useful phrases (1–6) with the phrases which show the meaning (a–f).

1 I'm really busy at the moment.
2 I don't know how to say this.
3 Good luck with that!
4 You're a legend!
5 I owe you one.
6 There you go.

a That isn't going to be easy.
b You are amazing!
c I must return the favor.
d I can't talk to you at the moment.
e I've finished.
f This is difficult for me to talk about.

B How do you say these useful phrases in your language?

PRONUNCIATION

Intonation and stress

1.12 A Listen and repeat the two questions in the table. Complete the headings with *falls* or *rises*.

1 Asking for help: intonation ________	2 Offering help: intonation ________
Can you lend me some clothes?	Can I help you with that?

1.13 B Listen, repeat and write down each question in the correct column. Practice the stress and intonation.

SPEAKING

A Work in pairs. You are going to write and perform a conversation where you ask a friend for help. Think about the following things:

- What sort of help do you need?
- Why do you need help?
- When do you need help?
- Who do you ask?

B PRESENT Write and practice your conversation. Then perform it for the rest of the class.

Ask for, offer and respond to help

➤ Turn to page 156 to learn how to write a report about trends.

10 COMMUNICATION   COMMUNICATION 11

Variety of English

The Glossary boxes on these pages point out differences between American English and British English.

Useful Phrases

The video also provides an opportunity to learn a variety of useful phrases that students can use to bring authenticity to their language output.

Pronunciation

Lesson 3 has a focus on stress and intonation. Students notice the stress and rhythm of British and American English pronunciation in the video before preparing to speak themselves.

Student's Book Hubs

Writing Hub

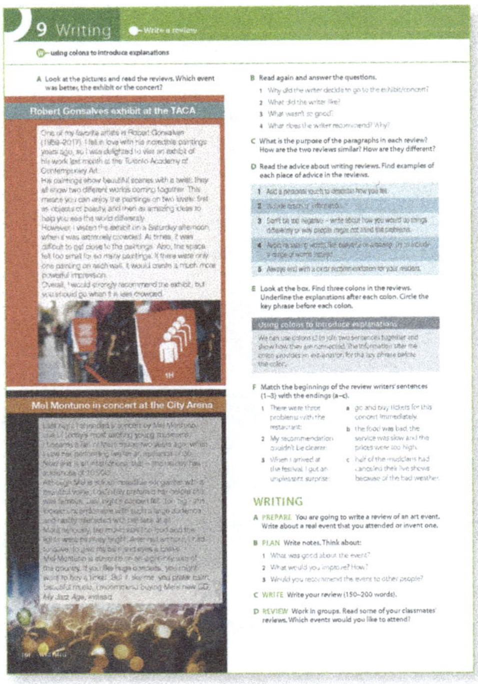
9 Writing

Robert Gonsalves exhibit at the TACA

Mel Montuno in concert at the City Arena

WRITING

The Student's Book has an individual writing page at the back of the book for each unit. Each writing lesson is aligned to the unit topic and teaches a different writing genre and writing skill. Students can see completed writing models to analyze before they begin to write their own work.

Grammar Hub

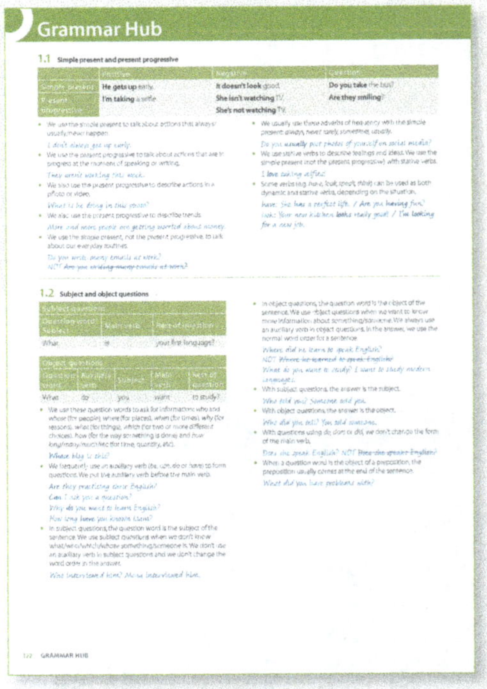
Grammar Hub

Clear explanations and further practice activities for each grammar point in the syllabus are provided at the back of the book. These can be used in class or set for homework to free up classroom time for communication.

Vocabulary Hub

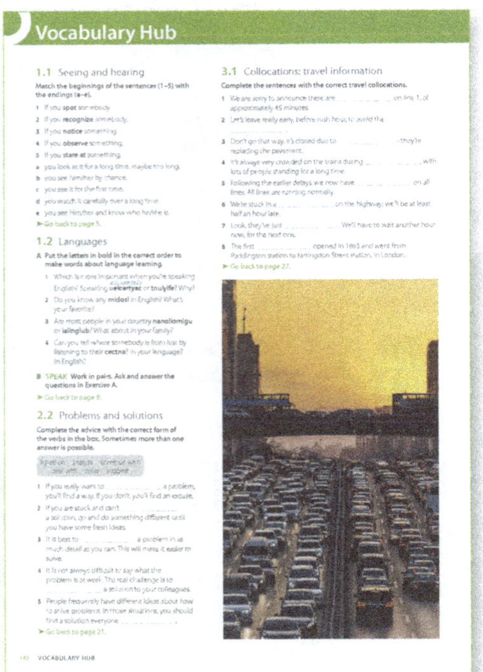
Vocabulary Hub

The Vocabulary Hub provides extra practice of key vocabulary presented in each unit. As with the Grammar Hub sections, these can either consolidate work done in class or be used for further self-study.

Communication Hub

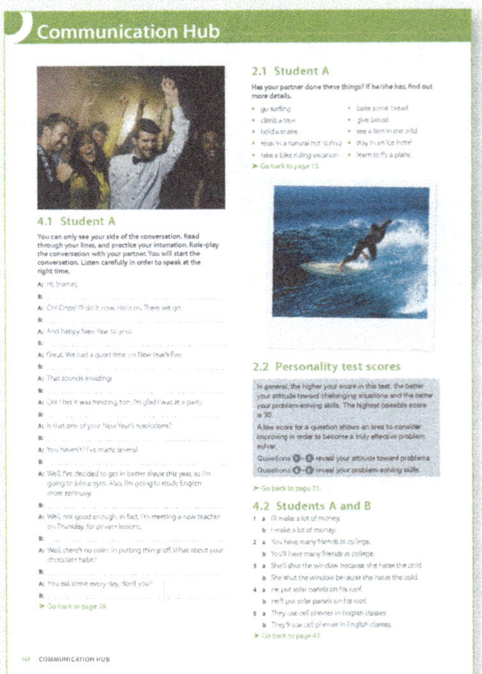
Communication Hub

The Communication Hub is used to set up longer communicative activities, such as information exchanges, quizzes and role plays.

Workbook

A Workbook is sold separately for American Language Hub. This includes 360 print activities practicing the language from the Student's Book. For each lesson there are corresponding practice exercises of grammar, vocabulary and pronunciation. There is further practice of the reading and listening skills from Lessons 1 and 2 and extension practice of the functional language from Lesson 3. There is also a page dedicated to the unit's writing genre and skill. All of these pages develop learning from the main lessons of the Student's Book.

Vocabulary and Grammar

The Workbook practices vocabulary and grammar that students have attended to in the Student's Book. By reminding themselves of the words and skills they have recently seen, students are better able to imbed learning and have it ready for recall during speaking practice.

Listening and Reading

The Workbook provides additional listening and reading texts that explore the topics in the Student's Book. These give students the opportunity to develop the key receptive skills from the unit.

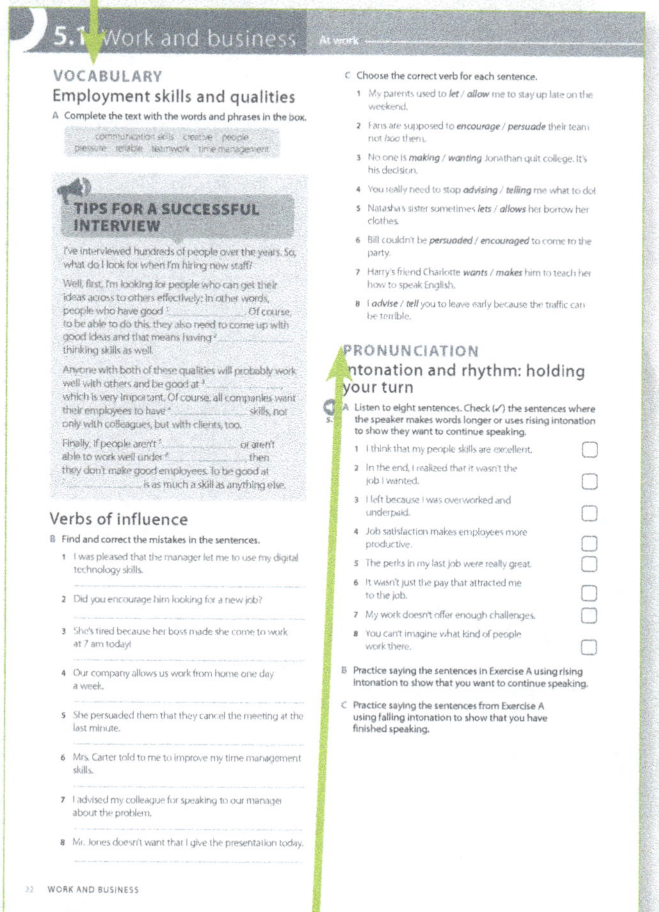

5.1 Work and business — At work

VOCABULARY

Employment skills and qualities

A Complete the text with the words and phrases in the box.

communication skills creative people pressure reliable teamwork time management

TIPS FOR A SUCCESSFUL INTERVIEW

I've interviewed hundreds of people over the years. So, what do I look for when I'm hiring new staff?

Well, first, I'm looking for people who can get their ideas across to others effectively; in other words, people who have good [1] ________. Of course, to be able to do this, they also need to come up with good ideas and that means having [2] ________ thinking skills as well.

Anyone with both of these qualities will probably work well with others and be good at [3] ________, which is very important. Of course, all companies want their employees to have [4] ________ skills, not only with colleagues, but with clients, too.

Finally, if people aren't [5] ________ or aren't able to work well under [6] ________, then they don't make good employees. To be good at [7] ________ is as much a skill as anything else.

Verbs of influence

B Find and correct the mistakes in the sentences.

1 I was pleased that the manager let me to use my digital technology skills.
2 Did you encourage him looking for a new job?
3 She's tired because her boss made she come to work at 7 am today!
4 Our company allows us work from home one day a week.
5 She persuaded them that they cancel the meeting at the last minute.
6 Mrs. Carter told to me to improve my time management skills.
7 I advised my colleague for speaking to our manager about the problem.
8 Mr. Jones doesn't want that I give the presentation today.

C Choose the correct verb for each sentence.

1 My parents used to *let* / *allow* me to stay up late on the weekend.
2 Fans are supposed to *encourage* / *persuade* their team not boo them.
3 No one is *making* / *wanting* Jonathan quit college. It's his decision.
4 You really need to stop *advising* / *telling* me what to do!
5 Natasha's sister sometimes *lets* / *allows* her borrow her clothes.
6 Bill couldn't be *persuaded* / *encouraged* to come to the party.
7 Harry's friend Charlotte *wants* / *makes* him to teach her how to speak English.
8 I *advise* / *tell* you to leave early because the traffic can be terrible.

PRONUNCIATION

Intonation and rhythm: holding your turn

A Listen to eight sentences. Check (✓) the sentences where the speaker makes words longer or uses rising intonation to show they want to continue speaking.

1 I think that my people skills are excellent. ☐
2 In the end, I realized that it wasn't the job I wanted. ☐
3 I left because I was overworked and underpaid. ☐
4 Job satisfaction makes employees more productive. ☐
5 The perks in my last job were really great. ☐
6 It wasn't just the pay that attracted me to the job. ☐
7 My work doesn't offer enough challenges. ☐
8 You can't imagine what kind of people work there. ☐

B Practice saying the sentences in Exercise A using rising intonation to show that you want to continue speaking.

C Practice saying the sentences from Exercise A using falling intonation to show that you have finished speaking.

32 WORK AND BUSINESS

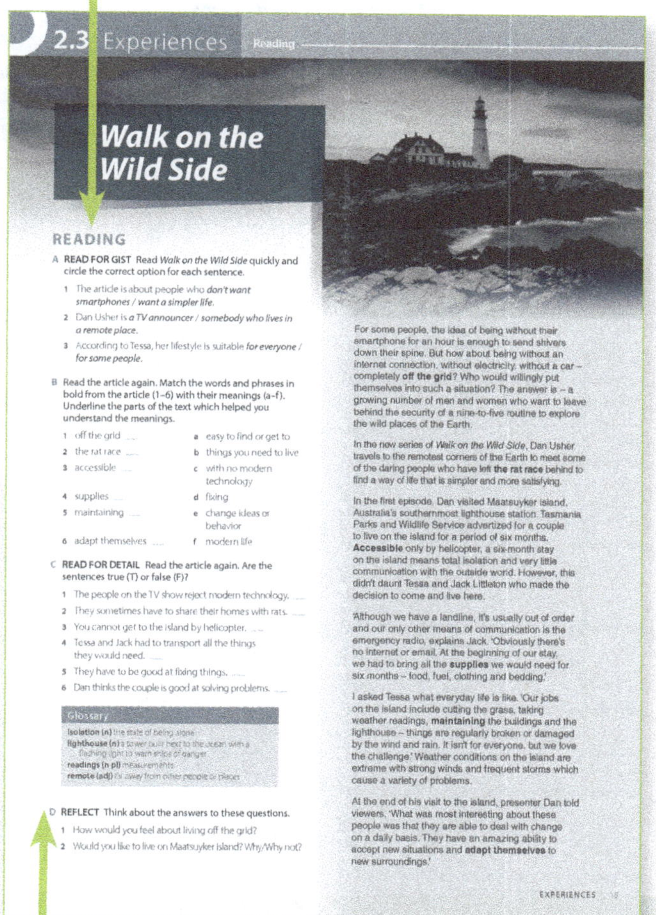

2.3 Experiences — Reading

Walk on the Wild Side

READING

A READ FOR GIST Read *Walk on the Wild Side* quickly and circle the correct option for each sentence.

1 The article is about people who *don't want smartphones* / *want a simpler life*.
2 Dan Usher is *a TV announcer* / *somebody who lives in a remote place*.
3 According to Tessa, her lifestyle is suitable *for everyone* / *for some people*.

B Read the article again. Match the words and phrases in bold from the article (1–6) with their meanings (a–f). Underline the parts of the text which helped you understand the meanings.

1 off the grid ___ — a easy to find or get to
2 the rat race ___ — b things you need to live
3 accessible ___ — c with no modern technology
4 supplies ___ — d fixing
5 maintaining ___ — e change ideas or behavior
6 adapt themselves ___ — f modern life

C READ FOR DETAIL Read the article again. Are the sentences true (T) or false (F)?

1 The people on the TV show reject modern technology. ___
2 They sometimes have to share their homes with rats. ___
3 You cannot get to the island by helicopter. ___
4 Tessa and Jack had to transport all the things they would need. ___
5 They have to be good at fixing things. ___
6 Dan thinks the couple is good at solving problems. ___

Glossary

isolation (n) the state of being alone
lighthouse (n) a tower built next to the ocean with a flashing light to warn ships of danger
readings (n pl) measurements
remote (adj) far away from other people or places

D REFLECT Think about the answers to these questions.

1 How would you feel about living off the grid?
2 Would you like to live on Maatsuyker Island? Why/Why not?

For some people, the idea of being without their smartphone for an hour is enough to send shivers down their spine. But how about being without an internet connection, without electricity, without a car – completely **off the grid**? Who would willingly put themselves into such a situation? The answer is – a growing number of men and women who want to leave behind the security of a nine-to-five routine to explore the wild places of the Earth.

In the new series of *Walk on the Wild Side*, Dan Usher travels to the remotest corners of the Earth to meet some of the daring people who have left **the rat race** behind to find a way of life that is simpler and more satisfying.

In the first episode, Dan visited Maatsuyker Island, Australia's southernmost lighthouse station. Tasmania Parks and Wildlife Service advertized for a couple to live on the island for a period of six months. **Accessible** only by helicopter, a six-month stay on the island means total isolation and very little communication with the outside world. However, this didn't daunt Tessa and Jack Littleton who made the decision to come and live here.

'Although we have a landline, it's usually out of order and our only other means of communication is the emergency radio,' explains Jack. 'Obviously there's no internet or email. At the beginning of our stay, we had to bring all the **supplies** we would need for six months – food, fuel, clothing and bedding.'

I asked Tessa what everyday life is like. 'Our jobs on the island include cutting the grass, taking weather readings, **maintaining** the buildings and the lighthouse – things are regularly broken or damaged by the wind and rain. It isn't for everyone, but we love the challenge.' Weather conditions on the island are extreme with strong winds and frequent storms which cause a variety of problems.

At the end of his visit to the island, presenter Dan told viewers, 'What was most interesting about these people was that they are able to deal with change on a daily basis. They have an amazing ability to accept new situations and **adapt themselves** to new surroundings.'

EXPERIENCES 15

Pronunciation

The Workbook also consolidates the pronunciation topics from the Student's Book through further controlled practice.

Reflect

Each reading and listening page has a Reflect section so that students can use their Workbooks in class if they wish to reflect on their learning with their peers.

American Language Hub for Teachers

Teacher's Book

Worksheets
The bank of communicative worksheets at the back of the Teacher's Book provide additional controlled and freer practice of every vocabulary and grammar section.

Extra activities
The Extra activity boxes help teachers extend the content of the lesson, both in and out of the classroom.

Interleaved pages
Every level of American Language Hub has a Teacher's Book interleaved with pages of the Student's Book. The answers to all of the Student's Book activities are annotated on the page so there is no need for teachers to flip back and forth to find information.

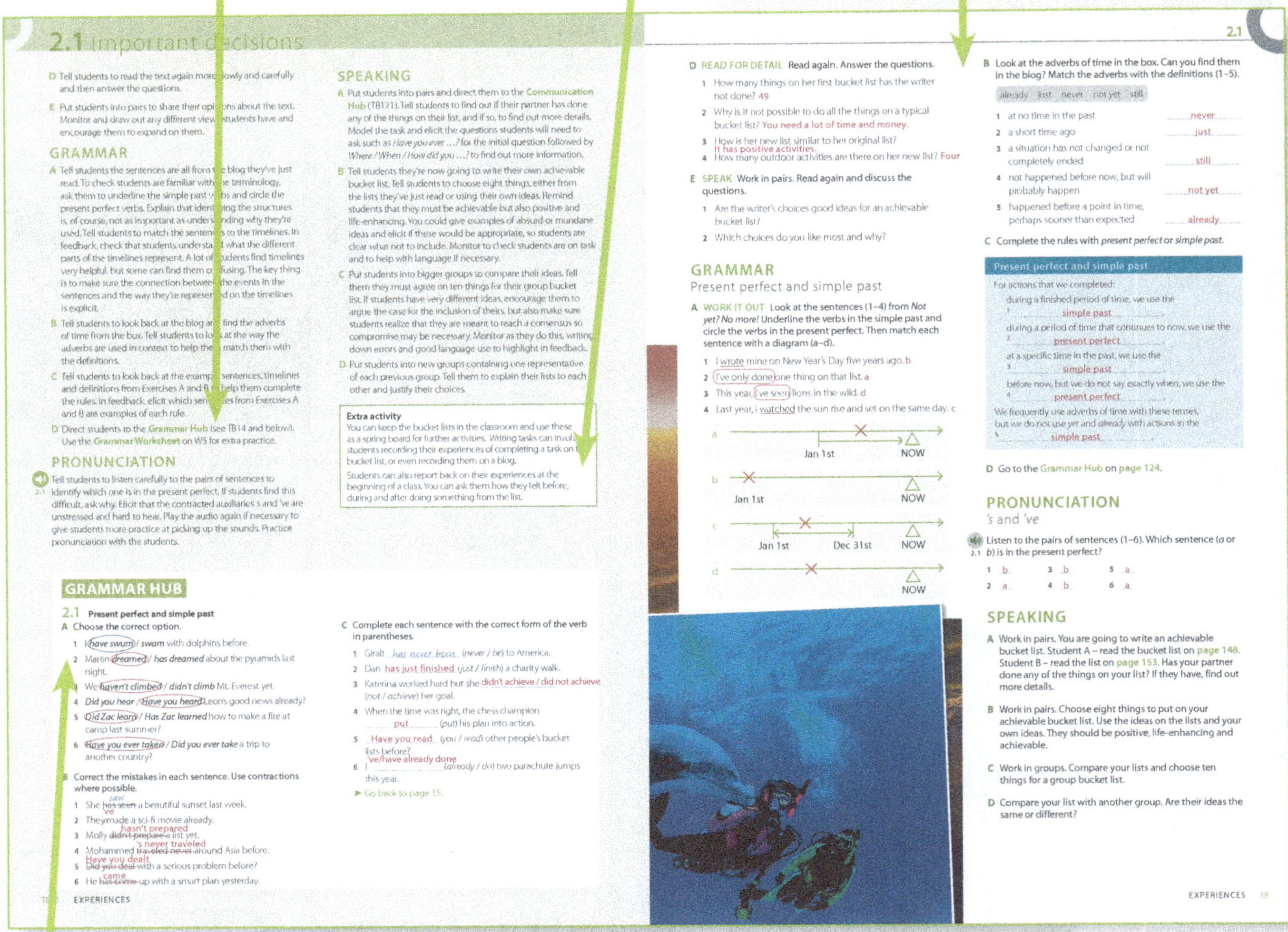

Grammar explanations
Where the Student's Book asks the students to look at the Grammar Hub, the teachers can find this already annotated on the Teacher's Book page. In this way teachers have everything they need at the correct point in the lesson, with the Grammar Hub reference activities from the Student's Book positioned close to the grammar sections they correspond to. This makes it easier for teachers to mark homework in class or refer to succinct grammar explanations.

Annotated answers
The answers to reading and listening exercises are annotated on the interleaved pages of the Student's Book. These provide a quick reference tool for teachers.

Teacher's Book: Macmillan Books for Teachers

Lead-in
Suggested lead-ins can be used to activate prior knowledge, generate interest in the lesson topic or focus on useful lexis.

Procedural notes
The lessons include procedural notes for teachers. These offer support to teachers on how to deliver the lesson rather than telling them how to teach. The notes are designed to be brief and easy to read.

4.1

READING

A Choose the correct sentence endings.

1 Self-help books …
a contain instructions for doing something, especially operating a machine.
(b) are designed to help you solve your own problems or improve your life.

2 Self-help books are usually written in …
a a formal style that is for experts only.
(b) an informal style for anyone.

B SCAN Read *Life Cycle* quickly. Match the phrases (1–5) with the topics (a–e).

1 Helena Schneiderlin — a a journey
2 *Life Cycle* — b the author's next book
3 Paris to Moscow — c the author's passion
4 cycling — d the author
5 *Inner Pedal Power* — e the author's first book

Life Cycle: How to find what you love and love what you find

About this book

Ex B Ten years ago, Helena Schneiderlin was a hard-working mom with no time for herself. Like many people, she didn't know what Ex B she really wanted to do with her life. Today, Schneiderlin is a cyclist who is well known for going on long and difficult journeys. Ex B She has ridden from Paris to Moscow by herself. She has also ridden across Australia, and last year she rode from the bottom of South America to the top.

Thanks to her cycling experiences, and the effect they have had on her life, Schneiderlin has also become a leading lifestyle expert. Her talks have been watched millions of times online, and she is regularly asked to speak at international lifestyle events and conferences.

Ex B In *Life Cycle*, which is her first book, she Ex B describes how finding her true passion changed her life, and explains how you can find yours.

'This isn't a book about cycling,' says Ex A Q1 Schneiderlin. 'It's a book about finding the thing that you enjoy doing most, and helping to make that thing benefit all other areas of your life.'

In *Life Cycle*, Schneiderlin uses her own story as an example for others to follow. She describes how she found her passion for cycling while on vacation with her family, and what it has taught her about commitment, sacrifice and success. She provides valuable advice and life Ex A Q2 lessons that apply to all of us, including chapters on getting rid of the things in life that aren't helping, and how to identify the things that make you feel better about yourself.

Schneiderlin says:

"I believe that everyone has a passion, but they may not know what it is. I also believe that when you find that passion, you should use it to improve every area of your life. In my case, it was cycling – but it could have been anything. What's important is finding the thing that you love, and then using it in the right way."

40 CHANGE

4.1 Personal change

READING

A With books closed, write the word *self-help book* on the board with some of the letters missing and replaced by a dash, e.g. *s___ h___ b___*. Explain the concept of a self-help book and try to elicit. To check the understanding of the concept, ask students what type of problems you might buy a self-help book to help with. Tell students to open their books and answer the questions.

B Tell students they're going to read about a self-help book. Tell them to look at the images and to predict what they think the book will be about. Elicit some predictions, then tell students to scan the text to match the phrases with the topics. Explain that scanning means reading quickly to find specific information, so students don't need to worry about unknown vocabulary to do this.

C Point out the strategies for summarizing in the box and make sure they understand the purpose of a summary. Tell students to read the two summaries and choose which is best and why, thinking about the summarizing strategies as they do this. Let students compare answers in pairs before checking answers as a whole class. Ask students to justify their choice with reference to the strategies.

1 repeats too many details, and some phrases are copied word for word. It doesn't give a clear overview of all of the information in the description.
2 is the best summary. It mentions all of the most important pieces of information from the book description but it doesn't copy the description word for word.

D Tell students to discuss with a partner whether or not they would like to read *Life Cycle* and why. Discuss as a whole class and ask if students have ever read any similar books to this. If they have, what did they think of them and would they recommend them.

TEACHING IDEA by David Seymour and Maria Popova

Topic: Hobbies

Use this activity to extend the topic.

(Arrange the students so that they are standing/sitting in a circle. Stand in the middle. Ask each of these questions to individual students at random. After they answer it, tell them to repeat the question to the next student and write a note of the student's answer. Indicate that they should continue the chain so the question progresses around the class. Meanwhile, introduce the other questions so that in the end there are a lot of questions moving around the class.)

What sports do you play, if any? How much time do you spend watching TV? Do you have a hobby? What hobby would you like to take up? What do you do on Sunday afternoons? How much free time do you have? What do you read for enjoyment? What hobbies did you use to have as a child? When did you last go to the beach and where was it located? What are the main recreational activities in your family?

Turn your notes into full sentences, e.g. *Maria wants to take up hang gliding.*

In small groups, discuss these questions.

What are the main recreational activities in the US/UK and in your country? What about other countries? What do you understand by the expressions quality time, work ethic and free time? How much quality time do you get? What do you think is the right balance between work and play?

TEACHING IDEA by David Seymour and Maria Popova

Topic: Free-time survey

Use this activity to extend the topic.

In small groups, find out who:

- watches TV the most
- has the most interesting hobby
- has had the most hobbies
- has been a collector of something

METHODOLOGY HUB by Jim Scrivener

The importance of skills work

Don't underestimate the importance of skills work. Not every lesson needs to teach new words or new grammar. Lessons also need to be planned to give students opportunities to practice and improve their language skills. Skills work is not something to add in at the end of a five-year course in English. There is no need to wait for extensive knowledge before daring to embark on listening, reading and speaking work. On the contrary, it is something so essential that it needs to be at the heart of a course from the start. Even a beginner with one day's English will be able to practice speaking and listening usefully.

CHANGE TB40

Teaching Idea
Tips and ideas from the *Macmillan's Books for Teachers* series are included in the teacher's notes to give some new ideas for instant communicative activities in the lesson. These can usually be used without paper preparation as warm-ups to get the class moving or as a flexible stage where there is time to fill.

Methodology Hub
Ideas for professional development from Jim Scrivener's *Learning Teaching, Third Edition* are presented in every unit to help new teachers pick up helpful tips to add to their repertoire or just reflect on a new way to use American Language Hub with their class.

Teacher's App

The American Language Hub Teacher's Book comes with a Teacher's App, which gives access to the Resource Center, Test Generator and Classroom Presentation Kit.

The Classroom Presentation Kit is designed to be displayed on an interactive whiteboard (IWB) or using a projector, it enables teachers to play video and audio or show interactive activities in class. It is not only user-friendly for the teacher but also for the student, with activities being clearly visible for the whole class. Answer-by-answer reveal enables teachers to elicit student responses and check answers one by one.

Tools

Embedded tools make it possible to highlight and annotate texts to prompt noticing or self-correction. Teachers have the option to turn on an audio script, which is timed to sync with the dialogue, when listening to audio.

Teachers can zoom into each activity with one click. Then they can either move smoothly through the activities or zoom out to see the whole page. They can also create a whiteboard area for additional notes.

Video

Teachers can also access the video and audio for the course, including the authentic video from *The Guardian*.

Homework

The app allows teachers to assign homework directly to their students' devices and alert them when they have activities to complete.

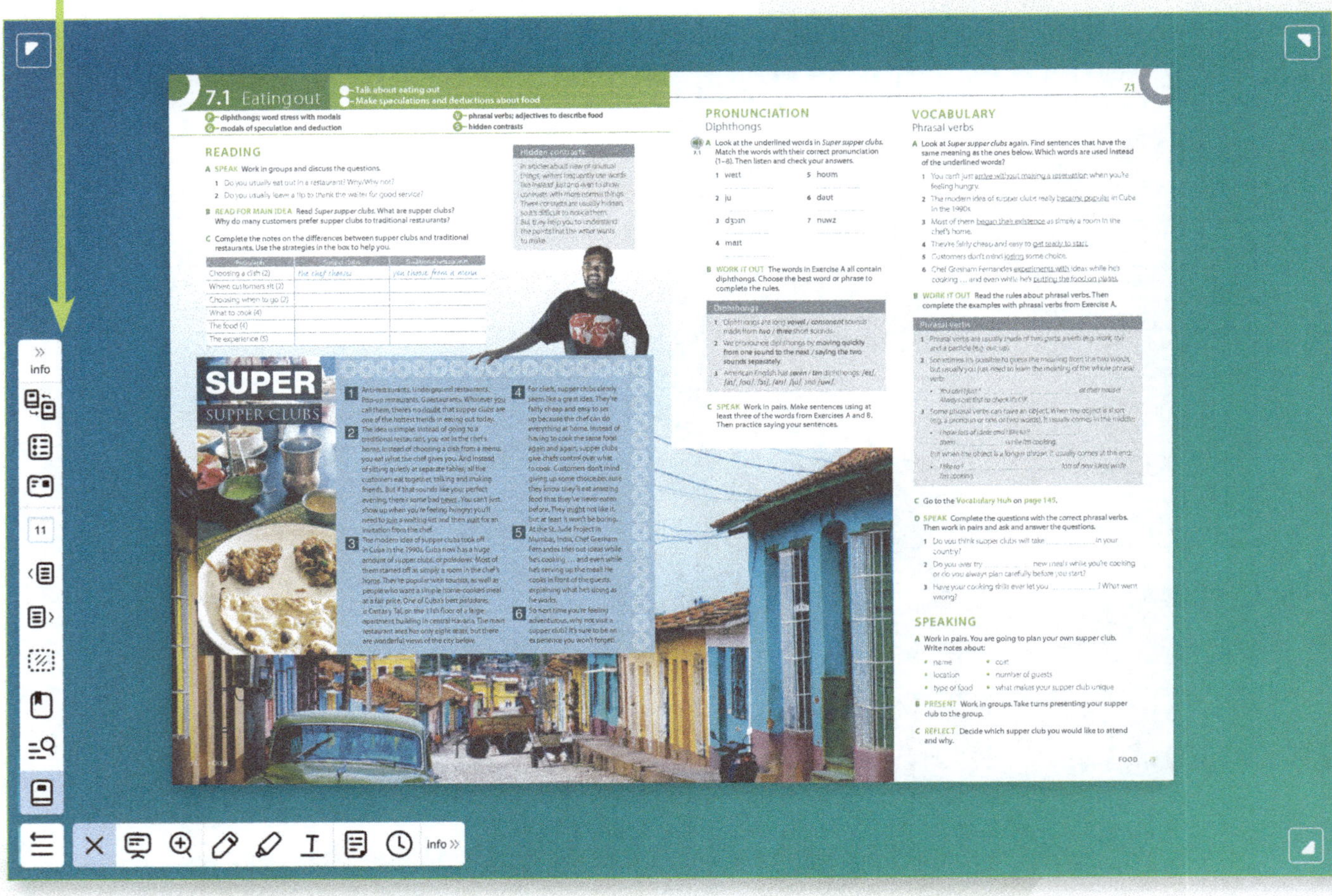

Preparation and Practice

Teachers can also configure student preparation and practice using the Teacher's App. Using the practice activities available, teachers can select and publish content to their students which they will receive through a push notification when they access their app. This enables teachers to personalize the amount and type of practice students do every week and to track their progress. Students can practice the grammar or vocabulary for the week before they go to class, allowing more time in the class for communication.

Test Generator

The Teacher's App also gives access to the Test Generator. In the Test Generator, teachers can create tests or use the pre-built tests for each level of the course and print these to assign to students. There are unit tests, mid- and end-of-course tests for each level, testing vocabulary, grammar and the four skills.

Student's App

Each Student's Book includes a code for the Student's App, to engage and encourage your students to practice their English on the move. Students can access grammar, vocabulary and pronunciation activities to prepare them for the lesson. Students are able to complete activities with varying levels of challenge and earn medals.

Preparation
Allows more time for communicative activities in the class by providing pre-lesson exposure to the language covered in the Student's Book.

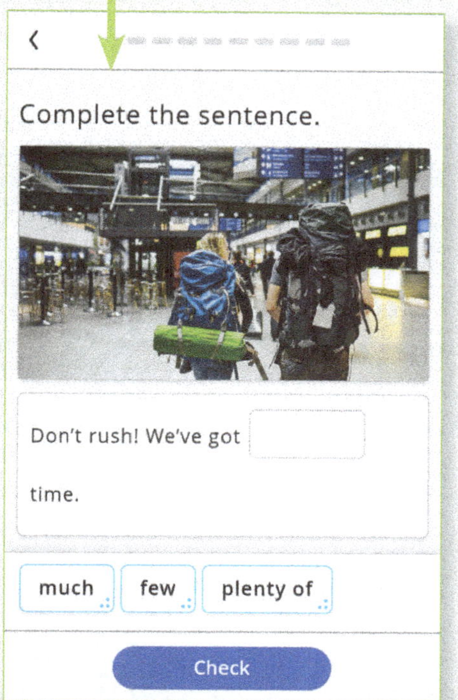

Practice
Provides additional practice to consolidate, review and extend areas covered in the Student's Book.

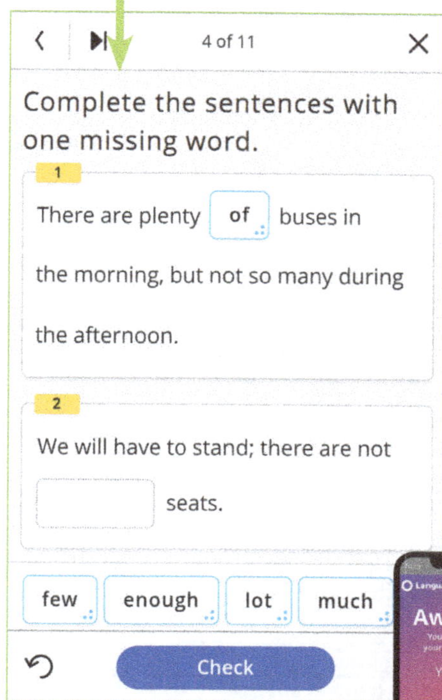

Rewards
A reward system helps to maintain student motivation.

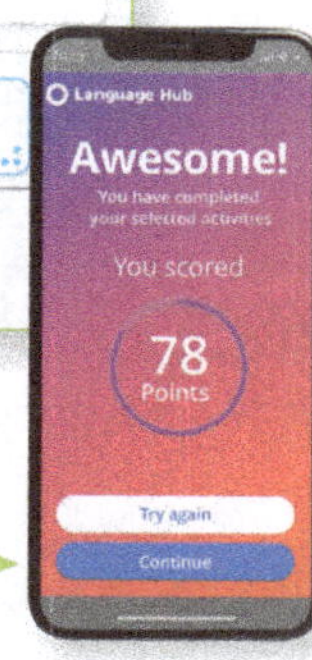

Video

Two types of video are available with the course. Café Hub is a situation comedy which models functional language. Video Hub uses content from *The Guardian* as a resource for authentic English. All the videos from the course relate to the unit topics, and offer listening practice and scaffolding for speaking output.

Video Hub

Café Hub

Contents

Welcome

GRAMMAR

Verb tenses and structures

A Choose the correct verb forms to complete the conversation.

A: Excuse me. I [1]*look* / *'m looking* for room 14. I have an English class today, but I [2]*don't know* / *'m not knowing* where to go.

B: Room 14? It's right here. It looks like we're [3]*being* / *going to be* in the same group. My name's Diego, by the way.

A: Hi, Diego. I'm Yulia. So [4]*did* / *have* you studied at this school before?

B: Yes. I [5]*was* / *'ve been* in the same group last year. The teacher, Helena, is really nice. [6]*You* / *You'll* like her, I'm sure. So … why [7]*did you decide* / *were you deciding* to join this school, Yulia?

A: Well, about two weeks ago, I [8]*'ve tried* / *was trying* to help my son with his English homework, but I couldn't remember anything! So I decided to come back to school, after all these years!

B Find and correct the mistakes in the sentences or questions. The first one has been completed as an example.

1 How ~~many~~ *much* time do you spend doing homework every day?

2 It's an online course, so all the answers are check(ed) by a computer.

3 Everybody make(s) mistakes when they speak English – even English speakers!

4 It's important to learn a lot of new words, but I don't really enjoy ~~to~~ study(ing) vocabulary.

C SPEAK Work in pairs and discuss the questions.

1 Why did you decide to join this class? Use the ideas from the conversation in Exercise A to help you.

2 What is the best way to learn English? Use the ideas in Exercise B to help you.

VOCABULARY

Describing places, illnesses and transportation

A Complete the table with the words in the box.

attractive bus ~~cold~~ ~~dirty~~ headache helicopter modern noisy ~~plane~~ temperature toothache trolley

Describing places	Illnesses	Transportation
dirty	a *cold*	a *plane*
attractive	a headache	a bus
modern	a temperature	a helicopter
noisy	a toothache	a trolley

Collocations

B Choose the correct words to complete the collocations.

1 Is it better if somebody helps you *by* / *for* / *to* / *with* your homework, or should you always work alone?

2 When was the last time you *did* / *made* / *took* / *went* a day off from school or work?

3 Are you good *at* / *in* / *from* / *on* cooking?

4 Is it better to *borrow* / *earn* / *lend* / *pay* money from your friends or from the bank?

5 Is it possible to *have* / *stay* / *make* / *play* in shape without spending a lot of time or money?

6 Do you prefer to pay *by* / *on* / *for* / *with* your shopping by card or in cash?

7 What is the best way to *fall* / *get* / *meet* / *win* a good job in your country?

C SPEAK Work in pairs. Ask and answer the questions in Exercise B. Ask your partner to explain his/her answers.

A: I think it's better to do your homework with someone.

B: Really? Why do you think so?

PRONUNCIATION

0.1 **Listen and choose the words you hear.**

1 *where* / *were*
2 *can* / *can't*
3 *work* / *walk*
4 *mouth* / *mouse*
5 *have* / *of*
6 *this* / *these*
7 *cap* / *cup*

FUNCTIONAL LANGUAGE

Match the sentences (1–9) with the responses (a–i).

1 My name's Adam, by the way.
2 What a nice surprise. Long time, no see!
3 What do you think I should do?
4 Would you like me to check it for you?
5 Are you doing anything this evening?
6 Do you feel like watching a movie this weekend?
7 I feel really sick today … and I have an exam later.
8 In my opinion, young people these days are incredibly rude.
9 It was really nice to see you again.

a Why don't you try to find a new job?
b Sounds great. I'll just check that I'm free.
c You, too. See you later. Take care.
d Nice to meet you.
e Some are, but then some adults are, too.
f No. Why? Should we go out?
g Oh, no! Poor you! That sounds terrible.
h Yeah, I know! What are you doing these days?
i Yes, please. That would be really helpful.

A young woman enjoys her walk outdoors.

Communication (n) the process of giving information or of making emotions or ideas known to someone. Synonyms: interaction (n), contact (n)

Plato means that people should more carefully consider what they choose to say and when they say it.

Plato (428–348 BCE) was a classical Greek philosopher. He was the founder of the Academy in Athens, which was the first higher-learning institution in the Western world.

OBJECTIVES

- update your status on social media
- make a short podcast
- plan and conduct an interview
- use rhetorical questions in a presentation
- ask for, offer and respond to help
- write a report about trends

Work with a partner. Discuss the questions.

1 How does 21st century technology make it easier or harder to communicate with other people?

2 Read the quote. To what extent do you agree with Plato?

3 Which forms of communication do you use most often: face-to-face or electronic; written or spoken communication? Which do you prefer and why?

COMMUNICATION 1

OBJECTIVES

Read the unit objectives to the class.

UNIT OPENER QUESTIONS

1 Focus students' attention on the picture to engage them in the topic and help generate ideas. Elicit one way in which 21st century technology makes it easier to communicate with other people and one way in which it makes 'real' communication harder. Put students into pairs to think of more ways before whole-class feedback.

2 Put students into pairs and encourage them to explain the meaning of the quote and to discuss if they agree with it. Ask one or two pairs to share their ideas with the class. Encourage the students to listen to each other and respond with their own ideas and opinions.

3 Elicit examples of the four types of communication mentioned in the question, e.g. instant messaging. Then ask students to discuss the question with their partner. Monitor and record any interesting vocabulary on the board. Give feedback at the end of the activity.

WORKSHEETS

Lesson 1.1 Communication today

Grammar: Simple present and present progressive (W1)

Vocabulary: Seeing and hearing (W2)

Lesson 1.2 Who owns English?

Grammar: Subject and object questions (W3)

Vocabulary: Languages (W4)

1.1 Communication today

- Update your status on social media
- Make a short podcast

G simple present and present progressive **V** seeing and hearing **P** schwa /ə/ **S** listening to check predictions

READING

A SPEAK Work in groups and discuss the questions.

1 Do you ever use social media sites? Which ones?
2 What sort of information do people usually post on social media?

B PREDICT Match the pictures (1–3) with the social media status updates (a–c). How do you think the people in the pictures are feeling? What can you guess about their lives?

a On my way to the top! Looking forward to an amazing view! 2
b Can't believe we're on vacation again! We're having a wonderful time! 3
c Our beautiful new kitchen! Looks good, doesn't it? 1

C READ FOR GIST Read the social media posts quickly to check your predictions from Exercise B. Write about the true stories behind the pictures.

D READ FOR DETAIL Read again and answer the questions.

1 How do Katia and Elisa know each other?
2 Why was Katia confused?
3 When did Katia go to the top of the mountain?
4 How does Katia feel about her new kitchen?
5 How does Katia feel about her 'boring' life?
6 Why doesn't Elisa post pictures when she isn't on vacation?

1

My *perfect* online life

@Katia … is feeling confused
6 hours ago

Had a very strange experience today. I met my old school friend **@Elisa** for the first time in eight years. 'You're so lucky!' she said. 'You have such a perfect life! I'm so jealous!' Ex D Q1

A perfect life? Me? I have a very normal life: I get up early every day, take the bus to work, watch TV … and that's all. In fact, Elisa seems to have a perfect life: her pictures always show her wonderful family relaxing in the sunshine on a beautiful beach. Ex D Q2

But now that I'm writing this post, I think I understand what happened: on social media, our lives look perfect, but the reality is very different.

For example, last week I posted a selfie from the top of a mountain. In the picture, you can see I'm smiling. But in fact, I felt absolutely exhausted and just wanted to go home as quickly as possible! But you can't see that in the picture! Ex D Q3

And did you see the picture of our new kitchen a few weeks ago? Well, yes, it's beautiful, but I didn't mention that it took six months to finish. Six months without a kitchen! And it cost us twice as much as we expected, so now we're getting worried about money. But no one ever talks about money problems on social media, do they? Ex D Q4

I'm not complaining, though. I'm very happy with my life! I love being normal … and I don't mind that my life is becoming a little boring! In fact, I'm thinking of staying at home this evening – just me, my husband and a takeout pizza! Perfect! Ex D Q5

Reply from **@Elisa**
4 hours ago

Hey, **@Katia**! Great to see you this morning. I know what you mean about our 'perfect lives'. I guess I need to explain about all those beach pictures. You see, I work really hard all year, and the only time I use social media is when I'm on vacation. That's why I'm sitting on the beach in all my pictures! It usually rains for most of the week we're on vacation, but of course we only take pictures when the sun's shining! Ex E Q6

Glossary

jealous (adj) unhappy because someone has something that you would like or can do something that you would like to do

2

1.1 Communication today

LEAD-IN

With books closed, put students into pairs and give them one minute to list as many means of communication as they can. The pair with the most wins.

READING

A If you ever use social media sites, tell the students which ones and what sort of information you post. If you don't, give an example about someone you know who does use social media. Ask students to do the same in pairs, telling each other about their social media habits and what people generally use social media for. As you monitor, encourage students to expand on their answers to generate plenty of interest in the topic.

B Ask students to look at picture 1 and yell out ideas about the man's feeling and life in general. Then ask students to work with a partner to discuss the other pictures and match them to social media updates. As a whole class, confirm the correct answers to the matching task but don't accept or reject any other predictions at this stage.

C Tell students they can now check their predictions as they read some social media posts by the two women shown in the pictures. Ask students to read and write some notes about the stories behind the pictures. Check with the class to determine which predictions were closest to the truth.

Picture 1: It took six months to finish and cost twice as much money as she expected.
Picture 2: Katia felt exhausted and wanted to go home.
Picture 3: Elisa only goes on vacation for one week per year, and it usually rains for most of the time.

D Tell students to work alone to read the text again to answer questions 1–6. Point out the glossary, with a definition of *jealous*, an important word to understand the text. Allow students to check their answers with a partner before checking as a whole class.

1 They were friends at school, but they last saw each other eight years ago.
2 Because she and Elisa both thought the other one had a perfect life.
3 Last week.
4 It's beautiful, but it caused a lot of problems.
5 She loves it.
6 She's too busy.

E You could tell students about the acronym FOMO (fear of missing out), which is common when discussing this topic. Ask if students have heard of this and if they ever have this feeling. Ask one or two pairs to share what they discussed, then encourage the rest of the class to say whether they have similar or different feelings.

Extra activity
The discussion questions could be used to introduce a short class debate on the theme of social media. For example, does social media make us more or less happy? Divide your class into groups. Ensure that students argue both for and against the motion, even if they aren't adopting their real position. Allow the class time to organize their arguments. Set a time limit on speeches. After the debate, students can vote on the motion.

METHODOLOGY HUB by Jim Scrivener

Activity road map

Here is a basic road map plan for running a simple activity. In some bigger activities, there may be a number of clearly separate 'sections' within the task, in which case you would go through steps 3, 4 and 5 a few times.

1 Before the lesson: Familiarize yourself with the material and activity; prepare any materials or texts you need.
2 In class: Prepare for the activity.
3 Set up the activity (or section of activity), i.e. give instructions, make groupings, etc.
4 Run the activity (or section): Students do the activity, maybe in pairs or small groups while you monitor and help.
5 Close the activity (or section) and invite feedback from the students.
6 Post-activity: Do any appropriate follow up work.

Here is some advice for step 1 in more detail:

1 Before the lesson:

- Familiarize yourself with the material and the activity.
- Read through the material and any teacher's notes.
- Try the activity yourself.
- Imagine how it will look in class.
- Decide how many organizational steps are involved.
- What seating arrangements/rearrangements are needed?
- How long will it probably take?
- Do the learners know enough language to be able to make a useful attempt at the activity?
- What help might they need?
- What questions might they have?
- What errors (using the language) are they likely to make?
- What errors (misunderstanding the task) are they likely to make?
- What will your role be at each stage?
- What instructions are needed?
- How will they be given (explained, read, demonstrated)?
- Prepare any aids or additional material.
- Arrange seating, visual aids, etc.
- Most importantly, you need to think through any potential problems or hiccups in the procedures. For example, what will happen if you plan student work in pairs, but there is an uneven number of students? Will this student work alone, or will you join in, or will you make one of the pairs into a group of three?

1.1 Communication today

GRAMMAR

A Do the first verb together as a class, before students work alone.

Simple present: have, get up, take, watch, seems, show, think, understand, look, talks, love, don't mind, know, mean, guess, need, see, work, use, rains
Present progressive: is feeling, 'm writing, 'm smiling, 're getting, 'm not complaining, is becoming, 'm thinking, 'm sitting, 's shining

B–C Put students into pairs to complete the exercises.

Suggested answers:

Rule 2: *Her pictures always show her wonderful family… / But no one ever talks about money problems…*
Rule 3a: *Katia…is feeling confused / I'm not complaining, though*
Rule 3b: *That's why I'm sitting on the beach in all my pictures! / …we only take pictures when the sun's shining!*
Rule 3c: *My life is becoming a little boring*
Rule 4: *I love being normal…and I don't mind that… / I guess I need to explain …*
Rule 5: *I think I understand what happened / I'm thinking of staying at home this evening …*

D Direct students to the **Grammar Hub** (see below).

E–F Put students into pairs then groups to complete the exercises. Use the **Grammar Worksheet** on W1 for extra practice.

SPEAKING

A Tell students to look on their phones for two or three pictures that might be posted on social media.

B Put students into groups to show their pictures to each other and discuss the questions.

C Monitor as the students are writing, helping if they need vocabulary.

D Either display the students' updates on the walls for students to walk around and read or pass them around so everyone gets a chance to read as many as possible. Tell students to think about whether the updates make their classmates' lives seem perfect or normal. In feedback, ask a few students to tell you which updates they found particularly interesting and why.

GRAMMAR HUB

1.1 Simple present and present progressive

	Positive	Negative	Question
Simple present	**He gets up** early.	**It doesn't look** good.	**Do you take** the bus?
Present progressive	**I'm taking** a selfie.	**She isn't watching** TV. **She's not watching** TV.	**Are they smiling**?

- We use the simple present to talk about actions that always/usually/never happen.
  I don't always get up early.
- We use the present progressive to talk about actions that are in progress at the moment of speaking or writing.
  They aren't working this week.
- We also use the present progressive to describe actions in a photo or video.
  What is he doing in this photo?
- We also use the present progressive to describe trends.
  More and more people are getting worried about money.
- We use the simple present, not the present progressive, to talk about our everyday routines.
  Do you write many emails at work?
  NOT ~~Are you writing many emails at work?~~
- We usually use these adverbs of frequency with the simple present: *always, never, rarely, sometimes, usually.*
  *Do you **usually** post photos of yourself on social media?*
- We use stative verbs to describe feelings and ideas. We use the simple present (not the present progressive) with stative verbs.
  *I **love** taking selfies!*
- Some verbs (e.g. *have, look, speak, think*) can be used as both dynamic and stative verbs, depending on the situation.
  *have: She **has** a perfect life. / Are you **having** fun?*
  *look: Your new kitchen **looks** really good! / I'm **looking** for a new job.*

1.1 Simple present and present progressive

A Choose the correct option.

1 Sarah *is showing* / *shows* me her vacation photos. They're amazing!
2 *Are they working* / *Do they work* today?
3 *Are you always getting up* / *Do you always get up* early on weekdays?
4 They *are relaxing* / *relax* on the beach in this picture.
5 We *are not usually* / *don't usually* watch TV but this show is really good!
6 I *am becoming* / *become* more worried about my social media posts.

B Complete the email with the correct form of the verb in parentheses. Use contractions where possible.

Hi Sarah!

We [1] 're having (*have*) a great time here in Spain! The sun [2] 's shining (*shine*) and the country is beautiful. We [3] have (*have*) a nice room in a little hotel with a view of the beach. I [4] 'm sitting (*sit*) on the balcony to write this email and I can see Paul down on the beach. He [5] 's playing (*play*) soccer with the boys on the sand. The children [6] like (*like*) it here – they say they [7] don't want (*not want*) to go home! Hope you [8] aren't working (*not work*) too hard!

See you next week!

Love, Mary

➤ Go back to page 3.

E SPEAK Work in pairs and discuss the questions.

1 Does your life look perfect on social media? What about your friends' lives?

2 Do you ever feel jealous when you see other people's status updates?

GRAMMAR

Simple present and present progressive

A Look at the underlined verbs in the social media posts. Which verbs are in the simple present? Which are in the present progressive?

B WORK IT OUT Match the sentences (a–f) with the rules (2–5).

a In the picture, you can see I'm smiling. rule 3 b

b I know what you mean about our 'perfect lives'. rule 4

c But now I'm writing this post, … rule 3 a

d You have such a perfect life! rule 5

e I get up early every day. rule 2

f So now we're getting worried about money. rule 3 c

Simple present and present progressive

1 Dynamic verbs (*talk*, *go*) usually describe actions.

2 We use the simple present with dynamic verbs to talk about actions that always, usually or never happen.

3 We use the present progressive with dynamic verbs:

a to talk about actions that are in progress at the moment of speaking or writing.

b to describe actions in a picture, video, etc.

c to describe trends (e.g. something is happening more and more these days).

4 Stative verbs (*want*, *seem*) frequently describe feelings and ideas. We use the simple present with stative verbs.

5 A few verbs (*have*, *look*, *speak*, *think*) have two or more meanings. They are sometimes dynamic verbs and sometimes stative verbs.

C Find at least one more example of each rule (2–5) in the posts.

D Go to the Grammar Hub on page 122.

E Are the verbs stative verbs (S) or dynamic verbs (D)?

1	contain	S	7	include	S
2	cost	S	8	mean	S
3	depend	S	9	own	S
4	deserve	S	10	relax	D
5	enjoy	D	11	seem	S
6	happen	D	12	shine	D

F SPEAK Work in groups and discuss the questions.

1 Why are you studying English? Why do you need English?

2 How is this week different from your normal weekly routine? What are you doing differently this week? What do you normally do?

3 What are people doing more and more these days? What are some trends in your own life?

SPEAKING

A Work in groups. If you have some pictures on your phone, choose two or three to discuss with your group. If you do not, think about some of your favorite pictures of you and your friends or family.

B Tell your group:

- What's happening in the pictures?
- Does your life seem perfect or exciting in the pictures? What's the real story behind the pictures?
- Do you have any pictures of you doing normal things, e.g. watching TV? Why/Why not?

C Write a short social media status update for one or two of your pictures. Decide whether to make your life seem perfect or normal.

Writing a status

We frequently leave out the subject and *be* from the beginning of status updates when it's easy for the reader to guess the missing words.

- *(It) Looks good, doesn't it?*
- *(I) Had a very strange experience today.*
- *(It was) Great to see you this morning.*

D Read some of your classmates' social media status updates. Do their lives look perfect or normal?

LISTENING

A SPEAK Work in pairs and discuss the questions.

1 What do you use your cell phone for?

2 How did people do those things before they had cell phones? What problems did they have?

B PREDICT Work in pairs. You are going to listen to *A week without phones!* Look at the pictures and discuss the questions. Use the strategies in the box to help you.

> **Listening to check predictions**
>
> Before you listen to something in English, it's always a good idea to predict what you will hear.
>
> If there's a title and pictures, you can try to predict the connection between them. Then you can listen to check your predictions.

1 Who are the people in picture a? What are they doing? brother and sister; making a podcast

2 What is the device in picture b? a voice recorder

3 What does the title mean? What's the connection with the people and the device? a week without using their cell phones, making a podcast about it

1.1 **C LISTEN FOR GIST** Listen to Part 1 of the podcast and check your answers to Exercise B.

1.2 **D PREDICT** Work in pairs and discuss the questions. Then listen to Part 2 and check your answers.

1 What went wrong when Olivia and Jackson tried to meet up on Monday? Jackson couldn't find Olivia because he usually uses his phone to get to places.

2 How did they solve the problem? Someone helped him and told him where Olivia was.

1.3 **E PREDICT** Work in pairs and discuss what you think Olivia and Jackson did differently on Tuesday when they met. Then listen to Part 3 and check your answer. Arranged a plan B: what to do if something goes wrong; Jackson wore a watch; Jackson checked a map before he left.

1.4 **F PREDICT** Work in pairs and discuss the questions. Then listen to Part 4 and check your answers.

1 Do you think Olivia and Jackson are enjoying the experiment? Yes

2 What do you think they're doing more or less of than usual? Looking around and thinking about their surroundings

1.5 **G LISTEN FOR DETAIL** Listen again. Choose the correct answers, a, b or c.

1 When is the last day of the experiment?
- a Tuesday
- b Thursday
- (c) Sunday

2 Why does Olivia decide to stop waiting outside on Monday?
- (a) She doesn't want to get wet.
- b She thinks Jackson isn't coming.
- c She knows the university closes at four o'clock.

3 How does Sebastian know Jackson and Olivia?
- a They study together at the university.
- b Olivia met Sebastian outside the bakery.
- (c) Sebastian has seen them before in pictures and videos.

4 Why is Olivia enjoying the concert more than usual on Tuesday?
- (a) She isn't recording it on her phone.
- b The audience isn't having as much fun.
- c Jackson isn't there with her.

5 On Thursday, why is Olivia surprised at the end of the podcast?
- a The university buildings are amazing.
- (b) Jackson doesn't usually talk so much.
- c She can't believe Jackson forgot his camera.

H SPEAK Work in groups and discuss the questions.

1 What problems did Olivia and Jackson have during the experiment?

2 What good things happened as a result?

3 Do you think Olivia and Jackson's experiment was a good idea?

4 Would you like to try a similar experiment? Why/Why not?

1.1 Communication today

LISTENING

A Put students into pairs to discuss the questions.

B Ask them to look at the strategies in the *Listening to check predictions* box. Put students into pairs to discuss the questions. Get feedback but don't confirm or deny anything yet.

C–H 1.1–1.5 Put students into pairs to make predictions and discuss questions. Allow them enough time to make predictions before playing tracks. Also for the last stage, ensure they have shared some ideas in pairs before opening up to a wider class discussion.

AUDIO SCRIPT

1.1

Listening, Exercise C
J = Jackson O = Olivia

J: Hello. Welcome to the Tec-cast. I'm Jackson, and this is my big sister, Olivia.

O: Hello. In this week's podcast, we're looking at phones. Or rather, we're not looking at our phones for a whole week!

Ex G Q1 **J:** Yes, that's right. Our experiment runs for seven days. We started on Monday and today's Thursday, so we're halfway through it.

O: Exactly. And instead of our phones, we're both carrying around one of these voice recorders all week, so we can record our experiences. And it's been an interesting week! I arranged to meet Jackson outside the university on Monday afternoon, but it didn't really work, did it, Jackson?

J: Uh, no. Sorry. Let's listen to our recordings from earlier in the week.

1.2

Listening, Exercise D
J = Jackson O = Olivia S = Sebastian

O: Hi. Olivia here. It's 4:20 on Monday afternoon and I'm waiting for Jackson. We arranged to meet here, outside the university, at four o'clock, but I can't see him and it's starting to rain. So it looks like he isn't coming and I'm not sure what to do. Hmm, I can't call him because I don't have my phone. (Ex G Q2) OK, I know. I'll go and wait in that bakery over there – at least I'll stay dry, and I'll be able to see Jackson through the window when he arrives.

Ex D Q1 **J:** Hi. This is Jackson. It's Monday afternoon and I'm late meeting Olivia. I think. I don't actually know the time because I never wear a watch; I always use the clock on my phone. Anyway, I missed my bus and I couldn't check the time of the next one – the timetables are all online now. So I decided to walk. But then I got lost because I didn't have a map – I usually use the map on my phone! And I couldn't call Olivia to tell her I'd be late. And now it's raining! OK, so I'm just arriving at the university now and I'm looking for Olivia, but I can't see her. Hmm, now I don't know what to do.

S: Excuse me. Are you looking for Olivia?

J: Uh, yes. Why?

S: Hi. I'm Sebastian. I'm a student here at the university. (Ex G Q3) I listen to your podcast every week, and I watch all your videos. I love them!

J: Really? Wow! Thanks. Uh … but how do you know I'm looking for Olivia?

Ex D Q2 **S:** I spotted her here a few minutes ago. I recognized her from your videos. She went into that bakery over there.

J: Oh, excellent. Thank you so much. Look, do you want to come and join us? I'll buy you a cupcake to say thank you, and you can tell us what you think of our podcasts.

S: Yeah, that sounds like a great idea. Thanks a lot.

1.3

Listening, Exercise E
J = Jackson O = Olivia

O: Hi. Me again. It's eleven fifteen on Tuesday morning, and yes, I'm waiting for Jackson, again. He's 15 minutes late, again, but it's OK because (Ex E) we arranged a plan B: what to do if something goes wrong. So I'm enjoying a nice outdoor concert in the park right now, by a really cool band. Maybe you can hear the music in the background. Our new friend Sebastian told us about the concert yesterday – he plays the guitar in the band, and he sounds really good. It's strange because all the other people in the audience are filming the concert on their cell phones, but I think they're missing half the fun! (Ex F Q1, Ex G Q4) I'm just listening and enjoying it – and it's much better. In fact, I think I'll stop recording now so I can listen!

J: Hi. It's Tuesday morning, and I'm late for a meeting with Olivia, again, but it's OK because we discussed where she'll be at 11, 11:30, 12:00 and 12:30. And yes, (Ex E) I'm wearing a watch today – an old one from when I was a teenager. It doesn't look great, but it's good for telling (Ex E) the time! Anyway, today, I decided to walk the same way I came yesterday – so I checked a map before I left home! I wanted to come back to this part of town because I noticed that the buildings are really beautiful and interesting. I don't normally look at the buildings around me – I usually just stare at my phone. (Ex F Q2) But it's really nice to look around and think about where I am and … how to get to the park from here. So I'm not exactly lost again; I'm just exploring the city a little more than usual.

1.4

Listening, Exercise F
J = Jackson O = Olivia

O: Hello again. So, as I said, it's now Thursday, and we're halfway through our experiment. How's it going for you, Jackson?

J: Surprisingly well! I mean, I think I'm seeing a lot more than usual – now I'm looking at the real world, not my phone all the time.

O: Yeah, me too. I really enjoyed observing all the people outside the university on Monday! So what about those amazing buildings? Did you take any pictures?

J: Uh, no. Because I didn't have my phone! But I can tell you about them, if you want.

Ex G Q5 **O:** Wow! You usually just show me your pictures. You see! We're talking more than before, too! Our experiment is working! So tell me about those buildings!

1.1 Communication today

VOCABULARY

1.6 **A** Tell students that all the sentences come from the podcasts they listened to earlier. Students first try to choose the correct verb before listening to check. Get feedback, but don't explain why any of the answers are correct or incorrect yet.

B Ask the class whether the eyes or the ears are used for each of the words, e.g. *hear* = *ears*. Students then use the symbols to work out the rules. As you monitor, direct them to the sentences in Exercise A to help them if necessary. Check answers with the class.

C Direct students to the **Vocabulary Hub** (TB121) for further practice of verbs of seeing and hearing. Allow time for students to compare answers in pairs before checking each exercise.

D Tell students to complete the questions with the verbs in the box. In feedback, check that students fully understand the meaning of the verbs and the differences between them.

E Put students into groups to discuss the questions. Get feedback from one or two students about the most interesting things they talked about. Use the **Vocabulary Worksheet** on W2 for extra practice.

PRONUNCIATION

1.7 **A** Focus students' attention on the information about the schwa, the most common sound in English. Model the sound so students know what it is, then tell them to listen and underline the schwas they hear in the sentences from the podcast.

B Tell students to practice saying the sentences in pairs. Encourage them to check and correct each other's use of the schwa. Join in yourself and make this light-hearted and fun. Point out how using the schwa is a very effective way to sound more natural, and therefore be more easily understood.

SPEAKING HUB

A Tell students that they're going to make a short podcast. Put students into small groups of three or four and tell them to choose one of the ideas in the box or to think of one of their own.

B Give the groups time to plan their podcasts. Encourage students to write notes, but not to write out the whole podcast word for word. Monitor and help with vocabulary and pronunciation as they do this.

C Students can either record their podcast and play it to the class or present it live. Encourage students to listen carefully to the other podcasts and think about whether they would like to try any of the experiments.

D Put students into groups to discuss the questions. Call on each group to say what they discussed and encourage other students to comment on what the group says.

E Put students into new groups to discuss what experiments they would like to try and whether they would want to make a real podcast.

Extra activity

You could encourage students to complete their experiment outside class. Before they start, students can make predictions about the outcomes of their experiments. Help students plan how they will carry the experiments out. Will they use a smartphone or voice recorder to record their impressions? Or will they keep a diary of their experiment?

After their experiment, students can reflect on whether their predictions came true and what they have learned from doing it. Finally, students can report back to the rest of their class about their experiment.

TEACHING IDEA by David Seymour and Maria Popova

Topic: Bare necessities

Use this activity to review the topic.

In pairs, brainstorm a list of the 20 most important things that you need on a day-to-day basis and put them in order from most to least important. See how your list and order compare with another pair.

What is the bare minimum that a person needs to survive? List a few other things that people say they need but might not in fact be necessary.

TEACHING IDEA by David Seymour and Maria Popova

Topic: World needs

Use this activity to review the topic.

Work in small groups and write five ideas under each of these headings:

- what the world needs now
- what things need doing to improve this town/country
- what people need in order to live in harmony

Discuss how the needs of different countries compare.

METHODOLOGY HUB by Jim Scrivener

Language skills

As well as working with the language systems (which we can think of as what we know, i.e. 'up-in-the-head' knowledge), we also need to pay attention to what we do with language. These are the language skills. Teachers normally think of there being four important macro language skills: listening, speaking, reading, writing. Listening and reading are called **receptive skills** (the reader or listener receives information but does not produce it); speaking and writing, on the other hand, are the **productive skills**. Skills are commonly used interactively and in combination rather than in isolation, especially speaking and listening. It's arguable that other things (e.g. thinking, using memory and mediating) are also language skills.

VOCABULARY
Seeing and hearing

A **Choose the correct verbs to complete the sentences from *A week without phones!* Then listen again and check your answers.** 1.6

1 In this week's podcast, we're ***looking at*** / *seeing* / *watching* phones.

2 It ***looks*** / *sees* / *watches* like he isn't coming, and I'm not sure what to do.

3 I'm ***looking*** / *seeing* / *watching* for Olivia, but I can't *look at* / ***see*** / *watch* her.

4 I *hear* / ***listen to*** / *sound* your podcast every week, and I *look at* / *see* / ***watch*** all your videos.

5 Yeah, that *hears* / *listens* / ***sounds*** like a great idea. Thanks a lot.

6 Maybe you can ***hear*** / *listen to* / *sound* the music in the background.

7 He plays the guitar in the band, and he *hears* / *listens* / ***sounds*** really good.

8 It doesn't ***look*** / *see* / *watch* great, but it's good for telling the time!

B WORK IT OUT **Complete the rules with the correct form of *hear, listen, look, see, sound* or *watch*.**

hear, listen, look, see, sound* and *watch

1 When you (eye) ___see___ or (ear) ___hear___ something, it just happens, not because you're trying to do it.

2 When you (eye) ___look___ *at* or (ear) ___listen___ *to* something, you do it because you decide to do it.

3 When you (eye) ___watch___ something, you look at it for a period of time, perhaps because it's moving.

4 When something (eye) ___looks___ good or (ear) ___sounds___ good, it probably is good, but you aren't sure.

5 When it (eye) ___looks___ like or (ear) ___sounds___ like something is happening, it probably is happening, but you aren't sure.

C **Go to the Vocabulary Hub on page 142.**

D **Complete the questions with the verbs in the box. There are two extra verbs.**

notice observe recognize spot stare

1 Do you ever sit in a café and ___observe___ the people through the window? Why do people enjoy doing this?

2 Are you good at remembering people's faces? Do you always ___recognize___ people when you meet them the second time?

3 When you're traveling around (e.g. by bus), do you usually ___notice___ the buildings around you?

E SPEAK **Work in groups. Ask and answer the questions in Exercise D.**

PRONUNCIATION
Schwa /ə/

Schwa /ə/

Schwa is the most common sound in English. We use it for most unstressed vowel sounds, especially in words like *a, the, of, to, and* and *but*.

A **Listen to the sentences from *A week without phones!* Underline all schwas. The numbers in parentheses tell you how many schwas to find. The first one has been done for you.** 1.7

1 We're not looking at our phones for a whole week! (3)

2 We arranged to meet here, outside the university, at four o'clock. (5)

3 It's Monday afternoon and I'm late meeting Olivia. (3)

4 I'll buy you a cupcake to say thank you, and you can tell us what you think of our podcasts. (7)

5 Yes, I'm wearing a watch today – an old one from when I was a teenager. (7)

B SPEAK **Work in pairs. Practice saying the sentences. Listen and check your partner's pronunciation.**

SPEAKING HUB

A **Work in groups. You are going to make a short podcast about an experiment. Choose one of the ideas in the box or use your own ideas.**

a week of doing something completely new every day
a week speaking only English
a week without complaining
a week without the internet/TV, etc.
a week without spending any money
a week of helping as many people as possible

B PLAN **Plan a short podcast (about two minutes). Imagine you are in the middle of your experiment. Write notes on:**

- what you can see and hear during your podcast.
- what's going well and/or badly with your experiment.
- what you're doing more or less as a result of your experiment.

C SPEAK **Record your podcast and present it to the class.**

D SHARE **After listening to the podcasts, discuss the questions.**

- Which group's experiment worked well?
- Which podcast did you enjoy most?

E REFLECT **Work in new groups and discuss the questions.**

- Will you try any of the experiments in real life? Why/Why not?
- Would you like to make a real podcast? What would your podcast be about?

— Update your status on social media

— Make a short podcast

1.2 Who owns English?

- Plan and conduct an interview
- Use rhetorical questions in a presentation

G – subject and object questions P – pronouncing questions V – languages S – rhetorical questions

LISTENING

A SPEAK Work in groups and discuss the questions.

1 Look at the infographic. What does it show? What do you know about the countries and the languages that people in those countries speak? Are you surprised by any of the numbers?

2 Who owns English? Who has the power to decide what's good and bad English?

1.8 **B LISTEN FOR MAIN IDEA** Listen to an interview about different types of English and answer the questions.

1 Why does Mona want to interview Juan?

2 Why did Juan enjoy his journey?

3 Where did Juan have problems with English?

4 How is Multicultural London English (MLE) different from the English we learn at school?

5 What's the connection between 'Standard English' and 'standard class' on a train?

6 Why is Standard English useful?

1.8 **C LISTEN FOR DETAIL** Listen again. Which person (Juan, Mona or Both) thinks …

1 traveling is a good way to practice your English? Both

2 it's difficult to understand people in England? Juan

3 MLE grammar contains mistakes? Mona

4 Standard English is boring but useful? Juan

5 it's sometimes better when you don't sound like a native speaker? Both

D SPEAK Work in groups. Look at the sentences from the interview. For each one, discuss what Juan and Mona were talking about. Do you agree with their opinions?

1 'Millions of people speak like that, so how can it be wrong?'

2 'There are hundreds of other forms of English all over the world … They're all different, but I think that's really cool!'

3 'Surely Standard English is better, isn't it?'

4 'We don't need to speak like native speakers. In fact … it's usually better when we don't speak like native speakers.'

1.2 Who owns English?

LEAD-IN

Ask students what they think the top ten English-speaking countries are. Students then open their books to check.

LISTENING

A Tell students to discuss the questions in small groups.

1.8 **B–C** Students can check in pairs before whole-class feedback.

1 *For a blog post. She wants to interview him about his experiences of using English during his trip across Europe.*
2 *He met a lot of great people and had amazing conversations.*
3 *In England*
4 *Mostly pronunciation but also some grammar differences.*
5 *On a train, first class is better than standard class. Juan thinks non-standard English is better (for some purposes) than Standard English.*
6 *Juan thinks it is useful for international communication.*

D Ask for feedback from groups and discuss suggested answers with class.

Suggested answers:

1 *They are discussing MLE. Juan doesn't think the grammar can be wrong as so many people use it.*
2 *They are discussing other non-standard forms of English, such as Jamaican English and Indian English.*
3 *Mona thinks it's better to use Standard English because it's good English.*
4 *Standard English is easier for non-native speakers to understand, so it's better to use this.*

AUDIO SCRIPT

1.8

Listening, Exercise B
M = Mona J = Juan

Ex B Q1 **M:** Hey, Juan. I'm writing a blog post for our website. I thought it might be nice to interview you. Can I ask you a few questions?

J: Yes, of course. Go ahead. But why do you want to talk to me? What do you want to talk about?

Ex B Q1 **M:** Well, I hear you've just returned from a trip across Europe. It'd be nice to hear about your experiences of using English during your trip.

J: Oh, right. Yes, no problem.

M: Great. I'll just turn on my microphone … OK, so thanks, Juan, for agreeing to talk to me today about your recent trip to Europe. Which countries did you visit?

J: Well, I started in Russia, and then I traveled through Belarus, Poland, Germany, the Netherlands and
Ex B Q2 England. It was a long journey, but I met a lot of great people and I had some amazing conversations. It was a good way to practice my English.

M: Yes, I'm sure it was! It sounds like a great way of practising. Was it hard to communicate in English?

J: No, actually I found it really easy to communicate all
Ex B Q3 the way from Russia to the Netherlands. But when I got to England … well, it was terrible!

M: Really? What happened in England?

J: Everybody spoke so fast! And they used really strange words and phrases – lots of idioms that I'd never heard before. Plus, the people had very strong accents, so I couldn't understand very much at all!

M: Oh, no! So what did you do?

J: I just asked people to slow down. 'Can you say that again, please?'; 'Could you speak slowly, please?', and so on!

M: And did that help?

J: Yes. I mean, the people were very nice, and they were happy to talk to me. But they speak very strange English! I guess it's because English is changing all the time.

M: Really? How is English changing? Can you give me an example?

J: Yes, of course. When I was in London, I heard many people speaking a new variety of English called MLE – Multicultural London English. It's becoming extremely popular.

M: Really? I've never heard of it. Who uses MLE?

J: Mostly young people in London.

M: So how is MLE different from normal English?

Ex B Q4 **J:** Well, it's mostly a question of pronunciation. But there are also grammar differences. For example, in MLE, they don't say 'you were'; they say 'you was'. 'I was', 'you was', 'he was', 'she was', 'we was', 'they was'. And then in negative sentences, it's 'I weren't', 'you weren't', 'he weren't', 'she weren't', and so on.

M: What? That's terrible! But isn't that a mistake?

J: Well, it isn't Standard English, of course. But millions of people speak like that, so how can it be wrong?

M: Hmm … what do you mean by 'Standard English'?

J: Well, Standard English is the form they use in books and newspapers. It's a kind of cleaned-up version of English. But it isn't the only form of English, and most native speakers don't speak Standard English – at least, not all the time. There are hundreds of other forms of English all over the world – like Jamaican English, Nigerian English, Indian English and so on. They're all different, but I think that's really cool!

M: OK, but isn't it just a question of good English and bad English? Surely Standard English is better, isn't it?

Ex B Q5 **J:** No. I don't think so. 'Standard' doesn't always mean 'the best'. When I traveled by train across Europe, I went by 'standard class', not 'first class'. And I think Standard English is like 'standard class' in a train: simple and basic, but a little boring. I think non-standard English is much more interesting.

M: So are you saying we need to learn non-standard English?

Ex B Q6 **J:** No, not at all. Standard English is perfect for international communication. As I say, Standard English worked well for me all the way from Russia to the Netherlands. I only had a problem when I got to England. So it depends what you need English for. I think for most learners of English around the world, it's better to learn Standard English. We don't need to speak like native speakers. In fact, as I learned on my trip, it's usually better when we don't speak like native speakers.

M: Wow! Yes, I see what you mean, and I certainly agree with you on that last point. OK, so thanks a lot for that interview, Juan. You've given me a lot to think about … and to write about on the blog.

GRAMMAR

1.9 **A–E** Go to the **Grammar Hub** (see below).

PRONUNCIATION

You can see the *Pronunciation* and *Speaking* activities on TB8.

GRAMMAR HUB

1.2 Subject and object questions

Subject questions		
Question word/ Subject	Main verb	Rest of question
What	is	your first language?

Object questions				
Question word	Auxiliary verb	Subject	Main verb	Rest of question
What	do	you	want	to study?

- We use these question words to ask for information: *who* and *whose* (for people), *where* (for places), *when* (for times), *why* (for reasons), *what* (for things), *which* (for two or more different choices), *how* (for the way something is done) and *how long/many/much*/etc (for time, quantity, etc).

  Whose blog is this?
- We frequently use an auxiliary verb (*be*, *can*, *do* or *have*) to form questions. We put the auxiliary verb before the main verb.

  Are they practicing their English?
  Can I ask you a question?
  *Why **do** you want to learn English?*
  *How long **have** you known Liam?*
- In subject questions, the question word is the subject of the sentence. We use subject questions when we don't know what/who/which/whose something/someone is. We don't use an auxiliary verb in subject questions and we don't change the word order in the answer.

  Who interviewed him? Mona interviewed him.
- In object questions, the question word is the object of the sentence. We use object questions when we want to know more information about something/someone. We always use an auxiliary verb in object questions. In the answer, we use the normal word order for a sentence.

  Where did he learn to speak English?
  NOT ~~Where he learned to speak English?~~
  What do you want to study? I want to study modern languages.
- With subject questions, the answer is the subject.

  Who told you? Someone told you.
- With object questions, the answer is the object.

  Who did you tell? You told someone.
- With questions using *do*, *does* or *did*, we don't change the form of the main verb.

  Does she speak English? NOT ~~Does she speaks English?~~
- When a question word is the object of a preposition, the preposition usually comes at the end of the sentence.

  What did you have problems with?

1.2 Subject and object questions

A Read the answers and write questions. Use the question words in the box.

how what where which who why

1 *Why are you taking an umbrella?* — Because it's raining!
2 Where is your house? — My house is close to the school.
3 What are you watching/doing? — I'm watching the news.
4 How do you get to work? — I get to work by bus.
5 Where do you want to visit? — I want to visit Poland.
6 Who is helping you? / What is David doing? — David is helping me.

B Put the words in order to make questions.

1 you / want / about / to talk / do / what / ?
What do you want to talk about?
2 I / am / pronouncing / right / this word / ?
Am I pronouncing this word right?
3 please / say / you / that again, / can / ?
Can you say that again, please?
4 usually / do / at work / use English / you / ?
Do you usually use English at work?
5 this / phone / whose / is / ?
Whose phone is this?
6 the graph / what / does / show / ?
What does the graph show?
7 you / me / help / this / article / with / can / ?
Can you help me with this article?
8 hours / how / you / English / study / week / do / many / each / ?
How many hours of English do you study each week?

C Correct the mistakes in each question.

1 How long you have your phone?
How long have you had your phone?
2 Where you are working right now?
Where are you working right now?
3 You understand these words?
Do you understand these words?
4 Who laptop is this?
Whose laptop is this?
5 Where you keep your English books?
Where do you keep your English books?
6 How many people do they speak English in the world?
How many people speak English in the world?
7 How long it takes you to get to work?
How long does it take you to get to work?
8 Who you met yesterday?
Who did you meet yesterday?
9 Where they are learning English?
Where are they learning English?
10 Does he uses the app to practice his pronunciation?
Does he use the app to practice his pronunciation?

➤ Go back to page 7.

GRAMMAR
Subject and object questions

1.9 **A** Put the words in the correct order to make questions. Then listen to the interview again and check your answers.

1. you / I / a / questions / ask / can / few / ?
   Can I ask you a few questions?
2. countries / did / which / visit / you / ?
   Which countries did you visit?
3. England / happened / what / in / ?
   What happened in England?
4. changing / English / is / how / ?
   How is English changing?
5. MLE / uses / who / ?
   Who uses MLE?
6. mean / do / 'Standard English' / by / you / what / ?
   What do you mean by 'Standard English'?
7. to / you / need / non-standard English / saying / are / learn / we / so / ?
   So are you saying we need to learn non-standard English?

B WORK IT OUT Match the questions (1–7) in Exercise A with the rules (a–c).

Subject and object questions

- **a** When we make questions in English, we usually put the auxiliary verb (*be*, *have*, *can*) before the subject. 1, 4, 7
- **b** In sentences with no auxiliary verb, we add *do*, *does*, or *did* when we make a question. 2, 6
- **c** When the question is about the subject, we use the same word order as in sentences. We don't add *do*, *does* or *did*. 3, 5

C PRACTICE Make questions about the missing information.

1. (Somebody) writes a blog for a website.
   Who *writes a blog for a website*?
2. Juan visited (a number of countries).
   How many countries did Juan visit?
3. You (can/can't) give me an example.
   Can you give me an example?
4. (A form of English) is becoming popular in London.
   Which form of English is becoming popular in London?
5. (A number of people) speak non-standard English.
   How many people speak non-standard English?
6. Most native speakers (speak/don't speak) Standard English.
   Do most native speakers speak Standard English?

D Go to the Grammar Hub on page 122.

E SPEAK Work in pairs. Student A – go to the Communication Hub on page 149. Student B – go to the Communication Hub on page 150.

PRONUNCIATION
Pronouncing questions

1.10 **A** Listen to two people asking questions from the interview. What differences do you notice in the way they speak? Who is easier to understand?

1. *Why do you want to talk to me?*
2. *What do you want to talk about?*

- **a** Which speaker joined the words together? Speaker 2
- **b** Which speaker is easier to understand? Speaker 1

B SPEAK Work in pairs. Read the information in the box. Then practice saying the questions. First, try to say them by joining the words together. Then try to say them as clearly as possible.

- What do you think?
- Do you want to talk about it?
- Where did you go?
- Why did you say that?

Pronouncing questions

Many English speakers join words together when they speak quickly. In questions with *do/did* + *you*, it can be difficult to hear whether the speaker is saying *do* or *did*.

- *What do you want to do?* /wɒdʒə wɒnə duː/
- *How did you travel?* /haʊdʒə trævəl/

1.11 **C SPEAK** Work in pairs. Listen to two people asking the questions in Exercise B. Which version is better for you to use, the first or the second speaker? Why? Tell your partner.

SPEAKING

A Work in pairs. You are going to interview another student about their experiences of using English and communicating with English speakers. Write five questions. Use the prompts to help you. You can also use your own ideas.

- frequently communicate / English speakers?
- using English in the classroom / in real life?
- for work / while traveling?
- problems: speaking/understanding?
- Standard/non-standard English?
- advice for others?

B Work in new pairs. Use your questions to interview your partner. Listen carefully and ask follow-up questions.

Follow-up questions

Really? Why?
What happened? What went wrong?
Can you give me an example?

C Work in groups and discuss the questions.

1. What was the most interesting thing you learned from your interview?
2. What advice can you give to other people about using English in real life?

READING

A SPEAK Work in pairs and discuss the questions.

1 Look at the title of the magazine article. What do you think it means?

2 Think of some examples where you can lose something if you stop using it. Have you ever lost a skill or an ability because you didn't use it?

B READ FOR GIST Read *Use it or lose it?* quickly and answer the questions.

1 Is the writer generally positive or negative about learning languages?

2 What's the connection between the pictures, the word cloud and language learning?

Use it *or* lose it?

1 What's the worst thing about learning a language? Is it the hundreds of hours you need to spend studying and practicing? No, although that's bad enough. In fact, the worst thing is how easy it is to forget everything!

2 How do I know? From bitter experience! Many years ago, I lived in Spain for a year and studied Spanish for hours every day. By the end of that year, I spoke Spanish fluently (but not very accurately). But now, 20 years later, it's all gone. My only evidence that I ever spoke Spanish is an old certificate.

3 So is there any hope for me and my Spanish? Recent research suggests that there is. Imagine your brain is like a big library. As you keep adding new information to that library, the old information doesn't disappear; it just gets harder to find.

4 How does this work in practice? When I see a dog, my English-speaking brain thinks of the word *dog*. But when I lived in Spain, my brain had two words to choose from, *dog* and *perro* (and yes, that's *dog* in Spanish!). My brain learned to block the wrong word: it blocked *dog* when I was speaking Spanish and *perro* when I was speaking English. Over time, my brain got very good at blocking words.

5 And what happened when I left Spain? The word *perro* stayed blocked. And, like a door that's been closed for years is harder to open, it became harder to unblock the word! Now, 20 years later, all those Spanish words are still in my brain. But they're blocked behind heavy old doors.

6 How can I open those doors? Two things: I need to make an effort to push the doors open again; and I need to keep the doors open by practicing regularly.

7 Is there anything good to say about this 'blocking' process? In fact, there's lots of evidence that it makes your brain work better. For example, look at the words in the box. As quickly as possible, say what color they're written in. Try it now. Did you notice how hard it was to say the color when the word itself was a color? That's because 'bad information' (the word on the page) blocked the 'good information' (the color of the word).

8 What's the connection with language learning? It turns out that bilingual people are much better at activities like this than monolingual people, because their brains are trained to block 'bad information' quickly and accurately. And in the modern world, where we have to deal with too much information all the time, the ability to block 'bad information' is the key to success.

9 What's the best thing about learning a language? Is it the ability to communicate with different people around the world? No, although that's amazing enough. In fact, the best thing is that it makes our brains more powerful.

1.2 Who owns English?

PRONUNCIATION

1.10 **A** Tell students they're going to listen to two questions from the interview. Tell them to listen carefully and think about questions 1 and 2.

B Ask students to read the information in the *Pronouncing questions* box. Model the pronunciation of the questions or play the audio again to ensure students understand. Tell students to work in pairs to practice saying the questions in two different ways and to discuss the questions.

1.11 **C** Tell students to listen to the different pronunciations of the questions from Exercise B and then to discuss the questions in Exercise C. Elicit answers and stress that there is no right or wrong answer here!

SPEAKING

A Tell students they are going to interview another student about their experience of using English. However, first, they need to work with a different student to prepare questions. Monitor to help with language.

B Give students a new partner and tell them they're going to ask each other the questions they have prepared. Before they do this, point out the *Useful language* for asking follow-up questions. Model the pronunciation of these and get students to repeat, focusing on sounding genuinely interested. Encourage students to use these follow-up questions in their interviews.

C Put students into groups to discuss the questions. Check answers and encourage students to expand on their answers.

READING

A Write *Use it or lose it* on the board and elicit what it means (that you may lose an ability to do something if you don't practice it regularly). Put students into pairs to think of examples and then elicit ideas from the class.

B Tell students that *Use it or lose it* is the title of an article about learning languages. Focus students' attention on the pictures and elicit what they show. Set a time limit and tell students to skim the text to answer the two questions. Point out the glossary, with the definitions of *block* and *evidence* which are important to understand the text. Explain that students shouldn't worry about any other unknown vocabulary or anything else that they don't understand at this stage, as they're going to read the text again more closely later. Stress that it wouldn't be possible to read the whole text carefully in the time limit, but it is possible to answer the two questions, which is all students need to do. Stick to the time limit. Allow students to check their answers with a partner before checking as a whole class.

1 *Positive (especially in the second half).*

2 *Library picture: Our brains are like a library. When we add more and more information, the old information is still there, but it gets harder to find it. That's why we feel like we forget languages that we once spoke.*
Door picture: When we don't use a foreign word for a long time, it becomes blocked by the word from our own language. After some time, it becomes hard to unblock that word, just like it's hard to open a door that's been closed for a long time.
Colorful words: This is an example of bad information (the words themselves) blocking the good information (the color they're written in), just like words in our first language block foreign words that we're trying to remember.

METHODOLOGY HUB by Jim Scrivener

Skimming and scanning

Many activities designed to increase reading speeds are variations on the following two ideas:

- Skimming = Read quickly to get the gist of a passage (e.g. to discover key topics, main ideas, overall theme, basic structure, etc). A typical skimming task would be a general question from the teacher, such as *Is this passage about Jill's memories of the summer or the winter?* or *Is this story set in a school or a restaurant?* The learners would attempt to find the answer quickly, without reading every word of the passage.
- Scanning = Move eyes quickly over the text to locate a specific piece of information (e.g. a name, address, fact, price, number, date, etc) without reading the whole text or unpacking any subtleties of meaning. A common scanning activity is searching for information in a flyer or directory, and a typical scanning task would be *What time does the train to Boston leave?*

Skimming and scanning are both 'top-down' skills. Although scanning is involved with finding individual points from the text without reading carefully through every word of the text, the way that a reader finds that information involves some degree of processing of the overall shape and structure of the text, moving his/her eyes quickly over the whole page, searching for keywords or clues from the textual layout and the content that will enable her to focus in on smaller sections of text that she is likely to get answers from.

METHODOLOGY HUB by Jim Scrivener

How do people learn languages?

If we want to plan lessons that are more than simply random entertainment, we need a clear idea of how we think people learn language. The activities we plan can then closely reflect those things that we believe are an important part of the learning process.

The following list charts one possible explanation of a student's progress when learning a new item of language:

1. The learner doesn't know anything about the item.
2. The learner hears or reads examples of the item (maybe a number of times), but doesn't particularly notice it.
3. The learner begins to realize that there is a feature he/she doesn't fully understand.
4. The learner starts to look more closely at the item and tries to work out the formation rules and the meaning, possibly with the help of reference information, explanations or other help.
5. The learner tries to use the item in his/her own speech or writing (maybe hesitantly, probably with many errors).
6. The learner integrates the item fully into his/her own language and uses it (without thinking) relatively easily with minor errors.

C Focus students' attention on the information about rhetorical questions in the box. Check that students understand what a rhetorical question is and elicit the first one in the text as an example. Tell students to find as many more in the text as they can. For weaker classes, you could tell students there are 12 and ask them to find them.

D Point out that each paragraph starts with a rhetorical question. Ask students to work in pairs to look again at the rhetorical questions in the text and discuss the answer. Check the answers as a class. Turn to SB8 where the answers are underlined.

E Give a personal example and elicit a few from the class. Put students into pairs to discuss the question. In feedback, encourage students to give their own ideas and examples.

VOCABULARY

A Focus students' attention on the sentences. Explain that the sentences come from the interview between Mona and Juan from earlier in the unit and from *Use it or lose it?*. Tell students to match the underlined words to the definitions. Check answers and check students fully understand the meaning of the words and the difference between *phrases* and *idioms*. Model and practice pronunciation.

B Direct students to the **Vocabulary Hub** (TB121) for further practice of vocabulary related to languages. Allow time for students to compare answers in pairs before checking each exercise. Use the **Vocabulary Worksheet** on W4 for extra practice.

SPEAKING HUB

A Put students into groups of three or four and tell them that they're going to give a presentation about learning and using languages. Tell each group to agree on a topic from the box or an idea of their own.

B Tell students to write three or four rhetorical questions about their topic. Give your own examples about a topic of your choice as a model. Tell students to think about how they could go on to answer the questions they write. Tell them to write notes, but stress that they shouldn't write out what they want to say word for word.

C Tell each group to give their presentation. Tell the groups who are listening to write down questions to ask the speakers after each presentation. During the presentations, write down a few instances in which students successfully used language and errors you could focus on in feedback.

D Put students into new groups to discuss the questions. Finish with whole-class feedback. You could ask whether rhetorical questions are as commonly used in the students' own language, and what students think about them as a rhetorical device.

TEACHING IDEA by David Seymour and Maria Popova

Vocabulary: Study skills

Use this activity to review the vocabulary.

In pairs, compare the way you study, including these categories:

notes, filing, dictionaries, other reference books, speaking in class, asking questions, handouts, vocabulary learning techniques

In small groups, discuss the advice you would give to a student who wants to learn a new language. Agree on your top ten suggestions for effective study, e.g. *Keep a vocabulary notebook using different colors for different parts of speech.* Ask the teacher if you do not understand something.

TEACHING IDEA by David Seymour and Maria Popova

Vocabulary: Class contract

Use this activity to review the vocabulary.

In small groups, make two lists of duties to help make a class effective: 1 students' duties and 2 the teacher's duties, e.g. *The students must arrive on time. The teacher must correct written work within a week.* Compare your lists with the other groups.

Which duties should go in a class contract? (Elicit ideas and write them on the board.)

TEACHING IDEA by David Seymour and Maria Popova

Speaking Hub: Languages

Listen to the countries and write the nationality and the language of each one. In small groups, compare your lists and write down any words that are new to you.

Germany (German – German)	Senegal (Senegalese – French, Pulaar, Wolof)
Peru (Peruvian – Spanish, Quechua)	Wales (Welsh – English, Welsh)
France (French – French)	Canada (Canadian – English, French, Indian)
Iran (Iranian – Farsi, Azerbaijani)	Kenya (Kenyan – English, Gikuyu, Swahili)
Holland (Dutch – Dutch)	Israel (Israeli – Hebrew, Arabic)
Japan (Japanese – Japanese)	Sweden (Swedish – Swedish)
Brazil (Brazilian – Portuguese)	Ethiopia (Ethiopian – Amharic, Tigrigna)
Turkey (Turkish – Turkish, Kurdish)	Ireland (Irish – English, Gaelic)
Switzerland (Swiss – German, French, Italian, Romance)	

C SCAN Read again. How many rhetorical questions are there? Use the information in the box to help you.

Rhetorical questions

A rhetorical question is a question that you ask when you don't expect other people to answer it. You usually answer the question yourself. It's a useful way of presenting information because it makes the reader or listener think about the answer.

When you read a rhetorical question at the beginning of a paragraph, always pause to predict the answer first. Then read the rest of the paragraph to check.

D Work in pairs. Look at the rhetorical questions at the start of each paragraph. Discuss the answers. Then read the paragraph again to check.

E SPEAK Work in pairs and discuss the questions.

What does the writer mean by 'we have to deal with too much information all the time'? Can you think of any examples from your own life?

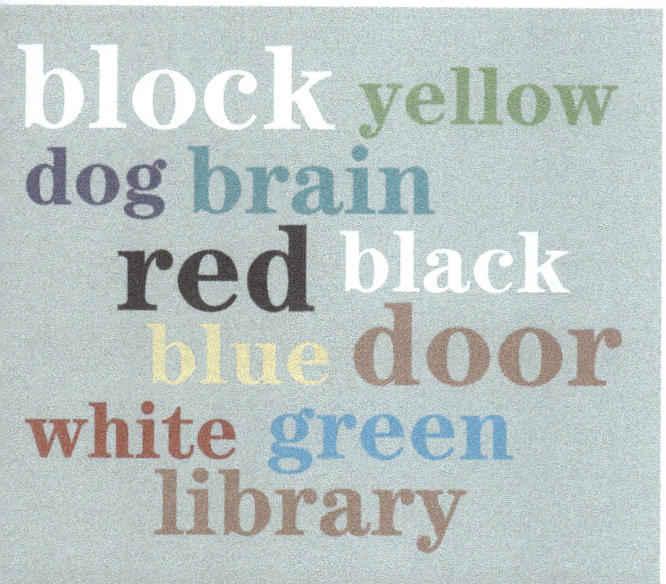

Glossary

block (v) to stop something from moving through something else

evidence (n) facts or physical signs that help to prove something

VOCABULARY

Languages

A WORK IT OUT Look at the sentences from the interview between Mona and Juan and from *Use it or lose it?* Then use the correct form of the underlined words to complete the definitions (1–5).

They used really strange words and phrases – lots of idioms that I've never heard before.

Plus, the people had very strong accents, so I couldn't understand very much at all!

By the end of that year, I spoke Spanish fluently (but not very accurately).

It turns out that bilingual people are much better at activities like this than monolingual people.

1 If you're __monolingual__, you only speak one language; if you're __bilingual__, you speak two languages.

2 A(n) __phrase__ is a group of two or more words that go together as a unit (e.g. heavy old doors).

3 Your __accent__ is the way you pronounce words. It sometimes shows which part of a country you are from.

4 A(n) __idiom__ has its own meaning (e.g. 'Use it or lose it'). It's usually hard to figure out the meaning just by looking at the words.

5 If you speak __fluently__, you don't pause to think in the middle of sentences. If you speak __accurately__, you don't make mistakes.

B Go to the **Vocabulary Hub** on **page 142**.

SPEAKING HUB

A Work in groups. You are going to give a short presentation about learning and using languages. Choose a topic from the list or use your own ideas. You can talk about English, your own language or both.

- accents
- standard and non-standard varieties
- advice on fluency and accuracy
- advice on how to practice
- how the language is changing
- why it's good to be bilingual

B PLAN Write three or four rhetorical questions about your topic. Then plan how you can answer those questions in a presentation. Write notes but do not write the answers down.

C PRESENT Give your presentation to the class. While you are listening to the other presentations, listen carefully and be ready to ask questions.

D REFLECT Work in groups and discuss the questions.

1 What did you learn from the presentations? What surprised you?

2 Will you use rhetorical questions again in your presentations or writing?

- Plan and conduct an interview
- Use rhetorical questions in a presentation

Café Hub

1.3 Welcome back

F – ask for, offer and respond to help P – intonation and stress

COMPREHENSION

A Watch the video. Complete the sentences with the names in the box.

Gaby Milly Neena Sam Zac

1. Sam owns a café.
2. Milly runs a vintage clothing shop.
3. Zac is Sam's best friend.
4. Neena lives with Gaby and Zac.
5. Zac is meeting Milly's mum tomorrow.
6. Sam agrees to lend Zac some clothes.
7. Gaby falls over and hurts her arm.

B Work in pairs and discuss the questions.

1. Why is Gaby taking pictures? For Sam's website
2. Why does Sam say 'Oh no Zac, I'm so sorry …'? He thinks Milly's mum/mom died
3. Why does Zac need to borrow some clothes? He is meeting Milly's mum
4. Why is Sam surprised when Zac asks for pants? pants are underwear - Zac means trousers/pants.
5. Why is Gaby worried about tomorrow? She has a photoshoot, but she has a broken arm

C Imagine you wanted to borrow the items in the box. Who would you ask and why? Tell your partner.

$10 $500 a belt a book a ladder a scarf a suitcase or backpack some shoes or boots

Glossary

flat **(n) (British)** = apartment **(n) (American)**
mum **(n) (British)** = mom **(n) (American)**
trousers **(n) (British)** = pants **(n) (American)**

FUNCTIONAL LANGUAGE

Asking for, offering and responding to help

A Complete the phrases with the correct form of *give*, *help* or *need*.

Asking for help

Could you [1] help me out?
Would you mind [2] giving me a hand?
Do you think you could [3] help me out?
I [4] need a favor. Can you lend me some clothes? Please? 1

Offering to help

I can [5] give you a hand with that. 2
I'd be happy to [6] help you with that.
Can I [7] help you with that?
Shall I bring some stuff round to the flat later? 4
Do you [8] need a hand? 6
Do you need any [9] help ?

Responding to help

Thank you so much, that would be great. 3
That would be awesome. 5
If you wouldn't mind.
I can manage. I'm OK. 7
It's OK – I can do it myself.
Listen, let me [10] help you. 8

B 01:01–03:40 Watch the last part of the video. Mark the eight phrases you hear in the order in which you hear them.

MILLY

SAM

NEENA

ZAC

GABY

USEFUL PHRASES

A Match the useful phrases (1–6) with the phrases which show the meaning (a–f).

1 I'm really busy at the moment.
2 I don't know how to say this.
3 Good luck with that!
4 You're a legend!
5 I owe you one.
6 There you go.

a That isn't going to be easy.
b You are amazing!
c I must return the favor.
d I can't talk to you at the moment.
e I've finished.
f This is difficult for me to talk about.

B How do you say these useful phrases in your language?

PRONUNCIATION
Intonation and stress

1.12 **A** Listen and repeat the two questions in the table. Complete the headings with *falls* or *rises*.

1 Asking for help: intonation rises.	2 Offering help: intonation falls.
Can you lend me some clothes?	Can I help you with that?
Could you help me out?	Do you need any help?
Would you mind giving me a hand?	Can I give you a hand?

1.13 **B** Listen, repeat and write down each question in the correct column. Practice the stress and intonation.

SPEAKING

A Work in pairs. You are going to write and perform a conversation where you ask a friend for help. Think about the following things:

- What sort of help do you need?
- Why do you need help?
- When do you need help?
- Who do you ask?

B **PRESENT** Write and practice your conversation. Then perform it for the rest of the class.

Ask for, offer and respond to help

➤ Turn to page 156 to learn how to write a report about trends.

1.3 Welcome back

LEAD-IN

Ask students to think about the last time they asked for or offered help. Ask them to give details about who, what, when and where. Give students a minute to write notes. Give an example of your own.

COMPREHENSION

A ▸ Explain that students are going to watch an episode of a video series. Tell students they will need to complete the sentences with the name of a character. Ask them to read through the sentences before listening.

B Tell students to discuss the questions in pairs.

C Tell students who you would ask to borrow $10 from, and model the question you would ask. Do the same for $500, using a more indirect question (as it's a larger amount and a bigger favor). Students then do the same in pairs with the other items.

FUNCTIONAL LANGUAGE

A Focus students' attention on the phrases. Tell students some of them come from the video they've just watched and ask them to complete the spaces with *give*, *help* or *need*. Point out that they will need to change the form of the verb in some of them. Check answers and refer back to the language the students used in the previous task, commenting on any similarities or differences between them.

B ▸ 01:01–03:40 Point out the boxes which follow eight of the phrases. Tell students these are the phrases that appear in the video. Tell them to watch again and number the phrases in the order they hear them.

USEFUL PHRASES

A Tell students the useful phrases were all in the video. Ask them to match each one with its meaning. Model and practice pronunciation of each phrase as you check the answers.

B Ask students to think how they would say these phrases in their language. For monolingual classes, students can decide together on the best translations. In multilingual classes, students can compare how similar or different the equivalent phrases in their languages are.

PRONUNCIATION

1.12 **A** Play the audio and tell students to repeat, paying careful attention to whether their voice falls or rises at the end of the questions. Tell students to complete rules 1 and 2. Emphasize the importance of sounding friendly and polite when asking for or offering help. You could demonstrate this to humorous effect by asking the questions again yourself with flat, uninterested sounding intonation and eliciting how effective that would be.

1.13 **B** Play the other questions and tell students to repeat. Students then copy the questions in the correct column.

SPEAKING

A Tell students to work in pairs and imagine a situation where they would ask a friend for help. Give them time to discuss the questions.

B Tell students to write out a script of their conversation. Monitor again to help with language input. Tell students to practice their conversation in pairs, especially the rising or falling intonation. Tell each pair to perform their conversation to the class.

▶ VIDEO SCRIPT

S = Sam **G** = Gaby **Z** = Zac **M** = Milly

S: Hey, I'm Sam. This is my café. This is Milly. She runs a clothes shop. She's dating Zac. He's my best friend.
This is Neena. She's a lawyer and she lives with Zac and … GABY! This is Gaby. She likes taking photos …
G: … And smile. Smile. Smile more … even more … EVEN MORE!
S: How's this?
G: Urgh, TOO MUCH! Stop. Good. Good! Perfect! These photos'll look great on your website.
S: Zac? Zac, hey, look I'm really busy at the moment, so …
Z: Sam, Sam! It's Zac!
S: Yeah I know! Look, I better get on …
Z: Sam! It's big news! Really big!
S: What is it?
Z: It's Milly's mom … I don't know how to say this, uh, she's … uh … she's …
S: Oh, no. Zac, I'm so sorry …
Z: She's coming to London. Tomorrow.
S: Oh, OK. You haven't met her yet, have you?
Z: No! We're meeting for lunch. Tomorrow!
S: OK, well. Good luck with that! Look, I better go now. I've got a lot of stuff to do.
Z: Wait! Listen, I need a favor, can you lend me some clothes? Please? I need to borrow a shirt, a smart jacket, some pants …
S: Pants?
Z: Oh, OK – trousers.
M: And a tie!
Z: Did you hear that?
S: What?
Z: And a tie! And some shoes.
S: You don't have any shoes?
Z: Well yeah, but … I need some smart shoes … Do you think you could help me out?
S: Sure, I can give you a hand with that.
Z: Thank you SO much, that would be great – you're a legend!
S: I am. Shall I bring some stuff round to the flat later?
Z: That would be awesome. I owe you one.
S: You owe me more than one. Gaby! Are you OK? Do you need a hand?
G: No, I can manage. I'm OK.
S: Listen, let me help you.
G: OK … I think it's OK.
S: Does this hurt?
G: No.
S: How about this?
G: ARGH!
S: There you go. Should be OK in a few days.
G: A few days … Oh, no! I've got a photo shoot tomorrow. What am I going to do?

Unit 1 Writing

1 Writing — Write a report about trends

W — using formal language in reports

A **Work in groups of three. Discuss the questions and complete the *Me, Partner 1* and *Partner 2* columns in the table.**

1 How much time do you spend doing each activity in the table each week?

2 Are you spending more (↑), less (↓) or the same (↔) time on each activity at the moment, compared to last year?

	Me hours	Partner 1 hours	Partner 2 hours	Average hours
checking social media				
sending instant messages				
studying online				

B **Now figure out the average number of hours spent doing each activity. Are people spending more or less time on each activity compared to last year? Complete the *Average* column of the table in Exercise A.**

C **Read the *Report about online trends* and answer the questions.**

1 What trends did the writer find? Did you find the same trends?

2 What was different?

3 What is the writer's main prediction for the future?

Report about online trends

[1]These days, online communication is more and more important in our daily lives. [2]But are we actually spending more time online? [3]This report examines the number of hours that people spend on various online activities and explores some recent trends. [4]I interviewed eight members of my English class about their online habits.

How much time do you spend checking social media?

The average number of hours in my group is just over one hour per day. This is surprising, as I expected the total to be higher. One possible reason is that several popular social media sites are showing more advertisements these days.

How much time do you spend sending instant messages?

The average number of hours here is approximately 1.5 hours per day. Almost everybody said that this number is increasing for them. It seems that many people are using instant messaging services for conversations that they had on social media before.

How much time do you spend studying online?

The average number of hours here was 4.3 per week. Two people in my group never study online, and this trend is not changing. Two people study online a lot: 12 and 15 hours a week. This trend is also not changing, as these people both study on long-term courses. However, the other three people's answers were especially interesting: they all spend two to three hours a week studying, but this is increasing very fast, from zero last year. They all use language learning apps to study for pleasure.

Conclusion

There certainly seems to be a trend away from social media and towards messaging apps. However, the main trend I noticed is the increase in online studying, especially the use of language apps. I expect this trend to continue into the future.

WRITING

D **Look at the introduction to the *Report about online trends*. Match the sentences (1–4) with the descriptions (a–d).**

4 **a** Explain where you got your information, e.g. *Who did you ask?*

2 **b** Ask a rhetorical question to make the reader think about the topic.

3 **c** Present your reason for writing the report: what does the report do?

1 **d** Start by introducing the general topic of your report.

E **Look at the box and complete the tips about using formal language in reports. Then find examples of each tip in the report.**

Using formal language in reports

We *use* / *don't use* contractions (e.g. *there's, isn't*).

In general, most sentences are fairly *long* / *short*.

Most sentences have ***a human subject, e.g. I, Two people*** / ***a non-human subject, e.g. It, This trend.***

F **Match the formal phrases (1–7), which are underlined in the *Report about online trends*, with the less formal phrases (a–g).**

d **1** This report examines …

f **2** various

c **3** One possible reason is that …

b **4** approximately

e **5** It seems that … / There certainly seems to be …

g **6** especially

a **7** However, …

a but

b more or less

c Maybe this is because …

d In this report, I look at …

e I think …

f a few different

g very

WRITING

A PREPARE **You are going to write a report about current trends in communication. What trends do you notice? You can use the ideas in Exercise A or your own ideas.**

B PLAN **Choose two or three points to include in your report. These will be your main paragraphs.**

C WRITE **Write your report (150–200 words). Remember:**

- to start with an introduction.
- when you present numbers, show what they mean and how they're connected together.
- to use formal language.
- to end with a conclusion.

D REVIEW **Work in groups. Share your reports. Who found the most interesting information? Were you surprised by any of the trends he/she found?**

Answers

1 *The writer found that the average amount of time people are spending on social media is one hour per day. The trend is that people are spending less time using social media. The average amount of time people are spending sending instant messages is 1.5 hours a day. People's usage is going up. The average amount of time people are spending studying online is 4.3 hours per week. For most people, there's no change, but for some people, the number is increasing fast. So overall, there's a small increase.*

3 *That people will use more and more online study, especially language learning apps.*

Refer students to this report as a model for the writing task.

Ask students to compare their reports in small groups.

WRITING

On the left-hand side of the board, write the following words randomly in a circle: *social*, *instant*, *study*, *messaging*. Then on the right-hand side of the board, write the following words in random order in another circle: *media*, *messages*, *online*, *app*. Give students a few seconds to pair the words up to make collocations (*social media*, *instant messages*, *study online*, *messaging app*). Then ask students to tell their partner if they do use these things and how much time they devote to them.

A Start by giving your own personal answers to the questions. Then put students into groups of three to discuss the questions and complete the table.

B Check that students understand the meaning of *average*, then ask them to complete the *Average* column of the table. Ask students to discuss any interesting findings.

C Check that students remember the meaning of *trends* from earlier in the unit and elicit an example of one. Tell students they're going to read a report about trends. Check understanding of *a prediction*, then ask students to read and answer the questions.

D Tell students to read the introduction (first paragraph) of the text again and to match the sentences labeled 1–4 to the descriptions a–d.

E Focus students' attention on the tips for using formal language in reports. Elicit the first answer and an example from the class. Tell students to complete the remaining tips and to find further examples of each in the report.

F Tell students that all the formal phrases are used in the report. Tell them to match each with the less formal equivalent.

WRITING TASK

A Give students some time to choose a trend to write about.

B Tell students to choose two or three main points to include. They should also write an introduction.

C Tell students to write their report.

D Put students into groups to share their reports. Finish with feedback on the content, organization and language in the reports.

Unit 1 Review

GRAMMAR

A Complete the social media update with the simple present or present progressive form of the verbs in parentheses.

I'm in Moscow! As you can see in the picture, I [1] 'm having (*have*) coffee with some of my new friends. I [2] 'm studying (*study*) here on a two-week intensive language course. I [3] 'm really enjoying (*really enjoy*) it so far. I [4] don't speak (*not speak*) very much Russian at all, so it was really difficult on the first day, but now it [5] 's getting (*get*) easier every day, and my teachers are excellent. Why Russian? Well, first, I [6] think (*think*) it's a beautiful language, and second, I [7] 'm considering (*consider*) studying at the university here next year.

B Read part of a report about social media trends. Then write questions about the underlined information in the report. Use the prompts to help you.

These days, more and more people [1]<u>are choosing to stop using social media completely</u>. I asked [2]<u>twelve people</u> about the way they use social media. [3]<u>Three people</u> said they never use social media, and [4]<u>two</u> are using it less and less. One student, Franek, believes social media is dangerous [5]<u>because it makes us feel jealous of other people's 'perfect' lives</u>. Another student, [6]<u>Lin</u>, thinks social media is useful for his work, but he never uses it with his real friends. He says his friends can speak to him face-to-face to find out his news!

1 What / more and more people / do / these days?
What are more and more people doing these days?

2 How many people / the writer / ask / about the way they use social media? How many people did the writer ask about the way they use social media?

3 How many people / say / they never use social media?
How many people said they never use social media?

4 How many people / use / social media less and less?
How many people are using social media less and less?

5 Why / Franek / believe / social media is dangerous?
Why does Franek believe social media is dangerous?

6 Who / think / social media is useful for work?
Who thinks social media is useful for work?

VOCABULARY

A Complete the sentences with the correct form of the verbs in the box.

hear listen look see sound watch

1 **A:** 'I think we should go soon.'
B: 'Yes, that sounds like a good idea.'

2 I prefer normal phone calls to video calls – it's better when the other person can hear you, but they can't see you!

3 Excuse me. I 'm looking for my dog. I can't find him anywhere. Have you seen him?

4 I usually listen to podcasts while I'm traveling to work.

5 Can I call you back later? I 'm watching a TV show and I don't want to miss the end.

B Choose the correct words to complete the conversation.

A: Oh, this is nice, just sitting outside a café and relaxing. I think it's really interesting to [1]*<u>observe</u>* / *recognize* / *stare* all the people on the street.

B: Yes, but be careful. It looks like you're [2]*noticing* / *spotting* / *<u>staring</u>* at other people a little too much. It's pretty rude.

A: Don't worry! They're too busy to [3]*<u>notice</u>* / *observe* / *recognize* me! They're all looking at their phones, anyway!

C Read about five English-speaking friends. Then answer the questions.

Angela only speaks English and no other languages.

You can hear that **Brian** is from New Zealand because of the way he pronounces *ed*.

When **Eryk** is speaking English, he doesn't make many mistakes.

Francesca speaks English as well as Italian.

George loves using phrases like 'use it or lose it' and 'plan B'.

1 Who speaks accurately? Eryk
2 Who's monolingual? Angela
3 Who likes idioms? George
4 Who's bilingual? Francesca
5 Who has a strong accent? Brian

FUNCTIONAL LANGUAGE

Complete the dialogues with the words in the box.

busy could favor hand help mind want

1 **A:** Hey, Gary, I need a favor. Do you have a few minutes?
B: Sorry, Paul, I'm really busy right now.

2 **A:** Do you think you could help me write this?
B: Sure, I can give you a hand with that.

3 **A:** Do you want me to take a look at that?
B: If you wouldn't mind.

4 **A:** Hi, Sam. If you aren't busy, I could use your help with my application letter.
B: Sure.

2 EXPERIENCES

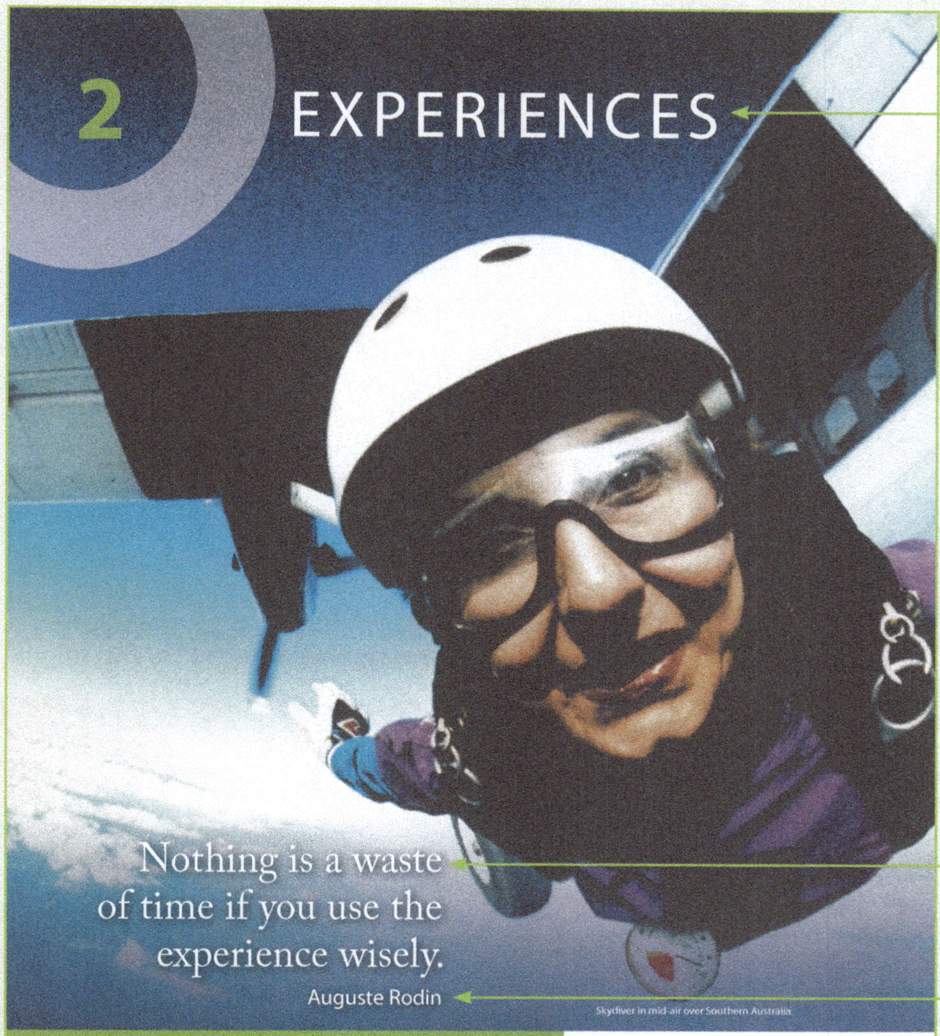

Nothing is a waste of time if you use the experience wisely.
Auguste Rodin

Skydiver in mid-air over Southern Australia

Experience (n) something that happens to you or a situation that you are involved in. Synonyms: situation (n), circumstance (n)

The quote for this unit is about learning from your experiences, whether they are positive or negative, and gaining wisdom as a result.

Auguste Rodin (1840–1917) was a French sculptor, most famous for the sculpture *The Thinker*. His style and ideas were ahead of their time, and he was involved in a lot of controversy during his life and career.

OBJECTIVES

- talk about past experiences and things you want to do
- talk about a life-changing decision
- talk about an inspirational person
- talk about solving a problem
- ask for, give and refuse permission
- write an informal email

Work with a partner. Discuss the questions.

1 Look at the picture. What do you think of the activity the person is doing?
2 Read the quote. What do you think it means?
3 Tell your partner about experiences you have had that were:

- incredible
- unusual
- risky
- memorable
- eye-opening
- thrilling

EXPERIENCES 13

OBJECTIVES

Read the unit objectives to the class.

UNIT OPENER QUESTIONS

With books closed, write the word *experience* on the board and elicit collocations. You could give an example of *an amazing experience*. When you have a few more on the board, put students into pairs to think of an example of each type of experience.

1 Focus students' attention on the picture and elicit their reactions. Have they ever done the activity shown? If so, did they enjoy it? Would they do it again? If not, would they like to try it? Why/Why not?

2 Tell students to read the quote and discuss in pairs what they think it means. Elicit answers, encouraging students to interpret the quote for themselves and in their own words. Ask if students agree with the idea expressed in the quote.

3 Check that students understand the adjectives. Give examples to help them understand where necessary. Tell students to tell their partners about their own experiences. Elicit ideas in open class. Pay attention to how confidently and accurately students use simple past and present perfect. This will indicate if students need a lot of clarification or just some consolidation when studying the grammar later in the unit.

WORKSHEETS

Lesson 2.1 Important decisions

Grammar: Present perfect and simple past (W5)

Vocabulary: Collocations: making big decisions (W6)

Lesson 2.2 You can do it!

Grammar: Present and past ability (W7)

Vocabulary: Dependent prepositions (verb/adjective + *for*/*of*) (W8)

2.1 Important decisions

- Talk about past experiences and things you want to do
- Talk about a life-changing decision

G – present perfect and simple past P – 's and 've V – collocations: making big decisions
S – listening for the main idea

READING

A Match the different types of lists (1–5) with the examples (a–e).

c **1** list of favorite things, e.g. movies, songs
a **2** shopping list
b **3** everyday to-do list
e **4** list of pros and cons
d **5** bucket list

a
- *bananas*
- *cheese*
- *yogurt*

b
1 Call Mom
2 Email the bank
3 Pay rent

c
1 Toy Story
2 X-Men
3 Beauty and the Beast

d
1 Swim with dolphins
2 Learn to surf
3 Do a parachute jump

e
For: cheaper / easy to find
Against: poor quality / ordinary

B SPEAK Work in pairs. How often do you make lists? What types of lists do you make? Why?

C READ FOR GIST Read *Not yet? No more!* and answer the questions.

1 Which sentence summarizes the blogger's opinion?

a A bucket list is a great idea, but remember that you probably can't do all those things in your lifetime.
(**b**) Make a list of things that are possible to do, rather than a list of dreams.
c People write bucket lists just for fun and to dream a little, not in order to actually do those things.

2 How many of the people commenting on the blog agree with the writer? two people - the first and third

Not yet? No more!

About me | Recent posts | Archive

posted by Julia
November 16 | Leave a comment

Have you ever written a bucket list? If so, have you done many of those incredible things on your list? I certainly haven't.

I wrote mine on New Year's Day five years ago, and I chose 50 things, like swimming with dolphins and climbing Mount Everest. However, after all these years, I've only done one thing on that list. Last year, I watched the sun rise and set on the same day. I still haven't swum with dolphins. I still haven't climbed Everest. And, I think I never will!

The problem is that you need an infinite amount of time and money to do all those incredible things or to learn those skills. I've simply never had that time and money. What is the point in making an unachievable list? How does that improve your life?

So, this is my achievable bucket list blog. The aim is still to do unusual things that are positive and life-enhancing, but without needing to be a millionaire or to have all the time in the world to achieve these goals.

Here's the start of my list. I haven't done any of these things yet, but I think I can in the future. What do you think? Achievable? Life-enhancing?

- Plant a tree.
- Do a charity walk or run.
- Write a poem.
- Learn how to make a fire in the wild.
- Ride a horse.
- Eat nothing but fresh food for a week.
- Stop using social media for two weeks.
- Learn and perform a magic trick.

Comments:

Yuka W

Thanks! Before I read this, my bucket list was only expensive travel ideas. I just wrote a new list of interesting but doable things! Ex C Q2

dream_catcher77

Actually, I think a bucket list should be about amazing things. I wrote mine last year and I've done half of it already. This year, I've seen lions in the wild and I've done a parachute jump. Next month, the Pyramids! All because they're on my list.

Robin Stannard

Also, sometimes those incredible things are not so great. I've swum with dolphins. It was garbage! I'd rather swim with my friends. Keep it simple – it's still special ;-) Ex C Q2

2.1 Important decisions

LEAD-IN

Elicit one example of a type of list. Tell students to think of as many more examples as they can in one minute.

READING

A Tell students to open their books and to see if any of their ideas are the same as those listed. Tell them to match the type of lists with the examples.

B Put students into pairs to discuss how frequently they make lists and which kind. Monitor and encourage students to explain why they do or don't make certain kinds of lists.

C Set a time limit. Make it clear that students don't need to read and understand everything at this stage. Students should just choose the correct summary and find out how many comments agree with the writer.

TEACHING IDEA by David Seymour and Maria Popova

Topic: Life plans

Use this activity to extend the topic.

Look at this pattern and write some more sentences that are true for you, e.g. *When it stops raining, I'll go out. As soon as he calls, I'll let you know.*

when	
as soon as	+ present perfect
until	
before	

Write some more examples using these verbs.

arrive, end (this lesson), start work, get up, finish job, go out, finish, be ready, get married, have dinner, do homework

In pairs, tell each other about your own expectations using *going to* for plans, e.g. *As soon as my English is good enough, I'm going to go back home and get a good job.*

In pairs, continue this sequence, e.g. *As soon as I pass my exams, I'll go to college. When I leave college, I'm going to go traveling. I'll keep traveling until my money runs out …* Try to make it go somewhere interesting, e.g. *into an extremely adventurous life, a lucky one*, etc.

pass exams –> leave college –> go traveling –> live in India …

GRAMMAR HUB

2.1 Present perfect and simple past

	Positive	Negative	Question
Present perfect	**Wilhelm has climbed** Mt. Everest before. **We've visited** the Pyramids already.	**I haven't been** sailing before. **Paula hasn't made** a bucket list yet.	**Have you** ever **met** a movie star? **Have they bought** the tickets already?
Simple past	**Wilhelm climbed** Mt. Everest last month. **We visited** Yosemite National Park a year ago.	**I didn't go** sailing last weekend. **Paula didn't move** out of her parents' house a week ago.	**Did you meet** a movie star yesterday? **Did they buy** the tickets?

- We use the present perfect for actions completed during a period of time that continues to now.

  *Juan **has been** in Asia for three months so far.*
  = He's still there.

- We also use the present perfect for actions completed before now when we don't say exactly when.

  *She **has** already **written** out a bucket list.*
  NOT ~~She already wrote out her bucket list.~~

- We frequently use time expressions such as *before, already, just* and *yet* with the present perfect.

  Have you finished your exams yet?

- We use the simple past for actions completed during a finished period of time or at a specific time in the past.

  *Did you **stop** using your social media account last week?*

- We frequently use time expressions such as *yesterday, two days / a week / a month ago, or last week/month/year* with the simple past.
- If we use a specific time reference, we usually use the simple past.

  *She's **just won** a free vacation. / She **won** a free vacation **a moment ago**.*

  *Henri has **already booked** a flight to India. / Henri **booked** a flight to India **yesterday**.*

D Tell students to read the text again more slowly and carefully and then answer the questions.

E Put students into pairs to share their opinions about the text. Monitor and draw out any different views students have and encourage them to expand on them.

GRAMMAR

A Tell students the sentences are all from the blog they've just read. To check students are familiar with the terminology, ask them to underline the simple past verbs and circle the present perfect verbs. Explain that identifying the structures is, of course, not as important as understanding why they're used. Tell students to match the sentences to the timelines. In feedback, check that students understand what the different parts of the timelines represent. A lot of students find timelines very helpful, but some can find them confusing. The key thing is to make sure the connection between the events in the sentences and the way they're represented on the timelines is explicit.

B Tell students to look back at the blog and find the adverbs of time from the box. Tell students to look at the way the adverbs are used in context to help them match them with the definitions.

C Tell students to look back at the example sentences, timelines and definitions from Exercises A and B to help them complete the rules. In feedback, elicit which sentences from Exercises A and B are examples of each rule.

D Direct students to the **Grammar Hub** (see TB14 and below). Use the **Grammar Worksheet** on W5 for extra practice.

PRONUNCIATION

2.1 Tell students to listen carefully to the pairs of sentences to identify which one is in the present perfect. If students find this difficult, ask why. Elicit that the contracted auxiliaries *'s* and *'ve* are unstressed and hard to hear. Play the audio again if necessary to give students more practice at picking up the sounds. Practice pronunciation with the students.

SPEAKING

A Put students into pairs and direct them to the **Communication Hub** (TB121). Tell students to find out if their partner has done any of the things on their list, and if so, to find out more details. Model the task and elicit the questions students will need to ask such as *Have you ever …?* for the initial question followed by *Where / When / How did you …?* to find out more information.

B Tell students they're now going to write their own achievable bucket list. Tell students to choose eight things, either from the lists they've just read or using their own ideas. Remind students that they must be achievable but also positive and life-enhancing. You could give examples of absurd or mundane ideas and elicit if these would be appropriate, so students are clear what not to include. Monitor to check students are on task and to help with language if necessary.

C Put students into bigger groups to compare their ideas. Tell them they must agree on ten things for their group bucket list. If students have very different ideas, encourage them to argue the case for the inclusion of theirs, but also make sure students realize that they are meant to reach a consensus so compromise may be necessary. Monitor as they do this, writing down errors and good language use to highlight in feedback.

D Put students into new groups containing one representative of each previous group. Tell them to explain their lists to each other and justify their choices.

Extra activity

You can keep the bucket lists in the classroom and use these as a spring board for further activities. Writing tasks can involve students recording their experiences of completing a task on the bucket list, or even recording them on a blog.

Students can also report back on their experiences at the beginning of a class. You can ask them how they felt before, during and after doing something from the list.

GRAMMAR HUB

2.1 Present perfect and simple past

A Choose the correct option.

1 I *have swum* / *swam* with dolphins before.
2 Martin *dreamed* / *has dreamed* about the pyramids last night.
3 We *haven't climbed* / *didn't climb* Mt. Everest yet.
4 *Did you hear* / *Have you heard* Leon's good news already?
5 *Did Zac learn* / *Has Zac learned* how to make a fire at camp last summer?
6 *Have you ever taken* / *Did you ever take* a trip to another country?

B Correct the mistakes in each sentence. Use contractions where possible.

1 She ~~has seen~~ saw a beautiful sunset last week.
2 They 've made a sci-fi movie already.
3 Molly ~~didn't prepare~~ hasn't prepared a list yet.
4 Mohammed ~~traveled never~~ 's never traveled around Asia before.
5 ~~Did you deal~~ Have you dealt with a serious problem before?
6 He ~~has come~~ came up with a smart plan yesterday.

C Complete each sentence with the correct form of the verb in parentheses.

1 Giralt has never been (*never / be*) to America.
2 Dan has just finished (*just / finish*) a charity walk.
3 Katerina worked hard but she didn't achieve / did not achieve (*not / achieve*) her goal.
4 When the time was right, the chess champion put (*put*) his plan into action.
5 Have you read (*you / read*) other people's bucket lists before?
6 I 've/have already done (*already / do*) two parachute jumps this year.

➤ Go back to page 15.

D READ FOR DETAIL Read again. Answer the questions.

1 How many things on her first bucket list has the writer not done? 49

2 Why is it not possible to do all the things on a typical bucket list? You need a lot of time and money.

3 How is her new list similar to her original list? It has positive activities.

4 How many outdoor activities are there on her new list? Four

E SPEAK Work in pairs. Read again and discuss the questions.

1 Are the writer's choices good ideas for an achievable bucket list?

2 Which choices do you like most and why?

GRAMMAR

Present perfect and simple past

A WORK IT OUT Look at the sentences (1–4) from *Not yet? No more!* Underline the verbs in the simple past and circle the verbs in the present perfect. Then match each sentence with a diagram (a–d).

1 I wrote mine on New Year's Day five years ago. b

2 I've only done one thing on that list. a

3 This year, I've seen lions in the wild. d

4 Last year, I watched the sun rise and set on the same day. c

a
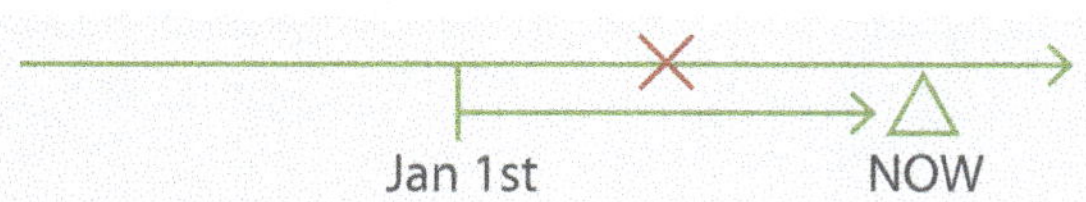

b

c
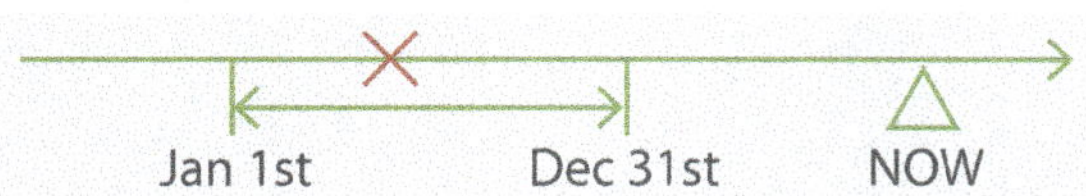

d

B Look at the adverbs of time in the box. Can you find them in the blog? Match the adverbs with the definitions (1–5).

already just never not yet still

1 at no time in the past ____never____

2 a short time ago ____just____

3 a situation has not changed or not completely ended ____still____

4 not happened before now, but will probably happen ____not yet____

5 happened before a point in time, perhaps sooner than expected ____already____

C Complete the rules with *present perfect* or *simple past*.

Present perfect and simple past

For actions that we completed:

during a finished period of time, we use the [1] ____simple past____.

during a period of time that continues to now, we use the [2] ____present perfect____.

at a specific time in the past, we use the [3] ____simple past____.

before now, but we do not say exactly when, we use the [4] ____present perfect____.

We frequently use adverbs of time with these tenses, but we do not use *yet* and *already* with actions in the [5] ____simple past____.

D Go to the **Grammar Hub** on **page 124**.

PRONUNCIATION

's and *'ve*

2.1 Listen to the pairs of sentences (1–6). Which sentence (*a* or *b*) is in the present perfect?

1 b 3 b 5 a

2 a 4 b 6 a

SPEAKING

A Work in pairs. You are going to write an achievable bucket list. Student A – read the bucket list on **page 148**. Student B – read the list on **page 153**. Has your partner done any of the things on your list? If they have, find out more details.

B Work in pairs. Choose eight things to put on your achievable bucket list. Use the ideas on the lists and your own ideas. They should be positive, life-enhancing and achievable.

C Work in groups. Compare your lists and choose ten things for a group bucket list.

D Compare your list with another group. Are their ideas the same or different?

a cruise along canals, freshwater, houseboat

b cross oceans, saltwater, yacht

LISTENING

A Match the words and phrases in the box with the pictures (a–b).

> cross oceans   cruise along canals
> freshwater   houseboat   saltwater   yacht

B SPEAK Work in pairs and discuss the questions.

1. Have you ever been on a boat? If so, what kind?
2. Which of the two boats in the pictures would you prefer to travel on?

2.2 **C LISTEN FOR GIST** Look at the pictures (a and b) and listen to a podcast interview with Emma. Complete the sentences with *a* or *b*.

1. Picture b shows Emma's ultimate dream.
2. Picture a shows Emma's current reality.

2.2 **D** Listen again. Which of the phrases (1–8) from the podcast are the main ideas of Emma's story? Use the strategies in the box to help you.

1. I love swimming
2. yachts are very expensive
3. (circled) to make a decision to put a plan into action
4. it won't take me around the world
5. (circled) to stay motivated and not lose heart
6. learning to live in a small space
7. (circled) doing something similar to my dream, it's a start
8. (circled) the hardest part of any journey is the first step

Listening for the main idea

To help you catch the main ideas of a conversation, listen carefully for common expressions that we use to introduce a main idea.

- *The most important thing here …*
- *Well, it is important to note …*
- *And I stress the importance of …*

Listen carefully for common words and phrases that we use to talk about things generally.

- *in general, overall, on the whole*

We usually speak more slowly or loudly when we want to emphasize a main idea.

2.2 **E LISTEN FOR DETAIL** Listen again. Find and correct six mistakes in the summary of Emma's story.

> Emma is ~~33~~ 35 and she works in ~~the sailing industry.~~ advertising. She loves swimming and ~~fishing~~ diving. For the last few years, she's been learning how to sail. Her dream is to live on a yacht and sail around the world. She hasn't bought a yacht yet because ~~she can't find one that she likes~~ they are expensive. She sold her house and bought a houseboat. The houseboat is an opportunity for Emma to learn to live on the ~~sea~~ water and move from place to place. She is happy with her decision to buy a houseboat because it means that she has 'made the break' from ~~the water to the land.~~ the land to the water

F SPEAK Work in groups and discuss the questions.

1. Do you agree that living on a houseboat will help Emma to achieve her ultimate dream? Give reasons.
2. What are the pros and cons of living on a houseboat compared to living on land?

2.1 Important decisions

LEAD-IN

With books closed, ask students to write down as many words connected to water as they can. You could help by giving prompts, e.g. types of water, ways of traveling on water, etc.

LISTENING

A Tell students to open their books and check if any of the words are the same as those the students thought of. Focus students' attention on the pictures and ask them to match the words and phrases to picture a or b. Check answers as a whole class. Practice pronunciation of *oceans*, *canals* and *yacht*.

B Put students into pairs to discuss the questions. Encourage them to ask follow-up questions to show interest in each other's comments and opinions. Do the same when you get feedback from the class.

2.2 **C** Tell students the pictures are related to a podcast. Ask them to listen and match the pictures to the sentences.

2.2 **D** Point out listening strategies to help understand the main idea of a conversation. Tell students some of the expressions were used in the podcast, so they should listen for them to help with the task. Ask students to read through the phrases and try to remember the main ideas of the story before they listen to the podcast again and check. In feedback, elicit not just the answers but what made the students decide they were the main ideas. You could practice pronunciation of these phrases, highlighting the intonation used. This will raise students' awareness of these features and start to build their confidence to use them in their own speaking.

2.2 **E** Tell students to read the summary and correct the six factual mistakes in it. They can then listen once more to check before you check answers as a whole class.

F Put students into groups to discuss the questions. Encourage them to give reasons to support their opinions. In feedback, record useful language that comes up on the board.

AUDIO SCRIPT

2.2

Listening, Exercise C
I = Interviewer E = Emma

I: Welcome to Dreams Come True, the podcast that finds out about people's life-long dreams and how they've turned them into reality. My guest in the studio today is Emma Sykes from New York.

E: Hello, thanks for having me!

Ex E Ex E **I:** Glad you could be here. Now, Emma, you are 35 and you are the owner of a successful advertising agency, is that right?

E: Yes, that's right.

I: So you've already had a lot of success in your life.

E: Yes, you could say that. I've worked very hard and the agency is doing well, but I still have dreams – well, one dream anyway.

I: And I believe that dream involves big plans on water! Tell us a little more about it.

Ex E **E:** That's right, John. Ever since I was young, I've been fascinated by the water. I love swimming and diving, and for the last few years I've been learning how to sail. My ultimate dream, the thing I've wanted to achieve my whole life, is to live on a yacht and sail around the world.

I: Wow, that's a big dream! And it doesn't sound easy. Tell us, just how have you made this dream a reality?

E: Well, that's the thing … I haven't. Not yet. Not completely.

I: So, you haven't sailed around the world?

Ex E **E:** No, I haven't. It's just not practical at this time in my life. Yachts are very expensive. I've saved a fair amount of money, but not enough yet. Plus, I don't have enough skills or knowledge yet to go sailing on my own across the oceans.

I: Well, that does sound very complicated! So how do you keep going with your plan when it seems so far away?

Ex D **E:** For me, the most important thing is to make a decision to put a plan into action. Once you've made the decision, you can set short-term and long-term goals that will help you achieve your dream.

I: I see. Yes, that's a good point. So what are some of your short-term goals? How are you going to work toward that ultimate goal?

E: Well, there's the sailing lessons, obviously. But actually, I've turned one part of the dream into reality already.

I: Really? What's that?

E: A year ago, I sold my house and used some of the money to buy a houseboat. It isn't a yacht, and it won't take me around the world, but it's a home and it's on the water. OK, I'm on freshwater, not saltwater, but I now live on a boat.

I: Wow, that's already a pretty big change! But does living on a houseboat really prepare you for sailing around the world?

Ex D **E:** Yes, I think so. The important thing here is to stay motivated and not lose heart, and this step helps me to do that.

I: And of course, you're getting some experience of what it's like to live on the water.

Ex E Ex D **E:** Exactly! I'm learning to live in a small space, and I'm also finding out what it's like to live in a home that can move from place to place. OK, I'm cruising along canals, not crossing oceans, but doing something similar to my dream – it's a start.

I: And now that you've made that start, do you think your plan to sail around the world is more achievable?

Ex D **E:** Absolutely. On the whole, I think the hardest part of any journey is the first step. Now that I've made the break from the land to the water, I'll be able to take the next step of my journey with more confidence.

I: Well, thank you for coming to talk to us, Emma. I hope you can join us again once you've achieved your ultimate dream. Will you do that?

E: Yes, of course. I look forward to it.

I: Thank you, Emma. Now, next up, I'll be speaking to …

2.1 Important decisions

VOCABULARY

A Tell students to look at the verbs and phrases and explain that they were all used in the podcast. Tell students to match each verb to a phrase and point out that one verb can be used twice. Check answers as a whole class, ensuring students understand the meaning of the phrases. The best way to do this would be to refer back to how they were used in the *Listening* to provide useful context to help students grasp the meaning. Tell students that these are all collocation words which are commonly used together. There isn't a rule for why certain words go together. Students should record collocations from here and elsewhere. They could experiment in recording them in different ways to see which method is most effective for remembering them.

B Tell students to look at the photos of the three people talking about a life-changing decision they've made. Tell students to fill in the blanks in the stories with the collocations from Exercise A.

2.3 **C** Play the audio for students to check. In feedback, use these new stories for further context to consolidate understanding of any items that students found difficult to understand at first. Practice pronunciation of the collocations either by modeling them yourself or using the recording.

D Put students into pairs to discuss which they think are the most and least achievable decisions. Monitor and encourage debate if students have different opinions. Use the **Vocabulary Worksheet** on W6 for extra practice.

SPEAKING HUB

A Tell students to think about a life-changing decision they have made, using either the ideas provided or their own. Check that they all understand the vocabulary, e.g. *healthier* and *retrain*.

B Give students time to plan what they're going to say, writing notes about each of the prompts. Be clear that students shouldn't write out what they're going to say word for word. Monitor to help with language input. Tell fast finishers to rehearse what they're going to say in their heads, referring to their notes.

C Tell students to interview their partner about their decision. Elicit how students can turn the prompts into questions to ask during the interview. Remind students about the methods of highlighting the main ideas of a story from the *Listening*. If time permits, change partners and tell students to interview each other again. Repeating a speaking task can build students' confidence. Students refine the language they use and speak more fluently once their ideas are consolidated.

D Put students into new groups to tell each other the decisions they heard about. When they have all shared the stories, ask them to decide which was the most life-changing and why. If a group reaches a consensus early, they can rank all the decisions. Monitor and get the class to share in any really positive experiences, giving them time to ask each other any questions they may have.

METHODOLOGY HUB by Jim Scrivener

Guidelines for listening skills work in class

- Keep the recording short: two minutes of recorded material is enough to provide a lot of listening work.
- Play the recording a sufficient number of times. (This is one point that teacher trainers and supervisors regularly comment on when they observe teachers' lessons: the teachers did not give the students enough opportunities to hear the recording. The students found the material a lot more difficult than the teacher realized.)
- Let students discuss their answers together (possibly in pairs).
- Don't immediately acknowledge correct answers with words or facial expressions; throw the answers back to the class: What do you think of Claire's answer – do you agree?
- Don't be led by one strong student. Have they all understood it?
- Try to get the students to agree together without your help, using verbal prodding, raised eyebrows, nods, hints, etc. Play the recording again whenever they need to hear it, to confirm or refute their ideas, until they agree.
- Play little pieces of the recording (a word, a phrase, a sentence) again and again until it's clear.
- Give help if they are completely stuck – but still with the goal of getting them to work it out if at all possible (e.g. *There are three words in this sentence* or *Listen to what she says here*) rather than giving them the answers.
- Consider giving the students control of the recording – to listen when and to what they wish.
- Don't cheat them by changing your requirements halfway, i.e. don't set one task, but then afterward ask for answers to something completely different!
- Don't let them lose heart. Try to make sure the task is just within their abilities. It should be difficult, but achievable. The sense of achievement in finishing a task should be great: *It was difficult, but we did it!*

VOCABULARY

Collocations: making big decisions

A Match the verbs (1–8) with the phrases (a–i) to make collocations that Emma used in her interview. One verb can be used twice. Use the audio script on page 167 to help you.

1 lose	a a decision
2 make	b a plan into action
3 put	c short-term and long-term goals
4 set	d toward a goal
5 stay	e a dream into reality
6 take	f motivated
7 turn	g the break/change
8 work	h the next step
	i heart

B Read the information from the people (1–3) about a life-changing decision. Fill in the blanks with collocations from Exercise A in the correct form.

2.3 **C** Listen and check your answers.

D **SPEAK** Work in pairs. Which decision in Exercise C do you think is the most achievable? Which is the least achievable? Give reasons.

SPEAKING HUB

A Think about a life-changing decision that you have made. Use the ideas below to help you.

- moving (changing cities/countries)
- studying (a new course, retraining, learning a new skill)
- a lifestyle change (becoming healthier, in better shape, more relaxed)
- turning a dream into reality

B **PLAN** Write notes about your decision. Think about:

- why you made the decision.
- how you put it into action.
- short-term/long-term goals.
- how you feel about the decision now.
- any advice you can give related to your decision.

C **SPEAK** Work in pairs. Interview your partner about his/her life-changing decision. Use your ideas in Exercise B to help you. Take turns.

D **REFLECT** Work in groups. Tell the group about your partner's decision. Then discuss all of the decisions. Whose decision was the most life-changing?

1

Lee, 31

The biggest [1] ___decision___ I've ever made was when I decided to move out of my parents' house. I was pretty scared at first, to be honest. But I soon found an apartment in the same town with a couple of friends. Thinking about it now, it was the right time for me to [2] ___make___ the change from living at home to living with friends.

2

Maki, 25

Three years ago, I decided to climb El Capitan in Yosemite National Park. It was always one of those things on my bucket list. Since I started to put the [3] ___plan___ into action, I've learned a lot about climbing and myself. My advice? Never [4] ___lose___ heart! If you are [5] ___working___ toward a goal, you'll achieve it in the end. I haven't gone to Yosemite yet, but I know I will!

3

Alessandra, 35

When I was a teenager, I wanted to be a famous movie star. But it didn't happen. My dream now is to be a chef. I've learned that the best way to [6] ___turn___ a dream into reality is to be realistic. Set short-term [7] ___goals___ to help you [8] ___stay___ motivated. Becoming a chef is going to be difficult, but I've already started a course and cook regularly for friends and family.

- Talk about past experiences and things you want to do
- Talk about a life-changing decision

2.2 You can do it!

- Talk about an inspirational person
- Talk about solving a problem

V – dependent prepositions; problems and solutions
G – present and past ability
P – word stress: verbs with two syllables
S – deducing the meaning of unknown words from context

READING

A SPEAK Work in pairs and discuss the question.

How do retired people typically spend their time in your country?

B Read the ad taken from a local newspaper. Then answer the questions.

1. What is unusual about the ad?
2. Why do you think he has written the advertisement?
3. How do you think people reacted to the ad?

C READ FOR GIST Read *89-year-old seeks job* and check your answers to Exercise B.

D Look at the words in bold in the article. What do you think they mean? Use the strategies in the box to help you. Then work in pairs and compare your ideas.

1. seeks
2. snaps him up
3. spotted
4. enable him to
5. role
6. taking on

89-year-old **seeks** job: café **snaps him up**

An 89-year-old has found a job after putting an ad in his local paper asking for part-time work to stop him from 'dying of boredom'. Joe Bartley, from Paignton, south Devon, is due to start working in a café next week in the town after the owners of the family-run business **spotted** his ad.

'Whatever your age or your background, you deserve a chance,' said Cantina Bar and Kitchen's co-owner Sarah Martin. 'Most people have something to offer, and Joe is someone who is eager, who is putting himself out there. What is not to like about that? A lot of people who come here don't just come for coffee – they come for a chat – so Joe is perfect.'

Ex B Q2 Bartley has lived alone since his wife, Cassandra, died a couple of years ago, and he has been lonely. 'I miss my wife dreadfully, when you live on your own there is no one to speak to. I like reading, and I'll watch a little television, but there's a lot of trash on these days. I just got bored stiff with nothing to do. I thought even though I am 89, I can still work. I can clean tables, do some gardening – anything really.'

Bartley put his advertisement in the *Herald Express* last month. 'The owner called me and she asked me to come in. So I arrived at the café, we had a little chat and shook hands.' He is now looking forward to earning his own money to **enable him to** pay his rent. 'I can't believe it really. I feel great about it,' he said.

Ex B Q3 Bartley told *The Guardian* that the media reaction has been incredible, adding that he is in danger of becoming a celebrity. 'When I first put in the ad, I thought it was just an old guy looking for work – I don't really see what is strange about that,' he said. 'But have I now reached celebrity status? That might worry some people, but it doesn't worry me.'

His new **role** in the café was not the only job offer he got. Glenn Rodgers, an independent baker in Barnstaple, north Devon, offered him a job, but the bakery was too far away for Bartley to travel.

Rodgers wanted to offer the senior citizen a job to put a 'smile on his face'. 'More employers should think about **taking on** older staff,' he added. 'Why not give him a chance? Also, it works both ways: employers are getting experienced reliable staff who really want to work.'

Bartley will get a ride to work with his new employer on Sundays, but will take a bus the rest of the week. 'He is delighted and we are looking forward to it,' said Martin. 'We think about these things all the time. We are never going to be rich, but we like to give something back to society.'

2.2 You can do it

LEAD-IN

Write the word *Work* in the middle of a circle and then draw some lines branching off in different directions. Put students into groups and give them three minutes to think of as many related words as they can. Elicit a couple of ideas (*job, part-time, full-time*) as a whole class to clarify the task.

READING

A Do this stage with books closed to prevent students from being distracted or influenced by the pictures. Put students into pairs and ask them to discuss how people in their country typically spend their time when retired. You could ask extra questions as well, e.g. *What age do people usually retire in their country, Are students looking forward to retiring (and why / why not)?* Get some feedback here, encouraging students to go beyond the most obvious or stereotypical ideas.

B In the likely event that students didn't say that they expect retired people to be looking for a job, pique their interest in the text by telling them they're going to read an unusual story about a retired person. Tell students to open their books, look at the ad and picture and discuss the questions. Get some feedback on students' predictions, but don't confirm or deny anything yet.

C Tell students to read the news article and check how accurate their answers in Exercise B were. Let students compare in pairs after reading, changing their answers together if necessary, before whole-class feedback.

1 *It is a little unusual for someone to place an ad looking for work. It is also unusual in the UK for that person to be 89 years old. The final sentence is very unusual in an ad related to work.*
2 *He wrote the ad because he was lonely and bored after his wife died. He felt he was still able to work.*
3 *People were impressed by the ad. He received two job offers. The media reported on the story. People wanted to help him. It was an opportunity for other people to do something positive and generous by offering him work.*

D Point out the strategies in the box for deducing the meaning of unknown words from context. Go through the first word *seeks* as an example, asking students each of the questions from the box before encouraging them to suggest what they think it means. Students can then work in pairs and follow the same steps for the other words. In feedback, ask students to tell you how they worked out the meaning of the words, again referring back to the questions in the box.

1 *looks for*
2 *employs him / gives him a job*
3 *saw/noticed*
4 *make it possible for him to*
5 *job*
6 *employing / giving someone a job*

TEACHING IDEA by David Seymour and Maria Popova

Topic: Job interview

Use this activity to extend the topic.

If you do not already know about the students' professions or future career plans, ask them to tell you the job they do, or the one they would like to do. Choose two or three students who do, or would like to do, the same kind of work and put them together to prepare for a job interview for a specific position of your choosing. They should write a list of their relevant skills and strengths.

The rest of the class works in two or three groups to write interview questions for this position. Applicant A is interviewed by the first group, while B is interviewed by the second. Then they swap places.

Interviewers: Who had the best certifications and experience? Who was the most relaxed and friendly during the interview? Who gets the job?

Applicants: How did you each feel about your interview? What did you think about the attitude of the different interviewers? Do you think you'll get the job?

TEACHING IDEA by David Seymour and Maria Popova

Topic: Project

Use this activity to extend the topic.

Look in the help wanted section of a newspaper and find a job advertisement to bring to the next class. In class, take a look at everybody else's ad and agree on the three or four most interesting ones. Work in groups, one ad for each group. Agree on a list of the skills and strengths needed for the job and discuss what research you could do on the company and the job before applying.

Write a cover letter for the job. (Elicit the layout and conventions for this kind of letter. Decide if the letter should simply request an application form, enclose a résumé or give additional information.)

Write your own résumé in English and bring it to class. Include the following information:

personal details, personal profile, education and certifications, employment history, other skills, hobbies/interests, references

In class, work in pairs or small groups. Look at another student's résumé and make suggestions for improving it.

E Tell students to read the comments and discuss which ones they agree or disagree with. You could also encourage them to discuss if they could imagine this situation happening in their country, and, if so, what people's reactions would be.

VOCABULARY

A Tell students that all the phrases come from the article and the comments they've just read. Check that students understand the meaning of the words in bold, and which ones are verbs or adjectives. Tell students to try to fill in each blank with a preposition. Students can then look back at the article and find the phrases to check their answers. Encourage students to think about how they would say the phrases in their own language and to notice any similarities or differences in the prepositions used.

B Tell students to fill in the blanks in the questions with a verb or adjective from Exercise A. You could make this more challenging by telling students to cover A while they do this, then uncover it to check when they've finished. Check answers as a whole class. Highlight that in question 4 *prepare for* was used as a verb in the comments, but here it's an adjective, *prepared for*.

C Tell students to discuss the questions with a partner. Encourage them to ask each other follow-up questions and to expand on their answers. These questions should produce interesting answers. Monitor and get students to share any particularly interesting answers with the whole class. Use the **Vocabulary Worksheet** on W8 for extra practice.

SPEAKING

A Tell students that they're going to choose someone to receive an award for inspiring others because of their special or unusual achievements. Give a personal example to further model the task. Tell students to work alone and think of three people who they think should receive the award.

B Tell students to work in pairs and explain who the people they've chosen are and what they've done to deserve the award. Tell students they have to agree on the one person who they think is the most inspirational and who they will nominate for the award.

C Put students into larger groups to give a presentation about their inspirational person and reasons why this person should win the award. Monitor and listen out for good examples of language used and errors that you could look at later in feedback. Once all students have made their presentations, tell them to vote in their group for who should win the award.

D Get feedback as a whole class. Each group should explain who their winner was and why they chose that person. If you have time, you could take a vote for the whole-class winner. Finish with some feedback on students' language use during the task. With some classes, peer feedback on language and delivery can be a useful way to round off a presentation activity. You should always handle this kind of feedback sensitively, though. One approach is to give students some areas to focus and write notes on: for example, pace, organization, etc. Ensure that feedback always focuses on some positive aspects of each presentation.

AUDIO SCRIPT

2.4

Listening, Exercise B
M = Matt S = Suzanna N = Nancy R = Roberto

M: You know, when you move away from home, arrive in a new place, there are lots of different challenges, and for me the biggest one was eating. Well, not eating, but cooking. (Ex C Q1) I mean, I could make a salad or a sandwich, but not cook anything, like, I couldn't boil an egg. I know that sounds silly, but I simply had no idea. Anyway, I looked at some books and (Ex C Q2) also found some excellent 'how to cook' videos online. To be honest, the books didn't help, but I started to teach myself with the videos. I wasn't very good at first – the first time, I didn't manage to make anything at all; I just watched the video and then ordered a takeout! But, I never gave up. I kept practicing. And when my parents came to see me six months later, I managed to cook them a really tasty meal. They were so surprised.

S: I really hate standing up in front of people to give a talk or a presentation. So, when (Ex C Q3) my brother asked me to make a speech at his wedding, I didn't know what to do. I couldn't say no to him. Luckily a friend of mine, an actor, helped me. Basically, we created a character for me to play when giving the speech, so that I didn't think it was actually me standing up to speak. (Ex C Q4) Also, I learned my speech by heart so that I didn't need to use any notes. Just like an actor. On the big day, I wasn't able to stop my hands from shaking, but I remembered everything and I played that character. And, incredibly, I was able to complete the speech. That was a big day for me, as well as for my brother.

N: I worked as a volunteer in a village school in China for about six months, and the language was my biggest problem. (Ex C Q5) I was able to speak very basic Chinese, but I couldn't remember many new words. I studied each day, but didn't achieve much – the words went in one ear and then straight out the other! Then, I had a great idea. I had my guitar with me, so I started to write simple songs with all the new words. They were kind of like children's songs. I asked a Chinese friend to check my grammar was correct, and then tried to learn the songs. And, you know what, it worked. Each day, I was able to remember those new words, and I even started singing the songs to the kids. I was actually pretty nervous the first time I sang to them, but (Ex C Q6) I managed to do it without mistakes, although I think my pronunciation was pretty poor, from the way the kids were laughing at me.

R: When I was a child, (Ex C Q7) I never learned to swim, and, when I started going on beach vacations, I really regretted that. My friends spent all day swimming in the ocean, but I wasn't able to swim. All I could do was sunbathe! So, I asked my sister to teach me. She was very patient, but, after a few months, I gave up because I still couldn't swim. Then, after another vacation just sitting on the beach, I decided to try again. This time, I paid for lessons at the local pool. And yes, after a few more months, I finally managed to swim 50 meters. That felt so good. And then, that next holiday, (Ex C Q8) I was finally able to swim in the ocean with my friends – that felt incredible. A real achievement!

Deducing the meaning of unknown words from context

When you do not know the meaning of words and phrases, you can use their context to help you understand them.

Think about:

- What type of word or phrase is it (noun, adjective or verb)?
- Does it have a prefix (*un-*, *im-*) or suffix (*-ment*, *-ion*)?
- Where is it in the sentence and what other words are near it?
- How does the word relate to the paragraph?
- What possible meanings of the word suit the topic of the sentence, paragraph and text?

E **SPEAK** Work in pairs. Look at the readers' comments on the article. Do you agree or disagree with them? Why?

Comments

Smart1

Joe is an inspiration to us all! He should be very proud of himself for getting a job that some would say is more suitable for a younger person.

ID2

If no one had replied to the ad, Joe could have thought about volunteering. Mind you, even those roles are hard to find these days!

Jan1003

The government should be more aware of this problem and work with communities to help people like Joe. Loneliness is a big problem nowadays.

4Kent

Though fairly typical of this newspaper, it's great that this issue is in the news. We need to prepare for our retirement now, so we can retire comfortably, not serve coffee in our old age.

VOCABULARY

Dependent prepositions (verb/adjective + *for/of*)

A Look at the phrases from *89-year-old seeks job* and from the comments. Are the words in bold verbs or adjectives? Complete each phrase with *for* or *of*.

verb **1** **look** __for__ work
verb **2** **prepare** __for__ retirement
adjective **3** **typical** __of__ this newspaper
adjective **4** **suitable** __for__ a younger person
adjective **5** **proud** __of__ himself
adjective **6** **aware** __of__ this problem
verb **7** **work** __for__ a café
verb **8** **ask** __for__ part-time work

B Complete the questions with a verb or adjective from Exercise A.

1 What do you __look__ for in an ideal job?
2 Do you think age ever makes people more or less __suitable__ for some jobs?
3 Which of your achievements are you most __proud__ of?
4 What big changes in your life are coming soon? How can you __prepare__ for them?

C **SPEAK** Work in pairs. Ask and answer the questions in Exercise B.

SPEAKING

A Think of three people who should receive an award for inspiring others because of their special or unusual achievements.

B Work in pairs. Discuss your choices and choose the most inspirational person. Write down some of your reasons for choosing that person.

C Work in groups. In pairs, give a short presentation about your inspirational person, explaining why the person should win the award. As a group, vote for who should win the award.

D Tell the class about your group's choice. Why did the group feel the person was special? Did everyone in the group agree with the vote?

1

2

3
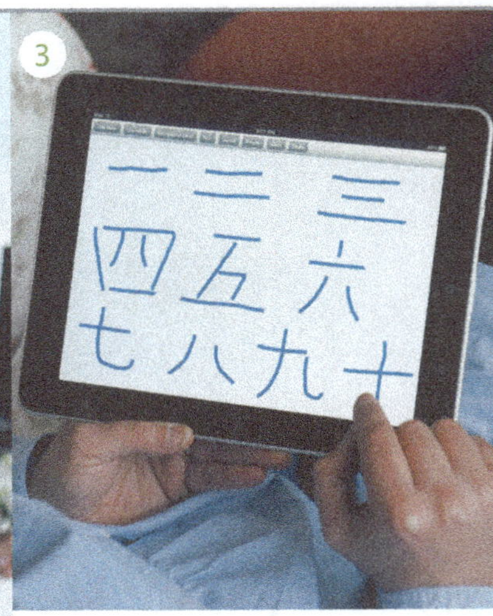

4

LISTENING

A SPEAK Work in pairs. Look at the pictures (1–4). What are the people doing? What problems could they have when they do these things?

2.4 **B** LISTEN FOR MAIN IDEA You are going to listen to four people talking about a challenge or problem. Complete the sentences (1–4) with the phrases in the box. There are four extra phrases.

> ~~by pretending to be a different person~~
> by spending a lot of money ~~by taking classes~~
> ~~by using a different skill~~ by using books during a vacation
> ~~on his/her own~~ with the help of his/her family

1 Matt solved a problem on his own.
2 Suzanna solved a problem by pretending to be a different person
3 Nancy solved a problem by using a different skill.
4 Roberto solved a problem by taking classes.

2.4 **C** LISTEN FOR DETAIL Listen again. Choose the correct words to complete the sentences.

1 Matt *knew* / *didn't know* how to cook simple hot food.
2 He found useful advice on *the internet* / *TV*.
3 Suzanna needed to give a speech at *work* / *a family event*.
4 She *read* / *didn't read* her speech aloud from a script.
5 Nancy *knew a little* / *didn't know any* Chinese.
6 She *made several* / *didn't make any* mistakes when she first sang to the children.
7 When Roberto was a child, he *tried* / *didn't try* to learn to swim.
8 He *has* / *still hasn't* swum in the ocean.

D SPEAK Work in pairs and discuss the questions.

1 Which of the four challenges do you think is the hardest?
2 What advice could you give to someone who can't do those things well?
3 Have you had any of these challenges yourself? What did you do to deal with them?
4 Is it more important to solve problems yourself or ask for help?

PRONUNCIATION

Word stress: verbs with two syllables

A Work in pairs. Look at the verbs from the listening below. Take turns saying the verbs and marking the stress.

1 achieve	3 complete	5 regret
2 arrive	4 create	6 study

B Does the stress normally come on the first or second syllable? the second syllable

2.5 **C** Now listen to the verbs. Check and repeat.

GRAMMAR

Present and past ability

A WORK IT OUT Look at the sentences (1–9). Write *a* if they are about having (or not having) a general ability or skill in the past. Write *b* if they are about doing something (or not doing something) on a particular occasion in the past.

1 I was able to speak very basic Chinese. a
2 I managed to cook them a very tasty meal. b
3 I was able to complete the speech. b
4 I couldn't boil an egg. a
5 I could make a salad. a
6 The first time, I didn't manage to make anything. b
7 I wasn't able to swim. a
8 I wasn't able to stop my hands shaking. b
9 I couldn't say no to him. b

B Choose the correct words to complete the rules.

> **Present and past ability**
>
> 1 When we talk about ability or skills in general in the present, we *use* / *do not use* *can/can't* or *(not) be able to*.
>
> 2 When we talk about ability or skills in general in the past, we *use* / *do not use* *could*, *couldn't* or *(not) be able to*.
>
> 3 When we talk about ability to do a specific task on a particular occasion in the past, we *use* / *do not use* *(not) manage to*, *(not) be able to* or *couldn't*. We do not usually use *could*.

C Go to the Grammar Hub on page 124.

LISTENING

A Point out the pictures and ask students to discuss the questions about what the people are doing. To encourage students to give more detailed answers, you could split the class into pairs or four groups and give each group or pair just one picture each to discuss. Get whole-class feedback, eliciting as many ideas from everyone as you can. Elicit the word *challenge* in relation to these activities at some stage during feedback.

2.4 B Tell the students they can now check their ideas as they're going to hear the people in the pictures talking about a challenge or problem they faced. Tell students to complete the sentences with the phrases from the box. Make sure students realize that they only need to use four of the phrases, and the other four don't match with any of the speakers. Check answers as a whole class but don't go into any more detail yet.

2.4 C Tell students they're going to listen again but before they do try to complete the sentences from memory. Students then listen again to check. This time, elicit more detail in feedback and ask students to explain their answers.

D Put students into pairs to discuss the questions. Discuss the questions as a whole class, encouraging students to expand on their answers, especially if they have personal experience of any of these situations.

PRONUNCIATION

A Tell students the verbs are all from the *Listening*. Model the first one, then tell students to pronounce them in pairs and mark where they think the stress is.

B Tell students to look over their answers and notice where they think the stress normally comes.

2.5 C Tell students to listen and check. Check answers as a whole class.

GRAMMAR

A Elicit that the sentences are all about ability. Use the first two sentences as examples to make sure students understand the difference between general ability and ability to do something on a particular occasion in the past. Then ask them to look at the other sentences.

B After checking the answers in Exercise A, tell students to use the sentences to help them complete the rules.

C Direct students to the **Grammar Hub** (see below and TB21). Use the **Grammar Worksheet** on W7 for extra practice.

GRAMMAR HUB

2.2 Present and past ability

can

	Positive	Negative
I/you/he/she/it/we/they	**Rosa can ride** a horse.	**They cannot drive.** **They can't drive.**

Question	Positive short answer	Negative short answer
Can you fish in the lake?	Yes, **I can**.	No, **I can't**.

***be able to* (simple present)**

	Positive	Negative
I/you/he/she/it/we/they	**I am able to book** a taxi online.	**Sven isn't able to fly** a plane.

Question	Positive short answer	Negative short answer
Are Tomas and Jaime able to work as volunteers?	Yes, **they are**.	No, **they aren't**.

***manage to* (simple present)**

	Positive	Negative
I/you/he/she/it/we/they	**He manages to remember** new words every day.	**We don't manage to meet** our friends very regularly.

Question	Positive short answer	Negative short answer
Does Laura manage to stay calm when she presents?	Yes, **she does**.	No, **she doesn't**.

- We use *can, can't, (not) be able to* and *(not) manage to* talk about our ability or skills in general in the present.

could

Subject	Positive	Negative
I/you/he/she/it/we/they	**I could cook** when I was young.	**Paolo couldn't take on** more work.

Question	Positive short answer	Negative short answer
Could your cousin swim as a baby?	Yes, **he could**.	No, **he couldn't**.

- We use *could, couldn't* or *(not) be able to* when we talk about our ability or skills in general in the past.
- We use *couldn't, (not) be able to* and *(not) manage to* when we talk about our ability to do a specific task on a particular occasion in the past. We usually do NOT use *could*.

We couldn't solve the problem at that time.
BUT NOT ~~We could solve the problem at that time.~~
We were/weren't able to solve the problem at that time.
We managed / didn't manage to solve the problem at that time.

- When a verb is followed by *-ing* or the infinitive, we can't use *can*. We use *be able to* instead.

Sebastian enjoys being able to cook.
NOT ~~Sebastian enjoys can cook.~~

D Model the game with your own personal example sentences before students write their own. Get some feedback on the most interesting stories.

VOCABULARY

A–C Put students into pairs to complete the exercises.

D Direct students to the **Vocabulary Hub** (TB121) for further practice of vocabulary related to problems and solutions.

E Tell students to complete the personality test for themselves. They should then check the **Communication Hub** (TB121) to see what their answers say about them.

SPEAKING HUB

A Elicit from students what typical questions they think are asked at job interviews. Tell students they're going to prepare to answer a question like this and ask them to read it.

B Tell students to work individually and write notes to prepare their answer. Monitor to provide language. Make sure students are not scripting their answer word for word.

C Tell students to ask and answer the question in pairs, writing notes about their partner's answer as they listen.

D Put students into new pairs to tell each other their previous partner's answer. Tell students to decide which answer they think was best and why. Conclude by discussing answers as a whole class. Focus on content and the language used.

GRAMMAR HUB

2.2 Present and past ability

A Complete the sentences with the words in the box.

can could couldn't manage managed wasn't

1 She didn't *manage* to make it to the interview on time.
2 Amazingly, Diego could read when he was two and a half years old.
3 They managed to find a solution to the complicated problem.
4 We were discussing something important, so I wasn't able to answer my phone.
5 Francisco couldn't stop his hands from shaking because he was so nervous.
6 Michela is amazing because she can work three jobs and not be tired.

B Put the words in order to make sentences.

1 can't / Helena / egg / an / boil
Helena can't boil an egg.
2 a / manage / I / cook / meal / didn't / tasty / to
I didn't manage to cook a tasty meal.
3 our / we / goals / long-term / were / to / able / achieve
We were able to achieve our long-term goals.
4 system / very / can / quickly / analyze / the / data
The system can analyze data very quickly.
5 manage / speech / to / give / Aisha / her / did / ?
Did Aisha manage to give her speech?
6 couldn't / easier / suggest / an / plan / they
They couldn't suggest an easier plan.

C Choose the correct option.

1 Marina ______ raise enough money for her trip.
a wasn't able b didn't manage **(c) couldn't**
2 Olaf ______ paint great pictures of animals.
(a) can b manages c is able
3 I ______ watch TV all day as a kid.
a was able b can **(c) could**
4 They ______ to deal with any more problems.
a couldn't **(b) weren't able** c can't
5 Hana ______ to find a good cooking video.
a can't **(b) didn't manage** c couldn't
6 She forgot her lines, but she ______ stay calm.
a could **(b) managed to** c was able
7 She ______ to find the theater with the help of her app.
(a) was able b manages c can't
8 Fred ______ sing to other people – he gets too nervous.
a couldn't b manages **(c) can't**
9 Poppy ______ work and study, but she's usually tired.
(a) manages to b able to c can't
10 I ______ take my English exam because I was on vacation.
(a) couldn't b didn't manage c wasn't able

➤ Go back to page 20.

D SPEAK Work in pairs. Play *True or false?* Follow the instructions.

1 Write two sentences for each idea (a–c). One sentence should be true and one should be false.

a something you can do now, but which you couldn't do five or ten years ago

b a problem you had because you weren't able to do something

c a particular time that you managed to do something that was difficult

2 Listen to your partner's sentences. Ask questions to find out more information, then guess which sentences are true. Take turns.

VOCABULARY

Problems and solutions

A SPEAK Work in pairs. How good are you at solving problems? Give yourself a score out of five. Explain your score to your partner.

B Look at the personality test. Complete the sentences with *problem(s)* or *solution(s)*.

How do you feel about difficult situations and problems?

Use this personality test to find out. How true are the following statements for you on a scale of 1–5?

1 = False	**4** = Mostly true
2 = Mostly false	**5** = True
3 = Sometimes true / Sometimes false	

1 If I can't **solve** a difficult __problem__, I don't give up. I keep trying until I find a __solution__.
1 2 3 4 5

2 I always try to **deal with** __problems__ because ignoring them only **causes** more __problems__.
1 2 3 4 5

3 When working in groups, I **suggest** a lot of __solutions__ to any __problems__.
1 2 3 4 5

4 When I have a __problem__, I look at it from different angles to **come up with** the best __solution__.
1 2 3 4 5

5 When I deal with a complicated __problem__, I **analyze** the possible __solutions__ with lists of their pros and cons.
1 2 3 4 5

6 I prefer to discuss a __problem__ with other people. Then we can **agree on** a __solution__ together.
1 2 3 4 5

C WORK IT OUT Match the verbs in bold in the personality test with the definitions (1–7).

1 to think of something such as an idea or a plan come up with

2 to study or examine something in detail in order to understand or explain it analyze

3 to decide together what will be done and how it will be done agree on

4 to offer an idea or plan for someone to consider suggest

5 to take action to do something deal with

6 to find a solution to something that is causing difficulties solve

7 to make something happen, usually something bad cause

D Go to the **Vocabulary Hub** on **page 142**.

E SPEAK Take the personality test. Go to the **Communication Hub** on **page 148** to see what your answers may show about you. Then work in pairs and discuss your answers.

SPEAKING HUB

A You are going to answer a question that employers frequently ask in job interviews to find out about problem-solving skills.

> Can you tell us about a time when you faced a challenge or a difficult problem that you successfully dealt with?

B PLAN Write notes about:

- the situation.
- what action you took to deal with the situation.
- what you learned from trying to deal with the situation.

C SPEAK Work in pairs. Ask and answer the question. Write notes about your partner's answer.

D REFLECT Tell a classmate what your partner said. Think about what you both heard. Whose answer was best?

- Talk about an inspirational person
- Talk about solving a problem

Café Hub

2.3 Picture this

F – ask for, give and refuse permission
P – intonation and stress in questions

COMPREHENSION

A 00:00–00:50 Watch the first part of the video. What wakes Gaby up? Someone knocking on the door.

B Work in pairs. The actual photo shoot is not successful. Look at the stills and predict the difficulties that Gaby has.

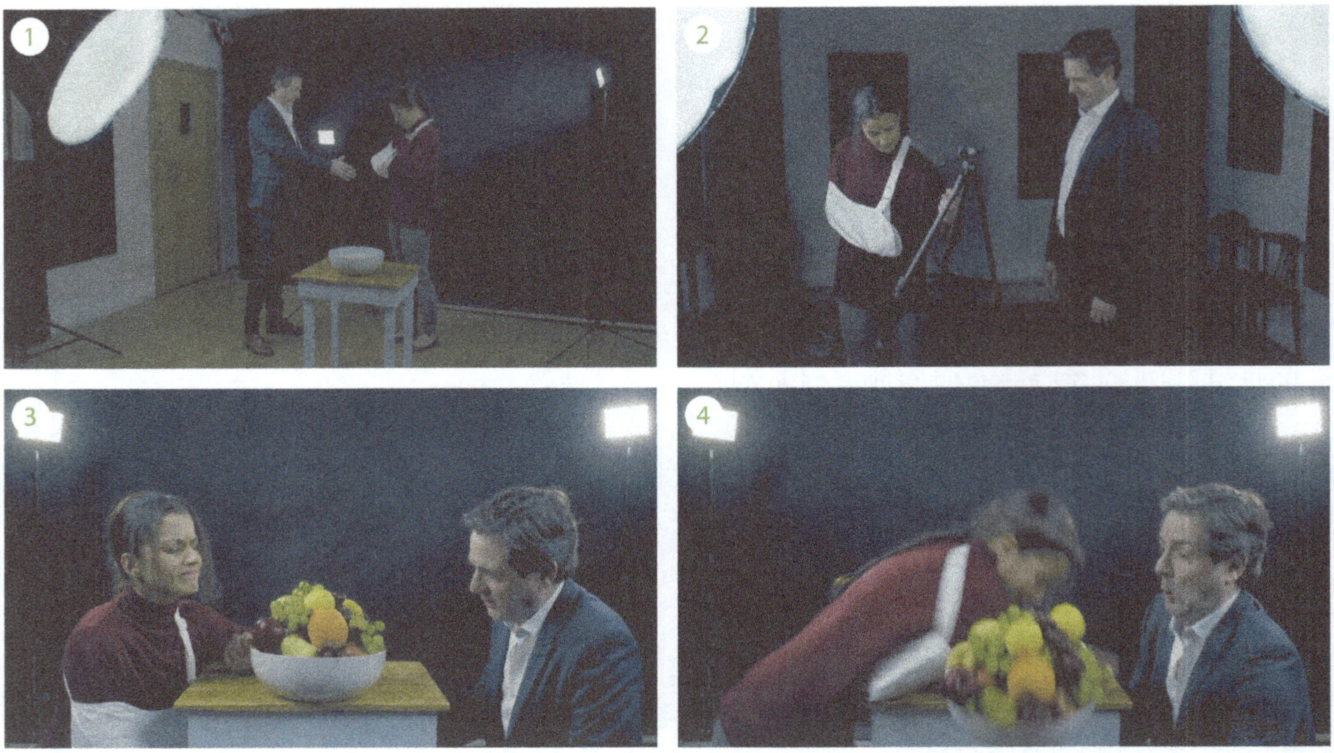

C 00:51–04:00 Watch the second part of the video and check your ideas. Then complete the sentences with *Gaby* or *Eric*.

1 Gaby gets Eric's name wrong.
2 Eric is in a hurry.
3 Gaby can't set up the tripod.
4 Gaby gets Eric's name wrong again.
5 Gaby drops the camera.
6 Eric fixes the camera onto the tripod.
7 Eric suggests more light on the bowl.
8 Gaby suggests putting fruit in the bowl.

FUNCTIONAL LANGUAGE

Asking for, giving and refusing permission

A Eric was in a hurry and wanted to start the photo shoot right away. Check (✓) the phrase he used.

Asking for permission

Can we start …	☐	Least formal
Could we start … right away?	☐	↑
May we start …	☐	
Is it all right if we start …	✓	
Would it be OK to …	☐	↓
Would you mind if we started …	☐	Most formal

Giving and refusing permission

Sure, I don't see why not.	I'm sorry, but …
No problem.	I'd like to help, but …
Yes, of course.	I'm afraid that isn't possible.

MILLY

SAM

NEENA

ZAC

GABY

B Write down phrases asking for permission in the following situations. Choose an appropriate level of formality.

1 It's very hot in the classroom. You want to open a window. Ask your classmates.

____

2 You have a dental appointment tomorrow. You want to leave work early. Ask your boss.

____

3 You are chairing a business meeting. You want to start. Ask everyone in the meeting.

____

4 It's a beautiful day and you're in a park. You want to sit on the grass. Ask the park ranger.

____

5 You're in front of somebody's house. You want to park your car there. Ask the home owner.

____

6 You're in a lecture with 200 other people. You want to ask a question. Ask the lecturer.

____

USEFUL PHRASES

A Choose the correct alternatives to complete the useful phrases. Watch the video again if necessary.

1 ***Call / Name*** me Gaby. = Please use the name 'Gaby' when you talk to me.

2 I can't thank you ***enough / at all***. = I am very grateful to you.

3 You ***must / should*** be Derek. = I am sure your name is Derek.

4 I don't have ***this / that*** long. = I have very little time.

5 We're ***almost / fairly*** there. = We have nearly finished.

B How do you say these useful phrases in your language?

PRONUNCIATION

Intonation and stress in questions

2.6 **A** Listen and repeat the questions. Does the intonation rise or fall after the main stress in the sentence?

1 Could I open the window? rises

2 Can I leave work early? falls

3 Is it all right if we start now? falls

4 Would it be OK to sit on the armchair? rises

5 Would you mind if I parked my car here? rises

6 May I ask you a question? rises

B Practice the stress and intonation in the questions in Exercise A.

SPEAKING

A Work in pairs. You are going to write a conversation in which you ask permission for something.

- Decide on the situation: why do you need permission and who from?
- Decide on the level of formality.
- Write your conversation.

B **PRESENT** Practice your conversation. Then act out your conversation for the class.

Ask for, give and refuse permission

➤ Turn to page 157 to learn how to write an informal email.

2.3 Picture this

LEAD-IN

Give students three minutes to think of as many words related to photography as they can. Elicit answers on the board and try to elicit *tripod* and *photo shoot*.

COMPREHENSION

A ▶ 00:00–00:50 Point out the pictures of the characters and elicit what they can remember about each. Students then watch and answer the question.

B Tell students to look at the pictures and predict what is going to happen, particularly why the photo shoot is unsuccessful.

C ▶ 00:51–04:00 Students watch the rest of the video to check their ideas. Let students compare in pairs after watching to complete the sentences. Play again if difficult.

FUNCTIONAL LANGUAGE

A Point out the phrases in the table, highlighting that they move from informal to formal. Ask students if they remember Eric's phrase.

B Tell students to imagine being in the situations and do the first one as a whole class. Students then discuss the others in pairs. Highlight to students that there may be several different correct answers for each situation.

USEFUL PHRASES

A Tell students all phrases were in the episode. Ask them to complete phrases with correct options. Play the video again if difficult.

B Tell students to think about how they would say these phrases in their own language.

PRONUNCIATION

2.6 **A** Tell students to listen and repeat, paying attention to intonation after the main stress. Point out that the main stress in a sentence is usually the final stressed syllable.

B Students practice asking the questions in pairs. Tell students to listen to their partner's stress and intonation and decide if it would make them likely to agree to the requests.

SPEAKING

A Students discuss the questions in pairs and then write the conversation. Remind them to refer to the phrases for permission as well as the useful phrases.

B Tell students to practice their conversations, paying special attention to their intonation. Students then act out their conversations for the class.

VIDEO SCRIPT

C = Client G = Gaby

C: These are excellent Gabriela. Excellent!

G: Please Derek, call me Gaby.

C: Yes of course, of course. Gaby – thank you. You've managed to capture the bowl perfectly. This is exactly what we were looking for! I can't thank you enough!

G: Come in. Hello. You must be Derek.

C: It's Eric actually.

G: Sorry, sorry! Of course. Eric. I'm Gaby.

C: Hi Gaby, nice to meet you. Is it alright if we start straight away? I haven't got that long.

G: Of course. No problem.

C: What's happened to your arm?

G: I fell over yesterday and hurt my wrist.

C: Oh no.

G: I've just got to set up the tripod and camera. It won't take long …

C: Erm … Can I do anything?

G: No, I'm fine.

C: I'm happy to help.

G: Actually, that would be great. Would you mind helping me with this?

C: Not at all. There you go.

G: Thanks, Derek.

C: Eric.

G: Eric! Sorry!

C: Are you okay?

G: Yes, I'm fine. Do you think you could help me with the camera as well?

C: Sure, no problem. That's all done.

G: Thank you so so much, it looks like we're ready to begin!

C: Would it be OK to have the light slightly brighter on this side?

G: Yes, of course.

C: These are definitely better. I think we're almost there. I feel like something's missing though. The shot feels a bit … Umm …

G: Empty …?

C: Yes.

G: How about adding some fruit?

C: Yes. Good idea. That would solve the problem. Yes, I think that looks good.

G: Maybe a few more grapes?

C: No, I think it's probably okay like that …

G: Come on. Just … one … more …

Z: Hey Gaby, how was the shoot?

G: A total disaster! I'm not sure photography is for me.

Z: I'm sure it wasn't that bad, I'll pick up some Pizza Roma to cheer you up!

G: Thanks, Zac.

2 Writing — Write an informal email

W – informal writing

A SPEAK Work in pairs. Read the email from Sophie to Marta. What is their relationship?

a family members
b new friends
c elementary school friends
d business colleagues

To: Marta
Subject: Hello and good news

Hi Marta,

How are you? I hope everything has been OK since you left New York. Did you have a good vacation with your family? I guess you're back at college now. Studying or partying hard? [1] b 🙂.

Sorry I haven't written sooner – I can't believe it's been two months since our course finished! I really miss New York. My English really improved, and I loved getting to know you, Sato and the others. [2] c

Anyway, I have some good news! I have a new job and I've moved to Paris. I'm working for a web design agency. I'm so happy. It's only a small company, but everyone's really nice and [3] a

So, how about coming to Paris to visit me? Would you like to? I remember that you haven't been to Paris before, so now's your chance. Come for a weekend and stay at my place – it's easy to get here from Rome! What do you think? [4] e

Let me know what you think, and let me know when you finally get on Facebook – [5] d

Hugs and all the best.
Sophie

B Read again. Answer the questions.

1 Where did Sophie and Marta meet each other? New York, during a course
2 When did they last see each other? Two months ago
3 Where do they live? Sophie–Paris, Marta–Rome
4 How has Sophie's life changed recently? She got a new job; moved to Paris
5 What does Sophie want Marta to do? To visit her in Paris.

C Complete Sophie's email with the sentences (a–e).

a I'm enjoying the work.
b Or both?
c Have you heard from anyone else from our class?
d I can't believe you haven't done that yet!
e I'd love to see you.

D Put the sections in the order they appear in Sophie's email.

telling Marta about what she has done recently	3
making a suggestion/plan for the future	4
asking about Marta's life	1
talking about a shared experience	2

E Look at the box. Find and underline features of informal writing in the sentences (1–4).

Informal writing

In emails and letters to friends and family, we usually use an informal writing style. We use:

- contractions, such as *You'll …*
- incomplete grammar, such as *How you doing?*
- informal words and phrases, such as *buddy* (= *friend*).
- informal punctuation, such as *!*, *–*.
- emojis/emoticons, such as 🙂.
- informal opening and closing expressions, such as *Hi*, *Hugs*.

1 I'm going on vacation soon – can't wait!
2 I've just passed my driving test 🙂.
3 All fine here. It's great to be back at college!
4 Big hug and say hi to your mom.

WRITING

A PREPARE You are going to write an informal email to a friend. Think of a friend you want to write to or imagine you are writing to a new friend.

B PLAN Write notes. Think about:

- What can you ask your friend about?
- What shared experience can you write about?
- What news do you have? What have you done recently?
- What suggestion or request can you make?

C WRITE Write your email (150–200 words). Use Sophie's email and the skills box to help you.

D REVIEW Work in pairs. Read your partner's email. Ask for more information about his/her news.

WRITING 157

Answers

1 *contractions: I'm, can't*
incomplete grammar: can't wait
2 *contractions: I've*
emojis/emoticons: 🙂
3 *contractions: It's*
incomplete grammar: All fine here.
informal punctuation: !
4 *informal grammar: say hi*
informal closing expression: big hug

Refer students to this email as a model for the writing task.

Remind students to use features of informal writing to make their emails sound more natural.

WRITING

With books closed, ask students to think of all the people they write emails to and the reasons they write to them. Ask the class to share some of their answers.

A Tell students to open their books and look at the photo of Sophie and Marta. Ask students what they think the relationship between them is. Tell students to read the email and check. Tell them to ignore the blanks in the email for now.

B Tell students to read the email again and answer the questions.

C Tell students to fill in the blanks in the email with the phrases. In feedback, elicit that the email is written in an informal style.

D Tell students that even though the email is informal, it is still well organized. Tell students to read it again and to put the sections in the order that they appear in the email. Point out that each of the first four paragraphs of the email is a section.

E Point out the features of informal writing in the box. Tell them to underline examples of these features in the sentences. In feedback, ask students if informal writing in their language follows similar conventions.

WRITING TASK

A Tell students to think of a friend they would like to write an informal email to. It could be a real friend or an imaginary new one.

B Tell students to write notes about the questions. Monitor to help with language input.

C Tell students to use their notes to write the email. Remind them to divide the email into paragraphs, one for each of the questions from Exercise B. Tell students to look back at Sophie's email and the features in the *Informal writing* box as well.

D Tell students to read each other's emails. Encourage them to ask each other questions to find out more information. Tell students to think about how well written the emails are in terms of style and organization. Finish with feedback both on the content of the emails and how successfully the students think the emails were written.

GRAMMAR

A Complete the comments (1–2) about achievable bucket lists with the correct form of the verbs in parentheses.

Comments

1 Maybe the best bucket list is a mixture of easy and hard to achieve . I [1] ___'ve done___ (*do*) both simple activities and bigger adventures. Both [2] ___have given___ (*give*) me great memories. I once [3] ___learned___ (*learn*) to bake a cake in the morning, and then [4] ___(I) did___ (*do*) my first bungee jump in the afternoon. The cake [5] ___tasted___ (*taste*) great after that! I [6] ___haven't done___ (*do*) a bungee jump since, but I [7] ___'ve made___ (*made*) plenty of cakes!

2 How about awesome adventures that also benefit other people or society? A few years ago, I [1] ___wanted___ (*want*) to ride an elephant, so I [2] ___found___ (*find*) a position as an international volunteer at an elephant conservation park. I [3] ___stayed___ (*stay*) there for two months. It [4] ___was___ (*be*) great to help a charity and do something on my bucket list. Since then, I [5] ___'ve done___ (*do*) loads of similar things.

B Find and correct the mistakes in five of the sentences.

1 When I was a kid, I could ~~to~~ swim. I learned as a baby.
2 They ~~wasn't~~ weren't able to score a goal. What a boring game.
3 I managed to finish everything. correct
4 I couldn't ~~to~~ ride a bike until I was 19.
5 I am able ^to dance fairly well.
6 I'm afraid you didn't ~~managed~~ manage to pass. You'll have to retake it.

VOCABULARY

A Match the sentence beginnings (1–5) and endings (a–e).

1 I don't believe in setting ___d___
2 It's easy to stay ___b___
3 I'm sorry you didn't get the job, but don't lose ___e___
4 When I moved to the countryside, I ___c___
5 I was nervous about taking ___a___

a the next step, but I knew it was the right time to make the change.
b motivated when you really enjoy what you do.
c turned my dream into reality!
d long-terms goals – I prefer to focus on my weekly plans.
e heart – there will be other opportunities.

B Complete the sentences with the correct form of the words in the box and *for* or *of*.

ask aware look prepare
proud suitable typical work

1 We're lost. We need to ___ask for___ help and get directions.
2 I ___'m looking for___ a new job. I check a few online agencies each week.
3 This behavior is ___typical of___ Jane. She has always been difficult.
4 She's giving a presentation tomorrow. She needs to ___prepare for___ that tonight.
5 Is this movie ___suitable for___ young children? I'd like to watch it with my niece.
6 We have both ___worked for___ the same company all our lives. That's very unusual.
7 Is your boss ___aware of___ all the problems with the project?
8 I'm very ___proud of___ my achievements. It's never too late to learn something new.

C Choose the correct words to complete the results of a personality quiz about problem solving.

The results show that when you try and [1]**deal** / **<u>solve</u>** a problem, you like to make quick decisions. This can be helpful, but sometimes you should take more time to [2]**<u>analyze</u>** / **come up with** the problem first. This will help when you have to [3]**<u>deal with</u>** / **suggest** complicated situations and need to [4]**<u>come up with</u>** / **cause** many different solutions.

The results also show that when you work on a team, you expect to [5]**solve** / **<u>agree on</u>** solutions quickly, and if you don't, you usually lose interest. However, if you don't take the time to look at the pros and cons of your solutions, this might [6]**<u>cause</u>** / **suggest** more problems.

FUNCTIONAL LANGUAGE

Put the dialogue in the correct order.

A: Alright, no problem. In that case could you lend me your phone? ___3___
A: Hey there, Pete. Would you mind if I borrowed your laptop? ___1___
B: I'm afraid I can't do that either – I'm expecting an important call. ___4___
B: I'm not sure to be honest – I have a lot of work to do today and I need it. ___2___
A: Yes, Arsenal is playing and I want to check the score! ___7___
A: OK, never mind. ___5___
B: Is it for something urgent? ___6___

View from Nelson's Column in Trafalgar Square towards Westminster, England.

On the move (phrase) traveling from place to place.
Synonyms: go (v), ride (v), commute (v)

The quote for this unit is humorous with Wilde implying that there is nothing more exciting to read than the story of his life while he is traveling.

Oscar Wilde (1854–1900) was an Irish poet and playwright. He wrote poetry and stories but is best known for his plays such as the comedy *The Importance of Being Earnest*.

OBJECTIVES

- talk about a difficult trip or travel experience
- talk about behavior on public transportation
- evaluate suggestions and justify a choice
- talk about why a plan didn't work
- tell a story
- write an email of complaint

Work with a partner. Discuss the questions.

1 Look at the picture. What different types of transportation can you see? How does the city's transportation compare to that in your own city?
2 Read the quote. How do you pass the time on public transportation?
3 Which types of transportation would you describe with the adjectives in the box?

convenient dangerous essential exciting expensive free fun noisy relaxing safe stressful tiring

ON THE MOVE 25

OBJECTIVES

Read the unit objectives to the class.

UNIT OPENER QUESTIONS

With books closed, write on the board *An advanced city is/has …* Put students into pairs and ask them to discuss different ways in which they would complete the sentence. Elicit students' ideas and write them on the board. Put students back into pairs to discuss which idea they agree with the most.

1 Tell students to look at the picture and elicit the different types of transportation shown (i.e. *bus, car, motorcycle*). Write the vocabulary on the board and practice pronunciation if needed. Put students into pairs to discuss how similar or different the public transportation in the city in the picture is to that in their own city, or nearest city.

2 Tell students to read the quote and discuss what they do while they are traveling. Share any interesting answers.

3 Check that students understand the adjectives, especially *convenient* (easy to use), *essential* (necessary) and *tiring* (making you feel tired). Practice pronunciation of all the adjectives. Ask students which methods of transportation they would describe with those adjectives. Elicit a couple of ideas as a whole class before students discuss them in pairs.

WORKSHEETS

Lesson 3.1 Travel experiences

Grammar: Narrative tenses (W9)

Vocabulary: Collocations: travel information (W10)

Lesson 3.2 Travel smart

Grammar: Articles and quantifiers (W11)

Vocabulary: Gradable and ungradable adjectives (W12)

3.1 Travel experiences

- Talk about a difficult trip or travel experience
- Talk about behavior on public transportation

G narrative tenses
P word stress in nouns ending in *-ion*
V collocations: travel information; nouns ending in *-ion*
S skim-reading to build a map of a text

LISTENING

A SPEAK Work in pairs and discuss the questions.

1 What types of transportation do you use? How often do you use them?
2 Which do you prefer and why? Which is your least favorite?
3 What problems might there be for each one?

3.1 **B LISTEN FOR GIST** Listen to a call-in radio show. What is the topic of today's discussion?

a bad or unusual trips to work
(b) bad or unusual trips in general
c bad or unusual trips on national holidays

3.1 **C LISTEN FOR DETAIL** Are the sentences true (T) or false (F)? Correct the false sentences. Then listen again and check your answers.

Junko's experience

1 There were no trains because ~~of the bad weather.~~ it was New Year's Day ___F___
2 She didn't sit at the bus stop for a long time. ___T___
3 ~~She stopped a police car to ask for help.~~ The police car stopped to ask if she needed help. ___F___
4 The police ~~found a taxi for her.~~ took her to her friend's house ___F___
5 She arrived at her friend's house in time for dinner. ___T___

Alan's experience

6 ~~He missed the first train because the taxi was slow.~~ The train was canceled. ___F___
7 The second train stopped moving after half an hour. ___T___
8 When the train reached its destination, he was ~~already two hours~~ an hour late for the interview. ___F___
9 Because the traffic was heavy, he ~~walked from the station to the office.~~ had to get out of the taxi and walk to the office. ___F___
10 ~~Another job candidate~~ The interviewer was late because of the train problems. ___F___

D SPEAK Work in pairs and discuss the questions.

1 What mistakes did Junko and Alan make? Who made the worst ones?
2 Who had the worst or most unusual trip? Why?

GRAMMAR

Narrative tenses

A Look at the pairs of sentences from the call-in radio show. In each pair, who is the speaker? Write J (Junko) or A (Alan). What tenses are the underlined verbs?

1 A: It was raining (past progressive) when I left (simple past). ___A___
B: It was snowing (past progressive). ___J___
2 A: I took (simple past) the next train, but after about 30 minutes, that train broke down (simple past). ___A___
B: I found (simple past) a bus stop and sat down (simple past). ___J___
3 A: A police car was driving (past progressive) by, when it suddenly stopped (simple past). ___J___
B: We were still not moving (past progressive), so I got out (simple past) and walked (simple past). ___A___
4 A: We arrived (simple past) about two hours late, and that meant I'd already missed (past perfect) the interview. ___A___
B: I'd arranged (past perfect) to go to a classmate's house for dinner. ___J___

B WORK IT OUT Complete the rules with *simple past, past progressive* or *past perfect*.

Narrative tenses

When we tell a story, we use a range of past tenses.

1 We use the ___simple past___ to describe the main events in a story, in the order that they happened.
2 We use the ___past progressive___ to describe a longer action that is interrupted by a shorter event. We also use it to describe a longer action that is not a main event in the story, such as the weather.
3 We use the ___past perfect___ to describe an event that happened before the main events in the story.

3.1 Travel experiences

LEAD-IN

Elicit an example of a reason why people make a trip. Write this on the board, then put students into pairs to think of more.

LISTENING

3.1 **A–C** Students work and check in pairs to complete the exercises. Monitor and encourage students to explain their opinions.

GRAMMAR

A Do the first one as an example to make sure students are familiar with the terminology.

B Tell students to use the example sentences from Exercise A to help them complete the rules. Use the **Grammar Worksheet** on W9 for extra practice.

AUDIO SCRIPT

3.1

Listening, Exercise B
B = Presenter (Bobby) J = Junko A = Alan

B: OK, our first caller is Junko. Hello, Junko.
J: Hello, Bobby. Well, my story happened some time ago, when I first came to the US to study English. I was only 18 then.
B: OK. Can I ask, where are you from, Junko?
J: Japan.
B: Japan? OK, but you aren't calling from there, are you?
J: No, no. I've lived here for ten years now.
B: OK. Well, Junko, thank you for calling. Tell us your story. What problem did you have?
J: Well, the problem was a public holiday. New Year's Day to be exact!
B: New Year's Day was a problem? That is pretty unusual. What happened?
J: Well, I'd arranged to go to a classmate's house for
Ex C Q1 dinner. Of course, I knew it was a holiday. But what I didn't know was there was no public transportation. So in the afternoon, I went to the subway station. It was snowing, not very heavily, but it was really cold. Anyway, the station was closed when I got there, so I couldn't get a train. I thought it was because of the snow, but the roads were OK, so I decided to try to get a bus.
B: But there were no buses either?
J: Mmm, exactly. But I didn't know. Anyway, I found a bus stop and sat down to wait.
B: Oh, no! Did you wait for long?
J: Actually, not so long. I was very lucky.
B: You got a taxi?
Ex C Q3 **J:** Not exactly. A police car was driving by when it suddenly stopped and one of the officers got out. She asked me if I was OK and explained there were no buses today. I felt so embarrassed and stupid. But then, guess what?
B: What?
J: She told me to get in the car. I was worried. Had I done something wrong? But they were both smiling, so I just asked why.
B: So then what?
Ex C Q4 **J:** They took me to my friend's place.
B: What? Like a taxi?
J: Exactly. I couldn't believe it. So kind. You know, we went right across the city. When I arrived, my friends hadn't started dinner. So, I wasn't late at all. Perfect!
B: How nice, Junko. I guess it was a quiet day for everyone, even the police. A great example of the New Year's spirit in action. Thank you. OK, now let's hear from Alan. Hello, Alan. Tell us your story.
A: Sure. Hi, Bobby. Yeah, so, I'd been out of work for a few months when I got this interview for a job in another city. I really needed the job, so I decided to leave really early – you know, I didn't want to be late and all that.
B: Not for an interview, no!
A: Right! Well, it was raining when I left, so I took a taxi to the station. That didn't take long, but when I got
Ex C Q6 there, I found out that they'd canceled my train. I wasn't too worried though – the next one was in half an hour, and I had plenty of time. So I took the next train, but after about 30 minutes, that train broke down and we were just stuck there. Not moving or anything. And, stupidly, I'd left my phone at home. Yes, I'd changed my jacket just before I left, and my phone was in that first jacket, so I couldn't even call the company.
B: How unlucky, Alan. So how long were you stuck there?
A: About an hour! And all that time I was getting more and more stressed. The train started moving again, but really slowly, and we arrived about two
Ex C Q8 hours late, and that meant I had already missed the interview by over an hour. So, I jumped in a taxi, but that only made things worse.
B: In what way?
A: The traffic was awful – you know, it was still raining.
Ex C Q9 We ended up stuck in a traffic jam. After about 20 minutes, we were still not moving, so I got out and walked. So, when I finally got to the office, I was really late, stressed and wet from the rain. I looked like a mess.
B: I can imagine. Nightmare! Did they still interview you?
A: Well, that's the funny thing. I was standing at the reception desk, waiting to make my excuses to the receptionist when this guy stepped in front of me. I was about to complain when the receptionist said 'Mr. Hammond, you've arrived. At last'. And, can you guess who he was?
B: Another candidate?
Ex C Q10 **A:** Oh, no, not another candidate. He was the manager, the interviewer! It turned out he'd been on the same train as me! I introduced myself immediately, and we had a laugh about the whole trip.
B: Amazing! What a coincidence. And so I have to ask: did you get the job?
A: Well, after all that bad luck, things had to change, and yes, I got the job.

C–D Put students into pairs to check answers when they have completed the exercises.

E Direct students to the **Grammar Hub** (see below).

F Direct students to the **Communication Hub** (TB121).

VOCABULARY

3.2 **A–B** Students check answers in pairs after completing the exercises.

C Direct students to the **Vocabulary Hub** (TB121) for further practice of vocabulary related to travel information.

D Put students into pairs to discuss the questions. Use the **Vocabulary Worksheet** on W10 for extra practice.

SPEAKING

A–C Students plan, share and decide on the best stories.

GRAMMAR HUB

3.1 Narrative tenses

	Positive	Negative	Question
Simple past	They **went** to Spain last year.	The train trip **didn't take** long.	Where **did** you **go** on vacation?
Past progressive	It **was raining** when we left the house.	Anna **wasn't enjoying** the trip.	Where **were you going** when I saw you yesterday?
Past perfect	I **had just arrived** at the hotel. We **had missed** the train.	Ben **hadn't arrived** at the office.	What time **had** they **left** the house? **Had** you ever **been** there before?

- We use the simple past to talk about finished actions or situations, and things that happened one after another.

  I waited at the bus stop until my bus came.
- We use the past progressive to describe the background to a story.

  It was snowing and the traffic was moving very slowly.
- When we are talking about two events in the past, we use the past perfect to show that one event happened before the other.

past ← *I had left the train station when I saw a bus.* → present

I left the train station. … I saw a bus.

- We use the past progressive for actions or situations that were unfinished at a past time and which were interrupted by shorter events (described using the simple past).

  While we were going through town, the bus started making a strange noise.

3.1 Narrative tenses

A Complete each sentence with the correct form of the verb in parentheses.

1. We got to the station but we *had already missed* (already / miss) the train.
2. When I arrived at the station, my cousin was waiting (wait) for me.
3. The car left the road and hit (hit) a tree.
4. Had you been (you / go) to Berlin before or was it your first time?
5. What did your friend say (your friend / say) when you finally arrived?
6. We had just arrived (just / arrive) at the station when we saw our train coming in.

B Choose the correct option.

1. We were excited because we *didn't visit* / *had never visited* South America before. [had never visited circled]
2. *Did anyone wait* / *Was anyone waiting* for you when you got there? [Was anyone waiting circled]
3. Tom arrived at the hotel and *had gone* / *went* straight to his room for a nap. [went circled]
4. The reason we were lost was that we *were taking* / *had taken* the wrong subway line. [had taken circled]
5. What *did you do* / *had you done* when you realized you'd lost your ticket? [did you do circled]
6. Didn't you know the train *was being* / *had been* canceled? [had been circled]

C Correct the mistakes in each sentence.

1. The accident happened because the driver had ~~fell~~ *fallen* asleep at the wheel.
2. I was late, but luckily for me the meeting ~~wasn't starting~~ hadn't started.
3. We missed the beginning because we ~~were getting~~ were stuck in a traffic jam.
4. They had already ~~went~~ been to Paris so they decided to go somewhere else.
5. I was worried because I ~~wasn't hearing~~ hadn't heard from my brother for several hours.
6. The traffic ~~didn't move~~ wasn't moving at all so we got out of the taxi and walked.

➤ Go back to page 27.

C Match the timelines (a–d) with the rules (1–3) in Exercise B.

2 a

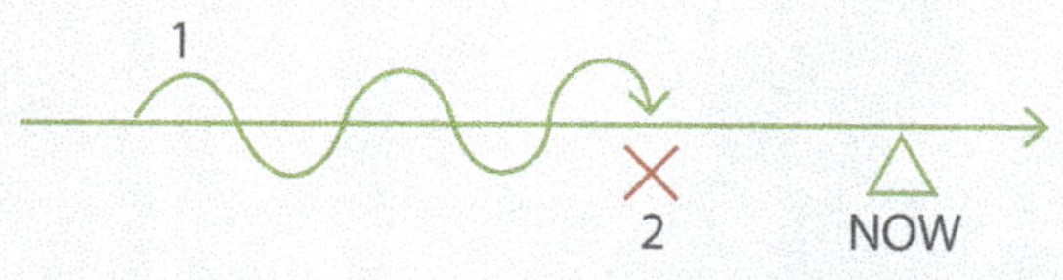

1 b

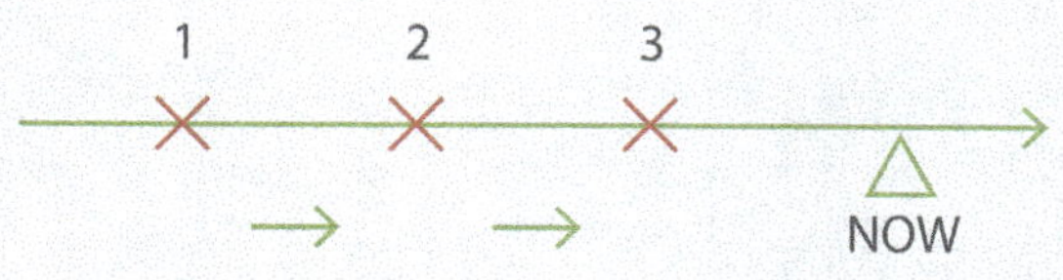

2 c

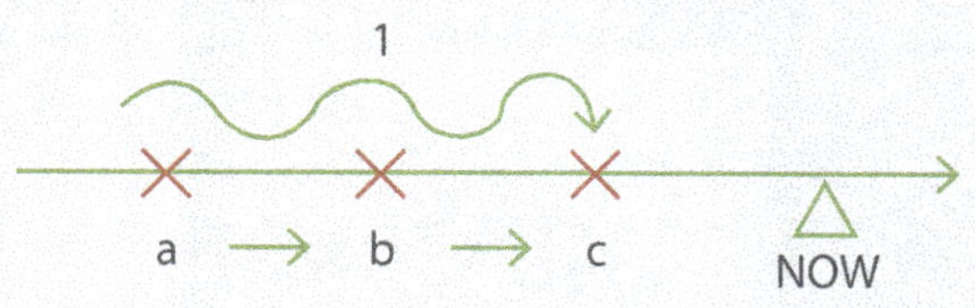

3 d

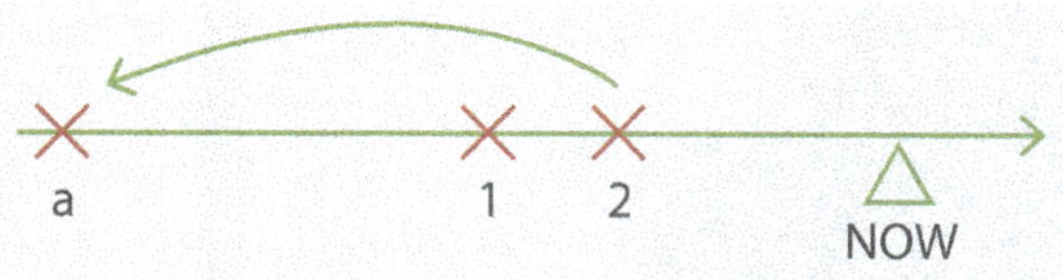

D PRACTICE Complete the stories with the correct form of the verbs in parentheses.

It [1] was raining (*rain*), and I [2] was driving (*drive*) at night in the countryside when a wild animal suddenly [3] jumped (*jump*) in front of me. I [4] managed (*manage*) to avoid hitting the animal, but I [5] went (*go*) off the road into a field and I couldn't move the car. Unfortunately, I [6] 'd/had forgotten (*forget*) to charge my phone, so I couldn't call for help. That was a long walk home!

I [7] was traveling (*travel*) to work on the train when a ticket inspector [8] asked (*ask*) to see my ticket. I [9] looked (*look*) everywhere, but I had no idea where I [10] 'd/had put (*put*) it. I emptied out my pockets but it [11] had disappeared (*disappear*) completely. There were two kids across from me, and while I [12] was paying (*pay*) the inspector, I [13] noticed (*notice*) they [14] were smiling and laughing (*smile and laugh*). They got off at the next station, and my ticket [15] was (*be*) on their seat. They [16] had found and hidden (*find and hide*) it.

E Go to the **Grammar Hub** on **page 126**.

F Work in pairs. Go to the **Communication Hub** on **page 149**.

VOCABULARY

Collocations: travel information

3.2 **A** Listen to a traffic news and travel update on a radio show. Answer the questions.

1 How many types of transportation do they mention?
three: cars, subway trains, trains
2 Which has the fewest problems?
the subway

3.2 **B LISTEN FOR KEY WORDS** Listen again. Choose the correct words to make the collocations used in the travel update.

1 rush *hour* / *job*
2 traffic *lights* / *jam*
3 road *sign* / *work*
4 severe *delay* / *problem*
5 slight *delay* / *interest*
6 good *conditions* / *service*
7 subway *station* / *line*
8 cancel *a train* / *an event*
9 heavy *rain* / *traffic*
10 overcrowded *trains* / *buses*

C Go to the **Vocabulary Hub** on **page 142**.

D SPEAK Work in pairs and discuss the questions.

1 When was the last time you were stuck in heavy traffic?
2 What do you think about traveling during rush hour?
3 Which is worse: being on an overcrowded train or in a traffic jam?

SPEAKING

A You are going to tell a story for a radio show. Think of either an interesting or a difficult trip that you have made. Write notes to help you plan your story. Think about:

- Background information (When? Where? Why?)
- What was the weather like?
- What happened on the trip?
- How did it finish?

B Work in groups. Share your stories. Ask and answer questions about the stories.

C Which story do you think would be best for the radio show? Which was the most interesting, unusual or difficult trip? Which was the funniest story?

READING

A SPEAK Work in pairs. Look at the pictures (a–c) and discuss the questions.

1 What are the people doing?

2 Which activities do you like / not like doing when you are traveling?

B SKIM Read the article quickly and answer the questions. Use the strategies in the box to help you build a map of the text.

Skim-reading to build a map of a text

You can build a map of a text by identifying the main topic and the paragraph topics.

Read the title and the first paragraph to find out what the main topic is.

Read the first sentence of each paragraph to find out what the paragraph's topic is. Make a note of the paragraph topics.

1 What is the main topic or idea in this text?
Talking to strangers on public transportation.

2 Match the headings (a–f) with the paragraphs (1–6).

4 a The details of what the research discovered
5 b Epley's conclusions regarding the research
6 c How the research changed Epley's life
1 d Avoiding conversations and reasons not to
3 e How the research was carried out
2 f The reason why Epley and Schroeder did the research

a

b

DAY2DAY SCIENCE Your source of science news

Is it time to start talking to strangers?

1 Using your cell phone. Putting on your headphones. Staring out of the window. Those are all classic ways to avoid talking to strangers on public transportation. However, this may not be the best thing to do for your well-being. Recent research by Nicholas Epley, a professor of behavioral science at the University of Chicago, and Juliana Schroeder, a PhD student, reveals that people are happier when they talk with other passengers rather than ignoring them.

Ex B Q1

Vocabulary, Ex A

2 The inspiration for the research came from Epley's own daily commute. Humans are, by nature, social animals, and being social is key to our happiness. However, the commuters that Epley saw every day were behaving in very antisocial ways, avoiding all communication as if they were sitting next to a rock. He wondered why nearly everyone acted against their social nature in this situation. Is talking to a stranger on a train truly less pleasant than sitting in silence? Or is everybody wrong?

3 To find out, Epley and Schroeder designed two experiments. In the first, Epley simply asked people to imagine starting a conversation with another passenger. Would it be a pleasant thing to do? Would they feel happy afterward? In the second study, they asked commuters to actually start conversations with strangers on their trip, and then to complete a survey about the experience.

4 His studies revealed a difference between people's expectations of talking to strangers and the reality. In the first study, people generally said it would neither be a pleasant thing to do nor increase their happiness. In addition, they felt that most strangers would not want to talk.
In contrast, the second experiment showed that people enjoyed their commute more when they talked to a stranger and their general level of happiness increased. It also revealed that the reaction was positive because they all took part in the conversations, even though they were not aware it was an experiment.

5 Based on the findings, Epley feels that passenger cars filled with silence, blank expressions and little eye contact are the result of basic misunderstandings and false expectations. Despite what everyone thinks, strangers are happy to talk and talking makes you happier. Once people make the decision to start a conversation, they find this connection to others improves their own lives.

6 Since publishing the research, Epley has put his findings into action and changed his own commuting behavior. He no longer uses his cell phone and he starts conversations with opening lines as simple as 'I like your hat'. He regularly finds himself sitting next to someone he has talked to before, which 'just makes it more pleasant'.'

READING

A Tell students to look at the pictures and discuss the questions in pairs. In feedback, elicit what they have in common – that they show people in public transportation and that the people aren't speaking to each other. Ask students if they think this is typical in their country and encourage them to share examples from their own experiences with the class, either traveling in their country or when traveling in another country.

B Tell students to read the strategies for skim-reading to build a map of the text. Ask students if they do any of these things already, either when reading in English or in their own language. Tell students to use these strategies to read the text and answer the questions. Students should work alone at this point but you can monitor and assist, particularly to ensure students have understood the box and are referring to it when answering the questions.

C Tell students to compare their answers in pairs and to discuss how much more information they can remember after their skim-reading. In feedback, elicit as much detail as you can about the text. Ask students if they found the skim-reading strategies effective. You can also ask them if they think they will use them again in the future.

D Put students into groups to discuss what they think about the results of the research described in the text. Encourage them to share their own experiences. If there is time you can let groups share their ideas with another group. Then discuss answers as a whole class and ask students to expand on their responses.

VOCABULARY

A Tell students that the article they've just read contains eight nouns that share the same suffix. Try to elicit what this is. Tell students to underline all eight examples in the text.

B Tell students to use the context in which the words appear in the article to help them work out the meaning of the nouns as they match them to the definitions. Do the first one as an example with the whole class.

C Direct students to the **Vocabulary Hub** (TB121) for further practice of nouns ending in *-ion*.

D Put students into pairs to discuss the sentences and to change them so they are true for them if they disagree. Monitor and encourage students to express different opinions.

Extra activity

As a way of extending the discussion about the topic, you could ask the following questions:

1 Have you ever talked to other passengers on public transportation?

2 What advice would you give to someone who would like to speak more frequently to other passengers?

3 Rank the following activities you can do while traveling in order of which you prefer most:

read a book or magazine, call friends or family, work or study, talk to other passengers, daydream, watch a movie, eat and drink, listen to music, sleep

TEACHING IDEA by David Seymour and Maria Popova

Topic: Reading habits

Use this activity to extend the topic.

How important is storytelling in your culture? Do you think it is important to tell young children stories? Why (not)? Find out about your partner's reading habits. Here are some questions to help you.

1 Are you reading a book in your free time? What's it about?
2 What kind of books do you usually read? Why?
3 What's the best book you've ever read? Why did you like it so much?
4 Are you a fast reader?
5 Do you read magazines or comic books? Which ones?
6 What do you think of e-books? Will they ever replace traditional books?

Estimate how much time you spend reading every day and how much time you spend watching TV. Write the times down on a piece of paper. Below that draw a pie chart including the following kinds of reading:

novels, 'quality' newspapers/magazines, comic books, signs/billboards, instructions, textbooks, computer screens

Mingle with the rest of the class and compare your notes and pie chart with other students.

TEACHING IDEA by David Seymour and Maria Popova

Topic: Public transportation

Use this activity to extend the topic.

How does the public transportation system here compare with the system in another city you know well? How do you travel to your class?

In small groups, discuss the advantages and disadvantages of bike riding and driving to work.

Agree on a list of ten transportation policies for a smoggy, congested, over-populated city. You will need to find a way of encouraging people out of their cars and onto public transportation.

METHODOLOGY HUB by Jim Scrivener

Creating a positive learning atmosphere

Below are some features that may be important in creating a positive relationship and a positive learning atmosphere. Decide which items are inborn and which could be worked on and improved. In a positive learning atmosphere the teacher . . .

really listens shows respect is fair
has a good sense of humor
gives clear and positive feedback inspires confidence
is, by and large, authentically her/himself is patient
empathizes with students/people trusts people
does not complicate things unnecessarily
is well organized is honest is approachable

PRONUNCIATION

3.3 **A** Tell students to listen carefully to the pronunciation of the words and to underline the stressed syllable in each one. If students struggle with this, play the audio again.

3.3 **B** When students have correctly underlined the stress, play the audio again and tell students to repeat them and think about how the stress pattern is similar. Ask students what is the same about the pronunciation of the final syllable of each word. Ensure that the students are pronouncing the nouns correctly. If necessary, correct and model the pronunciation.

The penultimate syllable is always stressed. The final syllable has a weak vowel sound: /ə/.

3.4 **C** Tell students to look at the nouns and underline where they think the stressed syllable will be. Play the audio for students to check and tell them to repeat the words as they hear them. Make sure students are repeating the words correctly. If necessary, model them again yourself. Check that students have noticed all nouns follow the pattern identified in Exercise B.

D Tell students to practice the pronunciation further in pairs and encourage them to correct each other if necessary. To provide more context, you could encourage students to put the words into sentences as they do this.

SPEAKING HUB

A Tell students to turn to the **Communication Hub** (TB121). Check understanding of *trash, coughing and sneezing, lining up, to board* and *to give up your seat*. Tell students to work individually first to rank the behavior on public transportation from one to ten in terms of how annoying it is for them personally.

B Put students into groups to compare their lists, explaining and justifying their reasons to each other. Tell students that their group is going to have to agree on the top three, so they need to try to persuade each other that their choices should be included. If some groups agree more than others, ask them to try to add more ideas to the list of annoying behavior on public transportation.

C Tell the groups that they need to agree on their top three most annoying things. If different groups have very different ideas, you could change groups again and encourage further debate. Ask groups to reveal their top three to the class. As a whole class, discuss further until a definitive top three is agreed upon.

Put students back into groups to think of ways to stop the annoying behavior from the top three. Elicit an example with the whole class, then monitor to help with language. When groups have their ideas, re-group students again to explain their ideas and again to try to agree on the best idea for each one. Finish with some discussion as a whole class with students explaining their choices. You could ask if students really believe this behavior can be changed. Finish with some feedback on students' language use during the task, focusing both on successes and errors.

METHODOLOGY HUB by Jim Scrivener

Give collocations rather than definitions

When a student wants to know what the difference is between *late* and *delayed*, it's usually hard to give a clear distinction of meaning. But there are clearly certain collocations and chunks that one is more likely to fit into than the other. When you want to make a sentence, knowing the typical collocations – and learning them, phrasebook-like – is probably going to be of more use than trying to select between two very similar meanings.

There are many games and activities specifically designed to work on collocational understanding. Here are three of my favorites:

Quick choices

Choose two or three nouns, e.g. food, cooking and meal, that have a number of (possibly confusable) collocations. In this case, the list might include baby, fast, slow, health, dog, home, evening, delicious, light, balanced, three-course, French, vegetarian, frozen, cat. Tell the students that you will read aloud the list item by item and they must indicate which of the two (or three) words is the best collocate, or if the item goes with more than one word. Decide on how students will indicate their choices. You could go for quiet ways, e.g. students write their answers in a list; noisy ways, e.g. students yell out their choice of words; physical ways, e.g. students point at the words written on a bulletin board; action ways, e.g. designate different parts of the room for different words and students run to the right part of the room (or between parts).

Guess the collocation

Divide the class into three or more teams. In each team, students are given a common word (e.g. town) and have to prepare a list of five common collocations (e.g. planning, hall, home, market, center). Each team has a different starter word. When everyone is ready, students read their lists aloud one item at a time and the other teams try to guess the original word. If the word is guessed immediately on the first clue, both teams (list-makers and word-guessers) get ten points; for each extra word, the points go down by one. This scoring system encourages list-makers to find the most likely and distinctive collocations.

Chunk watching

Students work in groups of three, two of whom face each other. The teacher gives them a topic to talk about and they simply chat naturally for a few minutes. The third person sits out of their line of sight and takes no part in the conversation, but listens carefully and writes notes of as many 'chunks' as he/she can catch. At the end of the time, the listener shows his/her list to the speakers and they go through and discuss the items.

C Work in pairs. Compare your answers to Exercise B. What other information can you remember from your skim-reading?

D **SPEAK** Work in groups. What do you think of the results of the research?

VOCABULARY

Nouns ending in *-ion*

A **WORK IT OUT** Look at *Is it time to start talking to strangers?* again. Find and underline nouns that end with *-ion*.

B Complete the definitions with nouns from Exercise A.

1 to have an __expectation__: to have a belief about what something will be like or what will happen

2 to have a positive __reaction__: to feel good as a result of something that happens

3 to make a __decision__: to choose something after thinking carefully

4 to have a __connection__: to have a relationship to something

5 to have a confused __expression__: to look like you don't understand something

6 to be in a difficult __situation__: to be doing something that is not easy

7 to be in __communication__: to be sharing information, ideas and feelings

8 to be an __inspiration__: to give you new ideas or the enthusiasm to create something with them

C Go to the **Vocabulary Hub** on **page 143**.

D **SPEAK** Work in pairs. Do you agree or disagree with the statements below. If you disagree with them, change them so they are true for you.

1 Communication with other passengers is a waste of time. I don't know them and I might never see them again.

2 How far you choose to live from work is a very important decision. There is a connection between everyday happiness and the length of your commute.

PRONUNCIATION

Word stress in nouns ending in *-ion*

3.3 A Listen to the pronunciation of the nouns ending in *-ion* and underline the stressed syllables. Some words may have two stressed syllables.

1 action 2 connection 3 communication

3.3 B Listen again and repeat the words. How is the stress pattern similar?

3.4 C Underline the stressed syllables of the nouns ending in *-ion*. Then listen and check your answers. Repeat the words.

1 decision
2 expectation
3 expression
4 inspiration
5 reaction
6 situation

D **SPEAK** Work in pairs. Practice saying the words. Listen and check your partner's pronunciation.

SPEAKING HUB

A Go to the **Communication Hub** on **page 154**.

B **SPEAK** Work in groups. Compare your lists and explain your reasons to each other.

C **DISCUSS** Decide on the top three most annoying things. Discuss ways of stopping that behavior. Compare your ideas with another group.

Talk about a difficult trip or travel experience

Talk about behavior on public transportation

3.2 Travel smart

- Evaluate suggestions and justify a choice
- Talk about why a plan didn't work

G articles and quantifiers **P** sentence stress: quantifiers **V** gradable and ungradable adjectives
S listening for signposting

READING

A SPEAK Work in pairs and discuss the question. Do you think there are too many cars on the road where you live or study?

B READ FOR MAIN IDEA Read *Whatever happened to Helsinki's Kutsuplus transportation service?* Match the headings (a–e) with the paragraphs (1–5).

a The advantages of Kutsuplus
b The disadvantages of Kutsuplus
c How Kutsuplus worked
d Was Kutsuplus a success?
e What was Kutsuplus?

Whatever happened to Helsinki's *Kutsuplus* transportation service?

1 e

A few years ago, Helsinki, Finland, decided it had a problem: there were **too many** cars. So the Helsinki Regional Transportation Authority decided to hold a three-year trial of an on-demand minibus service designed to reduce the number of cars on the road. It was called *Kutsuplus* and it allowed passengers to choose where they wanted to go. Ex C Q1

2 c Ex C Q2

Passengers went online and selected a start and end point for their trip. Rule 4; 1 They then paid online and went to their nearest bus stop. **A minibus** Rule 1 arrived and took them to the chosen end point. If other **people** wanted to Rule 2 go to the same area at the same time, no problem: there was **plenty of** Rule 3 space and they could share **the minibus**! Even if people wanted to go to Rule 2; 4 different places in the same area, **the online service** was able to choose Rule 3 the best route available, so everybody was happy!

3 a

For passengers, the key benefits of *Kutsuplus* were convenience and cost. They could choose where they wanted to go and they didn't have to wait long for the bus to arrive. During the time of the trial, the average *Kutsuplus* trip cost $5. In comparison, the average cost of a taxi ride started at $6, but could be much more expensive for longer trips. Surely this would make *Kutsuplus* a great success! Well, not really …

4 b

Although it was more convenient than a normal bus or the subway, unlike a taxi, the minibus wasn't able to take people exactly where they wanted to go. Passengers had to use the nearest bus stops as the start and end points of their trip. Another major problem was that there were very **few** buses in operation. By the end of the trial, *Kutsuplus* had 21,000 registered users, but only 15 buses. This would have a big effect on the result of the trial. Ex C Q3

5 d

In general, Helsinki residents had positive feelings about the service. **A lot of** them felt that it was convenient, especially for people who lived in areas where there wasn't **enough** public transportation. However, with **not enough** buses in operation, it wasn't convenient for everybody. In the end, city officials decided not to continue the service. Ex C Q4 Ex C Q5

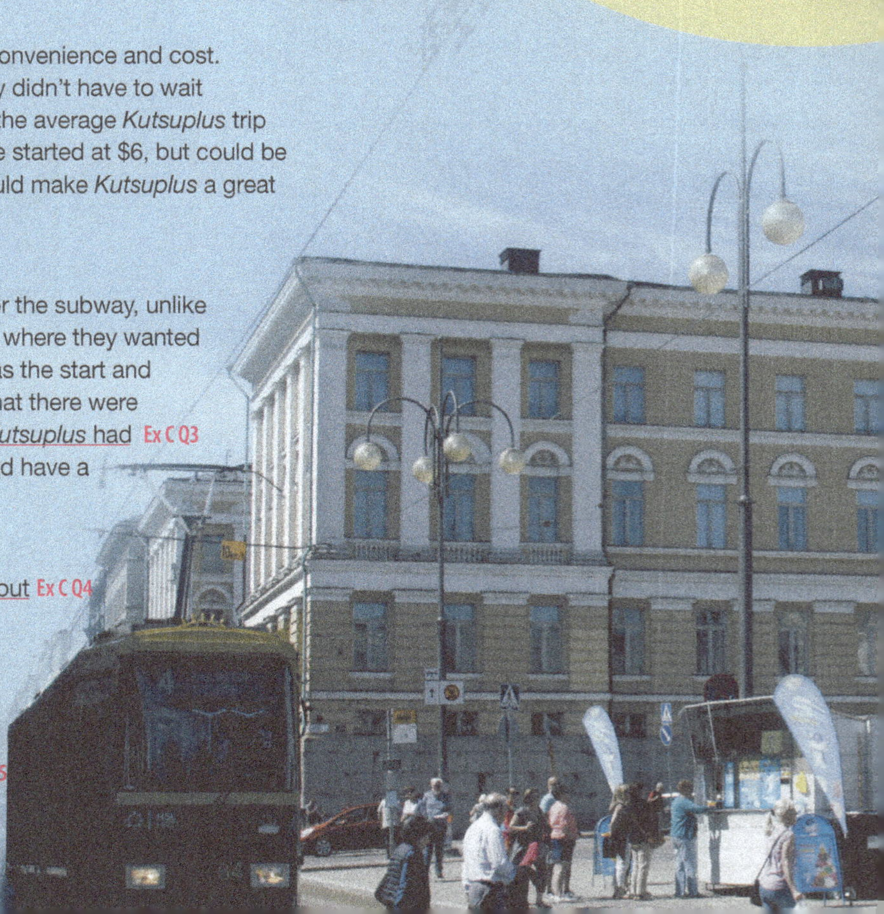

3.2 Travel smart

LEAD-IN

With books closed, elicit from students one positive thing and one negative thing they associate with cars and write these on the board. Put students into pairs to think of more before sharing answers as a whole class. Record useful ideas and language on the board.

READING

A Tell students to open their books and discuss the question. Monitor and make note of any errors for correction at the end of the lesson. Open the discussion to the whole class. Call on each pair to give their opinions. Encourage other members of the class to agree or disagree with the opinions given.

B Tell students to look at the pictures and tell them they are going to read an article about the Kutsuplus transportation service in Helsinki, Finland. Then tell students to read the article and match the five headings with the five paragraphs. Set a time limit to prevent students from reading in too much detail at this point, but tell them that they will have the chance to read again for more detail. Check answers as a whole class but don't go into in-depth discussion of the article yet.

C Tell students to read the article again in more detail to answer the questions. Encourage students to underline the parts of the text that help them find each answer. Ask students to justify their answers with reference to the parts of the text they underlined.

D Tell students to discuss the questions in pairs. You could also ask if they think the service would be popular in their country and if they think it could work.

GRAMMAR HUB

3.2 Articles and quantifiers

Articles

***a/an*, *the*, no article**

a/an	We use *a/an* the first time we talk about a singular noun.	I have **a ticket** for the train. There was **an accident** on the main road.
the	We use *the* when we have already mentioned the person or thing.	There was an accident. **The accident** wasn't serious.
	We use *the* with singular nouns when it is clear what we are talking about or when there is only one.	I usually take **the bus** that leaves at 6:15.
	We use *the* with plural nouns when it is clear what we are talking about.	**The trains** that leave in the mornings are overcrowded.
no article	We use no article with the names of people, companies, cities and countries (except *the UK*, *the US*, *the Netherlands*).	My cousin's name is **Sam**. He recently flew to **Colorado**, which is in **the US**.
	We use no article when we talk about things in general.	Do you like **traveling**? **Buses** are sometimes faster than **trains**.

- We use *an* before a vowel sound. We use *a* before a consonant sound, even if the word begins with *a*, *e*, *i*, *o* or *u*.

  an hour, an expensive trip, a university town
- We sometimes use *the* before a type of transportation.

  *We always take **the** bus / **the** train / **the** plane.*
- We use *the* before the names of oceans and rivers and countries whose names are plural.

  ***the** Atlantic Ocean / **the** Nile River / **the** United States / **the** Philippines*

Quantifiers

	Countable nouns	Uncountable nouns
Question	**How many people** use the subway?	**How much traffic** was there on the road?
Positive number	There are **a few people** on the train.	There is **a little ice** on the roads so drive carefully.
	There are **a lot of / lots of people** waiting for the bus.	There is **a lot of / lots of information** in this booklet.
	There are **enough seats**.	There is **enough space**.
	There are **plenty of buses**.	There is **plenty of time**.
Negative number	There are **few people** on the train.	There is **little chance** of us getting there on time.
	There aren't **many people** here.	There isn't **much traffic** today.
	There aren't **enough seats**.	There isn't **enough space**.
	There are **too many people** on this train. It's **too small**.	There's **too much noise** on the train. It's **too noisy**.

GRAMMAR

A Tell students to focus on the words in bold in the second paragraph of the text, and elicit that the connection between them is the use, or lack of use, of articles. Tell students to refer to these examples to help them complete the rules.

B Tell students to find and underline more examples of articles in the same paragraph of the text and to match each to the rules.

C Direct students to the **Grammar Hub** (see TB30 and below).

D–F Discuss as a whole class after students complete the exercises.

G Direct students to the **Grammar Hub** (see TB30 and below).

H Begin the task by giving some personal examples, modeling how you can use quantifiers in your answers. Use the **Grammar Worksheet** on W11 for extra practice.

PRONUNCIATION

3.5 **A–C** Put students into pairs to discuss their answers and practice.

SPEAKING

3.6 **A** Let students compare in pairs after listening. Monitor to check how well they understood. Check answers as a whole class.

The service was canceled because it was too expensive for the city to operate it. It needed more buses to be a success but this would have been a lot more expensive for the city.

B Put students into pairs to discuss what they think about the reasons given and if they agree with the decision.

C Put students into bigger groups to compare ideas. Ask students to expand on their ideas in feedback.

D Tell each group to discuss how they would either continue or adapt the service, either in Helsinki or in their own country. Finish with some feedback on students' use of language during the task.

Extra activity
For homework, students can research other ideas that cities or towns have used to solve car or traffic problems. Ask them to write notes on: key benefits, problems with the services, how residents felt about them. Review and discuss their research at the beginning of the next class.

GRAMMAR HUB

3.2 Articles and quantifiers

A Find eight more mistakes with articles and correct them.

The trip from my house to my office only takes me about half ^an hour. There is ~~the~~ a quicker way – I could take ^a/the bus – but I prefer to walk. There are many reasons for this. First, ~~the~~ walking is healthy and I find it puts me in ^a good mood. I usually arrive at ^the office awake and ready for work. Going by ~~the~~ bus, on the other hand, leaves me feeling tired and stressed before ~~a~~ the day begins!

B Write one word in each blank. Sometimes more than one answer is possible.

1 How __much__ time do we have before the train comes?
2 Sometimes we take __a__ taxi and share the cost between us.
3 There weren't very __many__ passengers on my bus this morning. I wonder why.
4 I find that bike riding is __an/one__ easy way to get through traffic jams.
5 Very __few__ people in the town have cars, so the bus service is really important to them.
6 There aren't __enough/many__ places to park, and that's why there are traffic problems.

C Check (✓) the sentences that are correct. Write *of* in the right place in the sentences that are incorrect.

1 There are very few buses that go near my house. ✓
2 It will take a little time for the public to get used to the new system. ✓
3 Not enough people used the bus service so they stopped running it. ✓
4 A lot ^of passengers complain of overcrowding on the buses.
5 I don't usually take taxis because they cost too much money. ✓
6 There are plenty ^of people who take their cars to work every day.
7 There are lots ^of taxis where I live.
8 There's plenty ^of money to improve the bus system.
9 There were few free seats on the train today. ✓
10 Is there too much traffic on our streets? ✓

➤ Go back to page 31.

C READ FOR DETAIL Read again. Complete the sentences by choosing a, b or c.

1 The long-term goal of *Kutsuplus* was to encourage people to stop …
- (a) driving cars.
- b using the subway.
- c hiring minibuses.

2 Passengers could choose the start and end point of their trips by …
- a asking at the bus stop.
- b calling the driver.
- (c) using the internet.

3 There were … registered users by the end of the trial.
- a a small number of
- b not enough
- (c) a lot of

4 Overall, people who lived in Helsinki thought the service was …
- (a) useful.
- b expensive.
- c unfair.

5 The local … stopped the service.
- a businesses
- (b) government
- c residents

D SPEAK Work in pairs. Do you think the *Kutsuplus* service was a good idea? Why/Why not?

GRAMMAR

Articles and quantifiers

A WORK IT OUT Look at the words in bold in paragraph 2 of *Whatever happened to Helsinki's Kutsuplus transportation service?* Then complete the rules with *a/an*, *the* or – (no article).

Articles

1 We use _a/an_ the first time we mention a person or thing.
2 We use _the_ the second time we mention the person or thing.
3 We use _the_ when it is clear who or what we are talking about.
4 We use _–_ when we talk generally about people or things.

B Find and underline other uses of *a/an*, *the* or – (no article) in the same paragraph and match them with the rules (1–4) in Exercise A.

C Go to the **Grammar Hub** on **page 126**.

D PRACTICE Choose *a*, *the* or – (no article) to complete the questions.

1 How long does *a* / *the* / – trip from where you live (or are staying) to where you study usually take?
2 Would you like to go by *a* / *the* / – different type of *a* / *the* / – transportation? If so, which one?

E SPEAK Work in pairs. Ask and answer the questions in Exercise D.

F WORK IT OUT Look at the quantifiers in **red** in the text. Then choose the correct words to complete the rules.

Quantifiers

1 We use quantifiers to talk about *amounts* / *qualities*.
2 Quantifiers go *before* / *after* nouns.

G Go to the **Grammar Hub** on **page 126**.

H SPEAK Work in pairs. What is the public transportation system like in your town? Does your town need more or fewer buses, trains or taxis? Why? Tell your partner.

PRONUNCIATION

Sentence stress: quantifiers

3.5 **A** Listen to the sentences from the article. Check (✓) the sentences you hear. Which words are stressed?

1 a A lot of them felt that it was convenient. ✓
  b A lot of them felt that it was convenient. ☐
2 a There were very few buses in operation. ☐
  b There were very few buses in operation. ✓

3.5 **B WORK IT OUT** Listen again and repeat the sentences. Do we usually stress the main noun or the quantifier? The quantifier

C SPEAK Work in pairs. Practice saying the sentences. Listen and check your partner's pronunciation.

SPEAKING

3.6 **A** Listen to an expert explaining why the *Kutsuplus* service was canceled. What reasons does the expert give?

B Work in pairs and discuss the reasons. Do you think the local officials were right to stop the service? Why/Why not?

C Work in groups. Summarize your discussion. Explain your opinions and listen to the opinions of others.

D Work in groups. Plan how you could continue the service or do it differently.

LISTENING

A SPEAK Work in pairs. Look at the poster and discuss the questions.

1 What event is the poster advertising?
2 What happens during that event?
3 Why do cities and towns hold these kinds of event?
4 Does your city or town hold similar events?

3.7 **B LISTEN FOR GIST** Listen to a city council meeting about Car-Free Day and answer the questions.

1 What is Alfred Shaw's view of the Car-Free Day?
2 Do the others at the meeting agree with him?
3 What is Alfred's opinion of cars generally?
4 What two events does Alfred suggest holding instead?
5 What reason does Alfred give for being at the city council meeting?

Glossary

ban (v) to say officially that someone is not allowed to do something
campaign (n) a series of actions intended to produce social change
pedestrian (n) someone who is walking, especially in a town or city, instead of driving or riding

3.7 **C LISTEN FOR DETAIL** Listen again and choose the correct answers.

1 Why don't annual car-free days reduce the amount of traffic?
 a The city has little public transportation.
 (b) Cars are the most effective type of transportation.
 c You need more than ten car-free days a year.
2 How do car-free days affect pollution levels?
 a They decrease the amount of pollution.
 b They increase the amount of pollution.
 (c) They do not change the amount of pollution.
3 What might increase the number of people buying electric cars?
 a Providing free electricity-charging stations.
 (b) Providing opportunities for people to test drive them.
 c Providing online videos showing their advantages.
4 Why do people prefer traveling by car rather than by bus?
 a There are not enough buses.
 b The buses are too slow.
 (c) The buses are dirty.
5 Why doesn't this city provide bicycles that people can rent?
 a The roads are not very safe.
 (b) The council has not discussed the idea.
 c It would be too expensive to do.

3.7 **D** Read the information in the box. Now listen again. For 1–7, put the signposting language you hear in the correct position.

Listening for signposting language

When giving a short talk, speakers use signposting language to show the order of points and make their argument easy for people to follow.

- First, I want to talk about the problems.
- 1 First of ___all___ …
- To start, …
- Finally, …

They can use it to introduce a new topic:

- Now, let's turn to the solutions.
- Moving on, I'll now discuss my ideas in more detail.
- 2 ___Let's___ look at …
- 3 I'll now ___move___ on to …

They can use it to introduce an extra point:

- In addition, …
- 4 Here's another ___reason___ why …
- 5 And ___another___ thing, …
- Also, …

They can also use it to finish a section of a talk or to finish the talk:

- That's all I want to say on that. Any questions?
- In conclusion, …
- 6 In ___short___, …
- 7 OK, to sum ___up___ …

E SPEAK Work in pairs. Discuss Alfred's arguments and claims. Do you agree or disagree with Alfred?

LISTENING

A Tell students to look at the poster and discuss the questions in pairs. In feedback, elicit students' opinions about car-free days. Do they think they are a good idea? Would it work in their country? Why/Why not?

B 3.7 Tell students they're going to listen to a city council meeting about a car-free day. Check that students understand that the *council* is the local government. Tell students not to worry if they don't understand everything as they just have to answer the two questions for now. However, draw their attention to the vocabulary in the glossary and check that students understand the concept of *ban* and *campaign* by eliciting examples of both.

1 *He thinks it is useless and won't solve the traffic problems.*
2 *No, they disagree.*
3 *He thinks they are great.*
4 *An e-car festival and Use Public Transportation Week.*
5 *He wants the city to be a great place to live.*

C 3.7 Tell students to read the questions and to try to choose the correct answer from memory. Play the audio again for students to check. Check answers as a whole class and ask students to justify their answer with reference to exactly what was said during the meeting.

D 3.7 Point out the strategies for listening for signposting language in the box. Explain that signposting language is used to organize a spoken or written text in order to make it easier to follow. Highlight the examples already filled in in the box. Tell students to read the strategies and try to add any words or phrases they remember hearing in the audio in the correct places. Then play the audio again for students to listen and check.

E Elicit Alfred's arguments against car-free days from the class. If students find this difficult, they could look at the audio script and identify the arguments there. Once the arguments are all clear, put students into pairs to discuss the question. Discuss the students' opinions as a whole class and encourage any further debate.

AUDIO SCRIPT

3.7

Listening, Exercise B
C = Chairperson A = Alfred C1 = Councilor 1
C2 = Councilor 2

C: OK, everyone, before we make our final decisions on this year's Car- Free Day, I'd like to invite some members of the public to give their views. First, let me introduce Alfred Shaw, a lecturer in business studies.

A: Thank you. OK, well, it's clear what most of you think about a car-free day. An absolutely wonderful idea, right? However, I'm here to disagree. Actually, it's a really terrible idea.

C1: What? You can't be serious!

C2: Nonsense, it's an excellent idea.

A: OK, you say that, but it really isn't. Let's look at the facts. First of all, they don't solve the traffic problem. And, anyway, cars are, very simply, great.

C2: Great? Come off it! We know they cause some awful problems.

Ex C Q1 **A:** OK, some things about cars are fairly bad, but they're clearly the best way to get around, and so they're never going to disappear. We've held this Car-Free Day 15 times before, but the rush-hour traffic jams have not gone away. Car-free days have a really tiny effect on driving habits, if any at all.

C1: But it's still better than doing nothing.

A: Is it? Here's another reason why we should think again. Car-free days don't even help the environment. Think about it. Although there may be no cars in the city
Ex C Q2 center for that one day, those cars are still out there on the roads, just on different roads. So, all you're doing is moving the pollution. And another thing, the car-free day causes massive traffic problems in the city, as drivers have to find other ways to go. Remember what happened last year, when that truck got stuck under the railroad bridge because we'd closed the main road? Because of that, there was an absolutely enormous traffic jam, trains were canceled and thousands of dollars of damage was caused. People were furious about that, and rightly so.

In short, car-free days are absolutely useless because they change nothing, and they create huge problems, not solutions. I'll now move onto what we should do instead.

C1: About time!

C2: Like what? A pedestrian-free day?!

C1: Ha ha. That's very funny.

A: Hmm, hilarious. You're clearly missing my point. We shouldn't ban anything, we should just improve everything.
First, we should start a campaign to encourage people to buy greener cars. Let's get more people using electric and hybrid cars. This may be extremely difficult, but it isn't impossible. We could hold an
Ex C Q3 e-car festival and give people a chance to try the cars out in order to see their benefits. That would be a superb way to change things.
Also, we need to improve public transportation and get people using it. We need more buses, and
Ex C Q4 cleaner buses – some of our old buses are really filthy, so it's no wonder people choose cars first. Let's invest some money, and then, why don't we run a 'Use Public Transportation Week', instead of banning cars for a day?

C1: Actually, that's a really good idea.

A: Thanks – an extremely good idea, I'd say. Finally, we should encourage a healthier and greener lifestyle all year round, rather than just for one day a year. Let's get people back on bikes. Let's teach people of all ages how to bike safely. Other cities have city bike
Ex C Q5 rental systems – why haven't we? We haven't even had a meeting to discuss it because you're too busy planning for Car-Free Day.
OK, to sum up, there are alternatives to car-free days that are actually better for the environment and that actually reduce car use. Let's try them out, instead of holding another useless car-free day. OK, any questions?

C2: Um, isn't it true that your brother runs an electric car dealership? Maybe that's …

A: Hey, what's that got to do with anything? Really! I just want our city to be a great place to live, that's all.

VOCABULARY

A Tell students the sentences here all come from the meeting they listened to. Tell students to underline the adjective in each sentence.

B Go through the information about gradable and ungradable adjectives in the box with the students. Use *bad* in sentence 1 as an example, eliciting from students that it's possible to say *fairly, very, extremely, a little, really bad*, and that it has a comparative form (*worse*), so therefore it is a gradable adjective. Tell students to look at the other adjectives from Exercise A and do the same to decide whether they are gradable or ungradable.

C Tell students to fill in the blanks with the adjectives from Exercise A. Do the first one as a whole class to make sure students are clear on the relationship between the adjectives in each pair.

D Tell students that there can be more than one ungradable adjective for a gradable adjective. Elicit that *wonderful* is a synonym of *excellent* from Exercise C, because both mean very good. Tell students to match the others.

E Direct students to the **Vocabulary Hub** (TB121) for further practice of gradable and ungradable adjectives.

F Put students into pairs and tell them to use ungradable adjectives to describe a recent experience, as in the example. To provide a clear reason to listen, you could tell students not to say what they're describing so that their partner has to guess. Use the **Vocabulary Worksheet** on W12 for extra practice.

SPEAKING HUB

A Check understanding of *mayor* and practice pronunciation. Tell students the local mayor has decided to cancel the city's Car-Free Day and now wants a new project and campaign to reduce the traffic problems and pollution. Tell students they are going to read three proposals that have been put forth. Turn to the **Communication Hub** (TB121).

B Tell students to read through the proposals in groups, then discuss the advantages and disadvantages of each one. Tell students to write notes as they do this, as they'll need to refer to them when they share and explain their ideas later. Encourage students to add more of their own ideas to each proposal as well.

C Tell students that they have to decide which proposal would be the best. Give each group time to decide and prepare to justify their choice.

An alternative way to do this would be to divide the class into three groups, assign one of the proposals to each group and tell them that they have to prepare to argue for their proposal to be chosen as the best.

D Ask students to share their ideas with the class and see how similar their thinking was. Encourage students to explain their reasons, and if there is disagreement, encourage debate. If the alternative option was chosen above in Exercise C, each group could present their ideas, either to the whole class or in smaller groups containing one or two members of each previous group. Tell students to put forth as many reasons as they can for why their proposal should be chosen. Finish with a whole-class vote on who had the best justifications for their choice; students can't vote for their own group!

TEACHING IDEA by David Seymour and Maria Popova

Vocabulary: Gradable and ungradable adjectives

Use this activity to practice the grammar.

In pairs, match an adjective from the first list with one from the second. What is the difference between the two lists? (Write the words from each box in two columns on the board. Re-order the adjectives in the second box when you write them; they appear here in the correct order.)

good, smart, small, hot, happy, cold, ugly, tired, difficult, hungry, funny, interesting, large

excellent, brilliant, tiny, boiling, thrilled, freezing, hideous, exhausted, impossible, famished, hilarious, fascinating, gigantic

Compare your answers with another pair.

Look at this conversation.
(Model the emphatic stress and ask the students to repeat it.)

A: This bedroom is rather small, isn't it?

B: Small? It's absolutely tiny!

In pairs, write similar short conversations with the words from the matching activity.
Invite pairs to read out some of their conversations.

Monitor and provide feedback on the emphatic stress. You can get pairs to swap their conversations for further practice. Finish with a class vote on the funniest conversation.

VOCABULARY

Gradable and ungradable adjectives

A **Underline the adjectives in the sentences from the council meeting about the Car-Free Day.**

1 Some things about cars are fairly bad.
2 That's very funny.
3 That's a really good idea.
4 This may be extremely difficult.
5 Car-free days have a really tiny effect on driving habits.
6 There was an absolutely enormous traffic jam.
7 People were furious about that.
8 Some of our old buses are really filthy.

B **Look at the adjectives in Exercise A. Which are gradable? Which are ungradable? Use the information in the box to help you.** G: bad, funny, good, difficult, old
U: tiny, enormous, furious, filthy

Gradable and ungradable adjectives

Gradable adjectives can be made stronger and weaker. We can use a range of adverbs to change their strength (*fairly, very, extremely, a little, really*). They have a comparative form.

Ungradable adjectives cannot be made weaker. They already mean *very* + adjective. We can use some adverbs to emphasise the adjective (*extremely, absolutely, completely, really*). They do not have a comparative form.

C **Write the adjectives from Exercise A in the correct place.**

1 very ___good___ → excellent
2 very small → ___tiny___
3 very ___bad___ → terrible
4 very angry → ___furious___
5 very ___difficult___ → impossible
6 very dirty → ___filthy___
7 very ___funny___ → hilarious
8 very big → ___enormous___

D **Match the ungradable adjectives (a–g) with some of the adjectives (1–8) in Exercise C.**

a wonderful ___very good___
b huge ___very big___
c fabulous ___very good___
d great ___very good___
e awful ___very bad___
f superb ___very good___
g massive ___very big___

E Go to the Vocabulary Hub on page 143.

F **SPEAK** **Work in pairs. Describe something you have bought, seen, eaten or done recently using ungradable adjectives.**

I saw an awful play last weekend. The lead actor was absolutely terrible. He kept forgetting his words!

SPEAKING HUB

A Go to the Communication Hub on page 151.

B **DISCUSS** Work in groups. Discuss the proposals and write notes on their advantages and disadvantages. Think of other ideas you can add to each proposal.

C **PLAN** Decide which proposal would be the best for the city and its people as well as being the best value for money.

D **REFLECT** Share your ideas with the class. Was your thinking similar or different?

- Evaluate suggestions and justify a choice
- Talk about why a plan didn't work

Café Hub

3.3 Getting there

F– tell a story   P– intonation in responses

COMPREHENSION

A Complete the personal information with *Milly* or *Zac*.

Name:	1 Zac	2 Milly
Nationality:	American	American
Home town:	Seattle	Seattle
Address:	London	London
Job:	makes video games	owns a clothing store
Hobbies:	playing video games	cycling

B Look at the picture. Where do you think Milly and Zac are going today?

C Watch the video and check your ideas. Then answer the questions.

1 Which famous people does the cabbie say have been in the back of his cab? Beyoncé, Jay-Z, Prince Harry, Wayne Rooney, Gérard Depardieu, Cristiano Ronaldo, guy out of Coldplay, all of One Direction

2 Why are Milly and Zac amazed at the cabbie's story about his American girlfriend? It is identical to their story.

3 How does the cabbie react when Milly asks, 'Are you sure this is the right way?' He's offended.

D Work in pairs. Discuss the last time you took a taxi.

- Where did you go from and to?
- How much did it cost?
- What did you talk about?

FUNCTIONAL LANGUAGE

Telling a story in five stages

A Work in pairs. Complete sentences (1–8) in the grey box with the endings (a–h). Then watch the video again and check.

a … went out with an American girl.
b … what happened the other day.
c … I was putting on a shirt and tie.
d … got my cab licence.
e … I miss you, Molly.
f … who I had in the back of my cab the other week.
g … she loved cycling.
h … she stopped answering my calls.

Telling a story in five stages

Introduction

1 You'll never guess … b
2 You won't believe … f
3 I once … a

Background

4 It was a few years ago now, when I … d
The funny thing was she hated driving.
5 It turned out … g
This is the best part: she used to run this fantastic little vintage clothes shop.

Problem

Well, a couple of months later, everything was going great, then one day, while I was watching the football, she said to me …
6 Before I knew it c
All of a sudden things started to change.

Resolution

7 In the end … h

Comment

8 I still love that girl … e

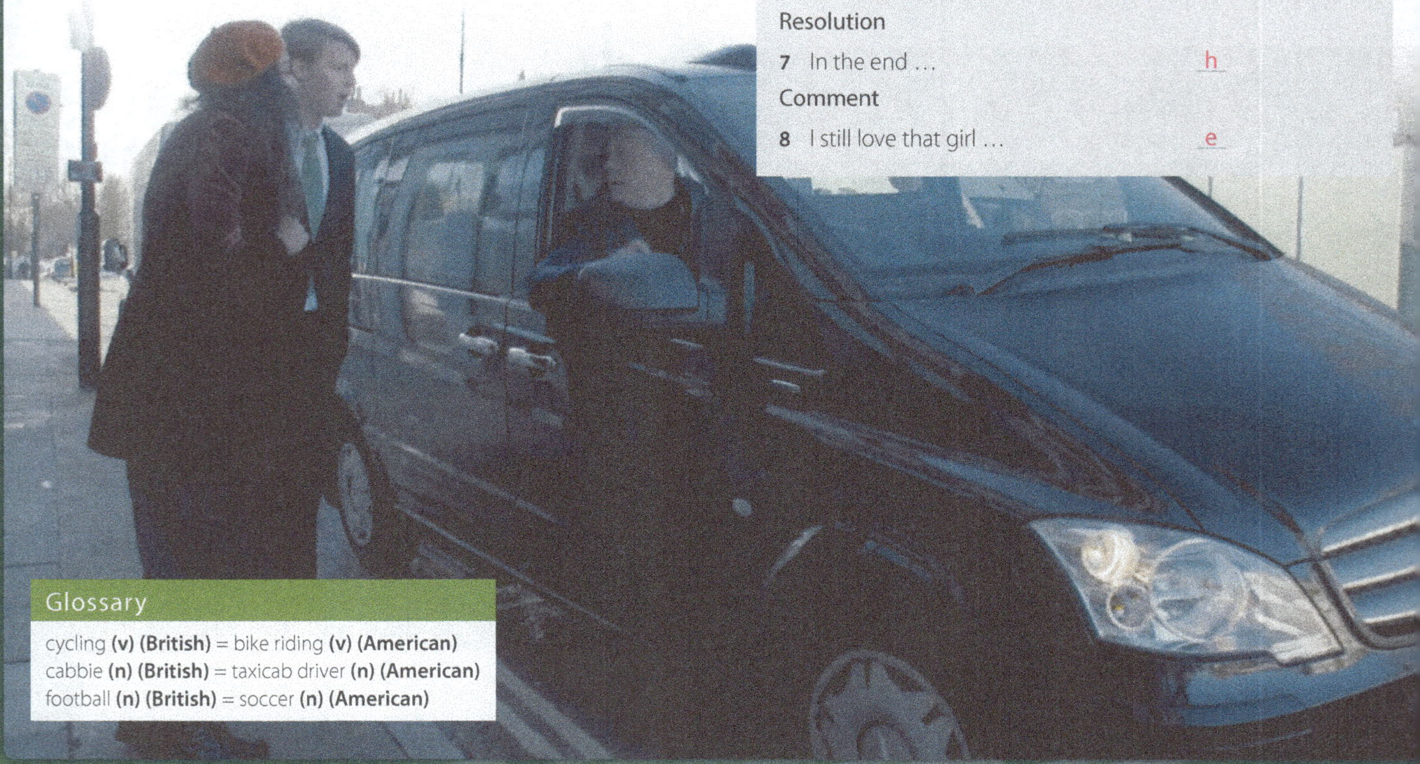

Glossary

cycling **(v) (British)** = bike riding **(v) (American)**
cabbie **(n) (British)** = taxicab driver **(n) (American)**
football **(n) (British)** = soccer **(n) (American)**

MILLY

SAM

NEENA

ZAC

GABY

B Work in pairs. Look at Milly and Zac's responses in the box. Student A – retell the cabbie's story. Student B – use the responses at an appropriate moment.

> No way! Really? That's awesome! Really? You're kidding! So what happened? That's tough.

C Work in pairs. Student A – use a prompt from the box or your own ideas to begin a conversation. Student B – respond appropriately.

> I found $50 in the street. I earned a perfect score in English. I got tickets to see my favorite band. I won a prize. My dog died. My father lost his job.

USEFUL PHRASES

A Complete the useful phrases with the correct form of the verbs in the box. There are two verbs you do not need.

> ~~be~~ do ~~joke~~ ~~jump~~ ~~let~~ make ~~take(x2)~~

1 Whatever, ___jump___ in the back, Jack.
2 Go on, ___take___ a guess.
3 Only ___joking___!
4 I'll ___take___ a short cut.
5 ___Are___ you two an item?
6 ___Let___ me tell you something.

B How do you say these useful phrases in your language?

PRONUNCIATION

Intonation in responses

3.8 **A** Listen and write the responses in the table below. Then listen and repeat the responses. Copy the stress and intonation.

B Which two types of responses have similar intonation?

Something is very good	Something is difficult	Something is surprising
Really? That's awesome!	That's tough.	I don't believe it!
Really? That's amazing!	That must be hard to take.	~~Really? You're kidding.~~
Wow! ~~That's impressive.~~	That's bad news.	No way!

SPEAKING

A You are going to tell your partner about somebody you used to spend a lot of time with, but now you do not. Answer the questions.

- Who is this person – a childhood friend, a neighbor, a relative?
- When and how did you meet him/her?
- How often did you use to see him/her?
- What sort of things did you use to do / talk about?
- Why did you stop seeing him/her so much?
- When was the last time you saw him/her?
- What is he/she doing now?

B DISCUSS Work in pairs. Take turns talking about the person. Use the functional language to structure your story, and if you are listening, respond in an appropriate way.

Tell a story

➤ Turn to page 158 to learn how to write an email of complaint.

3.3 Getting there

LEAD-IN

Ask students if they can remember a story and tell it to their partner.

COMPREHENSION

A Tell students to match the names with the fact files.

B Elicit a few ideas before students watch the video to check.

C ▸ Students discuss the questions in pairs.

D Tell the students about a taxi trip you've had, then ask them to discuss the questions in pairs.

FUNCTIONAL LANGUAGE

A ▸ Put students into pairs to complete the sentences, then play the video for students to watch again and check.

B Students retell the story, while their partner responds with the phrases. Then swap roles.

USEFUL PHRASES

A Ask students to complete the spaces with the correct form of the verbs. There are two verbs they won't need.

B Tell students to think about how they say the phrases in their own language. Are taxi drivers like that in their country?

PRONUNCIATION

3.8 A Play the responses to the story for the students to repeat, and put into the table.

B Check which two categories require similar intonation (*something is very good* and *something is difficult*).

C Tell students to practice with a partner by responding to the prompts in the box.

SPEAKING

A Tell students to think about the questions and write notes. Remind students to use some of the phrases for telling a story in five stages.

B Students talk about the person they chose with their partner. Remind them to respond appropriately while listening.

VIDEO SCRIPT

M = Milly Z = Zac C = Cabbie

M: Come on! We don't want to be late – You're meeting my mom for the first time …

Z: OK OK! I'm coming!

C: Jack?

Z: Zac.

C: Oh whatever, jump in the back, Jack. Afternoon! Americans?

Z: Uh, yeah …

C: Lovely! Let's go! You'll never guess what happened the other day? Go on then, have a guess … Only joking! So anyway. You won't believe who I had in the back of my cab the other week: Beyoncé and Jay-Z!

M: Really? You're kidding?

C: I'm not! They didn't say much though. I asked them to write a song about me. They stopped talking after that.

Z: Well …

C: I've had everyone you can think of in the back of my cab. I've had Prince Harry, Wayne Rooney … who's that French bloke er Gérard Depardieu … who else? Cristiano Ronaldo, that guy out of Coldplay, and even all of One Direction …

Z: You had Prince Harry in your cab?

C: Well … it looked like him. Probably was.

Z: Right.

C: Hmmm. Traffic jam. There'll be a slight delay, I'm afraid. Hang on, I'll take a shortcut. So, er, are you two an item?

M: A what?

C: IS HE YOUR BOYFRIEND?

M: Oh, err, yeah.

C: Luverly. Lovely stuff. I once went out with an American girl. It was a few years ago now, when I got my cab licence. The funny thing was that she hated driving! She wouldn't get into my cab!

M: No way!

C: Well, it wasn't too bad – it turned out she loves cycling. Everywhere. Absolutely. Everywhere. Even in the rain! Ah, she was hilarious … She actually taught me to cycle!

Z: Really? That's awesome.

C: Yeah … and this is the best part – she used to run this fantastic little vintage clothes shop. It was amazing, full of color – and she used to get me all these clothes! It was brilliant!

Z: So what happened?

C: Well, a couple of months later, everything was going great. Then one day, while I was watching the football, she said to me: 'I want you to meet my mum.' Before I knew it, I was putting on a shirt and tie and meeting up for lunch. She never liked me. Didn't even laugh at one of my jokes. Not even one of them!

Z: That's tough.

C: Yeah … all of sudden things started to change. She wasn't interested in me anymore – in the end, she stopped answering my calls. I still love that girl. I miss you Molly.

M: Milly?!

C: MOLLY. From Seattle.

M: Are you sure this is the right way?

C: Young lady, let me tell you something – I've been a cabbie all my life. My dad's a cabbie, my grandad was a cabbie, my great great … oh great! Here we are. That's er £9 please. Thank you. There you go.

M: Don't worry about it.

C: Have a lovely holiday!

Z: But we're not on holiday. Well then. Time to meet your mom. Let's do this …

3 Writing

Write an email of complaint

using adverbs to give emphasis

A Work in pairs. Add to the list of common causes of complaint for travelers.

- trash on buses and trains
- poor quality in-flight entertainment
- a lack of space
- delays due to technical problems

B Work in pairs. Have you experienced any of the problems you wrote down in Exercise A? Did you make a complaint? Why/Why not?

C Read Asaf King's email of complaint. Are the sentences true (T) or false (F)? Correct the false sentences.

1. When he made the reservation, Asaf paid more money to guarantee his seat. T
2. Asaf went quickly to check-in because he didn't have much time left. He arrived early F
3. There were no seats available on the flight to London. T
4. Asaf was not able to travel to Bangkok. Took a new flight F
5. Asaf did not tell the airline staff about his seat reservation. Staff ignored his reservation F
6. He wants the airline to give his money back and to pay extra for his problems. T

To: LuxAir Customer Services
Subject: A serious complaint:
Reservation Reference No. 589RT

Dear Sir or Madam,

a I am writing to complain about the mistakes your airline made with my reservation that meant I missed two flights and lost important business.

b On April 17, I made a reservation with your airline for flight Y33 from Dublin to London on May 23. I also paid extra to reserve my seat.

c I arrived at Dublin airport two hours before the flight and immediately went to the check-in desks. Since I had arrived early, I certainly wasn't expecting any problems, but sadly this was not the case. At check-in, I was told that the flight had been overbooked and was completely full, which meant I couldn't board the plane.

d This was extremely disappointing and incredibly inconvenient because it meant that I also missed my connecting flight, an international departure from London to Bangkok. The new flight to Bangkok cost me $500, and I missed an important meeting.

e The simple fact is that I had paid in advance to confirm my reservation, but you failed to hold my seat. I found your customer service at the airport completely unsatisfactory as your staff totally ignored my seat reservation.

f Because of the extra flight costs, my lost time and the effect on my business, I would like to ask for a full refund for my flight and for additional compensation.

I hope to hear from you soon regarding this matter.

Kind regards,

Asaf King

D Match the descriptions (1–6) with the paragraphs (a–f) in Asaf's email.

1. a detailed description of the main events c
2. the reason why you are writing the email a
3. the result you want from your email f
4. the key dates and places b
5. a summary of the main complaint e
6. the effects of the event and problems it caused d

E Look at the box. Then match the adverbs (1–3) with those that have a similar meaning (a–c). Use the email to help you.

Using adverbs to give emphasis

In the email, the writer uses adverbs to make a word stronger. An adverb usually goes before the adjective or verb that it describes.

- *The flight … was* ***completely*** *full.*
- *This was* ***extremely*** *disappointing.*

1 certainly — c definitely
2 extremely — a incredibly
3 completely — b totally

WRITING

A PREPARE Choose one of the situations to write an email about.

- Your recent flight was terrible.
- A member of staff gave you the wrong information.
- You experienced a long travel delay.

B PLAN Write detailed notes about what happened. Think about:

- where and when did it happen?
- what result do you want?

C WRITE Write a semi-formal email of complaint (150–250 words).

- Use Asaf's email and Exercise D to help you.
- Use adverbs to explain your problem.

158 WRITING

Remind students to use adverbs of emphasis to make their writing more powerful.

Refer students to this email as a model for the writing task.

If students don't have a real experience to write about, they could invent one.

WRITING

With books closed, elicit *complain* and *make a complaint* in relation to what people do when they aren't satisfied with a service. Put students into pairs to discuss if they have ever made a complaint about anything. If they have, how did they complain and what was the result? If not, why not? Ask students to share their most interesting stories. You could tell them that in some cultures, making a complaint can be fairly embarrassing, and ask if it is that way in the students' cultures.

A Tell students to look at the picture and elicit that it shows a bad traveling experience. Show students the list of common causes of complaint for travelers and ask them to add more. Discuss with the class and write any extra ideas elicited on the board.

B Give a personal example and then tell students to discuss in pairs if they have experienced any of the problems in the list. Ask them to also say if they made a complaint and why or why not.

C Tell students that they're going to read an email of complaint. Tell them first to decide if the sentences about the email are true or false and to correct the false ones.

D Tell students to read the email again, this time thinking about the way it is organized. Tell them to match the descriptions to the paragraphs.

E Point out the box and explain that adverbs are often used to give emphasis. Make sure students realize that the adverbs here are all used in the email. Tell them to look at how they are used to help them match those with a similar meaning.

WRITING TASK

A Tell students they're going to write their own email of complaint, either about a real experience they have had or an invented one. Tell students to choose one of the situations to write about.

B Tell students to plan their email by writing notes about the questions. Tell them that the notes should be detailed but stress that they shouldn't start writing out the email in full yet.

C Tell students to write their emails, using their notes and referring back to the paragraph structure and use of adverbs for emphasis from Asaf's email. If there are any fast finishers, tell them to read each other's emails and comment on how effective they are. Do they think the email would achieve the desired result, and why or why not?

Unit 3 Review

GRAMMAR

A Complete the story with the correct form of the verbs in parentheses.

We left home early in the morning because it [1] was snowing (*snow*) heavily. After we had found a parking space at the airport, we [2] went (*go*) straight to the check-in desk. That was when Kenny realized he [3] had forgotten (*forgot*) his passport. He thought he [4] had left (*leave*) it on the kitchen table!

I [5] decided (*decide*) to travel without him, but this made me nervous because I [6] hadn't flown (*not fly*) on my own before. Luckily, when I [7] was waiting (*wait*) in the line at the security checkpoint, Kenny [8] called (*call*) me with some excellent news.

He [9] had found (*find*) his passport in the car and [10] was walking (*walk*) back to the check-in desk.

B Correct the mistakes in the following passage by using *a*, *an*, *the* or – (no article).

Japan has ~~the~~ a famous network of bullet trains. ~~A~~ The network is the world's busiest and connects the major cities of the country. Like many ~~the~~ major train networks, it gets very busy at peak times. It is mainly a transportation system for long distances.

C Choose the correct quantifiers to complete the sentences.

1 The town center is full of traffic jams during the day. There are just *too much* / *too many* cars on the road.

2 Our city has a bicycle-sharing system. But at peak times it is difficult to get a bike because there are *not enough* / *too little*.

3 Overall, our town does not invest enough in transportation systems. This is because the council has *few* / *little* money for this.

4 How *many* / *much* of what the council says about the system is actually true?

VOCABULARY

A Choose the best words to complete the traffic reports.

Storm Anna is over, but there are still problems affecting roads and public transportation. You should only travel if it is essential. The central train station is closed, and they have [1]*canceled* / *delayed* all trains. Better news below the roads for the [2]*bus service* / *subway lines*. There [3]*is good service* / *are overcrowded trains* on all lines except for line 3. On that line, there are [4]*severe* / *slight* delays of about ten minutes. Traffic is building up on Bank Street due to the [5]*roadwork* / *rush hour* at the corner of Bank and Church Street. You can expect [6]*heavy delays* / *heavy traffic* all day there, and probably a [7]*slight delay* / *traffic jam* during [8]*heavy rain* / *rush hour*. That's certainly what happened yesterday.

B Complete the sentences with the nouns in the box.

communication connection decision
expectation inspiration situation

1 I don't like to make a decision too quickly as I may regret it later.

2 It is important to see the connection between the job you want and your own experience and knowledge.

3 Many jobs need strong communication skills because talking and writing to people is essential.

4 When your expectation is realistic, you are less likely to be disappointed.

5 When you cannot change a situation you are in, you can learn to accept it.

6 You can waste time waiting for inspiration to produce something. Sometimes it's best to take action.

C Find and correct the mistakes in four of the sentences.

1 Tell Stan that joke about the self-driving car. It's ~~very~~ hilarious.

2 I'm very angry. The train is late again!
correct

3 This road is very bad. They need to repair it.
correct

4 Sometimes, the old buses are ~~very~~ filthy.

5 These timetables are ~~very~~ impossible to understand.

6 The New York City bus tour was ~~very~~ excellent.

FUNCTIONAL LANGUAGE

Complete the dialogue with the words in the box.

~~awesome~~ ~~best~~ ~~couple~~ ~~dear~~ ~~guess~~
~~kidding~~ ~~sudden~~ ~~turned~~ ~~way~~

A: You'll never [1] guess what happened on my last trip with Kate. We got lost on a mountain without a map.

B: Really? You're [2] kidding!

A: No, I'm not! It was a [3] couple of months ago in Patagonia. I left the map in our hotel.

B: Oh [4] dear!

A: And even worse, it was dark when we got to the top. Then all of a [5] sudden Katie remembers she left the flashlight at the hotel, too.

B: No [6] way! I can't believe she did that.

A: Yeah, we were a little stupid. But we were lucky. We met two locals and they helped us get back. And you know the [7] best part?

B: What? Tell me!

A: They invited us for dinner. And it [8] turned out they owned the most expensive restaurant in town!

A: That's [9] awesome.

Old and new buildings contrast in modern day Hong Kong.

Change (n) a situation in which one person or thing is replaced by another. Synonyms: replacement (n), substitution (n)

The quote suggests that change is central to reality and is the only constant.

Heraclitus (c. 535–475 BCE) was a Greek philosopher. His work mainly survives as fragments that are quoted by other authors. He is known for his doctrine of universal flux – everything is constantly changing. His ideas were influential in philosophy.

OBJECTIVES

- talk about resolutions and plans
- talk about a life-changing book or movie
- make and discuss predictions
- discuss problems, reasons and consequences
- clarify and ask for clarification
- make and deal with complaints
- write a short essay

Work with a partner. Discuss the questions.

1 Look at the picture. What change does it show? Is it positive or negative?
2 Read the quote. Do you agree with it?
3 What have been the most important changes in your life?

CHANGE 37

OBJECTIVES

Read the unit objectives to the class.

UNIT OPENER QUESTIONS

With books closed, ask students what they associate with the word *change*. Are these associations generally positive or negative, and why?

1 Tell students to open their books and look at the picture. Elicit what kinds of change are shown. Ask students to discuss with their partner whether they think these changes are positive or negative. Monitor and provide language input. Elicit any interesting ideas and language on the board at the end of the activity. Is the class generally optimistic or pessimistic about how the world is changing?

2 Tell students to look at the quote and think about whether they agree or disagree with it. Give them a few seconds before speaking to write down a few ideas. They can also use this as an opportunity to request any new vocabulary. Ask students to discuss their opinion in small groups. Monitor and encourage debate if students have different opinions.

3 Tell students to tell each other about the most important changes in their own lives. Before they start, elicit a few ideas on the board of areas of change they could discuss (e.g. communication, fashion, shopping, studying, transportation, family, etc). Monitor to hear which students have experienced the most significant changes. Ask one or two to share them with the class.

WORKSHEETS

Lesson 4.1 Personal change

Grammar: Future forms (W13)

Vocabulary: Collocations: goals and resolutions (W14)

Lesson 4.2 Social change

Grammar: Making predictions (W15)

Vocabulary: Prefixes: *dis-*, *mis-*, *over-*, *re-*, *under* (W16)

4.1 Personal change

- Talk about resolutions and plans
- Talk about a life-changing book or movie

G – future forms
V – collocations: goals and resolutions
P – intonation for attitude and mood
S – summarizing

LISTENING

A SPEAK Work in pairs and discuss the questions.

1 Is New Year's Eve an important celebration:
- for you?
- in your country?

2 How do people celebrate the New Year in different parts of the world?

3 Why do people celebrate the New Year?

4.1 **B LISTEN FOR GIST** Listen to a video call between Julia and Shireen. Then answer the questions.

1 What is their relationship and where are they?

They are good friends. Julia is in Spain (Madrid). Shireen is in the US (New York City).

2 Check (✓) which of these topics they talk about.

a their New Year's Eve activities ✓
b moving ☐
c buying new clothes ✓
d making new friends ☐
e changing jobs ☐
f learning a language ✓

3 What do you think a New Year's resolution is?

It's a promise to yourself to make a positive change in your life.

4.1 **C LISTEN FOR DETAIL** Listen again. Are the sentences true (T) or false (F)? Correct the false sentences.

1 The weather was cold on New Year's Eve at Times Square in New York City. T
2 ~~Julia's boyfriend has always been very romantic.~~ He has decided to try to be more romantic in the future. F
3 Julia wants to do more physical exercise. T
4 ~~Julia can't speak Spanish.~~ She can speak Spanish, but wants to improve. F
5 ~~Julia is looking for a new teacher.~~ She has found a new teacher already. F
6 Shireen thinks Julia reads too many advice books. T
7 ~~Shireen agrees to stop eating chocolate.~~ She agrees to eat less. F

D SPEAK Work in pairs and discuss the questions.

1 Look at the list of the ten most common New Year's resolutions. Which do you think are the top three? Go to the **Communication Hub** on **page 147** to check your answers.
- get in shape and get healthy
- get organized
- enjoy life to the fullest
- change the foods you eat
- quit unhealthy habits
- help others achieve their dreams
- fall in love
- spend less, save more
- learn something exciting
- spend more time with family

2 What could people do to achieve these resolutions?

3 Which do you think are the hardest to achieve?

GRAMMAR

Future forms

A WORK IT OUT Look at the sentences (1–7) from the conversation between Julia and Shireen. Check (✓) the sentences in which the speaker made a decision or plan before this conversation.

1 Oh! Oops! I'll do it now. Hold on. ☐
2 I've decided to get in better shape this year, so I'm going to join a gym. ✓
3 I did get pretty cold. I'm going to look for a new hat tomorrow. ✓
4 Sophie's coming here to have lunch. ✓
5 I'm meeting a new teacher on Thursday. ✓
6 Make your mind up now! ☐
7 OK, OK. I'll stop eating it every day. ☐

4.1 Personal change

LEAD-IN

Put students into pairs to discuss which is their favorite day of the year and why. Share any interesting answers.

LISTENING

A Tell students to look at the picture and elicit where it is (Sydney Opera House / Sydney Harbour) and what is happening (New Year's Eve fireworks display). Put students into pairs to discuss.

4.1 **B** Tell students they're going to listen to a video call between Julia and Shireen. Focus them on the questions and have them apply check marks to correct boxes.

4.1 **C** Play the audio again. Students should correct any false sentences.

D Tell students to look at just Question 1 first. Encourage discussion in pairs and as a whole class before telling students to turn to the **Communication Hub** (TB121) to check their answers.

GRAMMAR

A Tell them to apply check marks to the sentences in which the speaker has made their decision or plan before speaking.

B Tell students to look at the sentences again and elicit the different ways they express the future. Tell students to look at the rules for using them and to fill in the blanks with the phrases, referring to their answers to Exercise A to help them.

C Direct students to the **Grammar Hub** (see TB39).

D Give students a chance to personalize the language by discussing the questions with their partner. Give a few personal examples to model the structures you would use to answer each question. Use the **Grammar Worksheet** on W13 for extra practice.

AUDIO SCRIPT

4.1

Listening, Exercises B and C
J = Julia S = Shireen

J: Hi, Shireen.
S: Hi, Julia. I can't see you; I don't think you've clicked the video button.
J: Oh! Oops! I'll do it now. Hold on. There we go.
S: That's better. Good to see you. Happy New Year!
J: And happy New Year to you!
S: How's everything going in Spain?
J: Great. We had a nice time on New Year's Eve; there's a real party atmosphere in Madrid. We were at a house party, and then out on the streets at midnight, eating grapes, dancing and drinking hot chocolate – just wonderful!
S: Well, lucky you! Sounds better than mine. We went to see the ball drop at Times Square in New York City.
J: But that sounds amazing!
S: Oh, I'm sure they were – it's just we never actually saw it.
J: Oh no! What happened? You didn't get lost again, did you?
S: Not exactly – we just weren't early enough. There was a massive crowd and we got stuck on a side road. We could hear the countdown, but couldn't see a thing.
J: Oh! I bet it was freezing, too. I'm glad I was at that party and had that hot chocolate at midnight.
S: Yeah, I can imagine. We were outside for hours, and I lost my hat. To be honest, I did get pretty cold. I'm going to look for a new hat tomorrow; Sophie's coming here to have lunch, and then we're going shopping.
J: That's nice. Is that one of your New Year's resolutions? Are you going to finally buy some new clothes? No more going out in your sister's old ones?
S: Haha, very funny. Actually, I've not made any resolutions yet.
J: You haven't? I've made several.
S: Really? What've you decided?
J: Try and guess.
S: OK, OK! Let me see. So, are you going to get married this year? Time to copy me?
J: Ooh, that's a big question to ask! No, no plans yet, but Alberto's said he's going to buy me flowers every month. He's going to try to be more romantic, for a change. *(Ex C Q2)*
S: That's great. He sounds sweet. Let's hope he keeps that one. So, what are yours?
J: Well, I've decided to get in better shape this year, so I'm going to join a gym. Also, I'm going to study Spanish more seriously. I find it pretty hard to follow Alberto's friends.
S: That's a surprise! I always thought your Spanish was really good. *(Ex C Q4)*
J: Well, not good enough. In fact, I'm meeting a new teacher on Thursday, for private lessons. *(Ex C Q5)*
S: Really? That's quick!
J: Well, there's no point in putting things off. Just get started and then stick to the plan. I was reading a self-help book about this the other day: *How to reach your goals and change your life.*
S: Another self-help book? I think you should make a resolution to stop reading them.
J: Well, I think you should read some. It'd be good for you.
S: Really? I'll leave that to you, I think.
J: Oh, come on – now's the time to make some resolutions. What do you want to achieve this year? Or change? What about your chocolate habit? Resolutions are a great way to quit bad habits.
S: My chocolate habit? What do you mean?
J: You eat some every day, don't you?
S: Well, just a little. At work, you know.
J: Shireen, I really think you should cut it out of your diet. I was reading about how we've all become sugar addicts and …
S: That's a surprise! Another book! But, yeah, I know what you mean. It's just that I get really bored at work. I don't think I can totally quit, but I'll cut down on the amount I eat. Happy now? *(Ex C Q7)*
J: Cut down by how much? There's no escape – make your mind up now!
S: OK, OK, I'll stop eating it every day. I'll have chocolate on Fridays only, as a treat.
J: Great, and I'll make sure you don't break that resolution.
S: Great, and how are you going to do that? Going to come to work with me each day?
J: Hmm, I'll put a webcam on your office desk.
S: Well, at least you can see how boring my job is then.

4.1 Personal change

PRONUNCIATION

A–C Monitor and give feedback as students complete the exercises.

4.2; 4.3

D Put students into pairs and direct them to the **Communication Hub** (TB121). When they seem ready, tell students to have the conversation and think carefully about their intonation.

VOCABULARY

A–B Put students into pairs to check answers before whole-class feedback.

C Direct students to the **Vocabulary Hub** (TB121) for further practice.

D Give a personal example as a model and then ask students to discuss the questions with their partner. Use the **Vocabulary Worksheet** on W14 for extra practice.

SPEAKING

A Put students into pairs and tell them to imagine they have agreed to make eight resolutions together. Tell them to turn to the **Communication Hub** (TB121).

B Tell students to follow the instructions, first making resolutions about their own topics, then making further resolutions about their partner's topics.

C Make bigger groups and encourage pairs to exchange ideas and discuss which resolutions will be easy or hard to keep.

GRAMMAR HUB

4.1 Future forms

- We use *will* when we make a decision at the time of speaking.

  I'll get my coat and we can leave now.
  I won't buy this dress because it's too small.

- We use *be going to* for our intentions (the things we want to do or have already decided to do).

  Salma is going to cut down on the amount of chocolate she eats.
  We aren't going to have a New Year's party this year.
  Are you going to keep your New Year's resolutions?

- We use the present progressive when we have made an arrangement for a certain time in the future, usually with another person.

  Aisa is going shopping with her sister tomorrow.
  He isn't coming out with us tonight.
  What are you doing on New Year's Eve?

Be careful!

- We don't use the present progressive for intentions that haven't been arranged yet. We use *be going to*.

  I'm going to write a book one day.
  NOT ~~I'm writing a book one day.~~

4.1 Future forms

A Match the sentences (1–6) to the answers (a–f) to make short dialogues.

1 The phone's ringing! d
2 Are you staying at home tonight? f
3 Would you like anything else? e
4 Josh is having a fireworks party tomorrow. c
5 I've lost my wallet! a
6 What time are you meeting the others? b

a Oh no! What are you going to do?
b Sometime tomorrow morning.
c Sounds amazing. Can I come?
d OK. I'll get it!
e Yes, I'll have a coffee, please.
f No, I'm having dinner with Kate.

B Choose the correct option.

1 A: 'I've just heard it's Dan's birthday today.'
B: 'Oh! *I'll get* / *I'm getting* him a present at lunchtime, then.'
2 Next year, I'm *going to try* / *trying* to keep my New Year's resolutions.
3 It's all arranged. *We'll move* / *We're moving* next Tuesday.
4 I made a big decision last week. *I'll* / *I'm going to* look for a new job.
5 A: 'I don't think I'll ever fall in love.'
B: 'Don't be silly. It's *happening* / *going to happen* soon, I'm sure.'

C Complete the dialogue with the correct form of the words in parentheses. Sometimes more than one answer is possible.

Ashanti: What are you doing on the weekend, Camilla?
Camilla: I [1] am/'m not doing (*not / do*) anything special. Why?
Ashanti: Well, I'm going to a two-day self-help course. Come with me!
Camilla: Self-help?
Ashanti: Yes. I've decided I [2] am/'m going to change (*change*) my life.
Camilla: It doesn't sound like my kind of thing. What time [3] are you leaving / (*leave*) tomorrow? are you going to leave
Ashanti: Early – at about eight o'clock.
Camilla: In that case, I definitely don't want to come! Tomorrow's Saturday and I [4] am/'m not working (*not / work*). I [5] am/'m going to sleep (*sleep*) until eleven o'clock and then have breakfast in bed!
Ashanti: All right. If you're sure. In that case, I [6] will/'ll call (*call*) you on Sunday evening and tell you all about it.
Camilla: OK. Have a good time!

➤ Go back to page 39.

B Complete the rules with the phrases in the box.

already | at a certain time in the future | at the time of speaking

Future forms

1 When we talk about future actions and events, we use ***be going to*** when we have ___already___ decided to do something.

2 We use ***will*** when we make the decision ___at the time of speaking___.

3 We use the present progressive when we have a planned arrangement ___at a certain time in the future___, usually with another person.

C Go to the **Grammar Hub** on **page 128**.

D SPEAK Work in pairs and discuss the questions.

1 What are you doing tonight?
2 Do you have any plans or arrangements for the weekend?
3 What do you intend to do over the next few months?
4 Imagine you have just realized you left your wallet at home. What will you do?

PRONUNCIATION
Intonation for attitude and mood

Intonation for attitude and mood

We change the tone of our voice to communicate our feelings about or attitude toward something. For example, interested/uninterested, surprised/unsurprised, positive/negative.

Our tone of voice can be in a high, mid or low position.

As we speak, our tone may rise and fall to show mood and attitude.

4.2 **A** Listen and write down the five words and phrases that you hear. They are in a neutral tone. 1. OK, OK. 2. Great. 3. Really? 4. Well, ... 5. That's a surprise.

4.3 **B** Listen to the same five words and phrases. Each phrase is said in two different tones. Match each tone (*a* or *b*) with the moods and feelings below.

1	very positive	a
	not very positive	b
2	excited	b
	unexcited	a
3	interested and surprised	a
	not interested	b
4	serious/determined	b
	unsure	a
5	pretty surprised	a
	not surprised at all (sarcastic)	b

4.3 **C** Listen again and repeat the sentences.

D SPEAK Work in pairs. Student A – go to the **Communication Hub** on **page 148**. Student B – go to the **Communication Hub** on **page 153**.

VOCABULARY
Collocations: goals and resolutions

A Match the phrases (1–6) with phrases with a similar meaning (a–f).

1	make a resolution	a	do less of something
2	keep a resolution	b	achieve something
3	break a resolution	c	set (yourself) a goal
4	quit a bad habit	d	not do what you promised
5	reach a target	e	stick to a plan
6	cut down on something	f	stop doing something that is not good for you

(Answers drawn: 1–c, 2–e, 3–d, 4–f, 5–b, 6–a)

B Choose the best words to complete the sentences.

1 I've made a resolution (*to learn*) / *of learning* ten English words a day.
2 He managed to keep his resolution (*by*) / *in* using a fitness app.
3 He quit (*smoking*) / *smoke* last year.
4 She wants to cut down on *drink* / (*drinking*) coffee.
5 His goals are not very (*realistic*) / *real*. They're too hard to achieve.
6 Stick to your plan (*until*) / *when* you reach your target.

C Go to the **Vocabulary Hub** on **page 143**.

D SPEAK Work in pairs. Discuss your experiences of making resolutions and achieving goals. Find out:

- about resolutions your partner has made, kept and broken.
- how your partner managed to achieve his/her goals and stick to his/her plans.
- if your partner has ever quit, or cut down on, doing something.

SPEAKING

A Work in pairs. It is New Year's Eve, and you have agreed with your friend to each make eight resolutions. Student A – go to the **Communication Hub** on **page 149**. Student B – go to the **Communication Hub** on **page 150**.

B Talk to your partner about your resolutions, and ask them to make a resolution for each of your topics.

C Compare your resolutions with another pair. Do you think the resolutions will be easy or hard to keep?

READING

A Choose the correct sentence endings.

1 Self-help books …

a contain instructions for doing something, especially operating a machine.

(b) are designed to help you solve your own problems or improve your life.

2 Self-help books are usually written in …

a a formal style that is for experts only.

(b) an informal style for anyone.

B SCAN Read *Life Cycle* quickly. Match the phrases (1–5) with the topics (a–e).

1 Helena Schneiderlin	a a journey
2 *Life Cycle*	b the author's next book
3 Paris to Moscow	c the author's passion
4 cycling	d the author
5 *Inner Pedal Power*	e the author's first book

Life Cycle: How to find what you love and love what you find

About this book

Ex B **Ten years ago, Helena Schneiderlin was a hard-working mom with no time for herself. Like many people, she didn't know what** Ex B **she really wanted to do with her life. Today, Schneiderlin is a cyclist who is well known for going on long and difficult journeys.** Ex B **She has ridden from Paris to Moscow by herself. She has also ridden across Australia, and last year she rode from the bottom of South America to the top.**

Thanks to her cycling experiences, and the effect they have had on her life, Schneiderlin has also become a leading lifestyle expert. Her talks have been watched millions of times online, and she is regularly asked to speak at international lifestyle events and conferences.

Ex B In *Life Cycle*, which is her first book, she Ex B describes how finding her true passion changed her life, and explains how you can find yours.

'This isn't a book about cycling,' says Ex A Q1 Schneiderlin. 'It's a book about finding the thing that you enjoy doing most, and helping to make that thing benefit all other areas of your life.'

In *Life Cycle*, Schneiderlin uses her own story as an example for others to follow. She describes how she found her passion for cycling while on vacation with her family, and what it has taught her about commitment, sacrifice and success. She provides valuable advice and life Ex A Q2 lessons that apply to all of us, including chapters on getting rid of the things in life that aren't helping, and how to identify the things that make you feel better about yourself.

Schneiderlin says:

> ***"I believe that everyone has a passion, but they may not know what it is. I also believe that when you find that passion, you should use it to improve every area of your life. In my case, it was cycling – but it could have been anything. What's important is finding the thing that you love, and then using it in the right way."***

READING

A With books closed, write the word *self-help book* on the board with some of the letters missing and replaced by a dash, e.g. *s___-h___ b___*. Explain the concept of a self-help book and try to elicit. To check the understanding of the concept, ask students what type of problems you might buy a self-help book to help with. Tell students to open their books and answer the questions.

B Tell students they're going to read about a self-help book. Tell them to look at the images and to predict what they think the book will be about. Elicit some predictions, then tell students to scan the text to match the phrases with the topics. Explain that scanning means reading quickly to find specific information, so students don't need to worry about unknown vocabulary to do this.

C Point out the strategies for summarizing in the box and make sure they understand the purpose of a summary. Tell students to read the two summaries and choose which is best and why, thinking about the summarizing strategies as they do this. Let students compare answers in pairs before checking answers as a whole class. Ask students to justify their choice with reference to the strategies.

1 *repeats too many details, and some phrases are copied word for word. It doesn't give a clear overview of all of the information in the description.*

2 *is the best summary. It mentions all of the most important pieces of information from the book description but it doesn't copy the description word for word.*

D Tell students to discuss with a partner whether or not they would like to read *Life Cycle* and why. Discuss as a whole class and ask if students have ever read any similar books to this. If they have, what did they think of them and would they recommend them.

TEACHING IDEA by David Seymour and Maria Popova

Topic: Hobbies

Use this activity to extend the topic.

(Arrange the students so that they are standing/sitting in a circle. Stand in the middle. Ask each of these questions to individual students at random. After they answer it, tell them to repeat the question to the next student and write a note of the student's answer. Indicate that they should continue the chain so the question progresses around the class. Meanwhile, introduce the other questions so that in the end there are a lot of questions moving around the class.)

> What sports do you play, if any? How much time do you spend watching TV? Do you have a hobby? What hobby would you like to take up? What do you do on Sunday afternoons? How much free time do you have? What do you read for enjoyment? What hobbies did you use to have as a child? When did you last go to the beach and where was it located? What are the main recreational activities in your family?

Turn your notes into full sentences, e.g. *Maria wants to take up hang gliding.*

In small groups, discuss these questions.

> What are the main recreational activities in the US/UK and in your country? What about other countries? What do you understand by the expressions quality time, work ethic and free time? How much quality time do you get? What do you think is the right balance between work and play?

TEACHING IDEA by David Seymour and Maria Popova

Topic: Free-time survey

Use this activity to extend the topic.

In small groups, find out who:

- watches TV the most
- has the most interesting hobby
- has had the most hobbies
- has been a collector of something

METHODOLOGY HUB by Jim Scrivener

The importance of skills work

Don't underestimate the importance of skills work. Not every lesson needs to teach new words or new grammar. Lessons also need to be planned to give students opportunities to practice and improve their language skills. Skills work is not something to add in at the end of a five-year course in English. There is no need to wait for extensive knowledge before daring to embark on listening, reading and speaking work. On the contrary, it is something so essential that it needs to be at the heart of a course from the start. Even a beginner with one day's English will be able to practice speaking and listening usefully.

LISTENING

4.4 **A** Tell students that they're going to listen to four people talking about a book or a movie that changed their lives. Tell them to listen and match each speaker to what they talk about. Remind students that they don't need to worry if they don't understand everything the speakers say and that they will be able to listen again for more information after completing this task.

4.4 **B** Before listening, tell students to look at the summaries of what each speaker said and to try to complete them with the words in the box. Play the audio again for them to check.

C Put students into pairs to discuss which of the books or movies they are most interested in and why. Encourage students to tell each other if they have read or seen any similar books or movies.

SPEAKING HUB

A Tell students they are going to talk about a life-changing book or movie. If students find this a little daunting, rephrase it to *a book or movie that had a big effect* on them. Tell students to read the questions and to write notes to prepare what they're going to say. Remind students specifically about the strategies for summarizing and elicit what makes a good or bad summary. Monitor as they prepare, helping with language as required and ensuring that students are just writing notes and not scripting exactly what they're going to say.

B Tell students to tell their partner about their chosen book or movie and to explain in as much detail as they can why it had such a big effect on them. Encourage students to listen carefully while their partner is speaking and to ask follow-up questions.

For further practice, you could put the students with a new partner to repeat the task. This time give a shorter time limit, but tell students they need to include all the key information. This would force students to think more carefully about the language they use to summarize the book or movie, and to be more precise in expressing how it affected them.

Conclude the activity by asking students which of their classmates' recommended books or movies they'd most like to read or see and why. Write any book or movie recommendations up on the board.

Extra activity

The list could be used to encourage extensive reading, as well as watching movies in English outside class. If any of the titles suggested are available in English, they could be added to a class list of reading materials. Also this class could be used to introduce any extracurricular book club that is planned. Students can be asked to bring in English books to share and discuss at the next class.

Either way as a follow-up activity, students can write up a brief book or movie recommendation based on the work they spoke about.

AUDIO SCRIPT

4.4

Listening, Exercise A
A = Announcer M = Maya L = Lukas J = Jody H = Hassan

A: Maya

M: I never usually bother with self-help books. I usually prefer fiction, especially things like sci-fi and fantasy. But last year, I read a book that totally changed the way I feel about myself. It's called *Life Cycle* and it's by a famous cyclist and lifestyle expert named Helena Schneiderlin. The book explains how you can find
Ex B Q1 the real you and be a happier person when you find your true passion. It gives you advice on how to find the thing that you love and how to use it to improve
Ex B Q1 the quality of your life. I followed the advice in the book, and since then I've become much happier. It's definitely changed how I feel about myself. It's
Ex B Q1 changed my life really. I'm much more confident now.

A: Lukas

L: I think the one thing that changed my life most of all was a book called *The Road*. It's by Cormac McCarthy
Ex B Q2 and it's about a father and son on a journey through a strange and unwelcoming place. It might be the future after a terrible event – the book doesn't say exactly. Really, I think it's about the relationship between the two characters. Even though their situation is very bad, the love they have keeps them strong. I'll never forget the first time I read this book.
Ex B Q2 It made me think about my own relationship with my father. We don't always get along, but I think *The Road* has helped me to understand him better.

A: Jody

Ex B Q3 **J:** There's a book called *Sapiens*. I only read it last year, but honestly, I can't think of another book that has
Ex C Q3 had such a strong effect on me. It's a history book, and it tells the story of the human race – everything, from how we started as hunters, and then became farmers, on to how we developed cities and industry. It's written by Yuval Noah Harari. He talks about
Ex B Q3 religion, money, countries, law – everything. It's a very impressive piece of work, and it really helped me to see things in context. I feel I have a better understanding about who we are now that I've read that book.

A: Hassan

H: Seeing *Hoop Dreams* was a life-changing moment for me.
Ex B Q4 It's a documentary about two teenagers in Chicago who want to be professional basketball players. It follows six years of their lives, as they try and make it to the top. Both boys come from poor backgrounds, and the film is about a lot more than just basketball. It's about society, and it's about how a life can
Ex B Q4 change in an instant. I was really into basketball when I was young, and I went into the movie theater that day wanting to be a basketball player, but by the time I walked out of the movie theater, I wanted to be a film-maker instead. And that's what I am now. *Hoop Dreams* inspired me to make documentaries.

C SUMMARIZE Read the two summaries of the book *Life Cycle*. Which is the best summary? Why? Use the strategies in the box to help you.

Summarizing

A summary gives a brief explanation of the most important parts of the text.

To write a summary, first identify the details in the original text that don't need to be included in a summary. Then find the main points in the original text. Finally, put these together to make a summary, but try not to copy word for word.

1 Helena Schneiderlin has gone on a lot of long bicycle journeys. Once she rode from Paris to Moscow. Another time she rode across Australia. She has also ridden all the way up South America. She is a mom. She is a lifestyle expert and lots of people watch her talks on the internet. This is her first book. This book is about lifestyle changes. This book is about finding the thing you enjoy doing most. It is not about cycling, but she does talk about how she found her passion for cycling while she was on vacation with her family. This book is also about improving your life.

2 Helena Schneiderlin is a top lifestyle expert and a well-known cyclist who has ridden across continents. In this, her first book, she explains how cycling led to a life change and self-discovery, and gives advice on how to find your true passion. Using her own story as a guide, the author explains what she has learned from cycling, and discusses how these 'life lessons' can apply to all of us, in all aspects of life.

D SPEAK Work in pairs. Would you like to read *Life Cycle*? Why/Why not?

LISTENING

A LISTEN FOR GIST 4.4 Listen to four people talking about books or movies that changed their lives. Write *Maya, Lukas, Jody* or *Hassan*.

Who talks about …

1 a non-fiction film? ___Hassan___
2 a fiction book? ___Lukas___
3 doing what the book suggested? ___Maya___
4 the whole of human history? ___Jody___

B LISTEN FOR MAIN IDEA 4.4 Complete the summaries (1–4) with the words in the box. Then listen again and check your answers.

advice characters confident documentary father history impressive journey passion society sport recently

1 Maya read a self-help book about finding your true ___passion___. She followed the ___advice___ in the book and now she feels happier and more ___confident___.

2 Lukas read a book about two ___characters___ on a ___journey___ in a strange place. The book made him think about his own relationship with his ___father___.

3 Jody learned a lot about the ___history___ of the human race in a book she read ___recently___. She thinks the book is very ___impressive___.

4 Hassan saw a ___documentary___ set in the US. He feels that the story is about more than a ___sport___; he thinks it also has an important message about ___society___.

C SPEAK Work in pairs. Which book or movie from the listening are you most interested in? Why?

SPEAKING HUB

A PLAN You are going to talk about a life-changing book or movie.

1 Choose a book or movie that had a big effect on you.
2 Think about how you can summarize the book/movie:
- What kind of book/movie is it?
- Who wrote/made it?
- What is it about?

3 Think about how it affected you:
- When did you read/see it?
- Why did you read/see it?
- How did it change the way you think/feel?
- Who else do you think should read/see it?

B SPEAK Work in pairs. Tell your partner about the book or movie that changed your life. Listen to his/her description. Ask and answer questions.

Talk about resolutions and plans
Talk about a life-changing book or movie

- Make and discuss predictions
- Discuss problems, reasons and consequences

G – making predictions
V – prefixes: *dis-, mis-, over-, re-, under-*
P – contraction of *will*; linking final consonant and first vowel sounds
S – paraphrasing

READING

A SPEAK Work in groups. Have you ever predicted something that later came true?

B Look at the headline of the article. Which word means:

a a person who has detailed knowledge about a subject? expert

b a person who talks about future events and situations? forecaster

C READ FOR GIST Read *How super-forecasters could replace professional experts*. Then choose the best summary.

1 Philip Tetlock carried out a study on why experts are good media guests, but make predictions that are generally less accurate than those made by most ordinary people.

2 Philip Tetlock carried out a research project to show that ordinary people who have particular thinking skills usually make better future predictions than experts.

How super-forecasters could replace professional experts

Katy Macnab

'Five minutes left, and Brazil is leading by three goals. They're going to win the World Cup again.' Apart from situations like this, the only certain thing about the future is that our predictions will probably be wrong.

In his early research, Philip Tetlock, of the University of Pennsylvania, showed that professional experts are only slightly better at predicting the future than monkeys. However, his most recent study is more hopeful.

This project involved thousands of ordinary people making predictions about social change. They used the internet, but they did not have detailed knowledge of a topic or access to secret data. Despite this, Tetlock found that 2 percent of them were rather good at it – better than both monkeys and professional experts. These 'super-forecasters' are smart, but not geniuses. However, they do have good thinking skills that anyone can develop.

Ex D Q2 Super-forecasters are analytical thinkers who update their opinion when they get new information, and they don't let their personal hopes affect their thinking. More importantly, they listen carefully to different views that they then use in their forecast. This perhaps explains why they make their most accurate predictions when working in teams of super-forecasters. Ex D Q3

Surprisingly, professional experts usually lack these qualities. They tend to work alone and have strong personal opinions that guide their thinking. They speak with great confidence, stressing they are totally certain: 'I'm sure all cars will be driverless', 'Robots are going to replace office workers', 'We won't have an early election'. This means they are great TV guests and bloggers, but not the best forecasters. Ex D Q1 Ex D Q4 Ex D Q6

Super-forecasters don't speak in a way that suits TV. They are more cautious: 'There may be an early election', 'People might stop reading newspapers', 'Chinese could become a global language'. They also use percentages to show how likely something is: 'I think this has an 80 percent chance of happening'. Ex D Q5 In this way, the team can discuss different ideas easily and make a final prediction.

Tetlock also identified three useful techniques, namely looking at current trends, comparing with past events and exploring the possible effects of a prediction: 'If everyone uses electric cars, how will we produce enough electricity?'

In the future, we will definitely develop better computers to make accurate predictions about our society. For now though, teams of super-forecasters are the best crystal balls we have.

Glossary

analytical (adj) using a method of separating things into their parts in order to examine and understand them

genius (n) someone who is much more intelligent or skilful than other people

tend (v) to usually do a particular thing

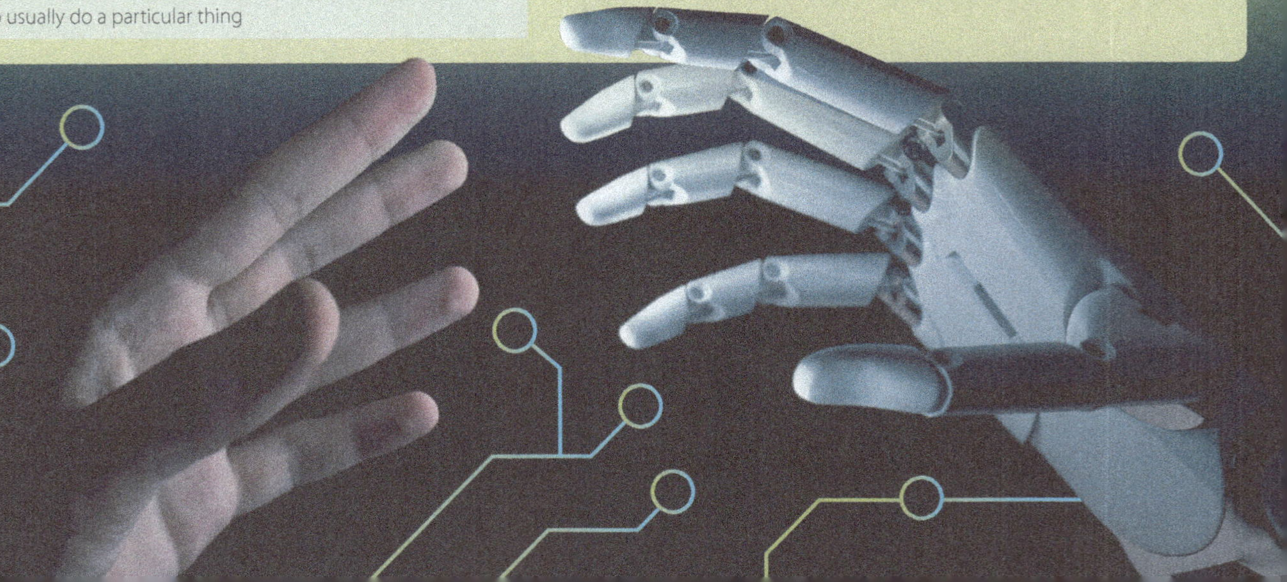

4.2 Social change

LEAD-IN

With books closed, ask students some simple questions about what they think will happen in the immediate future in relation to the weather, or a sporting event or any other topical issue they will know about. Elicit *prediction* by asking if their ideas are things that will definitely happen, or just their opinion.

READING

A Tell students to open their books and to discuss the question in groups. Share any interesting answers.

B Tell students they're going to read an article about predictions. Tell them to look at the headline and answer the questions.

C Set a time limit and tell students to read the article quickly and choose the best summary of it. Remind students that they don't need to read in detail or worry about unknown words at this stage. Reassure them that they will get a chance to read it again more carefully.

1 is a weak summary because it has the experts as the main topic, but in the article the ordinary people are the focus. Also, he was not studying why experts are good media guests. It's also incorrect that experts are worse at predicting than most ordinary people.

2 is the best summary as it identifies which ordinary people are good at predictions.

D Tell students they can now read the text more closely and decide if the sentences refer to professional experts (PE) or super-forecasters (SF). Tell students to underline the text that helps them to decide. Encourage students to check their answers with their partner. Check answers as a whole class, eliciting which sections of the text helped answer the questions.

E Look at the three different situations. For each situation, elicit some ideas on the board of things you would need to consider to help predict these things. For example, for the winner of a soccer competition, you might elicit ideas such as how many goals a team has scored this season, if their star player is injured, will they be playing at home or away, etc. Put students into pairs to discuss how easy it is to predict these things accurately and then to rank them. Elicit students' opinions.

b This is probably the easiest to predict because data on numbers of births allows sensible predictions.

a There may be a clear favorite, but in soccer you never know! There are plenty of examples of the underdog winning a tournament or competition.

c This is probably the hardest to predict accurately simply because of the length of time. However, it is sometimes surprising to note how little changes, even over 100 years.

TEACHING IDEA by David Seymour and Maria Popova

Grammar: Making predictions

2099

Write *2099* on the board. Ask students to imagine what the world will be like then. Offer some prediction of your own (People will live on Mars; Robots will do all the work; The oceans will be dead.) then get them to make predictions themselves.

Help with sentence beginnings (All children will …) or key vocabulary (extinct) where needed.

TEACHING IDEA by David Seymour and Maria Popova

Fortune-telling

Hand out a list of possible personal predictions (You will meet a tall handsome stranger; You will win a lot of money.) and check that students understand them. Make pairs – A is a fortune-teller and B is a visitor. A tells B their fortune, using ideas from the list and adding to them where possible.

GRAMMAR HUB

4.2 Making predictions

- When we are certain about a future event or situation, we can use either *be going to* or *will*.

  Panit is going to keep his New Year's resolutions.
  The company won't reach its sales target this month.
  Will the forecaster's predictions be accurate?

- Although there is little difference between the use of *be going to* and *will* for predictions, if there is strong evidence or a good reason for our prediction, we usually use *be going to* rather than *will*.

  Caitlyn is going to have a baby.
  NOT ~~*Caitlyn will have a baby.*~~

- To add even greater certainty to our prediction, we can use the adverb *definitely*.

  The other team has a lot of points – they're definitely going to win.

- We can use the adverb *probably* to show that we are not completely certain.

  I'll probably stay at home on New Year's Eve.

- We usually use these phrases with *will* when we're making a prediction: *I (don't) think …, I expect …, I'm sure …*

  I don't think the media experts will predict the election results accurately.

- When we feel that a future event is possible, but we are not completely certain, we use *could, may* or *might*.

  You could make some new friends by joining the gym.

Be careful!

- We put the adverbs *definitely* and *probably* after the auxiliary verb in sentences with *be going to* or *will*.

  They're definitely going to win the World Cup.
  NOT ~~*They're going to definitely win the World Cup.*~~
  I'll probably take part in the project.
  NOT ~~*I'll take part probably in the project.*~~

4.2 Social change

GRAMMAR

A Use sentence 1 to elicit that the speaker is 100 percent sure about this prediction before students complete the task.

B Tell students to look back at the sentences from Exercise A to complete the rules. Elicit which sentences from Exercise A are examples of each rule.

C Direct students to the **Grammar Hub** (see TB43). Use the **Grammar Worksheet** on W15 for extra practice.

PRONUNCIATION

4.5 A Elicit from students how *will* is usually said in natural, connected speech. Then play the audio for students to notice which sentence in the pair uses *'ll*.

4.6 B Tell students to listen again and repeat. Correct and model the pronunciation again yourself if they need extra practice.

C Tell students to turn to the **Communication Hub** (TB121). Tell one student to say a sentence, and their partner has to point at which one they think they heard.

SPEAKING

A Ask students to look at the topics in the box and choose three. They should then make two predictions for each topic. Next to each prediction, they should write a percentage to represent how likely they think their predictions are to come true. Ask students to write some note about their reasons.

B Explain that students are now a team of super-forecasters. Put students into pairs to discuss their predictions.

C Tell pairs to choose what they consider to be their four strongest predictions. When they have agreed on these, put two sets of pairs together to explain their predictions to each other. Tell them to think about how similar or different their predictions are, and if they agree with each other's ideas. Discuss these ideas as a whole class.

METHODOLOGY HUB by Jim Scrivener

Will: watch out for these problems …

Students at a low level overuse *will* as an 'all-purpose future' to the avoidance of all other ways of talking about the future:

✗ *It will rain.*

This is because it is met early on, it is quickly learned and then it is easy to place the single word into any sentence where they wish to convey a future meaning. Even if grammatically incorrect, it may frequently be a sufficiently successful piece of communication to encourage students to use it again and again.

GRAMMAR HUB

4.2 Making predictions

A Reorder the words to make sentences.

1 the future / for our children / is / going to / what / be like / ?
What is the future going to be like for our children?

2 probably / in college / study / Modern Languages / Gareth / will
Gareth will probably study Modern Languages in college.

3 going / she / buy / definitely / to / a new cell phone / is
She is definitely going to buy a new cell phone.

4 soon / will / he / sure / be here / I'm
I'm sure he will be here soon.

5 will / don't / to the party / Dimitris / I / come / think
I don't think Dimitris will come to the party.

6 Jamie / going / is / a new suit / to buy / for the interview / ?
Is Jamie going to buy a new suit for the interview?

B Write a word from the box in each blank to complete the sentences. Sometimes more than one answer is possible.

could definitely is might think won't

1 The score is 4-0 – they're __definitely__ going to lose.
2 She __could/might__ make a lot of money one day – anything's possible!
3 Don't worry – you __won't__ have any problems.
4 She __is__ going to compete in a national sports competition.
5 I __think__ she will need some help moving.
6 The weather's bad today; some people __could/might__ arrive late.

C Choose the correct option.

1 I'm sure people ________ fewer hours in the future.
a are working **(b)** will work

2 Hundreds of people ________ their jobs when the factory closes.
a are losing **(b)** are going to lose

3 Look out! That driverless car ________ crash!
a will **(b)** is going to

4 People ________ reading newspapers in the future, maybe, but I don't think they'll stop reading books.
a are stopping **(b)** will stop

5 I think Magda ________ a good mother when she's older.
(a) is going to be b is being

6 I don't expect that he ________ get good grades because he never studies.
(a) will b won't

➤ Go back to page 43.

D READ FOR DETAIL Read again. Match the sentences (1–6) to the professional experts (PE) or the super-forecasters (SF).

1 They generally work individually. PE
2 They change their ideas when they learn something new. SF
3 They make better predictions when in groups. SF
4 Their personal beliefs influence their thinking. PE
5 They use percentages to show how certain they are. SF
6 The way they speak shows they are really certain. PE

E SPEAK Work in pairs. How easy is it to accurately predict these things? Put them in order (1 = easiest, 3 = hardest). Give reasons for your decisions.

2 a the winner of a soccer competition
1 b the number of schools we will need in ten years' time
3 c what life will be like in 100 years' time

GRAMMAR
Making predictions

A WORK IT OUT Look at the words in bold in the sentences from *How you could become a super-forecaster*. Which words show that the speaker is less than 100 percent sure of a prediction? Which show that the speaker is 100 percent sure?

Language that shows you are 100 percent sure of a prediction: 1, 3, 5, 7

Language that shows you are less than 100 percent certain of your prediction: 2, 4, 6, 8

1 Brazil is leading by three goals. They**'re going to** win the World Cup again.
2 There **may** be an early election.
3 I'm sure all cars **will** be driverless.
4 Our predictions **will probably** be wrong.
5 Robots **are going to** replace office workers.
6 Chinese **could** become a global language.
7 We **will definitely** develop better computers.
8 People **might** stop reading newspapers.

B Choose the correct words to complete the rules.

Making predictions

1 When we feel certain about a future event or situation, we use / don't use *be going to*, *will* or *won't*.
2 To show stronger certainty, we can add *definitely* / *probably*.
3 To show we are confident, but not completely certain, we can add *definitely* / *probably*.
4 There is little difference between *will* and *be going to* for predictions. However, if the present provides strong evidence or reasons for our predictions, we usually use *be going to* / *will*.
5 When we feel a future event or situation is possible, but are not completely certain, we use / don't use *could*, *may* or *might*.

C Go to the Grammar Hub on page 128.

PRONUNCIATION
contraction of *will*

4.5 **A** Listen to five pairs of sentences. In each pair, which sentence (a or b) uses *'ll*?

1 a 2 b 3 a 4 b 5 b

4.6 **B** Listen and repeat the subject pronouns + *'ll*.

C SPEAK Work in pairs. Look at the audio script for Exercise A on page 148. Student A – say a sentence. Student B – point to the sentence. Take turns.

SPEAKING

A Follow the instructions.

1 Make two predictions for three of the topics in the box – one prediction for life in ten years' time, the other for life in 50 years.

education	housing and domestic life
free time	national culture
technology	the environment
transportation	work and employment

2 Give each of your predictions a percentage mark to show how likely you think it is.
3 What are the reasons for your predictions and percentages? Write notes.

B Work in pairs. Imagine you are a team of 'super-forecasters'. Explain and discuss your predictions. Practice using super-forecasting language from *How super-forecasters could replace professional experts.*

C Decide on your pair's strongest four predictions. Compare your predictions with another pair.

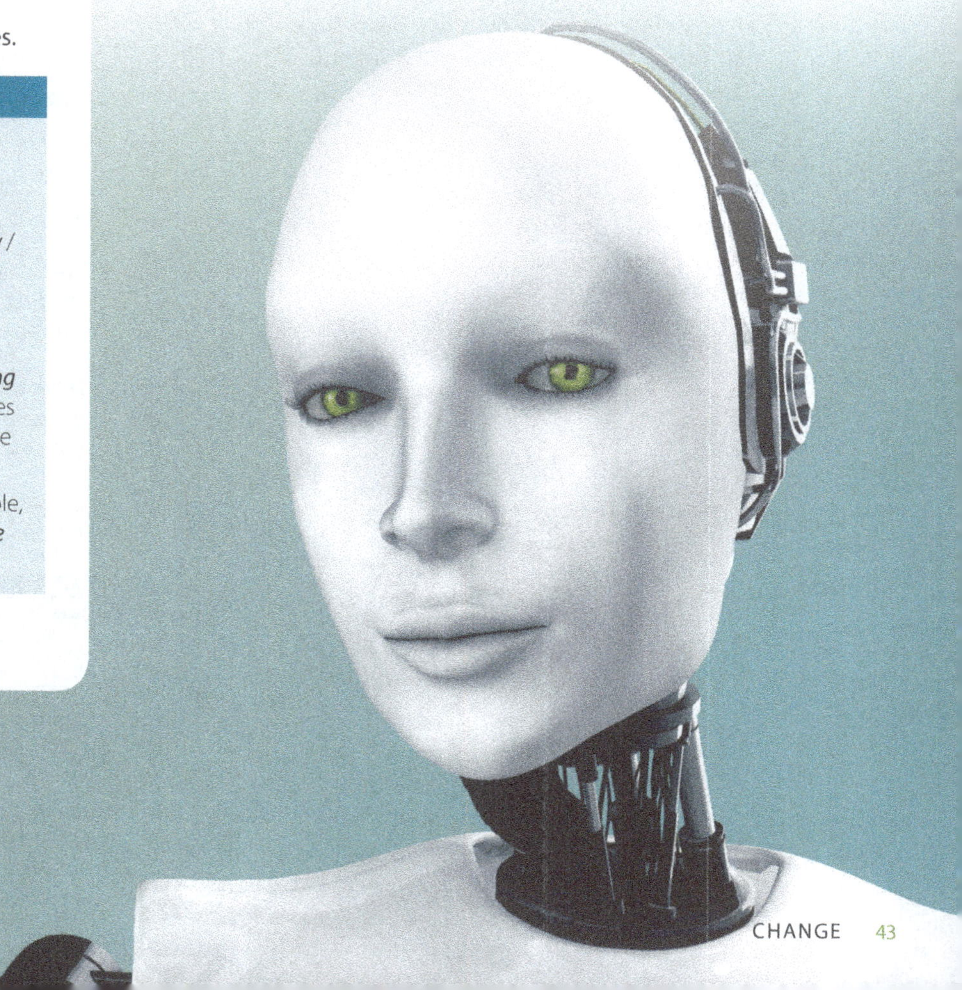

LISTENING

A SPEAK Work in pairs. Student A – describe picture a. Student B – describe picture b. Ask and answer the questions.

1 What are the positive things about living in this place?

2 What are the negative things about living in this place?

4.7 **B LISTEN FOR GIST** Listen to a current affairs radio show. Which is the best description of the show's main topic?

1 They are revealing why a negative prediction, about life in the countryside disappearing, is not very accurate.

2 They are describing the advantages and disadvantages of living in the countryside, in order to understand why the rural population is decreasing.

(3) They are reporting on how we can increase the number of people living and working in the countryside in order to stop villages from dying out.

Glossary

expense (n) an amount of money that you spend in order to buy or do something

resident (n) someone who lives in a particular place

4.7 **C LISTEN FOR DETAIL** Listen again. Complete the summaries with the missing word(s) and/or number(s).

Kamiyama, which is [1] ___far away___ from the city, offers a [2] ___super-fast internet service___ to attract new businesses. Toshi Asaka thinks working in Kamiyama doesn't have any [3] ___drawbacks or disadvantages___ and life is less expensive. Kamiyama is replacing old-style business with [4] ___modern___ companies.

Nakanoshima fishing village provides opportunities for [5] ___foreign visitors___ to live and work there for [6] ___six months___ and to discover a more traditional lifestyle. They get inexpensive accommodations and [7] ___part-time___ jobs with farmers and fishermen. Because of this program, residents start new businesses, and that helps keep [8] ___local (young) people___ in the area.

Mishima Island gives money to [9] ___single___ people to pay for romantic dates in the hope that they will stay on the island if they get married and start a family. All [10] ___new residents___ receive a young cow. The meat is valuable (it costs [11] ___$500___ per kilo), and these cows are [12] ___in danger of___ disappearing completely.

D Match the phrases (1–4) with phrases with the same meaning (a–d). Use the strategies in the box to help you.

Paraphrasing

When explaining and describing things, we sometimes paraphrase, which means that we repeat a point, but use different words. We paraphrase for various purposes:

- As the speaker, to make a point clear or to give it extra emphasis.
- As the listener, to check, or show that you understand the speaker's point.
- Both the speaker and the listener may paraphrase to sum up a few points or longer argument.

1 young people are relocating to urban areas
2 offering financial incentives
3 blue-sky thinking
4 these cows are in danger of extinction

a ideas that are different, fresh and unexpected
b they're going to the cities
c offering things like free or cheap housing
d of disappearing completely forever

E SPEAK Work in pairs. Can you think of any other ways to encourage people to move to the countryside?

PRONUNCIATION

Linking final consonant and first vowel sounds

4.8 **A** Complete the sentences from the radio show. Then listen and check your answers.

1 Oh yes, such ___as___ ?
2 Tell ___us___ more.
3 What's the next ___idea___ ?
4 That sounds like ___a___ fun thing to do.
5 But, is ___it___ such a good idea?
6 What ___else___ did you discover?
7 That isn't ___a___ lot of money, is it?
8 That's ___a___ lot of money!

4.8 **B** We usually link the final consonant sound of a word to the first vowel sound of the next word. Listen and repeat sentences 1 and 2 from Exercise A.

4.8 **C** Mark the links between the final consonant and first vowel sounds in Exercise A. Then listen again and check your answers. Repeat the sentences.

D SPEAK Work in pairs. Practice saying the sentences. Listen and check your partner's pronunciation.

LISTENING

A–D (4.7) Check answers and students' understanding in whole-class feedback as they complete the exercises.

E Ask each pair to share their best idea with the class.

PRONUNCIATION

A–D (4.8) Play the audio for students to check answers, listen and repeat. Help with and correct pronunciation where appropriate.

AUDIO SCRIPT

4.7

Listening, Exercise B
R = Rita Costa J = John Malone T = Toshi Asaka

R: Hi, I'm Rita Costa, and this is Rethinking the Future, when we look at how we can stop pessimistic predictions from coming true.
OK, so, today's prediction is that rural life has no future. Many villages and small towns are going to disappear, or only have older residents because young people are relocating to urban areas – that is, they're going to the cities to find work and a new, modern life. We've talked before about overpopulation in urban areas, but what about the problem of under-population in rural areas? Like many countries, Japan faces that problem, but it is trying to deal with it. Our reporter John has been there to find out more. Hi, John.

J: Hi, Rita. Yes, I visited several places and saw some great ideas for repopulating small villages, for getting people to exchange their life in the city for one in the country.

R: I guess that means offering financial incentives, you know, offering things like free or cheap housing, low business taxes and relocation expenses.

J: Yes, and some local governments are certainly doing that, but I'm talking about examples of blue-sky thinking, and by that I mean ideas that are different, fresh and unexpected.

R: Oh yes, such as?

J: Well, the fresh thinking involves foreigners, the internet, cows and love.

R: That sounds fascinating. Tell us more.

J: Sure. My tour started in the small mountain town of Kamiyama, where the city feels far away. (Ex C Q1) At first, it all seems very traditional and underdeveloped – you know, there are very few signs of modern life. However, to encourage companies to relocate from urban areas the town council provides a super-fast internet service, (Ex C Q2) faster than Tokyo's. And now, if you look inside some of those traditional buildings, you'll see signs of a growing digital start-up economy, teams of young designers and programmers working away on their computers.

R: Do you mean like small digital design and app companies? Like in those urban creative business centers?

J: Exactly. Here's Toshi Asaka, the owner of one.

T: I decided to move here from Tokyo because of the internet service. I can do my work anywhere, and here the quality of life is wonderful. There are no drawbacks, no disadvantages, (Ex C Q3) about living here– my employees don't feel underpaid now!

J: Kamiyama Council has managed to reinvent the local economy, moving from traditional to modern (Ex C Q4) digital business.

R: Right, using modern technology to create opportunities for young people. That makes sense. What's the next idea?

J: Well, other places are using tradition rather than technology to change their future. The small fishing village of Nakanoshima has its eye on young people, too, but not young Japanese. They offer special six-month Working Holiday Visas to foreign visitors (Ex C Q6; Q5) who want to experience a truly traditional Japanese lifestyle. You stay in cheap, shared accommodations, in a traditional building and do part-time (Ex C Q7) agricultural work, that is, you have a job in the farming or fishing industries.

R: That sounds like a fun thing to do. But is it such a good idea? I'm not sure it really helps the village to grow. I mean, the visitors only stay six months.

J: But then, new businesses like restaurants, cafés and language schools open up, and that encourages local young people (Ex C Q8) to stay and not go to the city, so the visitors are an opportunity for the locals.

R: OK, so the experience of the foreign visitors is only half the story. What else did you discover?

J: My final stop was Mishima Island. Like the other places, they provide financial help like cheap accommodations and relocation expenses, but if you are single (Ex C Q9) and looking for romance, they will also pay for your dates.

R: Pay for your dates? Cute, but, that isn't a lot of money, is it?

J: Well, perhaps you've misunderstood the goal of this plan… its intention. It isn't about attracting new people; it's about keeping them. What I mean is, they want people to move to their village, and to then stay forever. What better way to do that than to help them to find love and perhaps start a family. Isn't that both sweet and smart?

R: OK, I get it now, but what about married couples? It doesn't help them, does it?

J: (Ex C Q10) Not really, no, but they also give every new resident a young cow.

R: A cow? I'm not sure that will get me moo-ving there.

J: Oh, not just any cow. Mishima cows are extremely rare, and their beef is incredibly expensive, with a kilogram worth $500. (Ex C Q11)

R: That's a lot of money! I can't believe it.

J: Yeah, but it really is that expensive. And the thing is, just like the village life, these cows are in danger of (Ex C Q12) extinction, of disappearing completely forever, so they're another thing the new residents are helping to save.

R: The thing I love about the Mishima Island approach is that it creates emotional bonds to a place. What I mean by that is people soon make a strong connection to their new home, either through finding love or raising a cow. Definitely blue-sky thinking.

4.2 Social change

VOCABULARY

A Point out the information about using prefixes in the box, and check that students understand that certain prefixes have a particular meaning. Elicit the meaning of the three prefixes in the box. Tell students to look at the sentences from the *Listening* and to underline the prefixes.

B Tell students to look at the sentences from Exercise A again to help them match the prefixes with their meanings.

C Tell students to think about the meanings from Exercise B to help them add the correct prefixes to the words in bold.

D Direct students to the **Vocabulary Hub** (TB121) for further practice of prefixes.

E Tell students to look back at the sentences in Exercise C and think if they are true for them. If they aren't, tell students to rewrite them so that they are. Monitor and help with language if necessary here. Put students into pairs to compare their sentences and explain why they wrote what they wrote. Use the **Vocabulary Worksheet** on W16 for extra practice.

SPEAKING HUB

A Tell students to read the predicted future problems. Check that they understand them, and check pronunciation of *damage* and *privacy*. Tell students to think about the questions and to write notes about their ideas. Monitor and help with language if necessary.

B Put students into groups to compare their ideas and choose the best two solutions for each predicted problem.

C Regroup students so each new group has one or two representatives from a previous group. Tell the new groups to compare their solutions and to think about how similar or different their ideas are. Check that students understand the meaning of *blue-sky thinking* (creating completely new and highly original ideas). Tell them to try to agree on the best examples of blue-sky thinking. Conclude by briefly discussing their solutions as a whole class and giving some feedback on good language usage and any errors made during the task.

METHODOLOGY HUB by Jim Scrivener

Analyzing connected speech

In connected speech, the following things tend to happen:

- Unstressed syllables tend to have weak vowel sounds.
- Sounds get dropped (this is known as elision).
- Sounds get changed (this is known as assimilation).
- There may be additional sounds (linking or intrusive sounds) for bridging the space between words.

Your students probably need to be able to recognize and understand such sentences even if you don't want them to produce language like this. In fact, it's worth remembering that one of the main problems learners have with listening to English is that they can't recognize pronunciations that are entirely different from what they are expecting. For example, if a student expects to hear **/wɒt ɑː(r) juː/** (What are you…) but instead hears **/'wɒtʃə/** (Wotcha...?), they may well not register at all that it represents the same words. So a key point to remember is that it's vital to teach pronunciation – not just for the students' own speech production but to help them listen better.

METHODOLOGY HUB by Jim Scrivener

Ways of recording lexis

The action of writing down a list of lexical items is no guarantee that remembering will take place. Remembering involves four things: putting into storage, keeping in storage, retrieving, using

The following are alternative methods of recording items:

Lexical items lists

The table shows an alternative lexical item list that provides more information.

Lexical item	Pronunciation	Translation	Grammar	Collocations	Example
motorcycle /	'məutər saɪk(ə)ɪ/	*pikipiki*	*noun*	*ride a ~, get on my ~, ~maintenance, ~ race, ~ courier*	*She's just bought a 600cc Suzuki motorcycle.*

Labeling

Another way involves grouping of words so that a set is learned together. This is usually more effective than studying unrelated individual words. For example, you could present a set of words connected with kitchens by using a picture of a kitchen; the students each have a copy of the picture and write the words on it as they learn them.

Word or topic webs

A similar idea is to build a **word web** (or memory map or mind map) where connections in meaning or use between different words are visually indicated in the structure of the diagram.

Word page: collocations and chunks

This page is for recording lexical items that typically go together in patterns with a single keyword. The learner writes the keyword in the center box and then uses the columns before and after the box to write in phrases, sentences, chunks, etc.

Lexical item page: lexical item collector

This page can be used to record lexical items and then collect and relate items, classified as different grammatical types. For example, if the student has found *happy*, they could then go on to find and record *happiness* and *happily*.

VOCABULARY

Prefixes: *dis-*, *mis-*, *over-*, *re-*, *under-*

Using prefixes

We can add a prefix to a verb, noun or adjective to change its meaning. We use prefixes to show the opposite, to indicate a size or to show repetition. For example:

- *do – **un**do* *circle – **semi**circle* *organize – **re**organize*

A Underline the prefixes in the sentences from the radio show.

a Hi, I'm Rita Costa and this is *Rethinking the Future*.
b Many villages and small towns are going to disappear.
c We've talked before about overpopulation in urban areas …
d You've misunderstood the goal of this plan.
e My employees don't feel underpaid now!

B Match the prefixes in the box with their meanings (a–e).

dis- mis- over- re- under-

a bad or wrong mis-
b opposite dis-
c too little or too small under-
d again, but perhaps in a different way re-
e too much over-

C Complete the words in bold with the correct prefixes.

1 There are many things I _dis_ **like** about where I live. I'd like to move.
2 I know someone who usually _over_ **works**. They should relax more.
3 I regularly mis__ **place** things and waste time trying to find them.
4 There are some terrible buildings in my town that they should knock down and _re_ **build**.
5 I usually _dis_ **agree** with my parents, which sometimes leads to arguments.
6 I think that soccer players are _over_ **paid**. Some get millions of dollars a year. In contrast, I think nurses are _under_ **paid**.

D Go to the **Vocabulary Hub** on **page 143**.

E **SPEAK** Work in pairs. Rewrite the sentences in Exercise C so they are true for you. Then compare your ideas with your partner.

SPEAKING HUB

A Look at the predicted problems. Think of solutions to these problems. How can we stop this from happening? What could we do? How can we create a better future?

1 The use of robots and artificial intelligence will create massive unemployment because many jobs will disappear.
2 Across the world, air pollution will continue to increase and damage human health.
3 Using social media and digital services will lead to a near total loss of privacy, as companies and governments store and use all the data.

B **DISCUSS** Work in groups. Discuss your ideas. Choose the best two solutions for each problem.

C **REFLECT** Compare your group's solutions with another group. Are they the same or different? Which ideas are good examples of blue-sky thinking?

b

- Make and discuss predictions
- Discuss problems, reasons and consequences

Café Hub

4.3 Part-time

F– clarify and ask for clarification; make and deal with complaints
P– intonation and stress

COMPREHENSION

A 00:00–02:30 **Work in pairs. Watch the first part of the video without sound and guess the answers to the questions.**

1 How is Gaby feeling?
2 What does Sam suggest?
3 How does Gaby respond?
4 What do they decide?
5 What misunderstanding do they have?

B 00:00–02:30 **Watch the first part of the video with sound and check your ideas in Exercise A. What is the main reason Sam gives for taking Gaby on?**

C 02:30–04:49 **Watch the second part of the video and answer the questions.**

1 What does the customer complain about?
the coffee and croissant
2 What does the customer want Gaby to do?
give her her money back
3 How does Gaby react to the situation?
apologizes but then she becomes angry
4 Why does the customer ask to speak to Sam?
complain about the service
5 How does Sam deal with the situation?
Sam supports Gaby

FUNCTIONAL LANGUAGE

Clarifying and asking for clarification

A 01:48–04:49 **Complete what Gaby says with the correct form of *get*, *say*, *lose* or *catch*. Then watch the clip and check your answers.**

Clarifying and asking for clarification
1 What did you __say__?
2 Sorry, I didn't __catch__ that.
3 I don't __get__ what you're saying.
4 So you're __saying__ you want me to …
5 You've __lost__ me.
6 Why didn't you just __say__ that?

B **You are going to role-play a similar situation. Invent a conversation.**

Student A: You are Sam. Begin with '… And remember to put the plates under here.'

Student B: You are Gaby. Ask for clarification and use phrases from Exercise A.

MILLY

SAM

NEENA

ZAC

GABY

Making and dealing with complaints

C 02:30-04:49 Put the words or phrases in parentheses in the correct position to complete the sentences. Then watch the second part of the video to check.

Making a complaint	Finding out about a complaint	Apologizing
[1]I'm sorry to bother you, but *I'm afraid* there's a problem with … (*I'm afraid*)	[3]What is the problem? (*exactly*)	I'm sorry to hear that.
I want my money back, please.	What seems to be the problem?	[4]That's no problem. I'm sorry about that. (*so*)
[2]I'm not happy with the service. (*really*)		[5]I'm sorry for the inconvenience, madam; it won't happen again. (*terribly*)

USEFUL PHRASES

A Match the useful phrases in the box with the phrases before or after them from the video (1–6).

> How dare you! How's your first day going?
> Leave it to me. Something good will come along.
> The customer is always right. What's up?

1 What's up? / I don't know, Sam.

2 Something good will come along. / It always does.

3 How's your first day going? / Great so far.

4 Excuse me! Hello? Excuse me! / Leave it to me.

5 The customer is always right. / Unless the customer is wrong.

6 How dare you! / I want to speak to the manager.

B How do you say these useful phrases in your language?

Glossary

madam **(n) (British)** = ma'am **(n) (American)**

PRONUNCIATION

Intonation and stress

4.9 **A** Listen and write down three versions of the question 'What's the problem?'

1 exactly

What exactly is the problem?

2 seems

What seems to be the problem?

3 appears

What appears to be the problem?

B Practice the questions in Exercise A. Copy the stress and intonation.

SPEAKING

A Work in groups of three: the customer, the waiter, the manager. The customer makes one of the following complaints. Write a funny conversation.

- The soup is cold. (The customer has eaten the soup.)
- The steak is tough. (The customer has eaten the steak.)
- The pasta is too salty. (The customer has eaten the pasta.)

B **PRESENT** Perform your conversation in front of the class.

Clarify and ask for clarification

Make and deal with complaints

➤ Turn to page 159 to learn how to write a short essay.

4.3 Part-time

LEAD-IN

Elicit the verb *complain* and the corresponding noun *complaint*. Ask the students if they have ever made a complaint in a restaurant or a store and why.

COMPREHENSION

A ▶ 00:00-02:30 Tell students that they're going to watch part of the video without sound and to try to answer the questions. Let them compare ideas.

Suggested answers:

1 *miserable*
2 *That Gaby works part-time in the café.*
3 *She is apprehensive.*
4 *Sam will train her to work in the café.*
5 *Sam tells Gaby to put the glasses on top of the dishwasher, but he means on the top rack of the dishwasher.*

B ▶ 00:00-02:30 Play the video with sound for students to watch and check their ideas and to answer the extra question.

Sam was already thinking about advertising for some part-time help.

C ▶ 02:30-04:49 Tell students to watch the rest of the episode and to answer the questions.

FUNCTIONAL LANGUAGE

A ▶ 01:48-04:49 Ask students to fill in the blanks with the correct form of *get, say, lose* or *catch*. Play the video again for students to check. Elicit that the phrases are fairly informal.

B Put students into pairs and tell one to be Sam and the other to be Gaby. Tell the student playing Sam to give instructions and the students playing Gaby to ask for clarification.

C ▶ 02:30-04:49 Tell students to look at the words and to put the word in parentheses in the correct position. Watch the appropriate part of the episode again to check.

2 *I'm really not happy with the service.*
3 *What exactly is the problem?*
4 *That's no problem. I'm so sorry about that.*
5 *I'm terribly sorry for the inconvenience, madam/ma'am; it won't happen again.*

USEFUL PHRASES

A Point out the useful phrases and tell them to match each one with the phrase that came just before or after it.

B Tell students to translate the phrases into their own language. Ask students how often they use those phrases.

PRONUNCIATION

4.9

A Tell them to listen and to write down the question, putting the word given in the correct place. Elicit that adding the extra words makes the question softer and more indirect.

B Tell students to listen to the questions again and to copy the stress and intonation.

SPEAKING

A Put students into groups of three and tell them to each choose a role. Tell the groups to choose one of the situations given and to write a funny conversation about it. When the groups have finished writing their conversations, tell them to practice performing them.

B Tell each group to perform their conversation for the class. Tell the other groups to watch and write down something that they thought was really good about each conversation.

▶ VIDEO SCRIPT

S = Sam G = Gaby C = Customer

S: Hey.
G: Hey.
S: What's up?
G: I don't know, Sam. I don't have much work on at the moment and I'm totally broke …
S: Gaby! You're such a good photographer – the website photos you did for me are amazing! Something good will come along – it always does.
I've got an idea – why don't you help me out here? It's been very busy recently and I was already thinking about advertising for some part-time help.
G: Are you sure? I sometimes … drop … things …
S: Yeah … you do … but you're great with people! I'll train you! It'll be like the film *Rocky*, but with more coffee and less boxing.
G: OK! Let's do this.
S: … And remember to put the glasses on top.
G: What did you say?
S: Remember to put the glasses …
G: Sorry … I didn't catch that …
S: … on top …
G: On top of what? I don't get what you're saying?
S: The dishwasher.
G: So you're saying you want me to put the glasses on the top of the dishwasher? You've lost me.
S: No! On the top shelf of the dishwasher.
G: Ah! Sure, why didn't you just say that? Err, do you have any … glue?
S: So how's your first day going?
G: Great so far!
C: Hello? Excuse me!
G: Leave it to me!
C: Hello. I'm sorry to bother you, but I'm afraid there's a problem with the coffee AND with the croissant.
G: I'm sorry to hear that – what exactly is the problem?
C: I don't know! They just don't taste good. I want my money back please.
G: That's no problem. I'm so sorry about that, perhaps we … oh … but you finished them … both.
C: Well, yeah.
G: So they weren't that bad then?
C: What happened to the customer is always right?
G: The customer is always right. Unless the customer is wrong. Like now.
C: How dare you! I want to speak to the manager NOW!
G: Sam! You remember when you said I was good with people?
S: What seems to be the problem?
C: I'm really not happy with the service, this woman …
S: I'm terribly sorry for the inconvenience madam, it won't happen again.
C: Good.
S: … Because if you don't like it here, then you really don't need to come back. Thank you and have a nice day.
C: I have never … ever … ever … ever … ever … ever … ever.

4 Writing — Write a short essay

W — using linking words to introduce reasons and consequences

A Read the advertisement for a competition. What can you win? How can you win it? TINTO X cell phone; write a short essay.

Happy New Year with Digital Express and Tinto Phones

Enter our New Year competition and win a TINTO X cell phone.

Digital technology has already changed our lives in many ways, and this is going to continue in the future. We want to know how you think digital technology is going to change our lives over the next 20 years.

Write a short essay describing a change that digital technology will bring to our lives, explaining why this will happen and any consequences it will have.

The five winning entries will be published online.

B Read a competition essay entry. Put the paragraphs (a–d) in the correct order (1–4).

1 introduction (what the writer thinks the change will be) b
2 reason 1 d
3 reason 2 a
4 conclusion c

a Digital technology supports a sharing economy, and that means people will not need to buy so many things. Owning a car will not be necessary **as** you will simply use an app to book a driverless car when you need one. People will share things like bicycles and gardening equipment within their local community by using an app to find what they need. **As a result**, people will own fewer things, but they will have more contact with other people.

b People are always buying things **because** they want to get the latest products. However, in the future, people will probably buy fewer things **because of** the development of digital technology.

c To sum up, digital technology will definitely continue to change our lives, and one of those changes will be that we won't need to own so much stuff.

d In the past, new inventions brought many products into our houses, but digital technology usually replaces these things with a single device. For example, your cell phone can now be your television, radio, music player and alarm clock. In the future, children may play all their games on a phone or tablet, **and so** traditional board games will disappear. **Consequently**, people will have less stuff in their house, although they will spend a lot on digital services.

C SPEAK Work in pairs. Read again and discuss the questions.

1 What two reasons are given for why people will own fewer things?
2 How many examples illustrate each reason?
3 What other things will happen?
4 What do you think of the predictions?

D Look at the linking words in bold in the essay. Write them in the correct column.

Introduce a reason	Introduce a consequence
because, as, because of	As a result, Consequently, and so

E Look again at the linking words in bold in the essay. Write them in the correct place in the box. Use each of them twice.

Using linking words to introduce reasons and consequences

We use linking words and phrases to show the relationship between information and ideas.

1 Some linking words connect ideas inside one sentence. For example, because, as, because of, and so.
2 Some connect ideas across two sentences. For example, As a result, consequently.
3 Some linking words are followed by a clause (subject + verb). For example, as, as a result, because, and so, consequently.
4 Others are followed by noun phrases (such as the increase in pollution). For example, because of.

F SPEAK Work in pairs. Complete the sentences with your own ideas. Then compare your answers with a partner.

1 All cars should be electric because …
2 Children are using social media. As a result, …
3 Every year, more people are only paying for things electronically. Consequently, …
4 Cities are unhealthy places to live because of …
5 People are watching less TV as …
6 Online shopping continues to increase, and so …

WRITING

A PLAN Make a prediction about how digital technology will change the future. Think of the reasons why this change will happen and any consequences it will have.

B WRITE Write your competition entry (150–200 words).

C REVIEW Work in groups. Read and discuss your essays. Have a vote to decide on the two winning entries.

WRITING 159

Answers

1 *Digital technology usually replaces these things with a single device; digital technology supports a sharing economy.*
2 *Two examples per reason*
3 *People will spend a lot on digital services; they will have more contact with other people.*

Refer students to this essay as a model for the writing task.

Tell students to think about how the use of signposting language, such as linking words and phrases, can help them to transition between points.

WRITING

Ask students to tell their partner if they've ever entered a competition and if they've ever won anything.

A Tell students to look at the advertisement and answer the questions.

B Tell them to read and put the paragraphs in the correct order according to the paragraph structure given.

C Tell students to look back at the competition entry and to discuss the questions with a partner.

1 *Digital technology usually replaces these things with a single device; digital technology supports a sharing economy.*
2 *Two examples per reason*
3 *People will spend a lot on digital services; they will have more contact with other people.*

D Tell students now to look at the words in bold in the essay. Elicit that they are all linking words. Tell students to look back at the essay to help them work out the meaning of the linking words and to write them in the correct column.

E Tell students to look again at how the linking words are used in the essay and to complete the box.

F Tell students to work individually to complete the sentences with their own ideas before they compare.

Suggested answers:

1 *they are better for the environment.*
2 *they are not doing enough exercise.*
3 *cash will disappear.*
4 *the pollution.*
5 *they are spending time online and on social media.*
6 *traditional stores in town centers will close.*

WRITING TASK

A Tell students that they are going to write their own competition entry essay. Elicit some ideas from the class. Tell students to choose one of the changes and write some notes.

B Tell students to look back at the structure of the competition entry to help them organize their essay. Remind them to use but not overuse some of the linking words.

C Put students into groups and tell them to pass their essays around so everyone can read each other's.

GRAMMAR

A Choose the best verb form to complete the sentences.

1 I can't tonight, I'm busy. I can't call you tomorrow either. I ***'m visiting*** / ***will visit*** my parents all day. I ***'m calling*** / ***'ll call*** you when I'm free.

2 He ***'s going to*** / ***'ll*** do that this afternoon. It's next on his to-do list.

3 Can I borrow some money? You ***'re getting*** / ***'ll get*** it back tomorrow, if that's OK?

4 Well, let me check. Yes, I ***'m going to*** / ***'ll*** lend you $20. Here you are.

5 We're going now. We ***'re meeting*** / ***'ll meet*** Asif for dinner at seven. Bye!

6 Oh, look – it's raining. Change of plans! I ***'m not bike riding*** / ***won't bike*** today; I think I ***'m going to*** / ***'ll*** take the subway instead.

7 My sister's decided to go to Italy for her vacation this year. She ***'s going to*** / ***'ll*** visit Rome, Florence and Venice.

B Choose the correct words to complete the dialogues.

1 **A:** This game is terrible. Come on – let's leave early.
B: No, let's wait until the end.
A: But there's no point staying. We're losing 5–0. We [1] ***aren't going to*** / ***probably won't*** win.
B: But we [2] ***might*** / ***will*** score one at least. You never know!
A: There's no way that [3] ***may*** / ***will*** happen. Come on. Time to give up.

2 **A:** Flying cars? Of course, I can't say it will [4] ***definitely*** / ***probably*** happen, but it [5] ***definitely*** / ***probably*** will.
B: No, it [6] ***might not*** / ***won't*** happen. I'm sure. Think about it, what would happen if every car were a flying car? It would be too dangerous.
A: But people are definitely [7] ***going to*** / ***might*** want them in the future. The technology can't be far away. I'm sure we [8] ***'re going to*** / ***could*** have flying cars in the future!

VOCABULARY

A Which is the odd-one-out in each set of verb phrases? Why?

1 (a) achieve a target because the other two refer to making a plan
b make a resolution
c set a goal

2 a keep a resolution
b stick to a plan
(c) cut down on something because the other two refer to following a plan

3 (a) do less of something because the other two refer to stopping completely
b quit a bad habit
c stop doing something

4 (a) reach a goal because the other two refer to failing to achieve/to not reaching your goal
b break resolutions
c not do what you promised

B Look at the words in bold. Are the prefixes correct or incorrect? If they are incorrect, write the correct prefix.

1 The fire destroyed a lot of the building. We'll need to ~~mis~~ re **misbuild** it.

2 I'm definitely ~~over~~ under **overpaid**. Unless I get a pay raise, it'll be time to find a new job!

3 Some money has ~~re~~ dis **reappeared**. It's missing. No one is leaving until we find it.

4 Wait, let me help! It's heavy. Don't **overdo** it. I'll lift it with you. correct

5 And, don't ~~dis~~ mis **disbehave**! We want to impress our school visitors.

6 No, I didn't pass my exam, unfortunately. I have my ~~over~~ re **overtake** next week.

7 The answer is wrong. You made a **miscalculation**. Do the math again. correct

8 Urban ~~under~~ over **underpopulation** isn't a problem now, but it soon will be. The city's population is increasing rapidly.

FUNCTIONAL LANGUAGE

Choose the correct words to complete the dialogue.

A: Hi. I'm sorry to [1] ***excuse*** / ***bother*** you.
B: Not at all, sir. Please sit down. How can I help?
A: I took one of your courses, 'How to change your life in seven days'. I'm [2] ***afraid*** / ***not happy*** there is a problem with the course.
B: Oh, I'm sorry. Could I have your name first?
A: Jim Stevens.
B: Sorry, I didn't [3] ***take*** / ***catch*** the last part.
A: Stevens.
B: Great. What was the problem with the course?
A: I took the course ten days ago. But my life hasn't changed!
B: OK, I'm not sure I [4] ***have*** / ***get*** what you are saying. Do you mean the course was unhelpful?
A: Yes. I expect results for the price. And the teacher was always late.
B: I'm sorry to [5] ***hear*** / ***catch*** that. We will talk to the teacher. That won't [6] ***happen*** / ***bother*** again.
A: And the money?
B: So you're [7] ***saying*** / ***hearing*** you want your money back?
A: Exactly!
B: Ok, just let me check with my manager …

Designers making tough decisions at a studio in Berlin.

Work (n) activity that involves physical or mental effort.
Synonyms: labor (n), effort (n)
Business (n) the work of buying or selling products or services for money.
Synonyms: commerce (n), trading (n)

Henry Ford (1863–1947) is best known as the founder of the Ford Motor Company. He was also involved in the development of the assembly line, which made mass production possible.

The quote for this unit suggests that the purpose of a business should be to make people's lives better. It could also be interpreted as highlighting the need for social and environmental responsibility in business.

OBJECTIVES

- discuss and give advice about employment skills and career interests
- discuss and suggest workplace benefits and changes
- describe and evaluate a small business
- talk about environmental business ideas
- structure a presentation
- write a cover letter for a job application

Work with a partner. Discuss the questions.

1 Look at the picture. What do you think they are doing?
2 Read the quote. Do you agree that a business which makes money can still be poor?
3 What kind of business would you like to work for?

WORK AND BUSINESS 49

OBJECTIVES

Read the unit objectives to the class.

UNIT OPENER QUESTIONS

With books closed, ask students to discuss in pairs what they believe the purpose of a business is. While they're doing this, write on the board *A business that makes nothing but ____________ is a poor business.* Highlight the two meanings of *poor* (bad and not rich) that are played on in the quote. Elicit some ideas as a whole class and get them to guess the missing word.

1 Tell students to open their books and look at the picture. What do they think the people are doing? Elicit some ideas as a whole class.
2 Ask students to look at the quote again and discuss with their partner whether they think a business that makes money can still be poor. Monitor and provide language input.
3 Ask students to discuss what kind of business they would like to work for and why. Elicit some useful adjectives on the board for the type of attributes they would like to see in a company and in a boss.

WORKSHEETS

Lesson 5.1 At work

Grammar: Past habits and states (W17)

Vocabulary: Employment skills and qualities (W18)

Lesson 5.2 In business

Grammar: The passive voice (W19)

Vocabulary: Business collocations (W20)

5.1 At work

- Discuss and give advice about employment skills and career interests
- Discuss and suggest workplace benefits and changes

V – employment skills and qualities; verbs of influence
G – past habits and states
P – intonation and rhythm: holding your turn
S – following reference links in a text

a

teacher

b

restaurant manager

c

engineer

d

police officer

VOCABULARY

Employment skills and qualities

A SPEAK Work in pairs. Look at the pictures (a–d). What are the people's jobs? What skills do they need to do these jobs?

B SPEAK Work in pairs. Student A – go to the Communication Hub on page 152. Student B – go to the Communication Hub on page 147.

C Read the report about a business survey. Complete the phrases with *be* or *have*.

Many jobs require very specific skills and experience. However, there are also many skills and personal qualities that all employers are looking for. We surveyed **100 Human Resource Managers** to find out which are the most important general employment skills and qualities.

People should:

1 __be__ reliable. Student A, Q4
2 __have__ good communication skills. Student A, Q1
3 __have__ good digital technology skills. Student B, Q1
4 __be__ good at time management. Student A, Q2
5 __be__ good at team work. Student A, Q3
6 __be__ able to work well under pressure. Student B, Q2
7 __have__ creative thinking skills. Student B, Q4
8 __have__ good people skills. Student B, Q3

D SPEAK Work in pairs. Match the quiz questions in Exercise B with the employment skills in Exercise C.

E SPEAK For each employment skill in Exercise C, give yourself a percentage score to show your strength. For example, 100 percent = a great strength, no room for improvement. Then work in pairs and explain your answers.

LISTENING

5.1 **A** LISTEN FOR KEY WORDS Listen to the first part of a conversation between Fiona and Michael about work. Choose the correct answer for each question.

1 What is Fiona's job?
  a Human Resources Manager in a company
  (b) a career advisor
  c a psychologist
2 What is Michael's role in the bank?
  a head of the accounting team
  b a junior member of the property investment team
  (c) a member of the general management team
3 Why is Michael unhappy in his job?
  a He doesn't work closely with other people.
  (b) His work doesn't offer enough challenges.
  c He has to meet too many deadlines.
4 In which of these areas hasn't he worked?
  a fashion
  (b) sports
  c food and drink
5 Which of these things seem most important to Michael?
  (a) team work
  b digital technology skills
  c time management

5.1 **B** LISTEN FOR DETAIL Listen again. Are the sentences true (T) or false (F)? Correct the false sentences.

1 Michael has worked in ~~five different banks.~~ the same bank for five years. __F__
2 Michael currently uses the skills that the test showed as strengths. __T__
3 ~~Michael sometimes bought the clothes that he modeled.~~ They frequently gave him the clothes. __F__
4 Michael enjoyed working ~~as a waiter, but not~~ under pressure when it was ~~very~~ busy. __F__
5 Michael feels positively about training and coaching. __T__
6 Michael ~~is interested in setting up his own~~ wants to work for a good company. __F__

C SPEAK Work in pairs. Look at the pictures (a–d) again. Which job do you think Fiona will recommend for Michael? Why?

5.2 **D** LISTEN FOR DETAIL Listen to the second part of the conversation. Which job does Fiona suggest? Why?

5.1 At work

LEAD-IN

Put students into pairs and give them three minutes to think of a profession for every letter of the alphabet.

VOCABULARY

A Look at the pictures as a whole class and elicit the jobs shown. Put students into pairs to think of the skills needed for each.

B Tell students to work with a partner. Tell students to turn to the **Communication Hub** (TB121).

C–E Monitor the students as they complete the exercises and discuss the answers as a whole class. Use the **Vocabulary Worksheet** on W18 for extra practice.

LISTENING

5.1 **A** Tell students to read the questions and suggested answers before they listen and check understanding of *challenges*, *deadlines* and *property investment*.

5.1 **B** Tell students to look at the sentences and to try to remember if they are true or false. Play the audio again to check.

C Tell students to discuss which job Fiona will recommend.

5.2 **D** Tell students to listen to the end of the conversation to check their ideas.

Catering Manager: He has experience in the catering industry. His degree in business is useful for this job. She thinks the work will suit him: planning and running successful events. He has an interest in cooking and food. It should require good people, communication and time management skills. It should have a lot of variety and involve working on a team. It will give a sense of achievement.

AUDIO SCRIPT

5.1

Listening, Exercise A
F = Fiona M = Michael

F: Hello, sorry I'm late. You must be Michael. I'm Fiona.
M: Hi, Fiona. Nice to meet you.
F: Nice to meet you, and thank you for coming, and for waiting. I hope we can help you. So, I've had a quick look at your personality test and, in today's session, I'd like you to tell me why you're thinking about changing careers, and to find out more about the kind of work that you like doing.
M: Sure.
Ex B Q1 **F:** OK, so you're currently working in a bank. I see you've been there for five years, since leaving college, so why do you want to leave that behind?
M: Well, it's been a good job, but um, I just feel there's something missing. I studied business and finance in college, and getting a banking job seemed like the right thing to do at that time, but I'm not so sure now.
F: I see, and what is it that's missing exactly? Your personality test showed you have good people skills. Does your work involve using those much? And your organizational skills are strong. I'm sure that's important at the bank.
M: Yeah, absolutely. You definitely need to be well organized, to both meet deadlines and manage the money carefully. Um, I work in a local branch of the bank, so I have to deal with customers face to face, and I've recently been made assistant manager, so those people skills are important, and I do more general planning now, like team planning, you know, to make sure the work gets done – that sort of thing. I think the thing is that basically every day is pretty much the same. I rarely have to think on my feet, or deal with surprises.
F: OK, you want a little more variety in your work. So, this has been your only job since college. Did you have any part-time jobs before?
M: Well, this may surprise you, but I used to be a fashion model.
F: A fashion model? Well, now that you've told me, it isn't so surprising, I mean you look very neat and well-dressed.
M: Thank you. I didn't do it for long, um, but it was really fun. I really enjoyed the photo shoots. It's good doing something creative together; the teamwork
Ex B Q3 was good and important. And, well, they'd usually give us some of the clothes after the shoot, which was great for me as a student!
F: I can imagine, and also very different from working in a bank. Um, anything else?
M: The other thing was working as a waiter. I joined an agency for part-time catering work, so I used to serve food at conferences and events, or I'd work in a café or restaurant for a few days, you know, if their employees were sick or something.
F: Well, that's great experience to have. Did you like doing that?
Ex B Q4 **M:** Oh, yeah, for sure. You have to work hard. At busy times, you would always be under a lot of pressure, but in a good way. I liked helping the customers enjoy the event. I used to be tired but happy at the end of a day. But, you know, that was only student work for me. It did get me into food and cooking though; that's one of my hobbies now – home baking and stuff like that.
F: Well, it's certainly interesting to hear that you liked working under pressure. Um, you just mentioned hobbies. Do you have any other interests? Anything that might involve skills that you could use in a job?
M: Well, you obviously don't mean going to the movie theater. I love skiing. Um, before college, I was a member of a ski club at a local ski center. One thing then, I used to help new members, you know, I'd coach them a little, and just help them as they were learning. That was pretty rewarding. There was a nice sense of achievement, you know.
F: Is that feeling missing from your work in the bank?
M: In a way, yes. But I don't want to be a ski instructor,
Ex B Q6 you know, that's just like having your own business. I want a steady job, to have a career in a good company, but, well, just not in a bank.
F: Sure, sure. Well, from what you've said, I do have an early suggestion for you to consider.
M: Already? OK, well, what are you thinking?

AUDIO SCRIPT

5.2

Listening, Exercise D
F = Fiona M = Michael

F: Sure, sure. Well, from what you've said, I do have an early suggestion for you to consider.
M: Already? OK, well, what are you thinking?
F: Well, it's clear you like using your people and communication skills, and your personality test shows you're good at organization and time management.
M: That's all true, I think.
F: Yes, and you're looking for a job that has a lot of variety. And you enjoy working on a team.
M: Uh huh.
F: So, have you thought about a career in catering? Not as a waiter or chef, but as the person who organizes the catering at events. You used to work as a waiter at them, how about running them? A catering manager is a good career, and it requires all those skills.
M: Well, I don't know, um, sounds interesting, but, I mean, I don't have any training in that area.
F: But you do have experience of those events, and actually catering companies do look for people with a business studies degree.
M: Do they?
F: Uh huh. And I think that the work of planning and running an event should suit you and your skills.
M: And food and cooking is a hobby of mine.
F: Exactly.
M: OK, well, I'm interested. Let's find out more.

PRONUNCIATION

5.3 **A** Tell students to listen to the extracts from the conversation and to answer the questions.

1 Michael 2 Fiona 3 Fiona: word is longer with rise. Michael: word is shorter with fall.

5.4 **B** Tell students to read the information in the box about holding your turn. Tell them to read the other examples from the *Listening* and to underline the words the speaker makes longer.

C Tell students to work in pairs to practice saying the sentences with the same intonation as Michael and Fiona used.

GRAMMAR

A–B Allow students to check answers in pairs before whole-class feedback as they complete the exercises.

C Direct students to the **Grammar Hub** (see below and TB52).

D Give your own example for one of the topics as a model. Use the **Grammar Worksheet** on W17 for extra practice.

SPEAKING HUB

A Tell students that they're going to give and receive some career advice. Tell them to work alone and think about the questions, then to write down three jobs they would like to do.

B Tell students to prepare some interview questions that would be useful to find out about their partner's employment skills, interests and experience. Direct students to the **Audio script** at the back of their books to help them.

C Tell students to take turns interviewing their partner and write notes on their answers.

D Tell students to work alone. Tell them to look at their notes about their partner and to write down three jobs that they think would be suitable for them. Then tell students to show their partners the jobs they chose for them. After they've done this, students can tell their partners how similar the list is to the one they wrote in Exercise A.

GRAMMAR HUB

5.1 Past habits and states

	Positive	Negative
I/you/he/she/it/we/they	**I used to be** a waiter in a restaurant.	**They did not use to work** here. **They didn't use to work** here.

Question	Positive short answer	Negative short answer
Did you use to work from home?	Yes, **I did**.	No, **I didn't**.

- We use *used to* to talk about past situations that do not exist now. These include past habits and past states.

  *Past habit: We **used to meet** at the station on the way to work.*

  *Past state: He **used to be** a manager but he left his job.*

- We use *use to* with the auxiliary verb *did*.

  *I didn't **use** to work here.*
  NOT ~~I didn't used to work here.~~
  *Did you **use** to do voluntary work?*
  NOT ~~Did you used to do voluntary work?~~

- In the negative, we can also say *never used to*.

  *I **didn't use** to work here. OR I **never used** to work here.*

- We can use *would* when we talk about past actions. We do not use it for permanent states in the past.

  When I was younger, I would visit London regularly on business. NOT ~~When I was younger, I would live in London.~~

- We usually use *would* when we are telling a story or talking fondly about the past.

  Every year, the boss would take us all out to eat.

- When talking about the past, we rarely use *would* in the negative or question form.

  I didn't use to like it here. NOT ~~I wouldn't like it here.~~
  Did you use to work part time? NOT ~~Would you work part time?~~

PRONUNCIATION
Intonation and rhythm: holding your turn

5.3 **A Listen to Michael and Fiona saying *Nice to meet you.* Then answer the questions.**

1 Who sounds like they have finished speaking?
2 Who sounds like they are going to continue speaking?
3 What is the difference in how they say *you*?

Holding your turn

We can show that we are going to continue speaking by making a word longer, and sometimes, by using a rising intonation.

We show that we have finished speaking by using a falling intonation on our final word.

5.4 **B Read the box. Now listen to more examples from Michael and Fiona's conversation. Underline the words the speaker makes longer to show they want to keep speaking.**

1 I see you've been there for five years.
2 Well, it's been a good job, but um, I just feel there's something missing.
3 I see, and what is it that's missing exactly?
4 I've recently been made assistant manager, so those skills are important.
5 I mean, you look very neat and well-dressed.

C SPEAK Work in pairs. Practice saying the sentences in Exercise B. Listen and check your partner's pronunciation.

GRAMMAR
Past habits and states

A WORK IT OUT Look at the sentences from the conversation between Fiona and Michael. Which underlined verbs are state verbs and which are action verbs? Which words are used to show repeated actions and events in the past?

1 I used to be a fashion model.
State verb
2 They'd usually give us some of the clothes after the shoot.
Action verb
3 I used to help new members.
Action verb
4 At busy times, you would always be under a lot of pressure.
State verb
5 I used to be tired but happy at the end of each day.
State verb

B WORK IT OUT Choose the correct words to complete the rules. Then match the rules (2–5) with the sentences in Exercise A.

Past habits and states

1 We use ***used to*** and ***would*** to describe actions and states in the ***present*** / ***past***. These are likely to be actions and states that are finished.
2 To talk about repeated actions in the past, we can use *used to* ***and*** / ***but not*** *would*. 2, 3
3 To talk about temporary repeated states in the past, we can use *used to* ***and*** / ***but not*** *would*. 4, 5
4 To talk about permanent states in the past, we use *used to* ***and*** / ***but not*** *would*. 1
5 We usually use adverbs of frequency with ***used to*** / ***would***. 2, 4

C Go to the Grammar Hub on page 130.

D SPEAK Work in groups. Discuss some of these topics.

- your childhood vacations
- your grandparents' younger lives
- how you have changed over the years

SPEAKING HUB

A You are going to give and receive some career advice. Think about your employment skills, interests and experience. Then write down three jobs you would like to do.

- What strengths do you have?
- What skills have you used in work, college or your hobbies?
- What is important for you in a job or career?
- What types of work do you like doing?

B PLAN Write some interview questions that will help you find out about your partner's employment skills, interests and experience. Use the audio script on page 171 to help you.

C SPEAK Work in pairs. Interview your partner. Listen carefully and make a note of his/her answers. Take turns.

D DISCUSS Choose three jobs that you think match your partner's skills and experience. Are they the same jobs that your partner wrote down before?

READING

A SPEAK Work in pairs. Look at the pictures (a–c) and discuss the questions.

1. Which offices would you like to work in? Why?
2. Which wouldn't you like to work in? Why?

B READ FOR MAIN IDEA Read *Are we in the middle of a workplace revolution?* Which is the best subtitle? Why?

1. Why digital technology companies are so successful
2. Why office life is changing and how to manage it
3. Why modern offices and unusual benefits are bad for business

a

b

c

Are we in the middle of a WORKPLACE REVOLUTION?

Pool tables, nap-pods and free food. **They** sound like things at an all-inclusive vacation resort rather than in an office. However, digital tech companies have redesigned the office and provided unusual benefits to make the workplace a more pleasant and productive place to be. Ex D Q1 Need a massage to help reduce stress? Want to bring your pet to work? No problem. For these companies, the days of individual cubicles where people would work on their own for eight hours a day are no more.

This trend is now spreading outside Silicon Valley. Bob Randell, director of MiCareer, says, 'Everyone's realizing that tech companies don't provide fancy perks or game areas in order to seem cool and trendy. They want their staff to feel good about themselves and their jobs. Ex D Q1 Happy employees are less likely to leave to work for a competitor and, most importantly, they are more productive.'

This new kind of workplace also encourages people to collaborate and to be creative. Ex D Q1 Playing table tennis with a colleague you rarely work with can lead to new ways of working and fresh thinking. Thinking over a problem while lying in a hammock might be the best way to find **its** solution.

However, this doesn't mean employers should immediately offer free ice cream, replace desks with couches or let staff bring pets to work. 'Firms have to make sure their perks are of real interest to their employees, and that **they** can afford them for the long term. Ex D Q2 Ex D Q2 Ex D Q2 If a company stops offering a perk, staff happiness goes down and people are less satisfied,' says Anna Tang, head of HR at DigitalForest.

'We advise our managers to monitor the effects of the perks carefully. We now offer free breakfasts instead of free lunches. **This** persuades people to arrive early and to start work with good energy levels, which makes **them** more productive. Large free lunches just made them feel sleepy.'

This revolution in the workplace is unlikely to slow down. As Randell says, 'All businesses can improve by increasing creativity, collaboration and happiness at work. The most successful ones do exactly **that**, and which companies don't want to be successful?'

5.1 At work

READING

A With books closed, ask students what they think of when they think of offices. Do they generally have positive or negative associations for the students? Tell students to open their books, to look at the pictures and to discuss the questions. In feedback ask students if they were surprised by anything in the pictures.

B Tell students to look at the pictures in the article. Elicit what type of offices the students think the article will be about. Then tell students to read quickly and to choose the best subtitle for the article. Set a time limit and remind students that they don't need to read too closely or worry about unknown vocabulary in order to get the main ideas. Explain that students don't need to focus on the words in bold at this stage.

2 The article describes how trends have spread from digital technology company culture and the reasons for those trends. It also describes potential disadvantages and the need to think carefully before introducing these kinds of changes.

C Point out the tips for following reference links in a text. Look at the first word in bold in the text together as a whole class to demonstrate the reference link, then tell students to do the same with the rest. Check students' understanding by carefully eliciting how the words link back to the previously mentioned people, things or ideas.

D Tell students to read the article again, more closely this time, and to answer the questions. Tell students to underline the part of the text that helped them find their answers and elicit this when you check answers. If some students finish much faster than others, put the faster finishers together to prepare more comprehension questions for each other about the article.

E Elicit an example of one innovation or perk mentioned in the article (e.g. nap-pods, free food). Put students into groups to find and underline more and discuss what they think of them. Encourage students to expand on their answers by asking them the following questions: *Would you like to work in the types of offices described in the article? Why/why not? Are there offices like that in your country? If not, do they think there will be in the future?*

GRAMMAR HUB

5.1 Past habits and states

A **Complete the sentences with *used to* or *would* and the verb in parentheses. If both options are possible, write both.**

1. When I was younger, I *used to dream / would dream* of running my own business. (*dream*)
2. In my old job, I used to plan / would plan events. (*plan*)
3. The office has moved. It used to be closer to my home. (*be*)
4. I didn't use to think that management skills were important. (*not think*)
5. Joel used to love his job but he hates it now. (*love*)
6. Work used to start / would start at eight and nobody dared to be late! (*start*)

B **Make questions with *used to*.**

1. you / live / New York City / ?
   Did you use to live in New York City?
2. Sally / work / restaurant / ?
   Did Sally use to work in a restaurant?
3. things / be better / in the past / ?
   Did things use to be better in the past?
4. where / you / spend / your childhood vacations / ?
   Where did you use to spend your childhood vacations?
5. what / you / do / in your old job / ?
   What did you use to do in your old job?
6. when you walked to work / how long / it / take you / ?
   When you walked to work, how long did it use to take you?

C **Make sentences with *used to*. Put a check (✓) or an (✗) to show whether the same idea can be expressed with *would*.**

1. when / I / be / younger / I / have / my own business
   When I was younger, I used to have my own business. ✗
2. in the past / our manager / not have / good communication skills
   In the past, our manager didn't use to have (such/very) good communication skills. ✗
3. every afternoon / I / try / finish / all the letters
   Every afternoon, I used to try to/and finish all the letters. ✓
4. years ago / people / laugh / at the idea / computers in the home
   Years ago, people used to laugh at the idea of computers in the home. ✓
5. you / enjoy / your job / more / ?
   Did you use to enjoy your job more? ✗
6. we / not take / a summer vacation
   We didn't use to take a summer vacation. ✓

➤ Go back to page 51.

VOCABULARY

A Tell students to look at the sentences and explain that they were said by Sophia, the boss, to her employees Simon and James. Work through the first one as an example, eliciting which meaning is the correct description of what Sophia said. Tell students to do the same with the others.

B Direct students to the **Vocabulary Hub** (TB121) for further practice of verbs of influence.

C Show students the table. Give one or two personal examples about when you were younger to demonstrate how to create sentences, taking something from each column. Encourage students to ask you follow-up questions about your sentences, then ask them to do the same with their partner. Monitor students to check that they are using the verbs correctly, especially that they're using the base form of the verb after *let* and *make*. Share answers as a whole class and ask students to tell the class how similar or different their childhood and their partner's was and why. Use the **Vocabulary Worksheet** on W20 for extra practice.

SPEAKING HUB

A Tell students to look at picture b on page 52 and to imagine that they all work in an office similar to this. Tell them that they're going to have a meeting to discuss how to improve the workplace and employee motivation by redesigning the office and giving employees new perks. Elicit a couple of ideas from the group. Tell students to work alone and add more ideas to their list.

B Put students into groups to compare and explain their ideas. Encourage them to give as many reasons for their ideas as possible.

C Tell each group to agree on the best ideas and then to make a plan of their office redesign and list their chosen perks. Tell students to prepare to explain their ideas to the class. Monitor and help with language input if necessary.

D Tell each group to present their ideas to the class. Encourage the other groups to ask questions at the end of each presentation. Once all the presentations have been given and there are no further questions, tell students to vote on the best plan. Finish by giving some feedback on students' language use during the presentations.

TEACHING IDEA by David Seymour and Maria Popova

Topic: The job market

Do people spend too much of their lives working? What is the employment situation like in your country? What are the effects of globalization on the job market?

In small groups, tell each other about these jobs:

1 the best / worst / most interesting / most dangerous job you have done
2 the best / worst / most interesting / most dangerous job in the world

TEACHING IDEA by David Seymour and Maria Popova

Topic: Job description

Here are some important aspects of a job:

duties, pay, the boss, benefits, training, vacation days, health and safety, promotion, hours of work, experience, overtime, unions, job security

Ask me questions about these aspects of my job. (Pretend only to hear the grammatically correct questions.)

In pairs, use similar questions to interview your partner about his/her job. (If fewer than half the students work, put them in small groups. If no one is working, ask them to imagine a job they would like.)

TEACHING IDEA by David Seymour and Maria Popova

Topic: Globalization

Work in two groups of six. (If the class does not divide, make one or more groups smaller and take away one of the roles below.) Each of you choose a different number from 1 to 6. You are going to discuss the building of a clothing factory in a poorer country. I'm going to give you a role according to the number you chose.

In the richer country:	In the poorer country:
1 Businessman/investor	**4** Unemployed factory worker
2 Anti-capitalist protestor	**5** Politician
3 Factory worker	**6** Environmentalist

Take turns saying if you are in favor of the factory and how it will affect your life and the country if it is built. Assuming that the factory is going ahead, talk together as a group to negotiate the best possible deal for everybody concerned.

METHODOLOGY HUB by Jim Scrivener

Lexis and skills work

A great deal of lexis work in class occurs in relation to reading and listening tasks. There are definite advantages in this, most importantly because learners meet the language in realistic contexts and see how the items fit into the meaning and style of a whole text.

The text that immediately surrounds a lexical item is referred to as *co-text*. Co-text provides important exposure for learners to samples of language being used. This suggests why texts are usually more useful for teaching lexis than lessons that focus on lexis as separated, stand-alone items without such surrounding language.

When using reading or listening texts, a focus on lexis may occur before, during or after the students read or listen.

C Read again. What do the words in bold refer to? Use the strategies in the box to help you.

Following reference links in a text

We use pronouns (for example *it, them, this*) instead of repeating the same word many times. They usually refer to a person or thing, but they can also refer to ideas.

In order to improve your understanding of a text, it is important to understand which idea or thing the pronouns refer to.

1. Line 1: They *pool tables, nap-pods and free food.*
2. Line 21: Its a problem
3. Line 25: they firms
4. Line 31: This offering free breakfast
5. Line 32: them people
6. Line 37: that increasing creativity, collaboration and happiness at work

D READ FOR DETAIL Read again. Answer the questions.

1. According to the article, which of the following are advantages of modern office design and attractive perks?
   - (a) increasing the quality of work that people do
   - b attracting high quality people to the company
   - (c) encouraging sharing ideas with different people
   - (d) stopping people from leaving their jobs
2. What should companies who want to update their benefits and office design do?
   - (a) provide benefits that employees really want
   - (b) consider the future costs of extra benefits
   - (c) avoid canceling benefits
   - d offer different perks to other companies

E SPEAK Work in groups. Find and underline the innovations and perks in the article. What is your opinion of them?

VOCABULARY

Verbs of influence

A Look at what Sophia, the boss, said to her employees Simon and James. Match the pairs of sentences with the correct meanings (a or b).

1. Yes, of course, you can do that. a
2. Do it now! b
   - a She allowed him to do it.
   - b She told him to do it.
3. Of course, no problem. Feel free to do it. b
4. I'll explain why it's a good idea, and then you might change your mind. a
   - a She persuaded him to do it.
   - b She let him do it.
5. You must do it. If you don't, I will fire you! a
6. I think you should do it this way. b
   - a She made him do something.
   - b She advised him to do something.
7. Don't worry, I'm sure you are good enough. Try to do it. a
8. I would like you to do it, not her. b
   - a She encouraged him to do it.
   - b She wanted him to do it.

B Go to the **Vocabulary Hub** on **page 144**.

C SPEAK Work in pairs. Talk to your partner about when you were younger. Use the ideas below to help you.

When I was younger, ...		
my parents	didn't let	me ...
a friend	used to make	us ...
my teacher	encouraged	my parents ...
I	advised	a friend ...

SPEAKING HUB

A Look at picture b on page 52. Imagine that you work in an office similar to this. You are going to a meeting about improving the workplace and employee motivation. Make a list of ideas to take to the meeting.

B DISCUSS Work in groups. Compare your ideas, giving explanations for each one.

C ORGANIZE Choose the best ideas and make a simple plan to show your office redesign and list your chosen perks.

D PRESENT Show your plan to the class. Then take a class vote to decide which plan is the most popular.

- Discuss and give advice about employment skills and career interests
- Discuss and suggest workplace benefits and changes

- Describe and evaluate a small business
- Talk about environmental business ideas

G the passive voice V business collocations P silent consonants S listening for examples

READING

A SPEAK How much extra do you think you pay when you buy these products? Match the products (1–3) with the percentages in the box. There are two extra percentages. Then work in pairs and compare your answers.

~~40 percent~~ ~~300 percent~~ 600 percent 1,200 percent ~~4,000 percent~~

1. bottled water rather than tap water 4,000 percent
2. pre-cut vegetables and fruits rather than uncut 40 percent
3. takeout espresso coffee rather than making it at home 300 percent

B SPEAK Work in pairs and discuss the questions.

1. How often do you buy the items in Exercise A?
2. What's your opinion of these products and the prices charged for them?

C PREDICT You are going to read an article about a new company, Aethaer. Before you read, answer the questions below. Then work in pairs and compare your answers.

1. Look at the picture and the title of the article. What product does Aethaer sell?
2. Which four of the following topics do you think will be in the article?
   - a personal information about the owner of Aethaer
   - b the production method
   - c Aethaer's business model – product, price and target customers
   - d full details of how to order, including delivery costs
   - e information about other similar businesses
   - f why people buy the product

D READ FOR GIST Read *The new bottled water?* Check your answers to Exercise C. 1. It sells fresh air in jars. 2. b, c, d, f

Business Business

News and views on the business of doing business

The new bottled water?

AETHAER (MoreChaos Ltd)

At ***Business Business***, we are always looking for the next bottled water, and we think we have found it – bottled air.

Businessman Leo de Watts is selling jars of fresh air from Ex E Q1 the British countryside to the residents of polluted cities around the world. He claims Britain has 'designer quality' Ex E Q2 fresh air, and he sells Aethaer as a luxury product. Each jar costs a breathtaking £95.

Ex E Q3 The business was launched two months ago. Orders can Ex E Q4 be made online only, and already 200 jars have been delivered to China. Not many small businesses achieve sales of £16,000 in their first months, and none have a Ex E Q5 product that is so cheap to produce. With plans to start marketing Aethaer in India, Watts could be made a Ex E Q6 millionaire by selling almost nothing, nothing but air.

Ex E Q7 'Air-farming' is incredibly easy. The air is collected from different places in the countryside, from the seaside to the mountains, from the green hills to the forests. The glass jars are held high in the air, and are closed after a few minutes. That's it – the simplest production process ever. Ex E Q8 Next, a label saying where the air comes from is put on the jars. Then, after they have been packed for delivery, they are sent overseas. Job done.

There are currently 15 different 'airs' in the product range. Watts claims that each one has different qualities, depending on where they were collected. While some Ex E Q9 customers do buy the air to inhale, many people buy the jars as gifts that will be kept and won't be opened.

Aethaer air is sold as a luxury item for wealthy people, but other new businesses have started selling cans of compressed air for everyday or sports use. Ex E Q10 Each can contains 200 breaths of air, and they come with a face mask for efficient and easy use.

People laughed when bottled water was first sold in convenience stores, but now everyone buys it. With urban air pollution increasing, it may not be long until you buy a can of clean air as well as a bottle of water every day.

LEAD-IN

With books closed, ask students to think of a product that they consider to be good value for money, and one that they consider bad value for money. Ask students to explain their answers and try to elicit what students think it is that makes something good value for money.

READING

A Tell students to open their books and discuss the questions. Check the meaning of *pre-cut* and *uncut* and highlight the use of prefixes to create different meaning.

1 4,000 percent
2 40 percent
3 300 percent

B Tell students to discuss the questions with their partner. Ask students why they think people pay so much extra for these products and if they consider them a value for the money despite now knowing the price-percentage increases they saw in Exercise A.

C Tell students they're going to read an article about a new company called Aethaer. Tell them to cover the article below the title at first and just to look at the picture and title while they discuss the questions. Share students' predictions as a whole class before they read but don't confirm or deny anything yet.

D Tell students to uncover the article and to read it quickly to check their answers. Set a time limit to ensure students don't try to read in too much detail at this stage.

METHODOLOGY HUB by Jim Scrivener

Reading for detail

A lot of in-class reading work has traditionally been 'reading for detail' – or 'intensive reading', i.e. reading texts closely and carefully with the intention of gaining an understanding of as much detail as possible. Usually this is so that the student can answer comprehension questions (e.g. *Why did the three men go into the office?*). This is typically a stop/start kind of reading, involving going back over small pieces of the same text a number of times to find out more and more about it, making sure that the words have been correctly interpreted. This is how a competent language user might read an instruction manual for a piece of ready-to-assemble furniture or a booklet with guidelines on whether they have to pay income tax or not. It's not the way she/he would typically read a chapter from a novel or a magazine article, although, in classrooms, it is usually how students are asked to process such material (with true/false and other comprehension questions to check if they can pick up specific points).

In everyday life, we tend to do much more extensive reading, i.e. fluent, faster reading, usually of longer texts, for pleasure, entertainment and general understanding, but without such careful attention to the details. When we don't understand words or small sections, we usually just keep going, maybe only coming back when there has been a major breakdown in our understanding.

There is certainly a place for intensive reading in class, helping students to uncover and accurately understand details in a text – but this is by no means the only strategy that a good reader needs. Being able to read fast and fluently is also very important.

GRAMMAR HUB

5.2 The passive voice

	Positive	Negative	Question
Simple present	**I am expected** to work on weekends.	**You are not allowed** to take time off. **You aren't allowed** to take time off.	**Is he paid** a lot of money?
Present progressive	**The goods are being delivered** now.	**The workers are not being trained** right now. **The workers aren't being trained** right now.	**Is the product being sold** at full price?
Simple past	**I was told** to wait at the front desk.	**They were not asked** to work on weekends. **They weren't asked** to work on weekends.	**Were you given** instructions?
Past progressive	**The product was being used** all over the world.	**She was not being paid** very much. **She wasn't being paid** very much.	**Was bottled water being sold** here 30 years ago?
Present perfect	**The product has** just **been launched**.	**Your order has not been received**. **Your order hasn't been received**.	**Have the workers been told**?

- We use the passive voice when we don't say who or what causes the action (usually because the person or thing is not known, not important or obvious).

  *The business **was launched** last year.*

- We can sometimes say the same thing in the active or passive voice. The choice frequently depends on the topic we are talking about.

  *Active: The company **sells** the product as a luxury item. (The topic is the company.)*

  *Passive: The product **is sold** as a luxury item. (The topic is the product.)*

- We use *by* when we know who does/did an action and we want to mention it.

  *This product was bought **by** both young and old customers.*

- We can use the passive voice with modal verbs.

  *Orders **can be made** online or at one of our stores.*

  *The product **might be launched** in the New Year.*

- We don't use *by* + the agent unless it is important, useful information.

  The product is sold all over the world. NOT ~~The product is sold by store owners all over the world.~~

5.2 In business

E Ask students to read through the sentences, filling in any blanks with information that they remember and querying any unknown vocabulary. Then tell students to read the article again, more carefully this time, and to complete the sentences with a word or phrase from the article. Encourage students to compare answers when they've finished and to explain where in the text they found their answers. If students finish this task at very different times, monitor and check that the faster finishers have the correct answers and can explain how they found them. These faster finishers can then become your deputies, monitoring other pairs or groups and prompting them toward the answers. Elicit how and where students found the answers to ensure students have a good understanding of the text and the reading processes.

F Put students into pairs to discuss the questions. Encourage students to explain and expand on their opinions. Ask if they agree with the final sentence and if they think that fresh air in jars will one day become as popular as bottled water.

GRAMMAR

A Elicit that the sentences all come from the article the students have just read. Tell them to underline the main verb and to think about whether the sentences tell us who did the action. Do the first one together to check that students understand the task.

Sentences 1 and 5 say who did the action.

B Tell students to look back at the sentences in Exercise A to help them complete the rules. Check the answers as a whole class, referring back to the examples to check that students understand why the passive voice is used in each case. Ask students if they have a similar structure in their language and, if so, how often they use it. Point out that the passive voice is very common in English and used more frequently than it is in many other languages.

C Direct students to the **Grammar Hub** (see TB54 and below).

A way to make one of these exercises more fun would be to make it competitive. Divide the class into pairs or teams of three. Photocopy, and enlarge if possible, the exercise so there is one for each team. Have each one on different color paper as well if possible. Cut the exercise into strips to separate the questions, and attach them to a wall in the classroom, or in a hallway outside. Tell each team to choose one person who will be the runner. The runner has to run to their team's exercise, tear off the strip for question 1 and take it back to their team. They answer the question together and write the answer on the strip, then the runner brings it to you. If it is correct, tell the runner to take the next question from the wall and repeat. If it is incorrect, send the runner back to their team to try again. The first team to finish wins. Use the **Grammar Worksheet** on W19 for extra practice.

SPEAKING HUB

A Tell half the pairs to be student A and the other half to be student B and to turn to the **Communication Hub** (TB121).

B Tell students to look at their company profile and to work together to write notes to help them present the information to a new partner later. Monitor and help if needed.

C Re-pair students, so each pair contains one student A and one student B. Tell them to present their company to their new partner in as much detail as possible. Encourage them to ask each other questions if they don't understand something.

D Ask students first to discuss in pairs which of their companies should win the award, or whether Aethaer should win. Open this up to a whole-class discussion before taking a vote to establish the overall winner. Give feedback on students' language.

GRAMMAR HUB

5.2 The passive voice

A Correct the mistakes in each sentence.

1 The office [is] located in the center of Manchester.
2 The business was ~~start~~ started by two brothers in Cape Town in 2018.
3 The company is ~~knowing~~ known for its luxury goods and excellent website.
4 Is the plan ~~been~~ being considered right now or is there a delay?
5 The items you have ordered can [be] delivered within two working days.
6 The managers agreed. A decision was taken ~~by them~~ yesterday.

B Choose the correct option.

1 When will we ______________?
a paid (b) be paid c paying

2 My order ______________ yesterday.
(a) was made b is make c made

3 We ______________ what to do.
a haven't told b didn't tell (c) weren't told

4 When you called me, I ______________ for a job.
(a) was being interviewed b was interviewed c am interviewing

5 The food for tonight ______________.
a has been delivering (b) has just been delivered c was been delivered

6 Is everything ______________ in the box?
a provide (b) provided c providing

C Rewrite the sentences in the passive voice. Use *by* only when necessary.

1 They usually give us our tasks in the morning.
We are usually given our tasks in the morning.

2 The manager is studying Rob's business plan.
Rob's business plan is being studied by the manager.

3 They started the business last year.
The business was started last year.

4 They have only delivered three jars.
Only three jars have been delivered.

5 Matt presented details of the plan.
Details of the plan were presented by Matt.

6 When I started, they were making some big changes.
When I started, some big changes were being made.

➤ Go back to page 55.

E READ FOR DETAIL Read again. Complete each sentence with a word or phrase from the article.

1 Aethaer's customers usually live in polluted cities.
2 Aethaer air costs £95 per jar because it is a luxury product.
3 Leo de Watts started the business two months ago.
4 If you want some Aethaer air, you must buy it online.
5 There aren't any other businesses with such cheap production costs.
6 He may become a millionaire in the future.
7 Collecting the air is incredibly easy to do.
8 Before he puts the jars in boxes, Leo adds a label to each jar.
9 Some customers want to breathe the air, but many people never open the jars.
10 Aethaer's competitors want people to buy air for their everyday lives or when they are playing sports.

F SPEAK Work in pairs and discuss the questions.

1 Why does the article say bottled air is the new bottled water?
2 What do you think of the idea of buying a jar of air for £95?

GRAMMAR

The passive voice

A WORK IT OUT Look at the sentences from *The new bottled water?* and underline the main verb. Which sentences tell us who did the action?

1 Leo de Watts sells Aethaer as a luxury product.
2 The business was launched two months ago.
3 Orders can be made online only.
4 The air is collected from different places in the countryside.
5 Other businesses have started selling cans of compressed air.

B Choose the correct words to complete the rules.

The passive voice

We form the passive voice with *be* + the past participle of the main verb.

We use the passive voice when:

a we *know* / *don't know* or it is *important* / *not important* who or what did the action.
b it is *obvious* / *not obvious* who or what did the action.
c we *want* / *don't want* to focus on the person or thing affected by the action.

C Go to the **Grammar Hub** on page 130.

SPEAKING HUB

A You are going to choose a business idea as the winner of the *Business Business* Low-cost Business of the Year Award. Read the information about *Fall Memories* below, then compare it to the *Arctic Diamond* on page 152.

B PLAN Write notes to help you present the information in the company profile.

C PRESENT Work in pairs. Present the company to your partner. Then listen to your partner's presentation and write down the key information.

D REFLECT Take a class vote to decide which company (including Aethaer) should win the Low-cost Business of the Year Award.

Basic information

Country:	Canada
Business name:	Fall Memories
Slogan:	'Bring nature's beauty into your home'
Founded by:	Jessica Malone
Products:	Fall leaves in a gift box (Three leaves: 1 red, 1 yellow, 1 mixed)
Price:	$30

Production process

picked by hand / dried and pressed for ten days / wrapped in tissue paper / packed in a gift box

Sales

Online business:	130 orders in first three days / $12,000 in first year of business
Current customers:	People from hot, dry states in the US, e.g. Nevada, Texas
Future markets:	India / Saudi Arabia / Dubai

Fall Memories

REPAIR, REUSE OR RECYCLE

LISTENING

A SPEAK Work in pairs and discuss the questions.

1 How often do you buy new clothes?
2 Have you ever bought second-hand clothes?
3 Why do you think some people prefer to buy second-hand clothes?

5.5 **B LISTEN FOR GIST** Complete the sentences (1–3) with the words in the box. Then listen to the *Business Business* podcast and check your answers.

marketing outdoor second-hand

1 Patagonia is an __outdoor__ clothing company.
2 They launched a __marketing__ campaign called 'Worn Wear'.
3 It encouraged people to return old clothes and buy __second-hand__ clothes.

5.5 **C LISTEN FOR MAIN IDEA** Listen again. Are the sentences true (T) or false (F)? Correct the false sentences.

1 Patagonia makes ~~things~~ clothes that people ~~only~~ can wear ~~when they are at work or at home~~. and use outdoors. F
2 Patagonia is one of many companies in this sector. T
3 'Worn Wear' is a campaign that persuades people to ~~make their own~~ buy second-hand clothes. F
4 Customers are encouraged to give their old clothes to be sold second-hand. T
5 ~~'Worn Wear' is the only time Patagonia has launched an environmental campaign.~~ They also took out a full-page ad in The New York Times in 2011 encouraging people not to buy one of their jackets. F
6 As a company, Patagonia is concerned about its effect on the environment. T

5.5 **D LISTEN FOR EXAMPLES** Listen again. Complete the sentences (1–5) with the missing words and phrases. Use the strategies in the box to help you.

Listening for examples

In longer talks and discussions, speakers give examples to support their claims.

Here are some words and phrases that we usually use to introduce an example:

- *For example, …*
- *… like …*
- *… such as …*
- *As the survey(s) / results / sales figures show …*
- *Another instance …*

Paying close attention to the examples that follow these words will give you a fuller understanding of the speaker's main ideas.

1 There are lots of others, __such as__ North Face, Berghaus and Columbia.
2 'Worn Wear' encourages customers to buy second-hand Patagonia clothes, __like__ old jackets and T-shirts.
3 __As the results show__, their sales have increased because of campaigns like 'Worn Wear'.
4 __For example__, they made record profits on Black Friday.
5 __Another instance__ of this is when Patagonia took out a full-page ad in *The New York Times*.

E SPEAK Work in pairs and discuss the questions.

1 Why do you think the 'Worn Wear' and 'Don't Buy This Jacket' campaigns were a success for Patagonia?
2 Would campaigns like these encourage you to buy a company's products? Why/Why not?
3 Can you think of any other environmental business ideas like these campaigns? Give examples.

LEAD-IN

With books closed, ask students to tell you one thing they would buy second-hand and one thing they would never buy second-hand. Put students into pairs to think of more. Monitor and encourage students to ask questions or expand on their answers, especially if there are differences of opinion in the class.

LISTENING

A–D 5.5 Allow students to check answers in pairs before whole-class feedback as they complete the listening exercises. Then encourage them to share their opinions and talk about their own experiences in whole-class feedback.

E Put students into pairs to discuss the questions.

AUDIO SCRIPT

5.5

Listening, Exercise B
C = Clive E = Ella

C: Welcome to the Business Business podcast. Today, we're discussing environmental business ideas, and we're starting with the retail sector. I'm talking to our retail expert Ella Stevens.

E: Hello, Clive.

C: Ella, I understand you're going to tell us about a clothing company with some very unusual marketing ideas.

E: Yes. I'm talking today about Patagonia. It's an outdoor activities clothing company based in the US. It was started by Yvon Chouinard in 1973. He used to be a rock climber, and at first, Patagonia made climbing equipment. Since then, it has changed its focus to outdoor clothing.

C: So they make and sell clothing for activities like hiking and skiing, as well as climbing?

Ex C Q1 **E:** That's right. Patagonia is one of the largest brands in the outdoor clothing sector, but there are lots of others, such as North Face, Berghaus and Columbia. These brands are now so popular that you see people wearing their clothes all the time, not just when they are out in the country.

C: So what's different about Patagonia?

E: Well, a few years ago, the company launched a new marketing campaign called 'Worn Wear', which
Ex C Q3 encourages customers to buy second-hand Patagonia clothes like old jackets and T-shirts.

C: That is an unusual way to run a business. It's difficult for a clothing company to make a profit selling new clothes if everyone chooses to buy second-hand instead.

E: That's a good point, Clive, but Patagonia goes even further. They also actively encourage their customers to give them their old Patagonia clothes so that they can then sell them as second-hand items.

C: Really? Why are they doing this? There must be a good reason.

E: Well, Patagonia strongly believes in taking care of the environment.
They've built a brand based on respecting nature, and they are trying hard to reduce the negative impact that the company has on the world we live in. They believe that by encouraging people to repair their clothes and return them so they can be bought second-hand, they are helping the environment.

C: And is this strategy working for them?

E: Yes, it is, Clive. Patagonia is doing a good job of attracting new customers. As the results show, their sales have increased because of campaigns like 'Worn Wear'. For example, they made record profits on Black Friday a few years ago, and they donated the whole amount to environmental organizations.

C: That's incredible! And I imagine this helped them to make even more money in the long term.

E: It's certainly made their brand more attractive to customers who are concerned about the environment.

C: Is 'Worn Wear' the first time Patagonia has used such an unusual marketing campaign?

Ex C Q5 **E:** No, it isn't. Another instance of this is when Patagonia took out a full-page ad in *The New York Times* that encouraged people NOT to buy one of their jackets because of the damage it would do to the environment. Consequently, they got a lot of media attention.

C: I can imagine – that seems like a fairly risky strategy. Did they sell more jackets?

E: Probably, but there's no doubt that the company has helped to increase people's knowledge about the effect the clothing industry can have on the environment.

C: And it's a very interesting approach to building a brand. Thank you for coming in to talk to us today, Ella. Next on the podcast we're looking at …

5.2 In business

VOCABULARY

A Elicit that all the sentences are from the podcast. Tell them to choose the correct verb to complete the collocations, either from memory or according to which they think sounds right. Highlight that there is usually no rule or reason why certain words are frequently used together so students will just need to memorize collocations. You could briefly discuss different ways of recording vocabulary and get students to think about which methods are most effective for them.

B Highlight that these sentences are also from the podcast. Tell them to match the beginnings of the sentences with the endings. After checking answers, get students to work in pairs to test each other, with one student reading the beginning of the sentence and their partner trying to say the ending from memory. They can also test each other on the collocations from Exercise A, with one student closing their book and their partner reading the sentence without the verb. The student whose book is closed has to listen and say the missing verb.

C Direct students to the **Vocabulary Hub** (TB121) for further practice of business collocations.

D Students discuss the questions with a partner. Elicit some examples of companies that students will all be familiar with to get students started. Use the **Vocabulary Worksheet** on W20 for extra practice.

PRONUNCIATION

5.6 **A** Tell students to listen to the sentences from the podcast and to complete the missing word in each. Write the words on the board and ask students what the pronunciation of the two words has in common. Elicit that they both have silent letters. Elicit which consonant is silent in each one.

5.7 **B** Tell students all the words have a silent consonant. Ask them to underline which one they think it is in each word. Play the audio for students to check.

C Tell students to look at the sentences and to find and correct the spelling mistake in each one. Do question 1 together as a whole class. Elicit that the missing letter in each word will be a silent consonant like the *b* in *doubt*.

SPEAKING HUB

A Put students into pairs and make each one student A or student B. Ask student A to look at the box on the page and ask student B to turn to the **Communication Hub** (TB121). Tell them they're going to make a podcast and talk about an environmental business idea.

B Tell each pair to prepare and plan their talk by writing notes and thinking about all the points listed. Monitor and help with language input.

C Put students into new pairs with one student A working with one student B. Tell students to take turns presenting their idea as if they were presenting a business podcast. Encourage students to ask each other further questions about each idea.

D Tell each pair to discuss which idea they think is the best and why. Discuss as a whole class and ask students to explain their ideas and encourage further discussion here. Conclude the class with feedback on students' use of language during the task. Write on the board any interesting vocabulary that was requested earlier in the lesson.

Extra activity
For homework, students can research other environmental business ideas online. They should come prepared to share these ideas at the beginning of the next class.

TEACHING IDEA by David Seymour and Maria Popova

Topic: Public consultation meeting

Use this activity to extend the topic.

A paper factory is planned for your town, which is very beautiful but high in unemployment. There are concerns from the local community about pollution and the destruction of an ancient forest nearby.

In groups of eight, you are going to role-play a public consultation meeting to listen to local views. (Allocate these roles. If the class does not divide into groups of eight, drop one or two of the roles.)

In favor of the factory: the mayor, a representative of the paper company, the building contractor, an unemployed person.

Against the factory: a member of the Green Party, an environmental scientist, a local craftsman, a local hotel owner.

Before the meeting, discuss your arguments with the people who share your views, considering pollution, visual impact, tourism, jobs and effects on other businesses. Role-play the meeting.

TEACHING IDEA by David Seymour and Maria Popova

Topic: Eco-warrior

Use this activity to extend the topic.

What is an 'eco-warrior'? What kind of issues do they fight for and how do they fight for them?

In pairs, imagine a highway is being built through an area of outstanding natural beauty.

How would you oppose it if you were an eco-warrior?

What arguments would you make?

What arguments would you expect from the developer?

Role-play an interview between a journalist and an eco-warrior chained to a tree. Discuss the planned development, how long he/she has been there and what he/she plans to do when the bulldozers arrive.

PRONUNCIATION
Silent consonants

A Listen to the sentences from the podcast. Complete the missing words. Which consonant is silent? 5.6

1 Patagonia strongly believes in taking care of the e<u>nvironment</u>. Silent consonant: the second n

2 Is 'Worn Wear' the first time Patagonia has used such an unusual marketing c<u>ampaign</u>? Silent consonant: g

B Underline the silent consonants in each word. Then listen and check your answers. 5.7

1 climbing	3 high	5 knowledge
2 design	4 honest	6 write

C Find and correct the mistakes in the sentences.

1 There's no ~~dout~~ doubt the company sold a lot more clothes as a result of the magazine ad.

2 It's ~~rong~~ wrong to say that all businesses are only interested in profits.

3 To understand advertising, you need to understand people's ~~sychology~~. psychology

4 You can buy second-hand Patagonia clothes at any of their stores with a 'Worn Wear' ~~sain~~. sign

SPEAKING HUB

A You are going to talk about an environmental business idea in a podcast. Student A – read the box below about the company *REI stores*. Student B – go to the Communication Hub on page 153.

B PLAN Plan your talk:

- explain the idea.
- include examples and business collocations.
- be prepared to answer questions.

C SPEAK Work in pairs. Role-play presenting a business podcast. Listen to your partner and ask questions about his/her idea. Take turns.

D REFLECT Work in pairs. Which idea do you think is the best? Why?

Student A

Company:	REI stores, US
Retail sector:	Outdoor clothing and equipment
Environmental idea:	Close all stores on Black Friday (the busiest shopping day of the year in the US). Employees are paid to take the day off.
Reason:	To encourage people to spend more time outdoors.
Result:	700 organizations, and 8 million people supported the campaign via social media in its first few years.

- Describe and evaluate a small business
- Talk about environmental business ideas

VOCABULARY
Business collocations

A Choose the correct verbs to complete the business collocations in the sentences from the podcast.

1 The company *landed* / *<u>launched</u>* **a new marketing campaign** called 'Worn Wear'.

2 That is an unusual way to *<u>run</u>* / *do* **a business**.

3 It's difficult for a clothing company to *have* / *<u>make</u>* **a profit** selling new clothes.

4 They've *run* / *<u>built</u>* **a brand** based on respecting nature.

5 Patagonia is doing a good job of *<u>attracting</u>* / *adapting* **new customers**.

B Match the beginnings of sentences (1–5) with the endings (a–e).

1 Over the last few years, the company has **built**

2 When we **attract**

3 The company tries to **launch**

4 Like any business, we **make**

5 The best way to **run**

a new **investors**, we'll have more money.

b **money** by selling our products for a profit.

c its **reputation** successfully.

d **a company** is to hire good people.

e at least one new **product** every year.

C Go to the Vocabulary Hub on page 144.

D SPEAK Work in pairs and discuss the questions.

1 What can a retailer do to attract new customers?

2 What campaigns have companies that you know launched recently?

5.3 Major presentation

F – structure a presentation P – ordering adverbs

COMPREHENSION

A Work in pairs. Which of the following factors are most important for a successful business presentation?

- be nicely dressed
- have neat, organized handouts
- show interesting slides
- have a clear, confident voice
- be relaxed and in good shape
- be punctual

B 00:00–02:48 Watch the first part of the video. What problems does Matthew Williams have with his presentation?

C Predict what happens next. Do *Jobs, Jobs, Jobs and Jobs* get the contract?

D 02:48–04:53 Watch the second part of the video and check your ideas. Why does Neena smile at the end?

FUNCTIONAL LANGUAGE

Structuring a presentation

A Put the phrases in the box into a logical order in the table.

Do you have any questions? So first of all, I'd like to talk about
So, the next question is That brings us to
Today's presentation is all about

Structuring a presentation

Welcome

Good morning and thank you for coming.

Introduction

1 Today's presentation is all about how we can work together in Brazil.

Main points

2 So first of all, I'd like to talk about the benefits.
Let's take a look at the first slide.
We have a great deal of experience in the jobs marketplace.

3 So the next question is how to market ourselves in Brazil.

4 That brings us to the end of the presentation.

Questions

5 Do you have any questions?

Summary

Great. So to sum up, we see an exciting future …

B 00:00–02:48 Watch the first part again and check your answers.

C At what stage of a presentation would you expect to hear sentence beginnings 1–5? Use the headings in the box.

1 Let's move on now to look at … Main points
2 In conclusion, … Summary
3 The purpose of today's presentation is … Introduction
4 I'd like to finish with … Summary
5 The next point I would like to explore is … Main points

Glossary

pay rise **(n) (British)** = pay raise **(n) (American)**

MILLY

SAM

NEENA

ZAC

GABY

USEFUL PHRASES

A Rewrite the useful phrases from the presentation less formally. Use the words and phrases in the box.

agree   lots   write / right away

1 We have ~~a great deal~~ of experience …
We have lots of experience ...

2 If we can ~~come to an agreement~~ …
If we can agree ...

3 We can ~~put the contract together immediately.~~
We can write the contract right away.

B How do you say these useful phrases in your language?

PRONUNCIATION

Ordering adverbs

5.8 **A** Listen and write the ordering adverbs in the correct space.

1	First	4	Fourth
2	Second	5	Fifth
3	Third	6	Finally

B Work in pairs. Practice the adverbs in Exercise A. Student A – say a number. Student B – say the adverb.

SPEAKING

A You are going to give a presentation about a personal possession and explain why it is a good one to have. Choose from the personal possessions in the box or your own ideas.

my bag   my bicycle   my car   my coat
my laptop/computer   my cell phone

B Prepare your presentation. Make presentation slides if possible and think about the following:

- Give a 'history' of your personal possession – when, why, how did you get it?
- Talk about the advantages (and any disadvantages) of owning it.
- Say why it has been a good personal possession to have.
- Use at least six examples of functional language.

C PRESENT Give your presentation to the rest of the class.

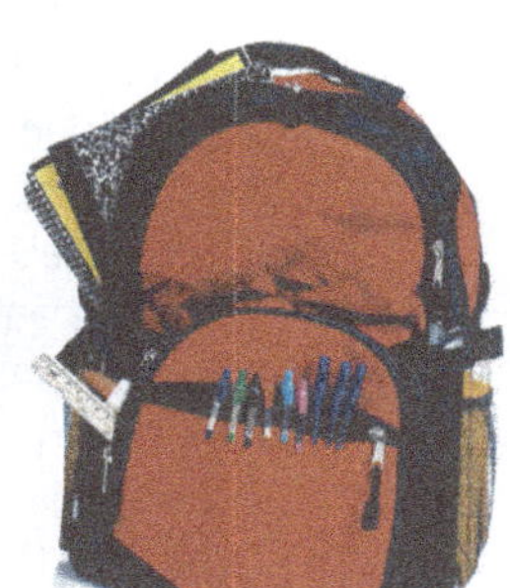

Give a presentation

➤ Turn to page 160 to learn how to write a cover letter for a job application.

5.3 Major presentation

LEAD-IN

Ask students to tell their partner about a presentation they gave. If they haven't done one, tell them to discuss what they think would make a successful business presentation.

COMPREHENSION

A Ask students to decide on which are the most important factors.

B ▸ 00:00-02:48 Tell students to watch the video and think about what problems there are with the presentation.

His tie is not on straight.
He is not well. He is coughing and losing his voice.
He arrives a little late and is not relaxed.

C Put students into pairs to predict what will happen next. Elicit some ideas but don't confirm or deny anything yet.

D ▸ 02:48-04:53 Tell students to watch the video to check their predictions and answer the question.

Neena thinks she is going to get a pay rise/raise.

FUNCTIONAL LANGUAGE

A Tell students to put the phrases in a logical order in the table.

B ▸ 00:00-02:48 Play the video for students to check their answers.

C Tell students to look at the sentence beginnings and decide what stage of a presentation they should be used in.

USEFUL PHRASES

A Tell students to rewrite the presentation phrases so they are less formal using the words and phrases in the box.

B Tell students to translate the useful phrases into their own language. Ask students in what situations they would use them.

PRONUNCIATION

5.8 A Tell students to listen and write the words they hear. Check answers as a class. Elicit the correct order they should be used in.

B Put students into pairs to practice saying the adverbs with one student saying the number from Exercise A and the other saying the corresponding adverb.

SPEAKING

A Tell students they can choose from one of the items in the box or use an idea of their own for their presentation.

B Make sure students follow the suggested steps as they prepare and remind them to use the phrases for structuring a presentation and the ordering of adverbs from earlier.

C Tell students to give their presentation, either in groups or to the rest of the class. Encourage the other students to listen carefully and to ask questions at the end of each presentation. Give feedback on students' language use, focusing on the organization of the presentations, pronunciation and any other useful language.

VIDEO SCRIPT

Ma = Matthew N = Neena Ms = Ms. Santos

Ma: Oh Neena! I'm so sorry I'm late!
N: That's okay. Are you alright?
Ma: Yes, yes, I'll be fine. Just a bit of a cold and a …
N: We're all ready to go and here's all the information. Ms. Santos will be here in about five minutes. Erm … tie?
Ma: What? Oh, yes, of course. Thank you. Good morning and thank you for coming. My name is Matthew Williams, I am a Director here at Jobs, Jobs, Jobs … Jobs. We've been finding jobs for people here in the UK since 2003 and we hope to do the same for people in Brazil in the future. Today's presentation is all about how we can work together in Brazil. So first of all, I'd like to talk about the benefits … Let's take a look at the first slide. We have a great deal of experience in the jobs marketplace … So, the next question is how to market ourselves in Brazil. Here at Jobs, Jobs … and Jobs … That brings … That bri …
N: That brings us to the end of the presentation … Do you have any questions?
Ms: Yes, thank you, Ms. …
N: Patel, Neena Patel.
Ms: Ms. Patel. And thank you, Mr. Williams, of course. First of all, what market share do you expect to have after the first year?
N: Well, from our forecasts, we expect around a 12% share of the market after the first year.
Ms: Really?
N: Yes, I can email you all the data this afternoon.
Ms: That's very good news. And secondly, how soon could you be ready to launch?
N: Realistically, by September, but perhaps earlier if we can come to an agreement in the next week or two.
Ms: Good. That's all the questions we have for now.
N: Great. So to sum up, we see an exciting future working closely together with Empregos, Empregos, Empregos e Empregos.
Ms: Thank you, Ms. Patel. Er … Can we have a moment to discuss?
N: Of course. Please say yes, please say yes!
Ms: Thank you for waiting. So moving onto my final question … when can we begin?
N: That's wonderful news! We can put the contract together immediately.
Ms: Perfect. I will send you an email later to sum up what we have decided today.
N: Thank you. We'll be in touch.
Ma: Well done, Neena. That was excellent work, excellent. Well, I'm sorry, I think I need to go home now.
N: Err … just a moment Matthew.
Ma: Yes.
N: Would now be a good time to talk about a pay rise?
Ma: No, now isn't a good time to talk about anything. Let's talk about it first thing in the morning!

5 Writing

Write a cover letter for a job application

W paragraph structure

A Read the job advertisement. Is it the type of work you are interested in? Why/Why not?

Events Team Assistant (Ref: 783G)
ICE: International Charity Events
This is an exciting opportunity to join our lively and dynamic Events Team. We organize and promote fundraising events and programs for charities across Europe. Typical events include sports, cultural events and adventure challenges and tours.
Essential requirements:
- excellent organizational, communication and marketing skills
- a great team player
- good digital technology skills
- able to meet deadlines

Desired experience:
- experience of working internationally

To apply, email a cover letter and résumé to Marta Safin: M.Safin@ice.nett

B Read Peter O'Malley's application. In which paragraph (1–4) does he cover each topic (a–d)?

- a why he is a good candidate for this job 2
- b when he is able to attend an interview 4
- c why he wants to work for this company 3
- d what job he is applying for and why 1

To: Ms. Safin
Subject: Events Team Assistant (Ref: 783G)

Dear Ms. Safin

Ex C

1 I am writing to apply for the position of Events Team Assistant, currently advertised on Euro_Recruit.com (Ref: 783G). I have attached my résumé. I recently graduated with a degree in Marketing, and I wish to start a career in events organization.

2 The experience and skills that I gained from college make me the perfect candidate for this role. I was a member of the Student Social Committee and I was responsible for our International Food Festival. This demanded excellent organizational skills and demonstrated my ability to meet deadlines. I also improved the marketing for the event, which led to the largest ever attendance at the festival. In addition, I attended frequent meetings, which required good communication skills and the ability to work on a team.

3 Working for your company would be a great opportunity for me to begin my career. I am interested in the wide range of events that you organize and I would love the opportunity to work for an international company.

4 Thank you for considering my application. I am available for an interview at any time, and I look forward to hearing from you.

Sincerely yours,
Peter O'Malley

C Look at the advice about writing a cover letter. Find and underline examples in Peter O'Malley's cover letter.

Writing a cover letter

Write in a professional, formal style that suits a business letter. Do not use informal language such as contractions. Follow a clear structure:
- If possible, address the letter to a named person. Use Dear Mr./Mrs. Do not use the person's first name.
- State where you saw the job advertisement and give its reference number.
- Show your interest in the position on offer and the company.
- Describe the key skills and experience that you have for the role and give examples to support your claims.
- Use standard closing sentences.

D Look at the box. Then read paragraphs 2 and 3 of the cover letter again. Identify the topic sentence and examples for each paragraph.

Paragraph structure

The paragraphs in the main body of a cover letter should focus on a single topic and be carefully organized and well structured. Always:
- start with a topic sentence that makes a clear, relevant point.
- support that point with examples to show how your skills and experience meet those listed in the job ad, or to show your genuine interest in the role.
- only add extra points if they relate to the topic sentence.

WRITING

A PLAN You are going to write a cover letter for the job advertisement below. Think about:
- what language style you need to use.
- the best way to organize the letter.
- what your topic sentences will be and how you will structure each paragraph.

This stage could also be modified to allow students to write cover letters for jobs they are interested in.

Refer students to this letter as a model for the writing task.

Catering Management Assistant (Ref: 812C)
SCC: Superior Conference Catering
High quality catering for events and conferences in the southeastern United States.
Essential requirements:
- excellent organization and time management skills
- excellent communication and team-working skills
- strong digital technology skills

Desired experience and interests:
- event organization
- food and drink
- languages

B WRITE Write the letter (150–200 words).

C REVIEW Work in pairs. Read your partner's letter. Has he/she covered the key points in the ad and organized the letter well?

WRITING

WRITING

With books closed, ask students what they would do and where they would look if they were trying to find a job. Elicit as many ways or places to find work as possible and write any interesting vocabulary on the board.

A Before they read, check students' understanding of *dynamic* and *fundraising*. Tell students to read the job advertisement and to discuss with a partner if they would be interested in the job and why or why not. Monitor and check that students understand all the information about the job.

B Tell students to read the application for the job and to match the topics (a–d) with paragraphs (1–4) in which they're mentioned.

C Point out the advice about writing a cover letter in the box. Ask students to find and underline examples of each tip in the letter from Exercise B.

D Point out the box about paragraph structure and check that students understand what a topic sentence is by eliciting an example from the letter. Tell students to read the letter again and identify the topic sentences and the examples that support them in paragraphs 2 and 3.

WRITING TASK

A Tell students they're going to write a cover letter for the job shown in the ad. Tell them to plan their letter, thinking about style, organization and structure as suggested. Monitor and help with language input.

B Tell students to write their letter. Monitor and provide help if requested.

C Tell students to swap letters with a partner and to read each other's. Tell them to give each other feedback on how successful the letter is in terms of style, organization and structure. Ask students if they think their partner would get an interview as a result of their cover letter.

Unit 5 Review

VOCABULARY

A Complete the interviewer's comments with the phrases in the box.

communication skills | creative thinking skills | people skills | reliable | teamwork | time management

1 Well, he arrived late, so he isn't very good at ___time management___.

2 I'd say she has poor ___creative thinking skills___ – she didn't offer any fresh ideas.

3 Her presentation showed she doesn't have good ___communication skills___ – it wasn't engaging, and her voice was rather flat.

4 I wasn't impressed by his ___people skills___; sometimes he looked annoyed by the questions, and he was a little rude once.

5 But will he be good at ___teamwork___? He's only been self-employed before, as a gardener. Not much group work there.

6 I don't think she is ___reliable___. She's left her last few jobs after only two months.

B Choose the best verbs to complete sentences. Use the correct tense.

At first, I didn't [1] ___want___ (*tell / want*) him to go on the rollercoaster, but he kept asking, and finally he [2] ___persuaded___ (*persuade / advise*) me to buy his ticket. I certainly didn't [3] ___encourage___ (*encourage / make*) him to do it, and I [4] ___told___ (*tell / let*) him to be careful. In the end, it was fine and he enjoyed it, so I [5] ___let___ (*let / persuade*) him go again.

My boss [6] ___made___ (*let / make*) my colleague work over the weekend. I couldn't believe it, but the boss is the boss. I [7] ___advised___ (*advise / let*) him to do it this time, but to say no the next time. My boss has [8] ___allowed___ (*allow / let*) him to have two days off later in the week, so it isn't so bad. Personally, I think that if they [9] ___want___ (*want / make*) us to work overtime, they could [10] ___persuade___ (*advise / persuade*) us by offering extra money!

C Complete the sentences with the nouns in the box.

customers | business | profit | campaign

1 The company made a big ___profit___ last year so employees received a bonus.

2 The key to running a successful ___business___ is to find the right employees.

3 The gyms have attracted ___customers___ because they offer excellent amenities.

4 The health stores launched a ___campaign___ about healthy eating.

GRAMMAR

A Find and correct the mistakes in the sentences.

1 A ~~few years ago, I would be~~ an accountant. I loved that job.
___A few years ago, I was an accountant.___

2 I'd to arrive early most days. I liked it when the office was quiet.
___I'd arrive early most days.___

3 So I use to have long lunch breaks.
___So I used to have long lunch breaks.___

4 He didn't used to be such a relaxed boss.
___He didn't use to be a relaxed boss.___

5 They would being very quiet when I returned to the office.
___They would be very quiet when I returned to the office.___

B Complete the text with the correct form of the verbs in parentheses.

Parmesan cheese, *Parmigiano-Reggiano*, [1] ___was created___ (*create*) over 1,500 years ago. It [2] ___has___ (*have*) a strong and complex savory taste, and its name [3] ___has been protected___ (*protect*) by EU law since 1955.

Parmesan cheese [4] ___is made___ (*make*) from cow's milk. The cows [5] ___are milked___ (*milk*) in the morning, and the milk [6] ___is put___ (*put*) into a large metal container. Key ingredients, such as whey, [7] ___are added___ (*add*), and then the mixture [8] ___is heated___ (*heat*) to 35°C. After 15 minutes, the temperature [9] ___is raised___ (*raise*) to 55°C for an hour.

FUNCTIONAL LANGUAGE

Complete the conversation with the missing words.

Ian: So, moving on to the next item on the agenda: the new office design. [1] ___First___ of all, does anyone [2] ___have___ any questions about the design? No? OK, so …

Kim: Um, just a [3] ___minute___. I just want to say that we should think again. Do we really need a Ping-Pong table?

Ian: I think we've heard enough, Kim. So moving [4] ___on___ to the next agenda item …

Kim: One minute – I have more to say!

Ian: Sorry, it's time to decide. Before we vote, let's [5] ___sum___ up what we decided. We're saying keep the table, but forget the fish tank, for health reasons and cost reasons. Who agrees?

Kim: No, Ian, you can't make decisions like this. And that [6] ___brings___ me to the next topic we need to discuss: how to make these meetings better.

A surfer rides the inside of a wave at End of the road Beach, Tahiti.

Sport (n) an activity in which players or teams compete against each other, usually an activity that involves physical effort.
Synonym: games (n)
Hobby (n) something that you enjoy doing when you are not working.
Synonyms: activity (n), amusement (n)

The quote for this unit is taken from *A Letter of Advice to a Young Gentleman Leaving the University Concerning His Behavior and Conversation in the World*, and suggests that the way someone reacts to winning or losing, and what they will do in order to win, reveals their true character.

Richard Lingard (1598–1670) was a professor of Divinity at the University of Dublin.

OBJECTIVES

- describe a sport or game
- give a short, persuasive talk
- talk about hobbies and free time activities
- discuss trying new things
- express your opinion
- write an article for a magazine

Work with a partner. Discuss the questions.

1 Do you agree with the quote?
2 Look at the picture. Why do some people take part in sports like this?
3 How interested are you in these free time activities?

team sports running music collecting

SPORTS AND HOBBIES 61

OBJECTIVES

Read the unit objectives to the class.

UNIT OPENER QUESTIONS

With books closed, elicit an example from the class of a good way to get to know what someone is really like. Put students into pairs to think of more ideas. Share answers as a whole class and elicit any useful language on the board.

1 Tell students to open their books and to read the quote. Ask students to discuss if they agree with it. Encourage students to support their opinions with reference to their own experiences.

2 Focus students' attention on the picture and elicit the name of the sport (*surfing*). Elicit a couple of reasons why people take part in sports like these, then put students into pairs to think of more reasons. In whole-class feedback, write any more useful language that students use to talk about sports on the board.

3 Tell students first to work individually to rank the free time activities in order of preference, then to compare their lists with a partner. Find out which is the most and least popular activity for the group and why.

WORKSHEETS

Lesson 6.1 Take part!

Grammar: Modals of obligation (W21)

Vocabulary: Adjectives ending in *-ive* (W22)

Lesson 6.2 Hobbies

Grammar: *had to* / *needed to* (W23)

Vocabulary: Hobbies and free time activities (W24)

6.1 Take part!

- Describe a sport or game
- Give a short, persuasive talk

G modals of obligation **V** adjectives ending in *-ive;* sports **P** rhythm: pausing
S listening for main and supporting points

COMPETITIVE SNOWBALL FIGHTING HITS SCOTLAND!

If you think snowball fights are just for school kids, think again. **Competitive** snowball fighting (*Yukigassen*) is a sport for grown-ups that has just arrived in Scotland.

It began as an official sport in Japan in 1987 and since then it has spread to countries such as Canada, Australia, Norway and Sweden. And this weekend sees the first ever matches in Scotland.

Angus Campbell, the captain of the Glasgow Ice Warriors, says 'I think *Yukigassen* is going to be **massive** here. We have the snow and it's a fun and **inexpensive** sport that's **attractive** to everyone. Each match only lasts nine minutes, so you don't have to be super athletic to take part in a game.'

The snowball fights take place on a small court (40 m x 10 m) between two teams of seven players – each team must include male and female members. To win a game, a team has to capture the other team's flag or take out all their opponents with direct snowball hits. If a player is hit, he or she has to leave the game.

The rules are fairly simple, but Angus insists that having an **effective** strategy is the key to success. 'You must work together as a team, be **decisive** and keep calm when under pressure from your opponents. You shouldn't just run for the flag – you'll soon get hit and be out. You need to be more **creative** than that. Your team only has 90 snowballs, which the referee gives you before the game. You must not make any more during the game.'

Six teams are taking part in the event this weekend, and there will be trial sessions for anyone who wants to try it out. 'It looks a little **aggressive** at first, but you shouldn't feel nervous. It's only snow, and all players have to wear a helmet, which we'll provide. However, you should bring some warm gloves!'

If you're interested in trying something **active** on these cold winter days, you simply must go. The games are **impressive** to watch, and great to play. After all, what's more fun than playing in the snow?

The first game starts at 2 pm, on Saturday, in the city park. Entrance is free. Families are welcome.

READING

A SPEAK Write down the names of the different sports you know in pictures 1–4. Then check with another student. What do you know about these sports? Tell your partner.

B READ FOR GIST Read *Competitive snowball fighting hits Scotland!* Where do you think the article comes from? Why?

- a a national newspaper
- b a sports science academic journal
- c a local news and information website
- d a travel blog

C READ FOR DETAIL Put the sentences in the order the information appears in the article.

- a New players do not need to bring any safety equipment. 6
- b There are two ways to beat the other team. 4
- c There are men and women on every team. 3
- d Generally, people think children, not adults, have snowball fights. 1
- e A good game plan is important. 5
- f Several countries play competitive snowball fighting. 2

D SPEAK Work in pairs. What is your opinion of *Yukigassen*? Would you like to play it?

6.1 Take part!

LEAD-IN

Ask students to write down one interesting fact about themselves (that no one in the class knows about them) on a piece of paper. Tell students to crumple up their pieces of paper into balls and imagine they're snowballs. Students have a snowball fight, first throwing their snowball at another student, then picking up and throwing another one. After one minute, tell students to pick up the nearest snowball to them and to read it. Students then have to find whose snowball they have by mingling and asking questions.

READING

A Tell students to look at the pictures and discuss the questions. Monitor and provide any vocabulary that is requested. Find out if any of the students have done any of these sports.

1 *ice skating*
2 *ski jumping*
3 *ice hockey*
4 *snowboarding*

B Tell students to read the article quickly and to decide where they think the article comes from. Tell students that they only need to skim the text in order to do this, but encourage them to think about the style in which it is written. Look at the four options (a–d) and quickly elicit what style of writing these would be.

c – The style and register is appropriate for this context, and the final sentence, with a reference to the city park, but not naming the city, suggests a local information site.

C Tell students to read the text again more carefully this time, so that they understand it in more detail. Tell them to look at the sentences and put them in the order the information appears in the article. Go through the example with the whole class, demonstrating how the information in the first paragraph is paraphrased in sentence d. Students then continue with the rest. Tell students to compare in pairs before feedback. Ask students to refer to the text to explain where they found their answers.

D Put students into pairs to discuss the questions. Encourage students to expand on their answers by monitoring and providing any language input they need.

TEACHING IDEA by David Seymour and Maria Popova

Grammar: Getting ready

Set the situation that a group is preparing to go on an expedition to the South Pole. They are discussing what they must do before they leave. Get students to talk and fill in endings for some written sentences (*We have to take …; The ship must …; We should tell …; We must not forget …; We will have to go …*).

TEACHING IDEA by David Seymour and Maria Popova

Grammar: Design the sign

Ask students to design a new sign for placing somewhere on the school premises where they are studying. Most signs contain implied modality (*No running = You must not run*) rather than explicit ones. Get students to think of a sign where they might need to spell out detailed rules saying what must/must not be done.

GRAMMAR HUB

6.1 Modals of obligation

should

	Positive	Negative
I/you/he/she/it/we/they	**I should choose** the best team.	**We shouldn't yell** at the players.

must

	Positive	Negative
I/you/he/she/it/we/they	**They must find** a better place to train.	**You must not be** so aggressive on the field.

have to

	Positive	Negative
I/you/we/they	**You have to wear** a helmet.	**They don't have to play** the game on the computer.
he/she/it	**She has to perform** well today.	**He doesn't have to win** every match.

- We use *should/shouldn't* when we describe what is or is not a good idea now, in the future or generally.
- We use *must* and *have to* when we describe rules and situations that are necessary.
- There is sometimes no difference between them. However, we usually use *must* and *must not* in written rules, and *have to* in speech.
- We use *must not* when we describe something that is not allowed.
- We use *don't/doesn't have to* when we describe things that aren't necessary, but you may still do them.
- There is a difference in meaning between *must not* and *don't have to*.

  must not = not allowed
  don't have to = not necessary
- In questions, we use *have to* instead of *must*.
- We can use *don't/doesn't need to* instead of *don't/doesn't have to* when we describe things that aren't necessary.

6.1 Take part!

GRAMMAR

A Do the first one together as a whole class, eliciting that it describes something 100 percent necessary so students should write *nc*. Tell students to complete the activity.

B Tell students to look back at the sentences in Exercise A to help them complete the rules. Use these sentences to provide context to check students' understanding.

C Direct students to the **Grammar Hub** (see TB62 and below).

D Put students into pairs and tell them to compare and contrast the rules of the sports. Do an example yourself, modeling how you could use modals of obligation to do this. Use the **Grammar Worksheet** on W21 for extra practice.

VOCABULARY

A Tell students to match the adjective with the definition, using the way the adjectives are used in the text to help them. Do the first adjective, *competitive*, as an example. Students then continue and complete the activity.

B Tell students to practice by completing the questions with an adjective from Exercise A. Check answers as a whole class, then tell students to ask each other the questions. Use the **Vocabulary Worksheet** on W22 for extra practice.

SPEAKING

A Model the task. Describe a sport with reference to the points listed in the task. Make sure it isn't too easy to guess what the sport is but not impossible either! When students have guessed correctly, tell them to work individually to do the same. Monitor to help with language if needed. Check that students have understood that they must not say the name of the sport.

B Put students into groups. Tell each student to read their sentences and the other students in the group to guess what the sport is. Tell students that they get six points if they guess correctly after the first sentence, five points if they guess correctly after the second sentence, four points after the third sentence and so on. Any fast finishers can move on to Exercise C.

C When all the sports have been guessed, tell students to discuss the questions in the same group. Discuss as a whole class and encourage students to expand on their answers. If some students have personal experience of a sport other students would like to try, take advantage of this to encourage further questions and discussion. Finish with feedback on students' language use during Exercises B and C, praising successes and correcting some errors.

GRAMMAR HUB

6.1 Modals of obligation

A Choose the correct option.

1 We *don't have to* / *must not* be competitive to have fun playing sports.
2 He *must* / *doesn't have to* wear a helmet. It's required.
3 I *must* / *must not* eat a massive meal before playing a sport.
4 They *shouldn't* / *don't have to* practice today because the coach isn't going to be here.
5 *Do you have to* / *Must you* train every day?

B Complete the sentences with the correct words and phrases from the box.

don't have · doesn't have · has · must not · don't need · should

1 You __don't need__ to buy a ticket. Dad's bought them already.
2 She __should__ ask her coach for advice on how to play better.
3 I __don't have__ to go to practice today. It's been canceled.
4 For a helmet to work, it __has__ to fit on your head properly.
5 You __must not__ run while holding the ball. It's against the rules.
6 He __doesn't have__ to wear protective gear because his sport isn't dangerous.

C Choose the correct option to complete the dialogue.

Anna: I'm excited about Saturday's game. It starts at 1 pm. I think we [1] ________ meet in front of the entrance, shouldn't we?

Vincenzo: I [2] ________ take my little sister to her lesson first, so I might be a little late. You [3] ________ wait for me outside. Just go on inside and I'll find you.

Anna: Well, I don't mind waiting for you outside. I [4] ________ be in my seat when the game starts. Besides, it's a big place. We [5] ________ go in together so we don't get lost.

Vincenzo: OK, fine.

1 a don't need to b must (c) should
2 (a) have to b should c don't have to
3 a must (b) don't have to c have to
4 a should b must (c) don't have to
5 a must (b) should c don't need to

➤ Go back to page 63.

GRAMMAR
Modals of obligation

A WORK IT OUT Look at the sentences from *Competitive snowball fighting hits Scotland!* Write *nc* (you have no choice, this is 100 percent necessary) or *c* (you have a choice, this is not necessary) next to each sentence.

1 All players **have to** wear a protective helmet. nc
2 You **don't have to** be super athletic. c
3 You **should** bring some warm gloves. c
4 You **shouldn't** just run for the flag. c
5 Each team **must** include male and female members. nc
6 You **must not** make any more during the game. nc
7 You **shouldn't** feel nervous. c

B Match the beginnings of the rules (1–4) with the endings (a–d).

Modals of obligation

b 1 We use *must / have to / need to*
d 2 We use *must not* when
c 3 We use *don't have to* when
a 4 We use *should / shouldn't*

a to talk about what is or is not a good idea.
b for rules and situations that are necessary (strong obligation).
c we describe things that are not necessary, but you may still do them.
d we describe something that is not allowed.

C Go to the **Grammar Hub** on **page 132**.

D SPEAK Work in pairs. Compare the pairs of sports below. How are they similar and different? Think about their basic rules and the qualities of good players and successful teams.

baseball and cricket   soccer and basketball
marathon running and running a 100 meter race   tennis and racquetball

VOCABULARY
Adjectives ending in *-ive*

A Look at the adjectives in bold in *Competitive snowball fighting hits Scotland!* Then complete the definitions with the correct adjective.

1 A __decisive__ person makes choices quickly and confidently.
2 A __competitive__ sport involves two teams trying to beat each other.
3 If something is __massive__, it is very big or, in informal English, very popular.
4 An __attractive__ suggestion or idea is one that people are interested in.
5 An __effective__ plan works well and produces the result that is wanted.
6 An __inexpensive__ activity doesn't cost a lot of money to do.
7 Having an __active__ lifestyle means you do not sit around all day.
8 __Aggressive__ behavior includes being rude or angry in order to get what you want.
9 You admire an __impressive__ performance because it is very good and shows a lot of skill.
10 A __creative__ person thinks of new or unusual ways to do things.

B SPEAK Complete the questions with adjectives from Exercise A. Then work in pairs and interview your partner. Take turns. Give reasons and examples to explain your answers.

1 What is the most ________ sport that you have played?
2 Are you a very ________ person? Why do you say that?
3 Which actors do you think are very ________?

SPEAKING

A You are going to write six sentences to describe a sport or game without naming it. Your classmates will try to guess what it is. Think about:

- reasons why you like it.
- the skills and qualities you need to play it well.
- how it is played and what you need to play it.

B Work in groups. Read your sentences to the group. Can your classmates guess the sport or game?

C Work in groups and discuss the questions.

1 Which of the sports and games described have you played? What do you think of them?
2 Which haven't you played? Would you like to try them?
3 Which is the most popular sport or game?

LISTENING

A SPEAK Work in pairs and discuss the questions. What are the pros and cons of playing video games?

6.1 **B LISTEN FOR GIST** Listen to a talk about eSports and choose the correct answers.

1 What is the best title for the talk?
 a Video gaming: is it good for you?
 b Video gaming: the professional sport of the future
 c Video gaming: nothing more than a free time activity
 (d) Video gaming: the next Olympic sport?
2 What is the purpose of the talk?
 a to give general information about eSports
 b to encourage people to watch and play eSports
 (c) to persuade people to agree with the speaker's opinion of eSports
 d to give a balanced analysis of eSports

6.1 **C LISTEN FOR DETAIL** Listen again to the introduction. What is the main idea of the talk? What are the supporting points? Use the strategies in the box to help you.

Listening for main and supporting points

When giving a talk, speakers usually give a main idea and then support it with detailed points, in the form of examples, statistics, names or dates.

Listen carefully to identify the main ideas and the supporting points that follow.

6.2 **D** Listen again to another part of the talk. What is the main idea? What are the supporting points?

6.1 **E LISTEN FOR DETAIL** Listen again to the whole talk and choose the correct answers.

1 The speaker thinks that many people in the audience …
 a play video games at home.
 b understand how popular eSports are.
 (c) don't realize that video gaming is played professionally.
2 She says playing video games is a sport because …
 a players practice a lot.
 b the games have clear rules.
 (c) there are winners and losers.
3 She says a great eSports player
 (a) has a strong mind and body.
 b plays other traditional sports.
 c spends all their time training.
4 She says eSports are different from traditional sports because …
 (a) they are growing in popularity.
 b young people like them.
 c people watch them online.
5 The Olympic Games wants to include sports that …
 a involve physical activity.
 (b) young people like.
 c have professional players.

F SPEAK Work in pairs and discuss the questions.

1 In your opinion, what is the difference between a sport and a game?
2 Do you agree with the speaker's arguments? Which of her points do you think are strong or weak?
3 Do you think eSports should be an Olympic sport? Why/Why not?

VOCABULARY

Sports

A Check (✓) the nouns that refer to people.

1	champion	✓	6	stadium	☐
2	coach	✓	7	fan	✓
3	final	☐	8	top player	✓
4	league	☐	9	tournament	☐
5	spectator	✓	10	trophy	☐

6.1 Take part!

LISTENING

A Tell students to look at the pictures and elicit their initial reaction to them. Divide the class into two groups. If there are clearly some students who like playing video games a lot, and others who strongly dislike it, group them together at this stage. Give some time for one group to think of pros and the other to think of cons. Monitor to help with language as they do this. Put students together with a partner from the other group and ask them to explain their lists to each other. Conclude by discussing this briefly as a whole class and write any useful language that comes up on the board.

6.1 B Tell students they're going to listen to a talk about eSports. Use the pictures from Exercise A to remind students what exactly eSports are. Tell students to listen and to choose the correct answers. Tell students not to worry if they don't understand everything the first time as they're going to listen again.

6.1 C Point out the strategies in the *Listening for main and supporting points* box. Tell students to listen again to the introduction and use these strategies to help them identify the main idea and supporting points.

Main idea: Soccer, basketball, golf and tennis are four of the world's most popular sports.
Supporting points: played by millions, watched by millions more, all in the Olympic Games

6.2 D Tell students to use the same strategies again to identify the main idea and the supporting points as they listen to another part of the talk.

Main idea: eSports are played in the same way as any other sport.
Supporting points: professional teams compete in large venues and stadiums, thousands of spectators, millions watch online

6.1 E Tell students to read the questions and to try to choose the correct answer from memory. Play the audio again for students to check their answers. Check answers as a whole class and ask students to justify their answers by telling the class exactly what the speaker said.

F Put students into pairs to discuss the questions. Share students' opinions as a whole class. Ask if anyone has changed the opinion they had in Exercise A after listening to the talk.

VOCABULARY

A Tell students to look at the nouns and to place a check mark next to the ones that refer to people. Check that students understand the meaning of the words by eliciting examples of each or an example sentence containing the word. Model and practice pronunciation of the nouns. Draw particular attention to the stress on the second syllable of *spectator* and on the first syllable of *tournament*.

AUDIO SCRIPT

6.1

Listening, Exercise B

Soccer, basketball, golf, tennis – four of the world's most popular sports. They are played by millions and watched by millions more, and all four are in the greatest festival of sports, the Olympic Games.
However, there is one sport that is just as popular as those, but it still hasn't been accepted in the Olympics, and indeed, many people say that it is not even a sport. What sport am I talking about? eSports. Yes, electronic sports, or competitive video gaming.
Ex E Q1 Now, I guess many of you think video games are just something people play at home or on their phones. In fact, they are played in the same way as any other sport, with teams competing against each other in large venues and stadiums, in front of thousands of paying spectators and with millions more watching online.
Even if you already know how massive eSports are, maybe many of you think gaming is not actually a sport. But I hope to persuade you that video gaming has all the features that we see in other sports.
Ex E Q2 First of all, it is clearly competitive. Players and teams compete in national and international tournaments, with a goal to win the final, lift the trophy and become the champions. The will to win is a key part of video gaming. Also, playing video games requires incredible mental strength and skill.
You need to focus for long periods of time and the games are very fast. eSports demand smart thinking, quick decision-making and great communication between team members, just like traditional team sports. Of course, some people argue that video gaming is not a real sport because it doesn't require physical strength. Now, I accept it isn't the same as soccer or football, for example, but, because the games are long and demanding, professional gamers have to be in
Ex E Q3 good shape. If your fitness levels are poor, so is your ability to concentrate. This is why the managers and coaches of professional teams make sure their players spend time training in the gym and have a healthy diet. That all sounds like a sport to me.
So, have I changed your mind yet? Do you now feel that
Ex E Q5 eSports should be in the Olympics? If not, remember that when they choose new sports for the games, they are looking for ones that are popular and have strong youth appeal. That sounds like eSports to me. Online eSports platforms have hundreds of millions of users
Ex E Q4 every week. While the numbers of people playing and watching traditional sports are declining, they are rapidly increasing for eSports, and most of those people are young people.
So, eSports are physically and mentally demanding. They attract young people like no other sport. They are popular all over the world, and, of course, anyone can take part. They have already become a professional success story, with famous top players, great teams and enthusiastic fans.
Video gaming is not a sport of the future; it is a sport of today, and so, eSports should, undoubtedly, be in the Olympic Games. Now, please excuse me, but I have a game to go and play. Thank you.

6.2

Listening, Exercise D

In fact, they are played in the same way as any other sport, with teams competing against each other in large venues and stadiums, in front of thousands of paying spectators and with millions more watching online.

B Tell students to complete the sentences with the correct form of a noun in Exercise A. Point out that they will need to make some words plural. Elicit the first answer as an example.

C Put students into groups to discuss the questions.

PRONUNCIATION

6.3 **A** Read the information aloud and demonstrate the use of pauses as you do this. Ask students if pauses are used the same way in their language. Tell students to listen to the beginning of the talk about eSports again. Point out how the first two examples of where the speaker pauses have been marked. Tell students to mark the other pauses as they listen and to think about which pauses are longer to add emphasis or drama.

6.4 **B** Tell students to look at the next part of the talk and to mark where they think the speaker will pause. Then play the audio for students to check.

C Put students into pairs to practice saying the extracts with the appropriate pauses. Tell them to listen carefully to their partner to check how well they do it.

SPEAKING HUB

A Tell students to choose one of the titles and write some notes about what they're going to say. Monitor to help with language input.

B Tell students to look at the tips for a persuasive talk and check that they understand all the points.

C Tell students to give their talks as persuasively as they can. Tell the students listening to write notes.

D Tell students to stay in their groups and to discuss which talks they agreed or disagreed with and which points were the strongest. Discuss as a whole class and encourage students to explain what made some talks especially persuasive. Finish with feedback on how well students organized and delivered their talks. Help them to record any other useful language that came up.

METHODOLOGY HUB by Jim Scrivener

Defining 'genre'

What does the word 'genre' mean? Why might 'genre' be an important consideration when teaching language?

In everyday life, people speak in a variety of ways, depending on who they are with, where they are, the nature of the situation, etc. To take two extreme examples, giving a presentation is a very different kind of speaking from inquiring about car insurance over the phone. These are two different genres.

A genre is a variety of speech (or writing) that you would expect to find in a particular place, with particular people, in a particular context, to achieve a particular result, using a particular channel (e.g. face to face, by phone).

A genre is usually characterized by specific choices about style, manner, tone, quantity, volume, directness, choice of words, formality, type of content, etc. Apart from the detailed content and specific words of the presentation or the phone call, there is likely to be a generally recognizable 'presentation-ness' about the presentation and an 'inquiry-on-the-phone-ness' about the call. That's not to say that we can't also knowingly choose to ignore or undermine the genre, e.g. by giving a presentation in the style of a comedy sketch (in fact, substituting one genre for another)!

METHODOLOGY HUB by Jim Scrivener

Varieties of speech genre

Make a list of about ten distinctly different real-life types of speaking, e.g. making a public speech. Some suggested answers:

- Giving an academic lecture
- Telling a joke
- Greeting a passing colleague
- Making a phone inquiry
- Chatting with a friend
- Explaining medical problems to a doctor
- Negotiating a sale
- Giving street directions
- Making a business presentation

Being more specific about genre

A term such as 'making a public speech' is still relatively imprecise. It could refer to a wide variety of very different kinds of tasks, from thanking some colleagues for a birthday present to standing up as best man at a wedding reception to presenting a one-hour talk at a conference of 3,000 people.

It is possible to specify types of speaking more precisely than by simply naming a genre if we add information about **why** the speaking is being done, **where** it is being done and **who** is listening or interacting with the speaker.

METHODOLOGY HUB by Jim Scrivener

Voice settings

One interesting approach to pronunciation may sound a little odd at first. It's based on the idea that, rather than work on all the small details of pronunciation (such as phonemes, stress patterns, etc), it might be better to start with the larger holistic picture - the general 'settings' of the voice. If you think about a foreign language you have heard a number of times, you are probably able to quickly recall some distinctive impressions about how the language is spoken - the sorts of things that a comedian would pick on if they wanted to mimic a speaker of that language; for example, a distinctive mouth position with the lips pushed forward, a flat intonation with machine-gun delivery, a typical hunching of shoulders, frequently heard sounds, a generally high pitch, etc.

Do your students have such an image about American speakers of English? Or Australians? Or Canadians?

One useful activity would be to:

1 watch one or more native speakers on video
2 discuss any noticeable speech features
3 try speaking nonsense words using this 'voice setting' ('comedian' style)
4 practice reading a simple short dialogue in as 'native' a way as they can. (This will probably seem very funny to your students, who will initially tend to do fairly bland copies, never fully believing that a voice setting may be so different or exaggerated compared to their own language; encourage them to risk looking and sounding just like a native speaker.)

B Complete the sentences with the correct form of the nouns in Exercise A.

1 In the Olympic Games, the winners receive a gold medal, not a ___trophy___.

2 Usain Bolt and Michael Phelps are two of the most famous Olympic ___champions___.

3 The FIFA World Cup is a soccer ___tournament___ that is held every four years.

4 If you are a Manchester United ___fan___, you should wear something red to the game.

5 The Camp Nou, in Barcelona, is the largest soccer ___stadium___ in Europe. It can hold nearly 100,000 ___spectators___.

6 ___Top players___ can earn a lot of money from advertising and sponsorship contracts.

7 If a team loses a lot of games, the ___coach___ usually loses his or her job.

8 Nothing in sport is certain – you don't always see the two best teams in a ___final___.

9 There are 20 teams in the national ___league___. Each team plays the others twice, so each team plays 38 games in a year.

C SPEAK Work in groups and discuss the questions.

1 What are the popular spectator sports and sports tournaments in your country?

2 Who are the top sportsmen and women in your country? What do you know about them?

PRONUNCIATION

Rhythm: pausing

Pausing

We use pauses to support the meaning of what we say, and to help the listener follow and understand.

- Use very short pauses to group words that go together in phrases or clauses. This is similar to using a comma in writing, but can be more frequent.
- Use short pauses at the end of sentences and paragraphs. This is similar to using a period in writing.
- Make the pauses a little longer to add emphasis or drama.

6.3 **A** Listen to the beginning of the talk about eSports. Mark where the speaker pauses. The first two pauses have been marked (/) to help you. Which pauses are longer to add emphasis or drama?

Soccer,/basketball,/golf/tennis/– four of the world's most popular sports./They are played by millions/and watched by millions more,/and all four/are in the greatest festival of sports/the Olympic Games.

6.4 **B** Where do you think the speaker pauses in the next part of the talk? Mark (/) each pause. Then listen and check your answer.

However,/there is one sport/that is just as popular as those,/but it still hasn't been accepted in the Olympics,/ and indeed,/many people say/that it is not even a sport./What sport am I talking about?/eSports./Yes,/ electronic sports,/or competitive video gaming.

C SPEAK Work in pairs. Practice saying the extracts in Exercises A and B. Listen and check that your partner pauses in the correct places.

SPEAKING HUB

A You are going to give a short persuasive talk (1–3 minutes). Choose one of the titles and write notes for your talk.

- eSports are not sports and should not be part of the Olympic Games.
- Playing video games is a good activity for children.
- Video games are generally more negative than positive.
- Professional athletes earn too much money. Their pay should be limited.
- ________ is the best sport to both play and watch.

B PLAN Look at your notes and use these tips on how to improve a persuasive talk.

- Have a good introduction and conclusion.
- Use confident language, e.g. *I strongly believe …; It's undoubtedly true that …*
- Use rhetorical questions, e.g. *Why should we do this?; I'm sure you agree, don't you?*
- Support your main points with good examples and arguments.
- Practice your pausing and rhythm when giving the talk.

C PRESENT Work in groups. Give your talks. Write down the main ideas and supporting points of the other talks.

D REFLECT Work in groups. Did you agree or disagree with the speakers? Which points do you think were strongest?

– Describe a sport or game
– Give a short, persuasive talk

6.2 Hobbies

- Talk about hobbies and free time activities
- Discuss trying new things

V – hobbies and free time activities
S – identifying tone
G – present perfect progressive; *had to* / *needed to*
P – *been*: unstressed

a

b

c

LISTENING

A SPEAK **Work in pairs and discuss the questions.**

1 Describe the pictures (a–e). What are the people doing?
2 Which free time activities are you most interested in? Why?

6.5 **B LISTEN FOR GIST** **Listen to a radio show about hobbies and free time activities. Match the pictures (a–e) with the guest speakers (1–5).**

1 d 2 b 3 a 4 e 5 c

6.5 **C LISTEN FOR DETAIL** **Listen again. Choose the best answers for each person.**

1 Speaker 1
a buys and sells new cars.
(b) spends a lot of money on his hobby.
c makes enough money from his hobby to pay for his vacations.

2 Speaker 2
a finds his hobby stressful at times.
b also works as a photographer.
(c) is learning how to do something new.

3 Speaker 3
a wants her husband to spend more time on his hobby.
(b) says her husband spends a lot of time on his hobby.
c shares her husband's hobby.

4 Speaker 4
(a) shares her interest with her friends.
b has her own social media site about her interest.
c regularly stays at hotels in Boston.

5 Speaker 5
a usually has a few hobbies at the same time.
b finds it hard to get interested in things.
(c) has had many different hobbies.

D SPEAK **Work in groups and discuss the questions.**

1 Are there any hobbies you would like to try? Which ones?
2 What are the benefits of having a hobby?

VOCABULARY

Hobbies and free time activities

A WORK IT OUT **Look at the three sets of verb phrases from the radio show. Match the beginnings of the phrases with the endings (a–d).**

1 join — a interest in a hobby
be — b a hobby
lose — c a society
take up — d my thing

2 be — a into something
be — b you in shape
keep — c of a singer
be a fan — d a member of a fan club

3 get — a relaxing
be — b from daily stress
collect — c you out of the house
escape — d something, like stamps or art

('get something' is also possible)

B **Complete the table with the verb phrases from Exercise A.**

Show enthusiasm for a hobby	Something you may do as part of a hobby	Benefits of a hobby	Start a new hobby
be into something	join a society	escape from daily stress	take something up
be my thing	collect something	be relaxing	
be a fan of something	be a member of a fan club	get you out of the house	
lose interest in something		keep you in shape	

C Go to the **Vocabulary Hub** on **page 144**.

D SPEAK **Rewrite these sentences so they are true for you. Then work in pairs and compare your answers. Give reasons and examples.**

1 I'm a big fan of the singer Ed Sheeran.
2 I need to find a way to get myself out of the house more frequently.
3 I've collected a lot of different things during my life.
4 I don't do much to stay in shape. I should do more.
5 I've never been a member of a fan club nor joined a society.
6 Cooking isn't really my thing.
7 I've had a few hobbies that I've lost interest in.
8 This year, I've taken up a new hobby.

6.2 Hobbies

LEAD-IN

With books closed, check understanding of *hobbies* and elicit an example. Put students into pairs and give each pair one of the following categories: indoor hobbies, outdoor hobbies, hobbies for young people, hobbies for older people, modern hobbies, traditional hobbies, educational hobbies, creative hobbies, physical hobbies, spiritual hobbies. Tell students to think of as many hobbies as they can for their category. Share ideas with the class and write any useful language that comes up on the board.

LISTENING

A Tell students to look at the pictures and discuss the questions. Elicit the names for the hobbies and free time activities shown in the pictures.

6.5 **B** Tell students they're going to listen to a radio show about hobbies and free time activities. Tell them to listen and match each speaker (1–5) to a picture (a–e) from Exercise A.

6.5 **C** Tell students to look at the questions and to try to choose the correct answer from memory. Play the audio again for students to check. Ask students to justify their answers with reference to exactly what each speaker said.

D Give a personal example answer for question 1, then put students into pairs to discuss the questions. Ask if any students have experience of the hobbies that their classmates would like to try. If they do, they can exchange helpful information.

VOCABULARY

A Elicit that the verb phrases were all used in the radio show. Tell students to match the beginnings with the endings. Check that students understand the meaning of the verb phrases by eliciting how they were used in the radio show and in relation to which hobby.

B Tell students to put the verb phrases into the correct column in the table. If students have difficulty with this, clarify the meaning of the verb phrases with further examples.

C Direct students to the **Vocabulary Hub** (TB121) for further practice of verb phrases related to hobbies and free time activities.

D Tell students to look at the sentences and to decide if they are true for themselves. Tell students to rewrite the false sentences so that they are true. Then put students into pairs to compare and explain their answers. Encourage students to expand on their answers and to ask each other follow-up questions. Use the **Vocabulary Worksheet** on W24 for extra practice.

Extra activity
Divide the class into two groups. Each group should write a list of five sports or hobbies. The groups exchange lists. One person from each group should describe or act out each word for their group to guess. Set a time limit of two minutes.

AUDIO SCRIPT

6.5

Listening, Exercise B
RP = Radio Presenter S1 = Speaker 1 S2 = Speaker 2
S3 = Speaker 3 S4 = Speaker 4 S5 = Speaker 5

RP: Hobbies. Interests. Pastimes. They're something more than watching TV, and something different from playing a sport. I'm Gavin Ross, and in this week's Human Behavior, we're asking you, the public, about what you like doing in your free time. What hobbies do you have? How long have you been doing them? Why do you have them? Let's hear from some of our listeners out on the streets in Boston today.

Ex C Q1 **S1:** I'm really into classic or vintage cars. I've been buying them since I was 18, when I first learned to drive and got my first one, a small 1960s sports car. Obviously, it isn't exactly a cheap hobby, what with buying and then repairing them. It means I don't go on expensive vacations like my friends, but I'm not going to give it up. I've just bought an old Mini, so I'll start working on that tomorrow.

S2: Arts and crafts are my thing – jewelry making, painting, woodwork.

Ex C Q2 I've had this interest since I was a child. For the last six months, I've been going to pottery classes. In fact, I've been working in the studio this afternoon – that's why my hands are so dirty. As a hobby, it's relaxing and a great escape from daily stress, and, you know, it makes time fly – a sure sign I'm enjoying myself.

S3: I don't really have a hobby, but my husband is an enthusiastic cyclist.

Ex C Q3 Actually, I think that cycling is an obsession for him, rather than a hobby. If he isn't out on a ride, he's cleaning the thing, or checking out the latest accessories online. He's been doing it since his teens, so I knew what I was getting when I married him. It isn't really my thing, so I leave him to it; it seems to keep him in shape and happy.

S4: I don't know if you can call this a hobby, but I spend most of my time following Danny CJ, the singer – I'm a massive fan. I've been a member of his fan club for a long time, I've been to a lot of his concerts and I collect everything I can about him: all the music, pictures, posters, calendars. It's great following him on social media, too. He even replied to one of my

Ex C Q4 tweets once. Whenever he comes to Boston, my friends and I all hang out outside his hotel. He's in there now – we've been waiting here all day, but we haven't seen him yet. Hold on, is that him? Danny! Danny! Over here!

Ex C Q5 **S5:** Do I have a hobby? Well, you might say my hobby is having hobbies. I tend to get really into something, like, at first, I get really obsessed with it, but then I soon lose interest. I don't know why. I've always been like this. Recently, I've been getting into bird watching – I've bought all the kits and a bunch of books, and I've joined two local societies. No idea how long this will last though.
I might start cooking classes soon, or take up sailing. Anything that gets me out of the house.

RP: Those are just some of the people I've met while making this show, and I'd like to hear from even more of you. Visit our show's website to see how you can take part in this series of Human Behavior. The address is www.radiotalk.nett/ humanbehavior …

6.2 Hobbies

GRAMMAR

A Do the first one together as a whole class.

B Tell students to look at the sentences in Exercise A again and to complete the rules.

C Direct students to the **Grammar Hub** (see below and TB68).

D Put students into pairs, one student A and one student B. Tell students to turn to the **Communication Hub** (TB121). As a class, share the most interesting answers and comment on how well students used structures.

PRONUNCIATION

6.6 A Tell students to listen to three sentences and to pay special attention to the pronunciation of *been*. Elicit that it rhymes with *thin*, not *seen*. Point out the information in the box, and check that students understand that *been* is an auxiliary verb and is normally unstressed and pronounced /bɪn/. Stressed words are usually main verbs and key information verbs, not auxiliary verbs. Elicit an example of each on the board and then practice pronunciation.

6.7 B Tell students to practice by listening and repeating the sentences.

SPEAKING HUB

A Tell students to think about the questions and to write notes. Monitor to help with language input.

B Tell students they're going to interview three or four of their classmates about their hobbies. Tell students to make sure they write notes about each person they speak to. Monitor as they do the interview and make sure both students in each pair get a chance to ask and answer questions.

C Tell students to sit down and then put them into groups with students they haven't worked with before. Tell them to use their notes to tell each other the most unusual/interesting/dangerous/expensive hobbies they heard about.

GRAMMAR HUB

6.2 Present perfect and present perfect progressive; *had to / needed to*

Present perfect

Positive	Negative	Question
I've joined a sailing club.	**They haven't made up** their minds about joining the league.	**Have you met** your opponent yet?

- We use the present perfect for actions completed during a period of time that continues to now.
- We also use the present perfect for actions completed before now when we don't say exactly when.
- See Grammar Hub 2.1 for more information about the present perfect.

Present perfect progressive

	Positive	Negative
I/you/we/they	**I have been collecting** stamps for years.	**We haven't been doing** our best in every game.
he/she/it	**She's been training** hard every single day.	**Zain hasn't been training** hard enough.

Question	Positive short answer	Negative short answer
Have they been playing tennis for long?	Yes, **they have**.	No, **they haven't**.
Has Anika been watching the game on TV?	Yes, **she has**.	No, **she hasn't**.

- We use the present perfect progressive to talk about an action that started in the past and continues in the present. It can be a single or a frequently repeated action.

  He has been cooking all afternoon.
- We can use both the present perfect and the present perfect progressive to describe a recently completed activity.

  She has posted the videos on social media. She has been posting the videos on social media all morning.
- We use the present perfect progressive to find out the duration of an activity.

  How long have you been waiting for your teammates?
- We do NOT use the present perfect progressive with state verbs.

  I have known my coach for years.

had to / needed to

	Positive	Negative
I/you/he/she/it/we/they	**They had to** practice for four hours each day.	**You didn't have to train** for the snowball fight.
	He needed to wear safety equipment.	**She didn't need to buy** a new helmet.

Question	Positive short answer	Negative short answer
Did you have to take a lesson first?	Yes, **I/we did**.	No, **I/we didn't**.

- We use *had to* and *needed to* to talk about things that were necessary in the past. They mean the same thing.
- We don't use *must* to talk about the past.

  They had to pay for the skiing lessons last winter.
- We use *didn't have to* and *didn't need to* to talk about things that were not necessary but possible in the past.

GRAMMAR

Present perfect progressive

A WORK IT OUT Look at the sentences from the radio show and choose the correct answers.

1 Which sentence describes a single action that continues up to now? b
Which sentences describe an action or activity that is frequently repeated up to now? a, c

- a He's been doing it since his teens.
- b We've been waiting here all day.
- c For the last six months, I've been going to pottery classes.

2 In each sentence, is the main verb a state or an action verb?

- a He's been doing it since his teens. action verb
- b I've had this interest since I was a child. state verb
- c I've been a member of his fan club for a long time. state verb

3 What are the recently completed actions in the sentences?
Which sentence focuses on the fact that the action is completed? b
Which sentence focuses on the duration of the action? a

- a I've been working in the studio this afternoon – that's why my hands are so dirty.
- b I've just bought an old Mini, so I'll start working on that tomorrow.

B Complete the rules (1–5) with the words in the box.

progressive long now past present repeated state

Present perfect progressive

1 We usually use the present perfect progressive to talk about an action that started in the ___past___ and is continuing ___now___. The emphasis is on the unfinished activity.

2 We also use it to talk about a past action that has just finished, but which has a ___present___ result.

3 We can use it to talk about ___continuous___ or frequently ___repeated___ actions.

4 We do not use the present perfect progressive with ___state___ verbs.

5 We use the present perfect progressive to talk about how ___long___ something has been happening.

C Go to the **Grammar Hub** on **page 132**.

D SPEAK Work in pairs. Student A – go to the **Communication Hub** on **page 150**. Student B – go to the **Communication Hub** on **page 155**.

PRONUNCIATION

been: unstressed

6.6 **A** Listen to three sentences. What do you notice about the pronunciation of *been* in each sentence? Does it rhyme with *seen* or *thin*?
Each time, *been* rhymes with *thin*.

been

In the present perfect progressive, *been* is an auxiliary verb and it is normally unstressed and pronounced /bɪn/.

The stressed words are usually the main verbs and key information words, not the auxiliary verbs.

6.7 **B** Listen and repeat.

SPEAKING HUB

A Choose one of your hobbies or free time activities and prepare to talk about it. Answer the following questions.

1 When did you take it up and why?
2 How much time and money do you spend on it?
3 What do you like about it?
4 Is there anything you dislike about it?
5 What benefits does it bring to you and your life?
6 Why would someone else enjoy your hobby?

B SPEAK Go around the class and interview three or four of your classmates about their hobbies. Write notes.

C DISCUSS Work in groups. Tell each other about your interviews. Which hobbies were:

- the most unusual?
- the most interesting?
- the most dangerous?
- the most expensive?

READING

A SPEAK Work in pairs. When was the last time you:

- tried a new food or drink?
- listened to a new singer or group?
- visited a new place?

B READ FOR MAIN IDEA Read the first two paragraphs of *My six months of trying new things.* Then complete the summary with a word in the box.

~~interesting~~ relaxing

Candie is not very active. She decided to spend the first six months of this year doing different activities because she wants to find a hobby that will make her free time more ___interesting___.

My six months of trying new things

By Candie Carmichael

July 15

I've never been the kind of person who does lots of exciting things in their free time. Paragliding, swimming with dolphins, climbing Mount Everest – not me! My idea of danger is to sit on the couch and watch the latest crime series on TV. The closest I get to nature is when I 'like' my friends' cat pictures on social media. As for climbing Himalayan mountains – forget it! I'd rather climb the stairs to bed.

But at one point toward the end of last year, I started to feel that my life was becoming a little … well … boring. I needed to take up a hobby. But which one? There are so many things out there – how do you know what you will enjoy? So I decided to spend the first six months of this year trying out a new hobby each month. I was a complete beginner at every activity I tried.

Here's what happened:

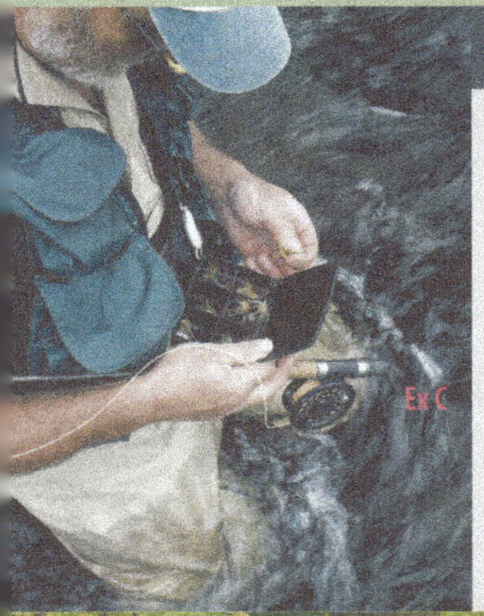

January: Fly fishing

The first thing I learned was that no flies are harmed in fly fishing. You make a pretty, artificial 'fly' and attach it to a hook on a fishing line. [1]___ When a fish takes a bite you … oh, I don't know. I did NOT do well at this. One month: lots of badly made 'flies', and ZERO fish (apart from the ones I got at the fish and fries place on my way home).

February: Stamp collecting

Why does anyone do this? [2]___ After a whole four weeks of attaching little squares of paper from around the world into a big book with blank pages, I still have no idea.

March: Ping-Pong

This one really surprised me. I'm actually good at it! I joined a club, and I didn't need to spend a lot of time practicing before I started winning games. After only a month, I was already one of the best players in the group. I really can't believe it. [3]___

April: Beekeeping

Surely all I had to do was keep some flying insects in a box? [4]___ About a hundred bee stings later, I realized that a lot can go wrong and beekeeping is a serious (and sometimes painful) business. I think I'll just get my honey from the grocery store in future.

May: Playing the ukulele

The ukulele is like a very small guitar. It has four strings. It makes you look like a giant when you play it. [5]___ I didn't have to be in great shape. It wasn't dangerous and it wasn't painful. And at the end of the month, I could play *Rivers of Babylon* all the way through. If that isn't success, I don't know what is!

6.2 Hobbies

READING

A Give a personal example, then put students into pairs to discuss the questions. Share any interesting answers with the class. Ask students to expand on why they tried these new experiences and how it made them feel.

B Tell students they're going to read about a woman named Candie who decided to try a lot of new experiences. Tell them to read the first two paragraphs and complete the summary with the correct word.

C Tell students to read the rest of the article and to match the activities with Candie's experiences. Tell them to ignore the blanks in the text at this stage. Ask students to explain which part of the text helped them find the answer.

D Tell students to read the text again and to fill in the blanks with the sentences. To make this more challenging for stronger students, tell them to cover sentences a–f and to try to predict the missing sentences. When the other students are almost finished, tell the stronger students to uncover sentences a–f and to put them in the correct blanks, comparing how similar they are to their ideas.

METHODOLOGY HUB by Jim Scrivener

Audience and purpose

When identifying tones, it is important to think about audience and purpose.

In real life, we can judge if our writing was successful by whether it did what we wanted it to do. For example:

- if we wrote a complaint email to an online bookstore, we would feel successful if they replied, seemed to understand our problem and took steps to deal with it;
- if we wrote a story about a happy incident in our childhood, we might feel we had succeeded if other people read it and enjoyed it and maybe wanted to talk to us about it and ask questions or respond with their own stories;

The fact that writing can achieve such things is part of what motivates us to put care into our writing. Good writers need to become careful readers of – and reflectors on – their own work. The existence of audience and purpose are worth bearing in mind in class.

METHODOLOGY HUB by Jim Scrivener

Some alternatives to reading aloud around the class

Here are some alternatives to try:

- You read.
- You read narrative, but students read character conversation.
- You (having read the chapter yourself before class) tell the story in your own words, without notes, in the most spell-binding way you can; later, you get students to do the same with other parts.
- Students read to each other in small groups or pairs, stopping, changing, discussing and helping each other whenever they want to.
- Students read silently, then, without discussion, act out, improvising a scene based on what happened.
- Students silently speed-read a text (say in two minutes), then report back, discussing, comparing, etc., before silently reading it more carefully.

GRAMMAR HUB

6.2 Present perfect and present perfect progressive; *had to / needed to*

A Choose the correct option.

1. I've never *played* / *been playing* racquetball before. Is it fun?
2. Have you *been watching* / *watched* sports on TV all day?
3. I've just *finished* / *been finishing* a really difficult exercise class.
4. Sorry about my appearance. I've *run* / *been running*.
5. Do you think he's *understood* / *been understanding* the rules yet?
6. Lee hasn't *worked out* / *been working out* for a long time but he's already *increased* / *been increasing* his muscle strength.

B Complete the sentences in the present perfect or progressive with the correct form of these verbs. Sometimes more than one tense is possible.

follow join stay lose play spend

1. Tom has ___lost___ interest in playing soccer.
2. The coach has ___spent / been spending___ a lot of time with the players lately.
3. Have you ___been following___ the tennis competition? It's getting good!
4. Georgia has ___been staying___ in shape these days using a new exercise program.
5. Eli and Greta haven't ___joined___ the club yet.
6. I've ___been playing___ this video game all day and there's still a lot left.

C Correct the mistakes.

1. He had to ~~left~~ leave the game because he broke his leg.
2. I ~~must~~ had to yell so the other players could hear me.
3. You ~~hadn't~~ didn't have/need to yell. I ~~couldn't~~ could hear you on the field.
4. I didn't ~~needed~~ need/have to tell my friend about the game.
5. **A:** Why ~~they didn't~~ didn't they have to buy a paddle?
   B: Because they already had one.

➤ Go back to page 69.

E Tell students to read the information in the *Identifying tone* box. Tell them to think about this information and to look at the highlighted phrases, words and punctuation in the article to decide what they think the author's tone is. Ask students to explain their answers and if similar techniques are used in their own language. Ask if students know any other ways in which this can be done.

They show us that the article has an informal tone. There are capitalizations for emphasis, exclamation marks and emphasizing adverbs and adjectives (still, actually, whole) that indicate the tone of this text is humorous and light-hearted.

F Put students into pairs to discuss which of the activities from the article they would choose to take up, if they had to choose one. If any students already have experience of any of the activities, ask them to share it with the class. Ask students to expand on their reasons for wanting or not wanting to try the activities.

GRAMMAR

A Tell students to read the sentences and to choose the correct words to complete the rules. Check understanding of *didn't have to* carefully by eliciting some personal examples. Ensure that students understand that it doesn't have the same meaning as *wasn't allowed to* or *shouldn't have*.

B Direct students to the **Grammar Hub** (see TB67 and 68).

C Put students into pairs to discuss the questions. Encourage students to expand on their answers. Use the **Grammar Worksheet** on W23 for extra practice.

SPEAKING HUB

A Tell students to think of one or two new activities they have tried.

B Tell students to look at the points in Exercise B and write notes to help them prepare to speak. Monitor to help with language input.

C Put students into pairs to tell each other about their experiences of trying a new activity. Encourage them to show interest in each other's stories and to ask further questions.

TEACHING IDEA by David Seymour and Maria Popova

Grammar: Desert island

Draw a desert island with one long-bearded inhabitant. Add a rescue ship arriving and a rescuer jumping off to greet Robinson Crusoe. Elicit some of their conversation *(How long have you been living here?; I've been eating coconuts for ten years)*. Challenge pairs to come up with three more present perfect progressive sentences.

TEACHING IDEA by David Seymour and Maria Popova

Invention

What does the saying `Necessity is the mother of invention' mean?

In small groups, brainstorm a list of ten important inventions. Pass your list to another group. Look at the list your group receives and next to each invention, write a sentence explaining why it was needed, e.g. the wheel – *It was invented because people needed to transport heavy loads.*

TEACHING IDEA by David Seymour and Maria Popova

Historical needs

In small groups, discuss what people needed and didn't need to do at these times, e.g. *People who lived 500 years ago needed to dry a lot of their food for the winter.*

50 years ago, 500 years ago, 5,000 years ago

Compare how things are different these days and write a few notes of your ideas, e.g. *Nowadays we don't need to dry things like fish because we can keep them refrigerated.*

METHODOLOGY HUB by Jim Scrivener

Grammar: Clarification

You have reached a point where you want your students to really focus in on a piece of grammar, to see it, think about it and understand it, to become much clearer on its form, meaning and use. This is what many teachers refer to as *clarification* or *presentation*. However, these are fairly broad headings; there is a significant difference between a presentation in which I give you a lecture for 60 minutes and one where I nudge and help you toward discovering much of the same information for yourself via a process of questioning and looking at suggested reference material. We could differentiate three general categories:

1 Teacher explanation

2 Guided discovery

3 Self-directed discovery

An example activity for each category is as follows:

1 Teacher explanation

You tell a story about your weekend. Every time you use a verb in the simple past, you repeat it and write it on the board. At the end, you write 'simple past' on the board and explain that you used all these verbs in the past because the story happened last Saturday.

2 Guided discovery

You hand out a list of 20 *if* sentences. You ask students to work together, discuss and find out what the 'rules' are.

3 Self-directed discovery

Students decide they want to learn about reported speech. They go to the library or on the internet and find out more.

C READ FOR KEY WORDS Read the rest of the article. Match the activities (1–6) with Candie's experiences (a–f).

1 fly fishing
2 stamp collecting
3 yoga
4 beekeeping
5 playing the ukulele
6 Ping-Pong

a This hobby caused her pain.
b She wasn't successful at all.
c She was able to complete a whole song.
d She was surprised by how good she was at this activity.
e She learned that she is not able to do this kind of thing well because she isn't athletic.
f She didn't understand why this is a popular hobby.

D READ FOR DETAIL Read again. Fill in the blanks in the article (1–6) with the sentences (a–f).

a Is this really a hobby? 2
b What could possibly go wrong? 4
c Maybe there's a chance for me to get in shape after all. 3
d Then you throw the line on the water. 1
e I really enjoyed this. 5
f I am not very flexible. 6

Identifying tone

An essay or serious news article will usually have a formal or serious tone. Other kinds of text, like emails between friends or some web or magazine articles, may have an informal or humorous tone.

You can identify a text's tone from the way it is written and the author's choice of phrases, adverbs and adjectives, capital letters and punctuation.

E Look at the highlighted words and phrases. What do the capital letters, punctuation and word choice tell us about the article's tone?

F SPEAK Work in pairs. If you had to choose one of these activities to take up for a month, which would you choose? Why? Tell your partner.

June: Yoga

Ouch! I thought yoga was relaxing. I didn't realize I had to be super athletic and flexible. After one month of downward dogs and (falling over!) tree poses, I learned some very important things about me: I am not Ex C very athletic. 6___ I do not like yoga.

GRAMMAR

had to / needed to

A WORK IT OUT Look at the sentences from *My six months of trying new things*. Then choose the correct words to complete the rules.

I needed to take up a hobby.

All I had to do was keep some flying insects in a box.

I didn't have to be in great shape.

I didn't need to spend a lot of time practicing before I started winning games.

had to / needed to

1 We use ***had to*** and ***needed to*** when we talk about things that were necessary in the *present* / *past*.

2 We use ***didn't have to*** and ***didn't need to*** when we talk about things that were *not allowed* / *not necessary but possible* in the past.

B Go to the Grammar Hub on page 132.

C SPEAK Work in pairs. Tell your partner:

- three things you *had to* / *needed to* do yesterday. Explain why.
- three things you *didn't have to* / *didn't need to* do yesterday. Explain why.

SPEAKING HUB

A Think of one or two new activities that you have tried. Use the list to help you or your own ideas.

get a pet
plant flowers or grow a plant
make a birthday present instead of buying one
try a new form of exercise
take language classes
make a photo album
learn a new board game

B PLAN Think about:

- how and why you did it.
- what was easy/difficult about it.
- the things you had to / needed to do.
- the things you didn't have to / didn't need to do.
- why you stopped/continued doing it.

C SPEAK Work in pairs. Tell your partner about the new activity you tried. Then listen to your partner and ask him/her questions about the activity.

- Talk about hobbies and free time activities
- Discuss trying new things

Café Hub

6.3 You got served

F – express your opinion P – intonation for expressing opinions

COMPREHENSION

A Work in pairs. Tell your partner how you prepare for exercising or playing sports. What do you do before you start?

B 00:00–00:32 Watch the first part of the video. Are any of the things you discussed in Exercise A in the video? Who do you think will win the game?

C 00:33–03:15 Watch the second part of the video. Check (✓) *Gaby* or *Sam* or both.

Gaby	Sam	
✓		thinks it's unusual to put butter on toast.
	✓	thinks British breakfast is more than buttered toast and milky tea.
✓		thinks Spanish food is better than English food.
	✓	thinks tortilla is boring.
✓	✓	changes their mind at the end.

FUNCTIONAL LANGUAGE

Expressing your opinion

A Complete the phrases in the table. Then watch the video again and check your answers.

Give an opinion	I [1] think that's very strange.
	[2] Don't you think that's horrible?
	I [3] reckon British food is better than ever these days.
	In my [4] opinion, British food is still really bad.
	If you ask [5] me, it's your opinion that's really bad.
	Spanish food is so much better. Don't [6] you agree?
	Do you know [7] what I think? Tortilla is a bit boring.
Give examples to support an opinion	[8] For instance, …
	To give you an example, …
Agree with an opinion	I agree.
	You are probably [9] right.
	Absolutely!
Disagree with an opinion	I disagree.
	I [10] really don't think that's true.
	Nonsense.
	To be brutally [11] honest, no!

B Work in groups. Decide which are the three countries with the best food in the world.

MILLY

SAM

NEENA

ZAC

GABY

USEFUL PHRASES

A Match the useful phrases (1–5) with the phrases that come before or after them (a–e). Then watch the video and check your answers.

1 Game, set and match – Sam!
2 Not hugely.
3 Wake up! Say something!
4 I didn't realize you were so passionate about food.
5 British food is average!

a So you don't like Spanish food?
b Sam, are you OK?
c I'm sorry! I got a bit angry.
d I was right!
e Nonsense!

B How do you say these useful phrases in your language?

PRONUNCIATION

Intonation for expressing opinions

6.8 **A** Listen and repeat the extracts from the video. Copy the stress and intonation.

A: In my opinion, British food is still really bad.
B: Well, if you ask me, it's your opinion that's really bad.
A: Spanish food is so much better – don't you agree?
B: To be brutally honest, no!
A: Do you want to know what I think? I think tortilla is a bit boring.
B: Boring!

B Work in pairs. Make similar conversations. Change the information.

SPEAKING

A Complete the statements with opinion phrases from Functional Language Exercise A.

… eat before exercising.

If you ask me, you shouldn't eat for one hour before exercising.

… do an hour of aerobic exercise every day.

… tennis is more exciting to watch than soccer.

… the gym is boring.

… female athletes should be paid the same as men.

… running is the best sport in the world.

… boxing is too violent.

… eSports are more exciting than real sports.

B **DISCUSS** Work in pairs. Take turns reading out your statements from Exercise A and agree or disagree with your partner's statements.

Express your opinion

➤ Turn to page 161 to learn how to write an article for a magazine.

6.3 You got served

LEAD-IN

Put students into two teams and give them a time limit of two minutes. They have to come up with a list of as many types of exercises and/or sports as they can. Check answers at the end. The team with the longest (and most accurate) list wins. Concept check any words that are new to the opposing team.

COMPREHENSION

A Elicit a couple of examples from the class and then put students into pairs to discuss the questions. Share ideas as a whole class and write students' ideas and any new or requested vocabulary on the board.

B ▸ 00:00-00:32 Tell students they're going to watch another episode of the video series. Ask students to listen and write down if any of their ideas from Exercise A were mentioned. They can use the list you wrote on the board to support them. They also need to think about who they think will win the game, and why. Check answers as a whole class.

C ▸ 00:33-03:15 Tell students to watch the rest of the episode and to apply a check mark next to the sentences that apply to Sam, Gaby or both of them.

FUNCTIONAL LANGUAGE

A ▸ Tell students to try to complete the phrases from the episode from memory. Tell them not to worry if they can't remember or have no idea, as they're going to watch it again. Monitor to check that all students have at least read all the phrases and check the meaning of *brutally* and *nonsense*. Play the video again for students to check their answers.

Make sure students understand that *nonsense* is very direct and informal and not to be used in formal situations or with people they don't know very well! Also point out that *reckon* is an informal word for *think*.

B Put students into groups to discuss which three countries have the best food in the world. Give students a couple of minutes to prepare their ideas before they speak and tell them to think about using some of the phrases from Exercise A. You could also ask them to try and choose one controversial food to elicit phrases of disagreement!

USEFUL PHRASES

A ▸ Tell students to match the useful phrases from the episode with the phrases that came before or after them. Play the video again for students to check. Check that students understand the phrases and how they should be used by referring to context in the video.

B Tell students to think about how they would say the useful phrases in their language. Ask if they use the same tennis reference for number 1. If not, do they use a reference from a different sport? Ask students if they use any other sporting phrases in everyday language.

PRONUNCIATION

A (6.8) Play the extracts from the video for students to listen and repeat. Tell students to listen carefully to the intonation and how some words are strongly stressed and to copy this. Ask students if they emphasize words with stress or show how they feel with intonation in the same way in their language.

B Write *In my opinion, British food is still really bad* on the board. Underline *my*, *British food* and *bad* and elicit words from the students that could be used to replace them in the sentence ensuring that it still makes sense. Put students into pairs to make conversations using the structure of the conversation from Exercise A but inserting different information. Monitor as students write their conversations and help them with ideas if they are struggling. Listen for appropriate stress and intonation when students practice their conversations and model if necessary. Choose one or two confident pairs to perform to the class.

SPEAKING

A Tell students to look at the statements and to complete them with an opinion phrase from *Functional Language* Exercise A. Point out the example and elicit which column it comes from in *Functional Language* Exercise A.

B Put students into pairs. Tell students to read their opinions and to agree or disagree with their partner. Encourage students to support their opinions with examples. If there is time, get students to swap partners and repeat the task. Monitor while students speak, writing down some good language to highlight and some errors for them to correct.

VIDEO SCRIPT

G = Gaby S = Sam

G: I'm hungry.
S: Really?
G: I haven't eaten anything.
S: I have to eat breakfast before a game of tennis in the morning. You should eat something.
G: I know, I just don't like the food you have for breakfast in England.
S: What? It's great.
G: You put butter on toast! I think that's very strange.
S: Strange? I really don't think that's true.
G: And you put milk … in your tea! Don't you think that's horrible!
S: No! Breakfast isn't just buttered toast and milky tea! People always say that British food isn't very good, but that's not true anymore! For instance, the food in my café isn't horrible, is it?
G: No, it's good – but what I mean is that in general British food is … average …
S: Nonsense! I reckon British food is better than ever these days.
G: In my opinion, British food is still really bad.
S: Well, if you ask me, it's your opinion that's really bad.
G: Ha! Spanish food is so much better, don't you agree?
S: To be brutally honest, no!
G: So you don't like Spanish food?
S: Not hugely.
G: Not even tortilla?
S: Do you know what I think? I think tortilla is a bit boring.
G: BORING!
S: It's just egg and potato.
G: AND … ONIONS! Sam! Are you ok? Sam? Sam! Wake up! Say something!
S: I didn't realize you were so passionate about food …
G: I'm sorry! I got a bit angry.
S: It's OK. I'm sorry, too. Your tortilla is really good.
G: Thanks … and you … are probably right. British food is good these days. What?
S: Haha, you said it – British food is good! I was right! Game, set and match – Sam! Yes.
G: OK. My serve.

6 Writing

Write an article for a magazine

introductory clauses

A Work in pairs. Read the magazine ad. Then look at the free time activities in the box. Which three do you think would be good subjects for an article? Why?

Share your stories with Life & *Style*.

In our Free time section, we're going to publish a new series of reader's articles, called *'Why everyone should ...!'*

Send us your short articles about ideas for free time activities and hobbies – things that you think everyone should try doing at least once in their lifetime.

arts and crafts · playing soccer · skydiving · stamp collecting · stargazing (astronomy) · team video gaming

B Read *Why everyone should ... go stargazing!*. Put the sentences (a–f) in the order they are mentioned in the article (1–6).

- **a** It is a good way to meet people. 4
- **b** It is a simple hobby to start. 1
- **c** Stargazing events at night are enjoyable. 6
- **d** Cellular digital technology is useful. 2
- **e** There is a place to go to use good equipment. 3
- **f** You can join a club. 5

Why everyone should ... go stargazing!

Wow! That's all I can say as I look at the rings of Saturn, or see a shadow pass across the sun. I'll never regret taking up stargazing.

Besides the wonder of discovering the universe, the great thing about stargazing is that it is an easy hobby to take up. You only have to look up into the sky at night and you've already become a stargazer. The cool thing is that there are many cell phone apps to help you when you start, telling you exactly what you are looking at. Ex D

It is also easy to visit your local observatory. The wonderful thing about going there is that you can use powerful telescopes to see deep into the universe. You'll see the mountains of Mars, the moons of Jupiter and the stardust of the Milky Way.

A nice thing about stargazing is that it is actually very sociable. There are local societies all over the country, and enthusiasts frequently meet up for 'star parties'. They are like having a picnic at night and are a lot of fun. One thing to remember is that you should bring hot chocolate rather than juice – it's important to keep warm!

Everyone wants to put a little 'wow!' into their lives, and stargazing is a surprisingly simple, inexpensive and enjoyable way to do that. There's so much to discover in the universe, so isn't it time to start exploring?

C Read the tips on writing articles. Then look at the article again. Which tips did the writer follow? Give examples.

Top tips for writing a magazine article

1. In the introduction, clearly give the topic, and grab the reader's attention and interest.
2. Use a more relaxed and personal style than in a newspaper report.
3. Show your passion for the subject.
4. Give each paragraph a clear topic.
5. Use direct quotes from interviews.
6. Use humor.
7. In the conclusion, summarize the key points in the article.
8. Finish with a memorable sentence, giving the reader something to think about.

D Look at the box. Find and underline the introductory clauses in the highlighted sentences in the article.

Introductory clauses

We can begin a sentence with an introductory clause that provides, and draws attention to, the topic for the rest of the sentence.

E Work in pairs. Complete the sentences with information about a hobby, sport or activity that you do. Then compare your answers with a partner.

1. One good thing about __________ is that __________
2. Something that I like about __________ is that __________
3. A good reason to __________ is that __________
4. One problem with __________ is that __________
5. One thing to remember is that __________

WRITING

A PREPARE You are going to write a short magazine article. Choose a hobby, sport or free time activity as the subject of your article. Why do you think everyone should try it?

B PLAN Write notes for your article. Read the tips in Exercise C again to help.

C WRITE Write an article (150–200 words).

D REVIEW Work in groups. Read the other students' articles. Which activities would you choose to do? Why?

WRITING 161

1 ✓ Topic: *Stargazing;* Grab attention: *Wow! That's all I can say ...*

2 ✓ *I'll never regret ...; The cool thing is that ...; ... isn't it time to start exploring?*

3 ✓ *I'll never regret ...; ... the great thing about ...; ... a lot of fun.*

4 ✓ *... it is an easy hobby to take up; It is also easy to visit your local observatory; ... it is actually very sociable.*

5 ✗

6 ✓ *... you should bring hot chocolate rather than juice ...!*

7 ✓ *Stargazing is a surprisingly simple, inexpensive and enjoyable way to do that.*

8 ✓ *There's so much to discover in the universe, so isn't it time to start exploring?*

Refer students to this letter as a model for the writing task.

WRITING

With books closed, ask students to think of a magazine that they read or have read. Tell students to tell their partner about it.

A Tell students to look at the magazine ad. Point out the pictures and make sure students understand what the activities are. Check the meaning of *stargazing*. Tell students to discuss and choose three free-time activities which would be good subjects for a magazine article.

B Tell students to read the article and to put the sentences in the order they're mentioned.

C Point out the tips in the box for writing a magazine article. Tell students to read the article again and to think about which tips the writer followed and to find examples to back up their answers. Do the first one together as a whole class.

D Point out the information in the box about introductory clauses. Tell students to look at the highlighted phrases in the article and to underline the introductory clause in each.

E Tell students to complete the sentences with information about a hobby, sport or activity that they do.

WRITING TASK

A Tell students to think about a hobby, sport or free time activity that they think everyone should try and why.

B Tell students to look back at the *Top tips for writing a magazine article* in Exercise C above and to write notes about the content and organization of their article.

C Tell students to use their notes to write the article. Remind students to use some introductory clauses as well as following the top tips.

D Put students into groups and tell them to read each other's articles. Encourage students to ask each other further questions.

Unit 6 Review

GRAMMAR

A Complete the conversation between a soccer coach and some new players with the correct modals of obligation.

Coach: The rules say so. You [1] must not touch the ball with your hands. It isn't allowed.

Player 1: But what about the goalkeeper? He sometimes [2] has to use his hand to stop a shot. I've seen it on TV.

Coach: OK, OK! Everyone except the goalkeeper [3] must / has to follow that rule. And you all [4] must / have to warm up before a game. I insist on that. If you don't warm up, you don't play.

Player 2: I can't get here until 6 pm.

Coach: That's a little late, the game starts at 6:15 pm. You [5] should start warming up at 5:45, by 6 pm at the latest. You bike here, don't you? If so, you [6] don't have to do a big warm-up. But you [7] have to / must be here by six, OK?

B Complete the TV interview with the present perfect or present progressive form of the verbs in parentheses.

Reporter: Hi, everyone. I'm with champion surfer Sally Gowen. Sally, [1] have you been surfing (*surf*) here all day?

Surfer: Hi, Maisie. Yes, I sure have. The water [2] has been (*be*) excellent all day. I love it here. I [3] have / 've been coming (*come*) here a lot recently.

Reporter: What [4] have you been practicing (*practice*) today? Some new moves?

Surfer: No, no. Nothing too special. OK, I'm going back on the surf now.

Reporter: Oh, I [5] haven't finished (*finish*) yet. Just one more … Sally? Sally! Oh, she [6] has / 's gone (*go*).

C Complete the text with *had to, didn't have to, needed to* or *didn't need to*. Sometimes more than one answer is possible.

I remember my first year at college well. It was so different from being at high school. Finally, we [1] didn't have to wear a uniform every day, and I [2] didn't need to / didn't have to tell my parents where I was all the time. I enjoyed that new freedom, and I [3] had to grow up quickly, too. I [4] needed to / had to take more responsibility for everyday things. I was lucky though because I lived in a student residence. I [5] didn't have to live there, but I chose to because I wanted to meet other people easily. It was a good decision. We [6] had to follow a few rules, but having a housekeeper was great. I mean, we still [7] had to wash the dishes and keep things clean, but a housekeeper every week was good.

VOCABULARY

A Choose the best adjectives to complete the sentences.

1 Don't delay any more. Make your mind up. It's time to be ***decisive*** / *aggressive*.
2 Stop yelling! You're being very *effective* / ***aggressive***.
3 He's very *creative* / ***competitive***. He hates losing.
4 eSports are already ***massive*** / *expensive*. They'll definitely be in the Olympics soon.
5 You won 7–2? That's ***impressive*** / *aggressive*!
6 Running with the ball is not very ***effective*** / *competitive*. It's better to pass it quickly.

B Complete the text about sports with the missing words.

I loved my time as a soccer player. I only played for one club in the national [1] league, but what a club! I had great [2] coaches who really improved my game, and our [3] fans were amazing, always singing and cheering us on. It was a great feeling walking into the [4] stadium, to hear that noise at the beginning of the game. And, of course, I played for the national team at three World Cup [5] tournaments, and the 2018 one was the highlight of my career. How can anything be better than winning the [6] final and lifting the [7] trophy, knowing you are the [8] champions of the world? I bet all the [9] spectators watching in the stadium and on TV were jealous! I think I can safely say I was a [10] top player. After all, I won the 'Player of the Year' award twice! I certainly miss those days. I don't get the same feeling from running a restaurant.

C Complete the radio vox-pop with the words in the box.

am been collect get joined lost took

Yes, I [1] collect stamps. I've [2] been into stamp collecting for a long time. I [3] took it up when I was just a kid. Some people think it is boring, but I have never [4] lost interest in it, and I'm 45 now. Of course, I [5] am a member of my local stamp collecting society. I [6] joined that ten years ago. The weekly meetings [7] get me out of the house.

FUNCTIONAL LANGUAGE

Complete the TV discussion with the correct phrases to express opinions.

Mario: Let's ask our panel of experts. You first, Tim, what do you think?

Tim: Well, in my [1] opinion, they should be banned.

Asif: If you [2] ask me, we shouldn't ban them.

Ana: As far as I'm [3] concerned, a ban is the answer.

Sue: I think we should do more research. Don't you [4] agree?

Tim: To be [5] honest, I disagree completely. We already know enough. To [6] give you an example, there were five different stories about them in the newspapers last week.

Lunch in Marrakesh: Rainbow salad bowl, falafel and mint tea.

Food (n) the things that people or animals eat.
Synonyms: meal, nourishment

The quote for this unit highlights the importance of food and suggests that as long as this basic need is met any other concerns are secondary.

Franz Kafka (1883–1924) was a German-speaking Jewish writer. His novels and short stories are concerned with the themes of social alienation, isolation and the harmful effects of bureaucracy on society.

OBJECTIVES

- talk about eating out
- make speculations and deductions about food
- compare different types of food
- compare a range of solutions and choose the best one
- make suggestions
- write a reply in an online discussion forum

Work with a partner. Discuss the questions.

1 Look at the photo. How many types of food can you name?
2 Read the quote. What do you think it means?
3 Do you think it is important to eat with your family or friends? Why/Why not?

FOOD 73

OBJECTIVES

Read the unit objectives to the class.

UNIT OPENER QUESTIONS

With books closed, put students into pairs. Ask what they think the best way to make a new friend or show what friendship is. Elicit an example, then tell students to think of more ideas with their partner. Elicit any new or interesting vocabulary on the board.

1 Tell students to open their books and look at the photo. Put students into pairs and give them two minutes to name as many foods as they can in the photo. Elicit and write any new vocabulary on the board at the end of the activity.

2 Tell students to read the quote. Put students into pairs to discuss what they think it means. Elicit ideas together as a whole class.

3 Ask students to discuss whether they think it is important to eat with their family or friends and why or why not. Ask them if they eat together with their family. You could also ask if they think this tradition varies at different ages, in different countries, etc. Another idea would be to ask them to talk about an occasion when they shared a special meal with their friends and/or family.

WORKSHEETS

Lesson 7.1 Eating out

Grammar: Modals of speculation and deduction (W25)

Vocabulary: Phrasal verbs (W26)

Lesson 7.2 Food fads

Grammar: Comparatives and superlatives; *the …, the …* (W27)

Vocabulary: Waste (W28)

7.1 Eating out

- Talk about eating out
- Make speculations and deductions about food

P diphthongs; word stress with modals
G modals of speculation and deduction
V phrasal verbs; adjectives to describe food
S hidden contrasts

READING

A SPEAK Work in groups and discuss the questions.

1 Do you usually eat out in a restaurant? Why/Why not?
2 Do you usually leave a tip to thank the waiter for good service?

B READ FOR MAIN IDEA Read *Super supper clubs*. What are supper clubs? Why do many customers prefer supper clubs to traditional restaurants?

C Complete the notes on the differences between supper clubs and traditional restaurants. Use the strategies in the box to help you.

Paragraph	Supper clubs	Traditional restaurants
Choosing a dish (2)	the chef chooses	you choose from a menu
Where customers sit (2)	together with other customers	quietly at separate tables
Choosing when to go (2)	join a waiting list; wait for an invitation	show up when you're feeling hungry
What to cook (4)	the chef has control	the chef cooks the same food again and again
The food (4)	amazing, but they might not like it	boring
The experience (5)	for all the senses; having fun	just food

Hidden contrasts

In articles about new or unusual things, writers frequently use words like *instead*, *just* and *even* to show contrasts with more normal things. These contrasts are usually hidden, so it's difficult to notice them. But they help you to understand the points that the writer wants to make.

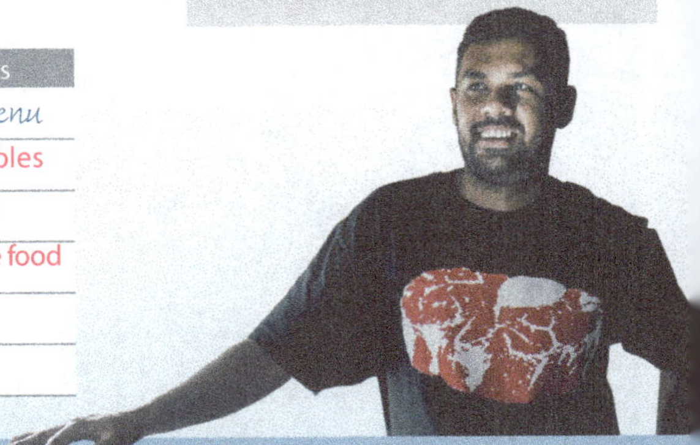

SUPER SUPPER CLUBS

1 Anti-restaurants. Underground restaurants. Pop-up restaurants. Guestaurants. Whatever you call them, there's no doubt that supper clubs are one of the hottest trends in eating out today.

2 The idea is simple: instead of going to a traditional restaurant, you eat in the chef's home. (Ex B) Instead of choosing a dish from a menu, you eat what the chef gives you. And instead of sitting quietly at separate tables, (Ex C) all the customers eat together, (Ex C) talking and making friends. But if that sounds like your perfect evening, there's some bad news. You can't just show up when you're feeling hungry; (Ex C) you'll need to join a waiting list and then wait for an invitation from the chef. (Ex C)

3 The modern idea of supper clubs took off in Cuba in the 1990s. Cuba now has a huge amount of supper clubs, or *paladares*. Most of them started off as simply a room in the chef's home. They're popular with tourists, as well as people who want a simple home-cooked meal at a fair price. (Ex B) One of Cuba's best *paladares* is Castas y Tal, on the 11th floor of a large apartment building in central Havana. The main restaurant area has only eight seats, but there are wonderful views of the city below.

4 For chefs, supper clubs clearly seem like a great idea. They're fairly cheap and easy to set up because the chef can do everything at home. Instead of having to cook the same food again and again, (Ex C) supper clubs give chefs control (Ex C) over what to cook. Customers don't mind giving up some choice because they know they'll eat amazing food that they've never eaten before. (Ex B) They might not like it, but at least it won't be boring. (Ex C)

5 At the St. Jude Project in Mumbai, India, Chef Gresham Fernandes tries out ideas while he's cooking … and even while he's serving up the meal! He cooks in front of the guests, explaining what he's doing as he works.

6 So next time you're feeling adventurous, why not visit a supper club? It's sure to be an experience you won't forget!

7.1 Eating out

LEAD-IN

With books closed, write on the board: *food, price, service, atmosphere, location*. Tell students that these are things people think about when choosing or rating a restaurant. Ask students if they can add any other categories and add them to the list. Put students into pairs to rank them in order of which is the most important to them in a restaurant. Get feedback and encourage students to expand on and explain their answers.

READING

A Check that students understand *leave a tip* by asking them if it is normal practice to do this in their country and who you might leave a tip for apart from a waiter. Tell them to open their books and to discuss the questions in small groups. Encourage students to ask follow-up questions. If your students are from different countries, explore different attitudes toward tipping here.

B Tell students to look at the pictures and elicit what they think about the places shown. Tell them they're going to read an article about supper clubs. Ask if any students have any idea what a supper club is. Check understanding of *supper* but point out that it is not very common in modern usage. Tell students to read the questions and to predict the answers based on what they can see in the pictures. Students can then read the article to check their answers.

Suggested answer: *They're restaurants in the chef's home. Many customers prefer supper clubs because they're a fair price, a simple home-cooked meal, the experience isn't boring and will be one they won't forget.*

C Point out the information in the box about hidden contrasts and ask students if they noticed the words *instead, just* and *even* in the text. Tell students to read the article again and to complete the table, paying special attention to how the writer uses those words to contrast supper clubs with traditional restaurants.

TEACHING IDEA by David Seymour and Maria Popova

Topic: Food survey

Use this activity to extend the topic.

I'm going to dictate one question to each person. Mingle and ask all the other students your question. Write notes about their answers. (Dictate each question quickly, but go through them two or three times so that students get another chance to write down their question. After the survey, elicit the results and write them on the board.)

How much tea or coffee do you drink every day?

Do you eat healthy food?

Have you ever tried Indian/Japanese/Greek food?

How often do you eat out?

What is your biggest meal of the day?

Do you like hamburgers and fries?

How much do you spend on food every week?

Do you prefer pizza or pasta?

What do you eat for breakfast?

Where do you buy your food?

Do you eat free-range eggs?

Do you eat a lot of chocolate?

TEACHING IDEA by David Seymour and Maria Popova

Topic: Restaurants

Use this activity to extend the topic.

Work in small groups. I'll give each group a different type of restaurant. Create a menu and include appetizers, main courses, side dishes, desserts and drinks. Don't forget the prices.

a steak house, a vegetarian café, an expensive French eatery, a highway service station restaurant, a seafood restaurant

In pairs, describe your last visit to a restaurant in detail.

- when and where
- the food and drink
- who you were with
- the décor
- the waiter
- the music
- what you talked about
- the other people there

If anyone has experience of working in a restaurant, answer questions about the job from the class.

METHODOLOGY HUB by Jim Scrivener

Lead-in Preparation

This may be to help raise motivation or interest (e.g. discussion of a picture related to the topic), or maybe to focus on language items (e.g. items of vocabulary) that might be useful in the activity.

Typical lead-ins are:

- Show / draw a picture connected to the topic. Ask questions.
- Write up / read aloud a sentence stating a viewpoint. Elicit reactions.
- Tell a short personal anecdote related to the subject.
- Ask students if they have ever been/seen/done, etc.
- Hand out a short text on the topic. Students read the text and comment.
- Play 'devil's advocate' and make a strong/controversial statement (e.g. *I think relaxing is better than exercise for your health*) that students will be motivated to challenge / argue about.
- Write a key word (maybe the topic name) in the center of a word-cloud on the board and elicit vocabulary from students which is added to the board.

7.1 Eating out

PRONUNCIATION

7.1 **A** Tell students to look at the underlined words in the *Super supper clubs* article and to match them with the correct pronunciation. If students are unfamiliar with phonemic script, point out that many of the symbols for consonant sounds are the same as the letters. When students have done this, play the audio for students to listen and check.

B Tell students that all the words contain diphthongs. Demonstrate the diphthong sound in the first word. Tell students to look at the words and to complete the rules. In feedback, highlight and practice pronunciation of all seven diphthongs again.

C Put students into pairs and tell them to make sentences using at least three of the words from Exercise A in each. Give an example, e.g. *I might wait at home*. Monitor to check that students are using the words appropriately. When all pairs have a few sentences, tell them to practice saying them. Monitor to check they're pronouncing the diphthong sounds correctly. You could then change partners and tell students to model and practice their sentences with their new partner.

VOCABULARY

A Tell students to look at the sentences, then to look at the article again and to find sentences with the same meaning. Tell them to replace the underlined words with the words used in the article.

B Elicit that all the answers to Exercise A were phrasal verbs. Tell students to read the rules and to complete the examples with some of the phrasal verbs from Exercise A. Make sure students realize that it's not possible to figure out the meaning of most phrasal verbs just from looking at the verb and the particle.

C Direct students to the **Vocabulary Hub** (TB121) for further practice of phrasal verbs.

D Tell students to cover the phrasal verbs in Exercise A and to complete the phrasal verbs in the questions. Let students uncover Exercise A to check. Ask students to discuss the questions in pairs. Encourage students to ask each other follow-up questions and to expand on their answers. Use the **Vocabulary Worksheet** on W26 for extra practice.

SPEAKING

A Put students into pairs and tell them that they're going to plan their own supper club. Tell them to think about the points and to write notes to help them present their ideas later. Monitor to help with language input. Check that students are just writing notes and not scripting every word that they're going to say.

B Put students into larger groups and ask them to take presenting their supper clubs. Encourage students to ask each other questions after each presentation.

C Ask each group to decide which supper club they would most like to attend and why. Ask one student from each group to explain to the class which supper club was the favorite and why. Finish with some feedback on students' use of language during their presentations and discussions.

Extra activity
You can extend the activity by making groups write a short menu or ad for their supper clubs. As well as listening to presentations, students can walk around and read the menus or ads before voting on their favorite supper club.

METHODOLOGY HUB by Jim Scrivener

Phrasal verbs

A phrasal verb expresses a complete meaning. The main verb on its own would not express the whole meaning. The meaning will usually not be guessable from the sum of its parts. For example, a learner might understand the separate meanings of gave and up – but still not be able to figure out the meaning of 'He gave up his job'.

Phrasal verbs are normal everyday language. Generally speaking, they are not slang, colloquial or lazy English.

In many cases, an equivalent single-word verb may sound over-formal when compared to the normal phrasal verb.

They put out the fire.

They extinguished the fire.

Watch out for these problems:

Students choose the wrong participle: *I turned ~~out~~ down his invitation.*

Students put a pronoun after a particle: *They looked ~~up it~~ it up in the library.*

Students use a transitive verb without an object: *We were excited about the party, but they decided to ~~put off~~ put it off till next week.*

TEACHING IDEA by David Seymour and Maria Popova

Call my bluff

Make small groups. Hand out four or five sentences with a phrasal verb (*The milk has gone bad.*) to each group and ask them to keep them secret from other groups. For each phrasal verb, the groups should prepare three definitions – two of which are untrue and one which is true ('gone bad' = (1) been spilled, (2) become bad, (3) been stolen). When students are ready, groups read out their sentences and each of their definitions. Students vote for which one they think is the correct definition / the group wins one point for every student who votes for one of the wrong definitions.

TEACHING IDEA by David Seymour and Maria Popova

Verb chain

Work in groups of four to six. Take turns giving a phrasal verb, alternately changing the particle and the verb, e.g. A – *Take off.* B – *Take up.* C – *Let up.* D – *Let down.* E – *Put down.* F – *Put on.*

If you can't think of one, you are out of the game. If you doubt another student's phrasal verb, challenge him/her to define it and give an example. If the student can't, he/she is out of the game. (Don't let students write during the activity, but write a note of the most useful phrasal verbs to review at the end.)

PRONUNCIATION
Diphthongs

7.1 **A** Look at the underlined words in *Super supper clubs*. Match the words with their correct pronunciation (1–8). Then listen and check your answers.

1 weɪt ___wait___
2 ju ___you___
3 dʒɔɪn ___join___
4 maɪt ___might___
5 hoʊm ___home___
6 daʊt ___doubt___
7 nuwz ___news___

B WORK IT OUT The words in Exercise A all contain diphthongs. Choose the best word or phrase to complete the rules.

Diphthongs

1 Diphthongs are long *vowel* / *consonant* sounds made from *two* / *three* short sounds.
2 We pronounce diphthongs by moving quickly from one sound to the next / saying the two sounds separately.
3 American English has *seven* / *ten* diphthongs: /eɪ/, /aɪ/, /oʊ/, /ɔɪ/, /aʊ/, /ju/, and /uw/.

C SPEAK Work in pairs. Make sentences using at least three of the words from Exercises A and B. Then practice saying your sentences.

VOCABULARY
Phrasal verbs

A Look at *Super supper clubs* again. Find sentences that have the same meaning as the ones below. Which words are used instead of the underlined words?

1 You can't just arrive without making a reservation (show up) when you're feeling hungry.
2 The modern idea of supper clubs really became popular (took off) in Cuba in the 1990s.
3 Most of them began their existence (started off) as simply a room in the chef's home.
4 They're fairly cheap and easy to get ready to start (set up).
5 Customers don't mind losing (giving up) some choice.
6 Chef Gresham Fernandes experiments with (tries out) ideas while he's cooking … and even while he's putting the food on plates (serving up).

B WORK IT OUT Read the rules about phrasal verbs. Then complete the examples with phrasal verbs from Exercise A.

Phrasal verbs

1 Phrasal verbs are usually made of two parts: a verb (e.g. *work*, *try*) and a particle (e.g. *out*, *up*).
2 Sometimes it's possible to guess the meaning from the two words, but usually you just need to learn the meaning of the whole phrasal verb:
- *You can't just* [a] ___show___ ___up___ *at their house! Always call first to check it's OK.*

3 Some phrasal verbs can have an object. When the object is short (e.g. a pronoun or one or two words), it usually comes in the middle:
- *I have lots of ideas and I like to* [b] ___try___ *them* ___out___ *while I'm cooking.*

But when the object is a longer phrase, it usually comes at the end:
- *I like to* [c] ___try___ ___out___ *lots of new ideas while I'm cooking.*

C Go to the **Vocabulary Hub** on **page 145**.

D SPEAK Complete the questions with the correct phrasal verbs. Then work in pairs and ask and answer the questions.

1 Do you think supper clubs will take ___off___ in your country?
2 Do you ever try ___out___ new meals while you're cooking or do you always plan carefully before you start?
3 Have your cooking skills ever let you ___down___? What went wrong?

SPEAKING

A Work in pairs. You are going to plan your own supper club. Write notes about:

- name
- location
- type of food
- cost
- number of guests
- what makes your supper club unique

B PRESENT Work in groups. Take turns presenting your supper club to the group.

C REFLECT Decide which supper club you would like to attend and why.

VOCABULARY
Adjectives to describe food

A Work in groups. Look at the pictures and discuss the questions.

1 Where do you think each dish is from?
2 What do you think it contains?

B Go to the Vocabulary Hub on page 145.

C Many food adjectives end in *-y* (e.g. *spicy*). Complete the sentences with the missing adjectives. Use the words in bold to help you.

1 I didn't think this soup would **taste** very nice, but in fact it's really ___tasty___!
2 Honey is very ___sticky___. It **sticks** to the bread like glue!
3 I really love ___cheesy___ pizza, so I always ask for extra **cheese** on the top.
4 This ___creamy___ sauce is too rich for me. How much **cream** did you put into it?

D SPEAK Work in pairs. Think of some types of food and drinks that these adjectives might describe. Use the glossary to help you.

buttery chocolatey fatty fruity oily meaty milky nutty peppery runny salty watery

E SPEAK Work in pairs. Use adjectives to describe:

1 your favorite soft drink.
2 your favorite flavor of ice cream.
3 your perfect breakfast.
4 your least favorite types of food.

LISTENING

A SPEAK Work in pairs. If you are invited to eat dinner at somebody's house, do you bring:

- flowers
- a gift
- something to drink
- dessert
- nothing

B Complete the description with the words in the box.

course dessert ~~dinner party~~ dishes host appetizer surprise

A [1] ___dinner party___ is an event where one person (the [2] ___host___) invites a group of friends to eat a meal at his or her house. At a traditional dinner party, the host cooks the food: an [3] ___appetizer___ and a main [4] ___course___. But the guests usually bring something to drink, and perhaps also a [5] ___dessert___. In a pot luck dinner party, everybody (the host and guests) prepares one or two [6] ___dishes___. It's called pot luck because it's always a [7] ___surprise___: nobody knows what the others will bring.

7.2 **C** LISTEN FOR SPECIFIC INFORMATION Listen to a conversation at a pot luck dinner party. Match the people (1–5) with the dishes (a–e).

1 Vicky (the host)
2 Charlie
3 Tina
4 Felipe
5 Markus

a cheesy chicken pasta surprise
b cream of chicken soup
c spicy buffalo wings
d cheese and chilli salad
e chicken curry in a creamy sauce

Glossary

allergic (adj) affected by an allergy (a medical condition in which you become sick or your skin becomes covered with red marks as a reaction to something you eat, breathe or touch)
buffalo (n) a large African animal similar to a cow, with curved horns
dairy products (n) foods that are made from milk (e.g. cheese, butter, ice cream)
spicy (adj) food that has a strong hot flavor

VOCABULARY

A Tell students to look at the pictures and elicit their reaction to the dishes shown. Put students into groups to discuss the questions. Share answers as a whole class and write any useful food vocabulary on the board. If any students are from a country where one of the dishes is from, ask them to tell the class more about it.

Picture a:
1 *Thai chicken green curry from Thailand*
2 *It contains chicken, red chilli peppers, curry paste, cooking oil, coconut milk, Thai fish sauce, sugar, etc.*

Picture b:
1 *Chilli con carne from Texas*
2 *It contains minced beef, red kidney beans, chilli peppers, tomatoes, sweet corn, onions, etc; it's served here with rice, lettuce and tomatoes.*

Picture c:
1 *Olivieh potato salad from Iran*
2 *It contains potatoes, eggs, chicken, mayonnaise, lemon juice, oil; it's decorated with cherry tomatoes, carrot, egg and peas.*

B Direct students to the **Vocabulary Hub** (TB121) to focus on adjectives to describe food. Check the meaning of *savory* (not sweet). Point out that it is not a synonym of *salty*. Elicit examples of foods for each adjective to consolidate understanding (e.g. *bread is savory but not salty*).

C Elicit the noun *spice* and the adjective *spicy* and how by removing the *e* and adding a *y* we make the adjective from the noun. Tell students to look at the sentences and fill in the blanks with an adjective formed from the words in bold.

D Write *buttery* on the board and elicit examples from the class of foods that are *buttery*. Put students into pairs to think of more examples of food that could be described with the other adjectives in the box.

Suggested answers:
buttery: cookies, pastry
chocolatey: cakes, cookies
fatty: meat, fries
fruity: tea, ice cream
oily: fish, salad
meaty: soup, pasta sauce
milky: coffee, white chocolate
nutty: cookies, chocolate bars
peppery: soup, omelettes
runny: soft cheese, eggs
salty: olives, chips
watery: soup, pasta sauce

E Put students into pairs to describe the different items. To make this more engaging, tell them not to tell their partner what it is they are describing. Students have to listen to their partner's description and guess what it is.

LISTENING

A Put them into pairs to discuss the question.

B Tell students they're going to read about an unusual type of dinner party. Tell them to read the description and to fill in the blanks with the words from the box.

7.2 **C** Tell them first to listen and to match the people with the dishes they bring.

GRAMMAR HUB

7.1 Modals of speculation and deduction

- We use *could*, *might* or *may* when we think something is possible, but we are not sure.
  This dish is very hot – it could contain a lot of chilies.
  Carla might be allergic to nuts – don't add any walnuts.
  Paul may want sugar in his coffee.
- In the negative, we use *might not* and *may not* but NOT *could not*.
  This restaurant may/might not be very good.
  NOT ~~*This restaurant could not be very good.*~~
- We use *must* when we are sure something is true because we have strong evidence for our belief.
  This cake is burned – it must taste horrible!
- We use *can't* when we are sure something is not true because we have strong evidence for our belief.
  These cookies are white – they can't be chocolate chip cookies.
- We don't use *must* and *can't* for facts we are 100% sure about.

7.1 Modals of speculation and deduction

A Decide if the statements are true or false.

1 'Kitty may serve fruit salad for dessert tonight.'
Dessert will definitely be fruit salad. True / (False)

2 'I've been invited to three pot-luck dinners. They must be popular.'
Pot-luck dinners are popular. (True) / False

3 'This can't be tomato soup – it isn't red!'
It almost certainly isn't tomato soup. (True) / False

4 'Bitter chocolate could be good in a cake.'
The speaker really doesn't like bitter chocolate. True / (False)

5 'If you left the milk out all night, it could be sour.'
It's possible that the milk is sour. (True) / False

B Choose the correct option.

1 **A:** 'Are you going to order soup?'
B: 'No, I'm very hungry and it ***must not*** / (***might not***) be very filling.'

2 **A:** 'Lara said she wants chicken.'
B: 'But she doesn't eat meat. She (***can't***) / ***must not*** want chicken.'

3 **A:** 'What's 'scampi'?'
B: 'I don't know really. It (***could***) / ***can*** be some kind of fish.'

4 **A:** 'Dinner is at seven tonight.'
B: 'I ***could*** / (***may***) not get there in time because I have to work late.'

5 **A:** 'Look at that man! He's ordered three pizzas!'
B: 'He ***can*** / (***must***) really like pizza!'

6 **A:** 'I've ordered sushi for lunch.'
B: 'Hector (***might***) / ***could*** not eat that but we'll see.'

➤ Go back to page 77.

D Tell students to try to complete the table from what they remember. Play the audio again for students to check. (7.2)

E Put students into groups to discuss the questions. Encourage students to expand on their answers.

1 The host and two guests are either allergic to, or don't like the food that has been made or brought.

GRAMMAR

A Tell students to choose the correct meaning of each sentence.

B Tell students to look at the sentences in Exercise A to help them complete the rules.

C Direct students to the **Grammar Hub** (see TB76). Use the **Grammar Worksheet** on W25 for extra practice.

PRONUNCIATION

A–D Monitor as students complete the exercises and model pronunciation where necessary. (7.3; 7.4)

SPEAKING HUB

A Monitor to help as students write their descriptions.

B Put students into groups to follow the stages and monitor to help.

C Ask one or two students from each group to tell the class about their party.

AUDIO SCRIPT

7.2

Listening, Exercise C
V = Vicky   C = Charlie   T = Tina   M = Markus

V: Charlie! You're here at last!
Ex D Q1 **C:** Hi, Vicky. Sorry I'm a little late.
V: No problem. You're only … 20 minutes late. Welcome to pot luck night.
C: Thanks. Am I the last person here?
V: No, actually, there's only one other person so far. He arrived half an hour early!
Ex D Q1 **C:** Oh, that must be Felipe, right? He's always early.
V: True. But it was good because he helped me make my dish: a cheese and chilli salad.
Ex D Q3 **C:** Ah … I'm allergic to dairy products. Oh, well. Never mind.
V: Hmm. Wow … those look delicious, Charlie. What are they?
C: Spicy buffalo wings. They're a traditional dish from New York made with a hot sticky sauce.
V: Wow. That's … different.
Ex D Q2 **C:** Yes, that's what I thought. Uh … can I heat them up in the oven? They just need 15 minutes.
Ex D Q2 **V:** Sure, but you'll have to wait ten minutes. I'm heating up Felipe's dish right now.
C: OK, no problem.
V: Great. Let me take your dish. Go and join Felipe – he's waiting in the backyard.
C: OK, thanks.
V: Aha … Tina. Welcome to pot luck night!
T: Thanks. Is everyone else here already?
V: No, not yet. But Felipe's here, and Charlie.
T: Those look nice. What are they?
V: Buffalo wings. Charlie brought them. Hmm … I've never eaten buffalo meat before. I wonder what it tastes like.
T: Hang on … that can't be right. They can't be buffalo wings. Buffaloes don't have wings!
V: No, you're right. But they're definitely wings. They could be chicken or something like that.
T: Aha … yes. Isn't there a city called Buffalo in New York? The name must come from the city, not the animal.
V: Good thinking. Anyway, what have you brought?
T: It's my own recipe. It's called cheesy chicken pasta surprise.
V: Oh, right. What's the surprise?
Ex D Q2 **T:** Ah … you'll have to wait and see. Can I just heat it up in the oven?
V: Well, uh … you'll have to wait for Charlie's dish … and Felipe's dish. It's chicken curry in a creamy sauce.
T: Oh, yes, so that's what smells so good. I love hot, spicy food.
V: Great. So let me take your dish to the kitchen. Go and join the others out in the backyard.
V: Markus! Great to see you. Come on in.
M: Thanks. I'm so sorry I'm late … again! You must think I'm so disorganized!
V: No, don't worry. Most of the others have just arrived, too. So … what have you brought?
M: Cream of chicken soup. I hope that's OK.
V: Uh … yeah, I hope so, too. But I don't have any soup bowls, so it might be a little difficult. I suppose we could drink it from cups. Uh … do I need to heat it up?
M: No, don't worry. I heated it up before I left. That looks great. What is it?
V: It's Tina's cheesy chicken pasta surprise.
M: Ah. It smells great, but … what are those red things?
V: They look like they might be chilies.
Ex D Q4 **M:** Oh, I hope not! I hate spicy food.
V: Well, they might not be chilies. They may be red peppers or something.
M: No, they're definitely chilies. Oh, well – hopefully there are some other dishes that I can eat.
V: Uh … you may have a problem there. We also have Felipe's spicy chicken curry and Charlie's spicy chicken wings.
M: Oh, no! Well, at least I have my chicken soup. And it means there'll be more food for you.
Ex D Q5 **V:** Uh … not really. I don't like chicken.

7.2 **D** Listen again. Check (✓) the correct name(s).

	Vicky	Charlie	Felipe	Tina	Markus
1 Who arrived late?		✓		✓	✓
2 Whose dish needs to be heated up?		✓	✓	✓	
3 Who is allergic to dairy products?		✓			
4 Who doesn't like spicy food?					✓
5 Who doesn't like chicken?	✓				

E SPEAK Work in groups and discuss the questions.

1 What went wrong with the pot luck dinner party?

2 Does it matter if some things go wrong at a party like this?

GRAMMAR

Modals of speculation and deduction

A WORK IT OUT Choose the correct meaning for the sentences from the conversation at the pot luck dinner party.

1 They **can't be** buffalo wings. Buffaloes don't have wings!

a Maybe they aren't buffalo wings.

(b) I'm sure they aren't buffalo wings.

2 They **could be** chicken or something like that.

(a) It's possible that they're chicken.

b It was possible that they were chicken.

3 You **must think** I'm so disorganized!

(a) I'm sure you think this.

b It's necessary for you to think this.

4 Well, they **might not be** chilies.

a It isn't possible that they're chilies.

(b) Maybe they aren't chilies.

5 Uh … you **may have** a problem there.

(a) Maybe you have a problem.

b I'm sure you have a problem.

B Look again at the sentences in Exercise A. Complete the rules (1–4) with the words in the box.

Modals of speculation and deduction

can't could may may not might might not must

1 We use ___must___ when we are sure something is true.

2 We use ___may___, ___might___ or ___could___ when we think something is possibly true, but we are not sure.

3 We use ___may not___ or ___might not___ when we think something possibly isn't true, but we are not sure.

4 We use ___can't___ when we are sure something is not true.

C Go to the Grammar Hub on page 134.

PRONUNCIATION

Word stress with modals

7.3 **A** Listen to the sentences (1–4) from the conversation at the pot luck dinner party. Then match the sentences with the rules (a–d).

1 Oh, that must be Felipe, right?

2 Hang on … that can't be right.

3 The name must come from the city, not the animal.

4 They might not be chilies.

a We usually place extra stress on the word *not* or a negative modal verb. 2, 4

b Modal verb + *be*: We usually stress the modal verb, not *be*. 1, 2

c Modal verb + main verb: We usually stress both verbs about the same. 3

d When we're speaking quickly, we usually don't pronounce the *t* in *must*. 1, 3

7.4 **B** Look at the highlighted words in the sentences below and underline the stressed words. Then listen and check your answers.

1 You're such a great host. You must have a lot of dinner parties!

2 'What's wrong with the oven?' 'I don't know. It might not be turned on.'

3 I made a lot of soup because some people may want two or three bowls.

4 Oh, no! Felipe can't be here already! The party doesn't start for another 20 minutes!

7.4 **C** Listen again and repeat the sentences. Then work in pairs and practice saying the sentences. Listen and check your partner's pronunciation.

D SPEAK Work in pairs. Make deductions and speculations about the people at the dinner party. Think about these questions.

1 How do they know each other?

2 What is the surprise in Tina's cheesy chicken pasta surprise?

SPEAKING HUB

A You have been invited to a pot luck dinner party. Write a short description of the dish you would like to bring.

B SPEAK Work in groups. Choose one person to be the host and give him/her your description. In your groups, decide:

- who brought which dish.
- which dishes you want to try.

C REFLECT Tell the class about your pot luck dinner party. Which dishes were the most popular?

○ Talk about eating out

○ Make speculations and deductions about food

- Compare different types of food
- Compare a range of solutions and choose the best one

G – comparatives and superlatives; *the …, the …*   P – vowel + *w*   V – waste   S – identifying people's opinions

READING

A SPEAK Read the definition of *fad*. Then work in pairs and discuss the questions.

> **fad** – definition and synonyms
> NOUN Pronunciation /fæd/
> 1 something that is popular or fashionable for only a short time

1 Can you think of any current food fads? Which foods are fashionable now?
2 Are there any food fads connected with different ways of cooking? Or different ways of eating?
3 Which older food fads have gone out of fashion?

B READ FOR GIST Read *Food fads* quickly. What is the writer's opinion about superfoods?

a They're just a fad – they aren't really very good for you.
b Expensive superfoods are much healthier than cheaper food.
c You don't need to spend a lot of money to buy some superfoods.
d Most superfoods are actually bad for your health.

FOOD FADS

Hi again! This week, I've decided to look at one of the biggest food fads of the 21st century: superfoods. Let's try to sort the facts from the fiction!

Quinoa has a long history as a superfood: it was known to the ancient Incas as 'the mother of all grains' because it was so healthy. Even today it's recommended by NASA as the perfect food for long space flights. Like all whole grains, it can help your body fight a variety of diseases, and it contains lots of vitamins, minerals and fiber. It's also one of the best sources of protein, so it's perfect for vegetarians and vegans, too. Amazing!

Goji berries are another great source of plant-based protein. These sweet berries have been used in China for centuries as a way to protect against illness. They contain less sugar than other fruits, so they're one of the healthiest snacks around. Unfortunately, they can be dangerous for some people, so always check with your doctor before eating them.

Açaí berries are perhaps the most successful superfoods of all: not long ago, they were unknown outside of Brazil. Now, açaí products are big business. Why are they so popular? Well, some people believe these berries will help them to grow old more slowly … or even to live longer. Like goji berries, they're full of chemicals which seem to protect our hearts and our brains. Sounds good, right?

Chia seeds are known as the healthiest food on the planet. The name 'chia' comes from the ancient Mayan word for 'strength'. Out of all the foods in the world, chia seeds contain some of the most nutrients for the fewest calories. They're also one of the best sources of fiber, which is great for your digestive system. Even better, they make you feel full … so you'll eat fewer snacks!

7.2 Food fads

LEAD-IN

With books closed, write on the board *one year ago, five years ago* and *ten years ago*. Tell them to think of something that used to be very popular at that time but isn't any more. Elicit a couple of examples to get them started. Put students into pairs to compare ideas. Share ideas as a whole class to see how similar everyone's answers are.

READING

A Point out the definition of a *fad* and use students' answers from the *Lead-In* to check understanding. Put students into pairs to discuss the questions. Get feedback and write any useful language that comes up on the board.

Suggested answers:

1 *non-dairy milk, e.g. almond milk; salted caramel*
2 *raw diets*
3 *low-fat diets*

B Tell students they're going to read a blog post about food fads. Set a time limit and tell students to read the post and to choose which sentence best describes the writer's opinion. Point out the glossary but tell students they don't need to understand every word to do this task.

GRAMMAR HUB

7.2 Comparatives and superlatives; *the …, the …*

Comparatives and superlatives

	Comparative	Superlative
Short adjectives (one syllable)	adj + *-er* (+ *than*) cheap → cheap**er**	*the* + adj + *-est* cheap → **the** cheap**est**
Longer adjectives	*more* + adj (+ *than*) popular → **more** popular	*the most* + adj popular → **the most** popular
Irregular adjectives	good → **better** (+ *than*) bad → **worse** (+ *than*)	good → **the best** bad → **the worst**
Adverbs	*more* + adv (+ *than*) quickly → **more** quickly	*the most* + adv quickly → **the most** quickly
Irregular adverbs	badly → **worse** far → **farther**/**further** fast → fast**er** hard → hard**er** well → **better**	badly → **the worst** far → **the farthest** / **the furthest** fast → **the** fast**est** hard → **the** hard**est** well → **the best**
Countable nouns	many nutrients → **more** nutrients few nutrients → few**er** nutrients	many nutrients → **the most** nutrients few nutrients → **the** few**est** nutrients
Uncountable nouns	much protein → **more** protein little fiber → **less** fiber	much protein → **the most** protein little fiber → **the least** fiber

- We use comparative adjectives and adverbs to say how two or more things or actions are different.
- We use superlative adjectives and adverbs to say that something is the top or bottom of a group.
- For adjectives ending in *-e* or *-y* the rules differ a little.

  Your meal is larger than mine, but Harry's is the largest.
  Carrot soup is tastier than pea soup, but chicken soup is the tastiest of all.
- For adjectives which end with one vowel and one consonant, we double the final consonant before adding *-er* or *-est*.

  These melons are ***bigger*** *than those ones.*
- To make negative comparatives and superlatives, we use *less* instead of *more* and *the least* instead of *the most*.
- We never use *more* or *the most* together with *-er* or *-est*.

  I think juice is healthier than coffee. NOT ~~I think juice is more healthier than coffee.~~
- We only use *than* when it is followed by the thing we are comparing.

  This dish is good but this one is better. NOT ~~This dish is good but this one is better than.~~
  This dish is better than that dish.

the …, the …

the + comparative adjective + noun, *the* + comparative adjective + noun	**The fresher** the ingredients, **the better** the dish.
the + comparative adjective + clause, *the* + comparative adjective + clause	**The more tasty** it is, **the more satisfied** they will be.
the + comparative adverb + clause, *the* + comparative adverb + clause	**The faster** it boils, **the more quickly** it will be ready.
the + *more/less* + noun + clause, *the* + *more/less* + noun + clause	**The more recipes** you learn, **the more food** you can cook.
the + *more/less* + clause, *the* + *more/less* + clause	**The more I practiced**, **the less I needed** a cookbook.

- We use *the …, the* to show that two changes are closely connected. As one thing changes, the other thing changes too.
- Sometimes we use the very simplest form of this structure, using comparative adjectives only, and no verb.

  The more, the merrier.
- We don't have to use only the forms shown in the table above. We can also combine different parts of the structures.

  The more complicated the recipe, the longer it takes.
  The less we spend on food, the more money we have.

7.2 Food fads

C Tell students to read the post again and to match the foods to the questions. Tell students to underline the sections of the text which helped them find the answer. Check answers as a whole.

D Put students into groups to discuss the questions. Encourage students to expand on their answers and talk about their own experiences with superfoods or healthy food.

GRAMMAR

A Tell students to cover the blog post and to look at the sentences. Tell them to try to complete the sentences with one word in each space, either from what they remember or by guessing. When all students have tried this, tell them to uncover the post and check.

B Direct students to the **Grammar Hub** (see TB78 and below).

C Put students into pairs to compare the ideas. Point out the example and elicit another from the class. If students have strong opinions about any of the topics, bring them up for debate with the class. Encourage students to use as many comparatives as they can when comparing or contrasting the ideas.

SPEAKING

Point out the example and elicit one or two more to make sure students are confident at forming questions with the superlative. Tell students to ask and answer more questions in pairs. Ask students to share the most interesting answers to their questions with the class. Finish with feedback on how well students used superlatives during the task praising good usage and working through any errors you noticed.

GRAMMAR HUB

7.2 Comparatives and superlatives; *the …, the …*

A Complete the sentences with the correct form of the adjectives and adverbs in parentheses.

1 The __fastest__ (*fast*) the pizza delivery man can get here is 15 minutes.
2 You can buy cheese __more cheaply__ (*cheaply*) in the street market than in the stores.
3 The food in the airport was bad, but the meal on the plane was __worse__ (*bad*).
4 I made the soup with __fewer__ (*few*) ingredients than it says in the recipe.
5 The __best__ (*good*) way to serve this dessert is with a little cream.
6 I would prefer to try a __milder__ (*mild*) sauce than the one you're eating.

B Complete the sentences with the words and phrases in the box.

less meat	more times	more quickly	the better
the more money	the sweeter	you disagree	

1 The __less meat__ you eat, the healthier it is for your heart.
2 The more sugar you add, __the sweeter__ the sauce will be.
3 The __more quickly__ you eat your salad, the sooner you'll have dessert!
4 The more __you disagree__ with me, the less likely I am to change my mind!
5 The __more times__ you reheat food, the more unsafe it becomes.
6 The less food we throw away, __the more money__ we'll save.

C Correct the mistakes in each sentence.

1 The peas will cook ~~more fast~~ faster than the potatoes.
2 I think the ~~most~~ sourest taste of any food is vinegar.
3 Salad is the ~~least~~ less filling than pasta.
4 First prize in the competition will go to the person who cooks the ~~more~~ most creatively.
5 I put very little sugar in Jim's coffee, but he wanted even ~~little~~ less!
6 Chia seeds have ~~much~~ more protein than some foods, but quinoa has the most.

D Write one word in each blank to complete the sentences.

1 Is fast food __more__ popular than home cooking in your country?
2 My old mixer worked fairly well, but this one works much __better__.
3 Water is the __least__ fattening drink you can have because it has zero calories!
4 Raw food is generally healthier __than__ cooked food.
5 All these curries are spicy, but this one is the hottest __of__ all!
6 The older the wine is, __the__ better it gets.
7 The salad plates are pretty large, but the dinner plates are __larger/bigger__.
8 Mmm! This is __the__ most delicious meal I've ever had!

➤ Go back to page 80.

C READ FOR SPECIFIC INFORMATION Read again. Write *A* (açaí berries), *B* (broccoli), *C* (chia seeds), *G* (goji berries) or *Q* (quinoa).

According to the blog post, which superfood …

1 isn't only eaten on our planet? Q
2 is much cheaper than other superfoods? B
3 might help you stay younger for longer? A
4 can help you digest your food more effectively? C
5 might not be safe for everybody? G
6 has become popular very quickly? A
7 helps you to eat less food between meals? C

D SPEAK Work in groups and discuss the questions.

1 Do you think it's worth paying more money for superfoods? Why/Why not?
2 Do you think it is more important for you to eat healthy food or tasty food? Why?
3 What are some simple ways that we can eat more healthily?

But before you all rush out to buy superfoods from your local health food store, remember that superfoods are usually super expensive, too! And do you know what? Strawberries are probably just as good for you as goji berries and açaí berries. Similarly, quinoa and chia seeds are great because they're whole grains. But you can get all that fiber far more cheaply by eating plenty of brown bread, brown rice and whole grain pasta. And what's the best superfood of all? Broccoli! It's cheap, tasty and incredibly good for you. It isn't as exciting as quinoa, but it's a lot less expensive! Ex C Q2

Glossary

fiber (n) the parts of fruit, vegetables and grains that your body cannot digest (= turn into substances it can use); it helps food to pass through your body
nutrient (n) a substance in food that plants, animals and people need to live and grow
protein (n) a substance in food, such as meat, eggs and milk, that people need in order to grow and be healthy

GRAMMAR
Comparatives and superlatives

A Cover the *Food fads* article. Complete the sentences with one word in each space. Then check your answers in the blog post.

1 This week, I've decided to look at one of ___*the*___ biggest food fads of the 21st century: superfoods.
2 They contain ___less___ sugar ___than___ other fruits, so they're one of ___the___ healthiest snacks around.
3 Chia seeds contain some of the ___most___ nutrients for the ___fewest___ calories.
4 Even better, they make you feel full … so you'll eat ___fewer___ snacks!
5 Some people believe these berries will help them to grow old ___more___ slowly … or even to live ___longer___.
6 It isn't ___as___ exciting ___as___ quinoa, but it's a lot ___less___ expensive!

B Go to the **Grammar Hub** on **page 134**.

C SPEAK Work in pairs. Compare each set of ideas.

1 quinoa vs white rice
2 broccoli vs ice cream
3 grocery stores vs health food stores
4 fast food vs superfoods
5 cooking vs eating out
6 eating alone vs eating in a large group

A: Quinoa is much tastier than white rice.
B: Yes, but it's a lot more expensive.

SPEAKING

Work in pairs. Use the superlative form of the words and phrases in the box to ask and answer questions.

bad expensive far (to travel for a meal) few ingredients little money (to spend on food) much time (to spend preparing a meal) spicy

A: What's the farthest you've ever traveled for a meal?
B: Not very far. I usually buy all my food in the local store. But once I spent an hour bike riding to the 'best ice cream store in town'. But it wasn't as good as I expected.

LISTENING

A Work in pairs. Take the **Reduce Your Waste** quiz. Then go to the Communication Hub on page 153 to check your answers.

7.5 **B** You are going to listen to part of a radio show about a family who is trying to waste less food. Look at the pictures (1–6) and guess the answers to the questions. Then listen and check your answers.

REDUCE YOUR WASTE

1 How long can you store these things before they go bad?

- a fresh milk in a fridge
- b frozen vegetables in a freezer
- c fresh bananas
- d dry food (e.g. pasta)
- e an opened bottle of apple juice in a fridge
- f a plate of leftovers in a fridge

2 True or false?

- a You can safely reheat food as many times as you like.
- b Most food is still safe to eat after it has passed its best if used by date.
- c You must eat rice within 24 hours of cooking it.

1 How much money does the average person lose from food waste every year?

2 Do ugly carrots taste as good as beautiful carrots?

3 What's the problem with growing lettuce in a greenhouse?

4 How many buckets of water does it take to make a loaf of bread?

5 What can you do with your leftovers if you don't want to waste them?

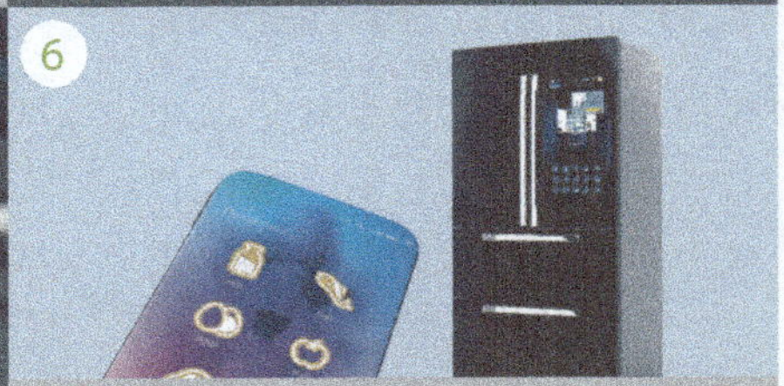

6 How can a cell phone app help us waste less food?

C Who expressed each of these opinions: *Mrs. Taylor, Mr. Taylor, Alison* or *Philip*? Use the strategies in the box to help you.

Identifying people's opinions

When you're listening, pay attention to whether people are just describing a situation or expressing an opinion about it. Adjectives like *great* and *awful* usually show that the person is expressing an opinion.

1 Food doesn't need to be beautiful. *Mrs. Taylor*

2 I like collecting and studying detailed information about our experiment. Philip

3 Food waste is bad for our planet. Mr. Taylor

4 I didn't like eating the same food the next day. Alison

5 I enjoy cooking meals to use up the food in the fridge. Philip

6 Money isn't the most important reason for reducing waste. Mr. Taylor

D SPEAK Work in pairs. How much food do you think you waste in your family?

GRAMMAR

the …, the …

A WORK IT OUT Look at the sentences from the radio show. Match the beginnings of the sentences (1–5) with the endings (a–e).

1 The more I researched the topic,
2 The less food we throw away,
3 The less we cook,
4 The longer we do it,
5 The more carefully you count things,

a the more normal it feels.
b the better.
c the more I realized that we aren't just throwing away food.
d the more accurate your results will be.
e the less we waste.

B Read the rule and complete the example. Use the words in parentheses to help you.

the …, the …

To show that two changes are closely connected, we use ***the*** + comparative, ***the*** + comparative. As one thing changes, it makes the other thing change.

As far as I'm concerned, the uglier *(ugly), the* better *(good)!*

C Go to the Grammar Hub on page 134.

LISTENING

A Put students into pairs to take the quiz. Check understanding of *leftovers, reheat* and *best if used by date*. Share some ideas as a whole class and encourage debate if they have very different answers. Don't confirm or deny any answers yet. Direct students to the **Communication Hub** (TB121) to check their answers. Ask students if they found anything surprising.

7.5 **B** Tell students they're going to listen to a radio show about a family who are trying to waste less food. Tell students to look at the questions and the pictures and to guess the answers.

AUDIO SCRIPT

7.5

Listening, Exercise B
H = Host MT = Mrs. Taylor Mr.T = Mr. Taylor
P = Philip A = Alison

H: Hello and welcome to The Food Fad Show. Today, we're talking about food waste. Did you know that globally, we waste a huge amount of the food we produce. The average person, just one person, wastes $200 of food every year. Can you believe that? $200!
In the studio today, we have the Taylor family. A year ago, they decided to reduce the amount of food they waste every year by 50 percent. Tell us more, Mrs. Taylor.

MT: Well, I've been interested in food waste for a long time. But the more I researched the topic, the more I realized that we aren't just throwing away food; we're also throwing away hundreds of dollars per year – enough to pay for a nice family vacation. That's when I decided we needed to cut our own waste dramatically.

H: OK, so what have you done to save money?

Ex C Q1 **MT:** Let me give you an example. Ugly carrots taste just as good as beautiful carrots, but in our local grocery store, they cost less than half as much. As far as I'm concerned, the uglier, the better! Also, my grocery store always lowers the price of meat or dairy products that are getting close to their best if used by date. So it's usually possible to buy food a lot more cheaply by checking those dates carefully. As long as you eat the food soon after buying it, it's completely safe.

H: Right. So it's all about money, then, Mr. Taylor?

Ex C Q6 **Mr.T:** No, not really. Food production has a massive impact on the environment: first to produce the food and distribute it, and then to get rid of any waste. I always thought the best way to save the planet was to reduce the amount of garbage we throw away and to reuse and recycle as much as possible. But in fact, the food itself has a much greater impact than the packaging it comes in. For example, throwing away a head of lettuce harms our planet 100 times more than throwing away the plastic bag. (Ex C Q3)

H: Really? That's amazing. Why?

Mr.T: Well, just think of all the water needed to grow it, the electricity to keep the greenhouse at just the right temperature, and then the environmental cost of keeping it fresh all the way from the farm to your fridge. It all adds up!

H: Wow! I'd never thought of that!

Mr.T: Here's another example. It takes 100 buckets of water to bake one loaf of bread. A hundred! Think about that the next time you throw away some one-day-old bread. If we could end all food waste around the world, it would be like taking one quarter of the world's cars off the roads. As far as I'm concerned, the less food we throw away, the better.

H: OK, so what have you done to cut down on food waste? Alison?

A: Yes, well, before our experiment, Mom or Dad always served up a large plate of food for each of us, but it was usually too much for me. So half of it always went in the garbage can. These days, we all help ourselves to food from a serving dish in the middle of the table. It's great because now we only take what we want – and we eat everything on our plates. It's much better because the less we cook, the less we waste.

H: OK, great. And what about leftovers?

A: When we started off, we had a rule that we had to eat yesterday's leftovers before any fresh food.
Ex C Q4 But it was awful, so we stopped it. I mean, yesterday's leftovers are disgusting! Who wants to eat those? But now we use those leftovers to make soup or a stew. It's still a little strange, but the longer we do it, the more normal it feels.

H: Yes, I'm sure. OK, and what about Philip? Can I ask you a question or are you too busy playing on your phone?

P: Don't worry – I'm not playing. I wanted to show you a cool cell phone app. It helps us keep track of exactly what food we have in the house – and when that food will go bad.

H: Oh, OK. Sorry. So … how does it work?

P: Well, you need to type in all the numbers whenever you buy – or eat – anything. Some people might find that to be a waste of time, but I like that sort of thing. Of course, you don't need to count every single potato, for example,
Ex C Q2 but the more carefully you count things, the more accurate your results will be. It's really fascinating when you study the numbers. Now, whenever we're in the grocery store, we can check what we need and what we don't. The app also sends us a notification when something is getting close to its best if used by date. That's really useful.

H: Yes, I'm sure.

Ex C Q5 **P:** And it even suggests delicious meal ideas to use up the ingredients we have, instead of buying new ones all the time. I never enjoyed cooking before, but thanks to the app, it's a lot more fun. And best of all, the app tells us exactly how much money we're saving every day.

H: Oh, yes. Tell us about the money, Mr. Taylor.

Mr.T: Well, so far, it's been a great success. According to Philip's app, we've managed to save $730 in food bills alone over the past year. And guess what? We're going on vacation next week to celebrate our fantastic achievement.

H: Wow! Congratulations!

7.2 Food fads

Use the pictures to make sure that students understand all the vocabulary in the questions. Elicit some ideas from the class but don't provide the answers yet. Ask students to listen to the radio show and check their answers. When checking answers, highlight the word *stew* (a dish made by cooking vegetables, and usually meat or fish, slowly in liquid), which is used in the answer to 5.

1 *$200*
2 *yes*
3 *It has a high cost to the environment because you need to keep the temperature just right.*
4 *100*
5 *You can make them into soup or a stew.*
6 *by helping us to check the best if used by dates of the food in our fridge; by suggesting ways of using the food we already have.*

C Point out the information in the box about *identifying people's opinions*. Tell students to look at the opinions and try to remember who expressed each one. Tell students to listen again and to check using the strategies in the box to help them.

D Put students into pairs to discuss how much food they think they waste in their family. Elicit some ideas as a whole class and find out the most common causes of food waste in the class.

GRAMMAR

A Elicit that all the sentences are from the radio show. Tell them to match the beginnings of the sentences with the endings.

B Tell students to look at the rule, and at the sentences from Exercise A, then to complete the example. Check that students remember the rules for how to form comparatives here as well.

C Direct students to the **Grammar Hub** (see TB78 and 79). Use the **Grammar Worksheet** on W27 for extra practice.

PRONUNCIATION

7.6 **A** Put students into pairs to pronounce the words above the box, using the information in the box. Play the audio for them to listen and repeat.

chew /tʃuː/
cow /kaʊ/
own /oʊn/
raw /rɔː/
stew /stjuː/

7.7 **B** Tell students to look at the words in bold in the sentences and to put them in the blanks in the box from Exercise A. Play the audio for students to check.

C Tell students to practice saying the sentences in Exercise B with a partner. Encourage them to say the sentences several times, getting a little faster each time. Tell them to make sure their partners are still pronouncing the words properly.

VOCABULARY

A Elicit that the words in the box are all connected to waste. Tell them to match the words to their definitions.

B Tell students to fill in the blanks in the questions with a word from Exercise A. Check answers as a whole class. Tell students to discuss the questions with a partner. Use the **Vocabulary Worksheet** on W28 for extra practice.

SPEAKING HUB

A Tell students they're going to think of ways to reduce food waste in their home by 50 percent. Elicit examples of how this could be done, then put students into pairs. Tell them to look at the suggestions and to write down notes about each one.

B Tell each pair to prepare their presentation, using the notes they made in Exercise A. When they are ready, tell each pair to make their presentation. Tell the other students to listen carefully and to think about how similar or different the other pairs' ideas are.

C Put students into groups to discuss the questions, using their notes to help them. When the groups have discussed all the questions, tell them to use those questions as criteria to choose the best two or three ideas.

D Put students into new groups to discuss the questions. Get whole-class feedback and find out which students are going to make the biggest changes to their lifestyle.

METHODOLOGY HUB by Jim Scrivener

Simple variations on well-known games are helpful in familiarizing students with phonemic symbols:

- **Phoneme bingo:** Hand out bingo cards with phonemes instead of numbers; call out sounds rather than numbers.
- **Anagrams:** Get students to work out anagrams of words using phonemes rather than normal alphabetic letters, e.g. /kbʊ/ (= book).
- **Category words:** Choose five or six categories – such as 'Food', 'Sports', 'Animals', 'Household objects', 'Clothing', etc – which students should write down. Students work in small teams. When you call out (and write) a phoneme, the teams must attempt to find a word containing that phoneme for each category. So, for example, if the phoneme is /iː/, a team could choose *cheese, skiing, sheep, teapot* and *jeans*. The teams then compare words and points are awarded.

PRONUNCIATION
Vowel + *w*

7.6 **A** **How do you pronounce these words? Use the strategies in the box to help you. Then listen and repeat the words.**

chew cow own raw stew

Vowel + *w*

Three vowels, ***a***, ***e*** and ***o***, when combined with ***w***, make a new sound. There are two possible sounds for ***e + w*** and ***o + w***.

a + w /ɔː/ for, draw, awful, ___awesome___, ___law___

e + w /juː/ you, few, view, ___few___

e + w /uː/ too, jewelry, threw, ___flew___, ___grew___

o + w /oʊ/ go, low, owe, ___flown___, ___throw___, ___know___, ___slowly___, ___grown___

o + w /aʊ/ out, how, wow, ___allowed___, ___flowers___, ___now___

7.7 **B** **Look at the bold words in these sentences. Write them in the correct place in the box in Exercise A. Then listen and check your answers.**

1 'Have you ever **flown** in a helicopter?' 'Yes, I **flew** in one a **few** weeks ago. It was **awesome**.'

2 You aren't **allowed** to **throw** away your trash here! Don't you **know** it's against the **law**!

3 The **flowers grew** fairly **slowly** at first, but **now** they're fully **grown**.

C **SPEAK** **Work in pairs. Practice saying the sentences in Exercise B. Listen and check your partner's pronunciation.**

VOCABULARY
Waste

A **Match the definitions (1–8) with the words and phrases in the box.**

garbage can cut down get rid of recycle reduce reuse garbage throw away use up ~~waste~~

1 to not use something that you could use ___waste___

2 a container for putting garbage in ___garbage can___

3 things that you throw away because they are no longer useful ___garbage___

4 to use all of something, so there's no waste ___use up___

5 to change waste materials such as newspapers and bottles so that they can be used again ___recycle___

6 to use something again ___reuse___

7 to use less of something ___cut down___, ___reduce___

8 to get rid of something that you no longer want ___get rid of___, ___throw away___

B **SPEAK** **Complete the questions with one word in each space. Then work in pairs and discuss the questions.**

1 Do you ___recycle___ plastic and glass containers so they can be turned into new products, or do you just get ___rid___ of them?

2 Do you ___reuse___ plastic bags again and again, or throw them in the ___garbage can___?

3 How could restaurants cut ___down___ the amount of ___waste/garbage___ they throw ___away___ each week?

SPEAKING HUB

A **Work in pairs. How could you reduce food waste in your home by fifty percent? Write notes about:**

- shopping habits (how often? how much?)
- meal planning (weekly menus)
- leftovers
- food storage (fridge? cupboard? special containers?)
- apps and gadgets

B **PRESENT** **Use your notes to prepare a short presentation on how you can help people reduce their food waste. Present your ideas to the class.**

C **DISCUSS** **Work in groups. Use these questions to compare your ideas from Exercise B. Then choose the best two or three ideas.**

- Which ideas will be easiest for people to understand and follow?
- Which ideas will make the biggest difference?
- Which ideas might cost people more money? Which ideas might save them money?

D **REFLECT** **Work in groups and discuss the questions.**

1 Are you going to try to reduce your own food waste? How?

2 Will you try to persuade others to cut their food waste? How?

Compare different types of food

Compare a range of solutions and choose the best one

Café Hub

7.3 Comfort eating

F – make suggestions P – suggestions

COMPREHENSION

A Work in pairs and discuss the questions.

What do you do when you're feeling upset or worried?

Do you cook, go for a run, call a friend, watch a good movie or something else?

B 00:00–01:30 Watch the first part of the video and answer the questions.

1 What is Gaby's big news? She really likes Sam.

2 What does Milly think about her news? She thinks it's great.

3 What is Gaby upset about? She left Sam a letter expressing her feelings for him and he hasn't mentioned it.

C 00:56–01:21 Find and correct five mistakes in the story that Gaby told Milly. What advice do you think Milly will give? Watch to check your answers.

It was about a week ago. Last ~~Wednesday,~~ Monday Sam had to leave work early and so he asked me to ~~look after~~ lock up the café. I had decided to tell him how I felt, and so before I locked up, I wrote a ~~poem~~ letter expressing my true feelings for him. ... And I left it on the ~~doormat~~ counter for him to find. He ~~can't~~ must have seen it.

FUNCTIONAL LANGUAGE

Making suggestions

A Match the two halves of the extracts from the video.

Making a suggestion

1 Have you tried
2 What about
3 The best thing might be
4 If I were you, I'd
5 Why don't we
6 We could

a cook something delicious.
b take some time to think about it.
c talking to him about it?
d put on some whipped cream and sprinkles?
e sending a text or an email or something?
f to just ask him if he got the letter.

B Complete the phrases in the table.

Saying no to a suggestion	Saying yes to a suggestion
No, I ___can't___. I don't know what to say.	That's a good ___idea___.
No, that wouldn't ___work___. To say what?	It's worth a ___try___.
That's a ___terrible___ idea. I'm already really embarrassed.	Good ___plan___.

C 01:21–04:13 Watch the second part of the video and check your answers to Exercises A and B.

MILLY

SAM

NEENA

ZAC

GABY

USEFUL PHRASES

A Match the useful phrases (1–4) with the screenshots (a–d).

1 What's up? a
2 Great timing! d
3 It'll help take your mind off Sam. c
4 He's been acting like nothing happened! b

a

b

c

d

B How do you say these useful phrases in your language?

PRONUNCIATION

Suggestions

7.8 **A** Listen to the extracts from the video and underline the stressed/key words. Does the intonation rise or fall at the end of each phrase?

Milly: Have you tried talking to him about it? (↑)
Gaby: No, I can't. I don't know what to say. (↓)
Milly: Or, what about sending him a text (↑) or an email or something? (↓)
Gaby: No, that wouldn't work. (↓) To say what? (↑)
Milly: I don't know exactly. The best thing might be to just ask him if he got the letter? (↓)
Gaby: No, no, no, no, no, no, no, no! That's a terrible idea. I'm already really embarrassed. (↓)
Milly: If I were you, I'd take some time to think about it. (↓)

B In pairs, practice the conversation. Copy the stress and intonation.

SPEAKING

A Work in pairs. Think about possible solutions to the problems below.

1 I'm having a dinner party, but I hate cooking.
2 I want to eat more healthily, but superfoods are too expensive.
3 I want to save some money, but I love going out to restaurants!
4 I frequently have leftover food, but I don't want to waste it.
5 I want to grow vegetables, but I live in an apartment.

B **DISCUSS** Take turns reading out a problem and make suggestions using the phrases in Functional Language Exercise A.

A: I'm having a dinner party, but I hate cooking.
B: What about getting takeout?

Make suggestions

➤ Turn to page 162 to learn how to write a reply in an online discussion forum.

7.3 Comfort eating

LEAD-IN

Put students into two teams. Give students cards with different emotions on them (i.e. *worried, sad, happy, stressed, embarrassed*). The student with the card has to act the emotion out for their team to guess.

COMPREHENSION

A Check the meaning of *upset* and then elicit one or two ideas of things students do to make them feel better.

B ▶ 00:00-01:30 Elicit what they can remember about Gaby, Milly and Sam. Tell them to read the questions, then watch and answer them.

C ▶ 00:56-01:21 Tell students to find and correct the five factual mistakes in Gaby's story. Ask them to discuss with a partner what advice they think Milly will give. Play the video again for students to check.

FUNCTIONAL LANGUAGE

A Tell students to match the two halves to complete the sentences.

B Tell students to complete the spaces in the phrases in the table. Point out that the phrases are all related to saying yes or no to suggestions.

C ▶ 01:21-04:13 Play the video once again for students to check their answers to Exercises A and B.

USEFUL PHRASES

A Tell students to match the useful phrases from the video with the screenshots.

B Tell students to think about how they would say these phrases in their language.

PRONUNCIATION

7.8 **A** Tell students to listen to the extracts from the video and underline the stressed/keywords. Tell them to listen carefully to decide if the intonation rises or falls at the end of each phrase.

B Put students into pairs to practice reading the conversation, paying careful attention to the stress and intonation.

SPEAKING

A Elicit some solutions to the first problem as an example with the class. Next, put students into pairs to think of possible solutions to the other problems. Share ideas as a whole class.

B Tell students to work in pairs and to take turns reading out a problem. After one student has read out a problem, the other has to make a suggestion. The first student can either accept or reject the suggestion. If they reject it, their partner has to make another suggestion. Continue until the first student is happy with the suggested solution.

VIDEO SCRIPT

M = Milly G = Gaby Z = Zac

M: So … I got your text. What's up?

G: Oh, Milly! It's big news.

M: Woah. You're starting to sound like Zac. What's going on?

G: Please – sit down.

M: So?

G: So … I like Sam.

M: So do I!

G: No, I mean, I really like Sam …

M: Oh … that's … great!

G: No. It's not great …

M: Why?

G: Well … It was about a week ago …
Last Monday, Sam had to leave work early and so he asked me to close up the café. I had decided to tell him how I felt, and so before I locked up, I wrote a letter expressing my true feelings for him.
… And I left it on the counter for him to find. He must have seen it.

M: So … What did he say?

G: Nothing. Nada. Zero. And all week, he's been acting like nothing happened!

M: Oh … Have you tried talking to him about it?

G: No … I can't, I … I don't know what to say … Anyway, he clearly doesn't feel the same, so … There's nothing to say …

M: Or … what about sending him a text or an email or something?

G: No, that wouldn't work … to say what?

M: I don't know exactly. The best thing might be to just ask him if he got the letter?

G: No no no no no! That's a terrible idea. I'm already really embarrassed. I'm not going to embarrass myself anymore.

M: Well … if that's how you feel …

G: I don't know Milly … I'm thinking about moving back to my parent's house in Madrid. You know, save up some money …

M: Well … If I were you, I'd take some time to think about it … Hey, I have an idea.

G: What?

M: You hungry?

G: A little.

M: Why don't we cook something delicious! It'll help take your mind off Sam!

G: OK. That's a good idea. It's worth a try.

M: OK … the recipe says it should be cooked by now.

G: Oh. It looks a bit sad. It looks like me.

M: We could put on some whipped cream and sprinkles?

G: And maybe some fruit on top?

M: Good plan.

G, Z, M (together): Ooooooooo!

Z: Great timing.

M: Ready?

G: GO!

7 Writing

Write a reply in an online discussion forum

comparing and recommending

A Work in pairs and discuss the questions.

1 Have you ever …
   a read an online discussion forum?
   b asked a question on an online discussion forum?
   c written a reply to somebody on an online discussion forum?
2 What kind of online discussion groups are you interested in? Use the ideas in the box and your own ideas.

current affairs · financial matters · food · health and fitness · music and movies · personal matters · product reviews and recommendations · travel

3 What's good about using these websites? What's bad about them?

B Read the forum post and the three replies. Which reply offers the best advice? What is the worst advice?

Possible answer:
The worst advice comes from Miss_Orange because she doesn't actually recommend one option and her comments are too obvious (i.e. expensive restaurants are expensive; fast food is fast). Stewpot and hungry_al both offer good advice.

Message from

Hi. We have some relatives from another country coming to stay next week. I want to take them out to eat when they arrive after their long flight. I'm not sure whether to take them to an expensive restaurant or a fast-food joint.

I've asked them which they prefer, and they say they don't mind … but maybe they're just being polite. What do you recommend?

3 Comments

Reply from Miss Orange

It depends. Expensive restaurants serve better food, but of course they're much more expensive than fast-food joints. On the other hand, I like fast food because it's a lot faster than food from a restaurant. Why don't you ask them what they want to eat? Or how about cooking a meal for them instead?

Reply from hungry_al

I strongly recommend taking them for a good meal at an expensive restaurant. It'll make them feel special and welcome, and it should make an excellent first impression on them. They might be stressed after their flight, so they might want to go somewhere quiet and relaxing. You could always take them to a fast-food joint later during their stay with you – it's a nice thing to do with somebody you already know well. But for that first meeting, an expensive restaurant is far better.

Reply from Stewpot

I think you should take them for some fast food. After a long flight, they'll be tired and hungry, so they'll want to eat as quickly as possible. Another thing to remember is that your visitors might not feel very fresh and clean after their flight, and they may not have suitable clothes for a fancy restaurant. So you'll have to take them home first so they can change their clothes … and that could take hours. It's much quicker and easier if you take them for some simple food at a fast-food joint. After all, you can always take them to your favorite restaurant the next day. Good luck!

Refer students to these forum posts as a model for the writing task.

162 WRITING

C Read again. Which reply or replies …

1 started with a clear recommendation? hungry_al; Stewpot
2 ended with a clear recommendation? hungry_al
3 introduced a third option? Miss_Orange
4 thought about how the visitors will feel after their trip? hungry_al; Stewpot
5 missed some important information in the original message? Miss_Orange
6 gave reasons to explain why their recommendation is better? hungry_al; Stewpot
7 suggested a way of using both options? hungry_al; Stewpot

D Look at the box. Choose *Do* or *Don't* for each rule.

Comparing and recommending

1 **Do** / **Don't** start with a clear recommendation. (I think you should …; I strongly recommend …)
2 **Do** / **Don't** say It depends. The writer is asking you for a recommendation, so don't make their decision more complicated.
3 **Do** / **Don't** use comparatives to show why your option is better. (It's much quicker and easier …)
4 **Do** / **Don't** just talk about what you prefer.
5 **Do** / **Don't** show that you have thought about the people in the situation. (They might be stressed after their flight, so …)
6 **Do** / **Don't** give reasons for your recommendation.
7 **Do** / **Don't** add extra suggestions.
8 **Do** / **Don't** end with a clear recommendation. (… is far better.)

WRITING

A PLAN Read the forum post. What are the two options? Write notes on some arguments for and against each option.

I want to organize a dinner party for about 20 people from work and their families. I like the idea of a pot luck dinner party, but I've heard they don't always work well. Maybe I should just cook all the food myself. What do you recommend?

B WRITE Which option will you recommend? Write your reply (100–150 words).

C REVIEW Work in groups. Read each other's replies. Did everyone follow all the rules in the skills box? Who wrote the best recommendation?

WRITING

Write *expensive restaurant* and *fast-food restaurant* on the board. Tell students to think of advantages and disadvantages of eating in each. Elicit an example, then put students into pairs to think of more.

A Put students into pairs to discuss the questions. Get answers from the class as a whole and encourage students to expand on their answers. If students have written on an online discussion forum, ask them to describe what they wrote about.

B Tell students to look at the picture and elicit what it shows. Tell them to read the forum post and replies and decide which advice they think is the best and the worst. Explain that *fast-food joint* is a more informal way of saying *fast-food restaurant*.

C Tell students to read the posts again and to match the replies to the questions.

D Tell students to use the replies to help them complete the *dos* and *don'ts* in the box. Elicit the first answer as an example, showing students that examples of this can be found in the posts that are more successfully written.

WRITING TASK

A Tell students to read the forum post and to find the two options. Establish that the two options are a pot luck dinner party or cooking all the food yourself for a dinner party. Put students into pairs to think of arguments for and against each option. Elicit ideas from the class as a whole to ensure everyone has a good number of ideas for the writing task.

B Tell students to choose which option they will recommend and write their reply. Tell them to refer to the *dos* and *don'ts* in Exercise D as they do this.

C Put students into groups to read each other's replies. Tell them to think about whether they agree with the suggestions and how well the writer has followed the *dos* and *don'ts*. Get some whole-class feedback on what are the best replies.

Unit 7 Review

GRAMMAR

A Choose the best words to complete the conversation.

A: Do you want some of this pot luck stew? I made it from all of last week's leftovers: fish curry, cheesy chicken pasta, spicy vegetables …

B: Yuck! That [1]*can't* / *might not* / *must* taste disgusting!

A: Well, no, it actually tastes very good. Try it – you [2]*can* / *might* / *must* like it.

B: Really? OK. I guess it [3]*couldn't* / *might not* / *must not* be so bad. But don't forget I'm allergic to peanuts.

A: Don't worry, it [4]*can't* / *may not* / *might* contain any peanuts. I never cook with them. But it [5] *couldn't* / *may* / *must* contain some other types of nuts – I'm not sure. Is that OK?

B: Yes, that's fine. Hmm … this [6]*can't* / *could* / *must* be a big mistake, but … OK, I'll try it.

B Complete the sentences with the correct form of the words in parentheses.

1 I want to cook the most food for the least (*little*) money. Any ideas?

2 Açaí berries are really good for you – they're much healthier (*healthy*) than I thought.

3 If you want to lose weight, you need to eat less (*few*) candy.

4 You should come to the restaurant on a Tuesday at lunchtime – that's the least crowded (*crowded*) time.

5 You baked this cake too quickly! Next time, try baking it more slowly (*slowly*).

6 Cooking for ten people is far more stressful (*stressful*) than cooking for one!

7 There's too much cream in this sauce. Can you make it a little less creamy (*creamy*) next time?

C Match the beginnings of the sentences (1–6) with the endings (a–f).

1 Bring all your friends to our dinner party – the more people who come,
2 The earlier you arrive at the restaurant,
3 The older I get,
4 The more sugar you add,
5 Natural food is much better for you; the fewer chemicals it contains,
6 Don't boil vegetables for too long; the longer you cook them,

a the more I prefer to stay in and cook at home.
b the less flavor they'll have.
c the more fun we'll have.
d the more likely you are to get a table.
e the sweeter it will be.
f the healthier it is.

VOCABULARY

A Complete the sentences with the correct form of the phrasal verbs in the box.

keep on   clean up   end up   put off   figure out

1 I can't figure out how to turn on the microwave. Can you help me?

2 Sorry to interrupt your meal, but I need to go out for a minute. Please keep on eating while I'm away.

3 I'm happy to cook dinner, but could you clean up the dirty plates afterward?

4 If you want to learn to cook, don't put it off! Join our cooking classes today!

5 I was planning to cook a big meal, but then the oven broke so I ended up buying takeout pizzas for everybody.

B Choose the best adjectives to complete the sentences.

1 I think we need to cook this meat a little longer – it's still *delicious* / *mild* / *raw* in the middle.

2 I don't really like sweet snacks. Do you have anything *bitter* / *rich* / *savory*, like a sandwich?

3 Don't worry. This soup is very *buttery* / *mild* / *spicy* – there are no chilies or strong flavors in it.

4 The food was great, but it wasn't very *chewy* / *filling* / *spicy*. We were still hungry at the end of the meal!

5 I don't like dark chocolate – it's too *fatty* / *bitter* / *creamy* for me. I prefer something sweeter.

6 If you want a cheap and *disgusting* / *sour* / *tasty* lunch, Kate's café is the best place to go.

C Complete the advice about food waste with words in the box. There is one extra word.

garbage cans   get   recycle   reduce   reuse   throw   use

Try these tips:

- Don't [1] get rid of yesterday's bread just because it isn't fresh. Make toast to [2] use up the last few pieces.
- Don't [3] throw old plastic away. You can [4] reuse the same shopping bags again and again.
- Use two (or more) [5] garbage cans : one for food waste and one for containers that you can [6] recycle .

FUNCTIONAL LANGUAGE

Find and correct the mistakes in the sentences.

1 I don't feel like cooking tonight. Why ~~we~~ don't ^we eat out tonight?

2 Yes, why not? What about go to The Food Zone?
What about going to The Food Zone?

3 Again? We went there last week. Could we going to that new supper club, The Spicy Kitchen, instead?
Could we go to that new supper club, The Spicy Kitchen, instead?

4 Good idea! The best thing might be call them. They might have a free table tonight.
The best thing might be to call them.

5 Yes, that's worth to try. Can you call them and ask?
Yes, that's worth a try.

A helicopter mechanic double checks some wiring, Germany.

Innovation (n) a new idea, method, piece of equipment. Synonym: breakthrough (n)

The quote suggests that you don't need anything very special in order to be an inventor except a good imagination. Check that students understand the meaning of *junk* (old, broken or useless things).

Thomas Edison (1847–1931) was an American inventor and businessman. Edison created over 1,000 inventions but one of his most famous was the light bulb. His inventions changed life all around the world.

OBJECTIVES

- explain how an invention works
- suggest and evaluate creative ideas
- use positive language to promote a new product
- give a friend advice about choosing a gadget
- give and follow instructions
- write a biography

Work with a partner. Discuss the questions.

1 Look at the picture. What characteristics would be helpful to have as a mechanic?
2 Look at the quote. Do you think you have to be imaginative to be an inventor?
3 Talk about a situation where you have been imaginative or innovative in your life.

INNOVATION 85

OBJECTIVES

Read the unit objectives to the class.

UNIT OPENER QUESTIONS

With books closed, write the word *innovation* on the board. Tell students they have one minute to make as many words as they can using only those letters. In feedback, find out who has made the most words, and who has made the longest. One of the longest possibilities is *ovation* with seven letters.

1 Tell students to open their books and to look at the picture. Elicit an example of how it could be considered creative or innovative. Practice pronunciation of both these words. Put students into pairs to think of more ways. Share any interesting answers as a whole class.

2 Tell students to read the quote and to discuss the questions. Elicit answers from the class and write any interesting vocabulary on the board.

3 Give a personal example of a situation where you have been imaginative or innovative. Encourage students to ask you follow-up questions. Put students into pairs to do the same. Share any interesting answers as a whole class.

WORKSHEETS

Lesson 8.1 Making a difference

Grammar: Adjective clauses (W29)

Vocabulary: Word families; creative thinking (W30)

Lesson 8.2 Must-have gadgets

Grammar: Zero and first conditionals (W31)

Vocabulary: Positive adjectives (W32)

8.1 Making a difference

- Explain how an invention works
- Suggest and evaluate creative ideas

V – word families; creative thinking
G – adjective clauses
P – adjective clauses
S – listening for problems and solutions

Eden Full Goh:

the inventor who is making a big difference

Eden Full Goh is perhaps not a name that you immediately recognize, but she is one of the most exciting and creative inventors of the 21st century.

Eden, who was born in Calgary, Canada, started to show talent at the age of nine, when she built a solar-powered toy car. That is where her interest in solar power began but certainly not where it stopped. She had not yet graduated from college when she came up with a very simple, but highly efficient, solar panel system that produces energy at low cost.

Eden's invention, which has won many prizes, is now used in 19 countries, where it makes a real difference to thousands of people's lives. Here is how to use it.

1. The SunSaluter is like a table. The top of the table is a solar panel, which can face in different directions.
2. Get up early in the morning when it's still dark. Fill one plastic bottle with sand and two more bottles with dirty water.
3. Attach the water bottles to the filter. At the bottom of the filter is a tube that takes clean water to a large container. At the top there's a hook that attaches the filter to the SunSaluter.
4. Hang the filter on one end of the SunSaluter, which will then go down. Hang the bottle that you filled with sand on the other end of the solar panel. Make sure the solar panel is facing the east, where the sun will rise.
5. At sunrise, when the sun comes up, the solar panel will start catching sunlight from the east.
6. During the day, the water will flow very slowly through the filter to the container, where it is stored. As the water bottles become lighter, the heavy sand bottle slowly pulls the other end of the SunSaluter down. At noon, when the sun is high in the sky, the solar panel will face upwards.
7. In the evening, when the water bottles are empty, the solar panel will face west. You can now drink the clean water that you collected during the day.

Glossary

solar panel (n) a piece of equipment that uses energy from the sun to create power

READING

A SPEAK Work in pairs and discuss the questions.

1. What famous inventors do you know? What did they invent?
2. What skills do inventors need?

B READ FOR GIST Read *Eden Full Goh: the inventor who is making a big difference*. What is special about Eden and her invention?

C READ FOR DETAIL Read again. Match the explanations (1–7) in the text with the pictures (a–g).

D SPEAK Make a list of your own life goals. Use the ideas in the box to help you. Then work in pairs and compare your lists.

awards and prizes · career · experiences · family · helping other people · certifications

VOCABULARY

Word families

A Read the box. Then complete the word families. Use *Eden Full Goh: the inventor who is making a big difference* to help you.

Word families

Word families can help you learn many words together, not just one at a time. Here's an example:

innovation (n) = a new idea or product
innovator (n) = someone who thinks of new ideas or products
innovate (v) = to invent or begin using new ideas or products
innovative (adj) = an adjective to describe an innovator or an innovation

Noun (thing/idea)	Noun (person)	Verb	Adjective
a success	a success	to succeed (in something)	1 successful
an 2 invention	an 3 inventor	to invent something	inventive
a design	a designer	to 4 design something	–
a product	a producer	to 5 produce something	productive
6 science	a scientist	–	scientific
engineering	an 7 engineer	to engineer something	–

8.1 Making a difference

LEAD-IN

Put students into pairs to discuss which recent invention has made the biggest difference to their lives and what future invention would make a big difference to their lives. Ask students to discuss the ideas with their partner.

READING

A Put students into pairs to discuss the questions.

B Tell students to look at the pictures and to predict the answers to the question then tell them to read the article and check their predictions.

Possible answer: *Eden is a successful inventor although she's young. Her invention is very simple but it has made a big difference to many people's lives.*

C Tell students to read the text again and match the explanations (1–7) to the pictures (a–g).

D Tell students to look at the ideas in the box and to make a list of their own life goals connected to them. Then put students into pairs to compare and explain their lists.

VOCABULARY

A Tell students to read the information in the box about word families. Tell them to look at the word families in the table and to fill in the blanks. Tell students all the words they need for this appear in the article about Eden Full Goh.

B Ask students to complete the sentences with words from the same family as the words in bold. Look at the example together and elicit that *successful* is the adjective and *succeed* is the verb. Use the **Vocabulary Worksheet** on W30 for extra practice.

METHODOLOGY HUB by Jim Scrivener

Model new words in context

When you teach lexical items, give students a chance to hear you saying the item naturally spoken in the context of a typical short phrase or sentence. Take care to stress naturally (rather than as a 'perfect' sentence). Allow students to repeat the phrase and give them honest feedback if there seem to be problems. If necessary, remodel it and let students work out what they are doing differently.

Modeling intonation

When you teach grammar, allow students to hear some typical examples of natural uses of the language. So, for example, when teaching the present perfect progressive, don't just teach it as dry examples, but model a typical real-life sentence or two yourself with real feeling, such as 'I've been waiting here for two hours!'. A loud, angry sentence like this will be much more memorable than a written example. Get students to repeat it to each other – and don't let them get away with flat, dull intonation. Encourage them to say it with real feeling.

GRAMMAR HUB

8.1 Adjective clauses

Essential adjective clauses

	Relative pronoun	
Person	who/that	The person **who/that** first had the idea was named Smith.
Thing	which/that	The thing **which/that** stops it being a success is the price.
Possession	whose	The man **whose** design won first prize was from China.
Place	where	The company **where** I work makes a difference to people's lives.
Time	when	Early in the morning is the time **when** I have my best ideas.

- We use an essential adjective clause to give information about and identify a noun (person or thing).
- We use *who* or *that* for people, and *which* or *that* for things.
- With *who*, *which* and *that*, we can leave out the relative pronoun if it's followed by a subject + verb rather than just a verb.

  The design (that) he suggested was very good.

- When the relative pronoun is the subject of the adjective clause, we don't add another pronoun.

  *Do you know the name of the man **who invented** this?* NOT ~~*Do you know the name of the man who he invented this?*~~

Non-essential adjective clauses

	Relative pronoun	
Person	who	Carol Taylor, **who** presents science programs, is a university professor.
Thing	which	The idea, **which** I first read about in the newspaper, is really very simple.
Possession	whose	Miriam, **whose** dad is a designer, would like to become an inventor.
Place	where	London, **where** her grandparents live, is where Sophie would like to find work.
Time	when	On Sundays, **when** Andrew isn't working, he likes to catch up with his reading.

- We use a non-essential adjective clause when we want to include two pieces of information in the same sentence. The adjective clause is usually an additional piece of information and is always separated by commas.
- We do not use *that* with non-essential adjective clauses.
- When we remove a non-essential adjective clause, the sentence still makes sense.

8.1 Making a difference

GRAMMAR

A Tell students to look at the article again and to decide what the highlighted words refer to. Go through the example with the students, demonstrating how *who* refers back to Eden.

B Tell students to read the rules about essential and non-essential adjective clauses and to complete the examples with adjective clauses from the article. Check that students understand the difference between the essential information, without which the sentence isn't complete, in the essential adjective clause, and the extra information, which could be removed, in the non-essential adjective clause.

C Direct students to the **Grammar Hub** (see TB86 and below). Use the **Grammar Worksheet** on W29 for extra practice.

PRONUNCIATION

8.1 **A** Play the audio and tell students to listen carefully to the different pronunciation of the two sentences. Ask students what they noticed. Play again if they are unsure.

*We pause before and after **non-essential** adjective clauses. Before each pause, our voice usually goes **down**.*

8.2 **B** Tell students to listen and repeat the sentences, paying special attention to the pauses and falling intonation.

C Put students into pairs for further pronunciation practice.

SPEAKING

A Ask students to work with a partner and write down three sentences using adjective clauses describing a famous person, a place and an object. Monitor, to help with vocabulary.

B Put pairs of students together so they are working in groups of four. The pairs should take turns reading aloud their sentences with the other pair guessing the missing information.

GRAMMAR HUB

8.1 Adjective clauses

A Choose the correct option.

1 There are a lot of students *which* / *who* have great ideas.
2 The last century was the time *when* / *where* technology really progressed.
3 The magazine *who* / *that* I like best is called *New Scientist*.
4 Princeton is the place *where* / *which* I studied for my degree.
5 I want to find a job *that* / *who* helps others.
6 John is the boy *who* / *whose* father is a doctor.
7 I don't know anyone *who* / *which* works in technology.
8 He was born at a time *when* / *where* computers didn't exist.

B Match to make sentences.

1 California is where b
2 The computer is an invention d
3 Steve Jobs was the person who a
4 The experiences e
5 Myra is the woman g
6 My phone is the one thing c
7 I really enjoyed the time f

a started Apple Computers.
b most software industries started.
c which I would hate to lose.
d which has changed many people's lives.
e that I had were more important than the money I made.
f when I was studying at college.
g who helped me choose my career.

C Join the two sentences to make one. Use non-essential adjective clauses.

1 My aunt is a scientist. She lives in Boston.
My aunt, who lives in Boston, is a scientist. / My aunt, who is a scientist, lives in Boston.
2 The invention is very simple. It has made a big difference to people's lives.
The invention, which is very simple, has made a big difference to people's lives.
3 Justin is 23. He has just won a prize.
Justin, who is 23, has just won a prize. / Justin, who has just won a prize, is 23.
4 Carl spoke to us from Lisbon. He lives there.
Carl spoke to us from Lisbon, where he lives.
5 The invention won first prize. It is sold in many countries. The invention, which won first prize, is sold in many countries. / The invention, which is sold in many countries, won first prize.
6 Marie loves inventing things. Her husband is also an engineer.
Marie, whose husband is also an engineer, loves inventing things.
7 Next week the results come out. We'll see if you win anything.
Next week, when the results come out, we'll see if you win anything.

➤ Go back to page 87.

B Complete the sentences with words from the same family as the words in bold.

1 You don't need to be **successful** every time. You just need to ___*succeed*___ in the most important things.

2 I could never **invent** something – I'm not a very ___inventive___ person.

3 You can only call yourself an ___engineer___ after studying **engineering** in college.

4 A ___designer___ should concentrate on **designing** things that work well. That's more important than making them look beautiful.

5 I always think like a **scientist**. Being ___scientific___ means checking the facts before making a decision, and not focusing on opinions and feelings.

C **SPEAK** Work in pairs. Which sentences in Exercise B do you agree or disagree with? Tell your partner. Then make the sentences true for you.

GRAMMAR

Adjective clauses

A **WORK IT OUT** Look at *Eden Full Goh: the inventor who is making a big difference*. What do the highlighted words in the article refer to?

1 who = ___*Eden*___
2 when = ___early in the morning___
3 where = ___the east___
4 which = ___Eden's invention___
5 that = ___the solar panel system___

B Read the rules and complete the examples with adjective clauses from the article.

Adjective clauses

Essential adjective clauses tell us which person, thing, place or time we are talking about. Without the adjective clause, the sentence isn't complete.

Eden Full Goh: the inventor [1] ___who is making a big difference___.

Non-essential adjective clauses give extra information about a person, thing, place or time. We can cut the adjective clause and the sentence is still complete. We use commas to separate the adjective clause from the rest of the sentence.

Eden's invention, [2] ___which has won many prizes___, is now used in 19 countries.

C Go to the Grammar Hub on page 136.

PRONUNCIATION

Adjective clauses

8.1 **A** Listen to the two sentences. What do you notice about the pronunciation of essential adjective clauses and non-essential adjective clauses?

1 The person who invented the SunSaluter has made a big difference to people's lives.

2 Eden Full Goh, who invented the SunSaluter, has made a big difference to people's lives.

8.2 **B** Listen and repeat the sentences.

1 Solar panels, which turn sunlight into electricity, are becoming cheaper all the time.

2 I've hidden my plans in a place where they'll be safe.

3 My favorite inventor is Mária Telkes, who created the first 100 percent solar-powered house in 1947.

C **SPEAK** Work in pairs. Practice saying the sentences in Exercise B. Listen and check your partner's pronunciation.

SPEAKING

A Work in pairs. Write down three sentences using adjective clauses. They should describe:

- a famous person
- a place
- an object

B Join another pair and take turns reading out your sentences, saying 'Beep' in place of the subject. The other pair must guess who, where or what you are talking about.

A: Beep, who is American, invented the light bulb.
B: Is it Thomas Edison?

Thinking outside THE BOX

Ex C Q1 Thinking outside the box means looking at a problem in a new way.
Ex C Q2 It means forgetting about 'the way we normally do things', taking away unimportant rules and experimenting with new ideas. So for example, in the 'nine dots' problem, we see 'rules' that don't actually exist. Who said your lines have to stay inside the red box? In fact, do the lines even need to go through the middle of each dot?

It's the same with the light bulb problem. We can't stop ourselves from thinking of a light bulb as something that we see with our eyes, as
Ex C Q3 something that can only be in two states, off or on. But what if we think of it as something we can touch with our hands? Are there still only two states?

Thinking outside the box also helps with brainstorming tasks, like the 'uses for old tickets' exercise. The key to successful brainstorming is
Ex C Q4 to break it into two stages: generating ideas in the first place, and then
Ex C Q5 evaluating those ideas to see if they're useful or not. We need to keep those stages separate; if we try to do both at the same time, we only generate boring, sensible ideas. But sometimes it's the silly ideas that help us to find excellent ideas. For example, a single bus ticket wouldn't make a great poster for your wall, but what about a poster made from 100 bus tickets from around the world?

READING

A SPEAK Work in pairs. How creative are you? Follow the instructions to find out.

1 Take an object from your pocket/bag (e.g. a used bus ticket). Try to think of as many different uses as possible for this object. Your ideas can be sensible or silly. What's your best idea?

A: We could cut it up to make a tiny jigsaw puzzle.
B: Why don't we write a short shopping list on the back?

2 Draw four straight lines to connect all the dots without taking your pen off the page. Now try again with only three straight lines.

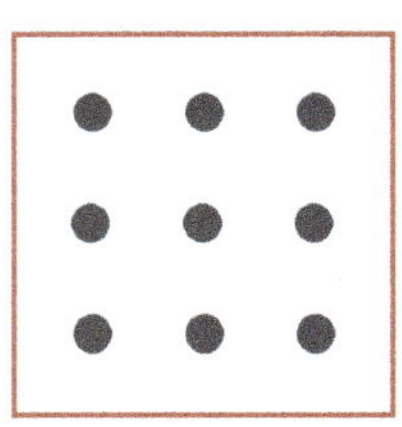

3 You're inside a room with three light switches on the wall. One of these switches turns on a light in a room on the other side of the house, but you don't know which switch. How can you find out? You can go to the other room to check only once.

B READ FOR GIST Read *Thinking outside the box.* How does it help with the questions in Exercise A?

C READ FOR DETAIL Choose *Do* or *Don't* for each piece of advice.

1 *Do / Don't* look at a problem in a new way.
2 *Do / Don't* do things the way you normally do them.
3 *Do / Don't* experiment with new ideas.
4 *Do / Don't* guess the rules and follow those rules.
5 *Do / Don't* evaluate ideas while you're generating them.

D SPEAK Work in groups. When do you need to brainstorm ideas? How could brainstorming silly ideas help you to think of useful ideas?

LISTENING

A SPEAK Work in pairs. The pictures show some techniques for becoming more creative. What do you think the techniques are?

B LISTEN FOR GIST 8.3 Listen to a conversation between two friends, Caroline and Toby, to check your answers to Exercise A. Number the pictures in the order they are mentioned.

Glossary

wander (v) if your mind or thoughts wander, you stop concentrating and start thinking about other things

8.1 Making a difference

READING

A–D Ask students to discuss ideas and check answers in pairs before whole-class feedback.

The first paragraph reminds us that our lines don't need to stay inside the red box or go through the middle of each dot.

The second paragraph reminds us we can touch the light bulb. Therefore, we can turn on the first two switches for a few seconds and then turn off the middle switch. Then the temperature of the bulbs when we go in the room will tell us if it is the first, middle or third switch.

The third paragraph shows us how silly ideas can lead to sensible ideas.

LISTENING

A Tell students to look at the pictures and tell them that they show techniques for becoming more creative. Put students into pairs to discuss what they think the techniques are. Elicit some ideas from the students but don't confirm or deny anything yet.

B (8.3) Tell students to listen to the conversation to check their ideas. Tell students that the speakers don't talk about the pictures in the same order as they appear in the book, so they need to number them in the order they are mentioned.

AUDIO SCRIPT

8.3

Listening, Exercise B
C = Caroline T = Toby

C: Hey, Toby. Do you want some coffee?
T: No, thanks. I'm in a hurry. I need to go to the library to work on my project for college.
C: Really? What's the project?
T: We have to invent 'something that will make a difference to people's lives'. But I'm terrible at coming up with ideas. They didn't teach us how to be creative in school when I was younger! But you, you're so creative. I mean, you write amazing stories; you design beautiful clothes. How do you do it?
C: Well, you can actually learn to use your imagination better. I've read a lot of books about creativity, and I've learned some great techniques from them. (Ex C Q1)
T: Really? Can you give me an example?
C: Well, whenever I feel like I have too much work, I always stop working for an hour or so.
T: But I don't have time to stop. I'm really busy!
C: I always thought the same. But when I tried it, I found that a break actually boosted my creativity. (Ex C Q2) When I'm relaxed, I have lots more creative ideas, and I'm much more productive after a break – I get more work done in less time. Tell me, how do you fill your time in the evenings?
T: Uh, I usually just watch TV or play games on my phone. I'm too tired to do anything else.
C: Aha. So that's what's blocking your creativity: you're filling your brain with information all the time. You need to unplug completely. Instead of watching TV, go for a run. (Ex C Q3) You need to let your mind wander freely.
T: OK, I guess I can watch less TV. But I hate running!
C: (Ex C Q3) Well, it doesn't have to be running. You could go dancing or swimming, or get some other type of physical exercise. They're all good for generating new ideas.
T: OK. I love swimming, so I guess I could go to the swimming pool once a week.
C: Great. Swimming's actually perfect because the water is blue.
T: Uh, sorry? What does that have to do with creativity?
C: (Ex C Q4) Well, I read recently that the color blue makes us more creative. Whenever I need to think outside the box, I go to the beach and look at the sky and the ocean. It always helps.
T: OK, but it doesn't really help me with my project. I need to start work on it right now. I'm actually getting stressed about it.
C: Well, maybe that's the problem: you're letting your emotions block your creativity. You should look at a problem from the outside, to take away the emotions. Then it's much easier to find a solution. That's why it's easier to solve other people's problems than your own – because you can focus on the problems, not the emotions.
T: OK, but …
C: So another good technique is to discuss your ideas with other people – and listen to what they say. The best solutions usually come from group discussions and brainstorming sessions. And if there's nobody you can talk to, you can imagine having a conversation with a friend. Look at the problem through someone else's eyes.
T: OK, yes, I know what you mean. But what about my project? I need to come up with an invention right now. But I don't have any ideas at all. My mind's gone blank!
C: Well, there's one last trick I usually use when I really have no ideas. I call it the alphabet technique. (Ex C Q5) OK, so tell me three letters of the alphabet.
T: Uh, W, G and P.
C: Perfect. So your invention needs to solve a problem, and that problem needs to start with your first letter, W.
T: Water? It isn't really a problem, is it?
C: Well, let's use your second letter to help us. What was it?
T: G – for grass. Hmm, water, grass. Aha, maybe the invention could be a better way of watering the grass in people's yards when they're away on vacation. I mean, just pouring water onto the grass all day and all night is really wasteful. But what's the solution?
C: I don't know. But it needs to start with your third letter, which was …?
T: P – for plastic bottles. Aha, I could use old plastic bottles, filled with water. Then I could make tiny holes in the bottles, so the water comes out really slowly, over a week or two.
C: Sounds good!
T: Hmm. I need to think about this carefully. OK, I'm going for a long walk along the beach to figure out the details. See you later.
C: OK. Call me if you need any help! Good luck!

8.3 **C** Tell students to read the information in the box about *Listening for problems and solutions*. Tell them to use the strategies in the box to answer the questions as they listen again.

D Put students into pairs to discuss which, if any, of Caroline's techniques they have used or might like to use in the future. Ask students who have used the strategies before to share their experiences. How successful were they? Would they recommend them to others?

VOCABULARY

A Elicit that all the sentences were used in the conversation between Caroline and Toby and ask if they remember hearing any of them. Tell students to match the beginnings of the sentences with the endings, either from memory or according to what they think makes sense.

B Put students into pairs to discuss what they think the words in bold from the sentences in Exercise A mean. As students do this, write the definitions on the board. Then ask students to look at the definitions and to match them with the words. This will make feedback clearer and more focused. Ask students if the definitions they thought of at first were similar to the ones on the board.

1. *coming up with new ideas = think of new ideas*
2. *use your imagination = be creative*
3. *boost your creativity = enhance your creativity*
4. *unplug completely = to completely relax, not to think about anything*
5. *let your mind wander freely = not to concentrate on one thing*
6. *generating new ideas = think of new ideas*
7. *think outside the box = think in a new way*
8. *block your creativity = stop yourself from being able to think of new ideas*
9. *look at a problem from the outside = think about a problem from a different perspective*
10. *my mind's gone blank = unable to remember or think anything*

C Tell students to choose the best words to complete the questions. Check answers, then put students into groups to discuss the questions. Share any interesting answers with the class.

SPEAKING HUB

A Put students into groups and tell them that they are going to create a website that will make a big difference to people's lives. Remind students about Caroline's alphabet technique from the Listening and tell them to discuss the questions in their groups.

B Tell students to brainstorm five ideas for each of the questions. Remind them to think outside the box. Monitor to help with language input.

C Tell groups to look at their ideas from Exercise B and the details about their website from Exercise A. Tell them they now have everything they need for an excellent idea. Tell students to choose the best ideas and to prepare to present them to the class. Again, monitor to help with language if needed.

D Tell each group to present their website to the class. Tell students to listen carefully and to ask questions at the end of each presentation. After all the presentations have been made, ask students which of the websites they would visit and which they think could be successful. Finish with feedback on students' use of language during the presentations.

Extra activity

For homework, students can write the *About us* page for their websites. You can give students the following points to help structure their writing:

- a summary or mission statement
- the story behind the website
- more detail on the problem you are trying to solve
- how you will solve it
- some personal details about your group

METHODOLOGY HUB by Jim Scrivener

Scaffolding

During a fluency activity, there may be a way to offer spontaneous correction that:

- does not interfere too much with the flow of conversation;
- offers useful language feedback;
- actually helps the speaker to construct his conversation.

'Scaffolding' refers to the way a competent language speaker helps a less competent one to communicate by both encouraging and providing possible elements of the conversation. It is the way an elementary school teacher might help a young child to communicate, or the way a talk show host might draw out a guest. The listener offers support – like scaffolding around a building – to help the speaker create his own spoken structure.

Scaffolding in class isn't a normal conversation in the sense that the teacher/listener is not meant to contribute any personal stories or opinions of her own; the goal of her own speaking is solely to help the speaker tell his story.

Scaffolding techniques

- Showing interest and agreeing: nodding, 'uh-huh', eye contact, 'yes', etc;
- Concisely asking for clarification of unclear information, e.g. repeating an unclear word;
- Encouragement echo: repeating the last word (maybe with questioning intonation) in order to encourage the speaker to continue;
- Echoing meaning: picking on a key element of meaning and saying it back to the speaker, e.g. 'a foreign vacation';
- Asking conversation-oiling questions (ones that mainly recap already stated information), e.g. *Is it? Do you? Where was it?* etc;
- Asking brief questions (or using sentence heads) that encourage the speaker to extend the story, e.g. *And then … He went … She wanted …* etc;
- Unobtrusively saying the correct form of an incorrect word (but only if having the correct word makes a significant positive contribution to the communication);
- Giving the correct pronunciation of words in replies without drawing any particular attention to it;
- Unobtrusively giving a word or phrase that the speaker is looking for.

8.3 **C** **Listen again. What was the solution to each problem? Use the strategies in the box to help you.**

Listening for problems and solutions

When you're listening, it's useful to organize information into a set of problems and solutions. This usually makes it easier to understand a lot of information and to remember it better later.

Listen carefully when you hear people talking about problems because they'll probably present a solution next.

1 You don't learn how to be creative at school.
  a Write stories and design clothes.
  b Go to creativity classes.
  (c) Read books about creativity.
2 You're too busy to stop working.
  (a) Take a break to make yourself more productive.
  b Work in the evenings so you can have a break during the day.
  c Relax – your work isn't as important as you think.
3 Your brain is filled with too much information.
  (a) Get some physical exercise.
  b Watch TV and play games on your phone.
  c Turn off your computer.
4 You need to think outside the box.
  a Go to the library to get some ideas.
  (b) Look at blue things.
  c Listen to some music.
5 You have no ideas at all.
  a Discuss your ideas with a group of friends.
  b Close your eyes for a few minutes.
  (c) Use letters of the alphabet to generate ideas.

D SPEAK **Work in pairs. Which of Caroline's techniques have you used? Which might you use in the future? Tell your partner.**

VOCABULARY
Creative thinking

A **Match the beginnings of the sentences (1–10) with the endings (a–j).**

g 1 I'm terrible at **coming up**
c 2 You can actually learn to **use your**
f 3 A break actually **boosted my**
i 4 You need to **unplug**
b 5 You need to **let your mind**
j 6 They're all good for **generating**
a 7 Whenever I need to **think outside**
d 8 You're letting your emotions **block**
h 9 You should **look at a problem**
e 10 **My mind's**

a **the box**, I go to the beach.
b **wander freely**.
c **imagination** better.
d **your creativity**.
e **gone blank**.
f **creativity**.
g **with new ideas**.
h **from the outside**.
i **completely**.
j **new ideas**.

B **Look at the sentences in Exercise A. What do the phrases in bold mean?**

C SPEAK **Choose the best words to complete the questions. Then work in groups and ask and answer the questions.**

1 Does your mind ever *boost* / *generate* / *wander* during boring activities? Think of some examples.
2 Is it possible to *come up* / *unplug* / *block* completely from the things that make you stressed? How can you do it?
3 What can you do when your *mind* / *creativity* / *imagination* goes blank in a stressful situation (e.g. when you're in an exam, giving a presentation or speaking English)?

SPEAKING HUB

A **Work in groups. You have decided to create a website that will make a big difference to people's lives. Use the alphabet technique to generate some ideas – silly or serious!**

Write down three letters of the alphabet.

- 1st letter: Who is your website for?
- 2nd letter: What problem do those people have?
- 3rd letter: How will you solve that problem?

B PLAN **Think of five ideas for each of the questions below. Remember to think outside the box!**

1 What will you call your website?
2 How can you make money from your website?
3 How will you tell the world about your website?

C ORGANIZE **Look at your ideas from Exercise B. Turn your silly ideas into excellent ideas. Choose your best idea.**

D PRESENT **Present your idea to the class. Which teams' websites would you visit?**

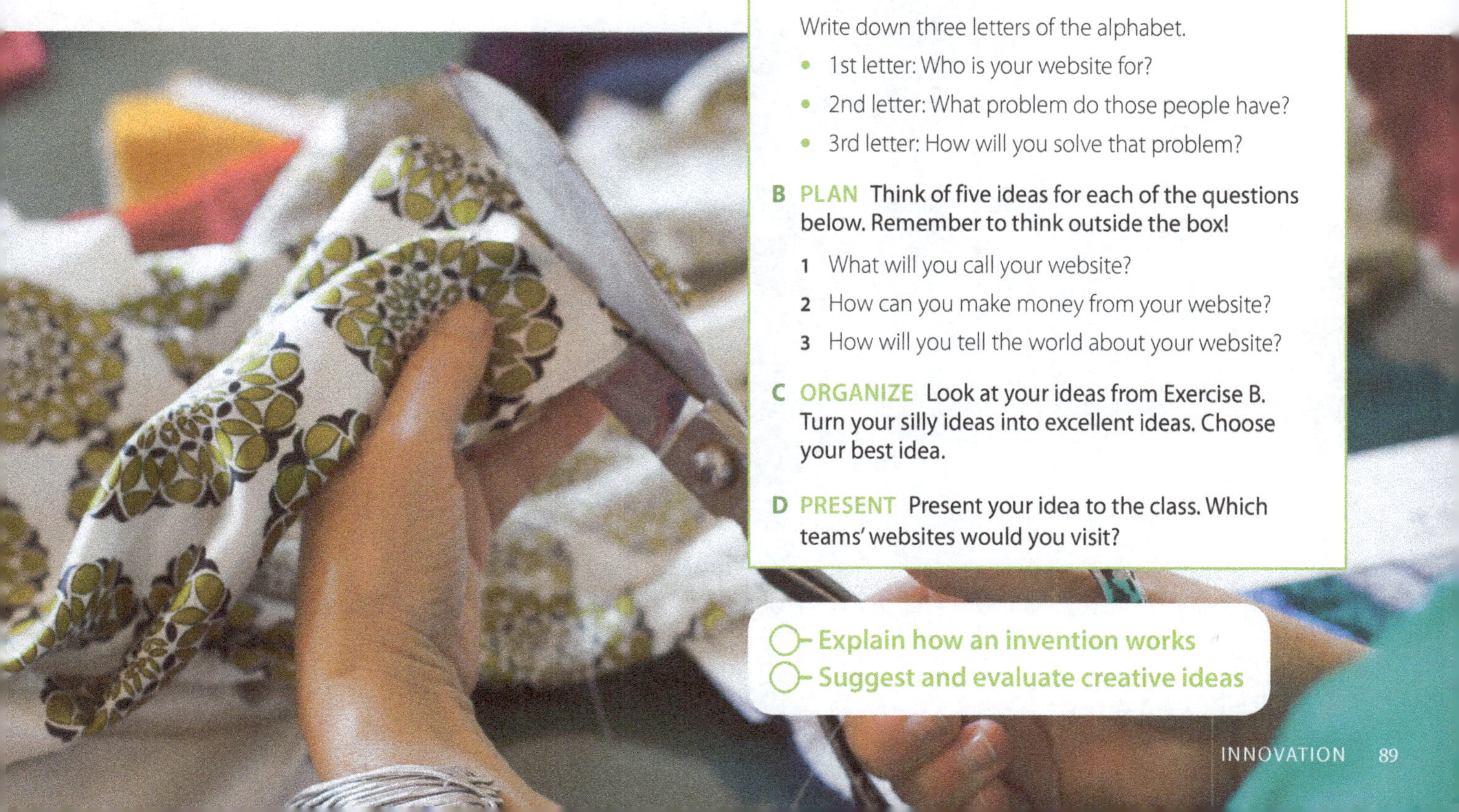

— Explain how an invention works
— Suggest and evaluate creative ideas

8.2 Must-have gadgets

- Use positive language to promote a new product
- Give a friend advice about choosing a gadget

V – positive adjectives
G – zero and first conditionals; conditionals with modals and imperatives
P – *'ll* and *won't*
S – topic sentences

LISTENING

A SPEAK Work in pairs. Look at the pictures of inventions (a–d) and discuss the questions.

1 What do you think the gadgets in the pictures do?
2 How useful are they?
3 Do you like gadgets? What gadgets do you own?

8.4 **B LISTEN FOR MAIN IDEA** Listen to a podcast about new gadgets and answer the questions.

1 Which gadgets from the pictures do the people discuss?
2 What is special about them?

8.4 **C** Listen again. Which gadgets do these sentences describe? Write *O* (Oombrella), *C* (CleverPet) or *B* (both).

1 It looks beautiful. O
2 It's connected to the internet. B
3 It sends messages to your phone. O
4 It's useful for many years. B
5 It gets more difficult to use over time. C
6 It can lead to a longer life. C

D SPEAK Work in groups and discuss the questions.

1 What is good about the two gadgets? Which one is more useful?
2 Who do you think will buy the gadgets? Why?

VOCABULARY

Positive adjectives

Using positive adjectives

As your English improves, try to avoid using words like *good* or *nice* too frequently. There are many other positive words that you can use like *amazing*, *excellent* and *wonderful*.

A Match the positive adjectives (1–10) with the meanings (a–j).

h 1 gorgeous
e 2 sensible
j 3 practical
f 4 unforgettable
a 5 impressive
d 6 unique
i 7 sophisticated
g 8 incredible
c 9 suitable
b 10 fascinating

a you admire it because it is very good, large or shows great skill
b making you very interested or attracted
c right for a particular purpose, person or situation
d not the same as anything or anyone else
e reasonable and practical
f will be remembered for a very long time
g surprising, or difficult to believe
h very beautiful
i complicated and advanced in design
j intended to be useful

B Go to the Vocabulary Hub on page 145.

C SPEAK Work in pairs. Write down the names of your favorite three possessions. Use positive adjectives to tell your partner why you like each one. Ask questions about your partner's possessions.

a

b

LEAD-IN

With books closed, write *Must-have*_____ on the board. Elicit ideas about how to complete the phrase (e.g. *must-have books*).

LISTENING

8.4 **A–D** Give students time to compare answers before whole-class feedback.

1 *They discuss the umbrella (Oombrella) and the dog bowl.*
2 *The Oombrella is connected to the internet. CleverPet entertains dogs and cats with puzzles – they have to press buttons to win food.*

VOCABULARY

A Tell students to match the positive adjectives with their meanings. Do the first one together as a whole class and practice pronunciation.

B Direct students to the **Vocabulary Hub** (TB121) for further practice of positive adjectives.

C Encourage students to ask their partner follow-up questions. Finish by commenting on how well students used the positive adjectives. Correct any inappropriate uses. Use the **Vocabulary Worksheet** on W32 for extra practice.

AUDIO SCRIPT

8.4

Listening, Exercises B and C
L = Leo T = Teresa

L: Hello, and welcome to this week's Must-have Gadgets podcast. I'm Leo Kovalski.
T: And I'm Teresa Martinez. Now, earlier this week, I went to the International Gadget Show, where I saw some really amazing gadgets. And I've brought two along today to show you, Leo.
L: Sounds great. So what do you have for us?
T: Well, let's start with a very sensible invention: the Oombrella. What do you think, Leo?
L: Uh … it just looks like a normal umbrella. I mean, (Ex C Q1) the design is gorgeous, really nice, but … it isn't exactly innovative, is it?
T: Oh! But this Oombrella is unique. (Ex C Q2) It's the world's first umbrella that's connected to the internet.
L: What? Why on earth do I need an umbrella that connects to the internet?
T: Well, did you bring an umbrella to work today?
L: No, unfortunately. I forgot to check the weather forecast, so I didn't know it was going to rain.
T: Aha. Well, you can borrow my Oombrella today. It'll check the weather forecast for you. If the forecast says it's going to rain later, Oombrella will send a message to your cell phone.
L: OK, but why do I need a special umbrella just to send weather forecasts to my phone?
T: Well, the Oombrella is especially suitable for forgetful people, like you, who forget to check the weather forecast on their phones.
L: Yes, well, I am a fairly forgetful person. But what do forgetful people do all the time? They leave their umbrellas behind in cafés, or on the bus! What if I lose your Oombrella tonight?
Ex C Q3 **T:** Well, if you leave it behind, you'll get a message on your phone. They call it the unforgettable umbrella because you can't forget it.
L: OK, yes, that is pretty practical, I suppose.
T: Yes. And the Oombrella also has lots of sophisticated electronics: if you go for a long walk in the rain tonight, the app will send you a weather report when you get home. So you can read all about the weather during your walk.
L: Hmmm … I'm not sure I need an Oombrella. I never go for a walk unless the sun's shining. The big question for me is: will it keep me dry if there's a storm tomorrow morning when I'm coming to work?
T: Absolutely! It's made of super-strong materials, so it (Ex C Q4) won't break. You'll be able to use it for years.
L: Really? Well, that is impressive. My umbrellas always break after five minutes in a storm. So if this Oombrella lasts for years, I'll be very happy.
T: Well, I only said you could borrow mine. I'd like to have it back tomorrow.
L: Oh, yes, of course. So … what else do you have?
T: Well, the second gadget is called CleverPet. It's a food bowl for dogs and cats.
Ex C Q2 **L:** Great. And don't tell me … it's connected to the internet, right?
T: Yes! How did you guess? Do you have any pets, Leo?
L: Yes, I have a dog named Henry.
T: And what does Henry do all day, while you're at work?
L: Uh … not much. He sleeps most of the day, but sometimes he chews the furniture in my apartment.
T: Well, that's because he's bored. Of course, he chews your furniture if he has nothing else to do all day.
L: OK. And what does this have to do with your incredible internet-connected dog food bowl?
T: Well, it isn't just a bowl. It's a puzzle.
L: A puzzle? For dogs?
T: Yes. There are three buttons with lights. When a light flashes, the dog has to press a button. If he presses the right button, the light goes on again and he wins something to eat.
L: OK.
Ex C Q4 **T:** Then, over the next few days, weeks, even years, the
Ex C Q5 puzzles get more and more difficult. The dog has to remember lots of information and press the buttons in the right order.
L: Oh, right. And, uh, do dogs enjoy puzzles?
T: Absolutely! They love them. It keeps them busy for hours, which means they never get bored. And if they don't get bored, they don't chew the furniture.
L: Well, I must admit, it sounds fascinating.
T: It is. And it really helps pets stay active. Scientists (Ex C Q6) have shown that pets stay healthier and they live longer if they keep busy. You should definitely get one for Henry.
L: Yes, I think I might!
T: Great.
L: OK, so that's all from today's podcast. We'll be back next time with more must-have gadgets. Thanks for listening.

8.2 Must-have gadgets

GRAMMAR

8.5 **A** Tell students to match the beginnings of the sentences with the endings. Play the audio for students to check their answers.

B Tell students to look at the sentences from Exercise A to help them complete the rules. When checking answers, ensure students understand that sentences 1 and 4 from Exercise A are zero conditionals and sentences 2 and 3 are first conditionals.

C Direct students to the **Grammar Hub** (see below and TB92). Use the **Grammar Worksheet** on W31 for extra practice.

PRONUNCIATION

8.6 **A** Point out the information in the box about *'ll* and *won't*. Tell students to listen to the sentences and to circle the words they hear.

8.6 **B** Play the audio again for students to listen and repeat the sentences. Focus on the contractions, practicing pronunciation of the contractions in isolation before building back up to the whole sentence. Tell students that they don't necessarily have to speak exactly like this but that an awareness of the pronunciation will help them understand natural speech more easily.

C Tell students either to show their partner a gadget they have on them or to invent one that they think their partner would be interested in. Choose an example as a whole class and elicit some examples of zero and first conditionals to describe the functions of your gadget and offer to lend it to someone in the class but with certain conditions. Put students into pairs to do the same. Ask the class to tell you about the most interesting gadgets and offers. Comment on any successful use of conditionals or any situations where students could have used them but didn't.

SPEAKING

A Tell students that they are going to invent a new gadget and then promote it to the class. Tell them to use the ideas in the table, ideas from the previous activity or new ideas of their own. Give students some time to work alone to think and write notes. Monitor and help them with any new vocabulary they need.

B Put students into groups to share ideas and to agree on which is the best gadget. When they have decided, tell each group to prepare to promote their gadget. Tell them to think about the questions and to write notes. Monitor to help with language input. When students have finished, tell them to practice making their presentation.

C Tell each group to promote their gadget to the class. Tell the other students to listen carefully and to think of questions to ask. At the end of each presentation, get the students to ask their questions.

D Tell each group to decide which gadget they think is the best. Tell them they can't vote for their own! Tell each group to vote, then congratulate the winner. Ask students which gadgets they would really buy, and which they think could become real products. Finish with feedback on students' use of language during the presentations and feedback.

GRAMMAR HUB

8.2 Zero and first conditionals; Conditionals with modals and imperatives

Zero conditional

Condition	Result
If **you listen**,	**you learn**.
If **you like** science,	**it helps**.

Question	Positive short answer	Negative short answer
If **I win**, **do I get** a prize?	Yes, **you do**.	No, **you don't**.
Does it help if you like science?	Yes, **it does**.	No, **it doesn't**.

- We use the zero conditional to talk about things that are always true.
- We can put the *if*-clause or the result clause first. The only difference is we do not use a comma if we begin with the result clause.
- We can use negatives and *unless* (which means *if not* or *except if*) in the zero conditional.

  If you don't pay attention, you make mistakes.
  = Unless you pay attention, you make mistakes.

First conditional

Condition	Result
If **you try** hard,	**you'll succeed**.
If **it doesn't work**,	**we'll start** again.

Question	Positive short answer	Negative short answer
If **we win** the award, **will we be** famous?	Yes, **we/you will**.	No, **we/you won't**.
Will we be famous if **we win** the award?		

- We use the first conditional to talk about possible situations in the future.
- We can put the *if*-clause or the result clause first. The only difference is we do not use a comma if we begin with the result clause.
- We can use negatives and *unless* (meaning *if not* or *except if*) in the first conditional.

  If you don't listen, you won't understand.
  = Unless you listen, you won't understand.
- We never put *will* in an *if*-clause.

Conditionals with modals and imperatives

- We can use other modal verbs (e.g. *can*, *could*, *might*, *should*) instead of *will*.

  *If you work hard enough, you **can** do it!*
  *I **might** visit the science museum if it's open tomorrow.*
- We can use an imperative instead of a result clause.

  *If you see smoke, **call** for help.*
  ***Call** me if you have any questions.*

GRAMMAR

Zero and first conditionals

8.5 **A** **Look at the extracts from the podcast about new gadgets. Match the beginnings of the sentences (1–4) with the endings (a–d). Then listen and check your answers.**

1 I never go for a walk
2 Will it keep me dry
3 If this Oombrella lasts for years,
4 Pets stay healthier and they live longer

a if there's a storm tomorrow morning?
b if they keep busy.
c I'll be very happy.
d unless the sun's shining.

B **WORK IT OUT** **Choose the correct words to complete the rules.**

Zero and first conditional

1 Conditional sentences usually have ***two*** / ***four*** clauses: the *if*-clause and the result clause.
2 When the ***if***-clause comes first, we ***always*** / ***never*** need a comma between the clauses.
3 We can use ***unless*** instead of ***if***. It means ***if not*** / ***because***.
4 We use the zero conditional to talk about things that are always true. We use ***past*** / ***present*** tenses in both clauses.
5 We use the first conditional to talk about possible situations in the ***future*** / ***past***. We usually use ***will*** in the result clause.

C **Go to the Grammar Hub on page 136.**

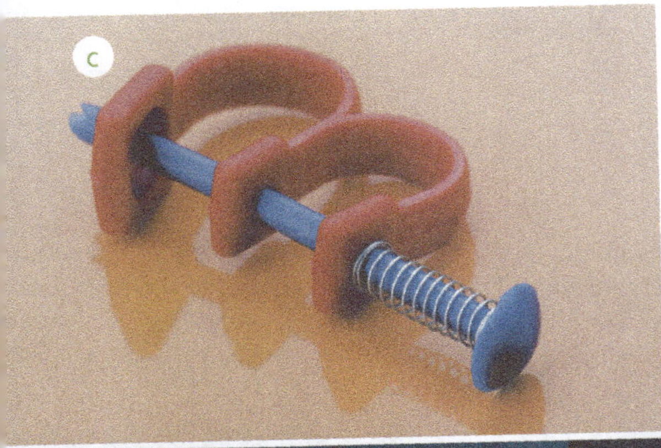

PRONUNCIATION

'll and *won't*

'll* and *won't

It's sometimes hard to hear the difference between words such as *you* and *you'll*, or *I* and *I'll*. It's also sometimes hard to hear the difference between *won't* and *want*. The rules for conditionals will help you figure out what you hear.

8.6 **A** **Listen and circle the words you hear.**

1 If you ***want to go*** / ***won't go*** to the grocery store, ***you*** / ***you'll*** need to bring a bag.
2 ***I lend*** / ***I'll lend*** you my raincoat if you ***want to borrow*** / ***won't borrow*** it.
3 If ***you*** / ***you'll*** like gadgets, ***you*** / ***you'll*** love this.
4 ***You learn*** / ***You'll earn*** a lot more if ***you*** / ***you'll*** listen carefully.

8.6 **B** **Listen again and repeat the sentences.**

C **SPEAK** **Work in pairs. Imagine you are going to lend your partner a gadget tonight. Follow the instructions.**

1 If you have a gadget with you (e.g. a phone, a smartwatch), show your partner what to do. Ask questions about your partner's gadget.
2 If you don't have a gadget, use an everyday object (e.g. a pen, your car keys) and pretend it's a gadget. Invent some cool functions for it.

SPEAKING

A **You are going to invent a new gadget and then promote it to the class. Use the ideas below and your own ideas to invent a gadget.**

What is it?	What's innovative about it?
a book, a chair, a food bowl, a hat, swimming goggles, a mirror, a light bulb, a plastic bottle, a puzzle, shoes, a toy, a TV, an umbrella	It can fly/talk/move by itself. It's connected to the internet. It contains a GPS device / a camera. It's for pets/birds/fish. It's very big/small.

B **PLAN** **Work in groups. Choose the best idea for your group's gadget and answer the questions:**

- What is special about your gadget?
- What problem does it solve?
- What else can you use to help you promote your gadget (e.g. pictures, stories)?
- What questions might people ask about your gadget?

C **PRESENT** **Promote your gadget to the class. At the end of each presentation, ask questions about other groups' gadgets.**

D **REFLECT** **Take a class vote to find out the most popular gadget. Would you like to buy the other groups' gadgets? Why/Why not? Do you think your gadgets could become real products?**

READING

A SPEAK Work in pairs. Look at the picture and answer the questions. Suggested answer

1 What do you think the people are doing? Why?
They're standing in line for something, e.g. to buy a new gadget such as a phone or to meet a famous movie star.

2 Have you ever done something similar? Why/Why not?

B PREDICT Work in pairs. Before you read *If you really can't wait …*, look at the five topic sentences (a–e) and discuss the questions. Use the strategies in the box to help you.

Topic sentences

The topic sentence is usually the first or second sentence in a paragraph. It tells you what the whole paragraph will be about.

You can usually understand a lot about a text just by reading and thinking about the topic sentences.

You can also use them to make predictions before reading the whole text to check.

a Marketers have a name for people who buy new gadgets before everyone else: innovators.
Why do you think marketers have a special name for these people? Why are marketers interested in them?

b A little further back in the line, I meet some fans who aren't just there to buy a phone.
Why do you think these fans are in the line?

c Near the back of the line, some people are feeling less positive.
Why do you think they're feeling less positive?

d It's five o'clock in the morning, and there are already over 200 people in the line outside the phone store.
Why do you think they're there so early in the morning?

e I decided to speak to some people in the line outside the phone store to find out … and I got a few surprises.
What surprises do you think the writer got?

If you really can't wait …

1 d It's cold and dark, but the people seem happy. In a few hours, the doors will open and they'll finally get their hands on the gadget of their dreams: a gorgeous new cell phone. Of course, if you don't want to stand in line all night, you can come to the store this afternoon when the lines will be gone. Even better, if you can wait six months or so, the same phone will cost half the price. But if you really need that phone right now, come and join the back of the line.

2 a I've always thought that was a terrible name – innovation normally means doing something extremely smart, like inventing a new machine. But what's innovative about buying expensive gadgets just because they're new? Of course, marketers love 'innovators' for two reasons: innovators are happy to spend a lot of money and they persuade the rest of us to buy those gadgets a few months later.

So why do they do it? 3 e The biggest surprise was that the people at the front of the line were actually being paid to be there. 'I work for a gadget store, Gary's Gadgets. My boss, Gary, is paying me,' said Bob, who is right at the front of the line. 'It's good for business because when the doors open, I'll be on TV around the world – wearing a T-shirt with the Gary's Gadgets logo.' Janice and Damian, who are second and third in the line, are also there for the money. (Ex D Q5) 'We came here ten days ago, just to make sure we were first,' says Janice. 'But then Bob offered us $2500 to move ahead of us.' (Ex D Q2)

(Ex D Q6) 4 b 'For me, it's a social event,' says a man named Mo. 'It's a great way to meet people who share my love of gadgets. (Ex D Q1) I've had some amazing conversations in this line. Many of us come every year, so it feels like meeting old friends.' (Ex D Q4) A woman named Ruby agrees, 'It's like going to a pop concert or a live sports game. I love the feeling of being at an important place at an important time.'

(Ex D Q7) 5 c 'I'm only here because of the special offer: 25 percent off for the first 200 customers,' explains a stressed-looking young woman named Lucy, 'so I'll be really annoyed if I'm number 201!' (Ex D Q3) Her best friend, Fiona, looks annoyed already. 'I'm only here to keep Lucy company,' she says. 'I actually think it's a waste of time and money. I've been here all night and I'm really cold. I mean, this new phone looks exactly the same as last year's!' But Lucy looks shocked. 'There's only one difference that counts: the difference between the best … and second best.'

8.2 Must-have gadgets

READING

A Check understanding of *standing in line*, then put students into pairs to discuss the longest they've ever stood in line for something. Give a personal example, explaining what you were standing in line for and why. Tell students to do the same with their partner. Get some feedback on the most interesting answers, then put them back into pairs to discuss the questions.

They're standing in line to buy a new gadget (e.g. a phone).

B Do not give them the answers below yet.

a *spend a lot of money, persuade us to buy gadgets*

b *social event, big occasion, special offer, gone with a friend, promoting a business*

c *miss out on the offer, waste a long time in the line*

d *to be the first to get the goods*

e *finding out that some people were paid to be there*

TEACHING IDEA by David Seymour and Maria Popova

Grammar: Functions

Use this activity to extend the grammar.

Here is a list of six functions. (Write them on the board.)

prediction, offer, warning, threat, advice, suggestions

I'm going to dictate six sentences. Write them down and decide which function they have. (Read aloud the sentences in a different order; they appear in the same order as the functions.)

1 If we don't leave now, we'll miss the train.
2 If you want, I'll do the dishes.
3 If you touch that wire, you'll get an electric shock.
4 If you don't stop doing that, I'll get angry.
5 If you explain why you did it, he'll understand.
6 If you turn it around the other way, it'll fit.

In pairs, compare your answers. Then write another conditional sentence for each function.

In groups, think of some situations where people make bargains with each other. Write an appropriate *If …* sentence for each. Read aloud your sentences for other groups to guess who is speaking to whom, e.g. If you're good, I'll buy you ice cream (parent to child).

TEACHING IDEA by David Seymour and Maria Popova

Grammar: Anxiety role plays

Use this activity to extend the grammar.

Work in pairs, A and B. Student A is very adventurous; Student B is very anxious. In your pairs, role-play a discussion between two good friends about the situation I give you, e.g.

A: I'm going to tour the Amazon.
B: What will you do if you catch malaria?
A: Don't worry. If I catch malaria, I'll go to see a local doctor.
B: But what if you're in the middle of the jungle?
A: If I'm in the jungle, I'll see an Amazonian Indian doctor.
B: What will happen if you get lost?
A: If I get lost …

1 You are going on vacation to South America, where you will spend six months taking photographs of the wildlife and landscapes, including the jungles, mountains, ocean and desert.
2 You are giving up a well-paid job to become an art student in Paris.
3 You are getting married to a singer in a rock and roll band that has a reputation for very bad behavior.

GRAMMAR HUB

8.2 Zero and first conditionals; Conditionals with modals and imperatives

A Find and correct the mistakes with the zero conditional.

1 If you ~~will~~ read a lot, you understand things better.
2 It's better if you ~~called~~ call me in the evenings.
3 Unless you ~~don't~~ try, you don't learn. If you don't try, you don't learn.
4 The roads ~~will~~ are more dangerous if it rains.
5 It doesn't work if you ~~won't~~ don't turn it on. It works if you turn it on.
6 ~~I'll never~~ I won't go out if it's cold.

B Complete the first conditional sentences using the information in parentheses.

1 The machine will not work *if you don't press this button.*
(*you / not / press this button*)
2 If you find it at the right price, will you buy it?
(*you / buy it?*)
3 What will we do if it doesn't / does not work?
(*it / not work?*)
4 How will you get home if you miss the bus?
(*you / miss the bus?*)
5 If it rains tomorrow, will you still play soccer?
(*you / still / play soccer?*)
6 If you take an umbrella with you, it'll / it will keep you dry.
(*it / keep you dry*)
7 I won't help him if he doesn't / does not ask. / unless he asks.
(*he / not ask*)

C Choose the correct option.

1 If you see Jimmy, ___
  a will give him this note.
  (b) give him this note.
2 You will save money if ___
  (a) you can wait a few months.
  b you will wait a few months.
3 If you don't like it, ___
  (a) you can go home.
  b will you go home.
4 If you have any problems, ___
  a will call me.
  (b) call me.
5 If I feel like it, ___
  (a) I might go to the pop concert.
  b I can go to the pop concert.
6 Ask me if there's anything ___
  (a) you don't understand.
  b you won't understand.
7 If you want to have a good time, ___
  a you will come and join us on Saturday night!
  (b) come and join us on Saturday night!

➤ Go back to page 93.

C Tell students to read the article and to match the topic sentences from Exercise B with each paragraph. Set a time limit and tell students not to worry if they don't understand everything.

D Tell students to look at the questions and to try to remember which person each question is about. Then tell students to read the article again to check. Tell them to underline the parts of the text where they find the answers. Elicit which part of the text provided the answers when providing feedback to the class.

E Put students into groups to discuss the question. Share answers as a whole class and encourage students to expand on their answers. If students don't agree that people who buy new gadgets are innovators, ask what kind of people they do think innovators are.

GRAMMAR

A Tell students to cover the article and to read the rules in the box. Tell them that the examples all come from the first paragraph of the article. Tell students to try to complete the sentences without looking back at the text. Encourage students to work in pairs or groups on this, then tell them to uncover the text to check. Remind students about the zero and first conditional structures they saw previously, and check they understand that these are used in the same situations and for the same reasons.

B Direct students to the **Grammar Hub** (see TB91 and 92).

C As a way to make a multiple-choice controlled-practice activity more varied and fun, you could play *Runaround*. Divide the class into as many areas as there are possible answers (in this case, just two) and label these areas A and B Read aloud the first half of the sentence, then read the two possible ways to complete it (A or B). Students have to run to the area of the class matches the letter which they think is the correct answer. Give a time limit for this, then give the correct answer. Students in the wrong area are out and can act as judges for the next questions.

SPEAKING HUB

A Put students into pairs and tell them to think of a gadget they both know well. Do an example together as a whole class to demonstrate the task. Elicit advice about the price, features and risks. Elicit some conditionals as you do this (e.g. *If you buy the most expensive one, you'll be able to …*) to model how students could do the same. Tell students to choose a gadget and write notes about their advice. Monitor as they do this to help with language input.

B Put students into new pairs to role-play the conversations, with first student giving advice to their partner, then changing roles. Next, put students together with a new partner to repeat the task.

C Move students back to their original partner and tell them to tell each other about the gadgets their other partners told them about. Ask them to report what the best advice they heard was. Tell them to decide which gadget they would be most likely to buy. Decide as a whole class on the most popular gadgets and the best advice given. Finish with feedback on students' use of language.

METHODOLOGY HUB by Jim Scrivener

Classifying conditionals

There are two different ways of analyzing conditional sentences.

Real/unreal

Grammar books tend to distinguish between real conditionals and unreal conditionals.

Real conditionals are made using exactly the verb tenses you would expect for the time they refer to.

If the children are playing in the yard, tell them to come in.

If you are going to fly to Paris, you'll need a new passport.

Unreal conditionals refer to unreal situations, i.e. when you are imagining impossible or unlikely futures or alternative possibilities for the past. These are made using special verb forms to indicate they are unreal:

Simple past = unlikely or impossible present or future

If human lived on Mars, do you think they'd get bored with the color red?

The sentence is about a possible but unlikely present or future. *Lived* is a past form. The speaker uses a past form to indicate (in his / her view) the unlikeliness or the remoteness of this idea ever becoming true.

Past perfect = an alternative past

If I hadn't gone to college, my life would be very different now.

The sentence is about something that didn't happen in the past. The speaker is imagining an alternative reality. The past perfect form is used to indicate that the event never happened.

First, Second, Third, Zero

Textbooks, teachers and students usually prefer a classification *into First conditional, Second conditional, Third conditional* and *Zero conditional* (also known as *Conditional Type 1, Type 2, Type 3 and Type 0*).

These are two different ways of dividing up and looking at the same cake. You'll have to decide which one is most suitable for you and your students. The first way is arguably more accurate and encompasses the wide variety of conditionals used in the real world. The other way is favored by many teachers because it allows for a more sequenced way of presenting and practicing a number of common types of conditional sentences.

C **READ FOR GIST** Read the article. Match the topic sentences (a–e) with the paragraphs (1–5).

D **READ FOR DETAIL** Read again. Write *B* (Bob), *J* (Janice), *M* (Mo), *R* (Ruby), *L* (Lucy) or *F* (Fiona).

Which person …

1 has met people from the line at events like this before? M
2 paid to be at the front of the line? B
3 doesn't want to buy a phone at all? F
4 compares the experience to other exciting events? R
5 arrived before anyone else? J
6 enjoys talking to other people about gadgets? M
7 is hoping to save some money? L

E **SPEAK** Work in groups. Do you think it is right to call people who buy the latest gadgets *innovators*? Why/Why not?

Glossary

gadget (n) a small tool or piece of equipment that does something useful or impressive, sometimes using new technology

innovative (adj) new, original and advanced

innovator (n) a person who invents or begins using new ideas, methods, equipment, etc.

GRAMMAR

Conditionals with modals and imperatives

A **WORK IT OUT** Read the rules. Then look at paragraph 1 of *If you really can't wait …* again and complete the examples.

Conditionals with modals and imperatives

Zero conditionals and first conditionals are very common. They can be very varied. Many patterns are possible.

For example, we can use imperatives in the result clause:

If you really need that phone right now, 1 come and join *the back of the line.*

We can use modal verbs (e.g. *should, might, can, must*) in the *if*-clause or the result clause:

If you don't want to stand in line all night, you 2 can come *to the store this afternoon.*

If you 3 can wait *six months or so, the same phone will cost half the price.*

B Go to the **Grammar Hub** on **page 136**.

C **SPEAK** Work in pairs. Write five pieces of advice for people who are thinking of standing in line for the latest cell phone. Use these ideas and your own ideas:

- If you want to be at the front of the line, you should …
- If you can't afford a new phone right now, …
- If somebody offers you $2500 for your place in the line, …

SPEAKING HUB

A Work in pairs. Choose a gadget you both know well (e.g. phone, camera, laptop, webcam). You are going to give some advice to a friend who wants to buy one of these gadgets. Write notes on:

- price (simple version / best version?)
- features (what must/should it have?)
- risks (what might go wrong with it?)

B **SPEAK** Work in new pairs. Take turns role-playing the conversation. Student A is the friend who needs advice. Student B gives advice.

A: I don't know anything about photography. Do you have any recommendations for a new camera?

B: Well, it does really depend on how much you want to spend …

C **DISCUSS** What was the best advice you received? Would you buy the gadget your partner recommended?

Use positive language to promote a new product

Give a friend advice about choosing a gadget

Café Hub

8.3 Flat-packed

F – give and follow instructions   P – sentence stress

COMPREHENSION

A Work in pairs and discuss the questions.

- Have you ever tried to build a piece of furniture or put up a shelf?
- How would you describe the experience – successful, frustrating, etc?
- Are you good at giving and following instructions?

B Match the words in the box with the tools in the pictures (a–d). Which tools do you think Sam and Zac will need to build a shelf?

allen key	drill	hammer	helmet
pliers	screwdriver	spanner	tape measure

a

b

c

d

C ▶ 00:00–02:53 Watch the first part of the video. How many tools do they use?
one - the screwdriver

D ▶ 00:00–02:53 Put the instructions in the correct order (1–5). Watch the first part again and check your answers.

2 Lay out all the pieces in a row.
5 Insert the screws on both sides.
4 Put the screws into the correct holes.
3 Take the packet of screws.
1 Organize all of the pieces into the correct order.

E ▶ 02:54–04:13 How is Sam feeling and why? Watch the second part of the video to check your ideas.

FUNCTIONAL LANGUAGE

Giving and following instructions

A ▶ 02:54–04:13 Complete the phrases with the words in the box. Then watch the second part of the video again to check your answers.

after	again	correct	do	how	let	sure	that	thing

Sequencing

1 The first ___thing___ to do is …
2 When you've done ___that___ …
3 ___After___ that, you …

Explaining

4 Make ___sure___ you …
5 ___Let___ me show you …
6 This is how you ___do___ it.

Checking

7 Sorry, can you say that ___again___.
8 Is this ___how___ you do it?
9 Are you sure this is ___correct___?

Glossary

allen key **(n) (British)** = allen wrench **(n) (American)**
flat-packed **(adj.) (British)** = ready-to-assemble **(adj.) (American)**
spanner **(n) (British)** = wrench **(n) (American)**

MILLY

SAM

NEENA

ZAC

GABY

B Work in pairs. Cover the functional language in Exercise A, and add sequencing phrases to the instructions in Comprehension Exercise D.

1 *The first thing to do is to organize all of the pieces into the correct order.*
2 After that, you lay out all the pieces in a row.
3 When you've done that, take the packet of screws.
4 After that, you put the screws in the correct holes.
5 Make sure you insert the screws on both sides.

USEFUL PHRASES

A Who says it? *Sam*, *Zac* or *Gaby*?

1 I know when something's wrong with you. concerned Zac
2 It's complicated. confused Sam
3 She's been acting strangely around me. puzzled Sam
4 A bit cold and unfriendly. upset Sam
5 Whatever! uninterested Gaby

B How would you describe how each person feels in Exercise A? Choose the most appropriate adjective for each phrase.

concerned confused puzzled uninterested upset

C How do you say these useful phrases in your language?

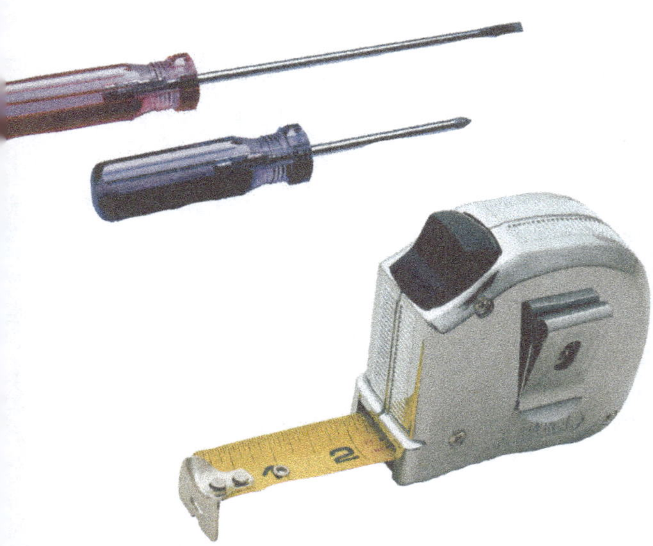

PRONUNCIATION
Sentence stress

8.7 **A** Underline the stressed words in the sentences (1–7). Then listen and check.

1 The first thing to do is to organize all of the pieces into the correct order.
2 Sorry, can you say that again?
3 What did you say?
4 When you've done that, take the packet of screws.
5 After that, you put the screws into the correct holes.
6 Is this how you do it?
7 Are you sure this is correct?

B Work in pairs. Practice saying the instructions in Exercise A, paying attention to the sentence stress.

SPEAKING

Work in pairs. Student A – go to the Communication Hub on page 155. Student B – go to the Communication Hub on page 151. Follow the instructions.

Give and follow instructions

➤ Turn to page 163 to learn how to write a biography.

8.3 Flat-packed

LEAD-IN

Put the students into pairs. Give one person a picture (of a house, for example) and the other person another picture (of an animal, for example). Tell the students not to show their picture to their partner but give them instructions on how to draw it. Their partner draws and they compare at the end.

COMPREHENSION

A Put students into pairs to discuss the questions.

B Put them into pairs to look at the picture and match the tools shown with the words in the box, and to discuss which tools Sam and Zac will need to build a shelf.

a allen key/allen wrench, drill, helmet, screwdriver
b tape measure
c spanner/wrench, pliers
d screwdriver, hammer

C Tell students to watch the extract from the video to check.

D ▶ 00:00–02:53 Tell students to look at the instructions and put them in order. Play the video for students to check.

E ▶ 02:54–04:13 Put students into pairs to discuss how they think Sam is feeling and why. Play the video for students to check.

He's feeling down/miserable/in a bad mood. You can tell because he's grumpy with Zac and tells him off for saying 'Right'. The problem is that he's in love with Gaby and she's acting cold.

FUNCTIONAL LANGUAGE

A ▶ 02:54–04:13 Elicit that all the phrases in the table were used in the video. Tell students to complete the phrases with the words in the box, then play the video again for them to check.

B Tell students to cover the Functional Language phrases from Exercise A and to look back at Comprehension Exercise D. Elicit the example, then tell students to put an appropriate sequencing phrase before the four remaining instructions.

USEFUL PHRASES

A Tell students to look at the useful phrases and to try to remember if each one was said by Sam, Zac or Gaby.

B Tell students to choose the adjectives that describe how each person was feeling when they said each of the phrases in Exercise A. Elicit that *puzzled* means confused.

C Tell students to think about how they would say the useful phrases in their language.

PRONUNCIATION

8.7 A Tell students to look at the sentences (1–7) and underline what they think are the stressed words. Play the audio for students to check. Let students compare in pairs before feedback.

B Practice pronunciation of the sentences with the class. Then tell students to practice further in pairs, paying special attention to sentence stress.

SPEAKING

A Put students in pairs and make one student A and one student B. Direct students to the **Communication Hub** (TB121).

VIDEO SCRIPT

S = Sam Z = Zac G = Gaby

S: So … Let's do this.
Z: WAIT!
S: Why?
Z: We need to prepare.
S: Prepare for what?
Z: Ready! You?
S: Ready. OK. The first thing to do is organize all of the pieces into the correct order.
Z: Sorry, can you say that again?
S: If you take your helmet off, you'll be able to hear better.
Z: Oh, sure. What did you say?
S: Just lay out all the pieces in a row.
Z: OK, right!
S: When you've done that, take the packet of screws.
Z: OK, right!
S: Are you going to keep doing that?
Z: OK, right!
S: Can you stop saying that?
Z: OK … wrong …?
S: Yeah. Let's just get this done.
Z: OK … then.
S: Right … after that you … put the screws into the correct holes which are …
Z: You what?
S: You just put it all together I guess?
Z: Let's follow the pictures.
S: Make sure you … insert the screws on both sides … before letting go.
Z: There must be some pieces missing.
S: I think if you put the screws in on the other side, it will hold together.
Z: What screws?
S: These screws.
Z: Is this how you do it?
S: No! Let me show you … This is how you do it. There you go. Perfect?
Z: Are you sure this is correct?
S: Probably. Oh, I don't know.
Z: Are you OK?
S: Yeah, I'm fine.
Z: I know when something's wrong with you man. What's up?
S: It's … complicated.
Z: What is?
S: Look. I really like someone and I thought that maybe she felt the same, but recently she's been acting strangely around me …
Z: Strangely?
S: Yeah, a bit cold and unfriendly and I don't know why. The big problem is that I'm in love with …
Z: GABY!
S: How did you know?
G: Know what?
S: Umm, er, I was just asking Zac how he knew … which screw to use.
Z: We're building some shelves.
G: Oh … cool. Whatever.

8 Writing
Write a biography

using linking words to show contrast

A SPEAK Work in pairs. Read the short biography *Sal Khan, founder of the Khan Academy.*

1 Who is Sal Khan?
2 What are the main events in his life?
3 How innovative is he? Why?

Sal Khan, founder of the Khan Academy

1 Sal Khan is one of the most innovative people in education today. The Khan Academy, which he started in 2006, makes free online videos to teach people around the world about math, science and many other things.
2 Sal was born near New Orleans, US, in 1976. After college, he found a well-paid job in finance. However, he soon realized there was more to life than money.
3 Sal's life changed in 2004, when he started giving math lessons to members of his family. To save time, he decided to record his lessons and post them on YouTube. Despite the simple quality of the videos, they soon became popular around the world. Suddenly, he was teaching millions of people and making a real difference to their lives.
4 Although Sal didn't invent video-based learning, he helped make it popular and successful. His main innovation was to give everything away for free. As a result, he can really help those people who need it.
5 Sal's story teaches us that we don't need to be an inventor to be innovative, and we don't need to be powerful to change the world. In fact, we just need to do something we love. Hopefully, we can help other people along the way.

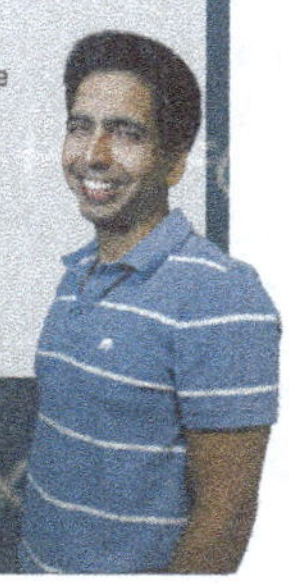

B Read again. Are the sentences true (T) or false (F)? Correct the false sentences.

1 You can only watch the videos in the US. ___
2 Sal's first job was as a teacher. ___
3 He made videos because he wanted to be famous. ___
4 Sal was the first person to teach using YouTube videos. ___
5 The writer thinks that Sal loves his work. ___

C A good biography usually has five sections. Match the sections (1–5) with the explanations (a-e). Use the biography of Sal Khan to help you.

1 introduction
2 backstory
3 turning point
4 impact
5 conclusion

a the story of the person's early life: family, education, first jobs, etc.
b why the person is special; how they changed the world
c lessons for our own lives
d who you are writing about and that person's biggest achievements
e something happened that changed the person's life

D Look at the box. Add an example of each linking word from Sal Khan's biography.

Using linking words to show contrast

We use linking words (*although, despite, however*) to link two different or contrasting ideas, one of which is unexpected, surprising or seems to be contradictory.

although + subject + verb
- ***Although*** *Sal Khan isn't an inventor, he's very innovative.*
- *Sal Khan is very innovative,* ***although*** *he isn't an inventor.*

1 Although Sal didn't invent...

despite + noun

2 Despite the simple quality...

despite + (*not*) + verb + *-ing*
- ***Despite*** *not being an inventor, Sal Khan is very innovative.*

despite the fact that + subject + verb
- ***Despite the fact that*** *he isn't an inventor, Sal Khan is very innovative.*

however
- *Sal Khan isn't an inventor.* ***However,*** *he's very innovative.*
- *Sal Khan is very innovative;* ***however,*** *he isn't an inventor.*

3 However, he soon realized...

E Complete the sentences with the correct linking words.

1 __Despite__ the fact that he had no experience as an engineer, he solved an extremely difficult engineering problem.
2 Nobody was interested in her ideas at first, __although__ they became a lot more popular later.
3 Her invention was gorgeous and extremely innovative. __However__, it was far too expensive at first.
4 She ended up changing the world __despite having__ some very serious challenges at the beginning.
5 __Although__ he was only 14 at the time, he managed to win the design competition.

WRITING

A PREPARE You are going to write a short biography of a famous innovator or an innovative friend or family member.

B PLAN Use the five-section plan in Exercise C to help you.

C WRITE Write your biography (about 200 words). Try to use linking words to show contrasting ideas. Use the skills box to help you. Check your grammar and spelling.

D REVIEW Work in groups. Read the other students' biographies. Which biography is about the most innovative person?

WRITING 163

Answers

1 *He's the founder of the Khan Academy, which uses videos to teach people.*
2 *He was born in 1976; he found a job after college; he started teaching in 2004; later, his videos became popular around the world.*
3 *Although he didn't invent anything, he is innovative because he decided to give away his lessons for free and this made a big difference to many people's lives.*

Answers

1 *F (You can watch the videos around the world.)*
2 *F (He first worked in finance.)*
3 *F (He made videos because he wanted to save time.)*
4 *F (He wasn't the first person to do this, but he helped make it popular and successful.)*
5 *T*

WRITING

Ask students to discuss in pairs if they have ever read biographies. If they have, tell them to tell their partner about an interesting biography they have read.

A Tell students they're going to read a short biography. Tell them to read the biography and answer the questions.

B Tell the students to read the biography and decide if the sentences are true or false. Tell them to correct the false sentences.

C Explain that a good biography often has five sections. Tell students to look back at the biography once again to help them match the sections with the explanations.

D Tell students to look at the information in the box about *using linking words to show contrast.* Tell them to complete each blank with an example of how each linking word is used.

E Tell students to practice the linking words by completing the sentences with a linking word from Exercise D.

WRITING TASK

A Tell students to think of either a famous innovator or someone they know who is innovative in some way. Tell them they're going to write a biography of this person.

B Tell students to look back at the five sections of a good biography in Exercise C to help them structure their biography. Give them time to write notes about what they could write for each stage.

C Tell students to write their biography. Encourage them to use some of the linking words to show contrasting ideas from the box in Exercise D. Advise them not to overuse them as this would result in a very unnatural piece of writing. Monitor to help and highlight issues with grammar and spelling for students to correct.

D Put students into groups and tell them to read each other's biographies. When they have read them all, ask them who they think the most innovative person in the biographies is, and why. Discuss as a whole class with one member of each group explaining their choice. Finish with feedback on the biographies, commenting on the organization and use of language.

Unit 8 Review

GRAMMAR

A Complete the dialogue with the adjective clauses in the box.

when which who

A: Hey, I like your watch. Is it new?

B: Yeah, I bought it last week [1] ___when___ I was in Boston. It has a built-in phone and a button [2] ___which___ you press to connect to the internet.

A: Cool. So what's the time?

B: Uh … I don't know. It worked for the man [3] ___who___ sold it to me, but when I took it home, it didn't work at all.

B Choose the correct words to complete the article.

The liter of light

If [1]***you want*** / ***you'll want*** to make a difference in people's lives, a good, simple idea is best. Brazilian engineer Alfredo Moser noticed that many people in his country live in houses with no electricity. Of course, if [2]***there'll be*** / ***there's*** no electricity, the houses are usually very dark. It's hard for people to read or study at home [3]***if*** / ***unless*** they have enough light. Alfredo's solution? Cut a hole in your roof and put a plastic water bottle through the hole. If [4]***you do*** / ***you'll do*** it properly, the light will fill your house.

C Match the beginnings of the sentences (1–5) with the endings (a–e).

1 If you can't think of any good ideas,
2 If you must have the new phone today,
3 If you wear your smartwatch in the bathtub,
4 You shouldn't watch TV all the time
5 Don't worry

a if you're late – I'll wait for you.
b it might stop working properly.
c if you want to be more creative.
d join the line outside the store.
e go for a long walk.

VOCABULARY

A Complete the sentences with the correct form of the words in parentheses.

1 My old website looked horrible, so I asked my sister to ___design___ (*designer*) a new one for me.
2 A great ___product___ (*produce*) is one that makes a difference.
3 This machine's broken again! Can you call an ___engineer___ (*engineering*) to come and fix it?
4 We've tried really hard, but we haven't had much ___success___ (*succeed*) yet.
5 You just copied all my ideas! That isn't very ___innovative___ (*innovate*), is it?

B Complete the advice with one word in each space.

Do you find it hard to come up [1] ___with___ new ideas? Try these techniques to boost your creativity!

- If your mind goes [2] ___blank___, you probably need to take a break.
- Too much TV can block your creativity. Try to [3] ___unplug___ completely.
- Try to relax and [4] ___let___ your mind wander freely.

- Don't follow rules that don't exist! Learn to think outside the [5] ___box___!
- Talk to a friend. This will help you to look at your problems [6] ___from___ the outside.

C Complete the sentences with the best adjectives from the box.

gorgeous impressive sensible sophisticated suitable unique

1 Each user has a ___unique___ username and password – it can't be the same as anybody else's.
2 **A:** 'I built a laptop computer in my garage when I was ten years old.'
B: 'Wow! That's ___impressive___!'
3 This camera isn't really ___suitable___ for taking underwater pictures. If water gets into the electronics, it might break.
4 The best thing about my watch is that it looks ___gorgeous___. Isn't it beautiful!
5 You can buy a simple microphone in the grocery store, but if you need something more ___sophisticated___, with lots more options, you need to go to a specialist store.
6 It's fine to use another person's computer, but you need to be ___sensible___. For example, don't use it to check your bank account.

FUNCTIONAL LANGUAGE

Correct the mistake in each part of the dialogue.

1 **A:** OK, here are the instructions for the table. Let's build this! The first thing ^to do is take everything out of the box.
2 **B:** After that, put the legs on. Careful ~~don't~~ not to lose the screws.
3 **A:** ~~This is~~ Is this how you do it?
4 **B:** No, no, no! Those are the wrong screws. Let ^me show you how to do it.
5 **A:** Are you sure this ^is correct ~~is~~? It looks wrong! Give me the instructions.

9 THE ARTS

The arts (n) activities such as art, music, movies, theater and dance considered together.

Art is unquestionably one of the purest and highest elements in human happiness.
John Lubbock

This is part of a longer quote where the author suggests art 'trains the mind through the eye, and the eye through the mind'. It suggests that art is more than entertainment but a means of achieving happiness by connecting and training both body and mind.

John Lubbock (1834–1913) was an English banker, politician and scientist. He was influential in establishing archeology as a science discipline and a law protecting archeological heritage.

A young man comes face to face with nature in a London gallery.

OBJECTIVES

- suggest improvements to a proposal
- plan an arts event
- report a conversation
- create a collaborative story
- talk about movies and books
- write a review

Work with a partner. Discuss the questions.

1 Look at the picture. Do you think this is art?
2 Look at the quote. Do you agree? Why/Why not?
3 Which of the arts do you like? What do you not like? Why? Are the arts important? Why/Why not?

THE ARTS 97

OBJECTIVES

Read the unit objectives to the class.

UNIT OPENER QUESTIONS

With books closed, write *Picasso* on the board. Elicit the names of other artists and their famous works of art and write these on the board, too. Ask students if they have ever seen any of the famous works of art and what they thought of them. Monitor and write any useful vocabulary on the board at the end of the activity.

Put students into pairs to discuss the questions. Discuss as a whole class and encourage students to expand on their answers and share experiences. Write further useful vocabulary that comes up on the board.

WORKSHEETS

Lesson 9.1 Art for everybody

Grammar: Second conditional (W33)

Vocabulary: The arts; verbal idioms (W34)

Lesson 9.2 Tell me a story

Grammar: Reported speech (W35)

Vocabulary: Reporting verbs (W36)

9.1 Art for everybody

- Suggest improvements to a proposal
- Plan an arts event

V the arts; verbal idioms **G** second conditional **P** /ʧ/, /ʃ/ and /k/
S using linking words to understand the writer's opinion

A NEW ARTS VENUE FOR THE CITY CENTER

After the recent closure of a furniture factory in the city center, the city council has become the owner of a large warehouse. Council members voted last week to turn the warehouse into a major public arts venue. There will be a competition to choose the best use of the space. Please visit the council website for information on how to submit a proposal.
The warehouse consists of a large empty hall (120 m x 150 m), with offices upstairs.

LISTENING

A Look at the picture and read the article above. What would you like to use the warehouse for?

9.1 **B** LISTEN FOR GIST Listen to the three finalists from the competition speaking at a council meeting. Match the finalists (1–3) with the pictures (a–c).

1 Leon MacGregor c
2 Violet Spring b
3 Florian Quirk a

9.1 **C** LISTEN FOR DETAIL Listen again. Choose the correct answers.

1 Who does Leon mostly want to help?
  (a) people who don't work now
  b professional musicians
  c people who go out frequently
2 What exactly is Leon's dream?
  a to teach people to play musical instruments
  (b) to bring people together to learn new skills
  c to make money by selling tickets to concerts
3 Why do people travel to other cities to visit the theater?
  a because they are open every day
  (b) because there's no theater in their own city
  c because they don't want to spend their money at the Grand Theater
4 What is special about immersive theater?
  a The audience is on the stage with the actors.
  b Tickets are a lot more expensive than for other plays.
  (c) The audience doesn't just watch the play.
5 Why does Florian think art is important?
  a It makes money that can be spent on roads and schools.
  (b) It helps you to understand new ideas.
  c It helps you to relax when you're stressed.
6 How will Florian's idea help the people of the city?
  a It will give them a place to perform.
  b It will help the city's artists to sell their paintings.
  (c) It will make them think in a different way.

D SPEAK Work in pairs. Which proposal sounds the most interesting? Explain why.

9.1 Art for everybody

LEAD-IN

With books closed, elicit some ideas from the class about what kind of services a community needs and write them on the board. If students don't suggest anything related to culture and the arts, add that to the list. Put students into pairs and tell them to rank the services on the board in order of their importance to a community. Discuss as a whole class and encourage students to explain their answers.

LISTENING

A Tell students to open their books and to look at the picture. Check understanding of *warehouse* (a big building where large amounts of goods are stored), then put students into pairs to read the article and discuss the question. Discuss as a whole class and compare students' opinions.

9.1 **B** Tell students they're going to listen to the three finalists from the competition speaking at a council meeting. Tell students to look at the pictures and elicit what they show. Then tell students to listen and to match the finalists with the pictures.

9.1 **C** Tell students to read the questions and to try to answer them from what they remember. Play the audio again for students to listen and check. Ask students to explain their answers with reference to exactly what the speakers said.

D Put students into pairs to discuss which proposal they think sounds most interesting and why. Discuss as a whole class and encourage students to give reasons for their answers.

AUDIO SCRIPT

9.1

Listening, Exercise B
C = Chair L = Leon V = Violet F = Florian

C: Welcome to the final of the Warehouse Project competition. Now, we received hundreds of excellent ideas, but there can only be one winner. Today, the three finalists are here to present their proposals before the public vote later this evening. But for now, let's hear from the first finalist, Leon MacGregor.

L: Thank you. I'd like to present my proposal to turn the warehouse into a community music center, with modern recording studios, rehearsal rooms and a performance area for live concerts. If the proposal is successful, people will be able to use the center free of charge. I believe music can make a big difference to our community, (Ex C Q1) especially for older people who have retired from work. If we open a community music center, it will change thousands of people's lives, by giving them opportunities to go out, meet new people and learn new skills. Won't that be wonderful for our city? (Ex C Q2) My dream is for the people of this city to join music classes with professional musicians, to learn how to sing or to play a musical instrument. They'll work together to form bands, orchestras and choirs. They'll have the space and equipment they need to rehearse and create new music. And they'll be able to perform live in front of an audience. If you share my dream, vote for my proposal to help it come true. Music … for the community.

C: Thank you, Leon. Our next finalist is Violet Spring.

V: Thank you. As an actor, I love the theater. And I'm not alone – tens of thousands of people all over the country visit the theater every day. But not in this city. (Ex C Q3) Since the Grand Theater closed down ten years ago, theater-lovers have had nowhere to go. They have to travel to theaters in other cities – and spend their money there instead of here. But I'm convinced that if we had a good, modern theater in this city, it would be extremely popular. What do I mean by a modern theater? Well, I firmly believe that the future is immersive theater. (Ex C Q4) Immersive theater is where the audience becomes part of the performance. There's no stage – just one shared space for actors and spectators alike. You don't just watch a play – you experience it. Immersive theater works best in a large open area, where groups of audience members can move around to watch different scenes of the play in different parts of the theater. And I think the city's warehouse would make a wonderful immersive theater. But it isn't just about art. Immersive theater is also a great business. The best shows attract rich international tourists who are prepared to pay premium prices. If we turned the warehouse into a theater, it would make a lot of money. This money could be spent on schools, roads and other important things for the city. If you like the sound of that, please support my proposal.

C: Thank you, Violet. Very interesting. Our final finalist is Florian Quirk.

F: Thank you. Let me ask you a question. What … is the purpose … of art? To keep bored people busy? To make money from rich tourists? No, I don't think so. (Ex C Q5) Art is about opening your mind to new experiences, new emotions. It's about losing yourself … and finding yourself. Great art makes you laugh; it makes you cry; (Ex C Q6) it makes you think. It helps you see things you've never seen, feel things you've never felt, understand things you've never understood. In short, the purpose of art … is to give a purpose … to life. That's why I'd like to turn the warehouse into a gallery of modern art. A place where audiences can view the works of today's best artists, including exhibits by some of the talented artists from this city. And if we make it free of charge, all the people of this city can enjoy the exhibits, displays and live performances. So if you really want to use this space for the arts, then forget about business plans and community projects. Let's create a gallery that will change the way the people of this city think … forever. Thank you.

C: OK, thank you. Well, I must say, all three proposals sound excellent! If the city council had three warehouses, maybe we could do all of those wonderful things. But we only have one warehouse, unfortunately, so we need to make a choice. Erm … I'd like to call a 15-minute break now so we can …

9.1 Art for everybody

VOCABULARY

A Point out that some words can go in more than one box. Monitor to help explain meaning.

Suggested answers:

Theater: a performance, to rehearse, a scene, a spectator, a stage

Art: a display, an exhibit, a gallery

Music: a choir, an instrument, a live concert, a musician, an orchestra, to perform live, a performance, a recording studio, to rehearse, a rehearsal room, a spectator, a stage

B Check answers by eliciting ideas from the class.

C Put students into pairs to discuss the questions.

GRAMMAR

A Put students into pairs to complete activities.

B Tell students to use the words in the box to help them complete the rules.

C Direct students to the **Grammar Hub** (see below).

D Put students into pairs to discuss the questions. Use the **Grammar Worksheet** on W33 for extra practice.

SPEAKING

A Put students into groups. Student A should look at the box on the page. Direct Students B and C to the **Communication Hub** (TB121).

B Pair student As and students Bs together and ask them to tell each other about the proposal they read about.

C Tell groups to decide which proposal should win and why. Share ideas as a class and ask students to justify opinions.

GRAMMAR HUB

9.1 Second conditional

Condition	Result
If **you submitted** a proposal,	**they would accept** it.
If **she didn't teach** music,	**she'd be** a full-time musician.
If **the show were** expensive,	**I wouldn't go** to it.
If **we didn't have** an art venue,	**we wouldn't see** much art.

Question	Positive short answer	Negative short answer
If **you had** more free time, **would you spend** it creatively?	Yes, **I would**.	No, **I wouldn't**.
Would you spend your free time creatively if **you had** more of it?		

- We use the second conditional to talk about present situations that aren't real and future events that are unlikely but possible.
- Although it uses the simple past, the second conditional is NOT about the past.
- We use *if* + simple past in the *if*-clause and *would* + base form in the result clause.
- We can use *might* or *could* in the result clause if we are not sure of the result.
  If she rehearsed every day, she might improve her skills.
  We could display community art if we had a local arts venue.
- With the verb *be*, we generally use *were* instead of *was* with all subjects, including *I*.

9.1 Second conditional

A Choose the correct option.

1 If I *knew* / *know* the words to the song, I would sing it.
2 If she had a better idea for the story, she *uses* / *would use* it.
3 If we *would hold* / *held* an art competition, many people would take part.
4 The public *liked* / *might like* his proposal if he presented it to them.
5 If you *invite* / *invited* Monique to the play, would she come?
6 If they allowed the public behind the stage, the actors *weren't* / *wouldn't be* pleased.
7 I'd study art at Kingston University if I *were* / *am* you.

B Correct the mistakes in these second conditional sentences.

1 If you ~~get~~ got rid of your guitar, you would miss it later.
2 If we bought cheaper tickets, we would save~~d~~ a lot of money.
3 If they ~~interact~~ interacted with the audience, the play would be more exciting.
4 I ~~won't~~ wouldn't be terribly upset if my bandmates and I didn't make up.
5 ~~Will~~ Would Chanda enjoy it more if she spent more time in her studio?
6 If the show took place outdoors, more people ~~can~~ could come.
7 Everyone would be very unhappy if it ~~rains~~ rained the day of the concert.

C Write the correct form of the verbs in parentheses. Use *would* if necessary.

1 If the city ___built___ (*build*) a new theater, many people would attend it.
2 If we rehearsed every day, we ___would become___ (*become*) the best!
3 If my favorite musician ___performed___ (*perform*) for free, thousands would go to see it.
4 Jean-Philippe ___would sell___ (*sell*) millions of copies if he recorded his songs.
5 The public would be disappointed if the gallery ___closed___ (*close*) its doors.
6 If I ___were___ (*be*) a famous artist, could I sell my paintings for $1 million?
7 If you ___told___ (*tell*) your story, I think people would show an interest in it.
8 Most people ___wouldn't like___ (*not like*) it if I sang in public!

➤ Go back to page 99.

VOCABULARY
The arts

A **Complete the table with the words in the box. Some words can go in more than one place.**

~~an audience~~ a choir a display an exhibit a gallery an instrument a live concert a musician an orchestra to perform live a performance a recording studio a rehearsal room to rehearse a scene a spectator a stage

Theater	Art (e.g. paintings)	Music
an audience		an audience

B **What other words can you add to each group? Think about people and places connected with each topic.**

C **SPEAK** **Work in pairs and ask and answer the questions.**

1 Do you ever rehearse what you are going to say before you say it? Think of examples.

2 Do you prefer to be a performer on a stage or a member of the audience? Why?

3 Can you play any musical instruments? Would you like to?

GRAMMAR
Second conditional

A **WORK IT OUT** **Work in pairs. Look at the sentences (a–d) from the council meeting and discuss the questions (1–3).**

a If we open a community music center, it will change thousands of people's lives.

b If we turned the warehouse into a theater, it would make a lot of money.

c If we had a good, modern theater in this city, it would be extremely popular.

d If the city council had three warehouses, maybe we could do all of those wonderful things.

1 Sentences **a** and **b** are both about the future. Which speaker is more certain that their plans will really happen? **a** uses *will* not *would*

2 In sentence **c**, does the city have a theater right now? *no*

3 In sentence **d**, does the city council have three warehouses? Can they do all three things? *no, no*

B **Complete the rules with the words in the box.**

could base past unreal were

Second conditional

1 Conditional sentences usually have two clauses: the *if*-clause and the result clause. To make second conditional sentences, we use *If* + simple ___past___ and *would* + ___base___ form of the verb.

2 With the verb *be*, we use ___were___ instead of *was*.

If I <u>*were*</u> *you, I'd vote for the first proposal.*

3 We use the second conditional to talk about ___unreal___ or impossible situations in the present or future.

4 If we are not sure of the result, we can use *might* or ___could___ instead of *would* in the result clause.

C Go to the Grammar Hub on page 138.

D **SPEAK** **Work in pairs and discuss the questions.**

1 How would you feel if somebody asked you to sing in public?

2 If you were a successful musician, what sort of music would you play?

SPEAKING

A **Work in pairs. Student A – read the box below. Student B – go to the Communication Hub on page 152. Student C – go to the Communication Hub on page 154. Read about one of the proposals for the Warehouse Project. Write about the advantages and disadvantages.**

Proposal 1: Community music center

Costs (= money going out)		Income (= money coming in)
Building work: $450,000	Employees: $50,000/year	None – everything will be free for community groups
Equipment: $350,000	Other costs (e.g. electricity): $100,000/ year	

- The community music center will save money by only opening for a few hours each day.
- Rehearsals/Workshops: Mondays, Wednesdays and Fridays, 10 am to 3 pm
- Concerts: Tuesdays and Thursdays, 12 pm to 2 pm
- Evenings and weekends: closed

B **Tell your partner about your proposal. Then discuss what you like about each one. Suggest some improvements.**

C **Decide which proposal should win the competition. Why? Then share your ideas with the class.**

READING

A SPEAK Work in pairs. Imagine you are watching a traditional play. What would you do if a character on the stage spoke to you? Would you be happy or would you feel uncomfortable?

B READ FOR MAIN IDEA Read the first paragraph of *The best (and the worst) of immersive theater*. Why has the writer written the article?

C READ FOR GIST Read the rest of the article. Match the recommendations (a–g) with the sections (1–6). There is one extra recommendation.

a Keep it simple. 3
b Tell a story. 5
c Make the audience feel special. 2
d Make it an experience for all the senses. 6
e Keep ticket prices as low as possible.
f Keep the rest of the audience out of sight. 4
g Make good use of the space. 1

The best (and the worst) of **immersive theater**

For most people, going to the theater is a chance to relax and let the actors do all the work. But in recent years, a new type of theater has appeared where the audience takes part in the play! When it works well, immersive theater can be breathtaking. But when it goes wrong, it can be awful. Here are my six recommendations based on my favorite (and least favorite!) immersive plays.

1 g

Sometimes the building itself is part of the Ex D Q1 experience. A good example is *Hotel Impossible*, which took place in a real hotel building. Similarly, *The Dark Tunnels* took place inside real tunnels, which created a very scary atmosphere. However, a great location isn't everything. *Dangerous Heart* was in a beautiful palace, but the play didn't really take advantage of the space.

2 c

In *Step by Step*, the audience was limited to 15, so we could interact one-on-one with the characters. During the play, the audience had to solve a crime, so we really had to pay attention to what we saw and heard. By the end, I was terrified and exhausted, but it was an unforgettable experience.

3 a

Some immersive plays feel far too complicated, with too many characters and storylines. For example, *Yellow and Blue* had amazing special effects, but I couldn't keep track of who was who. In *The Quiet* Ex D Q2 *Visitors*, however, there were only six characters in a large empty room. We had to use our imaginations, Ex D Q3 and the effect was incredibly powerful.

4 f

The worst thing about immersive theater? Other members of the audience! The play *Life with the Lions* got rid of this problem by making the audience wear animal costumes. I felt silly in my zebra costume, but at least we couldn't tell the difference between actors and spectators. In *The Dark Tunnels*, we all wore black clothes and masks so the members of the audience were almost invisible to each other.

5 b

Without a strong story, immersive theater can easily fall flat – it feels like something's missing. In *Hotel Impossible*, for example, lots of interesting things happened, but the whole play didn't really go Ex D Q4 anywhere. In *The Quiet Visitors*, however, there was a clear beginning, a middle … and a shocking surprise at the end.

6 d

It isn't just about what the audience sees and hears. The best immersive plays make use of the senses of taste, smell and touch, too. In *Dangerous Heart*, we enjoyed a delicious meal as part of the experience. Similarly, in *The Dark Tunnels*, the unpleasant Ex D Q5 underground smell added to the sense of danger. And in *The Quiet Visitors*, when the room suddenly went as cold as ice, the effect was terrifying. Ex D Q6

9.1 Art for everybody

READING

A Check understanding of *a play* and elicit some examples. Ask students if they enjoy watching plays and why or why not. Put students into pairs to discuss the questions. Share answers as a whole class and ask students to explain their responses.

B Point out the pictures and elicit what they show and how they could be connected to theater. Tell the students they are going to read an article about *immersive theater*. Elicit ideas for what they think *immersive theater* is. Tell students to read the first paragraph to check their ideas and to answer the question. Tell students not to worry about the highlighted and underlined words at this stage, as you're going to focus on them later.

Suggested answer: *To make recommendations for people who want to make immersive theater plays*

C Tell students to read the rest of the article and to match the recommendations with the sections. Point out that there is one recommendation that they don't need to use.

D Point out the information in the box about *using linking words to understand the writer's opinion* and tell students to look at the highlighted words in the article. Go through the first one as an example to show how *similarly* links one positive opinion to another. Tell students to use the same strategies to decide if the writer has positive or negative opinions about the other things. When checking answers, ask students to explain their answers with reference to how the linking words are used.

E Put students into pairs to discuss which of the plays from the article they would most and least like to see and why. Discuss as a whole class, encouraging students to explain their answers and express opposing opinions.

TEACHING IDEA by David Seymour and Maria Popova

Grammar: What if . . .

Use this activity to practice the grammar.

Supposing you could meet anyone you wanted, alive or dead, who would it be? Why? What would you say to him/her?

If you could live in another place and time in history, what would it be?

In small groups, brainstorm some endings for these sentences. Choose the best from your group and write the whole sentence down. (Ask the groups to read aloud their ideas and invite the class to choose their favorites.)

If the world was flat . . . If animals could speak . . . If we were all clones . . . If cows could fly . . . If you had two heads . . . If money grew on trees . . . If time travel was possible . . . If there was no money . . . If nobody knew how to read . . . If everyone was telepathic . . .

If I gave you one million dollars, what would you do with it? Write a list of five things. Read aloud your list. Who does the class think should get the money?

METHODOLOGY HUB by David Seymour and Maria Popova

Reading skills and exams

Reading texts do not necessarily need to be exam texts to practice key skills for exams such as IELTS and TOEFL. Here are two examples of reading skills which are crucial to exams, which can be practiced on many different types of texts, like the *The best (and the worst) of immersive theater.*

Reading for main information

On exams such as IELTS, candidates are sometimes required to extract the main information from a long text in order to complete a summary or notes on the text.

Students need to practice identifying the broad meaning of the text and the main points it contains, using, for example, the titles, introduction and conclusion, and topic sentences within the original article.

Reading for arguments

Reading texts on exams such as IELTS and TOEFL frequently contain more than just facts and information. Arguments and opinions are presented and the reader needs to be able to recognize these. Looking for keywords and phrases is an effective and efficient way to identify arguments and follow the logical connections the writer is making. Highlighting these words and phrases helps the reader to understand what is fact and what is argument or opinion.

METHODOLOGY HUB by David Seymour and Maria Popova

Lexical practice activities and games

Lexical practice activities and games

After students have seen and heard a new lexical item for the first time, they will need opportunities to become more familiar with it, to practice recognizing, manipulating and using it. Many simple lexical practice activities are based around the following ideas:

- discussions, communicative activities and role-play requiring use of the lexical items;
- making use of the lexis in written tasks.

There are many published exercises on lexis. These include:

- matching pictures to lexical items;
- matching parts of lexical items to other parts, e.g. beginnings and endings;
- matching lexical items to others, e.g. collocations, synonyms, opposites, sets of related words, etc;
- using prefixes and suffixes to build new lexical items from given words;
- classifying items into lists;
- using given lexical items to complete a specific task;
- filling in crosswords, grids or diagrams;
- filling in blanks in sentences;
- memory games.

Many such tasks seem to be designed for students working on their own, but can easily be used in class.

9.1 Art for everybody

VOCABULARY

A Point out the information in the box about verbal idioms, then direct students to the **Vocabulary Hub** (TB121). Tell students that the answers to Exercise A are all verbal idioms used in the article *The best (and the worst) of immersive theater*. Tell them to try to fill in the blanks without looking back at the text. When they have done this, tell students to look back at the text to check. Check answers as a whole class and check understanding of the idioms by eliciting personalized examples that will be relevant and memorable to the students. Students can then do Exercise B to focus on more verbal idioms.

B Tell students to work alone to complete the sentences so they are true for them. Then put them into pairs to compare and explain their sentences. To demonstrate, elicit an example from one student and ask the others to ask follow-up questions and react appropriately. Share the most interesting answers as a whole class. Use the **Vocabulary Worksheet** on W34 for extra practice.

PRONUNCIATION

9.2 **A** Point out the information in the box about the pronunciation of *ch*. Put students into pairs to discuss how they think the words are pronounced. Then play the audio for students to listen and check. Tell them to repeat each word as they hear it.

In charge and choice, ch is pronounced the usual way, /ʧ/.
In chef, it sounds like /ʃ/.
In character, choir and orchestra, it sounds like /k/.

B Tell students to find and underline *ch* in the sentences and decide on the pronunciation of *ch* in each case.

9.3 **C** Play the audio for students to listen and check. Then play it again for them to repeat the sentences. Repeat if necessary, or model and practice the sentences yourself if students need extra help with any words.

D Put students into pairs to practice saying the sentences. Encourage them to listen carefully to their partner to check their pronunciation. Monitor and help if any students are still having difficulty.

SPEAKING HUB

A Put students into groups and tell them they're going to devise their own immersive theater performance. Tell them to discuss the questions to help them brainstorm ideas for the story, the location and the interactive element. Tell them to think of as many ideas as they can at this stage. Monitor and help or prompt if necessary.

B Tell the groups to choose their best idea to make into an immersive theater performance. Tell them to look back at the article *The best (and the worst) of immersive theater* in their books for advice as they add details to their idea. Tell students they're going to present their idea to the class when they've finished preparing. Monitor to help with language if needed. When students have finished, tell them to practice making their presentation in their group.

C Tell each group to present their idea to the class. Tell the other groups to listen carefully and to ask questions at the end.

D Make new groups and tell students to discuss which of the immersive plays they would most like to watch, and why. Tell students it's not a competitive activity, so they can give their honest opinion and don't have to argue for their idea. Discuss as a whole class and find out which is the most popular idea. Ask students to explain their opinions. Finish with feedback on students' use of language during the presentation and reflection stages.

Extra activity

For homework, students can write a short advertisement for an immersive play. Without giving away the full plot, students should provide information about:

- the story
- the location
- how it is interactive or immersive
- why people should see it

TEACHING IDEA by David Seymour and Maria Popova

Topic: High culture

Use this activity to extend the topic.

What cultural activities do you take part in?

In pairs, tell each other about what you do and the places you go, e.g. movie theaters, theaters, galleries, museums, etc. (Ask students to specify movies, plays and exhibits.)

Mingle with the rest of the class and find out everyone's favorite painting, building and piece of music. Write down the name of anyone who shares your opinion. Did anyone find someone with the same three favorites?

TEACHING IDEA by David Seymour and Maria Popova

Grammar: Chain story

Use this activity to practice the grammar.

Tell a chain story about a boy named Tom who dreams of being an astronaut. *(If I were a grown-up, I'd become an astronaut. If I were an astronaut, I'd go to Mars. If I went to Mars, I think I'd meet some aliens. If I met them, we'd become good friends.)*

D Look at the highlighted words in the article. What is the writer's opinion? Use the strategies in the box to help you. Choose + (positive) or – (negative).

Using linking words to understand the writer's opinion

When you're trying to figure out the writer's opinion, don't just look for positive words (e.g. *amazing, interesting*) and negative words (e.g. *unpleasant, terrifying*).

Writers regularly use words like *for example, similarly* and *however* to link their opinions to earlier sentences.

1 the location for *The Dark Tunnels* + / –
2 the characters and story in *Yellow and Blue* + / –
3 the characters and story in *The Quiet Visitors* + / –
4 the story in *Hotel Impossible* + / –
5 the experience for the senses in *The Dark Tunnels* + / –
6 the experience for the senses in *The Quiet Visitors* + / –

E SPEAK Work in pairs. Which of the plays from the article would you most like to see? Which would you least like to see? Why? Tell your partner.

VOCABULARY
Verbal idioms

Verbal idioms

Verbal idioms are fixed phrases that work as verbs with a single meaning.

A Go to the **Vocabulary Hub** on **page 146**.

B SPEAK Complete the sentences so they are true for you. Then work in pairs and tell your partner what happened.

1 I had an opportunity to … but I didn't take advantage of it, because …
2 Everything went wrong when I …
3 I'm planning to get rid of …
4 I once tried to (tell a joke/story, etc.), but it fell flat, because …

PRONUNCIATION
/tʃ/, /ʃ/ and /k/

9.2 **A** How do you pronounce *ch* in these words? Listen and repeat.

character charge chef choice choir orchestra

ch

ch is usually pronounced /tʃ/ (as in *cheese*). But there are also a few words where *ch* is pronounced /ʃ/ (as in *mustache*) or /k/ (as in *chemist*).

B Find and underline *ch* in these sentences. Then write /tʃ/, /ʃ/ or /k/ above each example.

1 My children didn't go to school today – they both had bad stomachaches.
2 If I were a mechanic, I might be able to fix this machine, but I don't know anything about technology.
3 My sister is a chemist; she's doing some research into new techniques for recycling harmful chemicals.

9.3 **C** Listen and check.

D SPEAK Work in pairs. Practice saying the sentences. Listen and check your partner's pronunciation.

SPEAKING HUB

A Work in groups. Discuss ideas for an immersive theater performance. Think about:

- story: Will you use an existing story or create your own?
- location: Where will it take place? How could you make use of the location?
- interactivity: How will the actors interact with the audience?

B PLAN Choose your best idea and add more details. Follow the advice in *The best (and the worst) of immersive theater* on page 100.

C PRESENT Present your idea to the class.

D REFLECT Which immersive play would you most like to watch? Why?

Suggest improvements to a proposal
Plan an arts event

9.2 Tell me a story

- Report a conversation
- Create a collaborative story

G – reported speech   V – reporting verbs   P – using your voice to make a story more interesting
S – listening for definitions of new words

Francis Scott Key Fitzgerald (1896–1940) was one of the most important American writers of the 20th century. His best-known novel, *The Great Gatsby* (1925), is an American classic. It paints a powerful portrait of life in 1920s America, a period known as the Jazz Age. For many young people in America, this was a time for partying and having fun, with new types of music, new ways of dancing and new fashions.

READING

A Work in pairs. Read about F. Scott Fitzgerald and look at the pictures. Have you read *The Great Gatsby*? Why do you think it is 'an American classic'?

I haven't read the book but I have seen the movie starring Leonardo DiCaprio.

B 9.4 Listen to a conversation between two friends, Joe and Nadia. Answer the questions.

1. Who is Jay Gatsby?
2. Why doesn't Joe want to borrow the book? Why does he change his mind?
3. Why does Nadia like the book?

CHAPTER 3: I MEET GATSBY

PART 1

One day, I was invited to one of Gatsby's parties. As soon as I arrived, I began to look for Gatsby to thank him for his invitation. Ex C Q1 But no one knew where he was.

As I went to get a drink, I saw Jordan Baker. I walked toward her, glad to see someone I knew. Ex C Q2

'I thought you might be here,' Jordan said. Ex C Q3

We took our drinks and sat down at a small table under a tree. Jordan began to talk to a girl in a yellow dress.

'Do you come to these parties often?' Jordan asked her.

'I come when I can,' the girl said. 'No one cares what I do, so I always have a good time. Last time I was here, I tore my dress. Do you know, Gatsby sent me a new one! It cost him 265 dollars!' Ex C Q4

PART 2

Supper was now being served. Jordan and I left our table and went to look for Gatsby.

People were dancing now. The voices and the laughter were very loud. The moon was high in the sky.

Jordan and I sat down at a table with a well-dressed man of my own age. Ex D Q1 I was enjoying myself, now. The music stopped for a moment. The man at our table looked at me and smiled.

'I think I know your face,' the man said. 'Weren't you in France during the War?' Ex D Q3

'Yes, I was.'

'Me, too,' he said. We talked about the War for a few minutes. Then the man told me that **he had a new motorboat.**

'Want to go out with me in the morning, old sport?' he asked.

'Sure, what time?'

'Let's say nine o'clock.'

I looked at the yard and smiled.

'This is an unusual party,' I told the man. 'I haven't seen my host yet. Gatsby sent me an invitation this morning. I ought to thank him.'

The man stared at me in surprise.

'I'm Gatsby,' he said. 'I thought you knew, old sport. I'm not a very good host, am I?' Ex D Q2

Gatsby smiled. He had a pleasant smile. His smile made me feel important. I looked at Gatsby with interest. He was a tough-looking young man, but he had beautiful clothes and beautiful manners. Ex D Q1

PART 3

A few guests were standing near Gatsby. I went up to him to say goodbye.

'Don't forget we're going out in the boat, old sport,' he said. 'At nine o'clock.'

Gatsby smiled at me.

'Goodnight, old sport, goodnight.'

I walked across the lawn in the moonlight. The cars drove away. The yard was quiet and empty.

All alone, Gatsby stood on the white steps, waving goodbye.

Glossary

old sport (phrase) a popular way of saying 'my friend' in the 1920s

9.2 Tell me a story

LEAD-IN

Ask students to think of a classic book or movie from their country. Put students into pairs to discuss their choices.

READING

9.4 **A–B** Students work in pairs then individually to complete the exercises.

Joe: *Hey, Nadia, what are you reading?*
Nadia: *Oh, hi, Joe. It's The Great Gatsby – one of my favorite novels. Have you read it?*
Joe: *No. I've heard of it, but I don't know much about it. It's American, isn't it?*
Nadia: *Yeah. It's one of the classics of American literature. It was written in the 1920s.*
Joe: *So, what's it about?*
Ex B Q 1 **Nadia:** *Well, it's about a man named Jay Gatsby. He's rich and he has lots of amazing parties, but he has a hidden secret.*
Joe: *Really? What's the secret?*
Nadia: *I can't tell you. You'll have to read the book. Borrow mine when I finish.*
Ex B Q 2 **Joe:** *Um … How long is it? Classics tend to be very long, don't they?*
Nadia: *No, not at all, it's 180 pages.*
Ex B Q 2 **Joe:** *Oh, that's not too bad. So … why should I read it?*
Ex B Q3 **Nadia:** *Well, it's a great story – it's told by a man named Nick Carraway, who meets Gatsby at one of his parties, and then makes friends with him.*
Joe: *OK.*
Nadia: *But I think the best thing about the book is that*
Ex B Q3 *it really paints a picture of America in the 1920s. I really feel as if I'm there, inside the story. It's very well written.*
Joe: *Cool. I might read it. Can I take a look?*

GRAMMAR HUB

9.2 Reported speech

Direct speech	Reported speech
simple present	simple past
'**We enjoy** live concerts the best.'	They said (that) **they enjoyed** live concerts the best.
present progressive	past progressive
'**We are learning** how to write a short story.'	They said (that) **they were learning** how to write a short story.
will	*would*
'**I will** read my book later.'	She said (that) **she would** read her book later.
may	*might*
'**Elle may** sing in the play.'	He said (that) **Elle might** sing in the play.
can	*could*
'**We can** film our daily lives.'	They said (that) **they could** film their daily lives.
should	*should* (no change)
'**He should try out** for that role.'	She said (that) he **should try out** for that role.
For commands and instructions	*tell* + object (+ *not*) + infinitive
'**Rehearse** the scene again.'	He told them **to rehearse** the scene again.
'**Don't look** at the camera.'	She told me **not to look** at the camera.

- We use reported speech to report what people say. We use a reporting verb in the simple past (e.g. *said*, *asked*, *told*).
- When we report what someone says, the reported verb usually goes back one tense.
- When we report questions, the subject comes before the verb (the same as in sentences).
  *Alain: 'Where is **he acting**?' → Alain asked where **he was acting**.*
- With yes/no questions, we start the reported question with *if* or *whether*.
  *Chloe: 'Will Tom attend the show?' → Chloe asked **if/whether** Tom would attend the show.*
- We change some pronouns from direct speech to reported speech depending on the speaker (*I* to *he/she*, *you* to *me*, *my* to *his/her*, etc).
  *Kieran: 'I've given **you my** ticket already.' → He said **he** had given **me his** ticket already.*
- We sometimes also need to change words which refer to time and place.

Direct speech	Reported speech
tomorrow	*the next day / the following day*
today	*that day*
here	*there*
this	*that/the*

- We usually don't change the verb tenses if we are reporting facts that are still true in the present.
  *Our coach said that acting **requires** a great deal of time and effort.*

9.2 Tell me a story

C Tell students they're going to read an extract from the novel. Tell them to read part 1 first and to decide if the sentences are true or false and to correct the false ones. Let students compare with their partner before feedback.

D Tell students to read part 2 and to write notes on what they find out about Gatsby.

E Tell students to read part 3 and then discuss the question with a partner.

GRAMMAR

A Tell students to look at the phrase in bold in part 2. Ask if this is direct or reported speech. Tell students to complete the sentence for what they think Gatsby's exact words were. Elicit how the verb changes from direct speech to reported speech.

B Tell the students to read and complete the examples. Do the first one together as a whole class as an example.

C Direct students to the **Grammar Hub** (see TB102 and below).

D Tell students to report the sentences from *The Great Gatsby*. Elicit that they are all in direct speech. Tell students to change them into reported speech.

E Put students into pairs to imagine how the story continues. Tell them to write a conversation between Jay and Nick the following morning, using reported speech. Use the **Grammar Worksheet** on W35 for extra practice.

SPEAKING

A Tell students to think about the questions and write notes. Monitor and provide students with language they request.

B Put students into pairs to ask and answer the questions. Tell them to ask each other follow-up questions to find out as much information about each other as possible. To demonstrate this, start by eliciting some answers as a whole class.

C Put students with a new partner and tell them to tell each other as much as they can remember about their previous partner. Discuss as a whole class and find out who remembered the most and who was most accurate.

GRAMMAR HUB

9.2 Reported speech

A Choose the correct option.

1 Maya: 'I'm going to an outdoor concert tonight.'
She said she *is* / (*was*) going to an outdoor concert that night.

2 Dan and Tracy: 'We're rehearsing all day tomorrow.'
They said they ***were rehearsing*** / ***will rehearse*** all day the following day.

3 Joe to Lyn: 'I can give you my proposal.'
He said he ***can*** / ***could*** give her his proposal.

4 Nadia to me: 'I will ask the doorman to let you in for free.'
She said she ***asked*** / ***would ask*** the doorman to let me in for free.

5 The teachers: 'We've chosen a local warehouse.'
They said they ***will choose*** / ***had chosen*** a local warehouse.

6 Me: 'I'm not writing a review of the play this evening.'
You said you weren't writing the review ***this*** / ***that*** evening.

7 John to Isabel: 'Come to the concert hall at 7 pm.'
John ***said*** / ***told*** Isabel to come to the concert hall at 7 pm.

B Report the statements.

1 Hanna: 'I'm performing at the theater tomorrow.'
She said (that) she was performing at the theater the next/following day.

2 Alexis: 'I've never written a novel before.'
He said (that) he had never written a novel before.

3 Marcia: 'I'll buy my tickets online.'
She said (that) she would buy her tickets online.

4 Davide and Maria: 'We're meeting a famous actor today.'
They said (that) they were meeting a famous actor that day.

5 Anastasiya: 'I can't hear from the back row.'
She said (that) she couldn't / could not hear from the back row.

6 Hussein: 'I gave Sonia my seat.'
He said (that) he had given Sonia his seat.

C Choose the correct option.

1 Sara: 'When is the concert?'
She asked ______.
a if the concert was today
(b) when the concert was
c when is the concert

2 Elena to Jim: 'You'll love Paulina's performance.'
She promised that Jim ______ Paulina's performance.
a loves
b will love
(c) would love

3 Soraya to me: 'Have you read *The Great Gatsby*?'
She asked me ______ *The Great Gatsby*.
a whether I read
(b) if I had read
c why I had read

4 Georgia and Hans: 'Are our seats at the front?'
They asked ______.
a if our seats are at the front
b if our seats were at the front
(c) if their seats were at the front

➤ Go back to page 103.

C READ FOR DETAIL Read *The Great Gatsby*, Chapter 3, Part 1. Are the sentences true (T) or false (F)? Correct the false sentences.

1 Gatsby invited Nick Carraway (the storyteller) to his party. T
Nick did not know people at the party, and was glad to see Jordan.
2 ~~Nick already knew most of the people at the party.~~ F
Jordan expected to see Nick.
3 ~~Jordan was surprised to see Nick.~~ F
Gatsby spends a lot of money, and is generous with his money.
4 ~~Gatsby is very careful with his money.~~ F

D Read Part 2. What do we learn about Gatsby? Write notes on:

1 his appearance (= his clothes and the way he looks).
2 his manners (= the way he treats other people).
3 his background (= what he has done in the past).

E Read Part 3. Why do you think Gatsby has so many parties?

GRAMMAR
Reported speech

A WORK IT OUT Look at the phrase in bold from *The Great Gatsby*, Chapter 3, Part 2. What do you think Gatsby actually said?

Direct speech: 'I ___have___ a new motorboat.'

B Complete the examples in the correct tense.

Direct speech	Reported speech
Simple present 'My name's Jay Gatsby.'	**Simple past** He told me his name [1] ___was___ Jay Gatsby.
Present progressive 'I'm really enjoying the party.'	**Past progressive** I told him I [2] ___was___ really enjoying the party.
Present perfect 'I've never met Gatsby.'	**Past perfect** He said he [3] ___had___ never met Gatsby.
Simple past 'Gatsby sent me a new dress.'	**Past perfect** She said Gatsby [4] ___had___ sent her a new dress.
can 'I can't see the host.'	***could*** I told him I [5] ___couldn't___ see the host.
will 'We'll have a great time on my boat.'	***would*** He said we [6] ___would___ have a great time on his boat.

C Go to the **Grammar Hub** on **page 138**.

D Report the sentences (1–5) from *The Great Gatsby*.

1 'Do you come to these parties often?' Jordan asked her.
Jordan asked the girl if she came to these parties often.
2 'I come when I can,' the girl said.
The girl/She said she came when she could.
3 'I think I know your face,' the man said.
The man/He said he thought he knew Nick's/his face.
4 'This is an unusual party,' I told the man. 'I haven't seen my host yet.'
Nick/He told the man that it was an unusual party. He said he hadn't seen his host yet.
5 'Gatsby sent me an invitation this morning.'
Nick/He said that Gatsby had sent him an invitation that morning.

E SPEAK Work in pairs. Use your imagination to tell the next part of the story. Report the conversation between Jay and Nick the next morning.

SPEAKING

A Think about the questions below. Write notes.

1 Do you read a lot of novels? What sort of books do you enjoy? Which books would you recommend? Why?
2 Do you ever read books in English? What have you read? Did you find it easy or difficult? Do you need to understand every word or can you simply relax and enjoy the story?

B Work in pairs. Ask and answer the questions from Exercise A. Ask follow-up questions and give examples.

C Work with a new partner. Tell your new partner about your conversation.

LISTENING

A SPEAK **Work in groups and discuss the questions.**

1 What are some situations where people tell each other stories?

2 Are stories just for fun, or do they have a serious purpose?

3 Do you like telling stories? What kind of stories?

4 What skills do you need to tell great stories? When was the last time you told a story?

- Where were you?
- Who did you tell it to?
- Why did you tell it?
- What was the story about?

9.5 **B LISTEN FOR GIST** **Listen to the conversation between two friends, Zoe and Jacob. They are talking about storytelling. Put the pictures (a–c) in the order that they discuss them (1–3).**

1 b 2 a 3 c

Glossary

dice (n) a small block of wood or plastic with six sides marked with spots that you roll or throw to play a game

end up (with) (phrasal verb) to be in a particular place or state after doing something or because of doing it

a

b

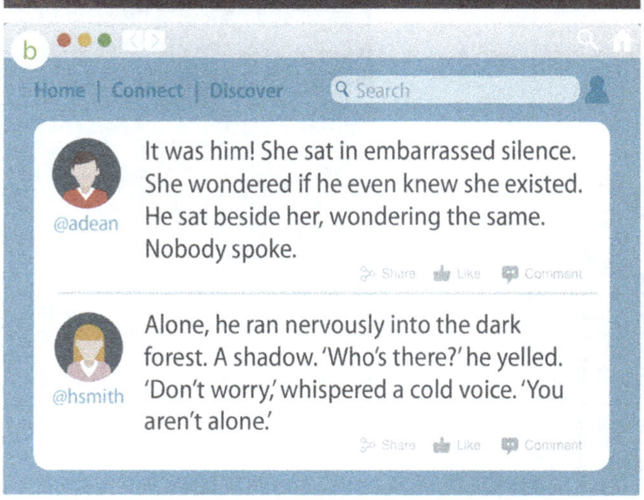

9.5 **C LISTEN FOR KEY WORDS** **Listen again and complete the definitions of the new words. Use the strategies in the box to help you.**

Listening for definitions of new words

Speakers usually pause before and after an important new word. They usually place extra stress on the word itself.

When you hear an important new word, listen carefully for a definition or explanation.

1 Flash fiction: A story with a word limit, usually 1,000 words.

2 Micro-stories: These are stories on social media sites (e.g. Twitter). A whole story told in a 140 -character message.

3 A twist: When something happens in the story that you didn't expect .

4 Collaborative stories: Stories that are created by a large group of people working together .

5 Pass the paper: You write one line of a story on a sheet of paper, fold it down and pass it to the next player, who writes the next line , and so on.

6 Add a word: You sit in a circle . The first person says the first word from a sentence, and then the next person says the next word.

7 Story dice: A set of 12 dice, and each one has six pictures , one on each side.

D SPEAK **Work in groups. Play *Add a word*.**

E DISCUSS **Work in groups and discuss the questions.**

1 Have you ever played any of the games or tried any of the story techniques mentioned in the conversation? Would you like to?

2 Do you think word limits make it easier or harder to write a good story?

3 Do you prefer working collaboratively or by yourself?

c

LISTENING

A Put students into groups to discuss the questions.

9.5 **B** Tell students to look at the pictures. Elicit what each one shows. Tell them to number the pictures in the order the friends discuss them.

9.5 **C** Ask students to explain what helped them work out the answers. Ask how useful they found the strategies in the box.

D Tell students they're going to play *Add a word*, one of the games described in the conversation. Choose a stronger student and do a quick example to model the task. Put students into pairs to do the same. Share stories as a whole class.

E Put students into groups to discuss the questions.

AUDIO SCRIPT

9.5

Listening, Exercise B
Z = Zoe J = Jacob

Z: So, Jacob, how's your creative writing class going?
J: Really well, thanks, Zoe. This week, we've been writing flash fiction. Ex C Q1 That's where you have to write stories within a word limit, usually 1,000 words. It's really difficult.
Z: Really? Why?
J: Because you have to make every word count. It makes you think hard, and that makes you more creative.
Z: Yes, I see what you mean, but 1,000 sounds very extreme.
Ex C Q2 **J:** Well, it isn't as extreme as micro-stories. They're stories on social media sites like Twitter. A whole story told in a 140-character message.
Z: You're joking, right?
J: No, I'm not. Do you want to hear one of my favorites? 'It was him! She sat in embarrassed silence. She wondered if he even knew she existed. He sat beside her, wondering the same. Nobody spoke.'
Z: OK. It isn't much of a story, is it? I mean, nothing happened.
J: No. But it's about creating a powerful scene, and characters with real emotions.
Z: Characters? You just said 'he' and 'she'.
J: Well, it's usually better if the writer provides less information, so that you, the reader, can create the missing information from your own imagination.
Z: Uh, OK.
J: OK, so here's another one. 'Alone, he ran nervously into the dark forest. A shadow. "Who's there?" he shouted. "Don't worry," whispered a cold voice. "You aren't alone."'
Z: Oh, that's better. I see what you mean about using your imagination. I like the twist at the end.
J: What do you mean by 'twist'?
Ex C Q3 **Z:** It's when something happens in the story that you didn't expect. I mean, you think he's alone, but then he isn't. It's really powerful, isn't it?!
J: Yeah, I think so. There are also some groups on social media that write collaborative stories: Ex C Q4 stories that are created by a large group of people working together. So, for example, I'll write the beginning of a story, in one 140-character message, and then you'll write the next part of the story, and so on. Eventually, we'll end up with an amazing story.
Z: Ah. It reminds me of a game we played when I was a child. We called it 'Pass the paper'. Ex C Q5 You write one line of a story on a sheet of paper, fold it down and pass it to the next player, who writes the next line, and so on. We could play it now, if you like. You'll enjoy it!
J: No, thanks. It isn't my kind of thing. But there are actually websites now that do similar things. You write a sentence online, and then someone else writes the next sentence, and so on. I know some people in my class use websites like those to give them ideas. Of course, most of the stories are trash, but it's all about opening your mind to new ideas.
Z: Yes, I'm sure.
J: And there's another one where each person can just write three words. Some of the stories are really funny.
Z: Oh, yes. That reminds me of another game we frequently played when I was a student in California, 'Add a word'. Do you know it? Ex C Q6 It's when a group of you sit in a circle. The first person says the first word from a sentence, like 'My'. And then the next person says the next word. For example …
J: Favorite?
Z: OK, yes. So, my – favorite, uh, frog.
J: Lives?
Z: Uh, under.
J: My.
Z: Uh, bed?
J: OK. Uh, because.
Z: He.
J: Can't.
Z: Afford.
J: A.
Z: Hotel?
J: Yeah, why not. Hey, that's a great game for collaborative stories, Zoe. You see! When you work together, you come up with ideas that you'd never have if you were on your own.
Z: Sure. So is that how you always come up with new ideas?
J: Not always, no. I sometimes use story dice.
Z: Story dice?
Ex C Q7 **J:** Yes. I have a set of 12 dice, and each one has six pictures, one on each side.
Z: OK.
J: So if I'm figuring out an idea for my story, I throw six dice. Then I have to use all six pictures in my story. Let's say the pictures on my dice show a castle, the color blue, an angry face, a bag of money, a motorcycle and a fish. So I have to write my story so that it includes all those things.
Z: Wow! So how about 'My fish was angry because he crashed his expensive motorcycle into a blue castle'?
J: Well, that's very creative, but it has to sound natural and believable. The story can have up to 1,000 words, remember.
Z: Cool. OK, I'm going to try to write it.
J: Great. It won't be easy … but it should be fun!

9.2 Tell me a story

VOCABULARY

A Tell students to look back at the examples of micro-stories in Listening Exercise B, picture b. Ask students what they notice about the verbs used. Elicit an example of a verb used instead of *say* or *think*, then put students into pairs to find more and to answer the question.

wonder (instead of think) and shout and whisper (instead of say) These verbs are more interesting and they allow you to communicate more information with a single word.

B Tell students to look at the information in the box about reporting verbs. Tell them to check the meaning of any verbs with a dictionary. Put students into pairs or threes to explain the meaning of some of the words together. Monitor and help with examples yourself as they do this. If the students speak the same language, and you speak the language as well, encourage translation of the verbs. Ask students if the verbs are used in the same pattern when translated into their language.

C Tell students to look at the sentences from the conversation between Zoe and Jacob. Tell them to choose the best reporting verb to complete each one. Do the first together as a whole class to demonstrate how students have to consider both the meaning of the verb and the pattern which follows it. When checking answers, use the context created by the sentences to further check and consolidate understanding of the meaning of the verbs. Use the **Vocabulary Worksheet** on W36 for extra practice.

PRONUNCIATION

9.6 A Tell students to listen to Jacob reading two micro-stories and to think about how he uses his voice to make them sound more interesting. Point out the ideas for students to think about as they listen.

Suggested answers: *In the first micro-story, he speaks fairly slowly and quietly, and his voice becomes very quiet at the end. He sounds excited at the beginning. He pauses a lot in the middle of sentences (e.g. after some verbs).*
In the second story, he speaks much faster and louder, but he becomes much slower and quieter at the end. His voice mostly expresses fear. He mostly pauses between sentences.

B Tell students to turn to the **Audio script** at the back of their books. Tell them to work in pairs and take turns reading the stories aloud. Remind them of how Jacob used his voice to make the stories sound more interesting and encourage them to do the same.

C Tell students to look back at the story they wrote earlier. Tell them to practice reading it together, trying to use some of the same techniques to make it sound interesting. Monitor to help if necessary. When students have had time to practice, tell each pair to read their story to the class. Tell the others to listen carefully and to think about how well the stories are told.

D Put students into new groups to discuss which story they thought was the best. Tell them to think about the content, how well the reporting verbs were used and how well the storyteller used their voice. Get feedback from the class on which stories the students liked best and why. Give your own feedback on what you liked about the stories and any way they could have been improved.

SPEAKING HUB

A Put the students into pairs. Direct students to the **Communication Hub** (TB121). Tell them to look at the pictures and to spend one minute thinking about the story the pictures tell.

B Tell students to take turns telling their story to their partner. Tell them to listen carefully to their partner and to help if they run out of ideas.

C Tell students to work together to improve and develop their stories. Tell them to try and combine them into one story if possible. Point out the suggested ideas to help with this. Monitor to help with language or ideas if needed. When students have finished, tell them to practice reading them aloud. Remind them of the strategies for using their voice to make it sound more interesting.

D Tell students to share their stories with the class, remembering to use their voice to try and make them sound as interesting as possible. Tell the others to listen carefully and to think about which is their favorite.

E Put students into new groups to discuss which story they liked best and why. As a whole class, decide who was the best storyteller. Finish with feedback on students' use of language in the stories.

Extra activity

As homework, this speaking activity can be extended into writing practice. Students can write up their stories. If the class were able to combine their stories into one version during the class, then students can compare their stories in the next class by asking:

How are they similar? How are they different?

METHODOLOGY HUB by Jim Scrivener

Speaking: Recognize the feeling

Write down four or five short spoken phrases on the left side of the board (e.g. *Where are you going?, Yes, please.*). Write down a number of 'moods' on the right (e.g. *angry, delighted, sarcastic*). Read aloud one of the phrases in one of the moods (adapting your intonation and stress to transmit a clear feeling). Ask students to compare ideas with each other and decide which was used. Later, learners can continue playing the game in small groups.

TEACHING IDEA by David Seymour and Maria Popova

Picture story

In four groups, choose one person to draw four pictures on separate pieces of paper: 1) an animate object, 2) an inanimate object, 3) a place, 4) an action. (Collect them all together and shuffle them.) Join another group so that there are two groups. Take half of the pictures each and use all the pictures your group receives to compose a story.

VOCABULARY

Reporting verbs

A Look at the examples of micro-stories in Listening Exercise B, picture b. Which verbs are used instead of *say* and *think*? Why?

B Look at the information in the box. Use a dictionary to check any new verbs.

> **Reporting verbs**
>
> Instead of using *say* and *tell*, we can use more interesting and descriptive reporting verbs.
>
> **verb (+ *that*) + reported speech:** *add, admit, agree, argue, explain, insist, mention, predict, promise, repeat, reply, say, yell, warn, whisper*
>
> **verb + somebody (+ *that*) + reported speech:** *advise, persuade, promise, remind, tell, warn*
>
> **verb + reported question:** *ask, explain, wonder*
>
> **verb + infinitive:** *agree, ask, promise, refuse*
>
> **verb + somebody + infinitive:** *advise, ask, persuade, promise, remind, tell, warn*

C Choose the best reporting verbs to complete the sentences from the conversation between Zoe and Jacob.

1. Zoe asked how Jacob's creative writing class was going, and he ***added / reminded / replied*** that it was going really well.
2. Zoe ***agreed / mentioned / wondered*** whether Jacob was joking about micro-stories.
3. Jacob ***persuaded / warned / whispered*** Zoe that it's usually better if the writer provides less information.
4. Zoe ***agreed / insisted / predicted*** that the second story was really powerful.
5. Zoe ***added / explained / persuaded*** how 'Pass the paper' works.
6. Zoe ***agreed / promised / yelled*** that Jacob would enjoy playing 'Pass the paper', but Jacob ***admitted / insisted / refused*** to play.
7. Jacob ***admitted / predicted / yelled*** that most of the stories are trash.
8. Zoe ***argued / explained / mentioned*** that she had been a student in California.
9. Jacob ***argued / predicted / reminded*** Zoe that the story could have up to 1,000 words.
10. Jacob ***insisted / warned / whispered*** Zoe that it wouldn't be easy to write the story.

PRONUNCIATION

Using your voice to make a story more interesting

9.6 **A** Listen again to Jacob reading the two micro-stories. How does he use his voice to make the stories sound more interesting? Think about:

- speaking quickly, slowly, loudly or quietly.
- showing emotions.
- pausing.

B **SPEAK** Work in pairs. Look at the audio script on page 176. Take turns reading the two stories aloud. Try to use your voice to make the stories sound more interesting.

C **SPEAK** Look at the story you wrote in Listening Exercise D. How can you use your voice to make it sound more interesting? Read your story to the class.

D **REFLECT** Work in groups. Which is the best story? Which storyteller used his/her voice most effectively?

SPEAKING HUB

A You are going to tell a story based on four pictures. Student A – go to the Communication Hub on page 147. Student B – go to the Communication Hub on page 154. Look at the pictures and spend one minute thinking about your story. Do not worry if your story is not very good yet!

B **SPEAK** Work in pairs. Take turns telling your story. While your partner is talking, listen carefully to his/her story. You can help if your partner runs out of ideas.

C **PLAN** Work together to improve your stories and make them longer. Can you join your two stories together into a single story? Use these ideas to help you:

- Who exactly were the people?
- What were the characters trying to do?
- How did they feel?
- What did they say?
- What happened next?

D **PRESENT** Share your stories with the class. Use your voice to make them as interesting as possible.

E **REFLECT** Work in groups. Which story did you like best? Why? Who was the best storyteller?

- Report a conversation
- Create a collaborative story

Café Hub

9.3 Leaving London

F – talk about movies and books   P – words connected to movies

COMPREHENSION

A Work in pairs and discuss the questions.

- What kind of movies do you like and dislike?
- Do you ever cry at movies? When was the last time?
- Do you prefer reading a book or watching the movie based on the book?

B Think of a movie you have seen recently and answer the questions.

1 What kind of movie was it? Romantic comedy, horror, etc?

2 Who was in it?

3 What kind of ending did it have?

C 00:00–03:36 Watch the first part of the video and answer the questions in Exercise B. Why is Gaby so emotional?

1. a sad, romantic film/movie, a tale of romance 2. Jessica Brune 3. A sad one.

D 03:36–05:03 Watch the second part of the video with the volume turned off. What do you think is happening? Discuss with a partner and then watch with the volume turned up and check your ideas.

FUNCTIONAL LANGUAGE

Talking about movies

Match the two halves of phrases you can use to talk about movies. Watch the video again and check your ideas.

Talking about movies

1 If you like sad and romantic films,	a sad ending.
2 It's got Jessica Brune in it,	b tearjerker.
3 It's a real	c where he writes the letter to her.
4 That was a really	d reading.
5 It's really worth	e amazing performance.
6 I thought the plot was good	f Oh really, she's a brilliant actor.
7 What an	g then this is the one for you.
8 I loved the scene	h and it felt like real life.

USEFUL PHRASES

A Match the useful phrases (1–6) with the phrases that have a similar meaning (a–f).

1 Yeah, right!	a There isn't always a happy ending.
2 Things don't always work out perfectly.	b I've almost done all my work.
3 There's something I've been meaning to tell you.	c We don't believe you.
4 We're going to miss you.	d I've been waiting for the right time to say this.
5 Do you want a hand?	e We don't want you to leave.
6 Just finishing up here.	f Can I help you?

B How do you say these useful phrases in your language?

Glossary

brilliant **(adj.) (British)** = great/fabulous/excellent **(adj.) (American)**
film/s **(n) (British)** = movie/s **(n) (American)**

MILLY

SAM

NEENA

ZAC

GABY

PRONUNCIATION

Words connected to movies

9.7 **A** These are some of the words connected to movies that appear in the video. Put them in the correct column according to the word stress. Listen and check your answers.

actor amazing brilliant comedy ending horror movie performance ~~review~~ romantic tearjerker terrible

oO	Oo	oOo	Ooo
review	movie	romantic	terrible
	horror	amazing	tearjerker
	brilliant	performance	comedy
	actor		
	ending		

B Work in pairs. Complete the sentences so that they are true for you. Compare with your partner.

1 The most terrible movie I've ever seen was …
2 My favorite comedy is …
3 The most fabulous actor in my country is …
4 I'd give the Oscar for the most amazing performance to …
5 The best place to read movie reviews is …

SPEAKING

A Think of your favorite movie of all time and write notes.

1 What's the title of the movie?
2 What kind of movie is it?
3 Who stars in the movie?
4 What happens and how does it end?
5 What do you particularly like about the plot and characters?
6 How did the movie make you feel?

B DISCUSS Work in pairs. Take turns describing your favorite movie.

Talk about movies and books

➤ Turn to page 164 to learn how to write a review.

9.3 Leaving London

LEAD-IN

Play a game of *Pictionary* with your students. Put them into two teams and give each team five movies to guess. Students take turns drawing the movie for their team until they guess.

COMPREHENSION

A Put students into pairs to discuss the questions. Discuss as a whole class and ask students to expand on their answers.

B Elicit the name of a movie some of the students have seen recently (maybe one that is currently out at the movie theater) and elicit some details about it. Then put students into pairs to tell their partner about a movie they've seen recently.

C ▶ 00:00–03:36 Tell students to watch an extract from the video series. Tell them to answer the questions from Exercise B and to find out why Gaby is so emotional.

D ▶ 03:36–05:03 Tell students to watch the next extract from the video series without sound. Put them into pairs to discuss what they thought was happening. Play the extract with the volume turned up for students to check.

Gaby says she's moving out. Neena and Zac are shocked. Zac calls Sam. Sam writes a letter and goes to mail it but then goes to their house and puts it through the mail slot.

FUNCTIONAL LANGUAGE

▶ Tell them to match the halves to complete the phrases, then play the video again for students to check. Check understanding of *tearjerker.*

USEFUL PHRASES

A Tell students to look at the useful phrases used in the video and to match them with their meanings.

B Ask students to think about how they would say these phrases in their language.

PRONUNCIATION

9.7 **A** Do one or two examples to check that students understand how the circles in the columns represent stressed and unstressed syllables. Then tell students to put the words into the correct columns according to where they think the stressed syllable is. Play the audio for students to check and tell them to repeat each word.

B Tell students to complete the sentences so that they're true for them. Then put students into pairs to compare and explain their answers.

SPEAKING

A Tell students they're going to tell each other about their favorite movie of all time. Tell them to look at the questions and to write notes. Monitor to help with language if needed.

B Put students into pairs to tell each other about their favorite movie. Encourage them to ask each other follow-up questions. If they've both seen the movie, tell them to say if they agree or disagree with their partner's opinion.

VIDEO SCRIPT

Z = Zac N = Neena G = Gaby S = Sam

Z: Big news. It's film night. So what are we watching tonight?
N: A film called 'Come Home' – I read the book a few years ago. The review in the paper says: 'If you like sad and romantic films, then this is the one for you. It's a modern tale of romance – two friends work together in London, they're both in love with each other, but they don't realize it.' Zac! Sit down!
Z: I think I have some work to do.
G: Zac! You made us watch that terrible horror movie for the last film night, so you have to watch this one now.
Z: OK …
N: Plus it's got Jessica Brune in it.
Z: Oh really! She's a brilliant actor.
N: Apparently it's a real tearjerker.
Z: Not for me! I never cry during movies.
G: Yeah right!
N: Here we go. Wow. What an amazing performance … I loved the scene when he writes the letter to her.
Z: Yeah … But she never got the letter. And so she never knew that he was also in love with her… And then she just left! Oh man, that was a really sad ending …
Neena – I have to admit, that was a really good movie.
N: See! I knew you'd like it! You should definitely check out the book. It's really worth reading.
Z: Sounds good. What do you think, Gaby?
G: I thought the plot was good and it felt like real life … because … that's what happens in real life. Things don't always work out perfectly and not everyone falls in love … it's sad. It's tragic. But it's true.
N: Maybe we should watch a romantic comedy next time?
Z: No, please no.
G: Oh … about next time. There's something I've been meaning to tell you.
Z: Oh, you won't be here for the next film night? Oh, that's OK, we can just …
G: No … I mean … I won't be here at all.
Z: Oh.
G: I'm moving back to Madrid. I love it here and I love living with you, but work isn't good and … and other things.
N: When are you thinking of leaving?
G: I've already booked my flight. I leave on Friday evening.
N: That's so soon!
G: I know. I'm sorry. I just want to go home now.
Z: We're gonna miss you, Gaby.
N: Yeah, we will.
G: I'm … going to do some packing.
N: Do you want a hand?
G: Yeah.
Z: Sam!
S: Hey buddy, just finishing up. What's going on?
Z: Sam … I have some … some big news.
S: What is it?
Z: It's Gaby – she's leaving London and going back to live with her parents in Madrid.
S: Oh … when?
Z: … Friday …
S: Look, I gotta go. I'll see you soon, OK?
Z: OK. Take care. Call me.
S: OK sure. Bye.

9 Writing — Write a review

using colons to introduce explanations

A Look at the pictures and read the reviews. Which event was better, the exhibit or the concert? the exhibit

Robert Gonsalves exhibit at the TACA

One of my favorite artists is Robert Gonsalves (1959–2017). I fell in love with his incredible paintings years ago, so I was delighted to visit an exhibit of his work last month at the Toronto Academy of Contemporary Art.

Ex E

His paintings show beautiful scenes with a twist: they all show two different worlds coming together. This means you can enjoy the paintings on two levels: first as objects of beauty, and then as amazing ideas to help you see the world differently.

However, I visited the exhibit on a Saturday afternoon, when it was extremely crowded. At times, it was difficult to get close to the paintings. Also, the space felt too small for so many paintings. If there were only one painting on each wall, it would create a much more powerful impression.

Overall, I would strongly recommend the exhibit, but you should go when it is less crowded.

Mel Montuno in concert at the City Arena

Last night I attended a concert by Mel Montuno, one of today's most exciting young musicians.

I became a fan of Mel's music two years ago, when I saw her performing live for an audience of 30. Now she is an international star – she usually has audiences of 10,000!

Although Mel is still an incredible songwriter with a beautiful voice, I definitely preferred her before she was famous. Last night's concert felt 'too big': she looked uncomfortable with such a large audience and hardly interacted with her fans at all.

Ex E

More seriously, the music was too loud and the lights were painfully bright. After half an hour, I had to leave, to give my ears and eyes a break!

Mel Montuno is currently on an eight-city tour of the country. If you like huge concerts, you might want to buy a ticket. But if, like me, you prefer calm, beautiful music, I recommend buying Mel's new CD, *My Jazz Age*, instead.

164 WRITING

B Read again and answer the questions.

1 Why did the writer decide to go to the exhibit/concert?
2 What did the writer like?
3 What wasn't so good?
4 What does the writer recommend? Why?

C What is the purpose of the paragraphs in each review? How are the two reviews similar? How are they different?
includes bad things; they don't both recommend

D Read the advice about writing reviews. Find examples of each piece of advice in the reviews.

1 Add a personal touch to describe how you felt.
2 Include practical information.
3 Don't be too negative – write about how you would do things differently or why people might not mind the problems.
4 Avoid repeating words like *beautiful* or *amazing*. Try to include a range of words instead.
5 Always end with a clear recommendation for your readers.

E Look at the box. Find three colons in the reviews. Underline the explanations after each colon. Circle the key phrase before each colon.

Using colons to introduce explanations

We can use colons (:) to join two sentences together and show how they are connected. The information after the colon provides an explanation for the key phrase before the colon.

F Match the beginnings of the review writers' sentences (1–3) with the endings (a–c).

1 There were three problems with the restaurant:	a go and buy tickets for this concert immediately.
2 My recommendation couldn't be clearer:	b the food was bad, the service was slow and the prices were too high.
3 When I arrived at the festival, I got an unpleasant surprise:	c half of the musicians had canceled their live shows because of the bad weather.

WRITING

A PREPARE You are going to write a review of an art event. Write about a real event that you attended or invent one.

B PLAN Write notes. Think about:

1 What was good about the event?
2 What would you improve? How?
3 Would you recommend the event to other people?

C WRITE Write your review (150–200 words).

D REVIEW Work in groups. Read some of your classmates' reviews. Which events would you like to attend?

Answers

The exhibit:

1 *The writer fell in love with the artist's paintings years ago.*
2 *the paintings*
3 *It was extremely crowded; the space felt too small for so many paintings.*
4 *Go when it's less crowded so you can get a better view of the paintings.*

The concert:

1 *The writer became a fan two years ago.*
2 *Mel is an incredible songwriter with a beautiful voice.*
3 *The concert felt too big; Mel hardly interacted with her fans at all; the lights were painfully bright and the music was too loud.*
4 *Buy her new CD instead of going to her concert if you prefer calm music.*

Answers

1 *One of my favorite artists is … / I fell in love with his incredible paintings years ago … / I was delighted …*
I became a fan of … / I definitely preferred …
2 *… at the Toronto Academy of Contemporary Art.*
… on an eight-city tour of the country.
3 *If there were only one painting on each wall, it would create a much more powerful impression.*
If you like huge concerts, you might want to buy a ticket.
4 *powerful; exciting; incredible*
5 *Overall, I would strongly recommend the exhibit, but you should …*
I recommend buying Mel's new CD, My Jazz Age, instead.

WRITING

A Tell students to look at the pictures and elicit what they show. Then tell to read and to decide which was better.

B Tell students to read the reviews again and to answer the questions.

C Elicit the purpose of the first paragraph of the first review to help students get started.

Paragraph 1: background (who, where, why, etc)
Paragraph 2 (the exhibit): good things/information about paintings
Paragraph 2 (the concert): good and bad things/information about the concert
Paragraph 3: bad things/information about the events
Paragraph 4: recommendation

D Do the first one together as a whole class to clarify the task.

E Again, elicit an example before students underline and circle.

F Tell students to practice by matching the beginnings of the sentences with the endings.

WRITING TASK

A Tell students they're going to write a review of a real art event they have been to. Tell them to choose a play, a concert, a music festival or an exhibit they'd like to write about.

B Tell students to write notes about the three questions. Monitor to help with language if needed.

C Tell students to look back at the advice about writing reviews in Exercise D and to follow it as they write their own review.

D Put students into groups to read each other's reviews. Encourage them to ask each other questions about the events they reviewed. As a whole class, discuss which events students would most like to attend. Finish with feedback on students' use of language in the reviews.

Unit 9 Review

A Correct the four mistakes in the sentences.

1 I'd feel really strange if one of the actors ~~start~~ talking to me.
I'd feel really strange if one of the actors started talking to me.

2 If I had a little more time, ~~I'll~~ come and watch the movie with you, but I'm much too busy.
If I had a little more time, I'd come and watch the movie with you, but I'm much too busy.

3 If ~~I'd know~~ the answer, I'd tell you, but I don't so I can't.
If I knew the answer, I'd tell you, but I don't so I can't.

4 You'd be a better actor if you ~~can~~ remember your lines!
You'd be a better actor if you could remember your lines!

B Change the direct speech into reported speech.

1 'My daughter is a talented artist.'
He said that his daughter was a talented artist.

2 'Immersive theater is becoming a lot more popular all the time.'
She said that immersive theater was becoming a lot more popular all the time.

3 'Do you prefer reading books or watching movies?'
He asked me if/whether I preferred reading books or watching movies.

4 'I can't paint, but I can draw fairly well.'
She told me she couldn't paint, but she could draw fairly well.

5 'How much will the tickets cost?'
She asked me how much the tickets would cost

6 'Be quiet! We're trying to rehearse!'
They told me to be quiet because they were trying to rehearse.

7 'Have you ever seen a famous band live in concert?'
He asked me if/whether I had/I'd ever seen a famous band live in concert.

VOCABULARY

A Complete the sentences with the words in the box.

choir display gallery orchestra scene spectators

Reviews

1 We went to an amazing classical music concert last week. The orchestra had over 50 musicians!

2 The play was very smart. There was an unexpected twist in the final scene.

3 The Japanese Culture Week ended with a wonderful display by a group of traditional dancers.

4 I'm a member of a choir. There are 30 of us, and we practice singing three times a week.

5 I'm really excited. There's going to be an exhibit of my paintings at the local gallery!

6 It was such an amazing tennis game. The spectators clapped for ten minutes!

B Read the conversation and choose the correct verb to complete the idioms.

A: So? What did you think of my short story?

B: Well, I thought it was a little too complicated. I couldn't [1]*stay* / *keep* track of who was who.

A: Really? So do you think I should [2]*get* / *go* rid of some of the main characters?

B: Yes, that would be much better. And some of your characters were too similar to each other. It needs to be much easier for the reader to [3]*tell* / *talk* the difference between them.

A: OK, that's a good point. I'll try to [4]*hold* / *pay* attention to things like that in future. Anything else?

B: The beginning was excellent, and I loved the fact that the whole story [5]*takes* / *starts* place on a train, but then you didn't really [6]*do* / *make* use of that idea later in the book. I think you should definitely try to [7]*take* / *make* advantage of the train trip more.

A: OK. What did you think of the ending?

B: I thought the ending was fairly weak, so the story kind of [8]*falls* / *keeps* flat at the end. But … apart from that, it was great.

(Answers: 1 keep, 2 get, 3 tell, 4 pay, 5 takes, 6 make, 7 take, 8 falls)

C Match the beginnings of the sentences (1–7) with the endings (a–g).

1 'Shhh! Don't talk during the play,' — g
2 'You must keep your promise and come to watch the show,' — d
3 'The gallery might be fairly crowded tomorrow,' — c
4 'Don't forget to buy a ticket,' — a
5 'Yes, you're absolutely right,' — f
6 'I didn't write my story – I copied it from the internet,' — b
7 'Where is everybody?' — e

a she reminded him.
b he admitted.
c she predicted.
d he insisted.
e she wondered.
f he agreed.
g she whispered.

FUNCTIONAL LANGUAGE

Choose the correct words to complete the conversation.

A: I want to go to the movie theater tonight, but all the new movies look a little boring.

B: Really? What about *Silly Story 2*? I thought the lead actor, Max Connor, was great [1]*at* / *in* / *on* / *with* it. If you like funny movies, it's definitely the movie [2]*by* / *for* / *of* / *to* you.

A: Oh, yes, I saw the ad for it. But I didn't like *Silly Story 1*. The plot was really difficult to [3]*follow* / *mention* / *predict* / *record*, and it was very sad at the end.

B: Yeah, I know what you mean. But this one's much better, and it really [4]*had* / *did* / *made* / *took* me laugh. And it has a really happy [5]*ending* / *finishing* / *starting* / *stopping*.

A: Don't tell me how it ends! You'll spoil it for me!

B: OK, sorry, but I think it's really [6]*worth* / *love* / *miss* / *recommend* seeing. Definitely watch this movie.

(Answers: 1 in, 2 for, 3 follow, 4 made, 5 ending, 6 worth)

10 PSYCHOLOGY

The purpose of psychology is to give us a completely different idea of the things we know best.

Paul Valéry

A hiker watches a storm approach in New South Wales, Australia.

OBJECTIVES

- talk about different versions of past events
- talk about past mistakes
- talk about your wishes and regrets
- plan a to-do list
- make and accept apologies
- write a report

Work with a partner. Discuss the questions.

1 Look at the picture. Where do you go when you want to think?
2 Look at the quote. Do you agree?
3 Work in pairs. Tell your partner what you do when you need to reflect on a problem.

PSYCHOLOGY 109

Psychology (n) the study of the mind and how it affects behavior.

The quote for this unit highlights the importance of psychology in giving us a fresh perspective on what we take for granted, for example, our own and other people's behavior.

Paul Valéry (1871–1945) was a French poet and well-known intellectual and public speaker.

OBJECTIVES

Read the unit objectives to the class.

UNIT OPENER QUESTIONS

With books closed, write on the board *The purpose of psychology is* ______________. Put students into pairs to discuss how they would complete the sentence. Get some feedback and write the different suggested endings on the board, correcting students' language as appropriate.

1 Tell students to open their books and look at the picture. Elicit that the person has gone somewhere peaceful to think. Ask students to tell their partner where they go when they want to think.

2 Tell students to read the quote and ask them if they agree or disagree with it. Ask if they prefer any of their sentences that they created at the beginning of the class to Paul Valéry's quote and why.

3 Put students into pairs and ask them what they do when they have a problem and they want to reflect on it. Give students a couple of minutes to write some notes on their own about their ideas. Monitor and assist with language input. When they are ready, ask them to share their ideas with their partner.

WORKSHEETS

Lesson 10.1 Making up your mind

Grammar: Third conditional; *would have* + past participle (W37)

Vocabulary: Expressions with *mind* (W38)

Lesson 10.2 Wish lists

Grammar: Hopes and wishes (W39)

Vocabulary: Staying organized (W40)

10.1 Making up your mind

- Talk about different versions of past events
- Talk about past mistakes

V – psychology verbs; expressions with *mind*
P – third conditional
G – third conditional; *should have* + past participle
S – listening for phrases that support an argument

READING

A SPEAK Work in pairs. Go the **Communication Hub** on **page 150**.

B READ FOR MAIN IDEA Read *Do you think you think rationally? Think again!* What is the connection between the three sub-headings and pictures 1–3 above?

C READ FOR DETAIL Read again. Are the sentences true (T) or false (F)? Correct the false sentences.

1. New research has shown that we're ~~good at making rational decisions.~~ much less rational than we think. F
2. After we've thought about a hook number, it's ~~easy~~ harder to think of a number that's a long way from that hook. F
3. We would probably make better decisions if we ignored hook numbers. T
4. If we were more rational, we ~~would~~ wouldn't worry ~~more~~ about buried costs. F
5. In the example about the weekend break, the money you've spent on the hotel and travel is a buried cost. T
6. Filtering involves presenting a situation in a way that makes it sound better (or worse) than it really is. T

D SPEAK Work in pairs. Can you think of any examples of hook numbers, buried costs or filtering from your own life? Tell your partner.

DO YOU THINK YOU THINK RATIONALLY? THINK AGAIN!

For centuries, psychologists assumed that people think rationally and make decisions based on facts. Ex C Q1 **But we're actually much less rational than we think.**

HOOK NUMBERS

Look again at the quiz. Question 1a is clearly nonsense: of course we have more than 70 thoughts per day! So it shouldn't affect our answers to question Ex C Q2 1b. But for most people, the number 70 acts as a hook. It encourages us to think of a number that isn't too far from 70. But if the hook number had been much higher, say 70 million, it would have made us think of a Ex C Q3 number in the millions. And if we hadn't seen a hook at all, we might have chosen a more likely answer: around 70,000 thoughts per day.

Sales people use hook numbers to persuade us to spend much more than we should, for example, by tricking us into believing a watch must be worth thousands of dollars.

BURIED COSTS

A buried cost is time, money or effort that we've already Ex C Q4 spent and can't get back. It would be rational to ignore buried costs when making decisions; they're gone, so we should forget about them. But for most of us, waste feels like physical pain, and we usually spend even more time, money and effort trying to avoid that pain. Ex C Q5 Look back at question 2 in the quiz. The money you've spent is gone. Instead of regretting the past, we should forget it and focus on the future. When you're sick, you should stay home and get better.

10.1 Making up your mind

LEAD-IN

Tell students to think of one moment in their life they would like to relive. Give a personal example, explaining why. Then put students into pairs to tell each other about their chosen moments.

READING

A Direct students to the **Communication Hub** (TB121) and look at the psychology quiz. Tell them first to read the quiz and think about their own answers, then put them into pairs to compare.

B Ask students what they think the connection is between the pictures and the three subheadings in the psychology quiz. Tell them to read the article and find out.

Suggested answers:

Picture 1 is connected to Hook Numbers. These are numbers that draw us toward them like how bait attracts a fish.

Picture 2 is connected to Buried Costs. Like the treasure chest buried beneath the ground, there is little chance of getting back money spent.

Picture 3 is connected to Filtering. Although the paintings are the same, different color filters make the paintings look better/worse. In the same way, words like pass and fail make the schools in question 3 sound better/worse.

C Tell students to read the sentences about the article and to try to remember if they're true or false. Then tell them to read the article again and check.

D Put students into pairs to discuss the questions. Monitor and assist as required. Ask students to expand on their answers and share experiences with the whole class.

TEACHING IDEA by David Seymour and Maria Popova

Grammar: If I hadn't done that …

1 Use pictures to build a situation of two friends, Jo and Tony, who can't decide what to do. There is a party tonight and a good show on TV. Establish that Jo decided to go to the party, while Tony stays at home.

2 It is two hours later. Draw Jo looking miserable at the party – and Tony looking miserable watching TV. Check that the students are clear what they chose and that they regret their choices. Elicit what they are thinking and feeling (If I'd stayed at home, I could have watched …; If I'd gone to the party, I could have …).

3 You could extend the situation to make more sentences if you wish (If I hadn't been so tired, I would've had a better time).

GRAMMAR HUB

10.1 Third conditional; *would have* + past participle

Third conditional

Condition	Result
I would have made a better decision	if **Daniel had done** the research.
If **I had known** all the facts,	**he wouldn't have made** his discovery.

Question	Positive short answer	Negative short answer
If **you had thought** about it more, **would you have made** the same decision?	Yes, **I would (have)**.	No, **I wouldn't (have)**.
Would they have passed the exam if **they had answered** correctly?	Yes, **they would (have)**.	No, **they wouldn't (have)**.

- We use the third conditional to imagine a situation in the past that didn't actually happen.
  *If I had set my alarm clock, I wouldn't have been late for work. (= I **didn't** set my alarm clock and I **was** late for work.)*
- As with other conditionals, we only use a comma when the *if*-clause comes first.
- We can use *could have* or *might have* instead of *would have* to express possibility.
  I could have answered correctly if I'd had more time.
- In answer to a third conditional question, we can use either *I would* or *I would have*
  Would you have made the same decision if you'd known all the facts?
  Yes, I would. / Yes, I would have. / No, I wouldn't. / No, I wouldn't have.

***would have* + past participle**

***should have* + past participle**

Positive	Negative	Question
I would have told her about my exam results.	**He wouldn't have bought** me such an expensive gift.	**Why would they have left** the house already?
She should have bought the first pair.	**You shouldn't have spent** so much money.	**Should I have changed** my mind?
They should have offered more choice.	**I shouldn't have bought** these shoes.	How much **should they have paid**?

- We use *should/shouldn't have* + the past participle of the main verb to talk about mistakes that we made in the past. We regret those actions and try to imagine how we could have acted differently.
  *She shouldn't have changed her mind. (= She **did** change her mind and this was a mistake.)*
- We always put the past participle of the main verb after *should/shouldn't have*.
  They should have thought about their decision more carefully. NOT ~~They should have think about their decision more carefully.~~

10.1 Making up your mind

VOCABULARY

A Tell students to find the verbs in the text and to think about what they mean. Then tell them to match the beginnings of the definitions to the endings.

B Tell students to choose the correct verb to complete the questions.

C Put students into pairs to discuss the questions in Exercise B.

GRAMMAR

A Tell students to look at the sentence and elicit that it's an example of the third conditional. Ask them to look at the sentence again in pairs and answer the questions in the box.

B Tell students to look back at the article to find and underline another example of the third conditional. Elicit that *might* is used instead of *would* because the writer is less sure about the result.

And if we hadn't seen a hook at all, we might have chosen a more likely answer: around 70,000 thoughts per day.

C Direct students to the **Grammar Hub** (TB110 and below).

D Write a personal example (e.g. *If I hadn't met …, I wouldn't have …*), then tell students to write three third conditional sentences that are true for themselves. Put students into pairs to compare and explain their sentences.

PRONUNCIATION

A (10.1) Tell students to listen and repeat the sentence. Ask students what they noticed about the pronunciation of the auxiliary verbs *had*, *would* and *have*.

had and *would* in third conditionals are frequently contracted and pronounced /**d**/.
have is usually pronounced /**əv**/ after modal verbs *like would*, *could* and *might*. It sounds the same as *of*.

B Put students into pairs to practice saying the sentences they wrote in Grammar Exercise D. Monitor and help if needed.

SPEAKING

Tell students a brief anecdote and then elicit a third conditional sentence to summarize the situation. Put students into pairs to discuss the questions. Monitor and write notes.

Extra activity

You can add to the two discussion questions with the following question or use it as a model for your anecdote:

Think of a time in the past when something bad nearly happened (e.g. somebody tried to trick you). What stopped the bad thing from happening? What might have been the result if it had happened? What did you learn from the experience?

I got an email from my bank last week telling me to click on a link to change my password. Luckily, I noticed that the link was to a completely different site, so I didn't click on it. But if I hadn't noticed …

GRAMMAR HUB

10.1 Third conditional; *Would have* + past participle

A Read the sentences and choose the option which is true.

1 He should have made a decision based on the facts.
 a He considered the facts. (b) He didn't consider the facts.
2 She could have avoided the other car if she'd stopped in time.
 a She avoided the other car. (b) She didn't avoid the other car.
3 If you had listened to me, you wouldn't have made a foolish decision.
 (a) You made a foolish decision. b You didn't make a foolish decision.
4 If David had gone to a smaller store, he would have felt less stressed.
 a David went to a small store. (b) David went to a big store.
5 You shouldn't have encouraged her to spend all that money!
 (a) She spent a lot of money. b She didn't spend a lot of money.
6 We wouldn't have bought this house if we'd known it was so noisy here.
 (a) We bought the house. b We didn't buy the house.

B Correct the mistakes in each sentence.

1 I shouldn't ^have paid so much for this cell phone.
2 If our teacher ~~gave~~ had given us time to review, we would all have earned better grades.
3 ~~Will~~ Would the show have attracted more people if we had advertised it better?
4 I'm sorry – I ~~would~~ should have listened to your advice.
5 If you ~~have~~ had bought your shoes in the first store, you would have saved time!
6 Should we have ~~count~~ counted the sunk costs?
7 Would you ~~had~~ have agreed to take part if you had known it was a trick?
8 I should ~~realize~~ have realized that the watch was made of plastic!

C Choose the correct option.

The sneakers were fashionable, attractive and cheap, so I bought them. However, I [1] ***(shouldn't)** / wouldn't* have been so easily influenced by the saleswoman. A few days later, I searched for that brand online and discovered that they were made by child workers! If I [2] ***(had known)** / would know* that they were made by children, I would never [3] *buy / **(have bought)*** them. In fact, I [4] *had avoided / **(would have avoided)*** that store completely! If I [5] *would discover / **(had discovered)*** the truth sooner, I would have complained to the store. And of course I [6] *hadn't encouraged / **(wouldn't have encouraged)*** my friends to buy them either! It's really important that, as shoppers, we act responsibly. I've found an online group which persuades customers not to buy products like these. I joined it right away. If I [7] ***(had heard)** / heard* about it sooner, I [8] ***(would)** / will* have joined months ago!

➤ Go back to page 111.

VOCABULARY
Psychology verbs

A Match the beginnings of the definitions (1–8) with the endings (a–h). Use *Do you think you think rationally? Think again!* to help you.

1 If something **affects** or **influences** you, g
2 If you **assume** that something is true, d
3 If something **attracts** you, h
4 If you **avoid** doing something, e
5 If you **encourage** or **persuade** somebody to do something, a
6 If you **regret** something, b
7 If something **tempts** you, f
8 If somebody **tricks** you into doing something, c

a you say something that makes him/her want to do it.
b you feel bad about something you did (or didn't do) in the past.
c they make you do it by lying or hiding the truth.
d you believe it although you haven't checked for sure.
e you are careful not to do it.
f you want it, even though it might be bad for you.
g it changes the way you think or behave.
h you like it and want to have it.

B Choose the correct verbs to complete the questions.

1 How do marketers and advertisers *avoid* / *tempt* us to buy things we don't really want or need?
2 When you go shopping, which things *attract* / *influence* your decision to buy something? Is it possible that the stores use psychological tricks to affect your choices?

C **SPEAK** Work in pairs. Ask and answer the questions in Exercise B.

FILTERING

In question 3 from the quiz, were you tempted by School A? That 75 percent pass rate sounds great, doesn't it? What about School B, with all those failures? No, thanks! Of course, your rational side knows that School B is better – a 20 percent failure rate means there's an 80 percent pass rate. But we can't help being influenced by Ex C 06 words like *pass* and *fail*.
We're strongly attracted to positive words like *success*, *save* and *free*. But negative words are even more powerful. We hate *losing*, *wasting* or *missing* things. So if you see an ad that warns, 'Don't miss your last chance to save,' remember that someone is trying to trick our irrational minds.

Glossary

bury (v) to put something in the ground and cover it with earth
filter (v) if you filter a photo, you change or improve the appearance of the image before posting it on social media
hook (n) a curved piece of metal or plastic fixed to a pole or with a handle at the other end, used for catching hold of something

GRAMMAR
Third conditional

A **WORK IT OUT** Work in pairs. Look at the sentence from *Do you think you think rationally? Think again!* Then choose the correct words to complete the rules.

If the hook number had been much higher, say 70 million, it would have made us think of a number in the millions.

Third conditional

1 We use the third conditional to talk about imaginary situations in *the past* / *the present*.
2 Conditional sentences usually have *two* / *three* clauses: the *if*-clause and the result clause. To make a third conditional sentence, we use:
if + past perfect, *would* + *have* + past participle
3 We *can* / *can't* use *might* or *could* instead of *would* in the result clause.

B Find and underline another third conditional sentence in the article.

C Go to the **Grammar Hub** on **page 140**.

D **SPEAK** Work in pairs. Write three third conditional sentences that are true for you. Tell your partner about the situations in your sentences.

PRONUNCIATION
Third conditional

10.1 **A** Listen and repeat the third conditional sentence. What do you notice about the pronunciation of *had*, *would* and *have*?

If I'd thought about it more carefully, I'd have made a better decision.

B **SPEAK** Work in pairs. Practice saying the sentences you wrote in Grammar Exercise D. Listen and check your partner's pronunciation.

SPEAKING

Work in pairs and discuss the questions.

1 Think of a time in the past when you paid too much for something or bought something you didn't really want or need. What happened? Why? What would have happened if you'd thought more carefully?
When I bought my first car, I thought it was perfect. But I didn't check whether it actually worked properly! In the end, I spent a lot of money fixing it and sold it again. If I'd …
2 Think of a time in the past when you made a bad decision because you didn't have enough information or experience. What would you have done differently if you'd known then what you know now?
I received an email from my bank last week telling me to click on a link to change my password. Luckily, I noticed that the link was to a completely different site. But if I hadn't noticed …

LISTENING

A SPEAK Work in groups and discuss the questions.

1 Do you find shopping relaxing or stressful? Why?

2 When you're shopping for clothes and shoes, do you find it easy to decide what to buy?

10.2 **B LISTEN FOR MAIN IDEA** Listen to a conversation between two friends, Robert and Vicky. What do they say about the items in the pictures (a–d)?

Glossary

common sense (n) the ability to use good judgment and make sensible decisions

paradox (n) a statement consisting of two parts that seem to mean the opposite of each other

perfectionist (n) someone who always wants things to be done perfectly

a

b

c

d

10.2 **C** Listen again. How does Robert support his arguments? Use the strategies in the box to help you.

Listening for phrases that support an argument

Sometimes when you listen, you need to decide how strong a person's arguments are. Pay attention to the techniques they use to support their argument.

Common sense:

- *Surely, Of course, Obviously, Clearly, As you can imagine, …*

Facts and statistics:

- *In fact, …; The researchers found that …*

Examples and details:

- *For example, …; For instance, …*

Expert opinions:

- *According to Professor Schwartz …; He's shown that …*

10.2 **D LISTEN FOR DETAIL** Listen again. Complete the notes about the conversation.

1 **The Paradox of Choice:** According to Professor Barry Schwartz (an __American__ psychologist), too many __choices__ makes us __stressed__.

2 **Shampoo company:** Cut choices from __26__ to __15__. Sales went up by __10__ percent.

3 **Robert's experience of buying a laptop:** He went to a small store with __three__ laptops to choose from. Took __five__ minutes to choose and buy a laptop.

4 **Perfectionists regret their choices:** Vicky bought __two__ different pairs of shoes, but took each pair back to the store.

5 **Quick deciders don't worry about perfection:** When Robert finds jeans that are __good__ enough, he buys them and stops worrying. Only takes them back to store if they're __damaged__.

E SPEAK Work in groups and discuss the questions.

1 Have you ever experienced the Paradox of Choice? Think about the following situations:
   - shopping
   - choosing what to watch on TV or online
   - making important life decisions
   - cooking or eating

2 Are you a perfectionist or a quick decider? What about other people in your family?

3 How can stores, websites and other businesses help us deal with the Paradox of Choice?

10.1 Making up your mind

LISTENING

A Put students into groups to discuss the questions. If any students have very strong opinions, encourage them to share and expand on them.

10.2 **B** Tell students to look at the pictures and elicit what they show. Tell students they're going to listen to a conversation between two friends. Ask them to listen for what they say about the items in the pictures. Point out the glossary but tell students not to worry if there are some words they don't understand at this stage.

Suggested answers:

a Vicky tried to buy a laptop but there were too many choices and she couldn't decide which one to buy. Robert bought his laptop easily because he only had three choices.

b A shampoo company cut the number of shampoo choices and sales went up.

c Vicky bought some shoes but she kept changing her mind.

d When Robert is buying jeans, he makes a quick decision and sticks with it.

10.2 **C** Point out the information in the box about *Listening for phrases that support an argument.* Tell students to listen again and to think about which of the strategies Robert uses.

Suggested answers:

He used all four techniques.

He used common sense to explain why having some choice is better than no choice.

He used facts and statistics to explain the example with shampoo.

He gave a well-known example (shampoo) as well as examples from his own life (his laptop, jeans).

He gave the opinions of Professor Schwartz.

10.2 **D** Tell students to look at the notes and to try to complete them with what they remember from the conversations. Play the audio again for students to listen and check.

E Put students into groups to discuss the questions. Briefly practice pronunciation of perfectionist /**pər'fekʃənɪst**/. Ask students to expand on their answers and ask each other follow-up questions.

AUDIO SCRIPT

10.2

Listening, Exercise B
R = Robert V = Vicky

R: Would you mind if I borrowed your laptop for a few minutes?
V: No, of course not. Go ahead. Just bear in mind that it's really slow and it keeps crashing all the time.
R: Sounds like you need a new one.
V: Yeah, I know. I'm trying to buy one, but … it's difficult.
R: What do you mean?
V: Well, I went to the electronics store last week. They had over 100 laptops to choose from. After about three hours in the store, looking at every single laptop, I found two that I liked, but I was of two minds and I couldn't decide which one to buy. It was horrible. In the end, I gave up! But never mind. I still have my old computer, so it isn't so bad.
R: Ah. Sounds like the Paradox of Choice.
V: What's that?
R: Well, the name comes from an American
Ex D Q1 psychologist, Professor Barry Schwartz. According to Professor Schwartz, most people assume that having lots of choices is always a good thing. But he's shown that in fact too many choices is bad for us. It makes us stressed, so we can't make decisions.
V: Uh … OK. So why do stores give us so many choices? Surely they'd sell more if they reduced the number of choices?
R: Exactly. The problem is, most companies still think more is better. But a few smart companies have realized that they'll sell more if they offer fewer
Ex D Q2 choices. I read recently that a shampoo company cut the number of shampoo choices from 26 to 15. Everyone thought they'd lose sales, but in fact, their sales went up by ten percent.
V: Really? Wow! So fewer choices is better.
R: Yes, in general. But of course, it's better to have fewer choices than no choice at all – that's just common sense.
V: Right.
R: So with your laptop, you should have gone to a smaller store. If you'd done that, you'd have had fewer choices, but your decision would have been
Ex D Q3 much easier. The store where I bought mine had just three laptops to choose from. One was too expensive; one was too basic; the third one was absolutely fine, so I bought it. It took me five minutes. And I'm very happy with it.
V: Wow! I could never do that. I'd be worried that I'd missed the chance to buy a better computer somewhere else.
R: That's because you're a perfectionist.
V: A perfectionist? What's that?
R: It's a person who always looks for the perfect thing to buy. You can't relax unless you're sure you've studied every option and chosen the best one. And even after you've made a decision, you still worry that you've made the wrong choice.
V: Yeah, that definitely sounds like me! For example, I went shopping for some new shoes last week. After about six hours, I finally bought a pair. But when I got them home, I regretted my decision
Ex D Q4 immediately. I realized that they weren't perfect and I shouldn't have bought them. So I took them back to the store to get my money back. Then I bought a different pair of shoes, but I took them back to the store a few days later. In the end, I bought the first pair again.
R: Yes, you're definitely a perfectionist. I, on the other hand, am what I call a 'quick decider'.
V: What's that?
R: It's a person who makes quick decisions without worrying about perfection. When I'm shopping for
Ex D Q5 new jeans, for instance, and I find some jeans that are good enough, I buy them and stop worrying about them. And I never take them back to the store – unless they're damaged, of course. Once I've made up my mind, I stick with my decision.
V: Wow! You're so lucky. I could never do that!
R: Well, you think it's impossible, but maybe it's all in the mind. I think you can become a quick decider – you just need to put your mind to it! It'll make life much easier.
V: Yes, you're right. I'll definitely do that! From now on, I'm going to be a quick decider. But, uh, what if I change my mind later?

10.1 Making up your mind

GRAMMAR

A Tell students to look at the sentences to complete the rules. Check students' understanding of the meaning.

B Direct students to the **Grammar Hub** (see TB110 and TB111).

A good way to consolidate students' understanding of the meaning and form of a structure like this is through translation. After feedback, when students all have the correct sentences, tell them to choose three sentences and to translate them into their own language. When they have done this, tell them to cover the original English sentence so they can only see their translation. Then tell students to translate the sentences back into English. Students can then look back at the original sentences and see how similar they are to their English version.

C Put students into pairs to discuss what Angela and Kasia should or shouldn't have done in the two situations. Use the **Grammar Worksheet** on W37 for extra practice.

VOCABULARY

10.2 A Elicit that all the sentences are from the conversation between Vicky and Robert. Tell them to try to fill in the blanks with the expressions in the box. Play the audio for students to check.

B Put students into pairs to discuss what they think the expressions from Exercise A mean. Tell them to look at the way the expressions are used in the sentences from the conversation to help them work out the meanings. Once students have discussed what they think, you could give them the definitions below on a handout or write them on the board and tell them to match the expressions to the definitions. Consolidate understanding of the meaning by eliciting personal examples that are meaningful to the students if necessary.

1 *Would you mind if (= Is it a problem if …)*
2 *bear in mind (= remember / be careful because …)*
3 *of two minds (= unable to make a decision)*
4 *never mind (= it doesn't matter)*
5 *made up my mind (= decided)*
6 *all in the mind (= something you imagine, not something in the real world)*
7 *put your mind to (= try hard / make an effort to achieve)*
8 *change my mind (= make a different decision later)*

C Put students into pairs to discuss the questions. Discuss answers as a class and find out how similar their ideas are. Use the **Vocabulary Worksheet** on W38 for extra practice.

SPEAKING HUB

A Tell students to read the sentences about regrets. Put students into pairs to discuss if they agree with the sentences.

B Tell students to think about two or three mistakes they've made in the past. Elicit an example as a whole class, then tell students to write notes about the questions. Monitor and help them correct their notes or provide requested vocabulary.

C Put students back into pairs and tell them to tell each other about their mistakes. Monitor and write notes to give as feedback at the end of the activity.

D Put students into different pairs to discuss the questions.

> **Extra activity**
> You can always extend a communicative activity like this one by asking pairs or groups to be ready to report back on their discussions to the whole class. Set a time limit to allow them to prepare. This actually provides further speaking practice, gives students time to structure responses and can usually encourage more thoughtful contributions.

METHODOLOGY HUB by Jim Scrivener

If I hadn't done that …

The following activity can also be extended to introduce *should have:*

1. Use board pictures to build a situation of two friends, Jo and Tony, who can't decide what to do. There is party tonight and a good show on TV. Establish that Jo decides to go to the party while Tony chooses to stay at home.
2. It is two hours later. Draw Jo looking miserable at the party – and Tony looking miserable watching TV. Check that students are clear what they chose and that they regret their choices. Elicit what the students are feeling and thinking *(If I'd stayed at home, I could have watched Spacecops. If I'd gone to the party, I could have met some nice people.)*.
3. You could extend the situation to make more sentences if you wish *(If I hadn't been so tired, I would have had a better time)*.

TEACHING IDEA by David Seymour and Maria Popova

The unreal past

In pairs, look at the following sentences and decide whether the people in each situation feel happy about what happened, unhappy about it or just neutral, e.g.

Ray went to the party. – *If Ray hadn't gone to the party, he wouldn't have met Maggie* (happy, because he met her). – *If he hadn't gone to the party, he would have felt better the next morning* (unhappy, because he went to the party and now he is tired). – *If Ray hadn't gone to the party, he'd have gone clubbing instead* (neutral, because he'd have spent the night dancing anyway).

> Terry moved to New York. He didn't know she was coming. James crashed his car. Vera lost her lottery ticket. Sonya went to Japan. Irene didn't have a spare key. Roger didn't pass the exam. Tracy couldn't sell her house.

Imagine you were the person in some of the situations. Work with a partner and write some sentences to express regret. Use *should (not) have done, e.g. I shouldn't have stayed up so late.*

GRAMMAR
should have + past participle

A WORK IT OUT Look at the sentences from the conversation between Vicky and Robert. Then choose the correct words to complete the rules.

So with your laptop, you **should have gone** to a smaller store.

I realized that they weren't perfect and I **shouldn't have bought** them.

> ***should have* + past participle**
>
> 1 We write *should* (*not*) + *have* + past participle / base form.
>
> 2 We use *should have done* to talk about mistakes that we *make* / made in the past and imagine how we could have avoided those mistakes.

B Go to the **Grammar Hub** on **page 140**.

C SPEAK Work in pairs. Use *should/shouldn't have done* to talk about these situations.

1 Angela went shopping for a new coat. She found a great coat in the first store, but she went to ten more stores to make sure it was the best one. When she went back to buy it, somebody else had bought it.

2 Kasia bought a used computer five years ago, but it didn't work properly. Although she had enough money to buy a new one, she kept using the old one for years.

VOCABULARY
Expressions with *mind*

10.2

A Complete the sentences (1–8) from the conversation with the expressions in the box. Then listen again and check your answers.

> ~~all in the mind~~ ~~bear in mind~~ ~~change my mind~~ ~~of two minds~~ ~~made up my mind~~ ~~never mind~~ ~~put your mind to~~ ~~would you mind if~~

1 Would you mind if I borrowed your laptop for a few minutes? (= Is it a problem if …)

2 Just bear in mind that it's really slow. (= remember / be careful because …)

3 I found two that I liked, but I was of two minds and I couldn't decide which one to buy. (= unable to make a decision)

4 But never mind. I still have my old computer, so it isn't so bad. (= it doesn't matter)

5 Once I've made up my mind, I stick with my decision. (= decided)

6 You think it's impossible, but maybe it's all in the mind. (= something you imagine, not something in the real world)

7 I think you can become a quick decider – you just need to put your mind to it! (= try hard / make an effort to achieve)

8 But what if I change my mind later? (= make a different decision later)

B SPEAK Work in pairs. What do you think the expressions in Exercise A mean?

C SPEAK Work in pairs and discuss the questions.

1 Quick deciders are generally less stressed, but there are some dangers connected with making quick decisions. What should they **bear in mind** before making a decision?

2 How long does it usually take you to **make up your mind** about whether you can trust somebody? What might make you **change your mind** about them?

SPEAKING HUB

A Read the sentences about regrets. Do you agree or disagree with them? Why?

1 You should never regret anything. Your mistakes are part of who you are.

2 You should regret the things you haven't done more than the things you have done.

B Think about two or three mistakes you have made in the past. What did you do? What did you not do? What should or should you not have done?

C Work in pairs. Tell your partner about some of the mistakes you have made. While your partner is talking, listen carefully, and then ask questions to find out more information.

> **Finding out more information**
>
> Really? So what did you do? Why did you do that?
>
> What do you think you should have done?
>
> But if you hadn't done that, what do you think would have happened?

D Work in pairs and discuss the questions.

1 What can you learn from the mistakes you have made in the past?

2 What would you do differently if you were in the same situation in the future?

3 Is it good to talk about past mistakes?

Talk about different versions of past events

Talk about past mistakes

10.2 Wish lists

- Talk about your wishes and regrets
- Plan a to-do list

V reflexive verbs; staying organized
S bridge sentences
P emphasis and reflexive pronouns
G hopes and wishes

LISTENING

A SPEAK Work in pairs and discuss the questions.

1 Do you have any habits that you'd like to stop?
2 Are there any good habits that you'd like to start?
3 How easy is it to change your habits?
4 Look at the diagram. What do you think it shows?

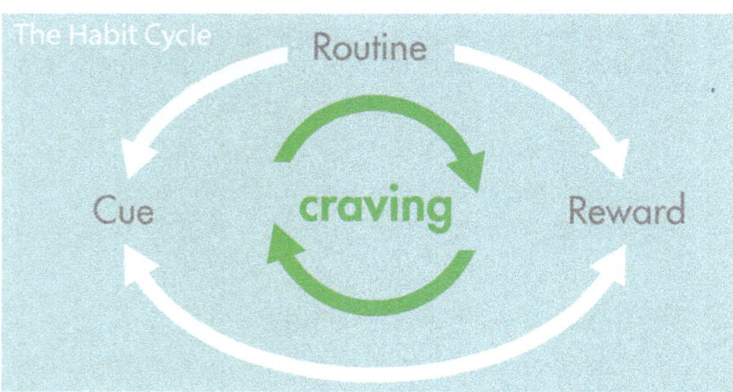

B LISTEN FOR GIST 10.3 Listen to a radio show about habits. Which habits in the pictures do the speakers talk about?
eating fast food, drinking coffee, drinking water

C LISTEN FOR DETAIL 10.3 Listen again and choose the correct answers.

1 What is David's main cue for eating fast food?
 a He sees a sign while he's driving.
 (b) He smells food in a shopping mall.
2 What happens when a routine is part of a true habit?
 (a) You can follow the steps without thinking.
 b You do it although you don't want to.
3 Why are cravings dangerous?
 a Because you don't want the reward any more.
 (b) Because you feel that you need the reward.
4 What's the only way to change a habit?
 (a) Change the routine.
 b Change the reward.
5 Why does Leo make coffee when he arrives at work?
 a Because he loves the taste of coffee.
 (b) Because he's tired and he needs a break.

D SPEAK Work in pairs and discuss the questions.

1 What are some cues for bad habits? What routines and rewards can we use to change those bad habits?
2 What cues and rewards can we use to start good habits?

VOCABULARY
Reflexive verbs

A 10.4 Complete the sentences from the conversation (1–8) with the words in the box. Then listen and check your answers.

blame control get help make reward set treat

1 When I drive past a sign for a fast-food restaurant, I ___treat___ myself to a snack from the package.
2 'Can I try one of those?'
'Sure! ___Help___ yourself.'
3 I wish I could stop, but I can't ___control___ myself.
4 I always ___make___ myself a cup of coffee before I check my emails.
5 I suppose I could ___get___ myself a glass of water.
6 I always ___set___ myself goals, but nothing seems to work.
7 First of all, Alice, don't ___blame___ yourself.
8 How will you ___reward___ yourself for being good?

Reflexive verbs

A reflexive verb is a verb + a reflexive pronoun (*myself, yourself, himself, herself, itself, ourselves, yourselves, themselves*).

Some reflexive verbs have a special meaning:

Help yourself! = Please take as much as you want; there's no need to ask.

10.2 Wish lists

LEAD-IN

Draw two columns on the board and write *Good habits* at the top of one and *Bad habits* at the top of the other. Students face the board in two lines by each column, and either write good or bad habits under the columns. The line that writes the most words wins. Give a time limit.

LISTENING

10.3 **A–D** Check answers and feedback as a whole class after students complete the exercises.

VOCABULARY

10.4 **A** Tell students to complete the sentences with the correct verb from the box. Play the audio again for them to check. Check understanding of the meaning of the verbs with reference to how they are used in the sentences and with further personal examples. Then point out the information in the box about reflexive verbs.

AUDIO SCRIPT

10.3

Listening, Exercise B
D = David B = Barbara A = Alice L = Leo

D: Hello, and welcome back to *All in the Mind*. On today's show, we're talking about habits. I'm joined by Professor Barbara Janovich, an expert in habits. Welcome to the show, Professor.
B: Thanks, David.
D: So, Barbara, why do we develop bad habits? And why are they so hard to break?
B: Well, the best way to understand habits is to break them into four parts. First, there's a cue, which might be something that you see or hear or feel. So in your example with fast food, the cue might be that you're driving in your car and you see a sign for a fast-food restaurant. Or maybe you're walking through a shopping mall and suddenly you smell the fast food.
Ex C Q1 **D:** Oh, yes. That smell always makes me want to eat fast food, even when I'm not hungry! I wish it didn't, but it does!
B: Exactly. So the next stage is the routine – the actions you always take. So this is where you go into the fast
Ex C Q2 food restaurant, order your food and eat it. In a true habit, you can do all of this without really thinking – it kind of happens to you, and your brain almost shuts off.
D: OK.
B: And then the third part is the reward: something nice happens. In this case, the sugar and salt in the food cause your brain to produce feel-good chemicals.
D: OK, so the cycle is cue, routine, reward. But you said there are four parts. What's the fourth part?
B: Well, this is the dangerous part: the craving. Let me explain. If you repeat the cycle a few times, your brain produces those feel-good chemicals earlier and earlier in the process. So instead of being part of the reward, you get that nice feeling at the cue stage – when you see the restaurant sign, for example, or you smell the food and you know the reward is coming soon. And now you have a
Ex C Q3 problem: you've had the good feeling, but you haven't had the reward yet. This creates the craving – a powerful need to get your reward. Now you can't relax until you have your reward.
D: Ah. I wish I'd known about all this a few years ago! But I guess it's too late for me now. Is there anything I can do to break the cycle?
B: Yes, but it isn't easy. You can't stop the cues, and you
Ex C Q4 still need the reward. So the trick is to change the routine. So, for example, I always keep a package of low-fat salty snacks in my bag. That means that when I drive past a sign for a fast-food restaurant, I treat myself to a snack from the package.
D: Uh, can I try one of those?
B: Sure! Help yourself. So the cue is the same, and the reward is similar – salty food – but I've changed the routine. Of course, salty snacks aren't perfect, but they're a lot cheaper and healthier than a burger and fries.
D: Sounds good. OK, so earlier we asked our listeners to call in to tell us about their bad habits. Our first caller is Leo. Leo, what's your habit?
L: Hello. Well, it's coffee. I drink about eight cups a day, but I don't even like it very much! I wish I could stop, but I can't control myself.
B: OK. Well, let's start with the first cup of coffee each day, Leo. What's your cue for drinking it?
L: It's when I arrive at work. I always make myself a cup of coffee before I check my emails.
B: How long does it take to get to work?
L: About an hour. Why?
Ex C Q5 **B:** Well, it sounds like the reward isn't really the coffee, but a five-minute break after your long, tiring trip.
L: Uh, yes, maybe.
B: So now we know the cue and the reward, the question is: is there a different routine that would give you the same reward after your trip to work?
L: I suppose I could get myself a glass of water and go for a quick walk around the office.
B: Sounds good.
D: OK, great. I hope your new routine works for you, Leo. I wish we had time to talk about your other seven cups of coffee, but we need to go to our next caller, Alice. What's your bad habit, Alice?
A: Well, actually, I'd like some help creating a new habit. You see, I wish I could run a marathon next year. I go running from time to time, but I want to get into the habit of running every day. I always set myself goals, but nothing seems to work. I really wish I were better organized.
D: Thanks for that, Alice. Professor?
B: Well, first of all, Alice, don't blame yourself. This is a very common problem. If you want to create a new habit, again you need to think about cues and rewards: what will make you remember to go running at the same time every day? How will you reward yourself for being good? So let's start by creating your cue, Alice. When would be a good time of day to go running?

B Direct students to the **Vocabulary Hub** (TB121) for further practice of reflexive verbs.

C Put students into pairs to discuss the questions. Monitor and give feedback on any really good or any incorrect use of reflexive verbs.

PRONUNCIATION

10.5 **A** Tell students to listen carefully to the sentences from the radio show and to decide if the reflexive pronouns are stressed or unstressed. Do the first one together as a whole class to demonstrate the task.

B Tell students to look back at the sentences from Exercise A to help them complete the rules about emphasis and reflexive pronouns. Check that students understand how sentence 3 is an example of emphasis. Model the pronunciation of sentence 3 again, exaggerating the stress at first, then more naturally.

C Put students into pairs to practice saying the sentences from Exercise A. Encourage them to listen carefully and check their partner's pronunciation. Monitor to check and help if necessary.

GRAMMAR

A Elicit that the sentences are also all from the radio show. Tell them to match the sentences with the explanations. Check answers and then point out the information in the box about hopes and wishes and the grammar box. Check that students understand the difference between *likely* and *unlikely*, and clarify that *hope* is only used for a likely situation and *wish* only for an unlikely or unreal situation. You could emphasize this by writing some negative examples (e.g. *I wish I'll pass the exam*) on the board and explicitly correcting them.

B Direct students to the **Grammar Hub** (see below and TB116).

C Tell students to practice by filling in the blanks with *hope* or *wish* and choosing the correct form of the verbs in bold. Use the **Grammar Worksheet** on W39 for extra practice.

SPEAKING

Put students into pairs to discuss the questions. If time allows, put students with a new partner to interview a different classmate. You could organize this with students arranged in an inner and an outer circle. After five minutes, tell all the students in the inner circle to move clockwise one place and speak to a new partner.

Finish with feedback on students' use of language during the conversations, especially how well they expressed their hopes and wishes.

GRAMMAR HUB

10.2 Hopes and wishes

wish + simple past	imagining a different present situation (unreal present)	**I wish she were** more organized. **I wish I weren't** so hungry! **He wishes he knew** the answer.
wish + past perfect	imagining a different past situation (unreal past)	**We wish our son had won** the race. **They wish they hadn't eaten** so much.
wish + *could*	imagining an unlikely future possibility (unlikely future)	**I wish I could stop** drinking coffee.
hope (that) + simple present/ present progressive	imagining a likely future possibility (likely future)	**I hope that you enjoy** yourself tomorrow. **I hope that you are enjoying** yourself on vacation! **We hope that she doesn't make** the wrong decision.

- We can use *wish* to talk about ourselves or other people.

  I wish I had more friends. / I wish Sarah had more friends. / Sarah wishes her brother had more friends.
- We usually use *were* instead of *was* after *I wish* or *He/She wishes*.

  I wish I were better organized.
- We use *wish* + *could* to talk about something that we want to be different in the future. However, by using *could*, we express a belief that our wish probably won't come true.

  I wish I could treat myself to a vacation. (= I know that I won't be able to do this because I don't have the money, time, etc.)
- Although *hope* refers to the future, it is followed by a verb in the present tense. You can include the word *that*, but it is usually omitted.

  I hope (that) the snacks aren't too salty.
  We hope (that) the fast food restaurant is open tomorrow.
- We use the negative for the verb which **follows** *wish* or *hope*.

  I hope it doesn't rain tomorrow.
  NOT ~~I don't hope it rains.~~
  I wish I hadn't spent so much money.
  NOT ~~I don't wish I had spent so much money.~~

B Go to the Vocabulary Hub on page 146.

C **SPEAK** Work in pairs and discuss the questions.

1 Where do you see yourself in ten years?
2 How do you amuse yourself when you're on a long trip?
3 Can you think of any situations where you can't trust yourself?

PRONUNCIATION

Emphasis and reflexive pronouns

10.5 **A Listen to the sentences from the radio show. For each sentence, decide if the reflexive pronouns are stressed or unstressed.**

1 I treat myself to a snack from the package. unstressed
2 I always make myself a cup of coffee before I check my emails. unstressed
3 Don't blame yourself. stressed
4 How will you reward yourself for being good? unstressed

B Now choose the best word or phrase to complete the rules.

Emphasis and reflexive pronouns

1 When a reflexive pronoun follows a verb, the pronoun **is / is not** usually stressed.
2 But when we want to emphasise the subject at the end of a clause, we **can / can't** stress the pronoun.

C SPEAK Work in pairs. Practice saying the sentences in Exercise A. Listen and check your partner's pronunciation.

GRAMMAR

Hopes and wishes

A WORK IT OUT Match the sentences from the conversation (1–5) with the explanations (a–d).

1 **I wish I'd known** about all this a few years ago! But I guess it's too late for me now.
2 **I hope your new routine works** for you, Leo.
3 **I wish we had time** to talk about your other seven cups of coffee, but we need to go to our next caller.
4 **I wish I could** run a marathon next year.
5 I really **wish I were** better organized.

a The speaker is talking about something that's likely to happen in the future.
b The speaker is talking about something that's unlikely to happen in the future.
c The speaker is imagining a different present situation.
d The speaker is imagining a different past situation.

Hopes and wishes

When we talk about hopes and wishes, we use very similar structures to the first, second and third conditionals.

	Conditional sentences	Hopes and wishes
Likely future	It'll be good if your idea works.	I hope your idea works.
Unlikely future	I'd be happy if I could find a new job. (or: … if I found a new job.)	I wish I could find a new job. (NOT: I wish I found a new job.)
Unreal present	It would be nice if I were taller.	I wish I were taller.
Unreal past	It would have been better if you'd told me.	I wish you'd told me.

B Go to the Grammar Hub on page 140.

C Complete the sentences with *hope* or *wish*. Then choose the correct words to complete the hopes and wishes.

1 I ___hope___ you *have* / *had* / *could have* a great time on vacation next week.
2 I started playing tennis last year and I love it, but I'm too old to become a top player. I ___wish___ I *start* / *started* / *'d started* playing when I was younger.
3 It's great that you're coming to my city next week. I ___wish___ I *met* / *could meet* / *'d met* you while you're here, but unfortunately I'll be away all week.
4 I'm a little worried about Frank and Donna. They should have arrived an hour ago. I ___hope___ they *arrive* / *'d arrived* / *arrived* soon.
5 I never have time to do all the things I need to do each week. Sometimes I ___wish___ there *were* / *are* / *had been* eight days in a week!
6 My main regret is that I didn't spend enough time with my children when they were younger. I ___wish___ I *don't spend* / *didn't spend* / *hadn't spent* so much time working in those days!
7 My dream is to be the first person to travel to Mars! I really ___wish___ I *went* / *could go* / *'d gone* there one day, but I know it's never going to happen.

SPEAKING

Work in pairs and discuss the questions.

1 Do you have any regrets about your habits? What do you wish you'd started earlier? What do you wish you'd never started?
2 What do you wish you could change about yourself?
3 What are your hopes for the future? Think about next week, next month and next year.
4 What are your dreams for the future? What do you wish you could do one day?

READING

A SPEAK Work in pairs and discuss the questions.

1 What is a to-do list? What information does it contain?

2 Why do you think psychologists are interested in to-do lists?

3 Do you keep a to-do list? Why/Why not?

B READ FOR GIST Read *The psychology of to-do lists*. Match the headings (a–g) with the paragraphs (1–7).

a Organization, motivation and satisfaction

b The benefits of forgetting

c Not as difficult as it sounds

d An experiment over dinner

e Keeping tasks small and simple

f Using to-do lists to cut stress

g The stress of not finishing things

The psychology of to-do lists

1 d

One day in the 1920s, a large group of psychologists were having a meal at their favorite restaurant. They were discussing the waiter's amazing memory: he always remembered everybody's orders perfectly, but he never wrote anything down. One of the psychologists, Bluma Zeigarnik, decided to try an experiment. She told everyone to cover their plates. Then she asked the waiter to come back to the table, and to try to remember what was on each plate. Amazingly, he couldn't remember anything, even though he himself had put the plates on the table only a few minutes earlier. How was it possible that a man with such an amazing memory had forgotten everything a few minutes later?

2 b

Zeigarnik realized that there was in fact nothing special about the waiter. In fact, we're all good at remembering current tasks – things that we still need to do. But as soon as they're finished, we forget all about them. The 'Zeigarnik effect', as it's now called, is our brains' way of cleaning up and sorting information. If we had to remember everything forever, our brains would soon run out of space.

3 g

But there's a dark side to the Zeigarnik effect. Studies have shown that people perform badly in tests when they're worrying about other unfinished tasks. It seems that we can't stop thinking about what we still need to do. This makes us stressed and prevents us from focusing on new tasks.

4 f

Is there anything we can do about this problem? Recent research suggests that we can reduce our stress levels by keeping a record of all our current tasks in a to-do list. This simple action tells our brains to stop worrying about the task, which means we can give our full attention to other tasks.

5 a

To-do lists have three additional benefits. First, they help us to stay organized. Second, they are a useful record of what we've achieved and when. It can be highly motivating to look back at our past achievements – especially because the Zeigarnik effect usually makes us forget them. However, the best thing about to-do lists is the satisfying feeling you get when you cross each item off the list.

6 e

The key to successful to-do lists is to break large objectives into smaller action points. Instead of writing 'Learn to drive' on your list, focus on small and practical jobs that you can achieve very quickly, such as 'Find a list of driving schools in my city' and 'Read a website with reviews of different schools'. The smaller the tasks, the better. Dave Allen, a time-management expert, also recommends an archive to store all the things you might need and a system of 43 folders to schedule when to do each task.

7 c

If that sounds like too much hard work, think again. With a good system, life is much easier. You can relax and enjoy the rest of the day, happy in the knowledge that everything is under control.

Glossary

archive (n) a place where you store documents and records

READING

A Put students into pairs to discuss the questions. Monitor and check that students have understood the concept of a *to-do* list (a list of things you have to do).

B Tell students to look at the pictures and ask what they think they have to do with the psychology of to-do lists. Tell students to read the text to check and to match the headings with the paragraphs. Point out the glossary but tell students not to worry if there are some words in the article that they don't understand. Tell students not to focus on the underlined words yet.

TEACHING IDEA by David Seymour and Maria Popova

Grammar: I wish and If only

Use this activity to practice the grammar.

In pairs, rewrite these sentences with *I wish / If only* in two ways, one with a past tense and the other with *would*, e.g. *It's raining.* – (1) *I wish / If only it wasn't raining.* (2) *I wish / If only it would stop raining.*

> She's singing that awful song again. I've had a nasty cold all week. You're unemployed. He's late for the meeting again. It's cold outside. They never write to us. The elevator is still not working. The streets here are filthy.

TEACHING IDEA by David Seymour and Maria Popova

Grammar: A better place to live

Use this activity to practice the grammar.

In pairs, write five sentences beginning *I wish . . .* about the town or city where you live in order to make it a better place to live, e.g. *I wish the buses ran all through the night so I didn't have to take a taxi home.*

Join with another pair. Discuss your sentences and decide which are the best five of your ideas from your combined lists. Then join with another group of four students and choose the best five ideas again. Choose someone from your group to write your ideas on the board. As a class, decide on the best five sentences.

(Variation: This activity also works well with ideas for improving the school.)

GRAMMAR HUB

10.2 Hopes and wishes

A Match the situations to the people's comments.

1 Brett's too short for the basketball team.
2 Dad is always losing his keys.
3 I don't know any of the answers.
4 Josh's drive to work takes 90 minutes.
5 I want to stop eating sugar completely.
6 Phoebe feels lonely.
7 Anna is really tired.

a 'I wish I didn't have to drive so far.'
b 'I wish I had studied more.'
c 'I wish I had more friends.'
d 'I wish I were taller.'
e 'I wish I hadn't stayed up all night.'
f 'I hope you achieve your goal.'
g 'I wish I wasn't so disorganized.'

B Choose the correct option.

1 I *wish* / *hope* to achieve everything on my to-do list.
2 Do you wish you ***don't give*** / ***hadn't given*** in to your cravings?
3 The children wish they ***could stay*** / ***stayed*** up late to watch the movie.
4 I wish I ***have*** / ***had*** more money to spend on clothes.
5 Kate wishes her husband ***is*** / ***were*** more focused on his career.
6 They wish they ***didn't live*** / ***couldn't live*** near a noisy shopping mall.
7 Jared ***wishes*** / ***hopes*** he could take a vacation.
8 I wish you ***didn't persuade*** / ***hadn't persuaded*** me to eat this burger – it's horrible!

C Complete the sentences with the correct form of the verb in parentheses.

1 I never have enough time. I wish there ___were___ (*be*) more hours in the day!
2 I hope this snack ___isn't___ (*not / be*) high in salt.
3 The children are full of energy. I wish they ___hadn't eaten___ (*not / eat*) so many sugary snacks!
4 My children wish I ___didn't work___ (*not / work*) such long hours.
5 I hope Pam ___doesn't change / hasn't changed___ (*not / change*) her mind!
6 Alisha wants to buy a laptop but wishes she ___knew___ (*know*) more about them.
7 I wish my best friend ___were/was___ (*be*) here to help me make the right choice!
8 She ___wishes___ (*wish*) she could give up drinking sugary drinks but says it's very difficult.

➤ Go back to page 115.

C Tell students to read the information in the box about bridge sentences. Remind students about topic sentences, which they saw in Unit 8 in the article *If you really can't wait …* about buying the latest gadgets. Put students into pairs to answer the questions.

Suggested answers: *The first sentence in a paragraph is usually both the topic sentence and a bridge sentence. But not always: some paragraphs don't have a bridge sentence (including the first paragraph); the topic sentence isn't always the first sentence. Bridge sentences refer back to the previous paragraph. Topic sentences introduce the main points of the current paragraph.*

D Tell students to read the first sentence in each paragraph and answer the questions. Do the first one together as a whole class. Put students into pairs to discuss the rest.

Suggested answers:

1. *'One day in the 1920s, a large group of psychologists were having a meal at their favorite restaurant.' This can't be a bridge sentence because it's the first paragraph.*
2. *'Zeigarnik realized that there was in fact nothing special about the waiter.' This is a bridge sentence. It refers to a contrast between what the people first thought (paragraph 1) and what was actually true (paragraph 2). The words Zeigarnik, nothing special* and *the waiter also refer back to the previous paragraph.*
3. *'But there's a dark side to the Zeigarnik effect.' This is a bridge sentence. But refers to a contrast between the positive things in paragraph 2 and the negative things in paragraph 3. The phrase the Zeigarnik effect also forms a bridge to the previous paragraph.*
4. *'Is there anything we can do about this problem?' This is a bridge sentence. This problem refers back to the problem described in paragraph 3.*
5. *'To-do lists have three additional benefits.' This is a bridge sentence. Additional refers back to the first benefit of to-do lists, which was described in paragraph 4.*
6. *'The key to successful to-do lists is to break large objectives into smaller action points.' This isn't a bridge sentence because the whole article is about to-do lists. This paragraph introduces a completely separate point about them.*
7. *'If that sounds like too much hard work, think again.' This is a bridge sentence. That refers back to Dave Allen's system from paragraph 6.*

E Put students into pairs to discuss the questions.

VOCABULARY

A Tell students to look at the underlined words in the article and to match them with the definitions. Tell students to read the sentences carefully to help them figure out the meanings of the words. Go through the example with the whole class to demonstrate how to do this, replacing the word in the text with different definitions until one makes sense. Consolidate students' understanding of the words by eliciting personal, more memorable examples.

B Put students into pairs to discuss the questions. If any students keep a record of tasks they need to do, encourage other students to ask further questions about how useful and effective they find it. Use the **Vocabulary Worksheet** on W40 for extra practice.

SPEAKING HUB

A Tell students to prepare a short wish list, either using the suggestions given or their own ideas. Elicit a few examples from the class for further guidance and inspiration.

B Put students into groups to share and explain their lists. When they have discussed all the lists, tell each group to choose the most interesting items and to create a to-do list. Tell them that they're going to present these lists to the class. Point out the tips and encourage students to follow them. Monitor to help with language if needed, and check students are following the suggested structure for their lists. When they've finished, tell them to practice presenting their list.

C Tell each group to stand up and present their list to the class. Tell the other students to listen carefully and write notes about any positive suggestions they could give to support and encourage their classmates with their plans.

D Put students into new groups to discuss the questions.

METHODOLOGY HUB by Jim Scrivener

Fluency and confidence

Fluency and confidence are important goals when considering speaking lessons. There is no point knowing a lot about language if you can't use it (which, sadly, has been the experience of many language learners in the past – able to conjugate a verb, but unable to respond to a simple question). To help achieve this goal, we usually want to find ways of enabling as many students as possible to speak as much as possible. Sometimes an all-class speaking activity is useful, but if it takes up the whole lesson, it actually offers very little speaking time to each individual student. It's usually a good idea to organize speaking activities in pairs, threes and small groups, as well as with the class as a whole.

TEACHING IDEA by David Seymour and Maria Popova

Grammar: Mountain rescue

Use this activity to practice the grammar.

(Write the sentences below in random order on the board.) These situations are all connected to the same adventure. Work in groups and put them in order. Imagine you were stuck on the mountain. Write two sentences for each situation, one using *If only / I wish …* and one using *should (not) have done.*

We didn't tell anyone at the hostel where we were going.

Leo forgot to pack a compass.

We left later than planned.

The cloud came down, but we decided to continue walking.

We lost the path.

Kathy fell and broke her leg.

No one had a cell phone or flashlight.

Ben tried to go back down the mountain.

What order did your group decide on? Talk together and decide what happened next. Did everyone survive?

C Read the box about bridge sentences. What is the connection between bridge sentences and topic sentences (see Unit 8)? What's the difference between them?

Bridge sentences

The first sentence in a paragraph is usually a bridge sentence, which shows how the paragraph is connected to the previous paragraph. For example, it might use words like *however* to introduce a contrast, or words like *another* to add extra information.

Not all paragraphs have a bridge sentence.

D READ FOR KEY INFORMATION Read the first sentence in each paragraph again. Which five are bridge sentences? Underline the words and phrases in the sentences that refer back to the previous paragraph. What exactly do they refer to?

E SPEAK Work in pairs and discuss the questions.

1 Have you ever experienced the Zeigarnik effect? Think about:
- preparing for a test.
- learning a speech, a song or a poem.
- remembering people's names and faces.

2 Do you ever look back at your past achievements? Would you find it motivating?

VOCABULARY
Staying organized

A Look at the underlined words in *The psychology of to-do lists*. Find words or phrases that mean the following.

1 a job that you need to do
a t a s k

2 to keep something in a safe place
to s t o r e something

3 to put things back in the right places
to c l e a n up

4 to plan exactly when you will do something
to s c h e d u l e something

5 a small thing that you're going to do
an a c t i o n point

6 to put things in the right order
to s o r t things

7 a large thing that you want to achieve
an o b j e c t i v e

8 to write something down
to keep a r e c o r d of something

B SPEAK Work in pairs and discuss the questions.

1 How many **tasks** are on your to-do list?

2 Do you **keep a record** of the tasks you need to do? Would you like to start?

SPEAKING HUB

A PREPARE Write a short wish list. Use the ideas below or your own ideas.
- a problem that you would like to solve
- a good habit that you hope you will start / wish you could start
- a way to become less stressed or better organized
- how you'll continue learning/using English after this course

B PLAN Work in groups. Discuss your wish lists. As a group, choose the most interesting items from your wish lists and create a to-do list. Try to:
- plan cues, routines and rewards for any habits you want to change.
- turn your objectives into tasks and action points.

C PRESENT Stand up and tell the class what you plan to do and when. When others are speaking, listen carefully and be positive about their plans.

D REFLECT Work in groups and discuss the questions.

1 How will you make sure you'll do the things on your list?

2 How will you motivate each other to do those things?

- Talk about your wishes and regrets
- Plan a to-do list

10.3 Come home

F make and accept apologies P vowel sounds

COMPREHENSION

A When was the last time you had to say goodbye to someone? How did you feel? How long was it before you saw that person again?

B Number the pictures in the order you think they happened. What do you think happened?

a 5

b 2

c 1
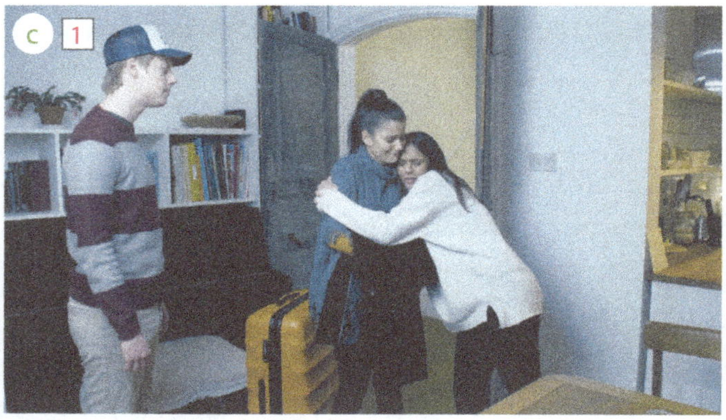

d 3

e 4

f 6

C 00:00–02:25 Watch the first part of the video and check your ideas. How do you think the video will end?

D 02:25–04:29 Complete the letter that Sam wrote to Gaby by choosing the correct words below. Watch the second part of the video and check your answers. Does the video end how you predicted?

1 leaving / in / over
2 words / time / pen
3 should / usually / never
4 city / life / home
5 business / Madrid / yourself

Dear Gaby,

I've just heard that you're [1] leaving London and ... I wish I had said this to you in person, but I just couldn't find the [2] words. I'm so sorry, but I [3] never know the right thing to say. I know you've already made your mind up about leaving, and I'm going to miss you so much. The thought of not having you in my [4] life hurts because ... I love you. I always have. I just didn't know how to say it before. Take good care of [5] yourself.

MILLY

SAM

NEENA

ZAC

GABY

FUNCTIONAL LANGUAGE

Making and accepting apologies

A Put the words in the correct order. Then put each phrase under the correct heading in the table.

1 quickly / leave / sorry / to / so / I'm / really
I'm really sorry to leave so quickly.

2 you'll / worry / be / don't / fine
Don't worry; you'll be fine.

3 apologize / need / no / there's / to
There's no need to apologize.

4 worry / don't / it / about
Don't worry about it.

5 just / things / of / those / one / it's
It's just one of those things.

6 OK / all / to / be / it's / going
It's all going to be OK.

7 my / it's / fault
It's my fault.

8 not / fault / fault / it's / it's / my / your
It's not your fault; it's my fault.

9 nothing / about / worry / there's / to
There's nothing to worry about.

10 great / is / this / to / be / going
This is going to be great.

Making an apology	Accepting an apology	Giving reassurance
I'm really sorry to leave so quickly. It's my fault.	There's no need to apologize. Don't worry about it. It's not your fault; it's my fault.	Don't worry; you'll be fine. It's just one of those things. It's all going to be OK. There's nothing to worry about. This is going to be great.

B Watch the video again and check (✓) each phrase as you hear it.

Glossary

housemate **(n) (British)** = roommate **(n) (American)**

USEFUL PHRASES

A Match the useful phrases (1–5) with the phrases that come before or after them (a–e).

1 It's time to go. c
2 I wish I had said this to you in person. d
3 I'm such an idiot! b
4 I've changed my mind about leaving. a
5 I'm scared. e

a What about your plane? You're going to miss it.
b I can't believe that I missed her.
c You'll be fine; don't worry.
d But I just couldn't find the words.
e There's nothing to worry about.

B How do you say these useful phrases in your language?

PRONUNCIATION

Vowel sounds

A Match words with the same vowel sounds from boxes A, B and C.

A airport roommate mind person sorry worry

B apologize guys hurt love strangely thought

C gone my of course paying under words

B 10.6 Listen, check and repeat the words. Copy the sounds.

SPEAKING

A Work in pairs. Write conversations about the following situations or your own ideas. Student A – apologize. Student B – accept the apology and reassure Student A.

arrive late / for meeting break / chair forget / to call miss / party spill / coffee

A: I'm really sorry about breaking your chair.
B: Oh, don't worry about it – it's not your fault. It's just one of those things.

B PRESENT Act out your conversations. Take turns being Student A and Student B.

Make and accept apologies

➤ Turn to page 165 to learn how to write a report.

10.3 Come home

LEAD-IN

Write the word *Goodbye* on the board. Put students into two teams. Give them a time limit of one minute to see how many different languages they know how to say *Hello* and *Goodbye* in.

COMPREHENSION

A Put students into pairs to discuss the questions.

B Elicit that the pictures are in the wrong order. Put students into pairs to put the pictures into the correct order. Tell them to discuss what they think happens.

C ▶ 00:00-02:25 Play the video and tell students to watch and check their answers. Encourage them to predict the ending.

D ▶ 02:25-04:29 Tell students to choose the correct words to fill in the blanks in the letter. Play the video for students to check, and to check if their predictions about the ending were correct.

FUNCTIONAL LANGUAGE

A Tell students to put the words in the correct order, then to put the completed phrases in the correct column in the table. Check understanding of *it's my fault* (I'm responsible for the bad situation) / *it's not your fault* (you're not responsible for the bad situation).

B ▶ Tell the students to watch the video one more time and to apply a check mark next to each phrase as they hear it.

USEFUL PHRASES

A Tell students to match the useful phrases from the video with the phrases that come just before or just after them.

B Tell the students to think about how they say the useful phrases in their own language.

PRONUNCIATION

A Read aloud all the words from boxes A, B and C in random order and get students to tell you which box they are in (i.e. *hurt–B, roommate–A*). Go through the example together to ensure students fully understand the task. Put students into pairs to group the other words according to their pronunciation.

10.6 **B** Play the audio for students to listen, check and repeat the words.

airport, thought, of course
roommate, strangely, paying
person, hurt, words
sorry, apologize, gone
worry, love, under

SPEAKING

A Put students into pairs and tell them they're going to write some conversations where people make and accept apologies. When students have prepared two or three conversations, tell them to practice acting them out. Tell them to change roles in each different conversation.

B Tell each pair to act out their conversations, taking turns being student A and student B. Tell the other students to listen and think about how appropriate the apologies and responses are. Ask students if they would have accepted the apologies, or if they would have been reassured by the replies.

VIDEO SCRIPT

G = Gaby Z = Zac N = Neena S = Sam

G: It's time to go … I think … Thanks. See you. Oh no.
Z: You'll be fine, don't worry.
G: Thanks, Zac. I'm really sorry to leave so quickly.
Z: There's no need to apologize!
G: I'll keep paying the rent until you get a new housemate. I'm sure you'll find someone soon.
N: Honestly, it's fine. Don't worry about it – it's just one of those things. I'm really going to miss you!
G: You have to come and visit me!
Z: Of course, we will!
N: Oh, this letter arrived for you.
G: Thanks … that's my taxi … well … goodbye.
S: Gaby?
Z: Whoa, you just missed her. What's going on?
S: It's from Gaby. I thought she'd been acting strangely.
N: What does it say?
S: That … that she's in love with me.
Z: But you're also …
S: Yeah, I know!
N: Oh, Sam!
S: And … she's gone.
Dear Gaby. I've just heard that you're leaving London and … I wish I had said this to you in person, but I just couldn't find the words. I'm so sorry but I never know the right thing to say. I know you've already made your mind up about leaving and I'm going to miss you so much. The thought of not having you in my life hurts, because I love you. I always have. I just didn't know how to say it before. Take good care of yourself.
Z: … She's probably getting to the airport about now …
N: Zac! I'm not sure that's helpful. Listen, Sam. It's all going to be OK.
S: I'm such an idiot! I can't believe that I missed her.
G: You didn't.
S: Gaby!
G: Hi … sorry, I forgot to leave my key …
S: I just found your letter! It was under the counter. I wish I'd known. It's my fault …
G: I thought you'd read it! Oh, Sam. It's not your fault. It's my fault – I should've said something.
S: Me, too.
G: I know …
S: … What about your plane? You're going to miss it?
G: I've changed my mind about leaving.
Z: Well … it seems like you guys have totally got this all under control, so we might …
N: … Yeah …
S: I'm scared.
G: Me, too. But there's nothing to worry about. This is going to be great.
S: Come here. Zac!
Z: Sorry!

10 Writing

Write a report

W– writing a report

A Work in pairs and discuss the questions.

1 Why do people write reports? What are some situations where non-business people write reports?
2 Why do people read reports? What information do they need?

B Read the *Report on charity auction* and answer the questions.

1 Why has the writer written the report?
2 What went well with the auction? What went wrong?
3 What did the writer learn from the experience?

REPORT ON CHARITY AUCTION

Summary:
On December 15, we held a charity auction to raise money for the local hospital. The auction raised less money than expected. This report explores what we did wrong.

Background:
We asked 24 local celebrities (e.g. sportspeople, TV presenters) to donate gifts for our auction. We received 55 gifts, including many valuable items (e.g. a signed soccer ball, a beautiful painting). We expected to raise around $5,000. 720 people attended our auction event. The auction only raised $322. Many of the items were not sold.

Analysis:
1 **Paradox of choice:** There were too many items, so people could not decide. If we had limited the auction to around ten items, we would probably have made more money.
2 **Hook numbers:** We wanted to attract large numbers of people to the auction, so in our marketing materials, we showed pictures of the best items with low starting prices, e.g. $2 for the signed soccer ball. We shouldn't have done this because it encouraged people to make offers of a few dollars, not hundreds of dollars.

Ex D

Recommendations:
- For future auctions, limit the number of items to around ten.
- In marketing materials, show the value of the items (e.g. *Worth over $500*) rather than the starting price.

Glossary
auction (n) a public occasion when things are sold to the people who offer the most money for them
donate (v) to give something such as money or goods to an organization, especially to a school, hospital, political party or charity

C Look at the box. Match the features of a report (1–8) with the explanations (a–h). Find examples in the report.

Writing a report
A report describes a past event or a present situation and ends with recommendations for the future.

1	title	d	5	numbered lists	e
2	summary	c	6	full forms	h
3	headings	f	7	facts and figures	b
4	bullet points	a	8	examples	g

a Use these small black circles to make it easier to read lists of items.
b Your report should include dates, names, numbers, etc.
c In the first paragraph, say briefly what happened and why you've written the report.
d The reader can see immediately what the report is about.
e You can use these to show that the order of items in a list is important.
f Use words like *Analysis* and *Recommendations* to show you're starting a new section.
g Include these to explain important points. You can put them in parentheses: (e.g. …).
h Reports are usually fairly formal, so it's best to write separate words (e.g. *do not*) instead of contractions (e.g. *don't*).

D Find examples of the third conditional and *would have* or *should have done* in the report. Which section are they in? Why?
analysis – thinking about what went wrong

WRITING

A PREPARE You are going to write a short report about an event where some things could have been better. Think about:

- will you write about a real event or will you invent one?
- what event will you describe? Something from your work or studies? An accident that you had?
- who will read your report? Why?

B PLAN Write notes under these headings:

- Background: What happened?
- Analysis: What went wrong? Why?
- Recommendations: What should happen differently in the future?

C WRITE Write your report. Remember to use headings, bullet points or numbered lists. When you finish writing the three main sections, write a short summary at the beginning.

D REVIEW Work in groups. Read some of your groups' reports. Do you agree with their recommendations?

WRITING 165

Answers

1 *explore what went wrong at a charity auction*
2 *well: received 55 gifts*
not well: only raised $322, too many items, showed best items with low starting prices
3 *Limit number of items, show value of items not starting price*

Refer students to this report as a model for the writing task.

Remind students to pay attention to whether they need to use the past, present or future tense in their writing.

WRITING

With books closed, tell students to imagine that they were asked to raise money for a local hospital. Put students into pairs to discuss how they would do this. Share the best ideas with the class.

A Tell students to open their books and to discuss the questions with their partner. Get some brief feedback as a whole class and ask students if they ever write or read reports and why.

B Tell students to read the report and answer the questions. Point out the glossary and check that students understand the words. These words are very important to understand the content of the report.

C Point out the information in the box about writing a report, then tell students to match the features of a report with their explanations. Tell students to find an example of each feature in the report about the charity auction.

D Tell students to find an example of the third conditional and of *would have* or *should have done* in the report. Tell students to think about which section these are in and why.

WRITING TASK

A Tell students they're going to write a short report about an event where some things could have been better. Tell them to think about the questions.

B Tell students to write notes under the headings.

C Tell students to write their report. Remind students about the features of a report to help them organize their writing appropriately. Tell them to go back and write a short summary at the beginning of the report when they have finished writing the three main sections.

D Put students into groups to read each other's reports. When they have read all the report, tell the groups to discuss if they agree with the recommendations and why, or why not.

GRAMMAR

A Complete the third conditional sentences. Use the correct form of the underlined verbs.

1 The waiter forgot our order because he didn't write it down.
If the waiter *had written* down our order, he *wouldn't have forgotten* it.

2 You didn't finish anything on your to-do list. Maybe it's because all the items were too big.
You might have finished some things on your to-do list if they 'd/had been a little smaller.

3 I saw a sign for a fast-food restaurant, so I felt a need to eat.
If I hadn't seen a sign for the fast-food restaurant, I wouldn't have felt a need to eat!

4 I didn't have time to try on these jeans, but I bought them anyway.
I wouldn't have bought these jeans if I 'd/had tried them on first! They're much too small!

B Write sentences with *should/shouldn't have done*.

1 I wish you'd been more careful.
You *should have been more careful*.

2 I regret buying these shoes.
I shouldn't have bought these shoes.

3 Why didn't they listen to us?
They should have listened to us.

4 It was a mistake to go out yesterday.
We shouldn't have gone out yesterday.

C Complete the conversation with the correct form of the verbs in parentheses.

A: Hey! I'm having a dinner party tomorrow night. I hope you 1 can come (*can come*). It's going to be excellent.

B: Oh, I wish I 2 could come (*can come*), but I can't. I have tickets for a soccer game tomorrow, and it's the final.

A: Oh, I didn't know it's the final tomorrow! I wish I 3 had/'d known (*know*)! I'd have arranged the party for a different night. Anyway, I hope your team 4 wins (*win*)!

B: Well, my team isn't in the final. I wish we 5 were (*be*)! But we lost in the semi-final last week. I wish I 6 hadn't bought (*not buy*) a ticket – then I could come to your party!

VOCABULARY

A Choose the correct verbs to complete the sentences.

1 I got an email from somebody who tried to *persuade* / *trick* me into giving my bank account number.

2 I didn't want to buy a camera at all, but the saleswoman *affected* / *persuaded* me to buy one.

3 Whenever I walk past a fast-food restaurant, I'm *regretted* / *tempted* to go inside.

4 For a long time, businesses *assumed* / *influenced* that more choice meant more sales.

B Find and correct one mistake in each underlined phrase.

1 Would you mind ~~that~~ if I asked you for some advice? You see, I want to go somewhere new this weekend, but I'm 2 of ~~three~~ two minds about where to go. This morning, I 3 made up my mind and decided to go bike riding in the forest, but then I heard the weather is going to be horrible, so I 4 changed ~~the~~ my mind and decided to go to the new museum instead. But ... I don't really like museums. What should I do? 5 Bear ~~to~~ in mind, I don't have a car, so it needs to be somewhere with good bus connections.

C Match the beginnings of the tips for staying organized (1–5) with the endings (a–e).

1 Don't do everything at once. Focus
2 Remember to schedule
3 Use a to-do list to keep
4 Break big objectives into smaller action
5 Use an archive to store

a a record of your tasks.
b important old documents.
c some time to relax!
d on one task at a time.
e points.

D Choose the correct reflexive verb to complete the sentences.

1 You shouldn't *blame* / *control* yourself. It's not your fault.

2 *Help* / *get* yourself to anything you want.

3 I always go into fast food restaurants when I see them. I can't *make* / *control* myself.

4 He's trained so hard for the race. Why doesn't he *treat* / *set* himself to a night off and just relax?

FUNCTIONAL LANGUAGE

Complete the conversation with the words in the box. There are two extra words.

about	apologize	blame	fault	not	so	those	worry

Dimitri: Hey, Igor! Have you eaten my pizza?

Igor: Don't 1 blame me! I've been out all day. I don't know anything about it.

Dimitri: Oh ... I'm 2 so sorry. I shouldn't have blamed you.

Igor: It's OK. Don't 3 worry about it. So I wonder who ate your pizza ...

Rob: Uh, sorry, but it's my 4 fault. I was really hungry when I got home last night and I hadn't gone to the store!

Dimitri: Oh, there's no need to 5 apologize. It's just one of 6 those things.

Vocabulary and Communication Hub

Contents

Vocabulary Hub

1.1 Seeing and hearing

Match the beginnings of the sentences (1–5) with the endings (a–e).

1 If you **spot** somebody, b
2 If you **recognize** somebody, e
3 If you **notice** something, c
4 If you **observe** something, d
5 If you **stare at** something, a

a you look at it for a long time, maybe too long.
b you see him/her by chance.
c you see it for the first time.
d you watch it carefully over a long time.
e you see him/her and know who he/she is.

➤ Go back to page 5.

1.2 Languages

A Put the letters in bold in the correct order to make words about language learning.

1 Which is more important when you're speaking English? Speaking ~~**uelcartyac**~~ accurately or ~~**tnulylfe**~~ fluently? Why?
2 Do you know any ~~**midosi**~~ idioms in English? What's your favorite?
3 Are most people in your country ~~**nanoliomlgu**~~ monolingual or ~~**ialinglub**~~ bilingual? What about in your family?
4 Can you tell where somebody is from just by listening to their ~~**cectna**~~ accent? In your language? In English?

B SPEAK Work in pairs. Ask and answer the questions in Exercise A.

➤ Go back to page 9.

2.2 Problems and solutions

Complete the advice with the correct form of the verbs in the box. Sometimes more than one answer is possible.

agree on analyze come up with deal with solve suggest

1 If you really want to solve / deal with a problem, you'll find a way. If you don't, you'll find an excuse.
2 If you are stuck and can't agree on / come up with a solution, go and do something different until you have some fresh ideas.
3 It is best to analyze a problem in as much detail as you can. This will make it easier to solve.
4 It is not always difficult to say what the problem is at work. The real challenge is to suggest a solution to your colleagues.
5 People frequently have different ideas about how to solve problems. In those situations, you should find a solution everyone agrees on.

➤ Go back to page 21.

3.1 Collocations: travel information

Complete the sentences with the correct travel collocations.

1 We are sorry to announce there are severe delays on line 1, of approximately 45 minutes.
2 Let's leave really early, before rush hour, to avoid the heavy traffic.
3 Don't go that way. It's closed due to roadwork – they're replacing the pavement.
4 It's always very crowded on the trains during rush hour, with lots of people standing for a long time.
5 Following the earlier delays, we now have good service on all lines. All lines are running normally.
6 We're stuck in a traffic jam on the highway; we'll be at least half an hour late.
7 Look, they've just canceled the train. We'll have to wait another hour now, for the next one.
8 The first underground/subway line opened in 1863 and went from Paddington station to Farringdon Street station, in London.

➤ Go back to page 27.

3.1 Nouns ending in *-ion*

Complete the sentences with the nouns in the box.

communication connection decisions expectation expression inspiration reaction situations

1 I think communication between the engineer and the passengers is important when a train is delayed.

2 In my country, there has been a negative reaction to driverless cars.

3 Environmental issues don't change the decisions that I make about transportation.

4 I think it is important to have a connection with the people you see every day.

5 There are some travel situations that make me annoyed or angry.

6 I generally have a blank expression when out in public. I never smile at others.

7 I find people that can talk to strangers an inspiration. I wish I were so confident.

8 When I was on vacation, the transportation system was better than my expectation.

➤ Go back to page 29.

3.2 Gradable and ungradable adjectives

Complete the sentences with the adjectives in the box.

enormous excellent filthy furious good hilarious terrible tiny

1 Your hands are absolutely filthy. Wash them before dinner.

2 Excellent work. You made no mistakes at all.

3 We had a really good time on vacation. We really didn't want to come back home!

4 Don't talk to him now. He's absolutely furious because you lost his bike. Let him calm down first.

5 Don't go to that restaurant. The food's really terrible.

6 Charlie thought the show was absolutely hilarious. He laughed from the beginning to the end.

7 The Gobi Desert is extremely large, but the Sahara Desert is enormous; it's seven times bigger!

8 Compared to Russia, the UK is absolutely tiny. Russia is 70 times bigger!

➤ Go back to page 33.

4.1 Collocations: goals and resolutions

Complete the sentences with the correct collocations.

1 He didn't stop drinking soda completely but he cut down to two cans a week.

2 When I make a plan I stick to it. I've kept the resolution(s) I made last year.

3 She finally reached her target of running for thirty minutes every day.

4 He quit eating sugary food three months ago and he already feels healthier.

5 He made a resolution to quit eating chocolate last New Year.

➤ Go back to page 39.

4.2 Prefixes: *dis-*, *mis-*, *over-*, *re-*, *under-*

Choose the correct prefix to complete the word.

1 I ***dis*** / ***mis*** like working late and try to make sure I finish on time each day. (dis circled)

2 I moved out of that city because it is ***re*** / ***over*** populated. There are just too many people. (over circled)

3 I didn't mean that. You ***mis*** / ***dis*** understood what I was trying to say! (mis circled)

4 Many people at the company feel they don't earn enough. Personally I agree that they are ***under*** / ***mis*** paid. (under circled)

5 I don't think this is the best strategy. We should ***under*** / ***re*** think this. (re circled)

➤ Go back to page 45.

Vocabulary Hub

5.1 Verbs of influence

A Match the beginnings of the sentences (1–4) with the endings (a–d).

1 My boss persuaded me c
2 My boss made me d
3 I told him a
4 My friend advised me not b

a to work on the weekend, but he refused.
b to work at home because I might feel lonely.
c to work overtime by offering me some extra money.
d apologize to the customer for being rude.

B Match the beginnings of the sentences (1–4) with the endings (a–d).

1 Our company lets us d
2 I want my boss c
3 My colleague encouraged me b
4 My company allows us a

a to use our personal social media at work.
b to apply for the job, and now I'm her boss!
c to go on vacation forever. I can't stand him.
d leave early on Fridays.

➤ Go back to page 53.

5.2 Business collocations

Which noun cannot be used to complete each sentence?

1 Over the last few years, the company has built its … very successfully.
a brand b reputation (c) customers

2 Recently, we have done a lot of … overseas.
(a) money b deals c business

3 The … was launched at the end of last year.
(a) reputation b product c campaign

4 The sales team are very good at making …
(a) business. b money. c a profit.

5 The media attention has helped us to attract new …
a customers. b investors. (c) expenses.

➤ Go back to page 57.

6.2 Hobbies and free time activities

Complete the texts with the verb phrases in the box.

collect escape from daily stress get you out of the house is a fan is into is relaxing isn't my thing joined a society keeps you in shape lost interest in took up

My brother [1] is into soccer. He [2] is a fan of Liverpool Football Club and he goes to almost all their games. To be honest, soccer [3] isn't my thing, so I've only been to one game with him. I like to [4] collect stamps. I've recently [5] joined a society for that, and I'm going to my first meeting with the other members now. Who says stamp collecting doesn't [6] get you out of the house?!

Last year, I [7] took up sailing as a hobby. I live in the city, and sailing is a great way to [8] escape from daily stress. Being out on the lake with the wind in your hair [9] is relaxing, and it [10] keeps you in shape too because you have to do a lot of physical work. I used to go to the gym, but I soon [11] lost interest in that. The running machines were too boring!

➤ Go back to page 66.

7.1 Phrasal verbs

Work in pairs. Match the underlined phrasal verbs (1–9) with the definitions (a–i) .

1 I can't figure out what ingredients you've used here. What are they? f

2 A: 'Maybe I'll start studying for my exams next week …' g
B: 'Don't put it off! Start today!'

3 We've eaten out every night this week. Let's stay in this evening and cook some food at home. e

4 Sorry to let you down, but I can't come to your party. i

5 I asked everybody to be quiet for a few minutes, but most people just kept on talking. a

6 Can you turn the oven down to 150°C in ten minutes? If you leave it at 220°C for too long, the food will burn. h

7 I don't mind cooking, but can you clean up afterward? d

8 Can you put your phone away, please! It's really rude to check your messages while we're eating dinner! b

9 Great job! Keep up the good work! c

a continue without stopping

b take something that's in the wrong place and put it in the right place

c continue at the same high level

d make everything clean and neat again after making a mess

e not go out

f find the answer by thinking carefully

g decide to do something later, not now

h make something lower/colder/quieter

i make somebody feel sad because you don't do something that you promised to do

➤ Go back to page 75.

7.1 Adjectives to describe food

A Complete the sentences with the adjectives in the box.

delicious disgusting filling mild savory sour

1 Our bakery sells a mix of sweet products, like cakes and fruit pies, and ___savory___ products, like bread and meat pies.

2 Do you prefer strong flavors or ___mild___ flavors?

3 Mmm … I love this meal. It's absolutely ___delicious___!

4 I love ___sour___ food like lemons, grapefruit and pickled cabbage.

5 Ugh! How long has this milk been in the fridge? Two weeks? It tastes ___disgusting___!

6 This meal is great but it's very ___filling___ – I feel completely full already.

B Label the pictures with the adjectives in the box.

bitter raw rich spicy

1

___bitter___

2

___raw___

3

___spicy___

4

___rich___

➤ Go back to page 76.

8.2 Positive adjectives

Choose the best adjectives to complete the sentences.

1 A: My dog pressed six buttons in the right order!
B: That's so *unique* / *impressive*!

2 I just want an umbrella that's *incredible* / *practical* – if it keeps me dry, I'm happy.

3 I read a *fascinating* / *gorgeous* article about the dangers of technology.

4 The party was *sensible* / *unforgettable* – I'll remember it for the rest of my life.

5 It's *unique* / *incredible* that people waste so much money on stupid gadgets!

6 It looks like a normal umbrella, but it contains very *sophisticated* / *gorgeous* electronics.

7 The CleverPet is *sophisticated* / *suitable* for small pets, like cats and dogs, but not large animals, like horses.

8 A: I lost my Oombrella. I forgot to take my phone with me.
B: Well, that wasn't very *sensible* / *unique*, was it?

➤ Go back to page 90.

Vocabulary Hub

9.1 Verbal idioms

A Complete the sentences with the underlined verbal idioms in *The best (and the worst) of immersive theater.*

1. I can't really **tell** the difference between immersive theater and interactive theater. Aren't they the same?
2. I tried to tell a joke, but it **fell** flat. Nobody understood it.
3. If you agree to help people all the time, they might **take** advantage of your kindness. You need to say 'no' more often.
4. Do you still have your old guitar, or did you **get** rid of it?
5. Immersive plays usually **take** place in unusual locations.
6. They have a nice big yard, but they don't really **make** use of it.
7. Six actors **took** part in the play: four adults and two children.
8. I always write down the money I spend to help me **keep** track of my finances.
9. Everything is **going** wrong today! My computer stopped working and my car broke down!
10. If you don't **pay** attention to your teacher, you won't learn very much.

B Complete the verbal idioms with the words in the box.

attention friends fun note sure true

1. I've always dreamed of being a chef, but I'm not sure my dream will ever **come** true.
2. You shouldn't **make** fun **of** other people's mistakes. They aren't funny at all.
3. When someone gives you good advice, always **take** note **of** what they say.
4. I **made** friends **with** Alissa when we were at school, and we've liked each other ever since.
5. I didn't notice the sculpture in the corner. They should put it in the middle of the room to **draw** attention **to** it!
6. I think I know the answer, but I need to check the internet to **make** sure.

➤ Go back to page 101.

10.2 Reflexive verbs

Complete the sentences with the correct reflexive pronouns. What do you think the reflexive verbs mean?

1. Can you all please behave yourselves! You're making too much noise!
2. Daisy bought herself a box of chocolates this morning and ate every single one!
3. Where do you see yourself ten years from now, Hannah? Will you still be doing the same job?
4. Many people find it difficult to express themselves when they're speaking a foreign language. They know what they want to say, but they can't say it.
5. Look at that dog! It's having a good time playing in the water! It's really enjoying itself!
6. I want to do some exercise every day, but I don't trust myself. I'll probably give up after a week!
7. I need to go out for half an hour. Can you all amuse yourselves while I'm gone?

➤ Go back to page 115.

1. If you behave yourself, you're good and you follow the rules.
2. If you buy yourself something, it's a present for you and you don't share it with others.
3. If you see yourself somewhere / doing something, you believe that's where you'll be / what you'll be doing at a point in the future.
4. If you express yourself, you speak/write clearly, so that others understand exactly how you feel.
5. If you enjoy yourself, you have fun.
6. If you trust yourself, you know you won't be tempted to break your own rules.
7. If you amuse yourself, you choose something to do so you don't get bored.

Communication Hub

4.1 Students A and B

The top ten most common New Year's resolutions (in descending order):

1 change the food you eat
2 get organized
3 spend less, save more
4 enjoy life to the fullest
5 get in shape and get healthy
6 learn something exciting
7 quit unhealthy habits
8 help others achieve their dreams
9 fall in love
10 spend more time with family

➤ Go back to page 38.

5.1 Student B

A Take the quiz. Choose the answer that is most true for you.

1 When you get a new piece of picture editing software or an app, do you
- **a** just use the basic functions?
- **b** teach yourself how to use all of its functions?
- **c** ask a friend to show you how to use it?

2 When your teacher suddenly tells you that you are going to do an important speaking test in the next lesson, do you
- **a** get nervous and make extra mistakes?
- **b** enjoy the challenge and do your best?
- **c** say it is not fair and ask to do the test the next day?

3 When you disagree with someone's suggestion, do you usually
- **a** say nothing?
- **b** explain your opinion clearly, and listen carefully to their views?
- **c** tell them directly that it is a bad idea?

4 If you are brainstorming ideas in a group, do you suggest
- **a** similar ideas to other people?
- **b** many, and usually different, ideas?
- **c** very little?

B Ask your partner the questions and take note of his/her answers. Then answer his/her questions.

C Go to **page 149** to find out your score and what it means!

➤ Go back to page 50.

9.2 Student A

➤ Go back to page 105.

4.1 Student A

You can only see your side of the conversation. Read through your lines, and practice your intonation. Role-play the conversation with your partner. You will start the conversation. Listen carefully in order to speak at the right time.

A: Hi, [name].

B: ______

A: Oh! Oops! I'll do it now. Hold on. There we go.

B: ______

A: And happy New Year to you!

B: ______

A: Great. We had a good time on New Year's Eve.

B: ______

A: That sounds amazing!

B: ______

A: Oh! I bet it was freezing, too. I'm glad I was at a party.

B: ______

A: Is that one of your New Year's resolutions?

B: ______

A: You haven't? I've made several.

B: ______

A: Well, I've decided to get in better shape this year, so I'm going to join a gym. Also, I'm going to study English more seriously.

B: ______

A: Well, not good enough. In fact, I'm meeting a new teacher on Thursday, for private lessons.

B: ______

A: Well, there's no point in putting things off. What about your chocolate habit?

B: ______

A: You eat some every day, don't you?

B: ______

➤ Go back to page 39.

2.1 Student A

Has your partner done these things? If he/she has, find out more details.

- go surfing
- climb a tree
- hold a snake
- relax in a natural hot spring
- take a bike riding vacation
- bake some bread
- give blood
- see a lion in the wild
- stay in an ice hotel
- learn to fly a plane

➤ Go back to page 15.

2.2 Personality test scores

In general, the higher your score in this test, the better your attitude toward challenging situations and the better your problem-solving skills. The highest possible score is 30.

A low score for a question shows an area to consider improving in order to become a truly effective problem solver.

Questions 1–3 reveal your attitude toward problems.

Questions 4–6 reveal your problem-solving skills.

➤ Go back to page 21.

4.2 Students A and B

1 a I'll make a lot of money.
  b I make a lot of money.

2 a You have many friends at college.
  b You'll have many friends at college.

3 a She'll shut the window because she hates the cold.
  b She shut the window because she hates the cold.

4 a He put solar panels on his roof.
  b He'll put solar panels on his roof.

5 a They use cell phones in English classes.
  b They'll use cell phones in English classes.

➤ Go back to page 43.

3.1 Students A and B

SPEAK Work in pairs. Put the pictures in the correct order and use them to retell the two stories.

Junko's story

Alan's story

➤ Go back to page 27.

1.2 Student A

A SPEAK Work in pairs. Ask and answer questions to complete the information about the percentage of people with English as a first language in different countries around the world.

Percentage of people with English as a first language		
Ireland	93 percent	
UK	92 percent	
New Zealand	86	percent
US	79 percent	
Canada	57 percent	
Singapore	37 percent	
Jamaica	17	percent
South Africa	9.3 percent	
Sierra Leone	8.5	percent
Pakistan	8 percent	

*Where **do** 93 percent of people **speak** English as a first language?*
*How many people in New Zealand **speak** English as a first language?*

B SPEAK Work in pairs. Are you surprised by any of the information?

➤ Go back to page 7.

5.1 Student A and B

Score 2 points for every time you chose answer b. Score nothing for all other answers.

6–8: You have a very good set of general skills and qualities for employment. Reflect on which are stronger than others, and look for jobs that use your clear strengths. What other employability skills do you have? Can you improve them?

2–5: You have some key skills that are important to employers, but there is room for improvement. Identify those skills, and find out what employers are looking for in those areas. What improvements could you make?

0–1: Employers want people to use their skills in certain ways in the workplace. Learn more about employability skills, and find opportunities to practice, for example group projects or leadership roles. Which skills could you focus on first?

➤ Go back to page 50.

4.1 Student A

A Make a resolution for each of these topics:

- studying English
- money
- food and diet
- house and home

B Tell your partner about your resolutions and why you have made them.

C Ask your partner to make resolutions for these topics.

D Make resolutions for your partner's topics.

➤ Go back to page 39.

1.2 Student B

A SPEAK Work in pairs. Ask and answer questions to complete the information about the percentage of people with English as a first language in different countries around the world.

Percentage of people with English as a first language	
Ireland	93 percent
UK	92 percent
New Zealand	86 percent
US	79 percent
Canada	57 percent
Singapore	37 percent
Jamaica	17 percent
South Africa	9.3 percent
Sierra Leone	8.5 percent
Pakistan	8 percent

*How many people in the UK **speak** English as a first language?*
*Where **do** 79 percent of people **speak** English as a first language?*

B SPEAK Work in pairs. Are you surprised by any of the information?

➤ Go back to page 7.

4.1 Student B

A Make a resolution for each of these topics.

- work or study
- physical fitness
- family and friends
- the internet and digital media

B Tell your partner about your resolutions and why you have made them.

C Ask your partner to make resolutions for these topics.

D Make resolutions for your partner's topics.

➤ Go back to page 39.

10.1 Students A and B

Take the quiz.

Psychology quiz

1 **a** Do we have more than 70 thoughts per day or fewer than 70?
b How many thoughts do we have each day?

2 You have paid for a weekend break in an expensive hotel. On the morning of your long journey, you feel sick and you just want to stay in bed. But it's too late to cancel your trip and get your money back. What do you do?

3 You're choosing a language school to help you pass an important exam. You know that 75 percent of School A's students passed the exam last year. You also know that 20 percent of School B's students failed the exam. Which school sounds better?

➤ Go back to page 110.

Suggested answers:

1 a more; b Some experts suggest we have around 70,000 thoughts per day, but it's almost impossible to count accurately.

2 The best thing to do is to stay in bed, but most people would feel bad about wasting the money, and many would choose to go on the weekend break.

3 School B is better (because 80 percent passed the exam), but School A probably sounds better (because of the words passed and failed).

6.2 Student A

Look at the table. Do you currently do these things? Complete the table so it is true for you. Then ask your partner questions and write down his/her answers.

	You		Your partner		
Activities	Yes/No?	How long?	Yes/No?	How long?	Other details
Use an app to study English					
Follow a celebrity on social media					
Regularly go to a favorite café					
Play a sport					
Collect something					
States					
Be a member of an online-only group					
Know someone from another country					
Have a desktop computer					
Have a car					

➤ Go back to page 67.

8.3 Student B

Use the pictures and notes to write instructions for making a paper heart. Use sequencing phrases. Then read out your instructions so that Student A can make a paper heart.

How to make a heart

You will need a square piece of paper.

Fold the piece of paper in half both ways, and unfold it so that you see the fold marks.

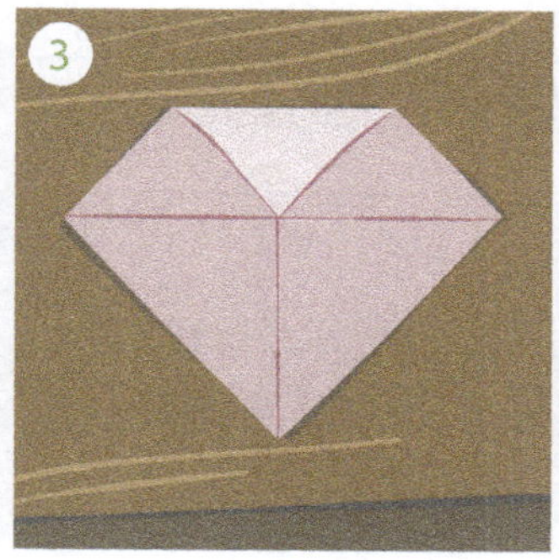

Turn the piece of paper around so that the point is at the top, and fold the top corner down to the middle.

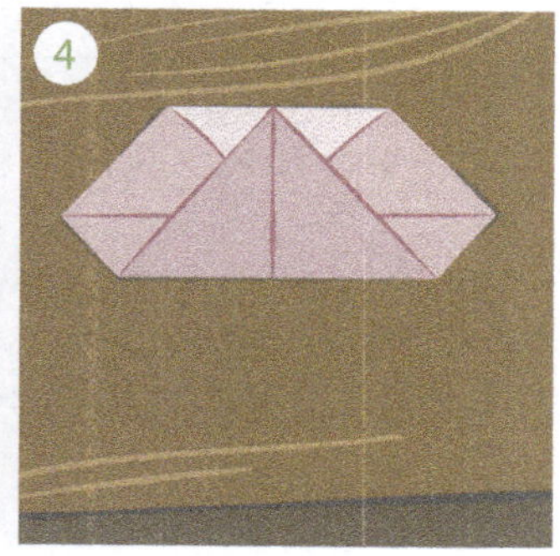

Fold the bottom corner to the top.

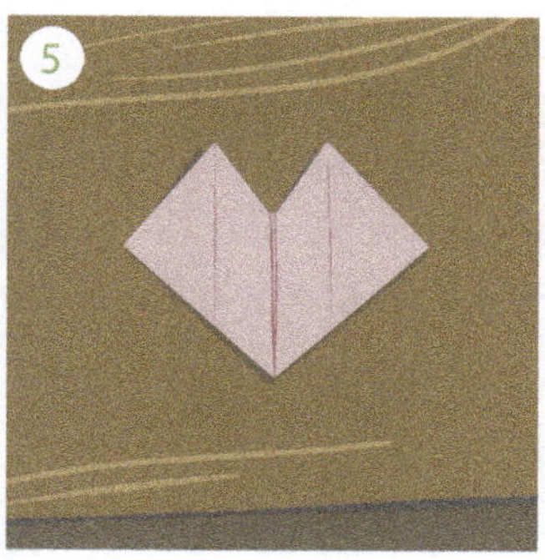

Fold the bottom edges to the middle.

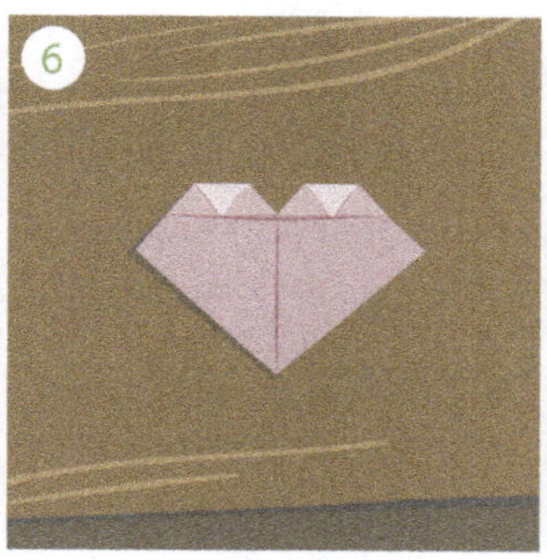

Turn the paper over and fold the two top corners down.

Fold the corners down on both sides.

The heart is ready.

➤ Go back to page 95.

3.2 Students

The local mayor has decided to cancel the city's Car-Free Day. She wants a new project and campaign to reduce the traffic problems and pollution. Read the proposals.

TRANSPORTATION PROPOSALS

1 Reduce your car use!

Encourage people to leave their car at home. Run a media publicity campaign to promote:

- shopping locally, not using out-of-town grocery stores.
- walking or biking for short trips.
- working from home.
- setting up a city council app for car-sharing on common trip.
- increasing city center car parking fees.

2 Go electric!

Encourage the purchase and use of electric cars:

- Install car-charging points around the city.
- Provide cheap loans for the purchase of electric cars.
- Allow free parking for electric cars.

3 A wheely good future!

Encourage biking:

- Run a media publicity campaign to promote riding your bike to work.
- Introduce a city bike rental system.
- Hold 'Bike Fun Days' in local park.

➤ Go back to page 33.

Communication Hub

9.1 Student B

Proposal 2: Immersive theater

Costs (= money going out)		Income (= money coming in)
Building work: $100,000	Marketing: $150,000/year	Ticket sales: $1,500,000/year
Equipment: $150,000	Other costs (e.g. electricity): $150,000/year	Sponsorship: $500,000/year
Employees: $500,000/year		

- Sponsorship: Companies pay for their names/logos to be in the theater, on posters, etc.
- Ticket prices: $50–$100
- 80–100 tickets/performance; 400 performances/year (evenings and weekends only)
- No plans to help the community (e.g. free tickets for schools)

➤ Go back to page 99.

5.1 Student A

A Take the quiz. Choose the answer that is most true for you.

1 When two friends are arguing about what to do on the weekend, do you
- **a** ignore them until they finish?
- **b** calm them down and help them decide?
- **c** tell them to stop and make the decision for them?

2 When you have many things to do next week, do you
- **a** start doing them this week and see how many you can finish?
- **b** make a plan before starting?
- **c** do nothing at first and then rush to do them late next week?

3 When you work on a group project, do you
- **a** focus on your personal tasks?
- **b** do your tasks and support others with theirs?
- **c** do little, and let others do a lot?

4 When you borrow a little money from someone and say you will return it the next day, do you
- **a** pay it back a few days later?
- **b** pay it back the next day?
- **c** need reminding to pay it back.

B Ask your partner the questions and take note of his/her answers. Then answer his/her questions.

C Go to page 149 to find out your score and what it means!

➤ Go back to page 50.

5.2 Students

Basic information

Country: Finland
Business name: Arctic Diamond
Slogan: 'Luxury chilling'
Founded by: Mika Hakala
Products: Ice cubes from the Arctic
Price: $50 for 100 grams

Production process

collected by hand / packed in freezer boxes / delivered by air and courier

Sales

Online business: 15 orders in first two weeks / $20,000 in first year of business
Current customers: European restaurants and bars, hotels in Abu Dhabi and Dubai
Future markets: China, United States

Arctic Diamond

➤ Go back to page 55.

4.1 Student B

You can only see your side of the conversation. Read through your lines, and practice your intonation. Role-play the conversation with your partner. Listen carefully in order to speak at the right time. Your partner will start the conversation.

A: ______

B: Hi, [name]. I can't see you – I don't think you've clicked the video button.

A: ______

B: That's better. Good to see you. Happy New Year!

A: ______

B: How's everything going in Spain?

A: ______

B: Well, lucky you! We went to see the fireworks.

A: ______

B: Yeah, it was great! Mind you, it was a long wait. We got there at nine.

A: ______

B: Yeah! Lucky you. I didn't have a hat or anything. In fact, I'm going to look for one tomorrow.

A: ______

B: Actually, I haven't made any resolutions yet.

A: ______

B: Really? What have you decided?

A: ______

B: That's a surprise! I always thought your English was really good.

A: ______

B: Really? That's quick!

A: ______

B: My chocolate habit? What do you mean?

A: ______

B: Well, just a little.

➤ Go back to page 39.

5.2 Student B

Company:	H&M stores, Sweden and worldwide
Retail sector:	Fashion clothing
Environmental idea:	Customers hand in their old clothes (even ones they didn't buy at H&M). The company either sells them as second-hand clothes from, or turns them into other clothing items.
Reason:	To stop old clothes from going to waste.
Result:	In a four-year period, the company received more than 40,000 metric tons of clothing items (enough material to make 150 million T-shirts).

➤ Go back to page 57.

2.1 Student B

Has your partner done these things? If he/she has, find out more details.

- go sailing
- climb a mountain
- hold a monkey
- relax on a beach all day
- take a camping vacation
- bake a cake
- give someone flowers
- see a tiger in the wild
- stay in an underwater hotel
- learn to drive

➤ Go back to page 15.

7.2 Students A and B

1 **a** about a week
b 8–10 months
c 4–5 days
d 18–24 months
e about 3 days
f about 2 days

2 **a** False. You should only reheat food once.
b True. After the best if used by date, the food may lose some taste or color, but it's probably still safe to eat for a little longer.
c True. Rice sometimes contains very strong bacteria which aren't killed by cooking. So after cooking, put any leftover rice in the fridge and eat within 24 hours.

➤ Go back to page 80.

9.1 Student C

Proposal 3: Modern art gallery

Costs (= money going out)	**Income (= money coming in)**
Building work and equipment: $150,000	Gift shop and snack bar: $150,000/year Sales of paintings, etc: $200,000–$500,000/year
Employees: $150,000/year	
Marketing: $50,000/year	
Other costs (e.g. electricity): $100,000/year	

- Two major exhibits each year (international artists, etc.)
- Smaller exhibits each month (local artists, etc.)
- Free entry for all people to all exhibits
- The gallery will take 40 percent of the sale price of any paintings (e.g. by local artists) that it sells.

➤ Go back to page 99.

3.1 Students

A Look at the list of annoying behavior on public transportation. Number them in order of how annoying they are (1 = most annoying, 9 = least annoying). Think about the reasons for your choices.

___ people talking loudly on the phone
___ people playing loud music and not using headphones
___ people walking too slowly
___ people eating takeout food
___ people not lining up or not waiting their turn to board
___ people leaving trash behind
___ people not giving up their seats to people who need them
___ people coughing and sneezing because of a cold
___ people trying to talk to me

➤ Go back to page 29.

9.2 Student B

➤ Go back to page 105.

6.2 Student B

Look at the table. Do you currently do these things? Complete the table so it is true for you. Then ask your partner questions and write a note of his/her answers.

	You		Your partner		
Activities	Yes/No?	How long?	Yes/No?	How long?	Other details
Use an app to order food					
Write a blog					
Regularly go to a favorite movie theater					
Play a musical instrument					
Work for a company					
States					
Be a member of a club or society					
Know someone famous					
Have a laptop computer					
Have a pet					

➤ Go back to page 67.

8.3 Student A

Use the pictures and notes to write instructions for making a paper airplane. Use sequencing phrases. Then read out your instructions so that Student B can make a paper airplane.

How to make a paper airplane

Put a piece of paper on the table.

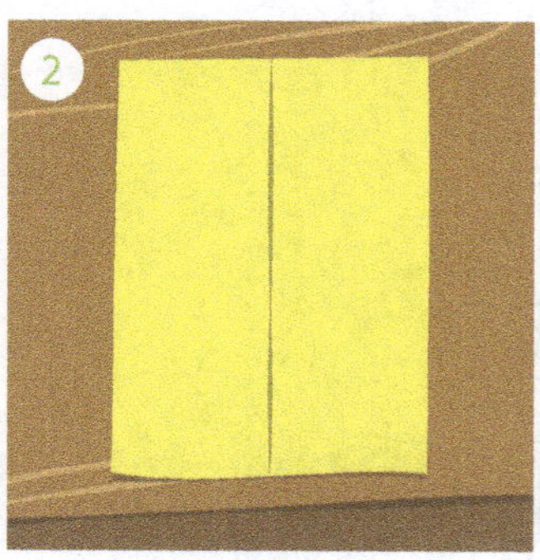

Fold the piece of paper in half lengthways, then unfold it.

Smooth it down.

Form a point at the top of the paper.

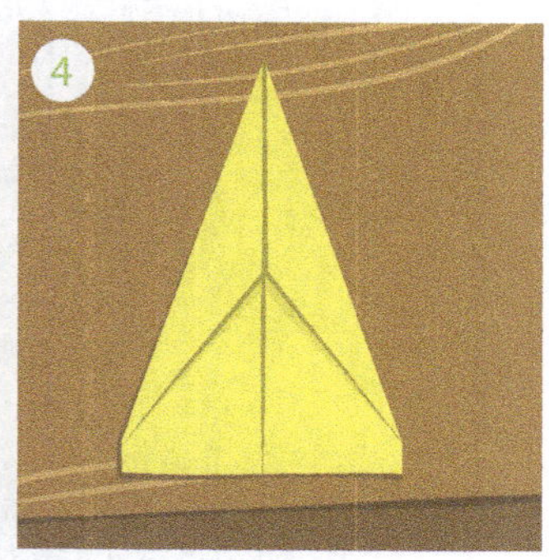

Fold the edges again.

Smooth down the edges with a ruler.

Fold the right side of the paper over the left side.

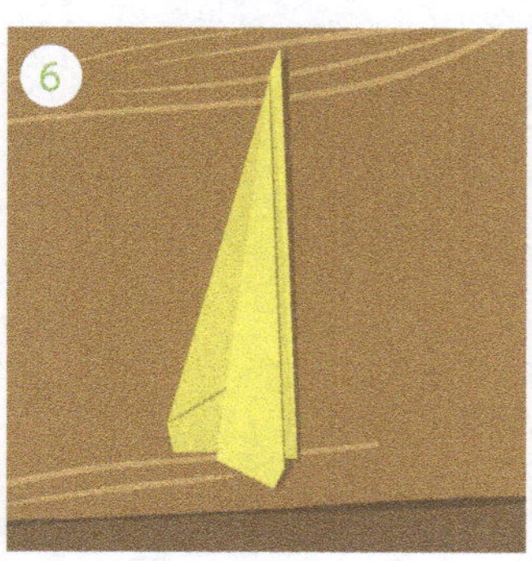

Create the wings.

Attach a paperclip to the nose of the airplane – it will make it fly better.

Unfold the wings and you're ready for takeoff.

➤ Go back to page 95.

Simple present and present progressive

A Read the blog post about Simon and complete the sentences with the simple present or the present progressive verb forms.

On Saturdays, I ________ (*play*) soccer with my brother in the park. I also try to exercise during the week because I'm ________ (*try*) to get in better shape. Right now, I am ________ (*learn*) Italian because I'm ________ (*go*) on vacation to Rome in two weeks – I can't wait! I'm probably most excited about ________ (*eat*) the food there – pasta, pizza … I really ________ (*like*) Italian food because it's delicious!

B Which questions would you need to ask to get the information in Exercise A?

1 What ________ on Saturdays?

2 When ________ exercise?

3 What ________ today?

4 Where ________ on vacation?

5 What ________ excited about?

6 What ________ Italian food?

C Work in pairs. Ask and answer the questions (1–6) in Exercise B.

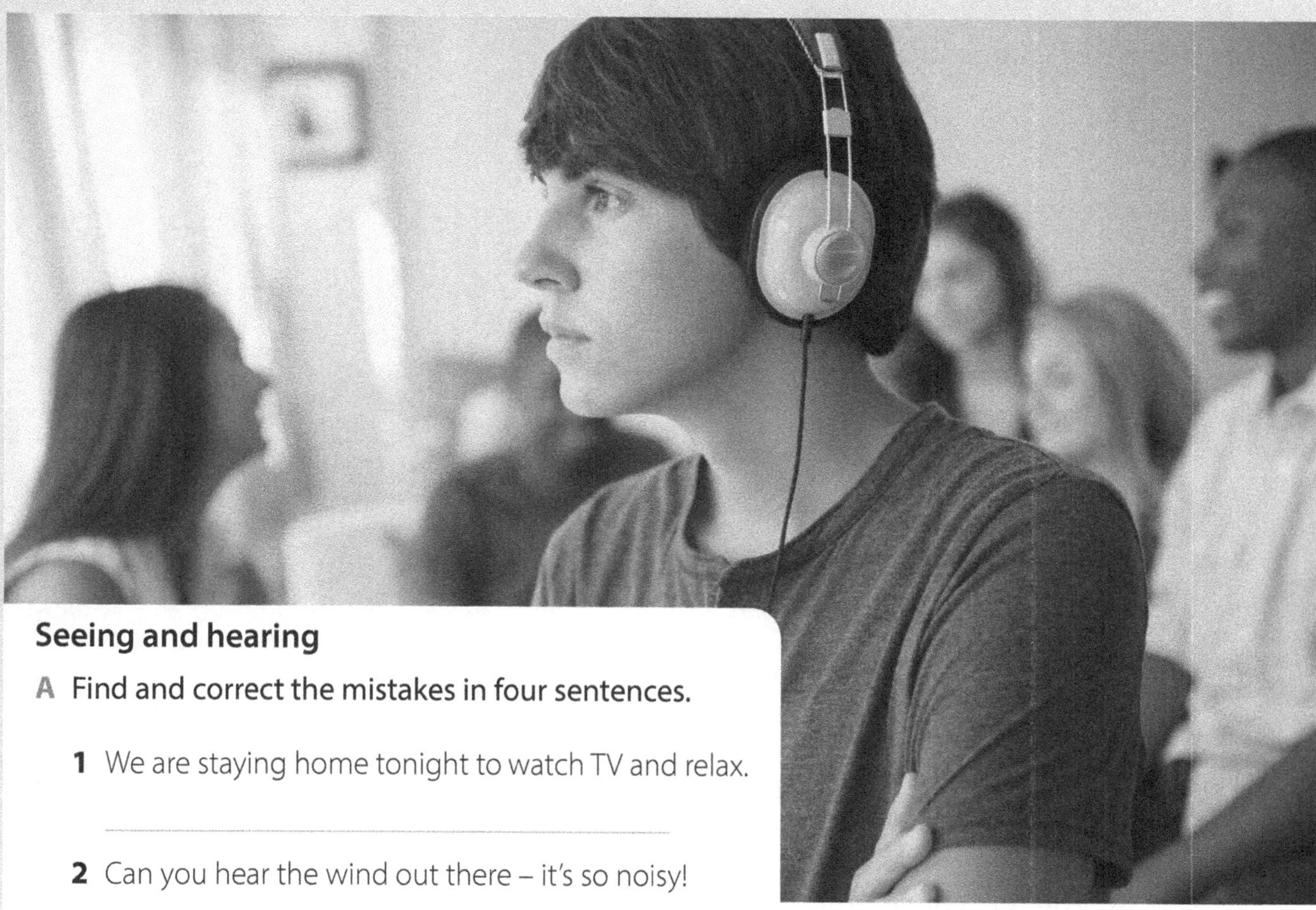

Seeing and hearing

A **Find and correct the mistakes in four sentences.**

1 We are staying home tonight to watch TV and relax.

____

2 Can you hear the wind out there – it's so noisy!

____

3 Thanks for inviting me. That hears great.

____

4 I'm going to watch the paintings at the exhibit on Tuesday.

____

5 It looks like it will rain.

____

6 His music listens amazing!

____

7 I don't think the food in that restaurant looks very good.

____

8 Where is my watch? I can't look at it anywhere!

____

B **What would you expect to see, watch, listen to or hear:**

- on a busy street
- on a plane
- at a party
- on the beach

Subject and object questions

Student A

A Complete the questions with the verb in parentheses.

1 What ______ you happy? (*make*)

2 Where ______ your best friend? (*meet*)

3 Who ______ the most time with? (*spend*)

4 Who ______ your name? (*choose*)

5 What ______ for your last birthday? (*get*)

6 What ______ you cry? (*make*)

7 Where ______ your shoes? (*get*)

8 Who ______ you to cook? (*teach*)

B What do you think your partner's answer for each question would be? Write it after the question, but don't ask your partner yet.

C Ask your questions to your partner. How many did you guess correctly?

Student B

A Complete the questions with the verb in parentheses.

1 What ______ you angry? (*make*)

2 When ______ your best friend? (*meet*)

3 Who ______ the most on the phone? (*speak to*)

4 Who ______ you the last present you received? (*give*)

5 Where ______ on your last vacation? (*go*)

6 What ______ you laugh? (*make*)

7 Why ______ those shoes? (*choose*)

8 Who ______ you to swim? (*teach*)

B What do you think your partner's answer for each question would be? Write it after the question, but don't ask your partner yet.

C Ask your questions to your partner. How many did you guess correctly?

Languages

A Read the information about the three different teachers and choose the correct words in bold.

Ana is from your country, but her parents are American so she's completely ***bilingual / monolingual***. She understands the problems you have with English, and sometimes she translates things to help you understand. When she ***speaks / talks*** English, she has a very strong ***idiom / accent***, which you find difficult to understand.

Chris is a native speaker. He loves teaching ***idioms / bilingual*** and modern, ***phrases / informal*** language, but he never gives you a very clear answer when you ask him questions about grammar. He doesn't speak your language and he doesn't like it when you try to ***accent / translate*** anything.

Diana has lived in a lot of different countries and speaks a lot of languages. She won't tell you exactly where she's from, but she speaks English very fluently with an American accent. She only lets you use a ***phrases / monolingual*** dictionary to look up words. Even though she says she ***talks / speaks*** your language, you've never heard her use it.

B Who would you prefer to be taught by? Why?

C Which of the following qualities of an English teacher are most important:

- being bilingual in your language
- having a native accent
- teaching informal language and idioms
- speaking many languages fluently

D What are the five most important qualities for you in a good teacher?

2.1 Grammar

Present perfect and simple past

A Make questions from the prompts below, using the present perfect or simple past.

1 plant a tree? *Have you ever planted a tree?*

2 get into trouble when you were in school? ____________________

3 ride a horse? ____________________

4 watch (a famous sporting event)? ____________________

5 meet (name of a famous person who is not alive)? ____________________

6 do a parachute jump? ____________________

7 have a big party on your 18th birthday? ____________________

8 swim with dolphins? ____________________

9 celebrate (an important event or national holiday)? ____________________

10 meet (a famous person who is still alive)? ____________________

11 go out last night? ____________________

12 write a poem? ____________________

B Work in pairs. Ask and answer six of the questions. For every question, you must answer 'Yes'. Ask your partner further questions to decide if they are telling the truth.

Collocations: making big decisions

A Read about an important career choice and complete the questions (1–6) with the correct form of the verb in parentheses.

I work as a chef in a restaurant. The hours are long and the work is usually very tiring but being able to create my own recipes and make food that I love helps me to stay motivated. One day, I dream of opening my own restaurant – I'd love to be able to turn that dream into reality. For now, my short-term goal is to finish my training and improve my skills as a chef, but in the future, I'd love to move to America. Leaving my old job to start a new career was the biggest decision I've made, but I think it's really important to try new things.

1 What ______________ (*help*) you stay motivated when you're working?

2 What's one dream you'd love to ______________ (*turn*) into reality?

3 What's one goal you're currently ______________ (*work*) toward?

4 What's one long-term goal you've ______________ (*set*) for yourself?

5 What's the last important decision you ______________ (*make*)?

6 What would make you lose heart if you were ______________ (*try*) to do something difficult?

B Work in pairs. Ask each other the questions (1–6). Then ask other questions to find out more information.

For example:

What else helps you stay motivated?

I like that I'm creative when I'm meeting goals.

Is that important for you?

Yes, but work hours are more important. I lose heart if I need to work long hours.

last year

today

Present and past ability

A Look at the pictures above. What couldn't the woman do last year that she can do today?

B Make sentences using phrases from the table and your own ideas.

Last year	I	could …
When I was ten	my parents	couldn't …
In the last century	my best friend	was / were able to …
Yesterday	my boss	wasn't / weren't able to …
Years ago	people	managed to …
Today	children	didn't manage to …
In my country	scientists	can …
	doctors	can't …
		am / are able to …

C Compare your sentences with a partner. Describe four things which you couldn't do in the past but you can do now.

Dependent prepositions (verb/adjective + *for*/*of*)

A Match the sentence halves, and add *for* or *of* between them to complete the sentences.

1 I'm looking

2 I don't want to work

3 Are you aware

4 I'm very proud

5 I don't think that would be suitable

6 Have you asked her

7 Are you prepared

8 My last job wasn't typical

a long hours?

b my certifications.

c a big company.

d the kind of thing I normally do.

e a new job.

f how important contacts are?

g me at all.

h a reference?

B The sentences are from a conversation between a career advisor and someone looking for work. Work with a partner and write the conversation, including the sentences above in the correct order.

C Join with another pair and perform your conversations to each other. How similar are they?

Narrative tenses

Work in groups. One person tosses a coin and moves one place for heads or two places for tails. They talk for one minute about the topic they land on. The other players ask further questions. Then the next person tosses the coin and moves from the previous player's position.

Tell your group about ...

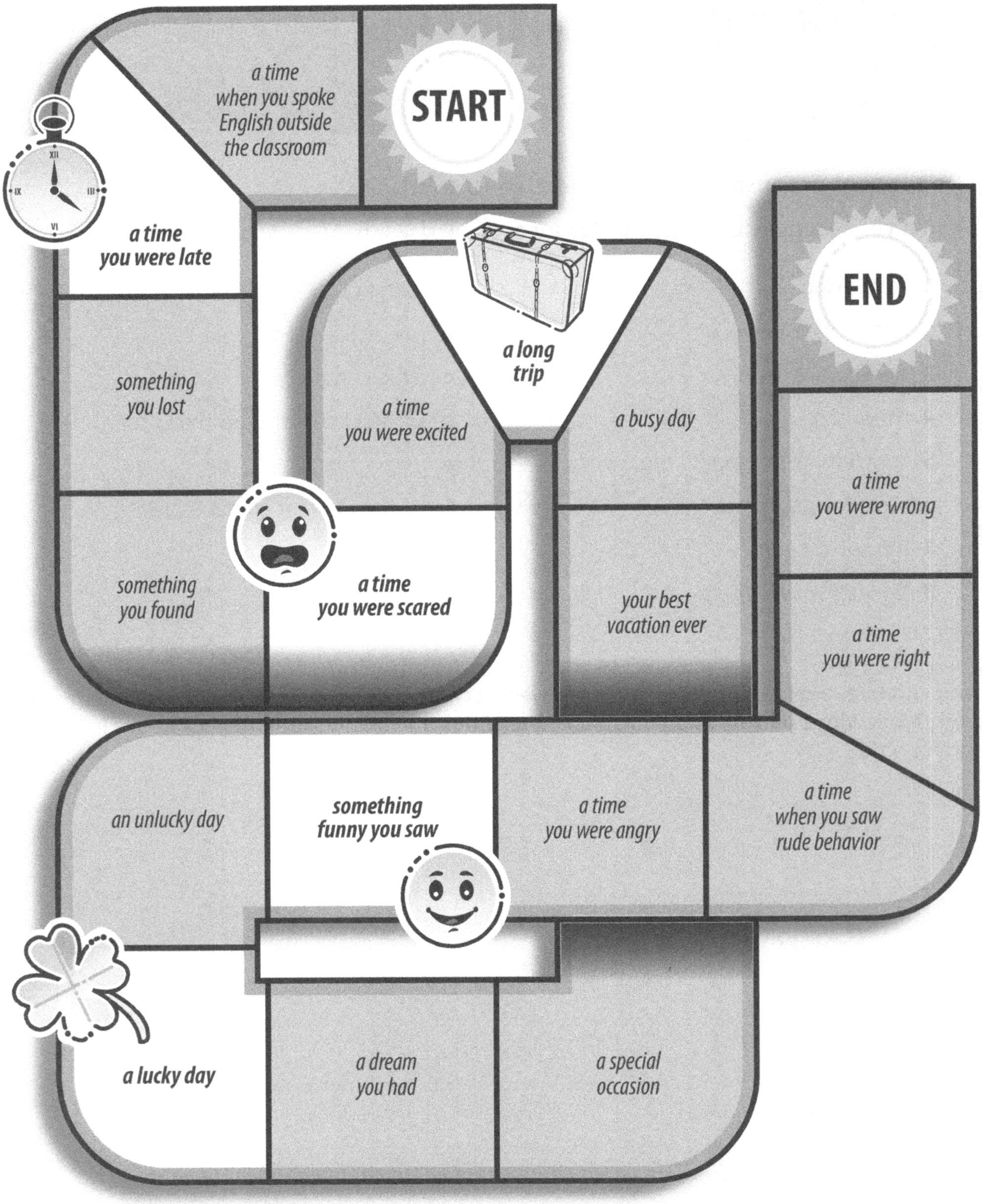

Collocations: travel information

A Correct any mistakes in the sentences.

1 There are usually severe delays on the trains.

2 I never travel in the busy hour.

3 There's always heavy traffic in the city.

4 I spend a lot of time stuck in traffic lines.

5 I hate waiting at the road lights when they're red.

6 There's usually good operation on the subway.

7 There is a lot of road work right now.

8 I don't like driving in heavy rain.

9 The buses are usually overbusy.

B Work in pairs and discuss which sentences are true for you, or true about where you live.

Articles and quantifiers

A **Read the article about Rio de Janeiro. Fill in the blanks (1–10) with *a, an, the* or – (no article) and choose the correct quantifier for each sentence.**

1 ***A lot of / few*** people visit Rio de Janeiro in ______________ February and March to celebrate Carnival.

2 ______________ costumes people wear are really amazing and colorful.

3 I felt that I should have brought ***more / less*** clothes with me on vacation so that I could have dressed up a little more.

4 ***Some / few*** people dance in ______________ street parade as musicians play samba.

5 ______________ atmosphere is amazing!

6 It's ______________ incredible experience to be able to celebrate with so ***many / a lot of*** people.

7 Another great thing about Rio is ______________ food!

8 My favorite dish is *feijoada*, which is ______________ stew made from ______________ black beans and ______________ beef or ______________ pork.

9 ***A lot of / few*** Brazilian people love this. In fact it is so popular that it is frequently considered ______________ national dish.

10 I wish I could stay in Brazil for longer – Rio is such ______________ wonderful city!

B **Work in pairs. Discuss a city you have visited that you thought was an amazing place. What did you like about it?**

Gradable and ungradable adjectives

A Read the reviews and change the gradable adjectives in bold to make the meanings stronger.

1 Although people had said the movie wasn't great, I didn't expect it to be so **bad**! The person behind me kept on kicking my seat and made me feel **angry**!

____

2 The new Japanese restaurant on Newport Street is **great**. I ordered sushi and it came with a lot of **good** side dishes. That was a **nice** surprise!

____

3 I'm not at all sure about her new album. I was a **big** fan of her earlier music, but then she got popular and her style changed. The new songs are just not the same. In fact, I'd say her new stuff is **bad**.

____

4 I didn't think I'd ever eat snails, but when I tried them I thought they were **good**.

____

5 I wasn't disappointed with this horror movie. It was frightening! The twist at the end of the story was unexpected and I was **scared**.

____

6 The first time I watched the show I thought it was boring. But after the third episode I was hooked. The main actor is **funny**.

B Work in pairs and talk about the following:

- a movie you've seen recently
- a meal you had in a restaurant
- a book which you read but didn't like
- your favorite singer or band

Future forms

A Read the conversation between two people who are going to a pop concert. Use *will*, *going to* or the present perfect progressive to complete the sentences.

Sandra: Have you heard the new Tamara Lopez album? It's great! I'm [1] __________ buy it today.

Henry: I know! Did you know she's [2] __________ perform at Radio City Music Hall in July?

Sandra: No? Are you [3] __________ go?

Henry: Yes, [4] __________ get you a ticket, if you like?

Sandra: Great! Thanks … oh, wait … did you say she's [5] __________ in July?

Henry: Yes.

Sandra: Oh. I actually don't think I'm [6] __________ be able to go. I'll be [7] __________ the UK in July.

Henry: Lucky you! That [8] __________ be wonderful! You [9] __________ have a great time!

B Choose one thing you want to achieve:

- learn a musical instrument
- learn a new language
- save money
- eat more healthily
- make more friends

C Now make a list of things you're going to do to achieve it.

Learn a musical instrument

- start lessons next week

Work in pairs. Tell a partner what you're going to do. Listen to their advice.

Collocations: goals and resolutions

A Complete the phrases in the table with the correct collocations below.

quit stick keeps reached cut down set breaks

Find someone who:	Extra information:
1 has ______ a bad habit Name:	
2 has ______ on something unhealthy Name:	
3 always ______ resolutions Name:	
4 finds it difficult to ______ resolutions Name:	
5 has ______ himself/herself an unrealistic goal Name:	
6 has almost ______ a target Name:	
7 always ______ to a plan Name:	

B Interview your classmates and find one person that each of 1–7 is true for.

C Tell the class about someone you spoke to. Include any extra information they gave on their goals and resolutions.

Ask them extra questions to get more information.

Making predictions

A Complete the sentences using the super-forecaster's phrases.

Over the next ten years:

My country's economy ________________ improve.

Unemployment in my country ________________ fall.

The world's population ________________ increase dramatically.

The world ________________ be more peaceful.

Technology ________________ make our lives better.

I ________________ make a lot of progress in my career.

My national soccer team ________________ win the World Cup.

People ________________ do more to protect the environment.

People ________________ eat more healthily.

The world ________________ end.

B Compare your predictions with a partner. Who is more optimistic about the future?

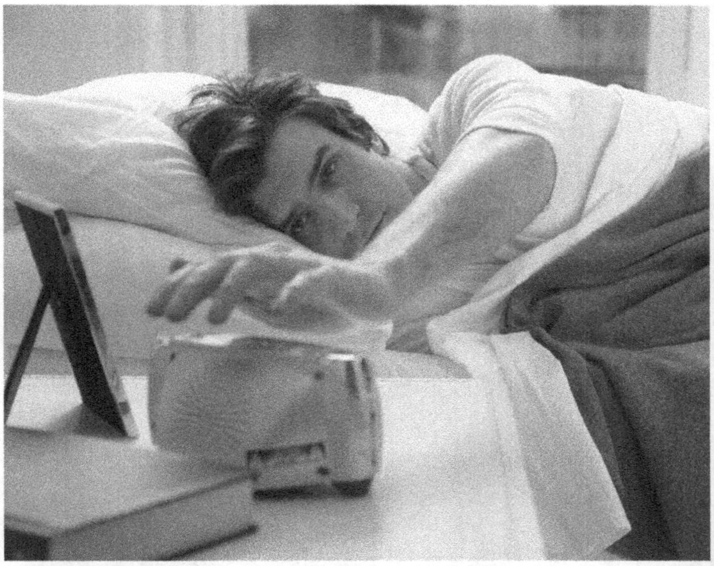

Prefixes: *dis-, mis-, over-, re-, under-*

A Add the correct prefix *dis-, mis-, over-, re- or under-* to the words in bold. Then complete the sentences with the correct form of the new words.

1	I can't believe I ______________ and missed my meeting.	**sleep**
2	There's no way that coffee costs $9! I must have been ______________.	**charge**
3	The man at the train station was really ______________! He was so rude.	**respect**
4	My keys can't have just ______________. They must be somewhere.	**appear**
5	I thought that was what she was saying, but I may have ______________.	**understand**
6	I just can't understand a word he says – he ______________ everything!	**pronounce**
7	This chicken is still pink. I definitely ______________ it.	**cook**
8	Are they planning ______________ the old school?	**build**
9	Ever since he ______________ his watch, he's late for everything!	**place**
10	There's always so much to do. We've been feeling a little ______________.	**work**

B Write five sentences about yourself using the words from Exercise A. Work in pairs. Tell each other your sentences. Ask questions to find out more information.

Past habits and states

A **Read the article about the people below and fill in the blanks in the sentences with *used to, would* or *didn't use to*.**

We both studied Medicine in college and I remember how we ________________ work in the library together to study for exams. We ________________ sit there for hours and hours, reading over our notes. We ________________ usually go out with our friends after lectures to discuss what we had learned. Because we were students, we ________________ have much money, so we cooked at home or went to our friends' houses. We ________________ make pizzas for everyone and we ________________ stay up fairly late, chatting and socializing. When I wasn't working, I ________________ get up very early. I always ________________ dream of becoming a doctor, but I didn't think about how much hard work it is! It's definitely worth it though. I love helping people.

B **Make sentences about your own past. Write two true sentences and one false sentence.**

C **Work in pairs. Tell each other your sentences and ask questions to guess the false sentence.**

Employment skills and qualities

A Match the sentence beginnings (1–7) and endings (a–g).

1 Is it more important for a boss to be __
2 Do you work better or worse when you're under __
3 Do all young people today have good digital __
4 In what jobs is it especially important to be good at team __
5 In what jobs is it not important to be good at time __
6 Did you learn creative __
7 Is having good communication __

a work?
b pressure?
c management?
d thinking skills in school?
e creative or reliable?
f technology skills?
g skills the most important quality today?

B Discuss the questions with a partner.

The passive voice

A Choose the best option to complete the sentences. Then work with a partner to guess what the product is.

This product is usually ***used in / made of*** various materials like plastic, glass and metal. It is currently ***bought by / sold in*** people across the world. It is ***made by / made of*** one of the biggest technology companies in the world. It is ***used for / known as*** staying in contact, taking photographs and searching online. It is ***found in / known as*** electronics stores and phone stores.

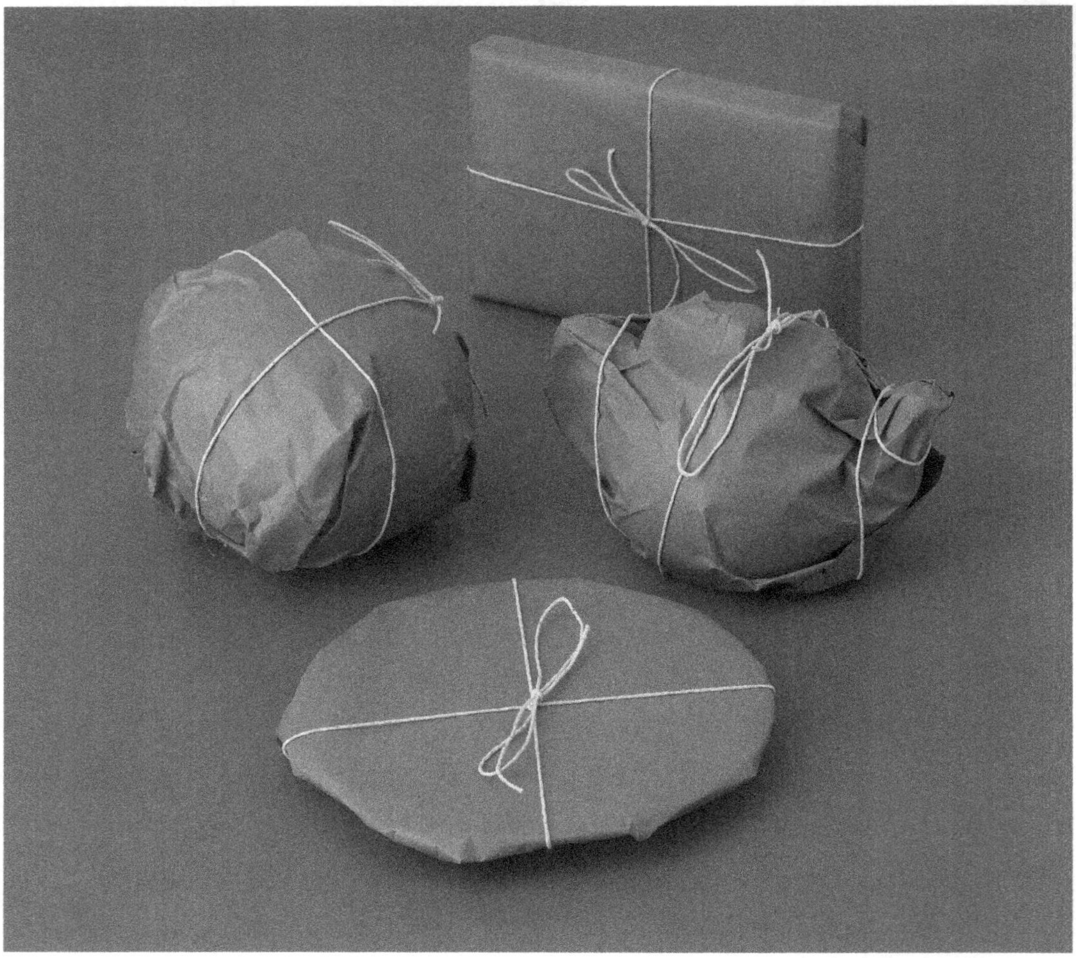

B Work in pairs. Choose a product and write five sentences to describe it. Use the phrases below and your own ideas. Write the first sentence so it is difficult to guess what the product is and make it easier with each sentence.

made of   made in   made by   used in   used by   used for   found in
known as   sold in   bought by   marketed as   loved by   watched by
eaten by   eaten with   served with   considered to be

C Work in pairs. Read your sentences to each other. Try to guess what your partner's product is before they read their last sentence.

Business collocations

A Put the nouns into the correct column to complete the table.

campaign investors deals money reputation

launch	run	build	make	attract
a product	*a company* *a business*	*a brand*	*a profit*	*customers*

B Cover the table. Complete the sentences with the correct form of one of the verbs.

Think of:

1 a company that ____________________ a good reputation.

2 a business you'd like ____________________.

3 an easy way ____________________ money.

4 a product that ____________________ recently.

5 something your school could do ____________________ more students.

C Work in pairs. Discuss the sentences (1–5).

Modals of obligation

A **Read the rules about playing basketball. Choose the best option to complete the sentences.**

The rules of basketball

1. Players ***must not* / *wouldn't*** walk or run with the ball for more than one and a half steps.
2. The referee ***has to* / *should*** disqualify a player who fouls five times.
3. Players ***should* / *shouldn't*** wear appropriate footwear.
4. A player ***must* / *shouldn't*** pass the ball to another player within five seconds.
5. Players ***must not* / *don't have to*** kick the ball to pass.
6. New players ***should* / *have to*** set goals to work toward so they can improve their skills.
7. Players ***need to* / *don't need to*** control their feet as well as their hands to play well.
8. You ***shouldn't* / *have to*** practice regularly if you want to improve your skills.

B **Work in small groups. Design a new sport. Write notes in the box below to help you organize your ideas. Then write ten rules for how to play your sport.**

NOTES:
equipment:
location:
players:
rules:
how to win:

C **Explain your sport to the other groups. Which sport do you like the most? Why?**

Adjectives ending in *-ive*

A Complete the questions with the adjectives in the box.

massive	attractive	decisive	active	competitive
effective	impressive	creative	inexpensive	aggressive

1 When you are trying to choose what to have in a restaurant, are you ________________?

2 Are you more ________________ at work or when you're playing a sport or a game?

3 What's a quality you find ________________ in a person?

4 What sports/song/band/movie is ________________ in your country right now?

5 Do you prefer to relax on vacation or stay busy and ________________?

6 How do you have an ________________ night out when you are saving money?

7 What's your most ________________ achievement?

8 What's the most ________________ way to stop hiccupping?

9 Are you an ________________ driver?

10 Are you a ________________ person that likes writing, painting or playing music?

B Work in pairs. Ask and answer the questions. How similar are you?

C Write five new questions using the adjectives above. Ask your partner.

had to / needed to

A Complete the sentences in the paragraphs below with the correct form of *had to* or *needed to.*

1 After I decided to take up running, I knew that I ________________ get in better shape. I was out of breath after just ten minutes – it was so embarrassing! I ________________ buy new running shoes because my brother had bought me some for my birthday, but I decided that I ________________ get a fitbit, to see how much my fitness improves.

2 I've always loved bike riding, so when I saw my friend's new road bike, I knew I ________________ get the same one. It was very expensive, so for a couple of months, I ________________ save money. I'm so glad that I did! It's the best thing that I've ever bought.

B Work in pairs. Student A, complete the sentences below about a sport you played. Student B, complete the sentences below about an event you went to. Don't say what the sport or event was.

Student A: a sport you played

I had to ________________ and I needed to ________________, but I didn't have to ________________ and I didn't need to ________________.

Student B: an event you went to

I had to ________________ and I needed to ________________, but I didn't have to ________________ and I didn't need to ________________.

C Read your sentences. Can you guess what sport or event your partner is describing?

Hobbies and free-time activities

A Read the two texts.
Complete each sentence with the correct form of one of the verbs in the box.

join be take keep escape lose get

1 Taking up bike riding

OK, so I've never ________ a member of a sports club before and team sports really ________ my thing. But last week, I ________ my college biking club. Best thing ever! It ________ you out of the house and ________ you active. It also helps you ________ weight. Win-win!

2 Taking up the guitar

I've always ________ a music fan. I think it helps you ________ reality and your daily stress for a little while. That's why I wanted to ________ up guitar. I've never ________ into piano and ________ interest with other instruments I tried to learn. But playing guitar ________ so relaxing. I don't think I'll ever get bored.

B Work with a partner. Make questions using the collocations from Exercise A. Discuss the questions with your partner.

1 Which club ________?

2 What hobbies ________?

3 Which instruments ________?

4 What do you do to ________?

C Work in groups of three. Each person chooses two hobbies from the list below. Tell your group about your choices. Then as a group, choose the best hobby to do together.

- flower arranging
- judo
- history of art
- salsa dancing
- sewing
- rock climbing
- foreign language conversation

7.1 Grammar

Modals of speculation and deduction

A Write a story. Write one sentence for each picture using the words below and describe what you think is happening.

may could might must can might not must not

Example: *I think he might be waiting for someone.*

B Work in pairs. Compare stories. How are they similar? How are they different?

C Work in groups. Choose the best version of the story to present to the class.

7.1 Vocabulary

Phrasal verbs

A Read the blog about a night market and replace each word in bold with a phrasal verb from the box.

show up   figure out   put off   keep up   stay up   stay in
start off   serve up   carry on   try out

Although I was tired from the long flight, I didn't want to **remain indoors**. I tried a tour of the night market in Chiang Mai. After we **found** the best route, we went straight there from our hostel. The great thing about the tour is you don't need to book it in advance, you can just **arrive without a reservation**. A variety of hot food is **put on plates** so you can **experiment** with the local specialities.

B Work in pairs. Choose four phrasal verbs and discuss your own experience of visiting a new place.

C Discuss the questions with a partner.

1 Do you usually go out or stay in on Saturday night?
2 What new experiences would you like to try out?
3 Have you given anything up for your work or studies?
4 How do you feel if someone shows up late for an appointment?
5 What's something you frequently put off doing?
6 Can you think of anything that has really taken off recently?
7 Would you like to set up a business? If so, what kind?
8 Do you prefer cooking or cleaning up?

American Language Hub Level 3 Teacher's Book.

Comparatives and superlatives; *the ..., the ...*

A Work in groups and find out who:

- has the biggest family.
- has the most pets.
- has the best phone.
- works the hardest.
- travels the farthest to get to work/school.
- has been to most countries.
- has known their best friend the longest.
- has the most pairs of shoes.
- is the best cook.
- can say the alphabet in English the fastest.

B Change groups. Tell your new group about your old group.

C Work in pairs. Find and correct the mistakes in five sentences.

1 The more friends you have, the happier you are.
2 The more expensive a restaurant, the more good it is.
3 The sooner you pay a bill, the better.
4 The slowlier you drive, the safer you are.
5 The more books you've read, the more interesting you are.
6 The more you sleep, the more tired you feel.
7 The more organized are you, the less time you waste.
8 The beautifuler someone is, the less interesting they are.
9 The unhealthier something is, the nicer it tastes.
10 The more early you get up, the more you achieve.

D Do you agree with the sentences? Why/Why not?

Waste

A Read the article and form collocations about waste from the letters in bold.

< >

Waste

Reduce

One way to **wnd ocut** on waste is to **deurce** amount of products you use. For example, you could use both sides of a piece of paper after you print something.

Reuse

Instead of **wringtho yawa** plastic grocery bags, why not **sreue** them? Then you don't have to buy another plastic bag when you go shopping. Cut down on the amount of packaging you **ret gio df** by reusing old jars and containers as storage containers.

Recycle

Rather than **gtering tid fo** all your trash in one **atrhs acn**, make sure that you separate glass, plastics and paper ready for **rgcecyinl**. Try to think of new ways to recycle old items – this will also save you money.

B Work in pairs and discuss:

- something you need to cut down on
- something you threw away recently
- something that can't be recycled
- something you usually reuse
- something that is frequently wasted
- something you usually use up
- something you'd like to get rid of

Adjective clauses

A Read the article. Choose the correct answers for the words in bold.

Leonardo da Vinci

Leonardo da Vinci is probably most famous for his painting of the *Mona Lisa* ***which/who*** is a unique work of art. But he was also a man ***who/which*** had a variety of other interests. Da Vinci had many ideas for inventions ***who/which*** became a reality in the future. His drawings of flying machines ***who/that*** looked like a mixture of a bicycle and a helicopter are just one example. These machines, ***where/which*** were designed to flap with wings like those of a bat, were not flown in his lifetime. However, he did design a hang glider ***who/that*** could have worked. Da Vinci, ***who/that*** was born to a poor family, had never received an education. His achievements were truly amazing.

B Work in pairs. Make sentences to describe an important inventor or invention. Use the phrases below to help you.

a person who …

an invention which …

a place where …

an object that …

Word families; Creative thinking

A Complete the questions (1–8) with phrases from the box. Use the correct verb form for each sentence.

come up with ideas	use your imagination	boost your creativity	unplug completely
let your mind wander freely	generate new ideas	think outside the box	
block your creativity	your mind goes blank	look at a problem from the outside	

1 Where's the best place to ____________________?

2 What's the best way to ____________________?

3 What's something that ____________________?

4 Who's someone who ____________________?

5 Who's someone who helps you ____________________?

6 Think of a time when ____________________?

7 Do you find it easy to ____________________?

8 How often does ____________________?

B Work in pairs. Ask and answer your questions.

C Work in groups. Choose one of the problems below or use your own ideas. Tell the group your problem and give each other advice to solve them. Then decide which is the best solution to each problem.

- you are stressed about a presentation
- you can't finish an essay
- you are too busy at work
- you are stuck with some creative writing
- your mind goes blank in interviews
- your mind wanders in lectures

8.2 Grammar

Zero and first conditionals

A Match the sentences (1–8) with (a–h).

1	If I win some money,	**a**	I'll pass the exam.
2	If he has time,	**b**	it boils.
3	If they buy a puppy,	**c**	drink it!
4	If my boss asks me,	**d**	I'll work overtime.
5	If she doesn't bring an umbrella,	**e**	she will get wet.
6	If you heat water,	**f**	he will finish the project.
7	If she buys you coffee,	**g**	they will walk it.
8	If I study,	**h**	I will give it to charity.

B Work in pairs. You are organizing an event for work. Read the tasks below. Decide which four tasks you most want to do:

- give a speech
- find speakers
- write a web page for the event
- create a poster
- find a venue
- figure out costs
- make a video for the event
- promote the event on social media

C Agree which four tasks you will do. Use the sentence below when agreeing on tasks.

I'll … if you … .

Positive adjectives

A Complete the reviews with the words from the box. More than one answer may be possible but use each word only once.

Fitness tracker

This ______________ device has an ______________ range of product features. It is ______________ among trackers because as well as checking weight, heart rate and steps, you can actually pay in stores with it. It looks good too with a ______________ design available in a wide range of colors. It is light but sturdy so it is very ______________ to use while exercising.

Wireless headphones

With so many features in one device, this product has a complex, ______________ design. But they are very easy to use, making them ______________ for anyone. They are not the most stylish option on the market, but their price and features make them a ______________ choice. The sound quality is excellent so they provides an ______________ listening experience.

gorgeous	sensible	practical	unforgettable	impressive
unique	sophisticated	incredible	suitable	

B Work in pairs. Choose positive adjectives from the box and describe:

- a person
- a place
- a building
- an event
- an experience
- a vacation
- a gadget
- a meal
- a piece of art
- a story in the news

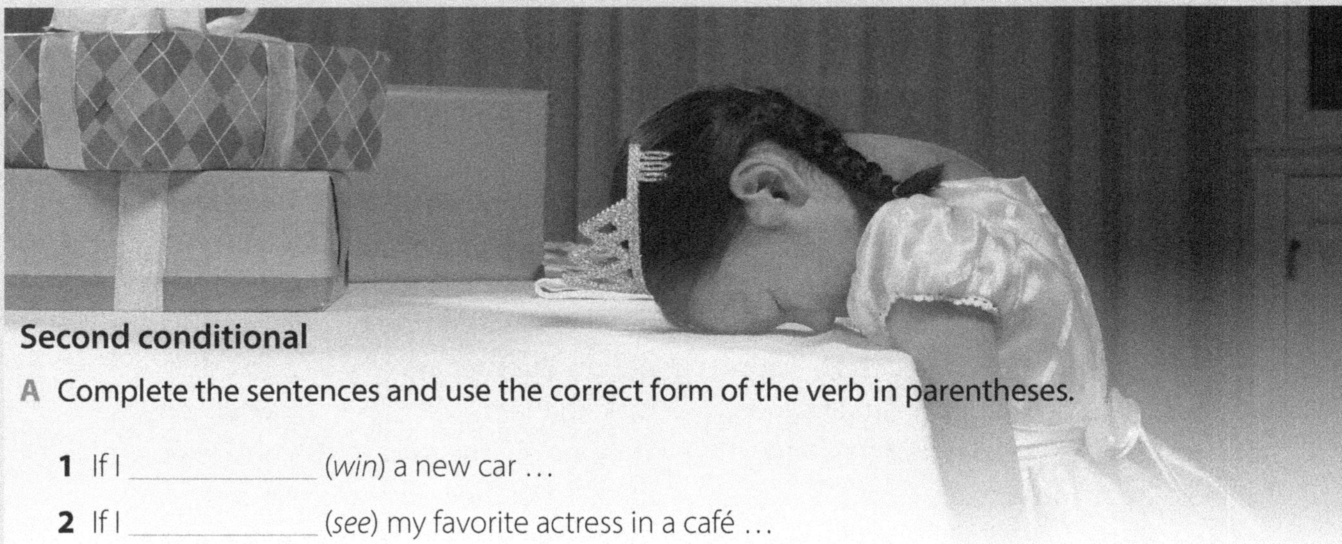

Second conditional

A Complete the sentences and use the correct form of the verb in parentheses.

1 If I ______________ (*win*) a new car …

2 If I ______________ (*see*) my favorite actress in a café …

3 If I ______________ (*buy*) someone a present they didn't like …

4 If I ______________ (*ask*) for money by someone on the street …

5 If I ______________ (*be*) late for work …

6 If I ______________ (*play*) the guitar …

7 If I ______________ (*be*) you …

8 If I ______________ (*speak*) …

B Ask your classmates: *What would you do if …?* and write down their answers in the column next to each question. Write their name next to their responses.

What would you do if …?	Answer	Name
1		
2		
3		
4		
5		
6		
7		
8		

C Discuss as a class. Whose answer did you like the most? Why?

The arts; Verbal idioms

A Find words in the word search to complete the sentences.

N	C	O	N	C	E	R	T	I	B
J	D	I	R	G	N	T	A	X	E
P	X	Y	R	E	L	L	A	G	P
T	O	C	N	A	E	H	U	D	B
I	Y	A	L	P	S	I	D	O	R
B	E	I	O	U	A	V	I	G	X
I	N	S	T	R	U	M	E	N	T
H	Z	T	R	X	W	T	N	A	M
X	H	U	I	A	E	X	C	C	Z
E	F	D	B	O	E	R	E	H	W
B	L	I	V	E	A	H	C	O	R
C	G	O	N	D	I	C	E	I	S
G	N	I	D	R	O	C	E	R	T

1 I'd love to be able to play an ______________ really well.
2 My dream would be to have a session in a recording ______________.
3 There's an ______________ going on right now that I'd really like to see.
4 I only ever go to a ______________ if it's free.
5 I prefer being at a ______________ to listening to music at home.
6 I used to sing in a ______________ when I was younger, but I don't have time nowadays.
7 It's really exciting to be part of the ______________ at the theater.
8 I saw an amazing fireworks ______________ once.

B Tell your partner if the sentences are true or false for you, and why.

9.2 Grammar

Reported speech

Without looking, each student in the class should choose one of the cards.

What's the first movie you ever saw at the movie theater?	What's the last movie you saw at the movie theater?	What's the longest book you've ever read?
What's the oldest book you've ever read?	What's your favorite scene from a movie?	Who's your favorite singer?
Who's your favorite actor?	Who's your favorite writer?	How much time do you spend watching TV?
Do you prefer watching a movie at home or in the movie theater?	How often do you go to the movie theater?	Have you ever written a poem?

A Ask your question to every student in the class. Write down their answers.

B Work in pairs. Can you remember the questions that your classmates asked you?

C Tell your partner the answers your classmates gave to the question you asked. Which answers were the most interesting?

Reporting verbs

A Choose the correct answers for the sentences (1–10).

1 Julie ***said / promised / argued*** Ben that she had turned off the oven.

2 Ben ***insisted / persuaded / wondered*** that they should go home and check.

3 Ben ***worried / argued / persuaded*** that the front door was unlocked.

4 Julie ***admitted / promised / insisted*** that they would miss their flight if they went home to check.

5 Julie ***refused / explained / persuaded*** to go all the way back home.

6 Ben ***explained / replied / agreed*** that there could be a fire in the house.

7 When they went home, Julie ***predicted /admitted / mentioned*** that she had forgotten to lock the front door.

8 After that, Ben ***warned / argued / mentioned*** that he had forgotten to turn off the kitchen faucet.

9 At the airport, they ***argued / shouted / reminded*** with the security officers.

10 Unfortunately, they ***whispered /insisted / mentioned*** that it was too late for Ben and Julie to get on their plane.

B Work in pairs and discuss:

- the last argument you had
- a time when you persuaded someone to do something
- the last prediction you made which came true
- a time when you warned someone about something

Third conditional; *would have* + past participle

A Work in pairs. Discuss two or three answers to the following questions.

What would have happened if ...

- you'd been born in a different country?
- you'd been born in a different era?
- you'd chosen a different English school?
- you'd decided to study something different?
- you hadn't started learning English?
- you'd gotten up earlier today?
- you'd worn a different pair of shoes today?
- you'd had a bigger breakfast?
- the internet had never been invented?
- your parents had never met?

B Compare your answers in a group. For each question, whose answer is the most realistic / the funniest / the most imaginative?

Expressions with *mind*

Student A

A Read these situations to your partner. Your partner will answer from one of the phrases on their paper.

What do you say if:

1 you're in a restaurant and you can't decide between the chicken or the fish?

2 someone is upset because they've missed the bus?

3 you've finally decided what to wear to a party?

4 you want to open the window on a train?

B Listen to your partner and choose which of the phrases below you would say in each situation.

I can if I put my mind to it | I've changed my mind | Bear in mind that you should … | It's all in the mind

C Act out each situation with a short conversation.

Student B

A Listen to your partner and choose which of the phrases below you would say in each situation.

I've made up my mind | I'm of two minds | Would you mind if I …? | Never mind

B Read these situations to your partner. Your partner will answer from one of the phrases on their paper.

What do you say if:

1 you were going to have chicken for dinner, but now you want fish?

2 you're trying to convince someone not to be afraid of the dark?

3 someone tells you something is impossible, but you don't believe them?

4 you're giving someone some advice about visiting your country?

C Act out each situation with a short conversation.

Hopes and wishes

1 ____________

2 ____________

3 ____________

4 ____________

5 ____________

6 ____________

A Match the pictures (1–6) to the words from the box below.

your house/apartment friendship family hobbies possession career

B Write sentences about these topics using the phrases below and discuss your ideas with a partner.

I wish I'd …

I wish I were …

I hope I …

I wish we had …

I wish I could …

Staying organized

A Read the article and replace the underlined definitions with a word or phrase which means the same from the box below.

tasks record plan motivated clean up objective schedule to-do list file

Ways to stay organized

The best way to keep on track and get everything done without missing deadlines is to first [1]get rid of, or throw away, anything you don't need, so that there is no clutter on your desk or workspace. This will make you less anxious and better able to work. [2]Put all documents away in folders, and then put these neatly away in drawers or cabinets.

Once you have done this, you can then write [3]a list of the things that you need to work on. After you have that down on paper, you can think about how to [4]divide your time or think ahead so what you need to do is achieved on [5]the date and time it is due. Keeping a [6]written document each day of what you have been working on will help you to meet the [7]main goal you are working toward. Dividing a large project into a series of smaller [8]jobs is a helpful way to stay on track with the work you need to finish, and you should also allow yourself time to see what you have achieved as this makes you feel [9]encouraged.

B Work in pairs. Do you agree with the advice in the article? What would you add to this?

Answer key

1.1 Grammar

A

1 play
2 trying
3 learning
4 going
5 eating
6 like

B

1 do you do
2 do you
3 are you doing
4 are you going
5 are you feeling / are you
6 do you like about

1.1 Vocabulary

A

1 –
2 –
3 Thanks for inviting me. That ~~hears~~ **sounds** great.
4 I'm going to ~~watch~~ **look** at the paintings at the exhibit on Tuesday.
5 –
6 His music ~~listens~~ **sounds** amazing!
7 –
8 Where is my watch? I can't ~~look at~~ see it anywhere!

1.2 Grammar

A

STUDENT A

1 makes
2 did you meet
3 do you spend
4 chose
5 did you get
6 makes
7 did you get
8 taught

STUDENT B

1 makes
2 did you meet
3 do you speak to
4 gave
5 did you go
6 makes
7 did you choose
8 taught

1.2 Vocabulary

A

Ana – bilingual, speaks, accent
Chris – idioms, informal, translate
Diana – monolingual, speaks

2.1 Grammar

A

2 Did you ever get into trouble when you were in school?
3 Have you ever ridden a horse?
4 Have you ever watched …?
5 Did you ever meet …?
6 Have you ever done a parachute jump?
7 Did you have a big party on your 18th birthday?
8 Have you ever swum with dolphins?
9 Have you ever celebrated …?
10 Have you met …?
11 Did you go out last night?
12 Have you ever written a poem?

2.1 Vocabulary

A

1 helps
2 turn
3 working
4 set
5 made
6 trying

2.2 Grammar

A

Last year the woman couldn't drive, today she can.

2.2 Vocabulary

A

1 e, for 2 c, for 3 f, of 4 b, of 5 g, for 6 h, for
7 a, for 8 d, of

3.1 Vocabulary

A

1 –
2 ~~in the busy hour~~ during rush hour
3 –
4 ~~traffic lines~~ traffic jams
5 ~~road lights~~ traffic lights
6 ~~operation~~ service
7 –
8 –
9 ~~overbusy~~ overcrowded

3.2 Grammar

A

1 A lot of, –
2 The
3 more
4 Some, the
5 The
6 an, many
7 the
8 a, –, –, –
9 A lot of, the
10 a

3.2 Vocabulary

A

Suggested answers:
1 **bad:** awful, terrible **angry:** furious
2 **great:** wonderful **good:** excellent **nice:** amazing
3 **big:** huge **bad:** terrible
4 **good:** delicious
5 **scared:** terrified
6 **funny:** hilarious

4.1 Grammar

A

1 going to
2 going to
3 going to
4 I'll / I will
5 playing
6 going to
7 visiting / going to
8 will
9 will / 'll

4.1 Vocabulary

1 quit
2 cut down
3 breaks
4 keep
5 set
6 reached
7 sticks

4.2 Vocabulary

1 overslept
2 overcharged
3 disrespectful
4 disappeared
5 misunderstood
6 mispronounces
7 undercooked
8 to rebuild
9 misplaced
10 overworked

5.1 Grammar

A

used to / would / would / didn't use to / used to / would / used to / used to

5.1 Vocabulary

1 e 2 b 3 f 4 a 5 c 6 d 7 g

5.2 Grammar

A

1 made of
2 bought by
3 made by
4 used for
5 found in

5.2 Vocabulary

A

launch: a campaign
run: a campaign
build: a reputation
make: money, deals
attract: investors

B

1 has built
2 to run
3 to make
4 has built a good reputation / has attracted customers
5 to attract

6.1 Grammar

A

1 must not
2 has to
3 should
4 must
5 must not
6 should
7 need to
8 have to

6.1 Vocabulary

A

1 decisive
2 competitive
3 attractive
4 massive
5 active
6 inexpensive
7 impressive
8 effective
9 aggressive
10 creative

6.2 Grammar

A

1 had to / needed to, didn't need to / didn't have to, need to
2 had to / needed to, had to / needed to

6.2 Vocabulary

A

1 been, aren't, joined, gets, keeps, lose
2 been, escape, take, gotten, lost, is

B

1 have you joined
2 have you taken up
3 can you play
4 escape reality

7.1 Vocabulary

A

remain indoors: stay in
found: figured out
arrive without a reservation: show up
put on plates: serve up
experiment: try out

7.2 Grammar

C

1 –
2 the ~~more good~~ better it is
3 –
4 the ~~slowlier~~ slower you drive
5 –
6 –
7 – The more organized ~~are you~~ you are
8 the ~~beautifuler~~ more beautiful
9 –
10 the ~~more early~~ earlier you get up

7.2 Vocabulary

A

Reduce: cut down, reduce
Reuse: throwing away, reuse, get rid of
Recycle: getting rid of, trash can, recycling

8.1 Grammar

which / who / which / that / which / that / who

8.2 Grammar

1 h **2** f **3** g **4** d **5** e **6** b **7** c **8** a

8.2 Vocabulary

Fitness tracker: incredible, impressive, unique, gorgeous, practical
Wireless headphones: sophisticated, suitable, sensible, unforgettable

9.1 Grammar

A

1 won
2 saw
3 bought
4 was asked
5 were
6 played
7 were
8 spoke

9.1 Vocabulary

A

1 instrument
2 studio
3 exhibit
4 gallery
5 concert
6 choir
7 audience
8 display

9.2 Vocabulary

1 promised
2 insisted
3 worried
4 insisted
5 refused
6 explained
7 admitted
8 mentioned
9 argued
10 insisted

10.1 Vocabulary

Student A

1 I'm of two minds.
2 Never mind.
3 I've made up my mind.
4 Would you mind if I …?

Student B

1 I've changed my mind.
2 It's all in the mind.
3 I can if I put my mind to it.
4 Bear in mind that you should …

10.2 Grammar

1 friendship
2 hobbies
3 family
4 your house/apartment
5 possession
6 career

10.2 Vocabulary

1 clean up
2 file
3 to-do list
4 plan
5 schedule
6 record
7 objective
8 tasks
9 motivated